T0202681

Lecture Notes in Computer Science 12214

More information about this series at http://www.springer.com/series/7409

Robert A. Sottilare · Jessica Schwarz (Eds.)

Adaptive
Instructional Systems

Second International Conference, AIS 2020
Held as Part of the 22nd HCI International Conference, HCII 2020
Copenhagen, Denmark, July 19–24, 2020
Proceedings

 Springer

Editors
Robert A. Sottilare
Soar Technology, Inc.
Orlando, FL, USA

Jessica Schwarz
Fraunhofer FKIE
Wachtberg, Germany

ISSN 0302-9743   ISSN 1611-3349   (electronic)
Lecture Notes in Computer Science
ISBN 978-3-030-50787-9   ISBN 978-3-030-50788-6   (eBook)
https://doi.org/10.1007/978-3-030-50788-6

LNCS Sublibrary: SL3 – Information Systems and Applications, incl. Internet/Web, and HCI

Foreword

The 22nd International Conference on Human-Computer Interaction, HCI International 2020 (HCII 2020), was planned to be held at the AC Bella Sky Hotel and Bella Center, Copenhagen, Denmark, during July 19–24, 2020. Due to the COVID-19 coronavirus pandemic and the resolution of the Danish government not to allow events larger than 500 people to be hosted until September 1, 2020, HCII 2020 had to be held virtually. It incorporated the 21 thematic areas and affiliated conferences listed on the following page.

A total of 6,326 individuals from academia, research institutes, industry, and governmental agencies from 97 countries submitted contributions, and 1,439 papers and 238 posters were included in the conference proceedings. These contributions address the latest research and development efforts and highlight the human aspects of design and use of computing systems. The contributions thoroughly cover the entire field of human-computer interaction, addressing major advances in knowledge and effective use of computers in a variety of application areas. The volumes constituting the full set of the conference proceedings are listed in the following pages.

The HCI International (HCII) conference also offers the option of "late-breaking work" which applies both for papers and posters and the corresponding volume(s) of the proceedings will be published just after the conference. Full papers will be included in the "HCII 2020 - Late Breaking Papers" volume of the proceedings to be published in the Springer LNCS series, while poster extended abstracts will be included as short papers in the "HCII 2020 - Late Breaking Posters" volume to be published in the Springer CCIS series.

I would like to thank the program board chairs and the members of the program boards of all thematic areas and affiliated conferences for their contribution to the highest scientific quality and the overall success of the HCI International 2020 conference.

This conference would not have been possible without the continuous and unwavering support and advice of the founder, Conference General Chair Emeritus and Conference Scientific Advisor Prof. Gavriel Salvendy. For his outstanding efforts, I would like to express my appreciation to the communications chair and editor of HCI International News, Dr. Abbas Moallem.

July 2020   Constantine Stephanidis

HCI International 2020 Thematic Areas
and Affiliated Conferences

Thematic areas:

- HCI 2020: Human-Computer Interaction
- HIMI 2020: Human Interface and the Management of Information

Affiliated conferences:

- EPCE: 17th International Conference on Engineering Psychology and Cognitive Ergonomics
- UAHCI: 14th International Conference on Universal Access in Human-Computer Interaction
- VAMR: 12th International Conference on Virtual, Augmented and Mixed Reality
- CCD: 12th International Conference on Cross-Cultural Design
- SCSM: 12th International Conference on Social Computing and Social Media
- AC: 14th International Conference on Augmented Cognition
- DHM: 11th International Conference on Digital Human Modeling and Applications in Health, Safety, Ergonomics and Risk Management
- DUXU: 9th International Conference on Design, User Experience and Usability
- DAPI: 8th International Conference on Distributed, Ambient and Pervasive Interactions
- HCIBGO: 7th International Conference on HCI in Business, Government and Organizations
- LCT: 7th International Conference on Learning and Collaboration Technologies
- ITAP: 6th International Conference on Human Aspects of IT for the Aged Population
- HCI-CPT: Second International Conference on HCI for Cybersecurity, Privacy and Trust
- HCI-Games: Second International Conference on HCI in Games
- MobiTAS: Second International Conference on HCI in Mobility, Transport and Automotive Systems
- AIS: Second International Conference on Adaptive Instructional Systems
- C&C: 8th International Conference on Culture and Computing
- MOBILE: First International Conference on Design, Operation and Evaluation of Mobile Communications
- AI-HCI: First International Conference on Artificial Intelligence in HCI

Conference Proceedings Volumes Full List

38. CCIS 1224, HCI International 2020 Posters - Part I, edited by Constantine Stephanidis and Margherita Antona
39. CCIS 1225, HCI International 2020 Posters - Part II, edited by Constantine Stephanidis and Margherita Antona
40. CCIS 1226, HCI International 2020 Posters - Part III, edited by Constantine Stephanidis and Margherita Antona

http://2020.hci.international/proceedings

Second International Conference on Adaptive Instructional Systems (AIS 2020)

Program Board Chairs: **Robert A. Sottilare, Soar Technology, Inc., USA, and Jessica Schwarz, Fraunhofer FKIE, Germany**

- Roger Azevedo, USA
- Brenda Bannan, USA
- Avron Barr, USA
- Michelle D. Barrett, USA
- Benjamin Bell, USA
- Gautam Biswas, USA
- Shelly Blake-Plock, USA
- Michael Boyce, USA
- Keith Brawner, USA
- Bert Bredeweg, The Netherlands
- Barbara Buck, USA
- Jody L. Cockroft, USA
- Brandt Dargue, USA
- Jeanine DeFalco, USA
- Lucio DePaolis, Italy
- Eric Domeshek, USA
- Dragan Gasevic, Australia
- Benjamin Goldberg, USA
- Art Graesser, USA
- Ani Grubisic, Croatia
- Andrew J. Hampton, USA
- Ioannis Hatzilygeroudis, Greece
- Ross Hoehn, USA
- Xiangen Hu, USA
- Jerzy Jarmasz, Canada
- Anne Knowles, USA
- Qiguang Lin, USA
- Robby Robson, USA
- Peder Sjölund, Sweden
- KP Thai, USA
- Richard Tong, USA
- Armon Toubman, The Netherlands
- Thomas E. F. Witte, Germany

The full list with the Program Board Chairs and the members of the Program Boards of all thematic areas and affiliated conferences is available online at:

http://www.hci.international/board-members-2020.php

HCI International 2021

The 23rd International Conference on Human-Computer Interaction, HCI International 2021 (HCII 2021), will be held jointly with the affiliated conferences in Washington DC, USA, at the Washington Hilton Hotel, July 24–29, 2021. It will cover a broad spectrum of themes related to Human-Computer Interaction (HCI), including theoretical issues, methods, tools, processes, and case studies in HCI design, as well as novel interaction techniques, interfaces, and applications. The proceedings will be published by Springer. More information will be available on the conference website: http://2021.hci.international/.

General Chair
Prof. Constantine Stephanidis
University of Crete and ICS-FORTH
Heraklion, Crete, Greece
Email: general_chair@hcii2021.org

http://2021.hci.international/

Contents

Designing and Developing Adaptive Instructional Systems

Sensor-Based Adaptive Instructional Systems in Live Simulation Training

Brenda Bannan[1]([⊠]), Elisa M. Torres[1], Hermant Purohit[1],
Rahul Pandey[1], and Jody L. Cockroft[2]

[1] George Mason University, Fairfax, VA 22030, USA
bbannan@gmu.edu
[2] The University of Memphis, Memphis, TN 38152, USA

Abstract. Sensor-based, mobile behavioral analytics have much potential for adaptive human-machine interactivity in team- and multiteam-based, live simulation training. This paper will explore a human-technology adaptive system where real-time data is generated from multiple sensor systems to inform multiteam-based training. Examples from first responder law enforcement training contexts will be discussed as well as the future potential of these sensor-based technologies to iteratively and adaptively inform both the smart technology system and the human system in a reciprocal learning cycle.

Keywords: Internet of Things · Sensors · Mobile behavioral analytics · Adaptive human-machine · Live simulation training · First responders

1 Introduction

Sensor-based, mobile behavioral analytics provide a new form of adaptive instructional systems for consideration by researchers and learning scientists. Real-time use of data from the Internet of Things (IoT) connected devices provide a system for processing data quickly and efficiently in dynamic, changing conditions such as live simulation training. Once these data streams are captured, they may be processed in real time leveraging artificial intelligence (AI) infused machine learning techniques such as deep learning and computer visioning. In this paper, we describe our conceptualization of an adaptive, human-machine instructional system incorporating IoT and video behavioral sensing of first responder teams engaged in a large-scale live simulation training exercise in an exploratory study research effort.

2 Adaptive Human-Machine Instructional Systems and Emergency Response Teams

Adaptive instructional systems are defined as "…artificially-intelligent, computer-based systems that guide learning experiences by tailoring instruction and recommendations based on the goals, needs and preferences of each individual learner or team in the context of domain learning objectives (p. 3)", (Bell and Sottilare [2]. When the domain is the complex system of multiple emergency response teams engaged in a

© Springer Nature Switzerland AG 2020
R. A. Sottilare and J. Schwarz (Eds.): HCII 2020, LNCS 12214, pp. 3–14, 2020.
https://doi.org/10.1007/978-3-030-50788-6_1

real-world live simulation training exercise, the adaptive instructional computer-based system may be conceived somewhat differently. A system consisting of sensor-based devices that seamlessly collect behavioral and environmental data in-situ (i.e., in the real world while live action typically unfolds) allows for the automatic processing and extraction of relevant data streams to inform learning and training in the simulation debrief or after action review. This integrated, seamless data collection from multiple sources can provide targeted, real time visualization of important temporal, behavioral, and environmental metrics to inform an iterative cycle of reflection, learning and improved performance for the first responder teams.

Specifically, this proposed human-machine iterative cycle represents a socio-technical system that incorporates adaptivity in the systems' ability to observe and sense the environment while leveraging machine learning algorithms to quickly interpret and process the contextual information from the building environment as well as the dynamic behavioral activity of the teams as it unfolds in real-time to provide human and machine feedback for learning. This adaptive and reciprocal feedback loop (see Fig. 1) provides the selection and visualization of the rich sensor-based information using machine learning algorithms and computer vision techniques. These advanced computational methods can help to better inform leadership, incident command and the first responder teams about their performance and environmental conditions in the simulated emergency context to provide situational awareness, contextual and tactical feedback to adapt their behavior for the next simulation run. These processed data streams individually and in combination can provide targeted, integrated information for enhanced human sensemaking of a complex and dynamic live action scenario with multiple teams and large amounts of behavioral and environmental data. Machine learning and computer visioning techniques support data-driven decision-making for the responder teams that goes beyond what is possible with human observation and feedback alone.

Currently, our work is situated in the multiteam emergency response training context. Emergency response multiteam systems are comprised of functionally distinct teams from different agencies who must engage in interdependent activity in order to ensure public safety [10]. The nature of emergency situations places a premium on not only effective coordination among members of the same team (or agency), but also effective coordination between these teams [9]. Our research program attempts to improve coordination within and between the first responder teams by utilizing a sensor-based adaptive instructional system.

This paper details our initial effort, focusing on response times of first responder organizations by providing a form of instant replay. This instant replay with various representations of video and sensor data permits enhanced feedback and research inquiry into the visualization of team and between team tactics as well as provides fine grain timing of important behavioral events. These analytics when visualized to participating first responder teams provide a new window and research investigation into how teams function together, team tactical strategy and incident command as well as potentially can improve the shared common operating picture and overall performance of the system. We see this as a human-machine interactive cycle seamlessly capturing team-based behavior and environmental data through sensor and video data devices during the live simulation training in real-time leveraging machine learning and computer visioning algorithms for processing, analysis and visualization of selected information for enhanced feedback. The adaptive socio-technical human-machine system works in a cyclical reflective process where the sensor and video data are processed in the cloud, continuously updated as each simulation run or exercise provides additional data from which the computational system adapts and learns providing rich information for the human system to adapt and learn.

3 Data Streams and User Studies in Emergency Response Simulation Training

When an emergency incident occurs, information from a variety of data sources are triggered that could potentially be mined with advanced computational techniques to inform emergency response and live simulation training. These data sources include: 1) public data streams such as television broadcasts, public radio communications, video, social media and physical sensing streams and consumer drone footage; 2) first responder data streams such as mission critical radio secure communications, wearable camera feeds, biometric data, emergency response robotic/drone information, and physical sensing devices such as blue force tracking or wearable cameras; and 3) building environment contextual data streams such as indoor location-based data, occupancy data, wi-fi detection, humidity, temperature, light, sound, carbon dioxide, organic gases barometric with data visualized and represented on a digital twin model of the building. These information data streams individually or in combination could potentially be tapped to inform incident response, team- and multiteam-based tactics, team- and multiteam-based learning and decision-making along with capturing the changing conditions of an emergency such as a fire, severe weather or active violence incident (AVI). These information streams may enhance the contextual and situational awareness of first responders, their leadership as well as the public when used in a secure manner. In simulated emergency conditions, these seamlessly captured and processed multimodal data streams can also provide access to important behavioral and environmental data for learning and training. Leveraging artificial intelligence (AI) advanced computational techniques to process and sift through massive amounts of this multimodal data permits the visualization of important metrics and data-driven analyses for first responder teams and their leadership immediate viewing. This creates an opportunity for a socio-technical, adaptive, and reciprocal *human-machine learning cycle*. Specifically, capitalizing on machine learning and computer visioning techniques can transform these large amounts of in-situ data into enhanced information for learning and training feedback with dynamic and actionable intelligence for first responders to improve individual and team and multiteam system response and behavior (see Fig. 1).

In addition to providing enhanced data-driven information to the first responder teams, an adaptive sensor-based instructional system can also provide citizens participating in the live simulation training exercise, an opportunity to experience and react to the use of various communication channels that incorporate these data streams to potentially provide enhanced information. Regarding the guided learning experience, researchers have noted that ineffective training tools used to assist training simulation instructors and trainees may result in suboptimal training effectiveness outcomes [4, 6]. For example, this system could include processed data and recommended evacuation routes that change as the dynamics of an emergency situation change. When new forms of communication and enhanced information are introduced to citizens in an emergency response simulation training exercise, these citizens can provide important input and guidance in iterative cycles of user studies to potentially improve the system. User studies provide an important iterative revision cycle evaluating the new forms of information and resulting communication from the first responder perspective as well as from the citizen user perspective.

Figure 1 below attempts to broadly capture this adaptive cycle of a human-machine, sensor-based instructional system for use in emergency response simulation training. The cyclical and iterative phases may be depicted from the start of an incident response, seamlessly collecting multiple described multimodal data streams (represented in graphic as buckets of integrated data streams) to be processed through machine learning and advanced computational techniques in the cloud and then visualized providing enhanced analytics and information for both the first responders and the public and improved through user studies (see Fig. 1).

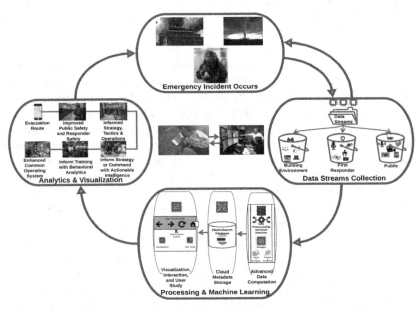

Fig. 1. Adaptive cycle of a human-machine, sensor-based instructional system for use in emergency response simulation training

4   Research and Development Targeting the Adaptive Human-Machine Iterative Experiential Learning Cycle

The sensor-based adaptive instructional system with seamless data collection described in this paper collects multimodal stream analytics from multiple data streams (e.g. sensing through video, audio, IoT building environment devices, media, social media, wearable technologies and represented on a digital twin representation of the building) to extract relevant information about the context of the simulated emergency and individual/team/multiteam behaviors. We propose a systematic approach to seamlessly collect this data related to the first responder team-based activity and the surrounding environment in the live simulation exercise in a dynamic and adaptive human-machine cycle to improve their learning and training. The selected data streams are efficiently processed for relevant patterns through advanced data computation and algorithms including machine learning and computer visioning techniques. These patterns are structurally stored with cloud metadata and processed with an elastic search database resulting in structured representation for targeted information retrieval on various types of visual interfaces such as time and behavioral data. Therefore, these computational techniques can efficiently process the multiple, multimodal and continuous data streams to identify important behavioral patterns and information (e.g. such as which persons were in a particular building location at a designated point in the action). The relevant information is visualized in real time for the first responder teams and their leadership to leverage for enhanced reflection and feedback based on this extracted information and used for teams to learn and adapt to the changing, dynamic conditions from run to run. The adaptive instructional cycle results from the capture, ingestion and advanced computation of multiple data streams that when automatically processed in real time provide insights into specific patterns of behavior immediately made available to the first responder leadership and to the participating teams for reflection and sensemaking in the debrief to provide a basis for experiential learning and behavior change.

4.1 Kolb's Experiential Learning Cycle

This type of experiential learning cycle aligns with Kolb's experiential learning theory [8]. This cycle may be described as "...the process whereby knowledge is created through the transformation of experience" and "...knowledge results from the combination of grasping and transforming experience" [7]. The sensor-based, adaptive instructional system grasps fine grain data from the first responder team's behavioral activity and environmental conditions of the simulated emergency transforming and processing it for enhanced situational awareness and reflection in the debrief or an after-action review. Two modes are described in Kohn's (1984) theory including the description of experiential learning in grasping experience through a cycle of initial Concrete Experience (CE) and Abstract Conceptualization (AC) – and transforming experience through Reflective Observation (RO) and Active Experimentation (AE). These first responder teams have initial concrete experience in the live simulation training exercise with capturing aspects of their experience that are transformed into data representations through visualization in an abstract conceptualization of that experience for reflective team-based observation and learning. As that learning and reflection occur with enhanced guidance from leadership and trainers, then it can be leveraged and acted up for active experimentation in the next simulation run. In this way, the human-machine dynamic and reciprocal feedback loop provide an iterative representation of an adaptive learning cycle that reflects Kohn's description of experiential learning. The system is adaptive by capturing dynamic behavioral information and ingesting the changing conditions of the emergency situation for processing to provide enhanced information for human interpretation and sensemaking. The computational part of the system autonomously captures this behavioral and contextual data to process and reveal select important aspects such as response time intervals or location and dispersion of personnel in the exercise to the first responder trainers and leadership for feedback. The human part of the system associates and interprets the behavior of the first responder teams and the contextual information from the building environment to provide additional guidance and support for team- and multiteam-based experiential learning such as would occur during instant replays for sports teams to improve their learning and performance in the next play.

4.2   Visualization of Information in the Sensor-Based Adaptive Instructional System

The visualized behavioral and contextual data are then incorporated into an enhanced common operating system and training system to provide contextual and behavioral intelligence for reciprocal human sense-making and machine computational analysis cycles that might adapt to each other. As the first responder teams view the processed information, they can reflect and make decisions for the next run based on the highlighted, processed, fine-grain data. For example, the computational vision algorithm may detect team behavioral patterns that are more efficient or less efficient in providing care to the injured simulated patients in the scenario. The behavioral and environmental conditions are visualized back to the teams for enhanced learning and feedback to potentially influence the next run.

In turn, the computational system can potentially learn with each run, the behavioral patterns of the teams such as who was near who at what point in time and in what part of the building, or were the first responders working well as a team or system of teams to care for all the simulated patients? This visualized information can illuminate, for example, the dispersion of team members and teams across the patient care needs in the situation and determine the timing of care by the responders to patients in need. If more responders react and begin to provide care on the first simulated patients they see initially and do not search for other patients in different parts of the building, outcomes for the later identified patients can be compromised. The system can spatially visualize location, occupancy of the first responders in specific parts of the building to demonstrate the results of in-situ decision-making influencing response times or behavioral patterns of teams. When this information is shown back to these teams, they can adjust their behavior. It is conceivable that over time, the computational system may be able to potentially learn these patterns of contextual information, behavior and related time intervals to iteratively progress to improve the information visualized for response and training. While our work has not yet fully matured to this level or the operational environment, we imagine a day when the fully integrated human-computational system may potentially learn dynamically and adaptively as it leverages sensor-based data capture and intelligence to track and update contextual conditions for adaptive recommendations and informed decision-making in this context.

5   Exploratory Study

In this paper, we detail our exploratory study, in which we focus on leveraging multimodal data stream analytics, visualization and machine learning algorithms to look at these unstructured, multimodal data streams to gain insight into the important timing, contextual information and team- and multiteam-based activity [13]. The human-machine adaptive cycle above employs a broad system perspective, which illustrates how information data streams from multiple, multimodal sources can inform an emergency incident. Specifically, these sensor data streams can provide important timing, contextual information and tactical, team-based information. These data analytics from multiple sources were processed with machine learning and computer visioning techniques to reveal and enhance the human experiential learning cycle visualizing team- and multiteam-based tactics and timing as well as providing cyclical input for the computational system to also potentially learn from each run. Improved selection, processing and enhancement of important sensor-based information including behavioral and environmental data provide enhanced information and visualization to prompt improved human sensemaking and contextual reasoning about the emergency training situation. The reciprocal loop between the computational system and the human system provided a form of socio-technical adaptivity in grasping experience through the seamless capture of continuous data streams of the sensor-based technologies and transforming the first responders' concrete experience into visual information for reflective observation of important behavioral and contextual data for use in the debrief and active experimentation based on this information in the next simulation run. This selective capture and visualization of information by advanced computation through machine learning and patterns contributed to the human sense-making and situational/contextual awareness to then potentially and adaptively contribute to experimentation and change of individual, team-and multiteam-based behaviors. This described human-machine adaptive cycle moves us closer toward the development of an enhanced decision support system that is informed by the continually changing dynamics of the situation.

5.1   Live Simulation Training Context

Live simulation training is a form of training which places learners in a realistic, immersive experience in the context with which the learner works. Simulation is an effective tool to develop complex skills across multiple contexts. In comparison to alternative training approaches (e.g., tabletop exercises, computer simulations), live simulation training exercises more fully replicate physical features of the real working environment by utilizing live actors and real equipment [5]. Within the emergency response environment, live simulation training is an important component of first responder preparedness. Live simulation training affords the first responders the opportunity to practice key processes including individual, team and system coordination, planning, and communication [1]. These processes are practiced within an environment that illicit similar physiological responses to what the first responders are likely to experience in a real emergency. Additionally, live simulation training helps to elucidate team and between-team coordination, communication, and knowledge-sharing issues in an environment where these human errors can have major negative consequences [3].

Due to the personnel and material resources required to implement live simulation training, there are several design components that must be carefully considered. It has been recommended that live simulations consider 1) instructional features embedded within the simulation, 2) the exercise scenarios are carefully crafted and contain opportunities for performance measurement and diagnostic feedback, 3) learning experience is guided (e.g., through timely facilitated debriefs), and 4) simulation fidelity is matched to task requirements [12]. Regarding the guided learning experience, researchers have noted that ineffective training tools used to assist training simulation instructors and trainees may result in suboptimal training effectiveness outcomes [4]. For example, much of the live simulation training debriefs are conducted using observation-based methods which may lose valuable information, therefore diminishing the quality of performance feedback delivered to the learners [11]. However, adaptive human-machine instructional systems may address some of these concerns and offer a more effective way to deliver quality feedback to the learners, facilitating the transfer of critical learning outcomes.

5.2 IoT Device Data Streams for Adaptive Instruction in Law Enforcement Training Example

Our exploratory research involved staging a live simulation active violence incident (AVI) in a large public arena building on a University campus in the mid-Atlantic region of the U.S. that included six separate first responder teams comprised of over 70 fire, EMS, law enforcement personnel, and volunteers. This exercise was a part of an ongoing research and development effort geared toward improved understanding of how the integration of multiple streams of data can be leveraged in a human-machine adaptive experiential learning cycle to enhance public safety training and response effectiveness in emergency situations. Specifically, the staged scenario provided a pilot test environment incorporating adaptive cycles of feedback through capturing individual, team- and multiteam-based experience, providing data-driven reflection and guidance with machine learning and computer vision techniques leveraging smart building and sensor-based technology systems that were targeted to support first responders tactics and experiential learning.

The live simulation exercise research pilot tested several technologies instrumented in the arena including video, location-based and occupancy sensors, and displays from a variety of technology innovators. Key technology partners developed the core IoT infrastructure, providing the analytics platform to utilize first responder team behavioral data and daily building environment operation data as well as a 3D digital twin visualization of the Arena to inform learning from emergency response simulation training. During routine operations, some of these smart building technologies were designed to improve the operational and energy efficiency of the arena, to enhance comfort and provide additional services to patrons. However, in the case of an emergency simulation exercise the 3D digital twin visualization, video and sensors can also be available to help responders more rapidly determine the location and type of emergency, help find victims more quickly, learn from their behavior and experience through mobile behavioral and building environment analytics to ultimately, save lives.

5.3   Sensor Systems and Displays

Specific sensors and displays included 24 sensor pods incorporating remote video capability, Wi-Fi detectors, blue-force tracking, LiDAR occupancy detectors, particulate and environmental sensors along with 2D/3D visualization tools. The analytics platform along with a digital twin of the facility, and Wi-Fi-based indoor location platform, allowed for rich information data streams to be captured along with real time first responder team tracking capabilities for review in the simulation debrief to enhance team and multiteam learning.

The live simulation-based exercise engaged the teams of first responders whom prior to the exercise, had never collectively engaged in a joint exercise together. The staged incident was an active violence incident mass casualty exercise in the large arena which required the joint efforts of local fire, EMS and law enforcement first responders. First responders were not provided the system interface with available data for use during the staged incident, such as the 3D digital twin of the building prior to arriving on scene. The first responder participating teams and simulated patient actors were also shown the technology system for adaptive instruction for input and evaluation. However, during a feedback session, leadership representing the participating agencies were presented with the opportunity to closely review the technology system and the first responder teams as well as the citizen volunteer simulated patients were interviewed about the adaptive system.

6   Data Analysis

We analyzed the captured video and sensor data displays during and after the simulation exercise deployment. We recorded, transcribed and analyzed the first responder debrief sessions to capture insights about the exercise itself. Then first responder teams were shown some of the captured and processed data for feedback. The expert panel provided rich feedback on the potential use of this type of system in their agencies.

7   Results

The teams and expert panel emphasized the desire for increased situational awareness for first responders. Members of the response agencies mentioned the usefulness of the 3D digital twin visualization in providing an enhanced and shared understanding of the operational environment, and for incident command responsible for managing the personnel and response efforts. This was deemed especially helpful for first responder teams who were unfamiliar with the layout and structure of the building, which is likely to be the case for real emergency events. Additionally, the occupancy and location-based sensors were seen as helpful data streams when engaging in search and rescue, after the exercise suspect was neutralized. The security of the collected data streams was also cited as an important consideration by all involved. As such, when designing the technology system, the security of data, and mitigation from cybersecurity attack or intrusion was highlighted as a critical component of the technology system developed. When instructed to record, all data collected via the technology system would be housed on a secure custom solution.

We designed and employed an initial prototype of an AI-infused system (see Fig. 2) which seeks to augment the learning experience of emergency responders in the live simulation training exercise. The AI-infused, adaptive instructional system was created to support training instructors with multimodal learning analytics for enhanced training debriefs (e.g., after-action reviews). The system applied AI methods of computer vision and machine learning to process the various multimodal data streams in near real-time, collected by the aforementioned state-of-the-art sensing technologies during the training exercise.

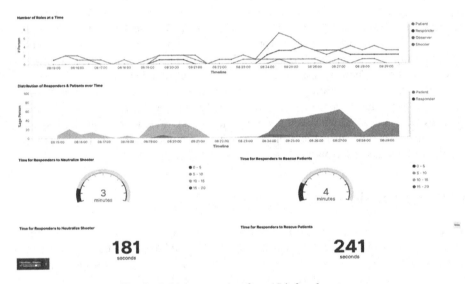

Fig. 2. Initial prototype of an AI-infused system

A core objective of the training simulation debrief after different scenario runs is to review and analyze the effectiveness of specific events of interest, such as the time differential between the response dispatch to the time of the neutralization of the shooter; or time of interaction between the responders and victims or patients. The AI-system provided first responders with an experimental user interface that displays information for these key indicators. Additionally, the AI-infused system provides a starting point for important insights for coordination activities within-teams, and between the different responder teams. This effort promotes the opportunity to facilitate both within- and between-team learning, which is an often neglected critical component of emergency response management operations. Future exercises will further explore the effectiveness of the technology and AI-infused system in initiating change in behavioral patterns, or coordinated dance, among the multiteam system composed of these brave first responder teams.

Preliminary insights from the training and initial exploratory research data analysis indicates that first responders and their leadership see significant value in this type of joint agency training event in building levels of trust amongst the different agencies that would respond and work together in an actual event. Situating the live simulation training and corresponding research cycles for evaluation of these emerging technologies, building intelligence and their security in a university setting provides a unique opportunity to explore new technologies, in-situ, incorporating direct insights from first responders in an applied research approach. The combination and integration of technology systems may provide enhanced situational awareness and security within a building, and first responder wearable devices for collecting sensor and environmental data to enhance actionable data for use in emergency preparedness training will also allow for researchers to study within- and between-team interaction and team and multiteam system learning with real-time data from these devices. Future training and research events are currently being planned.

8 Summary

In our work supporting the experiential learning of first responder teams, we connect their concrete experience captured through the seamless sensor-based data to the behavioral activity taking place in the real world which is then processed through advanced machine computational techniques and represented in an abstract conceptualization of team- and multiteam-based behavior for reflective observation and learning. This reflective human observation of the first responder teams and leadership leads to active experimentation by the teams in the next simulation run based on the learning and reflection on the processed, AI-infused data streams representing their prior team activity. Creating a reciprocal human-machine iterative loop and supporting their experiential learning cycle is the goal of this ongoing research and development. Positioning the described system as an adaptive instructional system in the sense that by ingesting dynamic information about the changing conditions of the simulated emergency situation for processing provides opportunities for enhanced human interpretation and sensemaking. The computational part of the system autonomously captures behavioral and contextual data to process in the cloud and artificial intelligence techniques help to reveal important aspects and timing information for shaping the emergency response multiteam system's future behavior. The human part of the system interprets this enhanced feedback in the debrief to potentially influence the experiential learning cycle and behavior of the first responder teams in an adaptive, real-time change cycle based on that data. This human-machine cycle may provide a novel conceptualization of adaptive instructional systems for future research.

Acknowledgement. This material is based upon work supported by the Center for Innovative Technology (CIT) and the Department of Homeland Security (DHS) Science and Technology Directorate. Any opinions, findings and conclusions, or recommendations expressed in this material are those of the author(s) and do not necessarily reflect the views of the sponsors.

References

1. Bannan, B., Dubrow, S., Dobbins, C., Zaccaro, S., Purohit, H., Rana, M.: Toward wearable devices for multiteam systems learning. In: Buchem, I., Klamma, R., Wild, F. (eds.) Perspectives on Wearable Enhanced Learning (WELL), pp. 79–95. Springer, Cham (2019). https://doi.org/10.1007/978-3-319-64301-4_4
2. Bell, B., Sottilare, R.: Adaptation vectors for instructional agents. In: Sottilare, R.A., Schwarz, J. (eds.) HCII 2019. LNCS, vol. 11597, pp. 3–14. Springer, Cham (2019). https://doi.org/10.1007/978-3-030-22341-0_1
3. Bond, W.F., et al.: The use of simulation in emergency medicine: a research agenda. Acad. Emerg. Med. **14**(4), 353–363 (2007). https://doi.org/10.1197/j.aem.2006.11.021
4. Buck, D.A., Trainor, J.E., Aguirre, B.E.: A critical evaluation of the incident command system and NIMS. J. Homel. Secur. Emerg. Manag. **3**(3), 1–27 (2006). https://doi.org/10.2202/1547-7355.1252
5. Cohen, D., et al.: Tactical and operational response to major incidents: feasibility and reliability of skills assessment using novel virtual environments. Resuscitation **84**, 992–998 (2012)
6. Feese, S., Arnrich, B., Troster, G., Burtscher, M., Meyer, B., Jonas, K.: CoenoFire: monitoring performance indicators of firefighters in real-world missions using smartphones. In: Proceedings of the 2013 ACM International Joint Conference on Pervasive and Ubiquitous Computing, pp. 83–92. ACM (2013)
7. Kolb, D.A.: Experiential Learning Experience as the Source of Learning and Development. Prentice Hall, Upper Saddle River (1984)
8. Kolb, D.A., Boyatzis, R.E., Mainemelis, C., et al.: Experiential learning theory: previous research and new directions. Perspect. Thinking Learn. Cogn. Styles **1**(8), 227–247 (2001)
9. Marks, M.A., DeChurch, L.A., Mathieu, J.E., Panzer, F.J., Alonso, A.: Teamwork in multiteam systems. J. Appl. Psychol. **90**(5), 964–971 (2005). https://doi.org/10.1037/0021-9010.90.5.964
10. Mathieu, J.E., Marks, M.A., Zaccaro, S.J.: Multiteam systems. In: Anderson, N., Ones, D.S., Sinangil, H.K., Viswesvaran, C. (eds.) Organizational Psychology: Handbook of Industrial, Work and Organizational Psychology, London, 2nd edn, vol. 2, pp. 289–313 (2001)
11. Purohit, H., Dubrow, S., Bannan, B.: Designing a multimodal analytics system to improve emergency response training. In: Zaphiris, P., Ioannou, A. (eds.) HCII 2019. LNCS, vol. 11590, pp. 89–100. Springer, Cham (2019). https://doi.org/10.1007/978-3-030-21814-0_8
12. Salas, E., Burke, C.S.: Simulation for training is effective when…. BMJ Qual. Saf. **11**(2), 119–120 (2002)
13. Sottilare, R.A., Schwarz, J.: HCII 2019. LNCS, vol. 11597. Springer, Cham (2019). https://doi.org/10.1007/978-3-030-22341-0

An Ambient and Pervasive Personalized Learning Ecosystem: "Smart Learning" in the Age of the Internet of Things

Anastasia Betts[1,2(✉)], Khanh-Phuong Thai[1], Sunil Gunderia[1], Paula Hidalgo[1], Meagan Rothschild[1], and Diana Hughes[1]

[1] Age of Learning, Glendale, CA, USA
[2] University at Buffalo SUNY, Buffalo, NY, USA
albetts@buffalo.edu

Abstract. Despite recent advances in technology, personalized learning to address diverse needs of students remains difficult to achieve at scale. With the availability and affordability of smart devices in the era of the Internet of Things, learners, parents, and educators are more "connected" than ever before. Education stakeholders and technology developers can leverage these advances to collect data about, inform, deliver, and improve education for all learners. In this paper, we review the core components of a Smart Learning framework and describe a personalized mastery-based learning system that leverages the framework to deliver personalized learning at scale. In the context of Smart Learning in the Internet of Things, we propose an Ambient and Pervasive Personalized Learning Ecosystem (APPLE), a learner-centered approach that uses Bloom's Four Agents of Change in the Internet of Things ecosystem to provide learners a comprehensive and personalized learning experience. This ecosystem uses people, processes, data, things, and networked connections to create new capabilities, richer learning experiences, and unprecedented educational opportunities for learners, educators, and families. We further discuss the challenges surrounding the implementation of such an ecosystem, specifically calling for applications of learning engineering approaches, the need of interoperability across systems and components, and the importance of ethical considerations.

Keywords: Smart learning · Internet of Things · Personalized learning · Adaptive instructional systems

1 Introduction

The K-12 student population in the United States is one of the most diverse in the world, and growing more so (de Brey et al. 2019; Geiger 2018; NCES 2019). Students arrive in the classroom from different cultural, socio-economic, and linguistic backgrounds, with varying degrees of prior knowledge, skills, aptitudes, and levels of parental or caregiver support. In recent years, learner diversity has experienced significant increases in levels of students living in poverty, students with learning

The original version of this chapter was previously published non-open access. A Correction to this chapter is available at https://doi.org/10.1007/978-3-030-50788-6_42

© The Author(s) 2020, corrected publication 2022
R. A. Sottilare and J. Schwarz (Eds.): HCII 2020, LNCS 12214, pp. 15–33, 2020.
https://doi.org/10.1007/978-3-030-50788-6_2

disabilities and/or learner differences, second language learners, students identified as gifted and talented, as well as students recovering from trauma (NCES 2019; Pape 2018).

Where learning takes place also varies. Many students no longer do most of their learning in formal learning environments (i.e., the classroom). Students have moved away from what has previously been estimated as a 90–10% split of formal to informal learning, and now are estimated to learn equally in formal and informal contexts (Kinshuk et al. 2016). Today's students are surrounded by technology and media they can learn from. The availability of information at the tap of a button, or a search on Google has widened already vast differences in student prior knowledge. It is impossible for teachers to know the depth or breadth of knowledge which students have gained outside of traditional school contexts, making it ever harder for teachers to design appropriate instruction that can keep students engaged and progressing efficiently.

These issues, among others, present a number of challenges for teachers and schools who have been tasked with increasing student performance as demonstrated on state, national, and international assessments of academic achievement. A review of the scores of U.S. students reveals the extent of the challenge, with more than 2 of every 3 fourth grade students not proficient in grade level expectations for reading, math, and science – an academic performance that does not improve as students move on to successive grades (de Brey et al. 2019).

Given the lack of achievement in the face of such extensive learner diversity, the current one-size-fits-all factory model of education, where a teacher provides the same content at the same pace to all students, is simply not working (e.g., Rose 2016). Personalized education is one key way to ensure that individuals students' needs are being met. Unfortunately, personalization remains very difficult to achieve at scale, especially in an educational context that has not changed much in the past century.

2   One-Size-Fits-Me: Personalization in the Internet of Things

The growth of personalization in the commercial sphere through the use of technology has increased in recent years, with consumers moving away from one-size-fits-all products and programs to one-size-fits-me-perfectly (Forbes Insights 2019). Media consumption is an illustrative example of this, as more consumers have cut the cord to television and cable services to embrace more selective, customizable streaming platforms that adapt to the individual consumer through recommendation engines and data collection on viewing practices. This kind of personalization is growing throughout the commercial sector. To wit, the number of personal health apps has exploded in recent years as consumers look for ways to use technology (e.g., smart phones, smart watches, activity trackers and other wearables, etc.) to provide more information about their personal health and wellbeing (Bakker et al. 2016; Lin et al. 2018). Apps that track heart rates, daily steps, nutrient consumption, workout regimens, blood sugar, and more, all collect personal user data, "talk" to one another to create personal profiles, and make relevant recommendations to the user (Rodrigues et al. 2018). Individually these apps are useful; combined they are far more than the sum of their parts. Working together, these apps empower more informed users who are then equipped with personal, meaningful knowledge about how to live healthier, active lives. Beyond providing relevant, personalized knowledge to the user, many apps and devices go even further, using principles of behavioral psychology to encourage and motivate users to change behavior, abandoning self-sabotaging habits for healthy ones (Bakker et al. 2016; Lin et al. 2018).

Personalization is big business, with one recent market research study reporting that the wearables market alone is projected to grow by more than 35 billion dollars by 2023 (Technavio 2019). The development of smart technologies that include hardware and software that collect, analyze, and make personalized recommendations based on the individual user's data, has led to what many in the field call the *Internet of Things* (IoT). IoT, a term first used by Kevin Aston in 1999 (Gabbai 2015), has alternately been called the Internet of Everything, the Internet of Anything, the Internet of People, the Internet of Data, and more (Bakarat 2016). Perhaps one of the best descriptions of the IoT defines it as bringing together *"people, processes, data,* and *things* to make *networked connections* more relevant and valuable than ever before—turning information into actions that create new capabilities, richer experiences, and unprecedented economic opportunities for business, individuals, and countries" (Evans 2012, p. 3).

At its simplest, IoT is the idea that all "smart" things are connected—laptops, smartphones, tablets, and other devices—such that they can communicate with one another, share and interpret information, make decisions about how and what information to present, and what suggestions to make to the user. Recent discussions surrounding the IoT have centered on ways to create Smart Cities, Smart Energy, Smart Transportation, Smart homes, and even Smart Security (Bakarat 2016). It seems there is no shortage of "things" that can be made "smart." Consequently, stakeholders in education have and continue to look for ways that the IoT can benefit students through Smart Learning. When considering the definition of the IoT shared previously, an important question for EdTech developers is: *how can we use people, processes, data, things, and networked connections to create new capabilities, richer learning experiences, and unprecedented educational opportunities for children and their families?*

Education stakeholders and technology developers have a powerful opportunity before them to leverage IoT to collect data about, inform, and improve the education of our children. Families and schools are more "connected" than ever before due to the prevalence of smart devices in the home and many 1:1 device programs in schools. Just as commercial technology has been designed to collect data about users' entertainment, media, or health habits, EdTech systems can be designed to collect meaningful data about learner performance, artificial intelligence (AI) can be used to both analyze that data and offer real time program changes in response to that data, and information systems can be designed to communicate data and responses to students, schools, and parents –connecting them in ways that have previously been unimaginable.

3 The Evolution of Smart Learning Programs

Over the past two decades, governments and school systems in various locales around the world have attempted to implement some version of Smart Learning, including Malaysia's Smart School Implementation in 1997, Singapore's Intelligent Nation

Master Plan in 2006, Australia's smart learning collaboration with IMB in 2012, South Korea's SMART education project, New York's Smart School program, Finland's SysTech program, the United Arab Emirates Mohammed Bin Rashid Smart Learning Program in the convening years (Zhu et al. 2016), and more. Each of these programs were considered by their developers to be "smart," yet the concept of what constitutes smart learning or smart education has varied widely across these and other contexts. What is or can be called "smart" is still too new to be fully understood by stakeholders, nor has it existed long enough for consensus to develop (Hoel and Mason 2018; Zhu et al. 2016). The widespread, and at times casual, use of the term has further complicated efforts to research, design, or implement solutions in the field (Hoel and Mason 2018).

Researchers have attempted to bring more coherence to the study and design of the Smart Learning Environments and systems through the development of common language and frameworks. For example, in the inaugural issue of the journal *Smart Learning Environments*, Specter (2014) argued that smart learning systems must be grounded in the philosophical, psychological, and technological domains. In each of these three areas Specter describes various characteristics of smart learning environments (e.g., such as the degree of adaptivity) as *necessary, highly desirable*, or *likely* (see Fig. 1).

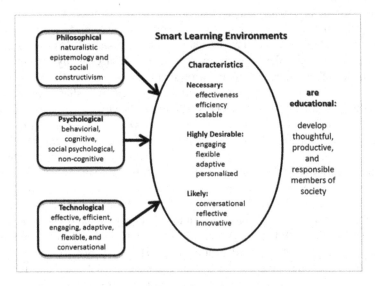

Fig. 1. "A Preliminary framework for smart learning environments" (Spector 2014, p. 8)

Kinshuk et al. (2016), provided additional context, explaining that Smart Learning moves education processes and pedagogy beyond simple technology-enhanced integration models, *to "enable the fusion of technology and pedagogy to create an ecosystem that involves active participation of teachers, parents and others in the learners' learning process... [and] also provide real-time and ongoing evidence of change in knowledge, instilling skills which are seamlessly transferred to learners as they move from one learning context to another" (p. 562).* The use of the word *ecosystem* is purposeful here, in that smart learning environments mirror the complex web of interconnectivity that permeates ecosystems in the natural world. In the natural world, every part of the ecosystem is connected; what impacts one part of the system almost surely will have consequences for other parts of the system (e.g., the butterfly effect, etc.). Beyond expansive interconnectedness, smart learning systems today have evolved to be omnipresent, empowering learners to access and interact with "just-right" learning resources at any time, in any place (Hwang 2014; Kinshuck et al. 2016).

Though various frameworks, terms, and definitions related to Smart Learning might differ, many "smart learning" systems today share three major components. Those components are (1) full context awareness, (2) big data and learning analytics, and (3) autonomous decision making and dynamic adaptive learning (Boulanger et al. 2015; Kinshuk et al. 2016). Across these three domains, Smart Learning environments *"facilitate just-in-time learning as they can provide various levels of adaptation and precision of diversified learning conditions (including curriculum, course content, strategy and support, etc.) for learners"* (Kinshuk et al. 2016, p. 565). We expand upon each of these three components and discuss how each support learning. We also argue for the importance of "small" data for Smart Learning in an IoT world.

3.1 Full Context Awareness

Full context awareness refers to the idea that computer systems have the potential to make sense of context and user behavior in order to provide information and/or services related to the tasks or goals of the user (Kinshuk et al. 2016). As technology has evolved, so has the idea of what it means for technology to be fully context aware. In Smart Learning environments, full context awareness may involve networks of people, processes, and things that combine to gather large amounts of information about the learners and their context in order to provide meaningful learning tasks, scaffolding, and feedback. In traditional learning environments, many learners are under the guidance of one teacher. This can make it difficult for the teacher to be fully aware of each child's performance; what the learner is learning in any given moment, what help or support the learner needs, or how well the learner is mastering the desired content may not be immediately apparent to the teacher. However, with Full Context Awareness, various *"learning management systems, mobile and ubiquitous learning systems, various artificial intelligence based adaptive and intelligent tutoring/learning systems"* (Kinshuk et al. 2016, p. 565) may work together to collect and analyze that data, providing valuable task-relevant information to the learner (through technology user interfaces) and to the teacher who may then take appropriate actions. If suitably advanced, the technology itself may make these adjustments in real time, based on information provided by the learner's behavior in the environment. For example, a Smart Learning system (i.e., synonymous with an adaptive instructional system or AIS) might capture data about the learner while engaged in playing a digital learning game. Based on that data, the system may automatically adjust the difficulty level of that game, while simultaneously providing information to the teacher about any misconceptions that the student might be demonstrating. With that new information, the teacher may conduct an intervention or mini lesson to address those misconceptions.

Full Context Awareness has the potential to empower teachers by helping them to conduct *"direct monitoring of the learning environment, understand learners' conditions and give learners real-time adaptive assistance, while at the same time facilitating independent learning for the learners"* (Kinshuk et al. 2016, p. 565). In sum, a fully contextually aware learning environment is one where processes and "things" are aware of themselves and each other. They are in continuous autonomous communication through active network communication, providing information and services to the entire network, as well as the people (users) who work with the system. As more things become "smart" and connected through networks, the opportunity to achieve Full Context Awareness becomes more possible.

3.2 Big (and Small) Data and Learning Analytics

For a Smart Learning environment to effectively serve the needs of individual students, it is important to collect and analyze data about each student's ongoing performance. Data collection serves a number of purposes, including tracking and drawing conclusions about student performance, making predictions about future learning performance, providing supportive feedback or scaffolding during moments of struggle, identifying student misconceptions that may be interfering with progress or comprehension, detecting and correcting counterproductive learning behaviors, adapting the content in order to personalize learning trajectories over time, and helping to keep students, parents, and teachers informed in real-time about student progress (i.e., Betts 2019; Hoel and Mason 2018; Kinshuk et al. 2016; Owen et al. 2019; Roberts-Mahoney et al. 2016).

Over the past decade, educational data collection has expanded dramatically. Student data bases today hold vast amounts of personal data including, *"student identification numbers, dates of birth, race, socioeconomic status, standardized test scores, attendance records, disciplinary records, health records, learning disabilities, homework completion, as well as student goals and interests"* (Roberts-Mahoney et al. 2016, p. 412). These demographic data can provide even more context about student learning capabilities and performance when combined with data collected during the process of learning. For example, it may be possible to detect that some young learners who have certain commonalities in their data (e.g., 4-year-old students from specific SES, backgrounds, regions or locales, with similar levels of prior knowledge) may perform similarly in a digital game-based Smart Learning system, and would benefit from specific types of support (e.g., receiving extra exposure and exploration on specific early math topics before beginning formal mathematics instruction) to ensure their most efficient pathway toward success (Betts et al. 2020). Powered by that information, student needs can be quickly identified, learning trajectories adapted, and support and scaffolding provided without delay.

As data is collected from thousands, tens, or even hundreds of thousands of individuals, trends and patterns emerge that combine with individual student performance data to create more powerful and precise predictive learning models that are personalized for each student. De Mauro et al. (2016) define Big Data as *"the information asset characterized by such a High Volume, Velocity and Variety to require specific technology and Analytical Methods for its transformation into Value"* (p. 131). Rich student interaction data from Smart Learning systems can support a broad range of analyses critical to understanding learning in the context of education. These large digital event streams enable the application of methods tailored to high-volume educational data, such as learning analytics and educational data mining (LA/EDM; Baker and Siemens 2014). These approaches empower the use of large educational data streams to mine organic learner patterns related to elements like student performance, affect, and behavior (Baker and Yacef 2009). In a wide range of other game-based research (e.g., Owen and Baker 2019), LA/EDM analyses have been used to uncover emergent learner patterns related to elements like strategy (e.g., Asbell-Clarke et al. 2013), student attrition (Hicks et al. 2016), player profiles (e.g., Slater et al. 2017), and learner affect (Kai et al. 2015; Rodrigo and Baker 2011). Rich event-stream data in game environments enables such investigations, which can inform potent data-driven design and personalized formative feedback (e.g., Ke et al. 2019).

It is also important to note that this embrace of "big data" does not mean that we ignore the importance of "small data" for Smart Learning in the IoT. On this topic, Lindstrom (2016) has aptly titled his book "Small Data: The Tiny Clues That Uncover Huge Trends". Not all questions, particularly those regarding causation, are answerable with big data. In education, small clues about the learning process and how to improve it can often come from data on a smaller scale: classes of students rather than whole grade levels, schools, or districts. Such data can be collected using formative assessments, human observations, face-to-face conversations, reflections and surveys, etc., revealing important information such as a student's confidence level when answering a question, their beliefs about the topics being taught, aspects of student-teacher personal interaction that may reveal important information like physical or mental health issues, problems at home, etc. that may more accurately support individual students' needs. These small clues are often hidden in the complex fabric of values, behaviors, and cultures that determine how teachers, learners, and parents interact. Understanding this complexity requires that we also be sensitive to small data.

3.3 Autonomous Decision Making and Dynamic Adaptive Learning

Another important key feature of Smart Learning systems is their ability to automatically collect data about each learner in the system. These data are likely to go beyond learning performance to include their socio-emotional behaviors as well. The data collected can be organized using AI algorithms to create a personalized profile of the learner. Based on the analysis of those data, a Smart Learning system makes inferences, draws conclusions, and makes decisions about what actions to take. Actions taken by the system may include a variety of things such as, adjusting the difficulty level, providing scaffolding or "just in time" feedback to help the learner get through a particularly challenging task, move the learner forward or backward within the system, notify the teacher of the need for remediation, or more.

This type of autonomous decision-making and dynamic adaptive learning is not limited to digital-only environments. For example, Kinshuk et al. (2016) point out that

Smart Learning environments that combine both digital and physical may benefit as well. Using collected data, some Smart learning systems can make recommendations to teachers about the types of interactions learners would benefit from most (e.g., reading specific books in the classroom library), or the best location for suggested activities (e.g., specific learners may improve their comprehension by engaging in a collaborative group reading), or even the types or problems that would most benefit the learner's progress at any given moment (e.g., learner "x" would benefit from more practice with multi-step word problems, etc.). This decision-making is autonomous, and the suggestions for how the learning environment might be adapted for student personalization are dynamic. Providing this type of guidance to teachers empowers them to extend the Smart Learning environment beyond the digital realm into the physical lives of children in and outside of the classroom.

4   The Learner at the Center of Smart Learning

Many existing Smart Learning systems (i.e., AISs) are mastery-based. The goal of mastery-based systems is to help learners master specific learning outcomes, usually through personalized learning trajectories that adapt based on the learner's existing levels of prior knowledge, learning pace, and need for remediation, support, or acceleration (Betts 2019). Mastery-based systems originally evolved from the work of Bloom (1984), who spent years studying the best practices of effective teaching and learning, and whose major contribution directly promotes personalization and learner variability. Bloom developed a framework for learning that goes beyond the immediate interactions of students and teachers, to include the other significant forces for learning in the learner's life. As Bloom (1984) described in his seminal work on mastery learning, there are Four Agents of Change: the *materials*, the *student*, the *teacher*, and the learner's *environment* (both inside and outside school), of which parents are a critical component – especially for young children. In order to significantly improve student learning, all four agents of change must be addressed.

Bloom's Four Agents of Change are particularly useful when viewed through the lens of Smart Learning, as Smart Learning systems have the power to integrate all four agents in ways that seamlessly work together to help the learner achieve learning outcomes. Additionally, Smart Learning systems that address Bloom's Four Agents of Change have the ability to do this at scale, for thousands of children simultaneously, which has been unobtainable through Bloom's mastery learning model alone (Betts 2019).

In a speculative article that echoes Bloom's framework, Ginsburg (2014) imagines a Smart Learning environment that would teach early childhood mathematics to the youngest learners. Beginning at age 3, the child would receive a personal tablet (which Ginsburg calls "Tubby") designed to function as a playmate of sorts for the child. Through Tubby, the child is presented with "microworlds" designed to sequence early childhood mathematics content in accessible and developmental ways. Through interactions with the child, Tubby collects data on what the child already knows, what the child needs to know, and what the child is most likely ready to learn next. It uses the algorithms of AI to test these "hypotheses," collect more data, and adapt to the child's individual need for support.

Ginsburg's vision goes beyond addressing only the learner and materials, and includes the important roles of teachers, and the environment beyond the school, reinforcing once again the need to consider Bloom's Four Agents of Change (Bloom 1984; Ginsburg 2014). Ginsburg describes a learning environment where people, processes, and things are fully connected, and where Tubby's operating system is engaged in ongoing, stealth assessment for the purposes of collecting data, feeding it to the teachers and parents, suggesting videos, books, and additional activities all at the child's just-right developmental level as part of a self-reinforcing cycle of progress through the desired content. At the time Ginsburg imagined this version of Smart Learning, it was perhaps still a fantasy (he even called it such in the title of his piece). However, advances in technology have made all that he imagined possible, and more.

5 A Personalized Mastery Learning System

Today, education technology developers seem closer to Ginsburg's dream than ever before, as they attempt to *use people, processes, data, and networked connections to create new capabilities, richer experiences, and unprecedented educational opportunities for children and their families.*

A contemporary example of how one EdTech developer is working to realize this vision is Age of Learning, Inc.'s Personalized Mastery Learning System (PMLS; Dohring et al. 2017) that uses the IoT (people, processes, data, things, & networks) as well as Bloom's Agents of Change to drive a multi-pronged approach to teaching early mathematics and reading skills to children 4–8 years old. The result is two independent personalized game-based learning systems, ABCmouse Mastering Math^{TM} and ABCmouse Mastering Reading^{TM}, designed to help young learners build a strong foundation of mathematics and reading, respectively.

Within PMLS, an evidence-centered design (ECD) approach (Mislevy et al. 2003) is used to structure embedded assessment in a game context, with an emphasis on aligning target knowledge, skills, and abilities with desired evidence and in-game assessment tasks designed to elicit such data. Such an approach provides context-rich interaction data streams that enable a broad range of analyses, including investigation of emergent learner patterns (Baker and Yacef 2009). Research has shown that ECD-based educational games can capture emergent, EDM-based insights with implications for iterative design (e.g., DiCerbo et al. 2015, Hao et al. 2016; Slater et al. 2017; Stephenson et al. 2014). When game-based assessment is a part of the development from conception, game design is founded in the consideration of learning evidence, which enable assessment to be embedded into the core mechanics of game play (Grace 2014). This integrated game-based assessment (iGBA; Owen and Hughes 2019) approach is core to the design and production of PMLS. The result is context-rich and detailed iGBA-based data that allow for iterative, data-driven design for improved learning and engagement via a range of methods, including evaluation of designed assessment, as well as broader explorations with LA/EDM to enhance intelligent system response in real time. These data also have implications outside the system, as event-stream insights can be surfaced to teachers to allow classroom-based intervention and student support, and to parents who receive (through a mobile application on their smart phone) both performance updates and recommendations regarding how best to support their learner with just-right activities at home.

While Mastering Reading has only just newly been released (early 2020), evidence suggests that Mastering Math (released in 2017) integrates well into formal learning environments, as recent classroom-based research suggests, providing promising learning results with PMLS and informing future development of the systems (Betts et al. 2020; Thai et al. 2019). Mastering Math currently features approximately 130 games, covering number sense and operations concepts and skills for pre-kindergarten through second grade. Consistent with good assessment practices, every game is designed with a clear learning objective, learning task, and evidence in mind; and each learning objective is supported by an interactive instruction level, as well as several layers of scaffolding and feedback. To support personalized instruction, the adaptive system decides what games to recommend and at which difficulty level using a pre-determined knowledge map of learning objectives and their prerequisite relationships (i.e., a node map). Adaptivity functions within individual games to provide scaffolding with each level of skill difficulty, between games to adjust to students' difficulty needs, and across the system to personalize learning trajectories for each learner based on performance (Betts 2019; Betts et al. 2020). Assessment is embedded throughout the play experience, including game-based pretests and final assessment tasks at a granular skill level.

To develop *Mastering Math*, Age of Learning implements a learning engineering approach (Thai and Rothschild, under review; ICICLE 2019) with a cross-disciplinary team of curriculum specialists, learning and data scientists, and professional game developers. This team collaborated to create a game-based learning solution built upon rigorous academic curriculum, developed with a high degree of polish and engagement value, and grounded in principles of evidence-centered design, game-based assessment, and educational data mining.

The PMLS, in real time, collects and interprets rigorous data in order to inform and modify content for students, as well as to inform teachers and parents. This system goes beyond mere information reporting, as it uses best practices in motivational digital content development to suggest, encourage, and motivate students, parents, and teachers to take action based on the information presented about each learner. This PMLS leverages smart tools (e.g., phones, tablets, laptops, etc.) to connect, in real time, the content to be learned (*materials*), the *student*, the *teacher*, and their parents (*environment*); in other words, the PMLS networks people, processes, and things to provide a context aware, personally adaptive learning experience that is driven by big data and small data, learning analytics and educational data mining (Owen and Hughes 2019; Betts 2019; Betts et al. 2020; Owen et al. 2019). Current ongoing research based on this system shows promising results and provides a basis for what Smart Learning might look like, or at least what it can look like right now, incorporating the tools and technology available to developers at this point in time.

Age of Learning is not alone in their efforts to move the field of Smart Learning forward. Similar efforts can be found with other research-based personalized learning frameworks such as the Generalized Intelligent Framework for Tutoring (GIFT;

Sottilare et al. 2012) and the Knowledge-Learning Instruction Framework (KLI; Koedinger et al. 2012) and LearnSphere (formerly PSLC DataShop; Koedinger et al. 2010).

6 What the Future Holds: Ambient and Pervasive Personalized Learning Ecosystem (APPLE)

The mastery-based Smart Learning systems taking advantage of the IoT available today are just the tip of the iceberg, though it is possible to imagine what such systems in the future might include. With that in mind, we propose a new vision for an Ambient, Pervasive, Personalized Learning Ecosystem (APPLE) that organizes Smart Learning and the IoT through the lens of Bloom's Four Agents of Change, in order to achieve a truly learner-centered framework founded on research-based best practices in teaching and learning (see Fig. 2). In this framework, people, processes, data, and things are networked in context from the learner outward. The learner, at the center of the framework, interacts with formalized learning materials presented through a variety of technology types (e.g., smartphones, tablets, computers, laptops, eReaders, etc.). These devices, along with the educational materials they supply, collect user data and provide information to the learner's educators. This information consists of meaningfully interpreted data, along with recommendations and suggestions for avenues of support, which may include additional scaffolding and/or remediation, or it may include extension, enrichment, or acceleration.

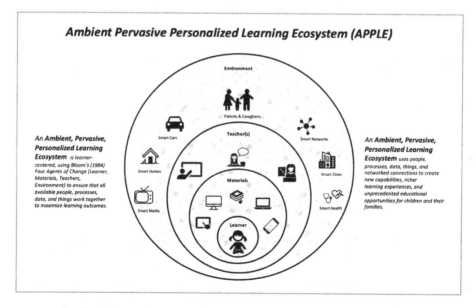

Fig. 2. APPLE: The Ambient Pervasive Personalized Learning Ecosystem

Beyond the formal learning sphere, the APPLE framework seeks to examine all the ways that the IoT present in the learner's environment can contribute to a more comprehensive and personalized learning plan. Data collected from the environment provides information about informal learning opportunities that can contribute to and further the learner's progress. For example, networked connections across the entire ecosystem allow for recommendations at the level where the child's learning can be maximized (i.e. the child's zone of proximal development; Vygotsky 1978). Video programs on media streaming services (e.g., Netflix, Amazon, YouTube, etc.) are recommended at an appropriate developmental level and on topics with which the learner has demonstrated high engagement; on Audible, books are recommended at the just-right listening comprehension level on topics known to be of high interest to the learner.

Behind the scenes, LA/EDM leverages AI algorithms to analyze and interpret data, to develop personalized predictive learning models, and direct the learning systems and materials to adapt in real-time with the learner's needs. Data collected from across a variety of formal and informal learning experiences as well as from a learner's passive consumption would be tracked and its impact on the child's learning trajectory evaluated, driving ongoing customization and adaptivity. In addition, such a comprehensive system could be used to identify, provide remediation and support for, and evaluate other learning needs, such as socio-emotional, metacognition, and executive function, etc. As an example of this, the Personalized Mastery Learning System discussed earlier is already beginning to do some of this work, through the use of data and AI algorithms that may be able to identify the need for additional executive function and fine motor coordination support in young children (Betts et al. 2020).

An APPLE approach would further allow for customization of collaborative learning. Children with similar needs could be grouped and encourage to engage in peer learning sessions. Specific content related to these groupings, or children grouped by interest or passion could be pushed through various smart devices or services (e.g., YouTube channels, etc.). The infrastructure to support these types of customized collaborative learning experiences does not yet exist, but the technology to build them does exist.

7 Challenges to Implementing APPLE

7.1 Evidence-Based Implementation

Enthusiasm remains high related to the ways in which technology might potentially transform education, and how the data created by all technology can bring about a new era of amazing personalized instruction. However, the history of technology in education suggests we need to be skeptical. The radio in the 1930's, film in the 1950's, television in the 1960's and 1970's, desktop computing in the 1980's and 1990's, mobile devices and smartboards in the 2000's, laptops and iPads in 2010's—each innovation had promised much, but never produced improved learning outcomes. For example, a 2007 congressionally mandated study by the National Center for Education Evaluation examined educational technology in 33 school districts and found no evidence that tech-enabled classrooms have helped boost student achievement (US Department of Education 2008).

In 2010's, the country of Peru, as part of the One Laptop per Child Initiative, spent $200 million to distribute laptops to 800,000 students, and found no evidence of improved learning (Horn 2012). Los Angeles Unified School District in California, one of the largest school districts in the US, spent more than one billion dollars to buy 650,000 iPads – one for every student in the district (Newcombe 2015). Program planners failed to consider critical infrastructure changes that might need to be implemented (e.g., not all schools had reliable internet connectivity making it difficult to access online curricula through the iPads), or how teachers might be sufficiently trained to effectively use these technologies (Newcombe 2015). The failure of the program resulted in ongoing lawsuits filed by the district against tablet curriculum providers and ultimately the resignation of the superintendent.

And here we are in 2020, embracing AI and IoT for Ambient, Pervasive, Personalized Learning Ecosystems (APPLE). What makes this time different? A key difference, if we choose to put it to work, is the availability of evidence-based principles from the learning sciences, and an increasingly robust learning engineering approach to apply those evidence-based principles and ideas, together with learner-center research methodologies and appropriate uses of data to drive iterative improvements in real-world settings (Saxberg 2017; ICICLE 2019). Doing this at scale is not at all trivial – requiring hundreds if not thousands of people to alter their thinking and practices around learning, making this a major change project on top of the new engineering challenges that evidence-based work creates. We must also consider carefully the interactions between (1) technology and teachers (how teachers are prepared, supported, and evaluated), (2) blending school and home (how the time a child learns in comfortable, personalized settings can be expanded), and (3) data and competency (how we collect and actually leverage data to systematically track mastery, give feedback, and inform the learning process) (Hess and Saxberg 2014). The good news is, there is a body of evidence available to tap. *Systematically* and *thoughtfully* taking advantage of that knowledge seems to be the key to making it work (e.g., Koedinger et al. 1997; Sottilare et al. 2013; Heffernan and Heffernan 2014; Saxberg 2017; The Learning Agency 2019; Hess and Saxberg 2014).

7.2 Interoperability

With the large amount of learning interaction that can take place in a Smart Learning network, existing industry standards are unable to support the interoperability of the information exchange within and among IoT components and systems, across different informal and formal, physical and virtual settings (Johnson et al. 2017; Thai and Tong 2019). Smart Learning in IoT has the potential to improve learning effectiveness across settings and devices, which involves a move from self-contained software to distributed AI-enabled cloud base systems. For example, the interoperability required to allow for a formal learning program like Mastering Reading to inform and leverage data from more informal learning opportunities such as listening to or reading an appropriately leveled book on Audible or Kindle (and vice versa) requires substantial infrastructure changes to networks, devices, and digital content, data collection, and data sharing protocols - more than exists at the present.

IoT includes all manner of objects and items made "smart," but until virtual infrastructures for data collection, aggregation, sharing, and analysis are built that extend across all of the "smart" things in our world, we will be unable to provide the unprecedented educational opportunities that such data might empower. This kind of holistic transformation of our smart systems requires transparency containing the operation, features, functionality, and use of AI in these systems for the benefit of the users (be it learners, parents, teachers, administrators, etc.). It also requires an exchange of data and semantic interoperability within and across learning and enterprise systems. In other words, machines must not only agree on what data look like, but also what they mean in a larger ecosystem. Such needs are driving recent efforts by the IEEE Learning Technology Standards Committee to provide standardized component definitions of systems and to establish a framework for the development of data interoperability standards (IEEE P2247.2).

7.3   Ethical Considerations

Smart Learning in the IoT raises an indeterminate number of self-evidenced but unanswered ethical questions. The first is about the data. As with mainstream AI, concerns exist about the large amount of data collected to support Smart Leaning, even when data are collected with the best of intentions (i.e., recording of student competencies, emotions, strategies, misconceptions, screen usage, etc. to better help learners learn). Who owns the data? Who can access them? What are the privacy concerns? How should data be analyzed, interpreted, shared? Who should be considered responsible if something goes wrong? As with healthcare, the use of personal data in education requires careful attention.

Another major ethical concern is the potential for bias, conscious or unconscious, that are incorporated into AI algorithms and models in working with large sets of data. Each decision that goes into constructing these algorithms and models might negatively affect the rights of individual students. For example, what happens if a child is unknowingly subjected to a biased set of algorithms (i.e., on the basis of gender, race, age, socio-economic status, income inequality, and so on) that impact negatively and incorrectly on their school progress?

These ethical concerns regarding data and bias are subject of many mainstream discussions, but other issues are possible, including those that are yet to be identified. For example, how does the transient nature of student goals, interests, and emotions impact the ethics of Smart Learning in the IoT? What are ethical obligations of private organizations (i.e., EdTech developers) and public authorities (i.e., schools involved in Smart Learning research?)? How might schools, students, teachers opt out from, or challenge, how they are represented in large datasets? Etc.

Strategies are needed to ameliorate risks of hacking and manipulation. Where Smart Learning interventions target learning, the entire sequence of pedagogical activity also needs to be ethically warranted. It is also important to consider the ethical cost of inaction and failure to innovate against the potential for innovation to result in real benefits for learners, educators, and educational institutions. Ethics of Smart Learning in IoT is complicated, but the potential benefits are paramount. We must all engage in productive dialogue to help ensure that the use of AI and the IoT for Smart Learning reaches its potential and has positive outcomes for all.

8 Conclusion: Summary and New Directions

In light of the stagnation in children's academic achievement as indicated on national and international assessments, combined with increases in learner variability that drive the need for more personalization, it is more critical than ever that we examine and explore the unique opportunities that advancements in technology might make possible in education. The field of Smart Learning and the IoT have advanced to the point where learning environments such as Age of Learning's Personalized Mastery Learning System and those implementing GIFT can *begin* to deliver on the promise of ambient and pervasive personalized learning. However, there is still a great deal of development needed before an ecosystem like APPLE, described in this paper, can come to fruition. Further advances are yet needed in standardizing component and system definitions in this ecosystem, and in the development of interoperability standards and the infrastructures to enable data exchange. In addition, specific challenges unique to the education sector, such as overcoming educator reluctance to implement technology solutions through proper training and implementation plans, as well as strategic plans for how the privacy of children's data will be handled, will need to be addressed.

As our population of diverse learners become ever more connected through personalized "smart" devices, it makes little sense to continue with an educational model based on a century old context. It also makes little sense to ignore the wealth of data that our learners are generating both in formal and informal learning environments, that might be put to use for their educational benefit. As education researchers and stakeholders, we have a role to play in helping to understand, define the scope of, and push the furtherance of the field. The field of Smart Learning, especially as it relates to efficacy and achievement gains is understudied and requires more attention. Our hope is that by establishing the APPLE framework rooted in learning engineering, we have provided a means for others to evaluate and insist on the development of more rigorous Smart Learning systems that utilize the IoT to produce learning outcomes at scale.

References

Asbell-Clarke, J., Rowe, E., Sylvan, E.: Assessment design for emergent game-based learning. In: MacKay, W.E., Brewster, S., Bodker, S. (eds.) Extended Abstracts on Human Factors in Computing Systems, CHI 2013, pp. 679–684 (2013)

Bakarat, S.: Education and the internet of everything. Int. Bus. Manag. **10**(18), 4301–4303 (2016)

Baker, R.S., Siemens, G.: Educational data mining and learning analytics. In: Sawyer, K. (ed.) Cambridge Handbook of the Learning Sciences, 2nd edn, pp. 253–274. Cambridge University Press, New York (2014)

Baker, R.S., Yacef, K.: The state of educational data mining in 2009: a review and future visions. J. Educ. Data Min. **1**(1), 3–17 (2009)

Bakker, D., Kazantzis, N., Rickwood, D., Rickard, N.: Mental health smartphone apps: review and evidence-based recommendations for future developments. JMIR Ment. Health **3**(1), 1–31 (2016)

Betts, A.: Mastery learning in early childhood mathematics through adaptive technologies. In: IAFOR (ed.) The IAFOR International Conference on Education – Hawaii 2019 Official Conference Proceedings. Paper Presented at the IAFOR International Conference on Education: Independence and Interdependence, Hawaii, pp. 51–63. The International Academic Forum, Japan (2019)

Betts, A., Thai, K.P., Jacobs, D., Li, L.: Math readiness: early identification of preschool children least ready to benefit from formal math instruction in school. In: IAFOR (ed.) The IAFOR International Conference on Education – Hawaii 2020 Official Conference Proceedings. Paper Presented at the IAFOR International Conference on Education, Hawaii, USA. The International Academic Forum, Japan (2020)

Bloom, B.: The 2-sigma problem: The search for methods of group instruction as effective as one-to-one tutoring. Educ. Res. **13**(6), 4–16 (1984)

Boulanger, D., Seanosky, J., Kumar, V., Kinshuk, Panneerselvam, K., Somasundaram, T.S.: Smart learning analytics. In: Chen, G., Kumar, V., Kinshuk, H.R., Kong, S. (eds.) Emerging Issues in Smart Learning. LNET, pp. 289–296. Springer, Heidelberg (2015). https://doi.org/10.1007/978-3-662-44188-6_39

Cavill, S.: The growing wearables market offers opportunities to engage consumers. Digital Marketing News, 9 July 2019. https://insights.digitalmediasolutions.com/articles/wearables-digital-marketing

de Brey, C., et al.: Status and trends in the education of racial and ethnic groups 2018 (NCES 2019-038). U.S. Department of Education. National Center for Education Statistics, Washington, DC (2019)

De Mauro, A., Greco, M., Grimaldi, M.: A formal definition of Big Data based on its essential features. Libr. Rev. **65**(3), 122–135 (2016)

DiCerbo, K.E., et al.: An application of exploratory data analysis in the development of game-based assessments. In: Loh, C.S., Sheng, Y., Ifenthaler, D. (eds.) Serious Games Analytics. AGL, pp. 319–342. Springer, Cham (2015). https://doi.org/10.1007/978-3-319-05834-4_14

Dohring, D., et al.: Personalized mastery learning platforms, systems, media, and methods: US Patent 10 490 092B2 (2017). https://patents.google.com/patent/US10490092B2/en

Dron, J.: Smart learning environments, and not so smart learning environments: a systems view. Smart Learn. Environ. **5**(25), 1–20 (2017)

Evans, D.: The Internet of Everything: How more relevant and valuable connections will change the world. Cisco (2012). https://www.cisco.com/c/dam/global/en_my/assets/ciscoinnovate/pdfs/IoE.pdf

Forbes Insights: The path to personalization. Forbes, 1 May 2019. https://www.forbes.com/sites/insights-treasuredata/2019/05/01/the-path-to-personalization/#609f9ada7a76

Gabbai, A.: Kevin Ashton describes "the Internet of Things": Innovator weighs in on what human life will be like a century from now. Smithsonian.com (2015). https://www.smithsonianmag.com/innovation/kevin-ashton-describes-the-internet-of-things-180953749/

Grace, L.D.: A linguistic analysis of mobile games: verbs and nouns for content estimation. In: Proceedings of the 9th International Conference on the Foundations of Digital Games, p. 8. FDG (2014)

Geiger, A.W.: 6 Facts about America's students. Pew Research Center, 7 September 2018. https://www.pewresearch.org/fact-tank/2018/09/07/6-facts-about-americas-students/

Ginsburg, H.: My entirely plausible fantasy: early mathematics education in the age of the touchscreen computer. J. Math. Educ. Teach. Coll. **5**(1), 9–17 (2014)

Gul, S., Asif, M., Ahmad, S., Yasir, M., Majid, M., Malik, M.S.A.: A survey on tole of internet of things in education. Int. J. Comput. Sci. Netw. Secur. **17**(5), 159–165 (2017)

Hao, J., Smith, L., Mislevy, R., von Davier, A., Bauer, M.: Taming log files from game/ simulation-based assessments: data models and data analysis tools, pp. 1–17. Educational Testing Service, Princeton (2016)

Heffernan, N.T., Heffernan, C.L.: The ASSISTments ecosystem: building a platform that brings scientists and teachers together for minimally invasive research on human learning and teaching. Int. J. Artif. Intell. Educ. **24**(4), 470–497 (2014)

Hoel, T., Mason, J.: Standards for smart education – towards a development framework. Smart Learn. Environ. **5**(3), 1–25 (2018)

Hess, F., Saxberg, B.: Breakthrough Leadership in the Digital Age. SAGE Publications, New York (2014)

Hwang, G.J.: Definition, framework, and research issues of smart learning environments: a context-aware ubiquitous learning perspective. Smart Learn. Environ. **1**(1), 1–14 (2014)

Horn, M.: No shock as Peru's one-to-one laptops miss mark. Forbes (2012). http://forbes.com

IEEE P2247.2 Interoperability Standards for Adaptive Instructional Systems (AISs). https:// standards.ieee.org/project/2247_2.html

IEEE Industry Connection Industry Consortium on Learning Engineering (ICICLE), December 2019. https://www.ieeeicicle.org

Johnson, A., Nye, B.D., Zapata-Rivera, D., Hu, X.: Enabling intelligent tutoring system tracking with the experience application programming interface (xAPI). Des. Recomm. Intell. Tutoring Syst. 41 (2017)

Kai, S., et al.: A comparison of video-based and interaction-based affect detectors in physics playground. In: Santos, O.C., et al. (eds.) Proceedings of the 8th International Conference on Educational Data Mining, pp. 77–84 (2015). http://www.educationaldatamining.org/ EDM2015/pro-ceedings/edm2015_proceedings.pdf

Ke, F., Shute, V., Clark, K.M., Erlebacher, G.: Designing dynamic support for game-based learning. In: Ke, F., Shute, V., Clark, K.M., Erlebacher, G. (eds.) Interdisciplinary Design of Game-based Learning Platforms. AGL, pp. 119–140. Springer, Cham (2019). https://doi.org/ 10.1007/978-3-030-04339-1_6

Kinshuk, Chen, N.-S., Cheng, I.-L., Chew, S.W.: Evolution is not enough: revolutionizing current learning environments to smart learning environments. Int. J. Artif. Intell. Educ. Soc. **26**, 561–581 (2016)

Koedinger, K.R., Anderson, J.R., Hadley, W.H., Mark, M.A.: Intelligent tutoring goes to school in the big city. Int. J. Artif. Intell. Educ. (IJAIED) **8**, 30–43 (1997)

Koedinger, K.R., Baker, R., Cunningham, K., Skogsholm, A., Leber, B., Stamper, J.: A data repository for the EDM community: the PSLC DataShop. In: Romero, C., Ventura, S., Pechenizkiy, M., Baker, R.S.J.d. (eds.) Handbook of Educational Data Mining, pp. 43–56 (2010)

Koedinger, K.R., Corbett, A.T., Perfetti, C.: The Knowledge-Learning-Instruction framework: bridging the science-practice chasm to enhance robust student learning. Cogn. Sci. **36**(5), 757–798 (2012)

Lin, Y., Tudor-Sfetea, C., Siddiqui, S., Sherwani, Y., Ahmed, M., Eisingerich, A.: Effective behavioral changes through a digital mHealth app: exploring the impact of hedonic well-being, psychological empowerment and inspiration. J. Mhealth Uhealth **6**(6), 1–13 (2018)

Lindstrom, M.: Small Data: The Tiny Clues that Uncover Huge Trends. St. Martin's Press (2016)

Mislevy, R.J., Almond, R.G., Lukas, J.F.: A brief introduction to evidence-centered design. Research Report-Educational Testing Service Princeton RR, 16 (2003). http://marces.org/ EDMS623/Mislevy%20on%20ECD.pdf

National Center for Educational Statistics (NCES): List of current digest tables (2019). https://nces.ed.gov/programs/digest/current_tables.asp

Newcombe, T.: A cautionary tale for any government IT project: L.A.'s failed iPad program. Governing: The Future of States and Localities, 13 May 2015. https://www.governing.com/columns/tech-talk/gov-tablets-los-angeles-ipad-apple-schools.html

Owen, V.E.: Learning science in data-driven adaptive design for young children (in press)

Owen, V.E., Baker, R.S.: Learning analytics for games. In: Plass, J.L., Meyer, R., Homer, B.D. (eds.) Handbook of Game-Based Learning. MIT Press, Cambridge (2019)

Owen, V.E., Hughes, D.: Bridging two worlds: principled game-based assessment in industry for playful learning at scale. In: Ifenthaler, D., Kim, Y.J. (eds.) Game-Based Assessment Revisited. AGL, pp. 229–256. Springer, Cham (2019). https://doi.org/10.1007/978-3-030-15569-8_12

Owen, V.E., et al.: Detecting productive persistence in an adaptive game-based learning system. Presented at the 12th International Conference on Educational Data Mining, Montreal, Canada, July 2019

Pape, B.: Learning variability is the rule, not the exception. Digital Promise (2018). https://digitalpromise.org/wp-content/uploads/2018/06/Learner-Variability-Is-The-Rule.pdf

Roberts-Mahoney, H., Means, A.J., Garrison, M.: Netflixing human capital development: personalized learning technology and the corporatization of K-12 education. J. Educ. Policy 31(4), 405–420 (2016)

Rodrigo, M.M.T., Baker, R.S.: Comparing learners' affect while using an intelligent tutor and an educational game. Res. Pract. Technol. Enhan. Learn. 6(1), 43–66 (2011)

Rodrigues, J., et al.: Enabling technologies for the internet of health things. IEEE Access Open Access J. 6, 13129–13141 (2018)

Rose, T.: The End of Average: How to Succeed in a World that Values Sameness. HarperOne, San Francisco (2016)

Saxberg, B.: Learning engineering: the art of applying learning science at scale. In: Proceedings of the Fourth ACM Conference on Learning @ Scale (L@S 2017), p. 1. Association for Computing Machinery, New York (2017). https://doi.org/10.1145/3051457.3054019

Slater, S., Bowers, A.J., Kai, S., Shute, V.J.: A typology of players in the game physics playground. Presented at the Digital Games Research Association (DiGRA), Melbourne, Australia, July 2017

Sottilare, R., Brawner, K., Goldberg, B., Holden, H.: The Generalized Intelligent Framework for Tutoring (GIFT) (2012). https://doi.org/10.13140/2.1.1629.6003

Sottilare, R., Ragusa, C., Hoffman, M., Goldberg, B.: Characterizing an adaptive tutoring learning effect chain for individual and team tutoring. In: Proceedings of the Interservice/Industry Training Simulation & Education Conference, Orlando, Florida (2013)

Spector, J.M.: Conceptualizing the emerging field of smart learning environments. Smart Learn. Environ. 1(1), 1–10 (2014)

Stephenson, S., Baker, R.S., Corrigan, S.: Towards building an automated detector of engaged and disengaged behavior in game-based assessments. Presented at the 10th Annual Games +Learning+Society Conference, Madison, WI (2014). http://radix.www.upenn.edu/learninganalytics/ryanbaker/GLS_Stephenson_v2.pdf

Technavio: Global wearable electronics market 2019–2023 (2019). https://www.technavio.com/report/global-wearable-electronics-market-industry-analysis?utm_source=pressrelease&utm_medium=bw&utm_campaign=t9_wk20&utm_content=IRTNTR31204

Thai, K.P., Li, L., Schachner, A.: Accelerating early math learning with a digital math resource: a cluster randomized controlled trial. Presented at the 2019 AERA Annual Meeting, Toronto, Canada (2019)

Thai, K.P., Tong, R.: Interoperability standards for adaptive instructional systems: vertical and horizontal integrations. In: Sottilare, R.A., Schwarz, J. (eds.) HCII 2019. LNCS, vol. 11597, pp. 251–260. Springer, Cham (2019). https://doi.org/10.1007/978-3-030-22341-0_21

The Learning Agency: Learning Engineer: It's a Game Changer (2019). https://www.the-learning-agency.com/insights/a-game-changer-lets-talk-about-learning-engineering

Dynarski, et al.: U.S. Department of Education: Effectiveness of reading and mathematics software products: Findings from the first student cohort. Washington, DC: Institute of Education Sciences, National Center for Education Evaluation and Regional Assistance (2008). http://ies.ed.gov/ncee/pubs/20074005/index.asp

Vygotsky, L.S.: Mind in Society: The Development of Higher Psychological Processes. Harvard University Press, Cambridge (1978)

Zhu, Z.-T., Yu, M.-H., Riezebos, P.: A research framework of smart education. Smart Learn. Environ. 3(4), 1–17 (2016)

Bridging Conceptual Models and Architectural Interchange for Adaptive Instructional Systems

Keith Brawner[(✉)]

Army Futures Command, Combat Capability Development
Command – Soldier Center, Orlando, FL, USA
keith.w.brawner.civ@mail.mil

Abstract. This paper serves to connect the papers between the AIS conceptual modeling group and the architectural interchange group by deriving requirements for the required components and the information that they need to exchange. It serves as an update to the original work on the subject, prior to the establishment of the conceptual modeling subgroup.

Keywords: Standards · Adaptive Instructional Systems · Competencies · Recommender systems · Interchangeable components

1 Introduction and Background

The Adaptive Instructional Systems core group divides up into three subgroups – the groups of conceptual modeling, interoperability, and evaluation. These groups are listed in order of the developmental order – defining the space, defining the parts, and evaluating the compliance and utility. The conceptual group has recently published a draft document standard for classification of adaptive instructional systems. The next steps for such a document, as it gels into standards documents, are to evaluate the component parts for the establishment of interoperability components. This paper performs this function.

The first major division that the AIS conceptual modeling paper makes is the division between the components of (1) the individual learner model, (2) adaptation model, (3), domain model, and (4) interface model. These divisions roughly align to the model put forth by Sottilare and Brawner (Sottilare and Brawner 2018), and (Sottilare et al. 2018), but also align to the Design Recommendations for Adaptive Instructional Systems book series (Sottilare et al. 2013; Sottilare et al. 2014; Sottilare et al. 2015; Sottilare et al. 2016), to the AutoTutor models (student expectation model, feedback model, content model, and tutor interface), the Yixue model (learner profile, adaptive engine, learning/content map, interface), and others. The author commends the conceptual modeling group for coming to a conclusion which encompasses many, if not all, of the existing systems; this eases the process of determining interchange and later evaluation.

These divisions then define what is contained within each of these models. A learner model shall have a structured representation of the learner's knowledge,

R. A. Sottilare and J. Schwarz (Eds.): HCII 2020, LNCS 12214, pp. 34–44, 2020.
https://doi.org/10.1007/978-3-030-50788-6_3

abilities, difficulties, etc. constructed of both raw and processed data. An adaptation model receives information from the learner and domain models to select/generate adaptions or recommendations, and may be performance-based (gating, looping), model-based (dynamic), or intelligent-based (self-improving), with various levels of adaptivity assigned to the various areas. A domain model contains the knowledge of what to teach (skills, knowledge), and the information about how to teach it (knowledge map, strategies/tactics). The interface model defines what is interchanged in between the student and the other system components, which is a relatively broad category intended to encompass both reading e-textbooks and flying hours in a physiologically monitored flight simulator.

This conceptual model of an adaptive instructional system defines where the interactivity points are defined – at the levels of [student->interface], [interface->domain], [domain->learner], [learner->adaptation], and [adaptation->domain‖interface]. Further, the draft document produced by the conceptual modeling group assists in defining the area where data about the various items should be stored and accessed. As an example, a pass/fail grading for a student should be part of a learner model. A record of instructional actions taken across a population of students is a requisite component for an adaptivity model. A game-based environment, regardless of its complexity, is an interface to the rest of the adaptive instructional system.

As the IEEE group continues to work to develop standards – this division into finite components by conceptual modeling is important, as it defines the boundaries of the respective systems. As an example, SquirrelAI Engine Ontology Layer has multiple components – a Content Map, Learning Map, Mistake Ontology, and Learning Goals. Under the definition put forth in the Conceptual Modeling subcommittee – these are all a domain model. A domain model of a competing product in the same domain may or may not have these components, as well as either a larger or smaller number of components, such as the addition of a Feedback Generation model, or the removal of the Mistake Ontology.

The IEEE AIS subgroup on interoperability, however, is charged with dealing with the *exchange* of information between the components defined in the conceptual modeling group. As such, there isn't, and more importantly, shouldn't, be a standard for the interchange of information between a Learning Map and a Content Map in the Squirrel AI system. In the Generalized Intelligent Framework for Tutoring (GIFT) system, there shouldn't be a standard for the interchange of information between the Assessment Model and the Domain Knowledge Map. In the AutoTutor system, there shouldn't be a standard for defining the difference between the expected student dialogue and entered student dialogue. These types of distinctions are left to the individual systems. Simultaneously, there should be a way to communicate the Squirrel AI progress on learning objectives, GIFT progress on learning objectives, and AutoTutor progress on learning objectives, as these parts of information are needed by the learner model portion of each of the systems – or the system is not compliant with the written standard as defined later by the evaluation AIS subgroup.

2   Overall Model

The AIS conceptual group, as part of P2247.1 Draft Version 19, has defined the following system components as follows:

- Individual Learner Model (IEEE-ILM)– states and traits that describe the critical attitudes, behaviors and cognition of an individual and serve as a basis for adaptation decisions by the AIS
- Adaptive Model (IEEE-AM) – logic that assesses the states and traits of the learner/team and the knowledge from the domain model in order to select content, generate feedback or generate recommendations tailored to that learner; the adaptive model combines features from the instructional model and the recommender to make instructional decisions
- Domain Model (IEEE-DM) – includes the knowledge model, learning objectives, content, feedback, question banks, and other information relevant to the subject or topical area.
- Interface Model (IEEE-IM) – technology (tools or methods) that support learner/team interaction with the other AIS functions

The above definitions are placed alongside a diagram which shows the Learner (learner states/traits) and Domain Model (learning objectives, knowledge) feeding information to the Adaptive Model (instructional decisions), and the Adaptive Model feeding information to the Interface Model (visual presentation, speech). The IEEE-ILM and IEEE-DM connect to the IEEE-AM which connects to the IEEE-IM. The below section considers the implications of this distinction between the Generalized Intelligent Framework for Tutoring (GIFT), AutoTutor (AT), Squirrel AI (SAI), Watson Tutor (WT), Traditional Model Tracing Tutor (TMT), and Adding a Tutorial Model (ATM) tutoring systems as examples of interchangeable systems, dialogue systems, model tracing systems, cognitive-based systems, service-API driven systems, and service collections. This maps to the following example systems in the following manners:

- Generalized Intelligent Framework for Tutoring (GIFT) has the following major components:
  - Domain Module (GIFT-DM), Learner Module (GIFT-LM), Sensor Module (GIFT-SM), Pedagogical Module (GIFT-PM), and Gateway Module (GIFT-GM).
  - These map approximately as follows:
    IEEE-ILM = GIFT-SM + GIFT-LM
    IEEE-AM = GIFT-PM
    IEEE-DM = GIFT-DM
    IEEE-IM = GIFT-GM
- AutoTutor has the following major components (Cai et al. 2019)
  - Conversation Module (AutoTutor-CM), Tutoring Interface (AT-TI), and Conversation Engine (CE). The Conversation Module is composed of a Main Question (CM-MQ), Ideal Answer (CM-IA), Expectations (CM-E), Misconceptions (CM-M), Hints (CM0H), and Agent Assignments (CM-AA)

- These map approximately as follows:

    IEEE-ILM = AT-CM

    - AT-CM assessment against IEEE-CM below

    IEEE-AM = AT-CE

    IEEE-DM = AT-CM

    - IEEE-DM = AT-CM (MQ, IA, E, M, H)

    IEEE-IM = AT-TI

- Squirrel AI Learning Engine has the following major components: Mistake Reasoning Ontology (SAI-MRO), Learning Map (SAI-LM), Content Map (SAI-CM), Goal Engine (SAI-GI), LRS (SAI-LRS), Profile (SAI-P), Recommendation Engine (SAI-RE), User State Evaluation Engine (SAI-USE), Diagnostic Engine (SAI-D), an outside system interface (SAI-I), and Realtime Classifier and Predictor (SAI-RCP) which has multiple subcomponents.
  - These map approximately as follows:

    IEEE-ILM = SAI-LM + SAI-GI + SAI-LRS + SAI-P + SAI-USE

    IEEE-AM = SAI-RE + SAI-D + SAI-RCP

    IEEE-DM = SAI-CM

    IEEE-IM = SAI-I

- Watson Tutor (WT) from IBM has the following major components, implemented as separate API services (Mukhi et al. 2017):
  - Tutor User Interface (WT-TUI), Next Best Action (WT-NBA), Response Analyzer (WT-RA), Hint Generator (WT-HG), Leaner Model (WT-LM), Feedback (WT-F), Question Recommender (WT-QR), and Conversation Engine (WT-CE)
  - These map approximately as follows:

    IEEE-ILM = WT-RA + WT-LM

    IEEE-AM = WT-NGA + WT-QR + WT-HG + WT-F

    IEEE-DM = WT-CE

    IEEE-IM = WT-TUI

- Traditional Model Tracing Architecture, as presented elsewhere (Heffernan et al. 2008) has the following major components:
  - Student Model (TMT-SM), Diagnosis (TMT-D), Feedback (TMT-F; buggy messages or hints), and a Tutor Response (TMT-TR) module where the student can place input.
  - These map approximately as follows:

    IEEE-ILM = TMT-SM + TMT-D

    IEEE-AM = TMT-F

    IEEE-DM = TMT-D

    - note – TMT-D contains both the content and the diagnosis of the student

    IEEE-IM = TMT-TR

- The Adding a Tutorial Model (ATM) Architecture grows the baseline TMT architecture to include more advanced components. The full list of the components is a Student Model (ATM-SM), a Tutorial Module (ATM-TM), and a Tutor Response (ATM-TR) module where the student can place input. The ATM-TM encompasses the TMT-D (ATM-D) as well as modules on Selection (ATM-S), Feedback (ATM-F), Reasoning (TMT-R), and Strategies (ATM-Strat)

– These map approximately as follows:

IEEE-ILM = ATM-SM + ATM-D

IEEE-AM = ATM-T = ATM-S + ATM-F + ATM-R + ATM-Strat

IEEE-DM = ATM-D

• note – ATM-D contains both the content and the diagnosis of the student

IEEE-IM = ATM-TR

Somewhat fundamentally, the author could continue to list systems and the mapping of systems against the conceptual model assembled in draft by the Adaptive Instructional Systems Conceptual Modeling group. However, the author believes that it is safe to say that the conceptual model components from the community map approximately against the models used in contemporary systems. It is relatively common for a system, based on models of dialogue (AT), cognition (TMT, ATM), architectural interchange (GIFT), service APIs (IBM), or service collections (SAI) to have the fundamental components defined in the modeling group. Among these systems there is only one point of less-than-perfect mapping – in the injection of content into architectural components.

At this point the author must declare his bias towards systems, such as GIFT and SAI, which can train many different domains without domain-specific configuration. However, there should be nothing in a standard which prohibits the creation of system-level components which are specific to the domain. Any standard should be sufficient to support both tutor-anything systems and tutor-something systems. A future vendor should be able to provide an instructional model for training a specific task, with future sales and marketing teams describing how their component was created and customized towards this task.

3   Learner Models (IEEE-ILM)

The conceptual model AIS group, at the time of writing, has written that "An adaptive instructional system (AIS) **shall** have a learner model.", and that the data within the IEEE-ILM is relatively free to vary. This data **may** include physiology, competency assertions, raw data, habits, misconceptions, learner attributes, history of actions, and many other forms of data – the conceptual model describes the learner model as an imperfect digital twin of the learner.

Conceptually – each of the GIFT, AT, SAI, WT, TMT, and ATM have a model of the learner. Many of these systems have multiple modules for input to the IEEE-ILM, such as GIFT, which has a Sensor Module and a Domain Module for the separation of physiological data (eye tracking, face movements) and domain-dependent data (performance, history).

In the IEEE-ILM, however, this information is communicated to the IEEE-AM. In GIFT, this information is communicated as a table of states, traits, and learner performance (at/above/under performance). In AT, this information is communicated as a list of misconceptions and conversational assessments - information as it relates to ideal answers. In SAI, this information is communicated as a "user state evaluation" fed from multiple sub-processes. In CT, this information is communicated as analyzed responses couple with learner model. In both TMT and ATM, this information is communicated as a student model coupled with domain assessment.

As such, the author proposes that the standard adopted contain information on:

- Learner States (unknown values possible)
- Learner Traits (unknown values possible)
- Leaner Performance on Learning Objects (unknown values possible)

Given that unknown values are possible, there is the ability for multiple systems/components to run multiple assessments and for configuration to trust certain systems more for certain items. In this way, an LRS-based Learner Trait information module can complement a physiological Learner State information module and a conversational assessment Learner Assessment module to be packaged into a single IEEE-ILM conformant with a standard. Given that the states, traits, and performance are calculated in very different manners by the differing systems, there is reason to believe that there isn't significant potential for standardization at the sub-component level, but the three values listed above and in the conceptual model align significantly to the various systems at the module level.

4   Adaptive Model (IEEE-AM)

The conceptual model AIS group, at the time of writing, has written that "An adaptive instructional system (AIS) *shall* have an adaptive model.", and that the data within the IEEE-ILM is relatively free to vary. Adaptations may include decisions about the learning experience (e.g., feedback, support, selection of different content), learner options, recommendations (e.g., next steps or future learning experiences), interaction with the current lesson, learning objectives, instructional resources, and methods of assessment (e.g., algorithms, gating, machine learning models, etc.). The draft standard expands on this by indicating that the IEEE-AM may be performance-based, model-based, multi-dimensional, learning, self-improving, or other types of implementation. What is not left to system designers is that the model must input information from the IEEE-ILM and output information to the IEEE-DM.

Conceptually, each of GIFT, AT, SAI, WT, TMT, ATM have an adaptive model. In GIFT, this consists of domain-general recommendations for scenario changes, feedback, and content presentation. In AT, this is the Tutoring Interface which presents hint/prompt/pump information. In SAI, these are recommendations, diagnostics, and groupings of students. In WT, these are generated hints, suggested next-actions, question recommendations, and feedback. In TMT, this is feedback. In AMT, this is expanded to include feedback as well as question selection, reasoning, and strategy selection.

As such, the author proposes that the standard adopted contain information on:

- Feedback (with levels)
- Next Steps (within problem/scenario)
- Next Steps (outside of problem/scenario)

Each system can find a mapping between their activities and the above actions for the system to take, while not every system performs each of these functions.

5 Domain Model (IEEE-DM)

The conceptual model AIS group, at the time of writing, has written that "An adaptive instructional system (AIS) *shall* have a domain model", and that the data within the IEEE-DM is relatively free to vary. That said, the data within the domain model is suggested to include, conceptually, the descriptions of good performance, descriptions of poor performance, content that the student should be able to know, and the maneuver space (feedback, changes) that the IEEE-AM can select from. In each of the systems, this maps in the manner described next.

GIFT has a Domain Module with a model of all of the content that can be presented within the content, assessments against the content, and feedback. AT has a description of the ideal answers, misconceptions, hints, and agent assignment. SAI has both content and classifier/predictor systems for goal management. WT has a conversational manager which has a model of content and assessment against it. Both TMT and ATM have models of tutor diagnosis and response which map roughly to the model of the domain.

As such, the authors suggest that, for the purposes of standardization, the stand should include:

- Content and delivery, provided via the tutor interface
- Assessment of Content, provided to the IEEE-ILM
- Deliverable Feedback, as requested from the IEEE-AM.

6 Interface Model (IEEE-IM)

The conceptual model AIS group, at the time of writing, has written that "An adaptive instructional system (AIS) *shall* have an interface model.". Somewhat fundamentally, however, the draft standard does not include any restrictions or requirements on the interface module. GIFT, AT, SAI, WT, TMT, and ATM all use *dramatically* different interfaces. Aside from the data which is interchanged as part as part of the IEEE-AM and the IEEE-DM, the IEEE-IM serves as an input function to the other core modules. GIFT has no standard interfaces, as it interfaces with dozens of systems, many of which are proprietary. AutoTutor operates similarly – interfacing with several base game engines. TMT/ATM systems are most frequently created through the use of the Cognitive Tutor Authoring Tools (CTAT) (Aleven et al. 2006) series of tools which creates interfaces at the same time as building systems (Tables 1, 2 and 3).

Table 1. Originally proposed module-level interoperability between systems (Brawner and Sottilare 2018)

Domain Model		
	Input	
		Requests for action (from Instructional Model)
		Feedback associated with concepts (optional field)
		A model of tasks and conditions, so as to generate Output
	Output	
		Learner Assessment (to Learner Model)
Learner Model		
	Input	
		Learner assessments for each learning objective or concept (from Domain Model)
		Sensor data (if applicable)
		Longer term data (if applicable)
	Output	
		Learner State representation (from Domain Model or derived from data)
Pedagogical Model		
	Input	
		Learning State representation (from Learner Model)
		Cognitive state of the learner (optional)
		Performance expectations (above, below, at) for each concept
		Predicted future performance based on competency model (optional)
		Physiological State representation (from Learner Model)
		Derived emotional, physical states (e.g., fatigue) (optional)
		Physiological stressors (optional)
		Behavioral State representation (from Learner Model)
		Derived attitudes or psychomotor performance based on primitive behaviors (optional)
		Longer term learner attributes (from Learner Model or LRS)
		Demographics and traits (optional)
		Historical performance (competency) (optional)
	Output (all optional)	
		Request for course direction
		Request for feedback
		Request for scenario adaption
		Request for assessment

Table 2. Changes from 2018 proposed (Brawner and Sottilare 2018) to align with conceptual modeling paper.

Domain Model
Input
Requests for action (from Instructional Model)
Feedback associated with concepts (optional field)
A model of tasks and conditions, so as to generate Output
Output
Learner Assessment (to Learner Model)
Learner Model
Input
Learner assessments for each learning objective or concept (from Domain Model)
Sensor data (if applicable) - Replaced with "Learner States"
Longer term data (if applicable) - Replaced with "Learner Traits"
Output
Learner State representation (from Domain Model or derived from data)
Pedagogical Model
Input
Learning State representation (from Learner Model)
Cognitive state of the learner (optional) - Replaced with "Learner State"
Performance expectations (above, below, at) for each concept
- Replaced with learner assessments per learning objective
Predicted future performance based on competency model (optional)
Physiological State representation (from Learner Model)
Derived emotional, physical states (e.g., fatigue) (optional) - Replaced with Learner State
Physiological stressors (optional) - Replaced with Learner State
Behavioral State representation (from Learner Model) - Replaced with Learner State
Longer term learner attributes (from Learner Model or LRS)
- Replaced with Learner Traits
Output (all optional)
Request for course direction - Replaced with 'next steps (outside)'
Request for feedback
Request for scenario adaption - Replaced with 'next steps (inside)'
Request for assessment - Removed

Table 3. Currently proposed starting place for standards among modules, bolded mandatory, non-bolded optional

IEEE-DM
  Input
    Requests for action (from Instructional Model)
    Feedback associated with concepts (optional field)
    A model of tasks and conditions, so as to generate Output
  Output
    Learner Assessment (to Learner Model)
Learner Model
  Input
    Learner assessments for each learning objective or concept (from Domain Model)
    Learner States
    Learner Traits
  Output
    Learner State representation (from Domain Model or derived from data)
Pedagogical Model
  Input
    Learning State representation (from Learner Model)
      Learner State
      Performance expectations (above, below, at) for each concept
      - Replaced with learner assessments per learning objective
      Predicted future performance based on competency model
    Physiological State representation (from Learner Model)
      Learner State
    Learner State
    Learner Traits
  Output (all optional)
    Request for feedback
    Next steps (inside of problem/scenario)
    Next steps (outside of problem/scenario)

7 Conclusions

In 2018 the author was involved in a paper trying to establish initial sets of compliance messages for module-level interoperability between systems (Brawner and Sottilare 2018). The table which was the primary output from that work is below, which reflects the thinking from 24 months ago.

Based on the information presented in the conceptual modeling paper, stripping the conceptual modeling paper of its optional fields, and stripping the above table of its optional fields, this would be updated to reflect the following tables, with changes tracked via strikeout and bold, and presented in summary. The below table in red marks the changes in the 2018 proposed standard to be updated with the current thinking of the AIS conceptual modeling group. The final table within this work proposes standards for communicating information in accordance with the conceptual modeling information presented and the information presented and mapped to various systems within this work. This work serves as a contribution to document the current thinking of the AIS groups – but also as a starting point for creating module-level standards of interchange.

References

Aleven, V., McLaren, B.M., Sewall, J., Koedinger, K.R.: The cognitive tutor authoring tools (CTAT): preliminary evaluation of efficiency gains. In: Ikeda, M., Ashley, K.D., Chan, T.-W. (eds.) ITS 2006. LNCS, vol. 4053, pp. 61–70. Springer, Heidelberg (2006). https://doi.org/10.1007/11774303_7

Brawner, K., Sottilare, R.: Proposing module-level interoperability for adaptive instructional systems. In: Artificial Intelligence in Education 2018 London, United Kingdom, p. 11 (2018)

Cai, Z., Hu, X., Graesser, A.C.: Authoring conversational intelligent tutoring systems. In: Sottilare, R.A., Schwarz, J. (eds.) HCII 2019. LNCS, vol. 11597, pp. 593–603. Springer, Cham (2019). https://doi.org/10.1007/978-3-030-22341-0_46

Heffernan, N.T., et al.: Expanding the model-tracing architecture: a 3rd generation intelligent tutor for algebra symbolization. Int. J. Artif. Intell. Educ. 18(2), 153–178 (2008)

Mukhi, N.K., et al.: Using a serverless framework for implementing a cognitive tutor: experiences and issues. In: Proceedings of the 2nd International Workshop on Serverless Computing (2017)

Sottilare, R., et al.: Exploring the opportunities and benefits of standards for adaptive instructional systems (AISs). In: Proceedings of the Adaptive Instructional Systems Workshop in the Industry Track of the 14th International Intelligent Tutoring Systems (2018)

Sottilare, R., Brawner, K.: Component interaction within the Generalized Intelligent Framework for Tutoring (GIFT) as a model for adaptive instructional system standards. In: The Adaptive Instructional System (AIS) Standards Workshop of the 14th International Conference of the Intelligent Tutoring Systems (ITS) Conference, Montreal, Quebec, Canada (2018)

Sottilare, R., et al.: Design Recommendations for Intelligent Tutoring Systems: Volume 3 - Authoring Tools and Expert Modeling Techniques (2015). www.gifttutoring.org

Sottilare, R.A., et al.: Design Recommendations for Intelligent Tutoring Systems: Volume 2 - Instructional Management. US Army Research Laboratory (2014)

Sottilare, R.A., et al.: Design Recommendations for Intelligent Tutoring Systems: Volume 1 - Learner Modeling. US Army Research Laboratory (2013)

Sottilare, R.A., et al.: Design Recommendations for Intelligent Tutoring Systems: Volume 4 - Domain Modeling. US Army Research Laboratory (2016)

Dewey's Ethics of Moral Principles and Deliberation: Extending IEEE's Ethics Initiative for Adaptive Instructional Systems

Jeanine A. DeFalco[1(✉)] and Andrew J. Hampton[2(✉)]

[1] US Army Combat Capabilities Development Command, Soldier Center, Simulation and Training Technology Center, Orlando, FL, USA
jeanine.a.defalco.ctr@mail.mil
[2] University of Memphis, Memphis, TN 38152, USA
Andrew.Hampton@memphis.edu

Abstract. This paper proposes an expansion of the classical ethical foundations as laid out by the IEEE's Global Initiative on the Ethics of Autonomous and Intelligent Systems that are of particular relevance for developers and interested parties concerned with establishing standards to inform the design and implementation of adaptive instructional systems. *Ethically Aligned Design* [1] argues for the value of integrating the following ethical traditions into either autonomous and intelligent systems public awareness campaigns or engineering or science education programs: virtue ethics, deontological ethics, utilitarian ethics, and ethics of care. Though these traditions cover a broad spectrum of important considerations, they lack specificity for adaptive instructional systems. We argue that an alternative, more manageable and particularly relevant framework should be considered: Dewey's notion of the ethics of moral principles and deliberation. Following from this framework, we also argue for the need to explore education of ethical thinking and related skills through the medium of adaptive instructional systems.

Keywords: Ethics · Artificial intelligence · Adaptive instructional systems · Dewey

> *Especially in times like the present, when industrial, political, and scientific transformations are rapidly in process, a revision of old appraisals is especially needed.*
> —John Dewey, *Ethics* (1932)

1 Introduction

1.1 An Exigent Need

Coinciding with the expansion of artificial intelligence and adaptive technology into daily life, we have seen an explosion of concern for the ethical implications surrounding research and development to ensure responsible implementation. However, most of this investigation has focused on the (admittedly valid) areas of existential threat, data privacy, and macroeconomic concerns such as job displacement. In

© Springer Nature Switzerland AG 2020
R. A. Sottilare and J. Schwarz (Eds.): HCII 2020, LNCS 12214, pp. 45–54, 2020.
https://doi.org/10.1007/978-3-030-50788-6_4

contrast, minimal effort has focused on the psychological perspective. How do these changes impact our perception of the world and how we interact with it? What price do we pay for these advancements (if such they are)? Have the developers even considered it? How does intelligent adaptivity change our assumptions and the ways in which we approach persistent challenges, such as learning and instruction? Some exploratory efforts have opened the door to broad areas of inquiry from this perspective based on particular applications and issues emanating from them [2]. Though critical to raising awareness and discussion of a substantial research gap, these case studies and thought pieces lack a unified ethical framework in the classical sense. As a result, logical conclusions drawn from bottom-up reasoning may fail to generalize to other domains or edge cases within adaptive instruction.

To address this gap, we propose an expansion of the classical ethical foundations as laid out by the IEEE's Global Initiative on the Ethics of Autonomous and Intelligent Systems that are of particular relevance for developers and interested parties concerned with establishing standards to inform the design and implementation of adaptive instructional systems. In *Ethically Aligned Design* [1], the authors note that there is value to be gained by integrating the following ethical traditions into either Autonomous and Intelligent Systems public awareness campaigns or integrated into engineering or science education programs: Virtue ethics, Deontological Ethics, Utilitarian Ethics, Ethics of Care. Though these traditions cover a broad spectrum of important considerations, they lack specificity for adaptive instructional systems. We argue that an additional, particularly relevant tradition should guide ethical standards, including recommendations for future research and instructional aims for adaptive instructional systems: Dewey's intertwining notions of the ethics of moral principles and methods of deliberation. This dual theoretical and methodological approach highlights the importance of extending learning platforms beyond mere instruments of measuring outcomes, advocating for additional considerations regarding devising conditions that aim at a broader purpose: sustaining democracy and education.

1.2 Standards

As noted by Winfield and Jirotka [3], standards represent either implicitly or explicitly a formalization of ethical principles that can be used to evaluate compliance or provide guidelines for designers on how to reduce the threat of ethical harm that could arise from innovative and novel products or services. IEEE's Global Initiative on Ethics of Autonomous and Intelligent Systems, produced from the work of 13 committees, sets forth guidance on how to embed and guide a range of AI concerns. The work encapsulates over 100 ethical issues and recommendations [3]. Specific objectives include ensuring personal data rights, promoting well-being through economic improvements, devising a legal framework for accountability, ensuring transparency and individual rights, and creating policies for education and awareness. Strategies for realizing these goals vary, but primarily rely on finding consensus principles from which developers, lawyers, or policymakers can make specific determinations. For example, the group advocates broadly inclusive well-being metrics as an objective tool for evaluation, but acknowledge that applications likely involve tradeoffs among various facets of the overarching construct. Similarly, the guidelines encourage value-based design methodologies aligned with the principle that machines serve human needs and not vice-versa.

The concerns that preoccupy the domain of AI have extended into the corporate domain. A 2018 study (sample population 305) notes that corporate AI adopters, which constitutes 72% of organizations globally, have ethics committees to review the use of AI (63%) and conduct ethics training for technologists (70%). However, their attempts to establish a governing set of ethical standards for AI systems have been oriented towards the notion of "do no harm," while explicitly seeking to develop prescriptive and technical guidelines that are transparent, secure, accountable, and oriented toward human values [4]. Their focus on prescriptive, universal guidelines presents a daunting task, viewed by some as an impossibility. Chatfield [5] argues that the impossibility arises "largely because there's no such thing as a single set of ethical principles that can be rationally justified in a way that every rational being will agree to." Acceding to this substantial difficulty without avoiding the exigent demand for ethical standards, we argue that the scope and orientation of the stated "need" is flawed as a premise.

The fundamental flaw with this premise of seeking to identify a single set of universally applied ethical principles is misguided precisely because the attempt to codify any possible ethical violation is not the answer to avoiding ethical violations. Indeed, the notion that the solution to avoiding ethical violations lay somehow in generating universal, static standards and statutes that will articulate every conceivable *do* and *don't* of ethical dilemmas is, we concede, an impossible task. It is impossible due to the infinite variety of unknown possible combinations of choices and circumstances that our future selves and future generations will devise. This impossibility does not preclude efforts to establish ethical *guidance* to stave off unintended consequences that can be harmful to individuals and society. The answer does not lay in implementing a *prescriptive* approach to devising ethical standards. Rather, as Dewey argues, the solution resides in an ongoing engagement in the establishing and constant re-evaluation of guiding ethical moral principles *and* the methods to continuously inform this guidance framework through cooperative, continual deliberation driven by discriminate intelligence [6].

2 Renewing Philosophical Traditions

2.1 Deweyan Ethical Framework for Adaptive Instructional Systems

We begin with an attempt to contextualize the argument for adoption of Dewey's ethical framework, which consists of values and methods. Dewey's philosophical foundations reside within the school of thought known as pragmatism, which he helped pioneer [7]. Among Dewey's contemporaries (and often attributed as a co-founder of pragmatism) was Supreme Court Justice Oliver Wendell Holmes Jr. The judicial philosophy he crafted from pragmatic principles provides an analogical touchstone for leveraging experience and discriminate intelligence to interpret broad principles (in his case, the Constitution of the United States) in novel circumstances.

Supreme Court Justice William J. Brennan, Jr. was among many justices strongly influenced by Holmes's approach to constitutional interpretation [8]. Brennan noted in his "Text and Teaching" symposium at Georgetown University [9], that the American

Constitution has been and continues to be for Americans "the lodestar for our aspirations" in creating a country "where the dignity and rights of all persons were equal before all authority." Yet, the Constitution is not explicit, or "crystalline" as to how to achieve and maintain these dignities and rights. Brennan notes [9], "[The Constitution's] majestic generalities and ennobling pronouncements are both luminous and obscure. This ambiguity of course calls forth interpretation, the interaction of reader and text." As a Supreme Court Justice, Brennan notes that the "burden" of his judicial career had been "to draw meaning from the text in order to resolve public controversies," [9].

Importantly, Brennan notes the social responsibility of interpreting the Constitution: "When Justices interpret the Constitution they speak for their community, not for themselves alone. The act of interpretation must be undertaken with full consciousness that it is, in a very real sense, the community's interpretation that is sought," [9]. Further, and relevant to this discussion, Brennan notes: "It is the very purpose of a Constitution—and particularly of the Bill of Rights—to declare certain values transcendent, beyond the reach of temporary political majorities," [9], and within the Constitution, there is embodied "substantive value choices; it places certain values beyond the power of any legislature."

There are two elements to highlight here: the first is that the Constitution is not an explicit set of prescriptive and technical guidelines to ensure that dignities and rights are sustained; and secondly, the Constitution's ambiguity requires the *interactive* engagement of the reader with the text. This mirrors precisely Dewey's notions of the ethics of moral principles:

> The fundamental error of the intuitionist is that he is on the outlook for rules which will of themselves tell agents just what course of action to pursue, *whereas the object of moral principles is to supply standpoints and methods which will enable the individual to make for himself an analysis of the elements of good and evil in the particular situation in which he finds himself.* No genuine moral principle prescribes a specific course of action; rules, like cooking recipes, may tell just what to do and how to do it. Moral principles, such as that of chastity, of justice or the Golden Rule, gives the agent a basis for looking at and examining a particularly question that comes up [...] A moral principle, then, is not a command to act or forbear acting in a given way: *it is a tool for analyzing a special situation*, the right or wrong being determined by the situation in its entirety, and not by the rule as such [10].

Importantly, Dewey's notion of ethics is less concerned with devising end-state goals regarding supreme ethical principles, but rather focuses his efforts on identifying a method for improving value judgments informed by moral principles [10]. It is important to note that Dewey defined moral principles outside of the constraints of institutional, religious doctrines. A moral principle is not a command, but rather it is a tool for analyzing novel situations [10]. Moral principles are standards that provide a consistent point of view to be taken in ethical deliberation. They leave room for discovery of new understandings of well-being and the future variety of circumstances that will yield even more refined solutions. Moral principles do not predetermine or prescribe precisely what will constitute the common good [10].

Further, Dewey identifies that there are common human values, e.g., belief in the value of human life, care of children, loyalty to tribal and community customs. Dewey notes that there are always opportunities to "widen and deepen the meaning of moral ideas. The attitude of *seeking* for what is good may be cultivated under any condition of race, class and state of civilization [...] The moral quality of knowledge lies not in possession but in concern with increase," and that to restrict moral knowledge and judgement to a definite realm limits our abilities to perceive unanticipated circumstances of moral significance [10]. And Dewey's answer to the methods through which we seek to continuously determine what is good, what is of value, what should define our moral principles resides in his notion of deliberation.

As a pragmatist, Dewey interest was rooted in the importance of employing reflective, discriminate intelligence to revise our judgments as a result of acting upon them—what Dewey termed deliberation. Deliberation, Dewey asserts, includes the "reflections when directed to practical matters to determination of what to do," [10]. Through deliberation, our judgments are formed to redirect actions when habits fall short—particularly in the context of solving novel problems. Essentially, Dewey's meta-ethic of value judgments derived from moral principles, and his notion of deliberation functioned as an iterative expression between thoughts and behaviors in much the same way Brennan [9] maintained we derived guidance from the Constitution to sustain our democracy.

Dewey conceptualized the primary concerns of his era in much the same way we do now—principally, the speed with which technological innovations were changing the landscape of the Western world. Indeed, there are many parallels between the concerns that shaped the philosophy and practical application of education reforms in the face of transformative emerging technologies of the early 20th century, and the concerns we face now. The primary distinction derives not from type but from scale, as the same technologies driving change have ensured global impact. Accordingly, Dewey's ethical framework of moral principles and deliberation, in addition to his overall philosophy of education, are ideally suited for the domain of the emerging field of adaptive instructional systems. Dewey is a particularly relevant figure as we grapple with the limitations and aims that should be integrated in the development and implementation of adaptive instructional systems.

While an established definition of the nature of an adaptive instructional system has yet to be codified and universally accepted, a working definition can be pulled from the ongoing efforts of the Adaptive Instructional Systems IEEE sub-working group (C/LT/AIS) P2247.1: "(adaptive instructional systems) are artificially-intelligent, computer-based systems that guide learning experiences by tailoring instruction and/or recommendations based on the goals, needs, preferences, and interests of each individual learner or team of learners in the context of domain learning objectives. Domains are topical areas of knowledge" [11].

Further, this sub-working group has adopted a working definition of "learning" limited to the field of adaptive instructional systems:

> Learning, within the context of adaptive instruction systems, is defined both within a historical domain framework as informed by John Dewey (1938) as well as by the National Academies of Sciences, Engineering, and Medicine (2018). Accordingly, we are proposing a definition of learning relevant to adaptive instructional systems hallmarked by a continuous process of reconstructing experience (Dewey 1938) that involves lasting adaptions of the learner in response to the interactive effects of external variables and individual factors [11].

Adaptive instructional systems, then, are distinguished from other AI-driven systems because of their aim to support learning. This is an important distinction because the values and ethical principles that should guide design and implementation should similarly be aligned with nature and purpose. It follows then, that if adaptive instructional systems guide learning experiences, then the guiding ethical principles should begin with whether or not the systems actually support learning. That is, does it afford a continuous process of reconstructing experience.

Digging deeper, it is worth reiterating what Dewey said about the moral nature of knowledge, activity, and education:

> What is learned and employed in an occupation having an aim and involving cooperation with others is moral knowledge, whether consciously so regarded or not for it builds up a social interest and confers the intelligence needed to make that interest effective in practice just because the studies of the curriculum represent standard factors in social life, they are organs of initiation into social values. As mere school studies, their acquisition has only a technical worth. Acquired under conditions where their social significance is realized, they feed moral interest and develop moral insight. Moreover, the qualities of mind discussed under the topic of method of learning are all of them intrinsically moral qualities. Open-mindedness single-mindedness, sincerity, breadth of outlook, thoroughness, assumption of responsibility for developing the consequence of ideas which are accepted are moral traits. [...] Discipline, culture, social efficiency, personal refinement, improvement of character are but phases of the growth of capacity nobly to share in such a balanced experience. And education is not a mere means to such a life. Education is such a life. To maintain capacity for such education is the essence of morals. For conscious life is a continual beginning afresh. [...] learning is the accompaniment of continuous activities or occupations which have a social aim and utilize the materials of typical social situations [...] All education which develops power to share effectively in social life is moral [12].

In this passage resides the guiding principle that should inform the ethical considerations of adaptive instructional system: whether the systems we devise and employ support the development of an individual's power to share effectively in social life. This is not to suggest that the traditional ethical foundations identified (i.e., Virtue, Deontological, Utilitarian, Care) identified in the IEEE work are unimportant or inapplicable, but rather Dewey's philosophy of ethics—and importantly, his views on the ethical nature of learning and knowledge—avoids the pitfalls of a merely prescriptive framework and gives us a context from which we can employ deliberation to determine whether adaptive instructional systems begin and support ethical considerations in learning. And this notion of deliberation is key to the Deweyan framework of ethics for adaptive instructional systems for it shifts the discussion from developing a prescriptive, rule-based approach toward a discussion that is rooted in developing the methods for deliberating the ethical aim and purpose of these systems.

It is the methods anticipating and reconciling ethical dilemmas—the continuous deliberation and refinement of values—that should guide the aim and purpose of AI and adaptive instructional systems: "conserving, transmitting, rectifying, and expanding the heritage of values we have received that those who come after us may receive it more solid and secure, more widely accessible and more generously shared than we have received it" [6]. In this way, as educators and policy makers, we need to focus both on developing systems by which we can execute purposeful deliberation of ethical considerations, as well as continue to address fundamental research as to the cognitive skills involved in ethical deliberation, or reasoning particularly as mediated through adaptive instructional systems.

2.2   Rigorous Deliberation and Implementation

This paper will not spend extensive time addressing the nature and scope of developing systems of ethical deliberation. However, irrespective of the ways in which we devise governing bodies, they would be well served by democratic principles that allow participants to safely engage in *parrhesia*.

The ancient Greek concept of parrhesia is defined as telling the truth as one sees it with honesty and integrity [13]. Foucault [14] argued that the qualities that constitute parrhesia are central and essential for both democratic and philosophical identities. These parrhesia qualities include engaging in dialogue, questioning, having a passion for public affairs and human equality, among many others [13]. Parrhesia requires intellectual courage and risk-taking in truth telling and pursuits of inquiry. Burch [13] argued that acts emanating from *parrhesiastic* modes of being are essentially acts of democracy and can be used to develop a coherent framework for democratic pedagogy.

Ancient Athenians eulogized parrhesia as a practice that promoted ideas of egalitarianism and a rejection of hierarchy and limitations set by superiors or history: "To say all, to speak freely was to uncover and thus to question what has been and to ignore the restraints of status," [15]. Burch [13] notes that the penultimate example of a *parrhesiastes* was Socrates: a person who dared to ask questions, expose the truth and contradictions of things, challenging assumptions and authority of the powerful, as well as identifying that which was still unknown. In essence, the speech-acts of parrhesia constitute democratic action, particularly as its original function was to expose and criticize authoritative deception [13].

In short, the parrhesia model can be used to inform the organization of ethical deliberation systems. This effort would begin with first establishing the values and qualities of parrhesia actions that promote and sustain a democratic society. Burch [13], note that these values and qualities include dialogue, questioning, initiative, a sense of equality, a concern for the common good, and passion for public affairs.

Essentially, the first task in devising an effective governing ethical body would include establishing these aforementioned elements of parrhesiastic values into protected procedural policies. In turn, these governing bodies could engage in ongoing deliberation as to whether innovations in adaptive instructional systems were aligned with a Deweyan framework of ethical principles. If learning is a social activity [12, 16], then *prima facie* there can be only limited learning if social activity is oppressively restrained, particularly if there will be retributive consequences for speaking truth to power on ethical issues. By insuring a protected governing body that can deliberate emerging ethical dilemmas driven by innovative AI technologies, we will safeguard the purpose of adaptive instructional systems: to support learning that ensures our systems develop the skills necessary for all learners to share effectively and meaningfully in social life.

3   Designing for Ethical Thinking and Reasoning

3.1   Learning to Train Ethical Thinking

Addressing the design of adaptive instructional systems to support ethical thinking and reasoning, we argue, is a topic of consideration for developing an ethical framework, falling under the umbrella of recommended practices. While there has been some work in determining the cognitive skills implicated in critical ethical thinking and reasoning, there is more work to be done as this effort relates to the adaptive instructional system domain. Arguably, ethics education and training should begin with an understanding of the relevant traits and cognitive skills implicated in ethical thinking and reasoning [17] —including moral imagination [18], problem representation and framing in decision making [19–21], interpretation, prioritization, bias identification, perspective taking, and emotional understanding [17].

An ongoing body of work seeks to unpack traits implicated in ethical thinking and behaviors [22, 23]. For example, there is evidence that personality traits—specifically low scores on the Honesty-Humility trait as measured by the HEXACO—are predictors of harmful and unethical behaviors [24] and lower learning outcomes in medical critical care education [23]. In terms of identifying relevant cognitive skills, there is evidence that creative thought and ethical thinking are closely associated, as both are characterized by uncertainty, and have multiple answers with multiple constraints [25]. In addition, there is evidence that working memory [26], cognitive interruptions [27], sense-making [25], and forecasting [28] play a role in ethical thinking—the latter two elements specifically implicated in developing mental models that allow individuals to discriminate critical causes and constraints in ethical dilemmas. However, what is missing is empirical evidence as to how adaptive instructional systems can be designed and deployed to support these relevant cognitive skills, determining if there are other skills latent in ethical decision making that are affected by mediation of adaptive instructional systems, and determining what and how individual traits can be used to inform adaptive instruction as it relates to supporting the development of ethical thinking and reasoning. While a daunting amount of work, we believe addressing these areas rises to the level of a social imperative. Not surprisingly, Dewey believed the same:

> A large part of the difference between those who are stagnant and reactionary and those who are genuinely progressive in social matters comes from the fact that the former think of morals as confined, boxed, within a round of duties and sphere of values which are fixed and final. Most of the serious moral problems of the present time are dependent for their solution upon a general realization that the contrary is the case Probably the great need of the present time is that the traditional barriers between scientific and moral knowledge be broken down so that there will be organized and consecutive endeavor to use all available scientific knowledge for humane and social ends [10].

There is also an opportunity to recommend to the adaptive instructional systems domain that designers, policy makers, and educators consider expanding their concerns from assessing only outcomes of learning, but consider how they are designing learning systems that contextualize outcomes within conditions that support the development of ethical citizens [29]. Goodlad [29] notes that when assessing the purpose of schools, there is a disconnect between teaching domain mastery of content areas and aligning these efforts to a broader purpose of education. He states:

> Most people have lofty goals for education. They talk about developing citizens, responsible workers, and good community members. But as your question implies, these ideals are very difficult to appraise, in part because we think we don't have a common set of values. The problem is that successful marks, grades, and test scores do not correlate with any of the virtues

that we set for the young. So we can measure fairly accurately whether a youngster is able to manipulate numbers, whether a youngster is able to read and write. But when it comes to civility, developing a test to be used in large quantities is a challenge. If we would move our attention away from thinking only of outcomes and think of conditions, then we could start examining whether the conditions are democratic, whether the conditions are caring, whether the conditions provide equity. I use a simple analogy: If you discover that in the population there's a great number of respiratory problems—colds, influenza—you might want to look at the conditions under which people are living. And if you provide for better conditions, you can't guarantee that people won't get sick. But you move a long way toward a healthier population.

Lastly, there is also an opportunity to recommend to the adaptive instructional systems domain that designers, policy makers, and educators consider expanding their concerns from assessing only outcomes of learning, but find ways to embed ethical considerations into instructional designs that would more explicitly link learning outcomes to real world conditions. This, we believe is a more fully realized Deweyan ethical framework that is desperately needed today.

3.2   Final Thoughts

Essentially, our effort to establish ethical framework standards that would provide some governance for adaptive instructional systems is not limited to the ethical design of these systems. Rather, it is our position that within these standards we provide recommendations to designers and educators to consider developing adaptive instructional systems that support the development of ethical thinking and reasoning, pursue fundamental research to unpack the relationship between ethical thinking and mediating effects of engaging with these systems, and consider expanding their preoccupation with simple learning outcomes to address broader ethical considerations of designing conditions that more explicitly link outcomes to promoting ethical agency.

References

1. IEEE: Ethically Aligned Design: A Vision for Prioritizing Human Well-Being with Autonomous and Intelligent Systems, 2nd edn. IEEE (2019)
2. DeFalco, J.A., Hampton, A.J.: On the frontlines of artificial intelligence ethics: machines like us?, Forthcoming
3. Winfield, A.F., Jirotka, M.: Ethical governance is essential to building trust in robotics and artificial intelligence systems. Philos. Trans. R. Soc. A: Math. Phys. Eng. Sci. **376**(2133), 20180085 (2018). https://royalsocietypublishing.org/doi/pdf/10.1098/rsta.2018.0085
4. SAS: Accenture Applied Intelligence, Intel with Forbes Insights: AI momentum, maturity, and models for success: based on findings from a global executive survey. https://www.sas.com/content/dam/SAS/documents/marketing-whitepapers-ebooks/third-party-whitepapers/en/ai-momentum-maturity-success-models-109926.pdf. Accessed 28 Jan 2020
5. Chatfield, A.: There's no such thing as 'ethical A.I'. Medium. https://onezero.medium.com/theres-no-such-thing-as-ethical-a-i-38891899261d. Accessed 27 Jan 2020
6. Dewey, J.: A Common Faith. Yale University Press, New Haven (1934/2013)
7. Menand, L.: The Metaphysical Club: A Story of Ideas in America. HighBridge Company, St. Paul (2001)

8. Schroeder, J.: The Holmes truth: toward a pragmatic, Holmes-influenced conceptualization of the nature of truth. Br. J. Am. Legal Stud. **7**(1), 169–203 (2018)

9. Brennan Jr., W.J.: The constitution of the United States: contemporary ratification. South Texas Law Rev. **27**, 433 (1985)

10. Dewey, J.: Ethics. In: Hickman, L., Alexander, T. (eds.) The Essential Dewey: Ethics, Logic, Psychology, vol. 2. Indiana University Press, Bloomington (1932/1998)

11. IEEE C/LT/AIS P2247.1: Adaptive instructional systems conceptual model. IEEE (forthcoming)

12. Dewey, J.: Democracy and Education. The Free Press, New York (1916/1966)

13. Burch, K.: Parhessia as a principle of democratic pedagogy. Philos. Stud. Educ. **40**, 71–82 (2009)

14. Foucault, M.: Fearless Speech. Semiotext (2001)

15. Saxonhouse, A.: Free Speech and Democracy in Ancient Athens. Cambridge University Press, London (2006)

16. Vygotsky, L.: Mind in Society: The Development of Higher Psychological Process. Harvard University Press, Cambridge (1978)

17. Schrier, K.: Designing and using games to teach ethics and ethical thinking. Learn. Educ. Games **1**, 141 (2014)

18. Whitaker, B.G., Godwin, L.N.: The antecedents of moral imagination in the workplace: a social cognitive theory perspective. J. Bus. Ethics **114**(1), 61–73 (2013)

19. Klugman, C., Stump, B.: The effect of ethics training upon individual choice. J. Further High. Educ. **30**(02), 181–192 (2006)

20. Lowenstein, J.: Thinking in business. In: Holyoak, K.J., Morrison, R.G. (eds.) The Oxford Handbook of Thinking and Reasoning, pp. 744–773. Oxford University Press, New York (2012)

21. Meisel, S.I., Fearon, D.S.: Choose the future wisely: supporting better ethics through critical thinking. J. Manag. Educ. **31**(1), 149–176 (2006)

22. Kavathatzopoulos, I.: Development of a cognitive skill in solving business ethics problems: the effect of instruction. J. Bus. Ethics **12**(5), 379–386 (1993)

23. DeFalco, J.A., Sinatra, A.M.: Adaptive instructional systems: the evolution of hybrid cognitive tools and tutoring systems. In: Sottilare, R.A., Schwarz, J. (eds.) HCII 2019. LNCS, vol. 11597, pp. 52–61. Springer, Cham (2019). https://doi.org/10.1007/978-3-030-22341-0_5

24. Marcus, J., Roy, J.: In search of sustainable behavior: the role of core values and personality traits. J. Bus. Ethics **158**(1), 63–79 (2019)

25. Bagdasarov, Z., Johnson, J.F., MacDougall, A.E., Steele, L.M., Connelly, S., Mumford, M.D.: Mental models and ethical decision making: the mediating role of sensemaking. J. Bus. Ethics **138**(1), 138–144 (2016)

26. Martin, A., Bagdasarov, Z., Connelly, S.: The capacity for ethical decisions: the relationship between working memory and ethical decision making. Sci. Eng. Ethics **21**(2), 271–292 (2015)

27. Stenmark, C., Riley, K., Kreitler, C.: Ethical decision-making interrupted: can cognitive tools improve decision-making following an interruption?. Ethics Behav. 1–24 (2019)

28. Stenmark, C.K., Antes, A.L., Wang, X., Caughron, J.J., Thiel, C.E., Mumford, M.D.: Strategies in forecasting outcomes in ethical decision-making: identifying and analyzing the causes of the problem. Ethics Behav. **20**(2), 110–127 (2010)

29. Tell, C.: Renewing the profession of teaching: a conversation with John Goodlad. Educ. Leadersh. **56**(8), 14–19 (1999)

Realistic and Relevant Role-Players
for Experiential Learning

Eric Domeshek[(⊠)], Sowmya Ramachandran, Randy Jensen,
and Jeremy Ludwig

Stottler Henke Associates, Inc., 1650 S. Amphlett Blvd.,
Suite 300, San Mateo, CA 94402, USA
domeshek@stottlerhenke.com

Abstract. Providing experiential training in complex tasks on an any-time anywhere basis—whether for individual or team tasks—often requires simulating interaction with non-player characters (NPCs): co-workers, superiors, subordinates, opponents, subjects, stakeholders, consultants, tutors, peers etc. Simulating all aspects of human behavior is overwhelmingly complex. Pursuing full human simulation is also needlessly costly and distracts from the task at hand, which is providing a learner with prompts and reactions supporting experiences that promote mastery of learning objectives and appropriate transfer. The question then is, *What techniques can be used to create relevantly realistic NPC agents to support desired learning outcomes?*

Rather than advance a one-size-fits-all silver bullet for instructional system NPC modeling, we advocate a flexibly configurable bag-of-tools approach. Using example systems that the authors have worked on, we discuss several different approaches to building NPCs for pedagogical effect. Choices of technologies to employ should be based on application requirements, considering issues such as: (1) content/authoring costs—both for achieving short term capability and for longer-term maintenance and scalability; (2) pedagogical approaches; and (3) relevant aspects of realism in behavior and interaction methods.

Keywords: Adaptive instructional systems · Experiential learning · Simulating non-player characters · Teammates · Opponents · Peers · Tutors

1 Simulation-Based Experiential Learning

Experience is the best teacher, and computers can be used to provide a wide range of simulated experiences. However, many skills and training approaches we might like to exercise in simulation also involve working with (or on, or against, or while supervised by) other people. It is possible to have multiple people participating in and/or supervising the same simulation, but there are good reasons why we might want to eliminate dependence on any human other than the trainee. Substituting simulated *Non-Player Characters (NPCs)* for humans can increase control of how exercises and training interventions play out. Use of NPCs can also increase the flexibility with which exercises can be delivered—allowing any volume of exercises to be mounted at any time and experienced from any location.

© Springer Nature Switzerland AG 2020
R. A. Sottilare and J. Schwarz (Eds.): HCII 2020, LNCS 12214, pp. 55–70, 2020.
https://doi.org/10.1007/978-3-030-50788-6_5

This paper discusses the use of NPCs as substitutes for live humans in simulations and their associated pedagogical interactions. In Sect. 2, we survey the range of roles that NPCs can play in experiential learning while introducing a set of sample systems used in later discussion. In Sect. 3, we use the sample systems to describe a range of technologies we have used to implement NPC behaviors supporting varied roles. In Sect. 4, we discuss the pros and cons of different NPC technologies in regard to costs (short and long term) and benefits (primarily pedagogical). Section 5 summarizes the issues discussed in the paper.

2   Non-player Character Roles

Depending on the kind of experience being created, the material to be learned, and the pedagogical approaches being used to support the learner, there can be a wide range of roles for NPCs. These include *in-scenario roles*, explicitly *pedagogical roles*, and a variety of possible middle ground *extra-scenario roles*.

In-Scenario Roles: In-scenario roles cover characters that are integral to the simulated exercise. NPCs playing in-scenario roles may be *teammates* (including *superiors* or *subordinates*); *adversaries*; *subjects* directly manipulated by actions; or *stakeholders* otherwise affected by actions. For instance, a system we built for the U.S. Navy (TAO-ITS; Stottler et al. 2007) supports exercises in which Tactical Action Officer trainees manage naval battles; this requires working with crew teammates and against active adversaries. A trainer we built for emergency room physicians (METTLE; Domeshek 2009) supports exercises in which the trainee must treat patients and coordinate with other medical staff. A Goal-Based Scenario (GBS; Schank et al. 1994) educational simulation we developed at Northwestern University to teach about the French Revolution (Invitation) included representatives of various social strata serving both as targets for persuasion and sources of information. Finally, in ongoing work for the U.S. Air Force (NSGC; Ludwig and Presnell 2019), we are developing an adversary that learns improved fighter jet piloting behavior.

Pedagogical Roles: Pedagogical roles are for characters that exist primarily to serve an instructional function and are generally outside the exercise scenario. NPCs playing pedagogical roles may be *instructors* (typically individual *tutors*), or they may be *peers*. Essentially all Intelligent Tutoring Systems (ITSs; Woolf 2010) include some form of simulated tutor to provide individually adaptive instruction. However, the focus and learner-visible behavior repertoire of such tutors can vary widely. TAO-ITS is typical of many tactical ITSs in that the tutor serves as coach and critic. In contrast, our ComMentor tactical decision tutors (Domeshek et al. 2004) engaged the student in a Socratic dialog to analyze tactical situations, highlight critical decision factors, and project plausible futures. Another system for the U.S. Navy (RASCAL; Luperfoy et al. 2004) used simulated peers to illustrate common misconceptions and provide context for explicit critique; the peers also aimed to enhance learner motivation through competition or reassurance that others also don't know everything. In other systems, peers have been used to provide a motivation for the learner to take on an instructional role, driving them to the kind of knowledge elaboration and organization that often comes only with attempts at explanation—whether self- or other-directed (e.g., Leelawong and Biswas 2008).

Extra-Scenario Roles: NPCs can serve as consultants or information sources more loosely tied to an exercise scenario. For example, we built an Advise GBS for Northwestern (Feeding Frenzy) where a set of simulated disciplinary experts offered advice on pending scenario decisions. In a similar vein, many GBS systems were paired with more general advisory sub-systems (Ask Systems; Ferguson et al. 1992). The Ask systems' automated advisors are not built to support any particular training scenario, but rather provide a wide range of domain-relevant advice.

In the following sections we will use the various systems briefly introduced here as examples.

Sec.	System	Developer	Customer	NPC Roles
3.1	Invitation	Northwestern	Arts & Sciences	Subjects and informants
3.2	Feeding Frenzy	Northwestern	Business School	Advisors
3.3	Ask Systems	Northwestern	Various	Informative conversation
3.4	ComMentor	Stottler Henke	U.S. Army	Socratic tutor
3.5	METTLE	Stottler Henke	U.S. Army	Subjects and stakeholders
3.6	TAO-ITS	Stottler Henke	U.S. Navy	Teammates, adversaries, & tutor
3.7	NSGC	Stottler Henke	U.S. Air Force	Adversaries

3   Non-player Character Technologies

Based on our experience, in this section we will describe seven different approaches to specifying the behaviors of NPCs. These approaches vary considerably in complexity and sophistication, and likewise in cost and applicability. Detailed discussion of tradeoffs is deferred to Sect. 4.

3.1   Branching/Collapsing Script Trees

Perhaps the simplest approach to controlling NPCs is to provide them with scripts that define their actions as direct responses to pre-enumerated user actions. The user and NPC take turns. On the user's turn, the system offers them a set of actions; each action, if taken, triggers a different NPC response; and those responses set up next user turn where a different set of actions is offered (with different possible NPC responses, and so on). The branching set of possible user actions and NPC responses forms a tree, where any path through such a tree, from root through branches, represents a possible sequence of interactions.

While simple, this approach can support both effective interactions and relatively straightforward authoring, so long as the trees remain shallow and/or behaviors and entire subtrees can be reused (perhaps with small variations). This approach makes a lot of sense when the NPC responses are not of the sort that can be generated, but rather require substantial production investment. For instance, in the *Invitation* system, each NPC behavior was actually a video snippet of a live actor.

One way to achieve shallow trees is to partition overall interaction into a set of disjoint episodes, each handled by a separate tree. Ideally, the path taken through one tree should not affect what happens in another tree at all. That idealized restriction can be relaxed to some extent. For instance, the path through an earlier tree might be reduced to one or more scores that have some simple effect on NPC reactions in later trees without changing the overall branching structure. Or in a learning system, if each tree is viewed as a standalone problem/exercise, assessments generated from a student path through one tree might be used to select a follow-up tree (next problem).

3.2 Conversational Association Graphs

When the primary purpose of one or more NPCs is to simulate conversations aimed at domain exploration, a theory of Conversational/Associational Categories (CACs; Schank 1977) can be used to structure NPC behaviors. A CAC theory defines a set of linkages between utterances intended to seem conversationally sensible, or—in the cases we care about—instructionally useful. For instance, a typical set of links used in instructional contexts includes four pairs: (Cleary and Bareiss 1995): **Refocusing** (General Context and Specific Details); **Comparison** (Analogies and Alternatives); **Causality** (Prior Causes and Later Results); and **Advice** (Opportunities and Warnings).

Compared to the script trees above, association-structured behaviors form a more general graph structure to be traversed during use. However, as with script trees: (1) each node in the association graph represents an NPC behavior; (2) each link represents a user action or choice; and (3) the system moves from node to node, carrying out NPC behaviors, based on user choices. Here the user choices are among follow-up questions associated with CAC links. In theory, CAC relations could be used to generate NPC behaviors off of an internal knowledge representation, rather than to choose pre-defined behaviors. However, this more complex approach has not been used in instruction.

Pre-defined CAC networks were the basis for *Ask Systems*, which (like *Invitation*) used recorded video of live humans as NPC behaviors. However, where the *Invitation* videos were used for in-scenario character NPC behaviors, the *Ask System* videos were of extra-scenario domain expert consultants providing information about relevant areas of expertise. GBS scenarios were often viewed primarily as providing context and motivation for users to explore the Ask resources.

3.3 Issue/Perspective Matrices

Another simple approach to controlling NPCs is to use a matrix structure (rather than a branching tree or a general graph). In one useful scheme, the rows represent issues or questions likely to be of concern to the user during a scenario, the columns represent several NPCs or advice perspectives, and each cell represents an NPC response to a question or issue. This scheme has been used to organize the actions of a panel of NPC experts, any of whom may have responses to a pre-enumerated set of scenario issues or user questions.

For instance, in the *Feeding Frenzy* system, the student was asked to prepare a report with recommendations for a decision about business internationalization. The system provided a panel of simulated experts on various aspects of doing business in emerging economies, e.g., politics, finance, logistics, etc. As with the previous systems, the NPC behaviors were pre-recorded videos of live humans (in this case, notable business experts recruited by the Kellogg School of Business at Northwestern University).

3.4   Socratic Argument Trees

The three approaches discussed so far all offer ways to organize pre-defined NPC behaviors so that they are easy to author, track, and select at runtime. They also each suggest pedagogical purposes for the NPC behaviors they organize—as in-scenario behavioral responses that advance the storyline, as extra-scenario domain discussion, or as issue-focused background and analysis keyed to scenario decisions.

Socratic argument trees, as discussed here, constitute a significant step up in complexity. The core structure is again a tree, but now the point of the tree is to define the behavior of a Socratic tutor NPC. Trees intended to capture arguments to be used by such a tutor require more elaborate structure and more complex interpretation rules.

First, there is the issue of controlling when to activate a tree. Each tree in Sect. 3.1 represents an episode within a scenario; episode tree activation is typically based on a higher level graph or tree structure, or perhaps just on simple user selection among available episodes. Each tree in an argument structure represents a major topic of discussion. For a Socratic tutor, choosing topics worth discussing is a significant NPC decision, and so there has to be logic to nominate and possibly prioritize topics (trees) for activation. In *ComMentor*, discussion topic activation was controlled by rule-based analysis of solutions to tactical decision game problems proposed by the student. Based on orders issued by a student, the tutor might, for instance, cue up discussion trees for topics such as *enemy intentions*, *likely enemy force locations over time*, the *pros and cons of a particular friendly force's positions or missions*, or the *possibility of friendly force fratricide*.

Next there is the issue of how to use a tree's content to support effective and naturalistic Socratic dialog. In an argument map (usually a tree structure; Van Gelder 2003), each node represents a claim—an actual or purported fact—about the scenario (or domain). In a Socratic argument tree, each node includes one or more questions the NPC tutor can ask to elicit student realization that the node's claim is, or is not, likely valid for the scenario or domain. For instance, if a tree is about *enemy intentions*, its root node might cue the question: *What do you think the enemy is trying to do?* The purpose of the question might be to get the student to understand and accept the claim that *the enemy is mounting an offensive to the east*.

Nested nodes of such argument trees are not necessarily alternate actions to be taken in response to student input, but pieces of an argument to support the parent node's claim. In the simplest case, the sub-nodes represent claims that together support the parent node. The sub-nodes of the root *enemy intentions* node might focus on establishing claims that (a) *the enemy is there in significant strength*; (b) *enemy forces are maneuvering in a way that would fit a thrust to the east*; and (c) *there is plausible motivation for the enemy to attack to the east.* In other cases, sub-nodes might capture different logical relations—e.g., disjunctions (enumerations of alternative claims), disjunctions of conjunctions (alternate conjunctive arguments), enumerations with negations (plausible but bad alternatives), and so on.

Given trees that represent arguments, the next issue is discussion control mechanisms. Discussion execution involves walking the argument tree, starting at the top. At each node, there are usually several questions available that the NPC tutor can use to elicit the node's claim from the student, typically organized to be progressively more leading. In the simplest case, if/when the student provides a response that acknowledges the claim, the tutor can close out processing of that node. Alternately, at some point(s) in the question sequence, the tutor can move down the tree to explicitly discuss the argument points that should get the student to see the validity of the parent claim. Other processing patterns are possible. For instance, enumeration nodes might seek to get the student to state a subset of reasons or examples rather than flesh out a logical argument. There may be a minimum number of sub-nodes the student must cover; there may be particular nodes treated as mandatory among that number; there may be nodes that represent bad (or "buggy") reasons or examples.

The levels of the argument tree can be thought of as inducing an argument topic stack. The tutor has to remain sensitive to the student providing input that matches a claim somewhere up or down the stack at any point. So, for instance, if the discussion has dived down into detailed argumentation supporting the claim that *the enemy is mounting an offensive to the east* and the student suddenly realizes (and states) that this is likely what's going on, the tutor can pop back up to that level of the argument. Conversely, if before even diving into that argument, the student has already observed (and stated) that *the enemy is there in significant strength*, there is no need to take the student through the nested node devoted to that claim.

Finally, there are a number of more advanced features that can usefully be incorporated into argument tree interpretation. For instance, depending on the nature of claims and student input mechanisms, it may be possible for the tutor to respond intelligently to underspecified and partially matching inputs entered by the student. For instance, if the student notes that *the enemy has reason to launch an offensive thrust*, but they do not specify *where*, the tutor might usefully seek clarification from the student to see if it can match the full claim: *there is plausible motivation for the enemy to attack to the east.*

3.5   Layered Rule Scripts

One natural way to think about a scenario with any number of NPCs is as a kind of dynamic theatrical *play*. Each NPC is following a *script* where they have a set of *lines* (or behaviors) they can enact, but the sequencing of scripted lines is not fixed. Rather, each script line is a kind of (contextualized) stimulus/response rule: the NPC will enact the behavior if they get the right stimulus in the right context. This is how we conceptualized the training scenarios in our *METTLE* system, focused on exposing doctors to rare emergency medical situations related to chemical, biological, or radiological threats.

There are several ways to think about context in such a scheme. One natural approach is to extend the play metaphor and divide the action into *scenes*; each NPC can be given a different bundle of lines available in each scene. A patient NPC in the initial scene may have different behaviors than the same patient NPC in a later scene, after their disease has progressed. Another form of context can be past behaviors or state established within a scene. For instance, a consulting physician NPC should give different responses after the student, acting as primary physician, has provided sufficient briefing on what is known about the patient. Other kinds of states are possible, including behaviors enacted by other NPCs, observed or inferred attributes (competencies) of the student, or even the simple passage of time in scenario play. Thus, behavior triggers need not be limited to immediate stimuli, but can be integrated over time.

When scenarios exist to provide training in some domain, it is common for there to be recurring NPC roles and scenes. In *METTLE*, *patient* was a commonly recurring NPC type, as was *nurse, consulting doctor*, and *hospital administrator*. One nice aspect of recurring NPC roles is that they tend to have associated recurring behaviors. For instance, any patient should be able to respond to a wide range of questions that a student doctor might ask as part of a diagnostic interview. It thus becomes possible to build up script components that are reusable across scenarios or scenes. In some cases, entire script lines (behaviors) can be reused, and, in others, line fragments might be reusable. For instance, we were able to establish a library of patient interview script lines with default (healthy) responses. Setting up any given simulated patient NPC then primarily required overriding the responses for those questions where their condition should result in non-standard answers. In addition, the NPC might need a few entirely new lines to respond to plausible follow-up questions the student might ask after unearthing the scenario's key diagnostic findings.

In *METTLE*, script lines could carry a wide range of other attributes that could be pre-authored and reused, overridden, and/or supplemented in different contexts (i.e., scenarios and/or scenes). For instance, many aspects of tutor behavior were tied directly to in-scenario NPC behaviors. This was a convenient way to tie coaching to potential student actions. A script line could carry expectations about when it would be most appropriate for the student to take its triggering action. It might also carry a set of hints suggesting the student take the triggering action when the expected conditions arise. It might further carry annotations tying appropriate performance or non-performance to curriculum objectives, providing a way to control updates to the student model. In this way, script lines in *METTLE* ended up combining scenario NPC behaviors and tutor NPC behaviors in one package.

3.6   Contextual Behaviors

When NPC behaviors require greater sensitivity to time-evolving context, we have found that a behavior rule representation based on finite state machines offers great flexibility and efficiency, while retaining comprehensibility for non-programmers. We have used Behavior Transition Networks (BTNs) for applications where contextual states may involve complex combinations of conjunctive, disjunctive, or sequential conditions as opposed to simpler enumerated or categorized conditions. Our implementation of BTNs is embedded in the open source SimBionic package (Fu and Houlette 2002) that combines the BTN behavior representation with graphical authoring tools, an efficient runtime, and integrated debugging tools.

BTNs derive from finite state machines in the sense of representing states, transitions, transition conditions, and a current state. BTNs, however, have additional capabilities. For example, software code can be associated with a transition and execute when the transition occurs. This allows BTN-driven agents to run fine-grained tests or take useful actions as needed. BTNs run very efficiently, so it is possible to have many of them running in parallel. The resulting collection of BTNs can simultaneously enact behaviors for multiple NPCs playing different roles, all watching and cueing off activity in the same simulation environment.

This kind of flexibility is particularly beneficial for training settings like tactical decision evaluation in realistic free-play simulations as it allows for triggering simulation events or behaviors while also evaluating student decisions. The best way to employ BTNs to monitor real-time tactical decision-making during mission execution is to have a large number operating in parallel where each looks at the situation and student's actions from the perspective of how they handle specific types of situations or apply specific types of principles.

For instance, in *TAO-ITS* the in-scenario NPC roles driven by BTNs provide simulated crewmember interactions for the trainee. These NPC behaviors can adapt based on both the scenario simulation state and student model instructional state—e.g., to help determine challenges to present to the trainee. For example, *TAO-ITS* teammate NPCs exhibit three levels of behavior depending on instructional and scenario state: perfect teammate behavior, errors of omission (remaining silent when an utterance should be transmitted), or errors of commission (taking incorrect actions). The latter two levels introduce conditions into the scenario that the trainee should recognize and remedy. Meanwhile, BTNs for *TAO-ITS's* pedagogical NPC (the tutor) evaluate student performance in the context of the same kinds of simulation and instructional state, augmented with the additional sensitivity to the student's observed actions and responses.

The generality of BTNs for student decision evaluation spans a continuum. In the extreme, a BTN may be designed to run in almost every scenario where the situation it is looking for might come up. At the other extreme, a BTN may be designed for exactly one scenario. BTNs will also fall between these two extremes. They may, for example, be designed for a family of similar scenarios, scenarios located in the same geographic area or country, scenarios with certain kinds of commander's instructions, or some other identifiable commonality. Generally, it is easier and quicker to develop specific BTNs for specific scenarios, but of course this effort has to be repeated often. Instructors or developers must decide when to spend more time on a BTN to make it applicable to more situations. How much more time will be required depends on the specifics of what the BTN is supposed to be evaluating and the logical complexity of that evaluation.

3.7 Learning Agents

Machine learning has been applied to many aspects of training systems development, including NPC behavior creation and refinement. This learning agents approach has received even greater attention with the recent successes of deep learning and big data. Here we briefly describe the *NSGC* example cited above, with its use of a particular kind of reinforcement learning.

The problem addressed in *NSGC* is development of adaptive adversaries for simulated air-to-air combat. The learning paradigm applied is known as *dynamic scripting*, a type of online reinforcement learning, which naturally applies to the problem of refining the behaviors of NPC adversaries. Dynamic scripting attempts to learn a subset of predefined behaviors (called actions) that allow the entity to perform well. The learned subset, chosen from the larger predefined set, is the script in dynamic scripting. In *NSGC*, the base behaviors were implemented as BTNs in SimBionic (discussed in Sect. 3.6). A special type of dynamic scripting node was introduced to indicate where dynamic scripting transition selection should be used rather than the standard SimBionic transitions (Ludwig 2008).

Overall, this approach has three potential benefits: (1) it exploits the graphical authoring tools and runtime efficiency of SimBionic; (2) it can learn rapidly from relatively little experience; and (3) it learns within a bounded space of human provided plausible behaviors. By learning a set of predefined actions that work well together, overall behavior improves but remains predictable and reasonable from an instructor's perspective. The goal is to learn behaviors for a realistic adversary, not to automatically learn the best possible fighter pilot behaviors.

4 NPC Technology Tradeoffs

The variety of NPC technologies sketched in the previous section do not cover the full gamut of approaches that have been used across the field. They do, however, serve to illustrate many of the concerns that drive decisions about which technologies to use in which situations. In our discussion, we focus on four sets of issues:

1. **Authorability:** How easy is it to arrange for appropriate NPC behaviors?
2. **Adaptivity:** To what extent (in what ways) do NPCs adapt to individual student actions and needs?
3. **IO Modalities:** What forms of input and output do different approaches best lend themselves to supporting?
4. **Pedagogical Impact:** How well can various kinds of NPCs achieve particular kinds of pedagogical effects?

4.1 Authorability

The past five decades have seen simulation-based education and training technology successfully developed and applied in many different areas. This has included proof of capability and utility for NPCs—for instance, the tutors in ITSs, and the autonomous actors in battlefield or social simulations (Lajoie and Lesgold 1989; Stottler et al. 2007;

Kim et al. 2009). Yet systems with intelligent tutors or other pedagogically useful agents have not achieved mass market penetration. A significant limiting factor has been the cost for their development.

Development costs can be conceived of as belonging to generic systems, to domain-specific applications of such a system, or to one or more scenarios developed within a domain. The system-level costs are tied directly to the complexity of conceiving, implementing, and proving the chosen agent technologies and related tools. While such costs may be high, they can generally be classified as research expenditures —often supported by governments, and plausibly amortized across a large number of applications. For instance, the costs associated with developing SimBionic were significant, but now SimBionic BTN-based agent technology is available in open source. The same is true for a wide range of Government-funded and/or university-developed technologies (e.g., GIFT: Sottilare et al. 2017; AutoTutor: Nye et al. 2014; CTAT: Aleven et al. 2009).

The costs standing in the way of widespread application of the technology, thus, are primarily those associated with building particular applications. Such costs can be lowered by using approaches and/or tools that ease creation and reuse of domain-specific content—especially if they enable that work to be done directly by domain experts or instructors, rather than by programmers or AI experts.

Some of the approaches discussed above are simpler to conceptualize and author, such as Sect. 3.1's *script trees* or Sect. 3.3's *issue/perspective matrices*. Limited structural forms (e.g., trees or matrices) ensure a clearer model of how the NPCs can behave and require fewer authoring decisions. Of course, it also limits the richness of the interaction that can be supported.

Some approaches are of intermediate complexity and authoring difficulty, such as Sect. 3.2's *conversational networks* and Sect. 3.4's *argument trees*. These more complicated network and tree structures tend to include more potential NPC behaviors and allow for more possible interaction paths. They afford greater opportunity for introducing variable or parameterized behaviors, such as bridging comments between conversational network elements, or answer clarification and general dialog management moves in Socratic discussions.

Some approaches are inherently more complex, such as Sect. 3.5's *layered rule scripts* or Sect. 3.6's *conditional behaviors*. These call for the authoring of sets of behaviors that may be automatically invoked at any time and in any order (perhaps within some limits, such as those imposed by scene and role packaging structure in the layered scripting approach). Tests and actions that control execution can include logical expressions akin to some kinds of restricted programming. For instance, *METTLE's* scripting language was built as a simple interpreter, with built-in primitives for basic logical (*and, or, not*) and control (*sequential, parallel, alternative*) ways to combine an extensible set of test and action operators. SimBionic offers a graphical BTN formalism, but it allows the tests and actions associated with graphical elements to include JavaScript and Java expressions.

The bottom line is that increased sophistication and flexibility of NPC behaviors leads to increased complexity of the behavior authoring and verification tasks. In addition, some general authoring wisdom emerges:

- Authoring tools should provide structure to guide author choices and validations to enforce rules for well-formed NPC behavior specifications;
- Authoring tools should integrate with some version of a runtime, so it is easy to see the student-visible behavior that will result from any content;
- Authoring tools should leave escape hatches for using more general and flexible programming constructs when needed to ensure appropriate or efficient behavior; and
- When experimenting with new approaches, needing new tools: a workable authoring tool today is often more useful than a great tool tomorrow.

4.2 Adaptivity

When we speak of agents carrying out "appropriate" behaviors, we are really speaking about adaptivity. Again, there are different degrees of adaptation we can aspire to. The ITS literature, with its focus on tutor NPCs, typically speaks of *micro* versus *macro* adaptation (Shute 1993) or *inner loop* and *outer loop* adaptation (Van Lehn 2006). Our broader view—including concern for authoring NPCs playing a wide range of pedagogically relevant roles—leads us to distinguish *scenario* adaptation, *context* adaptation, *student* adaptation, and *community* adaptation:

- **Scenario Adaptation:** NPC behaviors should be appropriate to the scenario. If a *METTLE* scenario is about a highly communicable disease, there should be behaviors related to quarantine. Specialized appropriate behaviors have to be authored and then assigned to a given scenario (or family of scenarios). This level of adaptivity can be achieved in any NPC control and authoring scheme.
- **Context Adaptation:** A system should select and adjust NPC behaviors to fit the particular circumstances that arise during any given execution of a scenario. If a *TAO-ITS* NPC crewmate is supposed to notify the student when an enemy aircraft poses a threat, whether, when, and how that notification is given will depend on the student's prior choices about how to maneuver the ship or deploy its sensors. Such context-specific adaptation is generally handled by the more complex NPC logic supported by the more complex behavior rule forms discussed above.
- **Student Adaptation:** NPC behaviors may be modulated to account for what is known about a particular student. A common case involves appealing to a model of the student's curriculum mastery to control the degree of scaffolding provided by pedagogical agents. Similarly, a tutor agent might adjust its choices of topics for Socratic discussion or after-action review based on a student model. This kind of adaptation may be effected by direct authoring of control logic, by authoring of general control flags that depend on policies embedded in the (pedagogical) behavior interpreter, or by use of automatically learned (data-driven) models (see next bullet).
- **Community Adaptation:** NPC behaviors may be adjusted over time as data accumulate regarding the student population's performance on certain scenarios/tasks or in response to particular NPC behaviors/interventions. This level of adaptation can exploit modern machine learning techniques that depend on large

volumes of data. The reinforcement learning technique discussed in Sect. 3.7 can be driven by student data but can also exploit NPC versus NPC competition data.

The first three kinds of adaptation are quite directly tied to authoring, as is the dynamic scripting approach to community adaptation. Achieving adaptivity depends on authoring the right content in the right way, and some levels of adaptation are hard or impossible to achieve with some NPC control techniques.

4.3   IO Modalities

Simulation environments aim to recreate aspects of real-world situations to support practice and learning. Despite some tendency to assume that higher fidelity simulations always produce better training and transfer, it has long been recognized that there are different aspects of fidelity and that different tasks may depend more on some forms than on others (e.g., Micheli 1972; Beaubien and Baker 2004; Norman et al. 2012). Thus, when considering simulation investments intended to enhance fidelity, it is best to think about tradeoffs between particular effects (and gradations of those effects) versus costs.

The modes in which a simulation-based training system can accept inputs and produce outputs is one of the most visible aspects of fidelity. When incorporating NPCs in simulations for training, there can be good reasons to want those NPCs to be able to interact in particular modalities, which in turn raise implementation challenges. Often, language—textual or spoken—is the primary real-world mode of interaction with other people involved in a task to be trained. When language is the medium, much is communicated not just by the content of what is written or said, but sometimes by choices of phrasing or diction. In writing, formatting and layout may be meaningful; in speech prosody may likewise carry significant task-relevant cues. In face-to-face settings, non-verbal aspects of human interaction can be important too—e.g., gestures, posture, eye shifts, or breathing changes may all matter, say, for an interviewing task. Other kinds of observation may be an essential part of some tasks—e.g., when managing others and judging how they are doing their jobs. And in some applications, physical interaction with other people (e.g., touch, or even smell) can be a key part of the task—e.g., palping a swollen area when diagnosing or treating a patient.

The techniques inventoried in Sect. 3 provide varying opportunities to control NPCs with respect to what they do or say, how they do or say it, and what other visual, behavioral, or physical cues (or surrogates thereof) they can produce. While it is rare to have a truly "free play" training simulation, there is a significant divide between techniques that encourage a sense of freedom and those that overtly constrain user choices. From a training perspective, explicit multiple choice input prompting can help model a space of reasonable actions, but it allows users to get by with recognition skills; less constrained input mechanisms require users to generate or recall potentially appropriate actions.

Script trees (3.1), *conversational graphs* (3.2), and *issue/perspective matrices* (3.3) are all overtly multiple choice setups. In this sense they provide very limited and unrealistic interaction. At the same time, however, that restriction on available NPC moves allows them to be (video) recordings of real people, which provides a relatively easy route to incorporating all the subtle aspects of human communication that go beyond the words actually said. Given current technology, it is hard to match that with computer-generated speech and animation.

Socratic argument trees (3.4) and *layered rule scripts* (3.5) are both based on explicit expectations, but at any given time, the number of such expectations and the ways they may be expressed in user actions or utterances can be quite large. In *METTLE*, there were often hundreds of active expectations, and they were not explicitly surfaced for the user as a comprehensive list of options. Instead, *METTLE* accepted text or speech input and echoed back a sorted list of closely matching expectations, letting the user select any that matched their intent, or reject all and try an alternate input. *ComMentor* accepted its inputs using an extensive form-centered system (that also recognized some gestures and text phrases) allowing expression of a wide range of command intents. If the task is reasonably constrained, then the fact that the system can only generate meaningful responses to what is expected may not be a problem—i.e., users may very rarely be frustrated by an inability to take unexpected actions because it very rarely occurs to them to consider or attempt such actions.

Contextual behaviors (3.7) are most appropriate when the aim is to approximate a free play simulation in a domain where NPC behavior more frequently depends on sequences of parameterized behaviors. As the *TAO-ITS* example suggests, tactical decision-making training is an ideal application. The user can take very many actions, in different orders, to varying degrees, and with varying timing. In general, tactical actions may be taken through manipulations of controls to some simulated system, or through NPC interactions, as text or speech inputs. The NPC behaviors can recognize sequences of such actions as falling into equivalence classes—e.g., across the many ways of failing to gather sufficient threat identity information, or of successfully responding to a threat in a timely manner. NPC behaviors can be generated in response. Since the user's tactical decisions are based more on the apparent facts of the situation than on how facts are communicated, there is generally no need to worry about controlling the non-verbal nuances of NPC communication.

4.4 Pedagogical Impact

The discussion of I/O modalities introduced some of the pedagogical tradeoffs that might be expected in adopting different NPC simulation mechanisms. For instance, that multiple choice schemes can help introduce and reinforce plausible response options; or that with fewer NPC behaviors, each behavior can potentially be richer (e.g., video of live people), allowing for incorporation of decision cues that might be hard to simulate by other means. In contrast, more open-ended schemes avoid constant user prompting, reducing reliance on the trainee's ability to recognize a good action, instead forcing them to recall or generate a response.

The higher-end simulation approaches that can handle a wider range of user inputs have other potential benefits. First, more sophisticated behavior schemes can be more generative. Parameterized rules can map situations and user inputs to a range of specific contextually appropriate NPC behaviors. While such rules may be expensive to author in the short run, they can lower long run costs if they can be reused across many scenarios. In the best case, they may allow automated generation of an unlimited set of variant scenarios. Second, scenarios that better approximate free play may be more engaging and promote higher user motivation. Together, more scenarios and greater motivation can provide an opportunity to capitalize on a core educational finding: that increased time on task predicts increased learning (Fredrick and Walberg 1980; Karweit 1984).

5 Conclusion

This paper presents a range of NPC technologies and applications, and discusses some of their pros and cons from a training system perspective—e.g., mechanisms and costs for creating NPC behaviors, ability of the resulting behaviors to cover the range of user activities and needs that might arise in training scenario execution, and ability to support particular pedagogical goals. The point has *not* been to argue that any of the presented technologies is best for some particular use, or that collectively they suffice for all uses. Rather, the point has been to discuss the kind of analysis that training system designers need to carry out when considering incorporation of NPCs, and to sketch part of a design trade space—at least as it exists given a set of current technologies.

Our suggestion is that designers consider choosing the least sophisticated NPC scheme that will satisfy training goals. For instance, if the goal is making students aware of a range of possible perspectives or critiques on an issue, then using an *issue/perspective matrix* approach may suffice. If the goal is allowing students to practice applying critiques, then using *Socratic argument trees* might be a more appropriate approach. If the goal is having students enact decisions based on assessing a situation (perhaps in light of a set of reasonably applied perspectives and critiques) then *layered rule scripts* or *contextual behaviors* may be needed.

The recommendation to "go low" is tempered by a reminder to consider both short- and long-term costs. If there will ultimately be a requirement for running very many scenarios (potentially automatically generating scenarios), then more sophisticated generative NPC behavior modeling and orchestration approaches may be justified, even if simpler schemes might meet other pedagogical requirements. On the other hand, if the content to be trained is expected to shift over time, that may suggest biasing towards less expensive individual scenarios. That is, unless the domain logic and its expected forms of drift allow for definition of rules that can be generalized and adapted to cope with change.

Finally, special circumstances may dictate other choices. If the goals of training include learning to attend to subtle interpersonal cues that cannot (yet) be simulated by generating NPC utterances and appearances, then producing videos with live actors may be required. The costs of such videos will constrain the number of possible NPC behaviors and hence the appropriate NPC control regimen. Likewise, if the training goal is to motivate exposure to experiences and war stories of expert practitioners, then again, videos clips packaged as NPC behaviors in a scheme based on *conversational associations* may be the best bet.

References

Aleven, V., Mclaren, B.M., Sewall, J., Koedinger, K.R.: A new paradigm for intelligent tutoring systems: example-tracing tutors. Int. J. Artif. Intell. Educ. **19**(2), 105–154 (2009)

Beaubien, J.M., Baker, D.P.: The use of simulation for training teamwork skills in health care: how low can you go? BMJ Qual. Saf. **13**(Suppl. 1), i51–i56 (2004)

Cleary, C., Bareiss, R.: Using points to construct browsing links in ASK systems. AAAI Technical report FS-95-03 (1995)

Domeshek, E., Holman, E., Luperfoy, S.: Discussion control in an automated socratic tutor. In: Proceedings of the Industry/Interservice, Training, Simulation & Education Conference (I/ITSEC 2004) (2004)

Domeshek, E.: Scenario-based conversational intelligent tutoring systems for decision-making skills. In: Proceedings of the Industry/Interservice, Training, Simulation & Education Conference (I/ITSEC 2009) (2009)

Ferguson, W., Bareiss, R., Birnbaum, L., Osgood, R.: ASK systems: an approach to the realization of story-based teachers. J. Learn. Sci. **2**(1), 95–134 (1992)

Fredrick, W.C., Walberg, H.J.: Learning as a function of time. J. Educ. Res. **73**(4), 183–194 (1980)

Fu, D., Houlette, R.: Putting AI in entertainment: an AI authoring tool for simulation and games. IEEE Intell. Syst. **17**, 81–84 (2002)

Karweit, N.: Time-on-task reconsidered: synthesis of research on time and learning. Educ. Leadersh. **41**(8), 32–35 (1984)

Kim, J.M., et al.: BiLAT: a game-based environment for practicing negotiation in a cultural context. Int. J. Artif. Intell. Educ. **19**(3), 289–308 (2009)

Lajoie, S.P., Lesgold, A.: Apprenticeship training in the workplace: computer-coached practice environment as a new form of apprenticeship. Mach.-Mediated Learn. **3**(1), 7–28 (1989)

Leelawong, K., Biswas, G.: Designing learning by teaching agents: the Betty's Brain system. Int. J. Artif. Intell. Educ. **18**(3), 181–208 (2008)

Ludwig, J.R.: Extending dynamic scripting. Doctoral dissertation, University of Oregon (2008)

Ludwig, J., Presnell, B.: Developing an adaptive opponent for tactical training. In: Sottilare, R. A., Schwarz, J. (eds.) HCII 2019. LNCS, vol. 11597, pp. 532–541. Springer, Cham (2019). https://doi.org/10.1007/978-3-030-22341-0_42

Luperfoy, S., Domeshek, E., Holman, E., Struck, D.: Synthetic dialog agents in simulated classroom discussion for case-method instruction. In: Proceedings of Behavior Representation in Modeling and Simulation Conference (2004)

Micheli, G.S.: Analysis of the transfer of training, substitution, and fidelity of simulation of transfer equipment (No. TAEG-2). Training Analysis and Evaluation Group (Navy) Orlando FL (1972)

Norman, G., Dore, K., Grierson, L.: The minimal relationship between simulation fidelity and transfer of learning. Med. Educ. **46**(7), 636–647 (2012)

Nye, B.D., Graesser, A.C., Hu, X.: AutoTutor and family: a review of 17 years of natural language tutoring. Int. J. Artif. Intell. Educ. **24**(4), 427–469 (2014)

Palinscar, A.S., Brown, A.L.: Reciprocal teaching of comprehension-fostering and comprehension-monitoring activities. Cogn. Instr. **1**(2), 117–175 (1984)

Schank, R.C.: Rules and topics in conversation. Cogn. Sci. **1**, 421–441 (1977)

Schank, R.C., Fano, A., Bell, B., Jona, M.: The design of goal-based scenarios. J. Learn. Sci. **3**(4), 305–345 (1994)

Shute, V.J.: A comparison of learning environments: all that glitters. In: Lajoie, S.P., Derry, S. J. (eds.) Computers as Cognitive Tools, pp. 47–74. Lawrence Erlbaum Associates, Hillsdale (1993)

Sottilare, R.A., Brawner, K.W., Sinatra, A.M., Johnston, J.H.: An updated concept for a Generalized Intelligent Framework for Tutoring (GIFT). GIFTtutoring.org (2017)

Stottler, R., Davis, A., Panichas, S., Treadwell, M.: Designing and implementing intelligent tutoring instruction for tactical action officers. In: Proceedings of the Industry/Interservice, Training, Simulation & Education Conference (I/ITSEC 2007) (2007)

van Gelder, T.: Enhancing deliberation through computer supported argument visualization. In: Kirschner, P.A., Buckingham Shum, S.J., Carr, C.S. (eds.) Visualizing Argumentation. CSCW, pp. 97–115. Springer, London (2003). https://doi.org/10.1007/978-1-4471-0037-9_5

Van Lehn, K.: The behavior of tutoring systems. Int. J. Artif. Intell. Educ. **16**, 227–265 (2006)

Woolf, B.P.: Building Intelligent Interactive Tutors: Student-Centered Strategies for Revolutionizing e-Learning. Morgan Kaufmann, Burlington (2010)

Learning Traces, Measurement and Assessment Templates for AIS Interoperability

Bruno Emond$^{(\boxtimes)}$ 📕

National Research Council Canada, Ottawa, ON K1A 0R6, Canada
bruno.emond@nrc-cnrc.gc.ca

Abstract. The current paper contains elements relevant for the conceptual modelling and interoperability of measurements and assessments across adaptive instructional systems (AIS). After an introduction, the first section presents a generic use case, where knowledge acquisition is supported by a sequence of training simulators of increasing complexity, and the need to capture regularity and variations in measurements and assessments across instructional systems. The second section briefly discusses the role of measurements and assessments as a core of functions of adaptive instructional systems. The section indicates that an adaptive instructional system needs minimally to capture references to learners' performance, knowledge components, learning tasks, and learning attempts. The third section maps the main Generalized Intelligent Framework for Tutoring (GIFT) components to a generic feedback control system model. The mapping makes explicit the dual interpretation of measurements and assessments as both results (learning traces) and functions (computation templates). The fourth section examines some non-proprietary frameworks in terms of their capability to support the interoperability of measurements and assessments across adaptive instructional systems. The section briefly discusses xAPI, the Competency And Skill System (CASS), the Evidence Trace File (ETF), the Training Objective Package (TOP), and the Human Performance Markup Language (HPML). The main contributions of the paper are: 1) an AIS conceptual model based on a feedback control system model, and 2) a brief review of learning data frameworks as they relate to measurements and assessments as both learning traces and computation templates.

Keywords: Adaptive Instructional Systems · Interoperability · Measurements and assessments · Generalized Intelligent Framework for Tutoring · Feedback control systems

1 Introduction

Adaptive Instructional Systems (AIS) cover a group of technologies ranging from intelligent tutoring systems, to adaptive multimedia and training content recommenders. A key factor affecting a larger adoption of adaptive instructional systems is the lack of interoperability standards [1] which limits the possibility of reusing AIS components such as domain content models, learner models, instructional models, and

© NRC Canada 2020
R. A. Sottilare and J. Schwarz (Eds.): HCII 2020, LNCS 12214, pp. 71–87, 2020.
https://doi.org/10.1007/978-3-030-50788-6_6

interface models. In addition to the issue of internal interoperability between these components, the interoperability between AIS and the learning technology ecosystem also needs to be specified [2, 3]. An IEEE working group is currently investigating the possible market needs for standards across this group of technologies [4]. The working group activities are organized in three subgroups: conceptual modelling, recommended practice for AIS systems evaluation, and interoperability.

A major incentive for learning technology interoperability and learning standards has been the need to support learning across a growing range of online opportunities, and the parallel move from training organizations to rely on a distributed ecosystem rather than LMS-centric silos for which data sharing is difficult [5]. Demands in training requires organizations to maximize access to adaptive training through high- and low-fidelity simulations. However, an increase of learning opportunities through simulations must also be associated with a high level of efficiency and efficacy of the training system as a whole [6]. The current paper contains elements relevant for the conceptual modelling and interoperability of measurements and assessments across adaptive instructional systems.

The first section discusses a generic use case, where knowledge acquisition is supported by a sequence of training simulators of increasing complexity. The section outlines the need to capture variations in measurements and assessments across instructional systems. Many areas of expertise require the acquisition of a combination of cognitive and psycho-motor skills. Marksmanship is an example where after mastering the basics, hundreds of hours of practice are required through various training systems [7]. Medical practice, tactical verbal procedures [8–10], and flight operations require a range of training systems including desktop, virtual reality, and high-fidelity training simulators. Providing a smooth transition between training systems raises the issue of between system adaptiveness and the sequencing of training content. According to Alessi's hypothesis [11], for each expertise level, there is a point where increasing perceived fidelity (hence human-machine interface complexity), might reduce and even be counterproductive in terms of learning effectiveness. Adaptive instructional systems conceived as organizational resources should allow to track knowledge components acquisition, as learning curves [12, 13] across instructional systems.

The second section briefly discusses the role of measurements and assessments as a core function of adaptive instructional systems. The essential functionality of any adaptive instructional system is the capability to measure and assess the level of proficiency of a learner in order to adapt the training and learning experience. According to the assessment triangle, every assessment, regardless of its purpose, rests on three pillars: a model of how students represent knowledge and develop competence in a subject domain, tasks or situations that allow one to observe and measure students' performance, and interpretation method for evaluating if knowledge has been acquired by inference from performance evidence process [14]. This model is articulated with more details in the Evidence Centred Design conceptual assessment framework [15]. The section identifies that a minimal representation for the purpose of measurements and assessments should include references to a knowledge component, a learning task, a learner, and his/her learning efforts (attempts).

The third section maps the main Generalized Intelligent Framework for Tutoring (GIFT) components to a generic feedback control system model. The mapping is done at the GIFT components level and ignores the cascading control systems of steps, tasks, and design loops in intelligent tutoring. The tutor interface model, training simulator, and sensors are grouped in the instructional system (target). The domain, learner, and pedagogical models as grouped in the adaptive instructional engine. The mapping introduces a measurement model as a transduction function, it also makes explicit the dual interpretation of measurements and assessments as both results (learning traces) and functions to compute results (computation templates).

The fourth section examines some non-proprietary learning data frameworks in terms of their capability to support the interoperability of measurements and assessments across adaptive instructional systems. The section briefly discusses xAPI, the Competency And Skill System (CASS), the Evidence Trace File (ETF), the Training Objective Package (TOP), and the Human Performance Markup Language (HPML). Almost all frameworks are equivalent representing measurement and assessment results as learning traces. However, only TOP and HPML offer the possibility of explicitly representing computations as computation templates.

The main contributions of the paper are: 1) an AIS conceptual model based on a feedback control system model, where the domain model (knowledge components), performance standards (learning objectives), and measurements and assessments are clearly distinguished; and 2) a brief review of learning data frameworks as they relate to measurements and assessments as both learning traces and computation templates.

2   Knowledge Acquisition Across Adaptive Instructional Systems

Demands in training require organizations to maximize access to adaptive training through high- and low-fidelity simulations. However, an increase of learning opportunities through simulations must also be associated with a high level of efficiency and efficacy of the training system as a whole [6]. To avoid the risk of creating a collection of practice simulators instead of objective-based training environments [16], training simulators must provide a precise yet comprehensible means to express and manipulate measurements, and assessments across a range of learning opportunities [17]. The risk of locking investments in learning design, measurements and assessments into specific customized training simulations is very high given the rate of technological changes. As new training technology emerges, reusing measurements and assessment specifications in new training environments allows for a higher return on investment on learning design.

Many areas of expertise require the acquisition of a combination of cognitive and psycho-motor skills. Marksmanship is an example where after mastering the basics, hundreds of hours of practice are required through various training systems [7]. Medical practice, tactical verbal procedures [8–10], and flight operations are also expertise that require a range of training systems including desktop, virtual reality, and high-fidelity training simulators. Although training content might be static at first, being focused on declarative knowledge, the full expertise in some domain area needs to be applied in a dynamic environment where decisions, procedural knowledge and psycho-motor skills applied in a time-sensitive manner. Sequencing simple to complex knowledge components is a key success factor for matching learners' states to learning conditions for different human competencies such as processing verbal information, intellectual skills, cognitive strategies, motor skills and attitudes [18]. Learning taxonomies have been proposed to identify both the hierarchical levels and the knowledge domain. Common taxonomies include the cognitive [19], affective [20], psychomotor [21], and team [22] taxonomies.

Even though the technology and computational power provide for new possibilities in training simulators with high-fidelity at a low cost, new features that make the tasks more complicated should not be included too early in the training. For example, gradually increasing functional fidelity during training improves the performance on later complex tasks, as compared to training the highest fidelity from the onset [23]. According to Alessi's hypothesis [11], see Fig. 1, for each of the expertise level, there is a point where increasing perceived fidelity (hence human-machine interface complexity), might reduce and even be counterproductive in terms of learning effectiveness. The example of overwhelming novices in high-fidelity simulators seems to be the worst case. As a student progresses in acquiring a set of competencies, there is a requirement to provide a seamless transition from low-fidelity to high-fidelity simulators [24]. Proving a smooth transition raises the issue of between system adaptiveness and the sequencing of training content conceived as including digital content and affordances provided by a training simulator user interface.

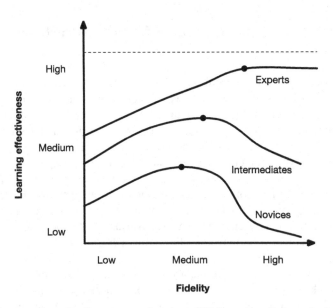

Fig. 1. Learning effectiveness as a function of fidelity: Alessi's hypothesis [11].

The current analysis and prior work [25] suggest that the question is not which level of simulator fidelity is best, but how a range of simulator fidelity can be introduced into a progressive training program to maximize the usage of training resources (external conditions) as a function of students' expertise level (internal conditions) [26]. An instructional design decision support system to allow for the proper alignment of training resources to training needs would need to conduct a continuous evaluation of the training system effectiveness based on evidence collected from student performance and learning over time. In practice, the sequencing of the external conditions (training scenarios and platforms) would be determined by an instructional design linking the assessment of students' prior knowledge and performance objectives and/or standards. Adaptive instructional systems conceived as organizational resources should allow to track knowledge components acquisition both as a short-term learning experience and longer-term knowledge proficiency across training opportunities [12]. Also, given that in the course of building a domain competency across instructional systems some knowledge components will be reassessed under different conditions, it appears that the interoperability of measurements and assessments is valuable for both training efficiency and cost reduction.

3 Measurements and Assessments as Core AIS Functions

The generic model of an adaptive instructional system (AIS) put forward by the IEEE working group [27] is presented in Fig. 2. The figure indicates that not only the instructional system adapts to the learner by providing feedback and selecting learning tasks at an adequate difficulty level, but the adaptive instructional engine is also subject to improvement by evaluating and adjusting its adaptive policies. At the core of AIS is the basic functionality to measure and assess the level of proficiency of a learner in order to adapt the training and learning experience.

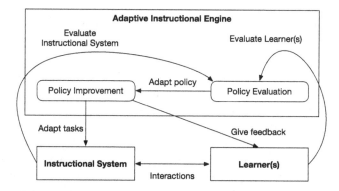

Fig. 2. Generic adaptive instructional system. Adapted from [27].

According to NRC's assessment triangle [14], every assessment, regardless of its purpose, rests on three pillars: a model of how students represent knowledge and develop competence in a subject domain, tasks or situations that allow one to observe and measure students' performance, and interpretation method for evaluating if knowledge has been acquired by inference from a performance evidence process [14]. Figure 3 presents a modified version of the NRC's assessment triangle [14]. In the figure, the original terminology for the triangle vertices are in parentheses (cognition, observation, and interpretation). A knowledge component (KC) is defined as an acquired unit of cognitive function or structure that can be inferred from performance on a set of related tasks [28]. The measurement vertex refers to the extraction of relevant training measures from a stream of events generated while an individual or a group of individuals is executing a task. The assessment vertex refers to the classification of measurements as they meet some criteria. For example, a set of aggregated performance measures on a set of questions will produce a score, and an assessment (interpretation) of this score will determine if the result is to pass or fail. In addition to the vertices, Fig. 3 also identifies objectives attached to each pair of vertices such as 1) the determination of which measurements, and tasks need to be used in order to elicit targeted knowledge 2) the application of criteria to measurements, and 3) the inference of knowledge acquisition from assessment results.

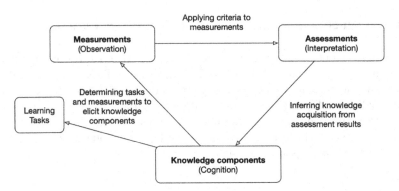

Fig. 3. Adapted assessment triangle from [14] showing the relationships between measurements, assessments and knowledge components. NRC's original terms are in parentheses.

A key principle is that assessment is always a process of reasoning from evidence, with the purpose to assist learning, measure individual and collective achievement, and to evaluate training sequences [14]. This model is articulated with more details in the Evidence Centred Design conceptual assessment framework [15]. The conceptual assessment framework specifies the information needed to perform measurement and assessments. The framework includes a model of learner proficiency, measurement and evaluation models, and a task model linking learners' productions to targeted proficiency [29]. The association between knowledge components and learning tasks is often referred to as a Q-matrix [30], and is particularly important for the evaluation of knowledge components models.

Establishing support for links between knowledge components models, learning tasks, learning sequences, and learner's performance can be associated to an instructional system design loop [31]. This loop requires data analysis methods like Bayesian knowledge tracing [13] or additive factor models [12] which rely on assumptions about knowledge components learning curves [32]. When looking at adaptive instructional systems, it is commonly recognized, at least for intelligent tutoring systems, that there are two other loop types [33]: 1) the step loop which provides a response to a learner action within an instructional task mostly in the form of a performance feedback or a hint, and 2) the task loop which provides a learner with a change of task, either to increase or reduce task difficulty depending on the task mastery assessment. Both of those loops rely on the measurement of the number of attempts. From the previous paragraphs it appears that a minimal representation for the purpose of measurements and assessments should include references to a knowledge component, a learning task, a learner, and his/her learning efforts (attempts).

4 Measurements and Assessments in Feedback Control Systems

Adaptive instructional systems, such as Intelligent Tutor systems (ITS), are typical artificial intelligence applications in education. The common analysis of adaptive instruction systems distinguishes four interacting components: 1) a model of the knowledge or skill domain, 2) a model of the learner(s), 3) a model for the pedagogical interventions, and 4) a user interface to the training system [34]. The domain model contains the specifications of the set of skills, knowledge, and strategies of the topic being tutored; the student model consists of elements of the domain model that are inferred from the performance of learners; the pedagogical model takes the domain and student models as input and selects tutoring strategies, steps, and actions to optimize students' learning, and tutor-student interface model presents and capture student interactions [35]. In addition, if the Generalized Intelligent Tutoring Framework (GIFT) architecture is taken as a reference model for the main components of an adaptive instructional system (see Fig. 4), sensors and a sensor model, as well as training simulations, or training applications can be added [36]. In this context, a training application provides the interface to the learning tasks, while the tutor-student interface would take charge of the communication between the tutor and the learner. The sensors and sensors model capture physiological and neurocognitive data relevant for the determination of the learners' cognitive and emotional states during learning. The GIFT architecture includes all the essential elements that are part of the measurements and assessments of knowledge components identified in the assessment triangle [36] and the conceptual assessment framework [15].

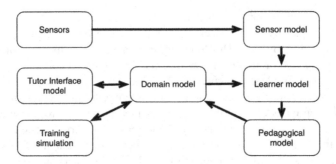

Fig. 4. Simplified version of the GIFT architecture from [36].

However, the current training simulation practice tends to embed measurements and assessments in the training simulation code, making it difficult to reuse those measures and assessments across instructional systems. Based on a generic feedback control model, the current section identifies the need for decoupling the training simulation code from the measurement. Figure 5 presents a block diagram of a feedback control system. The figure identifies the three main components, the target system to be controlled, the controlling unit (controller), and a unit design to transform signals received from the target system in a format suitable for the controller.

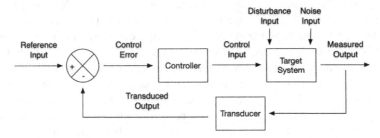

Fig. 5. Block diagram of a feedback control system [37].

Figure 6 presents a mapping of the GIFT architecture into feedback control system with an emphasis on the system elements related to the measurement and assessments of knowledge components. The reference input is associated to performance standards and assessment models; the control error to assessments (difference between measured performance and performance standards); control input is associated with the action of the adaptive instructional system on the instructional system; the controller is the adaptive instructional system; the disturbance and noise input are associated to the learners' interactions with an instructional system. The measured output is any logging of system events. The transducer is the process of transforming system events into a representation suitable for the comparison with the performance standard.

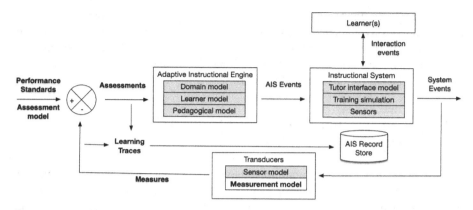

Fig. 6. AIS system as a feedback control system with an emphasis on the system elements related to the measurement and assessments of knowledge components (bold). The system elements in grey refer to the GIFT architecture of Fig. 4.

The system elements in grey refer to the GIFT architecture of Fig. 4. The mapping ignores the cascading control systems of steps, tasks, and design loops in intelligent tutoring systems that establishes the minimum information content of learning traces for the refinement of knowledge component models [35]. It focuses on the generic functions of performing measurements and assessments for the purpose of adaptation. In the figure, the tutor interface model, training simulator, and sensors are grouped in the instructional system (target). The domain, learner, and pedagogical models are grouped in the adaptive instructional engine. However, the insertion of GIFT components into a feedback control system are the introduction of a measurement model separates the performance standards (learning objectives), measurements and assessments from the domain model. The figure makes an explicit distinction between the identification of knowledge components in a domain, the assessments of proficiency for these knowledge components, and the measurements of relevant behaviour metrics from task execution. Figure 6 includes learning traces, as a general term to refer to time-based recording of measurements, assessments, and possibly other AIS events such as learner model updates, and pedagogical/tutor interventions, and tagged training simulation events for measurement of learners' behaviour. The need to capture in the same record store both learners and system behaviour, in particular anthropomorphic agents like a computer tutor, has been identified by other researchers [38]. The figure also includes an AIS record store to support offline learning analytics, similar to the xAPI learning record store [39–42].

Elements in bold in Fig. 6, which are directly related to measurements and assessments, are of two types: 1) results (learning traces), and 2) computations (models). Measures and assessments are the products of the respective application of measurement and assessment functions to data. Measurement models produce representations of system events suitable for assessments. Assessment models compare measured performances to standards in order to produce an assessment to be consumed by the domain, learner and pedagogical AIS models. If the objective is to allow for reusing and the interoperability of measurement and assessment models as computations, a useful format for their representation could be as computation templates, analogous to the lambda representation of a function with input parameters. The next section examines non-proprietary frameworks in terms of their capability to support the interoperability of measurements and assessments as results and computations across adaptive instructional systems.

5   Measurements and Assessments: Products and Computation Templates

The current section examines non-proprietary learning data frameworks in terms of their capability to support the interoperability of measurements and assessments across adaptive instructional systems. A good sample of these efforts includes xAPI [43], the Evidence Trace File (ETF) [29], the Competency And Skill System (CASS) [44], the Training Objective Package (TOP) [45], and the Human Performance Markup Language (HPML) [46].

Various efforts have been deployed to develop technology to support interoperable performance assessments, and more generally the recording of learning events in a sharable format so that the learning data can be decoupled from training applications that generate it. The xAPI framework [39–42] specifies how to encode and store a learning event in a standard format. xAPI proposes a simple format in the form of time-stamped "actor-verb-object" statements, with additional keys like "result", to add details to a measured outcome, or "context", which can contain relevant information to contextualize learning event statements [47]. The focus of xAPI is mostly on the encoding and storage of learning events, leaving the details unspecified on how measures, and assessments were computed to generate the recorded results.

The IMS Caliper Analytics [48] is another proposal to encode and manage learning events. IMS Caliper's main goal is to establish a way to capture and obtain measures from a set of learning activities, each having one or several associated metric profiles defining the information flow from a learning activity to competency assessments. IMS Caliper offers a set of structured templates/metric profiles while xAPI does not provide a similar set of statement types. However, the architecture is similar to xAPI, where a Caliper Event Store is used for storing metric profile instances independently of training applications. Caliper Analytics is a framework developed by the IMS Global Consortium [48]. The use of the framework requires a paid subscription to the IMS Global Consortium.

The Competency And Skill System [44] is a good example of a proposal focused mainly on the analysis of independently stored learning events. One use case for CASS is to access xAPI statements as an input for making competency assertions. However, the CASS architecture is mostly focused on the management of competency assertions and certifications issued by organizations, and on the encoding of detailed measurement and assessment statements. The management of competency statements across training systems and organization is an important interoperability issue.

Another less known approach to interoperable performance assessments is the Human Performance Markup Language (HPML), which aims at fulfilling the purpose of managing measurements, evaluations, and training objectives by providing a simple and reusable way to represent the performance of individuals and teams in those systems [49]. Other potential benefits of HPML include [6]: an increase in visibility and definition of measurement and evaluation requirements, reduced acquisition life-cycle costs in the long term, and increased technical quality of human performance assessment. HPML is currently being examined as a potential standard by a Simulation Interoperability Standards Organization (SISO) study group [46]. Starting in March 2019, version 6 of HPML is currently being developed with the objective of simpli-fying significantly the HPML 5 specifications to facilitate its adoption.

The Evidence Trace File [29] is intended to express learning events data in a way that meets the specific assessment needs. Figure 7 shows the structure of a generic data model for an evidence trace file. This structure is simple and could be used to encode both measurements and assessment information. By adding extended key-value pairs to refer to the item being processed as well as the knowledge component associated with the item, the structure includes the minimal information for processing real-time control loops as well as offline analysis to refine a domain model.

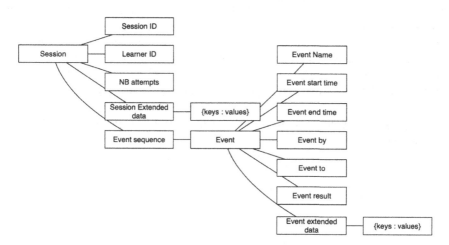

Fig. 7. Structure of a generic data model for an evidence trace file (ETF) [29].

However, it is worth nothing that the ETF structure of Fig. 7 could be easily expressed using xAPI or HPML. The xAPI framework is a very flexible representation system for capturing many types of learning events in different contexts using a simple syntax of learner-verb-object. The representation also allows to expand on the speci-fication of a context, which would be essential to include information regarding the specific knowledge components for the domain model, learning tasks, and tracking the learning efforts (learner identification and task attempts). There are some equivalences in expression capability and the decision to favour one or another could amount to ease of use and market acceptability.

The main issue regarding interoperability is the capability to reuse model specifi-cations in different training conditions. Learning traces allow the interoperability of measurements and assessments products, because they are decoupled from the systems that generated them. As encoding of learning events, they also support steps, tasks, and design loops. However, as products of models they are instances of structure templates or computation results. Most of the interoperability efforts have been focused on the results and not on making computation interoperable. Of the dual interpretation of assessments and measurements as results and as functions only the former has received most of the attention.

The Human Performance Modelling Language (HPML) is intended to cover all meaningful aspects of human performance measurements in various training and operational environments [46]. It is composed of schemas such as computations, measures, assessments, results, instances and periods. In the context of HPML, a computation represents an algorithm performing a mathematical, or logical operation. Measures represent the application of computations to data sources to produce measurements. Assessments are the assignment of measures to categories. Instances and periods represent the creation and use of measures and assessments for a given time and/or location context. Finally results refer to the output of both measure and assessment instantiations [50]. Figure 8 presents the dependencies between high-level HPML elements (A), and high-level XML schemas (B). HPML also has a JSON implementation. The boxes added to the figure on the left represent a grouping of measure and assessment specifications or templates (red), and measure and assessment instances, and results as a function of specific performance data in time periods. The right-hand side of the figure shows a detailed list of all high-level HPML schema elements, including ones for representing data requests, constants, actors (individuals or teams), training objectives and their links to measures and assessments (training objective packages). Each of these top-level schemas can be expanded to cover many human performance-modelling requirements.

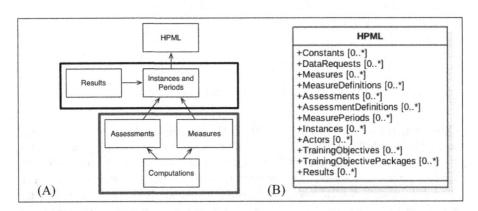

Fig. 8. (A) High-level HPML abstraction, and (B) HPML XML schemas. (Color figure online)

Another framework design to capture aspects of training in complex scenarios is the Training Objective Packages (TOP) [45]. The framework allows to organize objectives in a hierarchical manner and can attach measurement and assessment to each training objective. Extending HPML, TOP can also define behaviour envelopes which explicitly represent the bounds on desirable and undesirable behaviour given training conditions. Behaviour envelopes can also be applied across training scenarios, offering an efficiency proposition to instructional designers for reusing training objective definitions, measurements and assessments.

Table 1 summarizes the possibilities offered by interoperable assessments frameworks in terms of the AIS measurement and assessment components identified in the previous sections. The table identifies that all frameworks can represent measurements and assessments as results (learning traces), with the exception of CASS, which focuses on competency statements and their processing. As such, the CASS framework also provides some means to represent explicitly how to compute relationships between assessments regarding competency levels. The xAPI and ETF have very similar representation capabilities given the possibility offered by both frameworks to extend representation with contextual information for the results of measurements and assessments but none of them indicate in their specifications the representation of computations. The proposal that the generic data structure of an evidence trace file could serve as a way to communicate to software engineers what the training application should produce for the purpose of learning design [29], is illustrative of the lack of decoupling between the computer codes executing learning tasks, and the measurement and assessment computation specifications.

Table 1. Comparison of interoperable assessments frameworks in terms of AIS measurement and assessment components.

	As results		As computations		Performance standards
	Measures	Assessments	Measures	Assessments	
xAPI	X	X			
ETF	X	X			
CASS		X		X	X
HPML	X	X	X	X	X
TOP	X	X	X	X	X

6   Conclusion

The notion of interoperability, even though it appears as simply defined as a means to have separate systems function together, has many dimensions that quickly raise its complexity. Not only interoperability can be seen from a within and between systems point of view which can be addressed as a multilayered problem, but when the issue of interoperable content for adaptive instructional system is considered, it is not possible to only focus on the learning resources properties and resource distribution without considering embedded performance measurement and assessments. Providing a smooth transition between training systems raises the issue of between system adaptiveness and the sequencing of training content conceived as including digital content and affordances provided by the training simulator user interface. Adaptive instructional systems conceived as organizational resources should allow to track knowledge components acquisition, as learning curves [12, 13] across instructional systems.

The essential functionality of any adaptive instructional system is the capability to measure and assess the level of proficiency of a learner in order to adapt the training and learning experience. The mapping of AIS/GIFT into a feedback control system makes explicit the dual interpretation of measurements and assessments as results and as computations, and introduces a measurement component as a transduction function. A brief analysis of various efforts to develop technology to support interoperable performance assessments suggests that there are equivalences between proposals for the encoding of measurement and assessment results. xAPI, ETF, HPML, and CASS to a lesser extent, can all encode a binding between learning content, knowledge components, and variables relevant for the real-time processing of the steps and tasks control loops, as well as the refinement of knowledge component models in an offline design loop. However, the explicit representation of measures and assessments computations for interoperability seems to be only supported by the Human Performance Markup Language, and the Training Objective Packages.

The main contributions of the paper are: 1) an AIS conceptual model based on a feedback control system model, where the domain model (knowledge components), performance standards (learning objectives), and measurements and assessments are clearly distinguished; and 2) a brief review of learning data frameworks as they relate to measurements and assessments as both learning traces and computation templates. The capability to share and reuse measure and assessment computation specifications is a key feature that can support the interoperability of measurements and assessments across instructional systems. Frameworks focused on learning traces definitely provide an anchor for the determination of learner models so that their prior knowledge can be used as a training sequence increase complexity moving towards training simulators of high-fidelity. However, if some knowledge components need to be assessed under different conditions, then decoupling the measurement and assessment specifications from the device programming code provides means to refine and inspect the measurement and assessment resources without requiring a software engineering interpretation.

References

1. Santos, G.S., Jorge, J.: Interoperable intelligent tutoring systems as open educational resources. IEEE Trans. Learn. Technol. **6**, 271–282 (2013)
2. Sottilare, R.: Exploring methods to promote interoperability in adaptive instructional systems. In: Sottilare, R.A., Schwarz, J. (eds.) HCII 2019. LNCS, vol. 11597, pp. 227–238. Springer, Cham (2019). https://doi.org/10.1007/978-3-030-22341-0_19
3. Thai, K.P., Tong, R.: Interoperability standards for adaptive instructional systems: vertical and horizontal integrations. In: Sottilare, R.A., Schwarz, J. (eds.) HCII 2019. LNCS, vol. 11597, pp. 251–260. Springer, Cham (2019). https://doi.org/10.1007/978-3-030-22341-0_21
4. Adaptive Instructional Systems (AIS) Working Group: Adaptive Instructional Systems (C/LT/AIS) P2247.1. https://site.ieee.org/sagroups-2247-1/. Accessed 26 Nov 2019

5. Robson, R., Barr, A.: The new wave of training technology standards. In: Proceeding of the Interservice/Industry Training, Simulation, and Education Conference (I/ITSEC), pp. 1–11. National Training and Simulation Association, Orlando (2018)

6. Atkinson, B.F.W., Killilea, J.: A review of the potential return on investment benefits of a human performance measurement standard: lessons learned in the Navy aviation community. In: 2015 Fall Simulation Interoperability Workshop, SIW 2015. SISO - Simulation Interoperability Standards Organization, Orlando (2015)

7. Brawner, K.W., Goodwin, G., Regan, D.: Scaling Across Domains and the Implications for GIFT. U.S. Army Research Laboratory, Orlando (2016)

8. Emond, B., Kondratova, I., Durand, G., Valdés, J.J.: A multi-role reconfigurable trainer for naval combat information operators. In: Interservice/Industry Training, Simulation and Education Conference (I/ITSEC), p. 14. National Training and Simulation Association, Orlando (2018)

9. Emond, B., et al.: Adaptive training simulation using speech interaction for training navy officers. In: Interservice/Industry Training, Simulation, and Education Conference (I/ITSEC), pp. 2924–2934. National Training and Simulation Association, Orlando (2016)

10. Emond, B.: Interoperable assessments using HPML: a novice conning skills acquisition use case. In: Interservice/Industry Training, Simulation and Education Conference (I/ITSEC), p. 11. National Training and Simulation Association, Orlando (2017)

11. Alessi, S.M.: Fidelity in the design of instructional simulations. J. Comput. Instr. (1988)

12. Martin, B., Mitrovic, A., Koedinger, K.R., Mathan, S.: Evaluating and improving adaptive educational systems with learning curves. User Model. User-Adapt. Interact. **21**, 249–283 (2011). https://doi.org/10.1007/s11257-010-9084-2

13. Corbett, A.T., Anderson, J.R.: Knowledge tracing: modeling the acquisition of procedural knowledge. User Model. User-Adapt. Interact. **4**, 253–278 (1995). https://doi.org/10.1007/BF01099821

14. National Research Council: Knowing what students know: The science and design of educational assessment. National Academy Press, Washington, DC (2001)

15. Mislevy, R.J., Steinberg, L.S., Almond, R.G.: On the structure of educational assessments. Meas. Interdisc. Res. Perspect. **1**, 3–67 (2003)

16. Stacy, W., Merket, D., Freeman, J., Wiese, E., Jackson, C.: A language for rapidly creating performance measures in simulators. In: The Interservice/Industry Training, Simulation & Education Conference (I/ITSEC) (2005)

17. Stacy, W., Ayers, J., Freeman, J., Haimson, C.: Representing human performance with human performance measurement language. In: Proceedings of the Fall 2006 Simulation Interoperability Workshop, pp. 570–580. SISO - Simulation Interoperability Standards Organization (2006)

18. Gagné, R.M.: The Conditions of Learning. Holt, Rinehart and Winston, NewYork (1965)

19. Bloom, B.S.: Taxonomy of Educational Objectives, Handbook: The Cognitive Domain. David McKay, New York (1956)

20. Krathwohl, D.R., Bloom, B.S., Masia, B.B.: Taxonomy of Educational Objectives: The Classification of Educational Goals, Handbook II: Affective Domain. David McKay, New York (1964)

21. Simpson, E.J.: The Classification of Educational Objectives in the Psychomotor Domain. Gryphon House, Washington DC (1972)

22. Burke, C.S., Sottilare, R., Gilbert, S.: Leveraging team taxonomic efforts for authoring. In: Sottilare, R.A., Graesser, A.C., Hu, X., Sinatra, A.M. (eds.) Design Recommendations for Intelligent Tutoring Systems: Volume 6 - Team Tutoring, pp. 193–199. US Army Research Laboratory, Orlando (2018)

23. Hjelmervik, K., Nazir, S., Myhrvold, A.: Simulator training for maritime complex tasks: an experimental study. WMU J. Marit. Aff. **17**(1), 17–30 (2018). https://doi.org/10.1007/s13437-017-0133-0
24. Lathan, C.L., Tracey, M.R., Sebrechts, M.M., Clawson, D.M., Higgins, G.A.: Using virtual environments as training simulators: Measuring transfer. In: Stanney, K.M. (ed.) Handbook of Virtual Environments: Design, Implementation, and Applications, pp. 403–414. Lawrence Erlbaum, Mahwah (2002)
25. Brydges, R., Carnahan, H., Rose, D., Rose, L., Dubrowski, A.: Coordinating progressive levels of simulation fidelity to maximize educational benefit. Acad. Med. **85**, 806–812 (2010). https://doi.org/10.1097/ACM.0b013e3181d7aabd
26. Beaubien, J.M., Baker, D.P.: The use of simulation for training teamwork skills in health care: how low can you go? Qual. Saf. Heal. Care **13**, i51–i56 (2004). https://doi.org/10.1136/qshc.2004.009845
27. IEEE P2247 Working Group: Adaptive Instructional Systems (C/LT/AIS) P2247 Working Group. https://site.ieee.org/sagroups-2247-1/. Accessed 11 Dec 2019
28. Koedinger, K.R., Corbett, A.T., Perfetti, C.: The knowledge-learning-instruction framework: bridging the science-practice chasm to enhance robust student learning. Cogn. Sci. **36**, 757–798 (2012). https://doi.org/10.1111/j.1551-6709.2012.01245.x
29. Hao, J., Mislevy, R.J.: The Evidence Trace File: A Data Structure for Virtual Performance Assessments Informed by Data Analytics and Evidence-Centered Design. Wiley, Hoboken (2018). https://doi.org/10.1002/ets2.12215
30. Tatsuoka, K.K.: Rule space: an approach for dealing with misconceptions based on item response theory. J. Educ. Meas. **20**, 345–354 (1983)
31. Aleven, V., McLaughlin, E.A., Glenn, R.A., Koedinger, K.R.: Instruction based on adaptive learning technologies. In: Mayer, R.E., Alexander, P.A. (eds.) Handbook of Research on Learning and Instruction, pp. 538–576. Routledge (2016). https://doi.org/10.4324/9781315736419
32. Goldin, I., Pavlik, P.I.J., Ritter, S.: Discovering domain models in learning curve data. In: Sottilare, R.A., Graesser, A.C., Hu, X., Olney, A.M., Nye, B.D., Sinatra, A.M. (eds.) Design Recommendations for Intelligent Tutoring Systems: Volume 4 Domain Modeling, pp. 115–126. US Army Research Laboratory, Orlando (2016)
33. Vanlehn, K.: The behavior of tutoring systems. Int. J. Artif. Intell. Ed. **16**, 227–265 (2006)
34. Sottilare, R.A.: Developing standards for adaptive instructional systems: 2018 update. In: Proceedings of the 6th Annual GIFT Users Symposium, pp. 1–5. U.S. Army Research Laboratory, Orlando (2018)
35. Pavlik, P.I., Brawner, K.W., Olney, A., Mitrovic, A.: A review of learner models used in intelligent tutoring systems. In: Sottilare, R.A., Graesser, A., Hu, X., Holden, H. (eds.) Design Recommendations for Intelligent Tutoring Systems. Volume 1: Learner Modeling, pp. 39–68. US Army Research Laboratory (2013)
36. Sottilare, R.A., Brawner, K.W., Goldberg, B.S., Holden, H.K.: The Generalized Intelligent Framework for Tutoring (GIFT) (2012)
37. Abdelzaher, T., Diao, Y., Hellerstein, J.L., Lu, C., Zhu, X.: Introduction to control theory and its application to computing systems. Perform. Model. Eng. 185–215 (2008). https://doi.org/10.1007/978-0-387-79361-0_7
38. Hu, X., et al.: Capturing AIS behavior using xAPI-like statements. In: Sottilare, R.A., Schwarz, J. (eds.) HCII 2019. LNCS, vol. 11597, pp. 204–216. Springer, Cham (2019). https://doi.org/10.1007/978-3-030-22341-0_17
39. Rustici Software: What is xAPI (the Experience API) (2019)
40. Poeppelman, T.R., Ayers, J., Hruska, M., Long, R., Amburn, C., Bink, M.: Interoperable Performance Assessment Using the Experience API. Interservice/Industry Train (2013)

41. Hruska, M., Long, R., Amburn, C.: Human performance interoperability via xAPI: current military outreach efforts. In: Fall Simulation Interoperability Workshop 2014 Fall SIW, pp. 207–216 (2014)

42. Goodwin, G.A., Murphy, J.S., Medford, A.L.: Support for training effectiveness assessment and data interoperability. In: Interservice/Industry Training, Simulation, Education Conference, pp. 1–11 (2016)

43. Advanced Distributed Learning, ADLnet.gov: xAPI. https://www.adlnet.gov/xAPI. Accessed 19 May 2017

44. CASS Project: CASS Documentation. http://docs.cassproject.org/index.html. Accessed 09 Aug 2017

45. Stacy, W., Freeman, J.: Training objective packages: enhancing the effectiveness of experiential training. Theor. Issues Ergon. Sci. **17**, 149–168 (2016). https://doi.org/10.1080/1463922X.2015.1111459

46. Simulation Interoperability Standards Organization: Human Performance Markup Language (HPML) Development Group (PDG). https://www.sisostds.org/StandardsActivities/DevelopmentGroups/HPMLPDG-HumanPerformanceMarkupLanguage.aspx

47. Advanced Distributed Learning: GitHub - adlnet/xAPI-Spec. https://github.com/adlnet/xAPI-Spec. Accessed 09 June 2017

48. IMS Global Learning Consortium: Caliper Analytics. https://www.imsglobal.org/activity/caliper. Accessed 15 Sept 2019

49. Walker, A., Tolland, M., Stacy, W.: Using a human performance markup language for simulator-based training. In: Simulation Interoperability Standards Organization (SISO) Simulation Interoperability Workshop (SIW) Meeting. SISO - Simulation Interoperability Standards Organization, Orlando (2015)

50. Simulation Interoperability Standards Organization: Product Nomination for Human Performance Markup Language (SISO-PN-015-2016) (2016). https://www.sisostds.org/DigitalLibrary.aspx?Command=Core_Download&EntryId=43990

Supporting Different Roles and Responsibilities in Developing and Using Context-Based Adaptive Personalized Collaboration Environments Compliant to the Law

Mandy Goram[(✉)] and Dirk Veiel

Faculty of Mathematics and Computer Science, FernUniversität in Hagen,
58084 Hagen, Germany
{mandy.goram,dirk.veiel}@fernuni-hagen.de

Abstract. Developing context-based adaptive applications that are compliant to the law require experts from different domains, e.g. software designer, developers, legal professionals, providers and users, and a tight collaboration between them. Software providers must be assured that the applications they serve to users run compliant to the law. Additionally, it is important to support users to act according to the law, e.g. when they upload content which may concern the Copyright Law. This aspect is also relevant to providers, because they are responsible for users' legal breaches. To support users to act compliant to the law when using an application, it is important that they understand the current situation and the related consequences to the usage of the system. This paper presents a development and provisioning process for domain-specific context-based adaptive software applications. We define roles and responsibilities as well as artifacts that need to be specified in the different lifecycle phases of the process. Using the process, related stakeholders will be able to integrate legal regulations into context-based adaptive systems. We use a sample scenario, where Copyright Law and personalized explanations get relevant, to describe how legal experts support other stakeholders in the development process and how they can configure legal requirements and provide explanations. Our approach adds flexibility to the development and provisioning process, because only relevant regulations for a specific application have to be considered.

Keywords: Adaptive personalized environment · Compliance by design · Intelligent adaptive collaboration environment · Development process · Lifecycle

1 Introduction

Legal regulations demand that applications consider legal aspects of related application domains. Regulations equally concern software designer, developers, legal professionals (who check and confirm legal compliance), providers and users. The development of legally compliant software needs a tight collaboration between the above stakeholders. Software providers must be assured that the applications they use and

© Springer Nature Switzerland AG 2020
R. A. Sottilare and J. Schwarz (Eds.): HCII 2020, LNCS 12214, pp. 88–107, 2020.
https://doi.org/10.1007/978-3-030-50788-6_7

serve to customers or users run compliant to the law. For that, it is important to support users to act according to the law, e.g. when they upload content which may concern the Copyright Law. This aspect is relevant to providers, because they are responsible for users' legal breaches. But legal regulations are interconnected, even if there is no connection for the layman at first sight. In order to ensure legal conformity, it is therefore not sufficient to simply include a specific legal requirement in a system [1, 2].

1.1 Problem Statement

To support users to act compliant to the law when using an application, it is important that they understand the current situation and the related consequences to the usage of the system. Supporting users with explanations of the law and the related actions and consequences to the usage of the system is a big challenge. According to [3], the privacy control is strongly related to intelligible explanations. Therefore, it is necessary to explain system processes and data usage, to help users to better understand the current situation [4]. "The dynamic aspect of context implies that it is not possible to plan in advance the whole explanatory dialogue" [4, p. 123]. Personalized explanations shall "serve to clarify and make something understandable" [5, p. 498] to the user in a specific situation. When a user's action, e. g. affects the General Data Protection Regulation (GDPR) or the Copyright Law, the consequences of the usage of the system should be explained. To provide this support a more sophisticated system approach is necessary like a context-based adaptive system environment which is used to provide personalized support in the current situation. To address the aforementioned aspects, we have to answer three questions:

1. How to design a context-based adaptive software application which considers the concerning law?
2. How to support the different stakeholder of a software development process with compliance by design?
3. How to explain users what they must do to act in compliance to legal regulations in the specific situation?

1.2 Approach

We address the aforementioned questions and challenges by developing an intelligent context-based adaptive system environment, based on the CONtact platform [6], that enables us to develop or integrate context-based and/or adaptable applications. For that, we use a development and provisioning process presented in this paper. The involved stakeholders integrate technical, content and legal requirements in a common domain model [7]. This enables us to reuse our environment and to modify it according to required changes of the underlying four-layer context model (cf. [7]). We use the knowledge of domain experts to define rules for the specific application. In case of legal regulations, the context-based adaptive environment must know when and how it must do something. For that, a legal expert must predefine what needs to be considered and what action should be executed by the context-based adaptive environment. Legal experts should provide explanations for users and decide what data resp. information must be included in the declaration. Declaration is a concept of our domain model (cf. [7]) and its instances will be partially created by the so-called Template Builder, which conduct the structure of the explanatory dialog and the related information of the specific situation.

1.3 Contribution

This paper presents a development and provisioning process for domain-specific context-based adaptive software applications (cf. Sect. 4). We define roles and responsibilities as well as artifacts that need to be specified in the different phases of the process (cf. Sect. 5). Using the process, related stakeholders will be able to integrate legal regulations into context-based adaptive systems. We use a sample scenario, where Copyright Law, GDPR and personalized explanations get relevant, to describe how legal experts support other stakeholders in the development process and how they can configure legal requirements and provide explanations (cf. Sect. 6). With our approach we do not have to predefine all legal requirements. Only relevant regulations for a specific application should be integrated. This enables us to achieve more flexibility in the application of our context-based adaptive collaboration environment.

2 Prerequisite

Context: As defined by Dey [8], context includes all information that can be used to describe a situation, including information about the user, the technical and physical environment, as well as space and time. In our view, however, the description of a situation includes not only the socio-technical, physical and space-time information, but also the legal constraints that exist in the specific situation. These provide the necessary framework for action and the implementation of appropriate policies and interventions. This means that the situation must also include a proper evaluation of the legal facts that are needed to explain and support in the situation.

Application Domain: The application domain is the real-world environment and provides the setting in which a software application is used, e.g. online learning platforms, community applications, business or medical applications. Each of these domains (e.g. education, business or medicine) has special characteristics that do not exist in other areas. However, they also share a common basis which is necessary for IT-based support, e.g. recording, processing and changing data of objects or persons. Due to that, we call any application domain environment or system and the related requirements as domain-specific application or requirement.

Context-Based Adaptive Approach: We define a context-based adaptive approach as the provision of an environment that is able to perceive a situation, recognize the need for action and make an adequate adaptation of the system. This should support users in specific situations. In doing so, we address the individual needs of the users through personalized adaptations. In a group or collaboration situation, the system has to find a consent that takes into account the situation and circumstances of the individual group members.

Our context-based adaptive system is based on a formal model that we model using an ontology. We develop a core model with all necessary concepts and relationships which represents objects and functionalities within every supported application domain. This model will be extended for different scenarios and application domains at so-called extension points. It provides the basis to represent the context at runtime. For context modelling we use the Web Ontology Language (OWL) and the generic four-layer framework for modelling context in a collaboration environment and the related collaboration domain model presented in [9].

Four-Layer Framework: The generic four-layer framework for modelling context consists of the knowledge layer, the state layer, the contextualized state layer, the adaptation layer and related components to implement a generic adaptation process [9]. The knowledge layer describes a domain model with abstract (e. g. classes, properties) and concrete (e. g. individuals) predefined knowledge, mapped to corresponding concepts and relations. The sensing engine at the state layer uses sensing rules to instantiate related concepts and relationships from the domain model (cf. knowledge layer) to represent the current collaboration environment of all users. The contextualization engine at the contextualization layer applies contextualization strategies to extract a subset from the state (cf. state layer) and/or domain model (cf. knowledge layer) which are relevant for the current collaboration situation. This creates a contextualized state that we call the context. The adaptation engine at the adaptation layer evaluates the adaptation rules and executes applicable adaptation rules. This leads to the adapted state that is mapped to the collaboration environment.

Adaptation Cycle: Users interact with applications on the client side (cf. Fig. 1). Applications inform the Sensing Engine on the server side about these interactions. Using the above-mentioned sensing rules, the four-layer framework is used for Context Representation. After the updates have been applied to the formal Context Representation, the Adaptation Engine gets triggered. It uses the Context Representation to retrieve applicable Adaptation Rules (i.e. policies that can be mapped to actions of related applications), brings them into an Execution Order and notifies the related Adaptation Component(s) on the client side. The Adaptation Component applies the given adaptation actions (in order) to the corresponding Application(s) which triggers the next adaptation cycle.

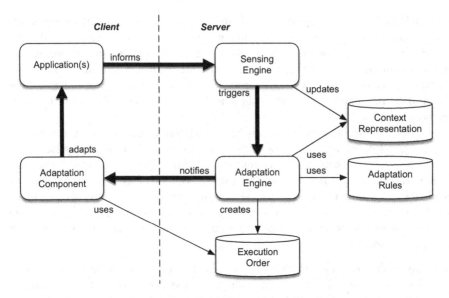

Fig. 1. Adaptation cycle of our approach.

eCBASE: extendable Context-based adaptive system environment, short eCBASE, is a common platform of functions and technologies for providing context-based adaptive and personalized software applications that can be made available for different domains. In the so-called core system, we model domain-independent and domain-specific objects and relationships as well as fundamental legal aspects, which must be considered in all future domain-specific applications. The design of the legal requirements is passed on to the responsible legal experts of the operating organization or the provider of a domain-specific application. eCBASE provides the necessary formal concepts and basic functions for this which are represented in a legal domain model.

CONTact: CONTact is a context-based adaptive system to support group collaboration and serves us as starting point for the development of an eCBASE platform. CONTact is based on a formal model that contains core concepts and relationships for domain-specific and domain-independent collaboration applications [6]. As part of our work, this system will be extended and adapted. This includes the development and integration of a domain model to represent legal requirements, as described in [7]. We use a self-developed and validated process model to extend and validate the existing domain model, but due to space reasons it is not subject of this paper.

3   Related Work

It is not known to us, that there is directly related work to our approach and the process and lifecycle we present in this paper. Due to our complex and interdisciplinary research on legal conformity in context-based adaptive personalized environments, there are relations into different research areas like legal domain modelling, context-based services, intelligible explanation of complex situations during the usage of an application as well as on the design and implementation of context-based adaptive personalized domain-specific applications, e.g. learning environments.

In the recent years, context-based adaptive and context-aware applications has been researched in several domain, e.g. distance learning [10], webservices [11]. The importance of legal conditions and user privacy is often mentioned [12], but not considered in the resulting methods, functionalities or formal models.

Nevertheless, there are approaches that take into account legal aspects of data protection. The GDPR, whose requirements for data collection and processing have been integrated into some approaches or were completely new developments, has also contributed to this. The classification of data protection-relevant functions and data at the source code level is a fundamental aspect to enable automated processing. This is intended to help users regain control over their privacy or to influence data processing. In the context-aware approach of [13], source-code-level annotations are used to classify personal and sensitive information for so-called "information spaces" by using privacy tags. The owners can decide who may access their information space.

The context-aware approaches of [11, 14] support the user's privacy while using webservices. They classify private and non-private data on the formal conceptual layer. An integrated adaptation mechanism uses Simple Object Access Protocol (SOAP) messages to realized user privacy preferences in context-aware webservices. Through [11] the policy language Consumer Privacy Language (CPL) is introduced and used to specify the user's privacy preferences. They are considered during the webservice invocation. Through an adaptation mechanism the privacy preferences are used to get access to context information on a per case basis. The mechanism is integrated into the presented webservice infrastructure that applies the user's privacy preferences and manages the service execution. The approach of [14] enhance and extend [11] but focus on the provider side. For that, they extended the privacy module of the Linked Unified Service Description Language (USDL). The USDL module is used to describe privacy policies for the use of any webservice. The extension can use and include existing privacy policies to answer questions about what personal data is collected from users, how the service provider uses the collected data and with whom it will be shared.

A whole formal ontology-based legal domain model for the GDPR is presented by [15]. The model contains the regulation with aspects of the basic data protection principals, the data processing rules, and the data subject's rights. They use the ontology to assist data controllers during the development cycle of software development. For that, they integrated the ontology in a Business Process and Model Notation (BPMN) workflow to express the GDPR requirements within the workflow. The data protection ontology of [15] was designed by a legal expert and could be integrated in our eCBASE core system to provide important concepts and relationships for the resulting domain-specific application. There is no process or description on how to develop or integrate the domain model into the BPMN or other workflows and applications in [15].

A more sophisticated regulatory ontology is presented by [16]. They are using ontologies to get a more flexible and modular system that allows to extend and adapt the concepts and relationships without losing the connection to the base system. They describe the regulatory Intellectual Property Rights ontology (IPROnto), allowing the combination of results from different areas or domains. The IPROnto contains a static and dynamic view to separate the design of the intellectual property regulation and its derived rights from the using of the defined rules and interdependencies. The static view describes legal concepts (defined by law), legal entities (possessing capacity in law) and the IP Law in detail. The dynamic view is used to create business models for its us in e-commerce applications. It contains events which represent the processes of the intellectual property right. For that they describe a content life cycle and sample events like the creation of origin contribution and its related law and rights of the legal entities. They also describe how they can develop and transfer their design on an ontology for the GDPR on base of their IPROnto framework. Although they have a content life cycle, the do not describe what is necessary to develop and implement an application using the ontology.

The presented related work describes the integration and the scope of data protection or the Intellectual Property Law in a specific area but do not take other regulations into account. The development of a common core system which transfers best practices to other areas, requires a common formal language [16]. For that, [11] creates the policy language Consumer Privacy Language (CPL) and an extended privacy module of the Linked Unified Service Description Language (USDL). But they do not foresee the use in a context-based adaptive system environment. Their approach contains the enhancement of web services with data privacy aspects. But a context-based adaptive system environment can also implement or trigger functionalities which do not interact on the basis of web services. Our context-based adaptive system environment approach could consider a bunch of legal regulations. Furthermore, it is important to provide intelligible explanations about protection of privacy and privacy control to the users. Explanations are needed to help users to understand why and how their data is used in the system and to whom it will be accessible [17]. For the representation of different legal areas and the provision of personal explanations for users, we developed a specific legal domain model, which is not in the scope of this paper.

4   eCBASE Lifecycle

For the development of a context-based adaptive system environment and the provision of a domain-specific context-based software applications we identified three phases. The overall lifecycle is illustrated in Fig. 2 and contains the phases (1) Core eCBASE, (2) Legal Framework Extension and (3) Domain-specific Application Extension. The rectangles show the result of the specific phase of the lifecycle and the added text a short description of the specific phase.

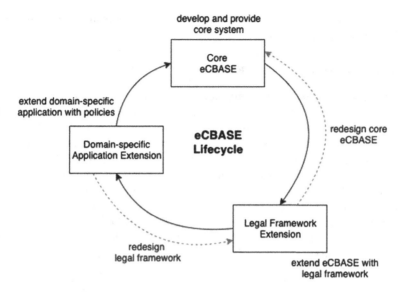

Fig. 2. eCBASE Lifecycle to provide compliant context-based adaptive applications.

4.1 Phase 1: Core eCBASE

In the first phase, the core system with a common model and core functionalities is developed. It follows a typical software development lifecycle to identify the specific requirements for scenarios which have to be supported. We us our four-layer framework to develop a context-based adaptive application. For that, we have to design and test a core domain model with all relevant concepts and relationships of a context-based adaptive system. Based on this core model we have to identify and define the domain models for specific application domains, e.g. adaptive personalized learning environments or adaptive personalized community applications. The core model also contains relevant and common legal requirements which must be considered in all application domains, e.g. a request approval for personal data usage or a functionality for data usage explanations.

The result of the first phase is a domain independent core eCBASE which can be extended with domain-specific applications by domain experts. The core eCBASE has to be extended with new and not yet considered concepts of new domains, e.g. medical adaptive personalized applications. Over time the core eCBASE becomes more mature and provides flexible and extendable services and functionalities. For that, we combine different technologies and use a loosely coupled software architecture which is independent from a specific implementation.

We use different extension points to extend the core model with more specific services. The core model itself is stable and can be used without any extension. The provision is independent of a specific provider or organization who offers and uses the end-user applications. For the extension of eCBASE with the legal framework and the domain-specific adaptation policies special user interfaces are provided. They give an overview of available data and application functionalities together with explanations about the usage and legal advice.

4.2   Phase 2: Legal Framework Extension

The second phase builds on the provided core eCBASE. In that phase the legal framework is implemented and tested for specific scenarios. The legal framework is specific to a provider and/or an organization. It contains legal requirements for the specific usage. The core eCBASE provides common legal requirements which are covered by the concepts *dm:Requirement* and its subclass *dm:legal* (cf. [7]). Furthermore, we use a more flexible approach to define and integrate legal requirements into the end-user application. We think, only a responsible legal professional of the particular provider of a context-based adaptive application can decide how the system has to act in certain situations. Our core model can be extended with specific requirements of other organizations, branches and countries. The core model supports the integration with a structural concept of law texts and the consequences for the specific application environment. In the end, the responsible legal professional should decide what legal requirements must be considered and with what consequences for the usage of the application.

The legal consequences will be integrated as legal policies which must be considered at runtime by the domain-specific application. It is the basis for the design of the end-user application. When the integration of the legal framework needs more concepts or executable actions within the core model (cf. Fig. 2, arrow to step one *Core eCBASE*), then it must be extended and updated. Best practices of legal requirements can also be integrated into the core model as an extension which is available for other organizations. Changes at the core concepts or the integration of new available application functionalities within existing context-based adaptive applications need a revision and release of the legal framework. That should support the compliance by design process and the controlled feature extension.

4.3   Phase 3: Domain-Specific Application Extension

The last phase is to extend the domain-specific application with the context-based adaptive functionalities of eCBASE. Besides the functionalities of the core system and its special domain extensions, the legal framework for creating the domain-specific application is also available. The rule designer, who should be a domain expert, can extend the domain-specific end-user application for the target group based on the application functionalities and objects provided by eCBASE. To do this, he or she determines which functionality and content will be provided for the individual users.

Adaptation policies are used to determine how the software application should act in specific situations, e.g. providing help texts when a task is processed in the application. In the phase of extending the domain-specific application, no extensions are made to eCBASE itself, so no software developers are involved.

If it becomes necessary to support scenarios that cannot be supported with the current functional scope, the core system must be adapted according to the scenario (cf. Fig. 2, redesign core eCBASE). This leads to the life cycle being run through again. As soon as it becomes clear that legal regulations are missing in the extended domain application, the legal framework has to be adapted (cf. Fig. 2, redesign legal framework). When this not be possible, it is necessary to return to the development phase of eCBASE (cf. Fig. 2, redesign core eCBASE).

5 Roles and Responsibilities

This section introduces the roles and responsibilities within the eCBASE lifecycle. Within each phase of the lifecycle we use a typical software development process. Due to the tightly coupled work of the different stakeholders an agile or scenario-based development is required. The scenario-based approach [18, 19] fits to our user-centered design and development, because our research focus on intelligent and assistive socio-technical applications. Some roles exist in more or all lifecycle phases. In our approach the provider takes care of the project management (i.e. managing the lifecycle).

5.1 Roles

Analyst (ANA): As in classical software development processes, the analyst is responsible for the collection and specification of requirements [20]. For this, he or she creates various detailed use cases which are used to determine the functional and technical requirements for the context-based adaptive system. This contains requirements for the core eCBASE as well as for the domain-specific applications.

Legal Professional (LPR): The legal expert supports the development process of the eCBASE platform by providing advice on how to realize legal requirements and explains how system functionalities can be implemented and used in a law compliant manner. He or she notes which functionalities or data must be signalized and documented in the system. A legal professional is also responsible for the specific configuration of the legal framework. For that he or she designs the legal policies which must be considered in specific situations and while using application functionalities from eCBASE. A special user interface shows all application functionalities and legal implications which were identified be a legal expert in the first phase of the eCBASE lifecycle. The legal professional is responsible for the release of the legal framework.

Designer (DSG): The designer is responsible for the design and the high-level architecture of eCBASE. For that he or she can use established processes and modelling languages, e.g. Unified Modeling Language (UML) and BPMN. The designer has to consider classical aspects like modularity, usability, fault-tolerance, performance, portability and security. In a tight collaboration with the legal professional he or she creates a solution design which considers legal aspects and contains legal advices and explanation components. While our system operates on a formal model, the designer should at least create the domain-specific requirements within an existing domain model or create new domain models which are added at the related extension point. We use OWL 2 for modelling, so in our case the designer models the domain and legal requirements with OWL 2.

Developer (DEV): Developers check the technical requirements and implement the requirements in eCBASE. They are responsible for the integration of the formal model, e.g. the OWL 2 file(s). Furthermore, the developers implement and extend the sensing and adaptation engine of eCBASE (e.g. by supporting sensing rules and/or adaptation actions through adaptation interfaces). Domain-independent adaptation policies will be defined and implemented by the developer. Developers are responsible for the implementation of legal compliant data processing and must consider legal advices of the legal professional. Due to that, they have to annotate source code sections, data fields and functions which use or store personal data. Any application functionality which concerns the GDPR (personal data processing, profiling etc.) must have an explanation which contains the reason of data storing and processing, the purpose, the storage duration and what other functionalities or services are used for data processing, especially the transfer to third party services and tools.

Tester (TST): Based on scenarios and the functional design description, tester check and test the eCBASE domain-independent and domain-specific modules and functionalities. For that they use white box and black box testing, as well as mocked up user interfaces. While testing the extended legal framework (phase 2) and domain-specific application (phase 3), the testers check if the defined policies are executed as intended.

Rule Designer (RUD): Rule designers are experts in their field. They are specialized in designing and integrating adaptation policies into eCBASE. They use a special user interface to develop adaptation rules for the policy at hand. The adaptation rules get active during runtime. Rule designers are part of the second and third phase of the eCBASE lifecycle. During the Legal Framework Extension phase a legal professional take over the role of a rule designer and build up the legal framework which contains the adaptation policies and explanations about them. He or she is involved in testing the developed adaptation rules and is responsible for the release of the framework and the eCBASE functionalities.

Provider (PRV): A provider is either a single person or an organization. The provider is responsible for the extension and elaboration of the legal framework as well as for the provision and the hosting of the domain-specific application. The provider is responsible for the software and the content, if available in a public (e.g. public available content on websites and forums) or semi-public (e.g. community system with access to content after user authentication) space. For that, the provider has a specific frame of legal and/or organizational policies which must be reflected in the domain-specific application. Due to that, the provider or legal professional who is in charge must decide how to deal with the legal requirements, e.g. allow the usage of a content upload functionality or not which may concern the intellectual property law and data privacy law.

DevOps (DOP): The DevOps are responsible for the maintenance of the domain-specific application and support users and rule designers.

User (USR): Users interact with the domain-specific application. They should be supported by adaptive personalized functionalities while using the application. The user will be informed by explanations about the current situation and related policies. This should create awareness that actions in and handling of the system are subject to legal regulations, for which the user is responsible, e.g. using a location-based service needs an approval of personal data usage, i.e. the location. Due to that, the application provides advices how to deal with the related situation.

5.2   Artifacts

Use Cases (UC): They are created from domain-independent and domain-specific requirements. Responsible role to create the artifact: Analyst.

Legal Checklist (LC): The checklist contains requirements for the design and development of eCBASE and the domain-specific applications that have to be considered according to legal requirements, e.g. data privacy and the resulting data processing requirements. The checklist is based on the use cases and the domain-specific situation descriptions. Responsible role to create the artifact: Legal Professional.

Functional Design (FD): The artifact contains the classical aspects of the functional design of the required or extended software application. Responsible role to create the artifact: Designer.

Technical Design (TD): The technical design document contains the classical aspects of the technical design of the required or extended software application and uses the functional design document. Responsible role to create the artifact: Designer.

Domain Model (DM): The domain model is the formal description of the concepts and relationships of eCBASE and its domain-specific extensions. Part of the modeling is the logical validation (reasoning) to check the model for errors and incomplete information. Responsible role to create the artifact: Designer.

Software (SW): The implementation of the requirements results in a software application or a software module, which can be tested and deployed. Responsible role to create the artifact: Developer, Rule Designer.

Test Protocol (TP): The test protocol describes the scenarios to be tested and the test cases which have been created and executed. Based on the results, previous steps must be repeated (e.g. due to errors or incorrect specification) or a release is made. Responsible role to create the artifact: Legal professional, Tester.

Acceptance Report (AR): The acceptance report is the confirmation that all functional and legal requirements for the developed software and the legal framework are fulfilled. Responsible role to create the artifact: Legal professional.

Legal Report (LP): The legal report based on the analysis of the use cases, the legal checklist and the provider-specific legal requirements, e.g. when using a context-based adaptive learning environment in a public university. For that, the report describes legal conditions which get relevant when extending and using the domain-specific application. The legal report also contains explanations for legal related actions and restrictions as well as case scenarios of the legal intended results. Responsible role to create the artifact: Legal Professional.

Recommendation for Action (RA): Based on the legal report, the legal professional makes recommendations for action on the integration and operation of the application functionalities. The regulations and their consequences for users and providers are explained and integrated into the legal framework. Responsible role to create the artifact: Legal Professional.

Legal Policies (LP): The legal policies contain decisions on how to deal with certain situations and under which circumstances the functions can be used. The LPs are used to create the adaptation rules within the legal framework. Responsible role to create the artifact: Legal Professional.

Release Note (RN): The release notes contain information about the added or changed components and policies of eCBASE (phase 1). These will be extended by additional information about changes in the legal framework (phase 2) and the domain-specific application (phase 3). Responsible role to create the artifact: Legal Professional.

Adaptation Policies (AP): Adaptation policies contain a formal description on how actions are triggered in eCBASE. For that, they contain the circumstances when the action gets relevant (condition) and will be executed, and what the result of the action should be. Responsible role to create the artifact: Rule Designer.

6 Supporting Stakeholder in extendable Context-Based Adaptive Systems

In this section we illustrate our development and lifecycle approach. For that, we use a scenario when eCBASE must be extended with new functionalities which are required in the domain-specific application meinDorf55+ (a novel community support system for elderly). For that, a content upload functionality to upload documents, pictures and photos into a private space or group space is needed.

6.1   Phase 1 – Core eCBASE

The users of the app meinDorf55+ would like to upload documents to their account and make them available to other users. This is currently not possible, because the app was previously designed to distribute and organize events that were created right in the app. To make the new functions available, eCBASE must be extended. Firstly, the requirements must be analyzed, which is why the process starts with the requirements analysis.

Analyst: The analyst found out that video, pictures, text documents in different formats should be uploaded in the application environment.

Legal Professional: The legal professional analyzed the scenario and mentioned that all kind of uploaded documents needs information about the origin author(s), the upload date, the usage (private/public) and a published state. In case of pictures there must be a separation into pictures and photos. An uploaded photo must have information about the content, especially if it shows any other person different to the uploading user or any others property, and in case of persons depicted the subject. The legal professional point out that the uploading user needs the permission of the depicted persons in the photo before he or she could make it accessible in a public space of the software application. That makes it necessary to provide an approval mechanism.

Designer: The eCBASE designer creates design of the upload functionality and take into account the legal advices. He or she models additional concepts and relations for core concepts by using related extension points to integrate application functionalities. The upload service can process documents which must be separated as document, picture and photo. Whereby the document upload is the general function. The picture upload is a subclass of is it. The photo upload is a specialization of the picture upload, because it needs additional information and processes (approval or permission when it pictures persons) for a proper legal mapping into a software application.

Developer: The developer implements the concepts and relationships, extends the sensing and adaptation engine. Due to respect the legal advice he or she classifies the upload functionality with the tags "IPLaw", "GDPR". The code annotations are used to check the documentation for completeness and are needed for data processing. The legal professional has to provide explanations and an overview of related or may concerned law while using the upload functionality. These will be reflected in later steps to explain the functionality and maybe necessary actions. For that, legal requirements and explanations must be integrated before using the application functionality.

Tester: The tester checks the sensing and adaptation engine based on the created domain-specific policies. He or she tests whether or not the content upload and all related specializations run according to the predefined situations in a policy-specific manner. In addition, the requirements of the legal expert are used to check the documentation and annotation in the source code. When all tests succeeded the modifications get deployed. After that the tester runs a post-test to unsure a correct deployment (Table 1).

Table 1. Roles and Responsibilities of the phase Core eCBASE.

Step/ Role	Analysis	Design	Development	Test	Deployment
ANA	Requirement analysis; Input: Require- ments Output: UC				
LPR	Legal advice; Input: UC Output: LC	Legal advice	Legal advice	Check implemen- tation Input: UC, LC Output: AR	
DSG		Application Design Input: LC Output: FD, TD			
DEV		Feedback technical requirements	Implementation Input: TD, LC Output: DM, SW	Pre-tests; Defect analysis	
TST				Testing Input: UC, LC, FD, TD Output: TP	Post-test Input: TP Output: RN

6.2   Phase 2 – Legal Framework Extension

After the requirements for a content upload have been implemented and tested in eCBASE, the legal framework must be extended in the second phase.

Legal Professional: The legal professional analyzes the use cases and legal advices from the first phase to create a legal report (LR). Based on the LR, he or she creates recommendations for actions (RA) for the integrating and running of the content upload function. In our scenario the RA says that the content upload is allowed and includes photos. The RA are used to develop the legal policies (LP). The LP say that, when photos are uploaded in a public or group space, they must be approved by the con- cerned persons. Furthermore, the uploading person is fully responsible for the content and violations (if he/she makes false statements) against the policy. The adaptation policies can be integrated as adaptation rules into the legal framework by the legal professional or the rule designer. The LPR tests the integrated policies and their completeness. After the tests, the legal professional has to release the legal framework.

Rule Designer: The rule designer creates the adaptation rules of the legal framework based on the legal policies. The adaptation rules could by describe as follows: (1) When photos for public or group spaces are uploaded, then the application must provide an approval dialog with legal implications and consequences. (2) When asking for per- mission, then the concerned person must be informed with an approval request dialog (assuming that these affected persons use this or a linked application). The rule designer could be a legal professional or have deeper knowledge about the legal conditions. He or she supports the tests of the legal framework.

Tester: Based on the use case scenarios of the domain-specific application specification and the legal advices the testers check the provided application and policies. Through the legal framework from the second phase, he or she gets explanations and personalized adaptations as an end-user of the application. The explanations contain the legal interconnection, their consequences and the needed or triggered actions from the user interface. The tester then checks if the required action has been triggered and applied correctly (Table 2).

Table 2. Roles and Responsibilities of the phase Legal Framework Extension.

Step/ Role	Analysis	Design	Development	Test	Deployment
LPR	Analyze functionalities; Analyze facts of the use cases; Input: UC Output: LR	Create recommendations for action Input: LR Output: RA	Create adaptation policies; Integrate and configure adaptation policies Input: RA Output: LP	Scenario testing (checking adaptation policies) Input: UC, LP Output: TP	release integrated policies Input: TP Output: AR, RN
RDG			Create adaptive rules; Integrate and configure adaptive rules Input: RA Output: LP	Scenario testing Input: UC, LP Output: TP	
TST				Scenario testing Input: UC, LP Output: TP	

6.3   Phase 3 – Domain-Specific Application Extension

In the third phase new functionalities will be integrated into the app meinDorf55+.

Analyst: The domain-specific analyst checks the upload functionalities and the legal conditions to prepare the extension of the App meinDorf55+. For that, he or she creates use cases and describe how to use the upload functionalities and for what situations.

Legal Professional: The legal professional advises in the analysis of use cases and in the development of adaptation rules in order to integrate the new functionalities compliantly. Once the rules have been implemented, he or she checks them for conformity and releases the changes for the app (Table 3).

Table 3. Roles and Responsibilities of the phase Domain-specific Application Extension.

Step/ Role	Analysis	Design	Development	Test	Deployment	Usage
ANA	Requirement analysis; Input: Requirements Output: UC					
LPR	Legal advice; Check Use Cases for legal concerns	Legal advice	Legal advice		release application and policies Input: TP Output: AR, RN	
RDG		Design adaptation policies Input: UC Output: AP	Integrate adaptation rules Input: AP Output: SW	Scenario testing Input: UC, AP Output: TP	Post-tests Input: TP Output: TP	
TST				Scenario testing Input: UC, AP Output: TP		
PRO						provide domain-specific eCBASE
DVO					deploy application Input: AR, RN Output: SW	run and support extended CBASE
USR						Use domain-specific application

Rule Designer: He or she creates the adaptation rules of the domain-specific application based on the use cases and the functional design. The adaptation rules could by describe as follows: (1) When a user will upload a file, then the application provides an upload dialog with explanations about legal implications and consequences. (2) When a user will publish a photo, then he or she gets an approval request dialog with explanations about legal implications and consequences. The rule designer supports the tests of the domain-specific application.

Tester: To support the testers during the last eCBASE lifecycle phase (*Domain-specific Application Extension*), he or she gets an overview of the functionalities and its related legal implications. Based on the use case scenarios of the domain-specific application specification and the legal advices the testers check the provided application and policies. Through the legal framework from the second phase, he or she gets explanations and personalized adaptations as an end-user of the application. The explanations contain the legal interconnection, their consequences and the needed or triggered actions from the user interaction interface. The tester then checks if the required action has been triggered and applied correctly.

Provider: The provider takes over the changes into the running meinDorf55+ application.

DevOps: The DevOps deploy the changes into the running application and support the users of the meinDorf55+ application.

User: Users can use the content upload functionality to upload their documents in a private or public space. If they upload a photo with other persons or other persons property, they have to make an approval request. The application supports the user with a call to action and provides an approval request dialog.

7 Discussion

In order to support different stakeholders in the development and provision of a legal compliant context-based adaptive application, we presented a generic lifecycle with the three phases Core eCBASE, Legal Framework Extension and Domain-specific Application Extension. Every phase has specific tasks for the different stakeholders. For that we described what roles are needed in the process and what are their responsibilities and the important artifacts of the phases. Based on an example scenario we could show the tightly coupled tasks and the interdisciplinarity of the development and provision of context-based adaptive applications. The legal professional has an important role within the eCBASE lifecycle and supports nearly every task at least in a consultative way. In the phase *Legal Framework Extension*, he or she is responsible for the analysis of domain-specific scenarios and the development of legal policies which must be considered during the relevant scenarios.

With our generic lifecycle we can plan and develop our core system. The integration and extension of the legal framework through a user interface is not yet supported and part of future work. Nevertheless, we pointed out the responsibilities and the required artifacts which are needed in our eCBASE lifecycle phases.

8 Conclusion and Future Work

In this paper we presented a development and provisioning process for domain-specific context-based adaptive software applications. We defined roles and responsibilities as well as artifacts that need to be specified in the different phases of the process. Using the process, related stakeholders will be able to integrate legal regulations into context-based adaptive systems. We used a sample scenario, where Copyright Law, GDPR and personalized explanations get relevant, to describe how legal experts support other stakeholders in the development process and how they can configure legal requirements and provide explanations.

The presented solution enables us to address all three questions we introduced in Sect. 1 as follows. Using the presented process, involving different stakeholders, defining related roles and responsibilities and creating the above-mentioned artifacts, enables the development and provisioning of domain-specific context-based adaptive software applications according to the legal regulations (answer to questions 1 and 2). In addition, our approach can support users to comply with the law when using related functionalities of the application at hand by generating personalized explanations (answer to question 3). For that, we use the specific context to generate explanations containing the legal interconnection, their consequences and the required or triggered actions from the user interface.

Future work should give answers to the question on how to design a user interface for integrating legal and domain-specific policies into the legal framework and the domain-specific adaptive application without changing source code. This user interface should enable legal professionals and rule designers to integrate the relevant policies into eCBASE. We plan to use focus groups to evaluate the user interfaces. Later on, we try to support good or best practices using than existing legal policies. Therefore, we plan to use domain experts for finding and validating good or best practices. Additionally, the design and evaluation of personalized explanations to support users' in specific situations is topic of further research.

Acknowledgment. This work was supported by the Research Cluster Digitalization, Diversity and Lifelong Learning. Consequences for Higher Education (D^2L^2) of the FernUniversität in Hagen funded by the Ministry of Culture and Science of the German State of North Rhine-Westphalia. The App meinDorf55+ is supported (was supported) by funds of the Federal Ministry of Food and Agriculture (BMEL) based on a decision of the Parliament of the Federal Republic of Germany via the Federal Office for Agriculture and Food (BLE) under the rural development program.

References

1. Baumann, C., Peitz, P., Raabe, O., Wacker, R.: Compliance for service based systems through formalization of law. In: WEBIST (2), pp. 367–371 (2010)
2. Casellas, N., et al.: Ontological semantics for data privacy compliance: the Neurona project. In: 2010 AAAI Spring Symposium Series (2010)
3. Dey, A.K., Newberger, A.: Support for context-aware intelligibility and control. In: Proceedings of the SIGCHI Conference on Human Factors in Computing Systems, pp. 859–868. ACM (2009)
4. Brezillon, P.J.: Contextualized explanations. In: Proceedings of International Conference on Expert Systems for Development, pp. 119–124. IEEE (1994)
5. Gregor, S., Benbasat, I.: Explanations from intelligent systems: theoretical foundations and implications for practice. MIS Q. **23**(4), 497–530 (1999)
6. Veiel, D., Haake, J.M., Lukosch, S., Kolfschoten, G.: On the acceptance of automatic facilitation in a context-adaptive group support system. In: 2013 46th Hawaii International Conference on System Sciences, pp. 509–518. IEEE (2013)
7. Goram, M., Veiel, D.: Supporting privacy control and personalized data usage explanations in a context-based adaptive collaboration environment. In: Bella, G., Bouquet, P. (eds.) CONTEXT 2019. LNCS (LNAI), vol. 11939, pp. 84–97. Springer, Cham (2019). https://doi.org/10.1007/978-3-030-34974-5_8
8. Dey, A.K.: Understanding and using context. Pers. Ubiquit. Comput. **5**(1), 4–7 (2001)

9. Haake, J.M., Hussein, T., Joop, B., Lukosch, S., Veiel, D., Ziegler, J.: Modeling and exploiting context for adaptive collaboration. Int. J. Coop. Inf. Syst. **19**(01–02), 71–120 (2010)
10. Abarca, M.G., Alarcon, R.A., Barria, R., Fuller, D.: Context-based e-learning composition and adaptation. In: Meersman, R., Tari, Z., Herrero, P. (eds.) OTM 2006. LNCS, vol. 4278, pp. 1976–1985. Springer, Heidelberg (2006). https://doi.org/10.1007/11915072_106
11. Kapitsaki, G., Ioannou, J., Cardoso, J., Pedrinaci, C.: Linked USDL privacy: describing privacy policies for services. In: 2018 IEEE International Conference on Web Services (ICWS), pp. 50–57. IEEE (2018)
12. Perera, C., Zaslavsky, A., Christen, P., Georgakopoulos, D.: Context aware computing for the internet of things: a survey. IEEE Commun. Surv. Tutor. **16**(1), 414–454 (2013)
13. Jiang, X., Landay, J.A.: Modeling privacy control in context-aware systems. IEEE Pervasive Comput. **1**(3), 59–63 (2002)
14. Kapitsaki, G.M.: Reflecting user privacy preferences in context-aware web services. In: 2013 IEEE 20th International Conference on Web Services, pp. 123–130. IEEE (2013)
15. Bartolini, C., Muthuri, R., Santos, C.: Using ontologies to model data protection requirements in workflows. In: Otake, M., Kurahashi, S., Ota, Y., Satoh, K., Bekki, D. (eds.) JSAI-isAI 2015. LNCS, vol. 10091, pp. 233–248. Springer, Cham (2017). https://doi.org/10.1007/978-3-319-50953-2_17
16. Delgado, J., Gallego, I., Llorente, S., García, R.: IPROnto: an ontology for digital rights management. In: 16th Annual Conference on Legal Knowledge and Information Systems, JURIX, vol. 106 (2003)
17. Bellotti, V., Sellen, A.: Design for privacy in ubiquitous computing environments. In: de Michelis, G., Simone, C., Schmidt, K. (eds.) ECSCW 1993, pp. 77–92. Springer, Dordrecht (1993). https://doi.org/10.1007/978-94-011-2094-4_6
18. Sutcliffe, A.G.: Convergence or competition between software engineering and human computer interaction. In: Seffah, A., Gulliksen, J., Desmarais, M.C. (eds.) Human-Centered Software Engineering – Integrating Usability in the Software Development Lifecycle. HCIS, vol. 8, pp. 71–84. Springer, Dordrecht (2005). https://doi.org/10.1007/1-4020-4113-6_5
19. Carroll, J.M. (ed.): Scenario-Based Design: Envisioning Work and Technology in System Development. Wiley, Hoboken (1995)
20. Murch, R.: The Software Development Lifecycle-A Complete Guide. Richard Murch (2012)

Experiential Instruction of Metacognitive Strategies

Andrew J. Hampton[⊠] and Andrew A. Tawfik

University of Memphis, Memphis, TN 38152, USA
andrew.hampton@memphis.edu

Abstract. Learners often have metacognitive deficits that limit their ability to select material at appropriate levels in independent studying situations. The increasing prevalence of intelligent recommender systems can assume this role, while also fostering a kind of experiential meta-instruction. The creation of hybrid tutors (federated systems of both adaptive and static learning resources with a single interface and learning record store) provides an opportunity to test this experiential instruction of metacognitive strategies. As a test case, we examine the hybrid tutor ElectronixTutor, which has two distinct intelligent recommender engines corresponding to distinct use cases. Each of these constitutes a method of providing scaffolding to learners so that they can internalize the principled, theoretically informed reasons for the order of their progression through learning content. However, the learning described is speculative and requires evaluation. By examining expected efficacy, perceived efficacy, actual efficacy, and especially the relationships among these three concepts, actionable insights should arise pertaining to adaptive instructional system design, learning science generally, and other areas.

Keywords: ElectronixTutor · Intelligent recommender · Hybrid tutor

1 Introduction

1.1 Metacognitive Deficits

Progressing through a federated learning environment via adaptive recommendations may constitute experiential learning of metacognitive strategies. Intelligent, personalized recommendations attempt a delicate task otherwise incumbent upon learners. That task depends upon metacognitive processes and awareness which are deficient in (or potentially foreign to) many learners [1]. To compensate for the paucity of those skills, conventional independent learners have rigid lesson plans, at best. Such plans fail to provide many aspects of an experiential process identified by many as critical to knowledge construction [2–4].

Appropriate recommendations—human or otherwise—may complement explicit content instruction by scaffolding how to learn complex topics beyond the immediate application or solution. However, this meta-instruction works best when learners understand the essential logic of artificially intelligent recommendations—that their past performance and personal characteristics inform what should come next. The

© Springer Nature Switzerland AG 2020
R. A. Sottilare and J. Schwarz (Eds.): HCII 2020, LNCS 12214, pp. 108–116, 2020.
https://doi.org/10.1007/978-3-030-50788-6_8

challenge then becomes how to introduce and reinforce the complexities and relationships among these variables through interactive experience, and how to evaluate whether or not such instruction has taken place.

Experiential instruction relies largely on emotional engagement and dynamism. Graesser [5] argues that emotions are the "experiential glue" of learning environments. To accomplish this engagement, adaptive instructional systems sometimes must operate in open defiance of the user experience design principle that cognitive load should be minimized. A cognitively demanding state of confusion may serve as an effective emotional and experiential tool to establish or correct mental models of the domain, as well as the learner's understanding of his mastery status within it [6]. Naturally, this state of confusion may also lead to frustration and in turn disengagement. This risk necessitates a balance, maintained by accurate assessment of the learner's status on multiple dimensions.

Further complicating the high-wire act, learners need some degree of understanding of the intelligent recommendations that guide their interaction with the system. Jackson, Graesser, and McNamara [7] argued that the accuracy of expectations of the learning technology constitute stronger predictors of actual learning than prior knowledge, initial motivation, and technological proficiency combined. As learners are unlikely to differentiate between the production quality of individual learning resources and the federated learning system generally (with special emphasis on the intelligent recommender), a holistic measure of expected efficacy compared to actual efficacy may prove strongly predictive of the latter.

1.2   Hybrid Tutor

Effective instruction of complex domains naturally progresses and varies along multiple dimensions to instill complex understanding. For example, Ohm's Law in electrical engineering logically precedes calculating voltage of series and parallel circuits, because those calculations frequently rely on Ohm's Law. Complementing that linear progression, alternation between applied, conceptual, and formalized denotation can provide symbiotic advancements. Applied mathematical problems may contextualize the need for Ohm's Law to find a solution. A subsequent conceptual exercise may demonstrate why voltage increases with current and decreases with resistance, and in what proportions. Understanding those in succession can concretize formulaic problems and foster a learning environment tied to practice. This constitutes an authentic learning experience, critical in developing meaningful skill acquisition [8]. For these reasons, comprehensive content instruction of complex domains nearly *requires* the availability of learning resources targeted at various levels and perspectives.

In this manuscript, we refer to a class of learning environment called a *hybrid tutor* [9]. These systems combine static learning resources, like text or videos, with adaptive resources such as intelligent tutoring systems or interactive assessments. Hybrid tutors incorporate these disparate resources within a single interface and provide intelligent recommendations based on progress across the various components.

The hybrid tutor we use for illustration is called ElectronixTutor [10, 11]. This system subsumes several independently developed learning resources pertaining to electrical engineering principles and application. These include static conventional texts, dialogue-based conceptual interactions, stepwise formulaic progressions, tiered multiple-choice questions, and comprehensive diagrammatic problems, among others.

These resources serve as the raw material from which to construct holistic content instruction and meta-instruction through two distinct intelligent recommendation pathways (one unconstrained, the other instructor-driven). Both pathways leverage the same comprehensive model of progression and perspective. They both produce individualized assessment of performance that recognizes (via distinct methods) deficiency and excellence. We leverage the construction and evaluation of ElectronixTutor to examine in context the relevant issues of sequential progression, diversity of perspective, experiential instruction, intelligent recommendation, and the relationship between learner expectation and learning outcomes.

2   Designing for Experiential Learning

2.1   Adaptive Recommendations

Adaptive instructional systems are generally advantageous, relative to non-adaptive learning tools [12]. However, methods of implementation for adaptivity vary widely, as does the relative advantage bestowed on the learner. The relatively novel architecture of hybrid tutors requires similarly novel construction of adaptive recommendation engines. Recommendations need to function simultaneously within-resource and between-resource. The system must translate progress in an independently developed learning resource into a holistic understanding of the learner [13, 14]. From there, the system must make determinations based on learning theory that account for the learner and domain considerations noted above. Based on those determinations, the system then identifies the learning resource and individual item that best matches the needs of the moment.

The complexity of this decision-making process leaves considerable room for variation. ElectronixTutor includes two distinct methods of constructing adaptive recommendations. These follow from two basic use cases. In the first case, independent learners wish to increase their knowledge of the domain. This likely does not involve any structure outside of that suggested by the domain itself, and recommendations follow accordingly with adaptivity derived from the individual's historical performance data. In the second case, the system functions as a classroom companion learning tool. There, instructors may wish to have a degree of control over the content order and availability, to more closely follow existing syllabi and lesson plans.

Historically Derived. In the case of an independent learner, ElectronixTutor leverages all data collected about the learner throughout all historical interactions [15]. These data reside in the learning record store, from which the system calculates performance on several dimensions, including performance within that topic, within that resource, recent versus historical average, etc. From there, the system generates potential recommended items using considerations influenced by learner characteristics and experiential factors. For example, the system may use historical performance information to infer that the learner is particularly motivated based on extended time spent on problems without giving up. In that situation, pushing the envelope may be the ideal approach.

This recommendation engine provides three options to the learner, from which they can select freely. These options may all come from the same learning resource or not. If the engine identifies more than three appropriate items, it performs conflict resolution based on historical performance within that learning resource and topic. Low performance triggers a zone of proximal development strategy [16], wherein the candidate problem's difficulty suggests a learner should be able to successfully complete it with some structural support. High performance triggers a "pushing the envelope" strategy, with advanced difficulty. This strategy allows the system to "catch up" to advanced students quickly. If performance is average, the recommendation engine defaults to random selection among the candidate problems. Figure 1 illustrates the process.

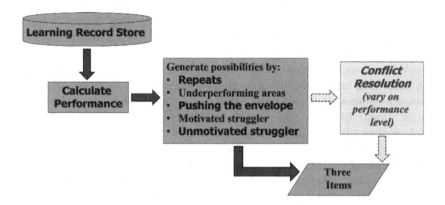

Fig. 1. A simplified depiction of historically derived intelligent recommendations, with sample considerations illustrating how possible items are generated.

Instructor Circumscribed. In the case of a hybrid tutor being deployed as a classroom companion learning tool, instructors will likely want some degree of control over content ordering and availability. To accommodate that, while still leveraging the intelligent adaptivity afforded by the medium, ElectronixTutor incorporates a second recommendation engine. In this engine, instructors designate on which of the topics (e.g., Ohm's Law, parallel circuits, transformers) learners should focus during a designated time frame. This singular recommendation (as opposed to the three generated by the historically derived engine) appears under the label "Today's Topic".

Because of the restriction to a single topic, and further because that topic is likely new to the learner, the system has substantially fewer datapoints from which to calculate recommendations accurate to the individual's needs and idiosyncrasies. Also, the instructor may prefer a relatively explainable procedure for determining if learners have reached a set level of mastery on that topic. For these reasons, instructor circumscribed recommendations rely on a decision chart rather than complex calculations.

This process may vary slightly among topics (depending on the breadth of resources available), but typically proceeds as follows. First, the recommendation engine directs learners to a topic summary, with text providing an overview of the new topic, including hyperlinks to external resources (e.g., Wikipedia). Learners then progress to conversational reasoning questions. These questions provide substantial diagnosticity as they contain multi-part answers and account for the level of fluency with which the learner was able to produce each part [17]. Based on this nuanced performance evaluation, the system leads learners to advanced, remedial, or roughly equivalent problems across all learning resources. Basic adaptivity (i.e., correct responses lead to more difficult problems and vice versa) complements a bias toward variability in learning resources presented.

This process continues until two conditions have been met. First, the learner's overall performance within the topic reaches a "mastery threshold". This score updates with every completed item and includes weightings relative to difficulty and scope. The instructor can determine the numeric value of the threshold (represented between zero and one), to allow added control over learner requirements. Second, the learner must have completed items in at least three learning resources. This ensures breadth of understanding, as different learning resources have distinct focus areas and approaches (e.g., conceptual versus mathematical versus practical).

Using this approach, instructors can assign homework that biases fluency with the content, rather than interaction with a set amount of content. Both historically derived and instructor circumscribed recommendation engines appear in the top-left portion of the screen, emphasizing their importance to the learning process (see Fig. 2). By default, both are available. The instructors may disable the historically derived option (as well as the self-directed learning option, shown below the other two options) to have added control over the content. In the case of an independent learner unaffiliated with a class, the instructor circumscribed recommendations proceed through the 15 topics in order, with each successive topic unlocked by completion of the previous one.

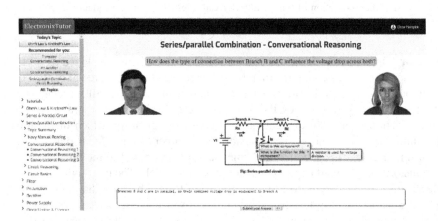

Fig. 2. The ElectronixTutor interface with a conversational reasoning question.

2.2 Scaffolding

In addition to providing flexibility in learner use cases, the two recommendation generation methods described provide distinct opportunities to scaffold metacognitive strategies. The experience of receiving personalized recommendations acts in the traditional role of a tutor, and "serves the learner as a vicarious form of consciousness until such time as the learner is able to master his own action through his own consciousness and control" [18] (p. 24).

In historically derived recommendations, a complex combination and processing of information yields three appropriate options for next steps. As detailed above, this goes significantly beyond questions becoming harder after a successful completion. The system demonstrates how to properly balance approaches rather than binging on a single learning resource. Detection of frustration within problems should lead to relatively easier problems that build confidence. Ideally this also avoids disengagement by virtue of variety. Repeated, but not exclusive, exposure to problem areas reinforces the need for persistence balanced against diversity.

The ability to select from three options emphasizes these principles by tripling the number of exposures to metacognitively aware decisions. A list of three conversational reasoning recommendations could highlight that the learner has been avoiding that resource, or that he lacks conceptual understanding. And the act of choosing creates a closer link between the artificial intelligence and the acts it is scaffolding.

In instructor circumscribed recommendations, a relatively restricted state space reduces the number of possibilities to a level that the learner may find more manageable. Consistency at the beginning of a topic (*Topic Summary* followed by *Conversational Reasoning*) demonstrates important principles in addressing content—first refresh yourself on the big picture then check for conceptual understanding. Subsequent recommendations reinforce the importance of diversity or perspective and of holistic understanding, while progression to harder or easier content provides implicit, high-level feedback on performance. Finally, completing a topic upon reaching the mastery threshold correlates successful content fluency with a specific metacognitive status.

3   Proposed Evaluation

In theory, interacting with the prescribed recommendation engines constitute a means for scaffolding metacognitive awareness. However, their effectiveness in this regard relies on learners understanding that intent and evaluating the proffered information accordingly. How much learners fulfill this requirement, or indeed are aware of its existence, remains largely in doubt. Scaffolding typically assumes explicit instruction, as opposed to the experiential and implicit method described in the hybrid tutor. We conclude our discussion with a proposal of methods to evaluate the degree to which, and mechanisms by which, experiential learning provides instruction related to metacognitive awareness and strategies.

3.1   Expected Efficacy

Following the findings of Jackson, Graesser, and McNamara [7], we anticipate learner expectations to strongly predict learning outcomes. However, these findings have not yet been replicated in metacognitive awareness and strategies—they applied to learning outcomes of the target domain. Adapting the approach appears relatively straightforward.

A survey of participants before interacting with the system could illustrate expectation for how adaptive instructional technologies generate recommendations.

Some difficulty arises in avoiding biasing subsequent interactions with the system. For example, asking "What factors do you believe will influence how the system generates recommendations for you?" may cause the participant to search for intention most diligently than he would have otherwise. Further, it may bias him toward belief that the recommendations are genuinely artificially intelligent. This may not have been the default position. To avoid this, acquiring a general sense of the participant's views on personalized adaptivity may prove less problematic. People commonly interact with applications that claim to learn their preferences (e.g., Nest smart thermostats), daily routine (e.g., Google Maps), language use (e.g., auto-complete text generation) etc. A broad trust or frustration in these technologies likely correlates highly with their expected efficacy of intelligent recommendations in learning technology. Complementing this subtlety is the structure of the hybrid tutor itself, where the focus lies primarily on the learning content, not elements of progression through them.

This aspect of the evaluation has two benefits. First, it expands the research on the link between learner expectations and learning outcomes to include metacognitive learning through experiential instruction. Second, it may provide valuable context for the mechanisms by which intelligent recommendations lead to (or fail to lead to) metacognitive benefits with respect to learning. If the effect does extend to this application but metacognitive learning outcomes are hindered by inaccurate expectations, the intervention to remedy the situation becomes clearer. Effort spent in optimizing the recommender engines may be more efficiently deployed in conveying their capabilities to the learners.

3.2   Perceived Efficacy

A measure of perceived efficacy would complement the expected efficacy survey. Following completion of the testing, a survey would measure perception of the hybrid tutor's intelligence and the appropriateness of its adaptivity. This would provide a direct measure of the match between actual capabilities and its perceived capabilities. This directly impacts our understanding of experiential instruction of metacognitive strategies. If learners did not notice any reason for the recommendations, then they are unlikely to have absorbed the lessons implicit within them.

Comparison to the previous survey could also demonstrate the effect of bias on perceptions of intelligent adaptivity. This could potentially have far-reaching implications for any kind of artificially intelligent adaptivity. Trust in automation constitutes a large research field with immediate economic concerns such as the public's willingness to cede control to self-driving cars. Improvements to the automation systems themselves may be tempered by bias that negates or ignores tangible advances.

3.3   Actual Efficacy

Finally, we come to a direct examination of the potential for experiential instruction of metacognitive strategies through intelligent recommendations. This will require a degree of deception. As stated, instructing these strategies requires learners to understand that recommendations are adaptive to the learners, based on past performance and individual characteristics. A proper control group requires the absence of that understanding.

Randomly dividing the participant population, half should proceed normally through the hybrid tutor for some amount of time enough to encounter as many iterations of the recommender(s) as is feasible. The other half of the participants should follow the same procedure, except they should be under the impression that the order of learning resources and items is predetermined. The experimenter should show them a checklist of items through which they will proceed one at a time. Almost certainly, the participant will glance at this (preferably inscrutable) list and then disregard the specifics. From there, the experimenter simply pretends to read from the checklist while in fact instructing the participant to continue using intelligently generated recommendations. Further, the label "Recommended for you" should be altered to "Random practice" to avoid implications of intelligence.

During or after the task, one or more established methods of metacognitive assessment [19] can provide empirical validation of the approach. Think-aloud protocol and reflecting when prompted are both common, though with some concern that they interrupt the learning process [20]. Alternatively, following completion of the task, all participants could take a survey. This should include self-assessment of their mastery of topics encountered (which can be compared to calculated values), impression of the relative values of learning resources (e.g., conceptually-oriented versus mathematically rigorous), and their mastery of each of the learning resources (again, comparing to calculated values). This between-participants experimental approach could rigorously test the impact of experiential instruction on metacognitive strategy learning.

3.4   Conclusion

Deficiencies in metacognitive strategies and awareness mean that learners appropriately selecting content without the benefit of expert supervision is unlikely. Because of this, intelligent recommendations provide an invaluable service to learners in adaptive instructional systems. Beyond the act of substituting for experts, those recommendations may provide meta-instruction by virtue of scaffolding understanding of the mechanisms at play in deciding the best way forward.

Principles of experiential learning and scaffolding of instruction suggest that this may be the case. Hybrid tutors provide a viable testing environment, with differential methods of intelligent recommendation helping to ensure sufficient breadth to generalize any findings. Evaluating the extent to which and mechanisms by which this proves effective could have far-reaching impacts. Comparisons among the expected, perceived, and actual efficacy of intelligent recommendations can inform learning science, trust in automation, and adaptive instructional system design principles.

References

1. Baker, L.: Social influences on metacognitive development in reading. In: Cornoldi, C., Oakhill, J. (eds.) Reading Comprehension Difficulties: Processes and Intervention, pp. 331–352. Lawrence Erlbaum Associates, Inc., Mahwah (1996)

2. Dewey, J.: Democracy and education. In: Boydston, J.A. (ed.) The Middle Works of John Dewey, vol. 9, pp. 1899–1924 (1966)
3. Kolb, D.: Experiential Learning: Experience as the Source of Learning and Development. Prentice-Hall, Upper Saddle River (1984)
4. Reigeluth, C.M., Carr-Chellman, A.A. (eds.): Instructional-Design Theories and Models: Building a Common Knowledge Base, vol. 3. Routledge, Abingdon (2009)
5. Graesser, A.C.: Emotions are the experiential glue of learning environments in the 21st century. Learn. Instr. (in press)
6. Tawfik, A.A., Gatewood, J., Gishbaugher, J.J., Hampton, A.J.: Toward a definition of learning experience design. Technol. Knowl. Learn. (in press)
7. Jackson, G.T., Graesser, A.C., McNamara, D.S.: What students expect may have more impact than what they know or feel. In: Dimitrova, V., Mizoguchi, R., Du Boulay, B., Graesser, A.C. (eds.) Proceedings of 14th International Conference on Artificial Intelligence in Education. Building Learning Systems that Care: From Knowledge Representation to Affective Modelling, pp. 73–80. IOS Press, Amsterdam (2009)
8. Jackson, L., MacIsaac, D.: Introduction to a new approach to experiential learning. In: Jackson, L., Caffarella, R. (eds.) Experiential Learning: A New Approach, pp. 17–28. Jossey-Bass, San Francisco (1994)
9. Hampton, A.J., Graesser, A.C.: Foundational principles and design of a hybrid tutor. In: Sottilare, R.A., Schwarz, J. (eds.) Proceedings of the First International Conference, AIS 2019, Held as Part of the 21st HCI International Conference, Orlando, FL, pp. 96–107 (2019)
10. Graesser, A.C., et al.: ElectronixTutor: an adaptive learning platform with multiple resources. In: Proceedings of the Interservice/Industry Training, Simulation, and Education Conference (I/ITSEC 2018), Orlando, FL (2018)
11. Graesser, A.C., et al.: ElectronixTutor: an intelligent tutoring system with multiple learning resources for electronics. Int. J. STEM Educ. 5(1), 15 (2018)
12. Graesser, A.C., Conley, M.W., Olney, A.: Intelligent tutoring systems. In: Harris, K.R., Graham, S., Urdan, T., Bus, A.G., Major, S., Swanson, H.L. (eds.) APA Handbooks in Psychology®. APA Educational Psychology Handbook. Application to Learning and Teaching, vol. 3, pp. 451–473. American Psychological Association (2012)
13. Morgan, B., et al.: ElectronixTutor integrates multiple learning resources to teach electronics on the web. In: Proceedings of the Fifth Annual ACM Conference on Learning at Scale, pp. 1–2 (2018)
14. Tackett, A.C., et al.: Knowledge components as a unifying standard of intelligent tutoring systems. In: Proceedings of Artificial Intelligence in Education 2018, London, UK, p. 33 (2018)
15. Graesser, A.C.: ElectronixTutor recommender system (2017). Privately shared Google Doc. Accessed 24 Feb 2020
16. Vygotsky, L.: Interaction between learning and development. Read. Dev. Child. 23(3), 34–41 (1978)
17. Hampton, A.J., Wang, L.: Conversational AIS as the cornerstone of hybrid tutors. In: Sottilare, R.A., Schwarz, J. (eds.) HCII 2019. LNCS, vol. 11597, pp. 634–644. Springer, Cham (2019). https://doi.org/10.1007/978-3-030-22341-0_49
18. Bruner, J.: Vygotsky: a historical and conceptual perspective. In: Wertsch, J.V. (ed.) Culture, Communication, and Cognition: Vygotskian Perspectives, pp. 21–34 (1985)
19. Israel, S.E., Bauserman, K.L., Block, C.C.: Metacognitive assessment strategies. Think. Classr. 6(2), 21 (2005)
20. Bannert, M., Mengelkamp, C.: Assessment of metacognitive skills by means of instruction to think aloud and reflect when prompted. Does the verbalisation method affect learning? Metacogn. Learn. 3(1), 39–58 (2008)

Falling Forward: Lessons Learned from Real-Life Implementation of Adaptive Learning Solutions

Alysson Hursey, Kathryn Thompson, Jill Wierzba, Elizabeth Tidwell, Joyner Livingston, and Jennifer Lewis[✉]

SAIC, Reston, VA 20190, USA
jennifer.e.lewis@saic.com

Abstract. To meet modern organizational job performance needs, effective training solutions must accelerate student learning while simultaneously maintaining exceptionally high standards for learner knowledge and skill proficiency. As organizations seek to revitalize traditional training programs to fit the needs of next-generation learners, innovation incubators allow for the exploration of new technologies to facilitate adaptive learning solutions. Transitioning traditional training programs through an innovation phase and toward cohesive, results-based adaptive learning solutions is a complex undertaking. This transformation is neither a simple nor painless process, and as such it presents many complicated and unexpected challenges. The key to a successful implementation of an adaptive learning program is a structure that allows for extensibility and reproducibility. These characteristics are supported by the adoption of a well-defined process maturity model and a deliberate instructional systems design framework based in human performance improvement and learning science and ensure the deliberate application of learning technologies. To mitigate challenges and ensure quality for future adaptive learning design efforts, SAIC presents a phased roadmap that describes programmatic structure required for success.

Keyword: Adaptive learning

1 Introduction

1.1 Information Age Learning

The vitality of a modern organization depends on the ability of its workforce to adapt to the pace and direction of an ever-evolving body of information technology. A majority of organizations rely on future-proofing their Information Age workforce with learning programs that are founded on traditional, one-size-fits-all Industrial Age learning methodology, technologies, and product management processes. Up to this point, Industrial Age methodologies and technologies have worked fine, but fine is no longer good enough [1].

Rapid advancements in technology have enabled constant access to information. Both the global data body and information delivery infrastructures are expanding, in progression and complexity, at an exponential rate. As such, a modern workforce has

© Springer Nature Switzerland AG 2020
R. A. Sottilare and J. Schwarz (Eds.): HCII 2020, LNCS 12214, pp. 117–129, 2020.
https://doi.org/10.1007/978-3-030-50788-6_9

more to learn, at a faster pace, in more breadth and depth than ever before; their needs have outgrown traditional learning models. As organizations seek to revitalize their training programs to answer Information Age demands, they must capitalize on the mass influx of data and emerging technologies to make their organization-specific job performance improvement and maintenance topics relevant and readily available. Additionally, the method and model of information delivery must be adapted to learners of this era. With infinite amounts of knowledge a simple click or tap away, learners have the luxury of controlling what, when, and how they learn. Because of the amount and complexity of available information, learners need content that is tailored to them and their job performance specifics. This results in a "just-in-time" learning paradigm to which modern Information Age learners have become accustomed.

Organizations that are seeking to modernize are looking towards innovative solutions to accelerate student learning while simultaneously maintaining exceptionally high standards for learner knowledge and skill proficiency. Revitalizing learning programs requires organizations to update learning engineering architectures, learning resource media, delivery modalities, and the process standards to which the learning is built.

1.2   Adaptive Learning Solutions

In recent years, adaptive learning has remained among the most sought after Information Age-sensitive approaches to performance improvement. For the purposes of this paper, adaptive learning is computerized learning that personalizes learning experiences on the fly to meet specific learner needs. Functionally, individual learner experiences are driven and/or performance analyzed by a combination of subjective, deterministic influencing factors and objective, AI/ML-driven logic. Adaptive learning capitalizes on the Information Age paradigm by deliberately balancing the timing and quantity of information delivery to enable the maximum amount of performance-gap-targeted learning to occur in the minimum amount of time.

Many organizations are seeking adaptive learning solutions to revitalize their learning programs—learners need to learn better, faster, and sooner than traditional methods can accommodate [2]. Adaptive learning puts an initial focus on the learner rather than the curriculum itself [3], which is a drastic shift from the rigid, curriculum-driven, linear approaches to learning utilized during the Industrial Age. Personalized, learner-centric training allows learners to get the information they need, when they need it, and get back to the real work they need to do, with the ability to immediately apply what they have learned to improve their job performance and efficiency.

However, the "why" of adaptive learning program implementation is much clearer than the "how." Simply purchasing an off-the-shelf adaptive learning design tool and expecting to plug and play legacy learning resources into it as a means to transforming an Industrial Age learning program overnight is highly unrealistic. Successful adaptive courses cannot be standalone; they must be components of an adaptive instructional system architecture characterized by the application of learning sciences and complex human-centered engineering design, which enables data-informed decision making that can be used to improve human performance [4]. Effective adaptive instructional systems serve up multi-modal, device-agnostic, mindfully created modularized content at the most effective time, which can be adapted to fit individual and organizational needs; this can be a tall order for learning, technology, and interoperability engineers.

Until adaptive instructional systems become more commonplace, standing up an adaptive learning capability requires organizational investment in research, experimentation, and incubation; particularly if the desired solution is competency-based, features a high degree of AI/ML capability, and/or requires the learner to perform psychomotor activities to demonstrate mastery. Keeping track of advances in technology, adjudicating custom features to meet specific organization and industry requirements, and the logistics associated with curating the kind of interdisciplinary team required to emplace and test such a system are all considerations that further complicate implementation. The technical and instructional approaches certainly require considerate planning and analysis; after all, one of the key benefits of adaptive learning is that, by design, it enables data-driven and results-based organizational decision-making around performance. However, it is the ability to lay a foundation for implementation and to define and document the approach via process and procedure management activities which make adaptive learning programs scalable and repeatable, therefore salable. Many organizations, including SAIC, have gained this knowledge the hard way—through deliberate experimentation, failing fast, adapting to lessons learned, and falling forward into both technical and program management practices tailored to adaptive learning program development.

2 Implementation of Adaptive Learning Solutions

2.1 Challenges

Prior to taking on a large-scale, adaptive training renovation, SAIC anticipated encountering a wide variety of technical challenges, particularly related to the complexity of interoperability between disparate hardware and software. A talent management plan was put in place to address these anticipated challenges, and agile development methodologies and a matrix operating model were utilized. As the project progressed, many of the challenges faced were actually less related to the technical work necessary to create a data-driven, results-based adaptive learning solution, and more related to organizational culture. SAIC's evaluation revealed that many technical challenges could be attributed to the fact that the organizational culture was—to a degree—actually more resistant to change than they realized. Adaptive learning efforts require *breaking* institutional paradigms as innovation and a holistic revitalization of training occurs.

2.2 Lessons Learned

The following are the most insightful and helpful lessons learned:

Adaptive Design and Development Standards. Employing adaptive design and development standards is critical because they illuminate the path for technical teams to conduct their work. They also provide an organized method that can be used to clearly communicate with the customer about the depth and degree of technical work required to achieve the ultimate goal of truly adaptive, data-driven learning. Without design and development standards, both the technical teams and the customer suffer. Identifying and adopting adaptive design and development standards is currently difficult for several reasons. First, the field of adaptive learning engineering is an emerging field in and of itself and governing bodies are still in the process of developing said standards [5] The body of knowledge is continuously evolving, particularly as related to building context around data. Unlike other industries that have clear definitions, applications, and specific use cases, adaptive capabilities within the edtech industry have no specific guidelines, taxonomies, or even a common vernacular for how various adaptive capabilities are described [6]. This makes it difficult to trust the "adaptive" learning technologies on the market. What we found is that a majority of vendors marketing adaptive learning solutions did not actually have a robust adaptive solution, particularly those vendors who were marketing AI/ML capabilities. Second, the current lack of common standards meant we went into our project without clear guidelines to assist us in steering customer requests towards the ultimate goal of scaling a robust adaptive learning solution. Third, in the absence of confirmed industry-wide standards, we relied on standards from each of the interdisciplinary fields that made up our technical teams—information technology, data science, software engineering, learning engineering, training development, human performance, serious games development, and multimedia design. Though each of these disciplines has useful and appropriate design and development standards, this heterogeneous conglomeration of standards was not appropriately tailored to meet our specific requirements or circumstances and resulted in interoperability difficulties that lead to a cumbersome user experience—both from a learning and technology standpoint.

To synchronize technical teams, Agile Project Management was employed to facilitate the application of these multidisciplinary standards in an integrated way that allowed for rapid, aggressive innovation that remained sensitive to final product priorities. Agile processes were leveraged to facilitate effective communication between technical teams, and also as a way to communicate to the customer the reality of technical depth necessary to bridge the digital divide between the legacy content that was inherited and the vision and goals of the stakeholders. As per the Agile Manifesto [7], formal, comprehensive documentation was not a priority so technical documentation was used for communication between technical teams. The speed of development hindered the creation of a formal living document, which had pros and cons. Under innovation-minded, post-industrial style leaders and middle-management, agile processes allowed for extremely creative innovations in a matter of weeks and months rather than years, albeit at the expense of scalability since prototypes were never finished before moving on to the next innovation. In contrast, after project handover to a more conservative, industrial-style leadership team, this agile methodology was not as effective and more formal documentation was required which led to a more clear scalability plan at the expense of innovation and experimentation with cutting edge technologies.

Stakeholder and Technical Team Concurrence. A consistent shared vision amongst all stakeholders and technical developers is of critical importance to maintaining unified efforts and complementary development. Agreement on actionable, measurable milestones is a critical step in empowering both the customer and the technical teams as they work towards a clear, shared vision. As technical subject matter experts were given their piece of the puzzle and empowered to move development forward at an alarmingly rapid rate, desired end-states quickly became convoluted as they pushed innovation boundaries. Technical teams became hyper-focused on milestones within their own area of expertise, but at the expense of how those milestones overlapped and interacted with milestones within other discipline areas as well as the impact upon the ease with which everything converged into one single adaptive learning solution. Development efforts such as Single Sign-On (SSO) capabilities, data visualizations, and learning analytics suffered greatly as technical team milestones drifted further and further apart. As siloed efforts persisted, a Scaled Agile Framework (SAFe) [8] was introduced as a means to heighten communication between stakeholders and technical teams. This helped to minimize disjointed development efforts and allowed innovation to continue and technical teams to flexibly adjust milestones within the larger learning ecosystem in a ways that were beneficial to all stakeholders and technical discipline areas. The necessity to continually assess and reassess milestones as they related to a clear, shared vision cannot be overstated.

One of the largest technical hurdles was related to the adaptation of legacy curriculum and training methodologies to fit into a data-driven adaptive instructional system. Industrial Age training curriculum has be developed using traditional instructional design theory and methodologies, and as a result have produced terminal and enabling learning objectives that are not granular or descriptive enough to be easily ingested into an adaptive learning instructional system. Depending on how recently curriculum has been updated, there is also a lack of clear job-performance indicators and behavioral markers that can be directly tied to proficiency data which can then be used to inform and adapt training based on an individual's performance needs. In many cases, curriculum needs to be completely decomposed and realigned with an appropriate learning taxonomy (e.g., revised Bloom's taxonomy) to ensure that an AI/ML-based adaptive instructional system can appropriately adapt individual learning journeys. This process takes time and is often overlooked—sometimes completely ignored—but is foundational to the efficacy of adaptive learning solutions. By developing internal processes to decrease the time this foundational curriculum decomposition takes, the technical teams can utilize this information to make intentional choices regarding the types and interoperability functionality to various technologies within the larger learning ecosystem; this enables a unified solution in the vision of both stakeholder and technical developers.

Cross-Functional Communication Processes and Tools. As the emerging field of adaptive learning engineering is itself an inter- and intra-disciplinary field, the necessity for many technical functional areas to communicate and collaborate with ease is essential. Cross-functional communication standards enable knowledge sharing and expectation management, which is essential in mitigating technical risks and challenges. The further you get into the development of an adaptive learning solution, the more complicated the development becomes, and communication becomes increasingly important. However, communication does not always happen naturally—typically a symptom of how busy and task-saturated everyone is. For example, with so many technical development meetings on the calendar, it is easy to tune out the seemingly inefficient use of time; in most cases, technical developers would rather be developing than talking about developing. However, if during that meeting a quick two minute conversation about a technical specification can avoid two days' worth of technical work to fix an interoperability issue due to lack of a quick discussion between technical developers, the communication time investment is well worth it! Regular and prioritized sync sessions to communicate efficiencies and technical issues are a necessity, even if multiple, daily synchronization meetings seem inefficient or ineffective. This habitual battle rhythm helps technical teams put out metaphorical fires before they even start.

Having processes for communication is important but so too is having the right tools for technical task efficiency. The introduction of emerging technologies (e.g. design and development software, IT firewall exceptions for developers, etc.) to streamline workflow efficiencies to create "less busy" people, which facilitates better communication overall, both internally for technical teams and with customer stakeholders. Functional roles and responsibilities dynamically change throughout the design, development, and implementation processes and ensuring that technical team members have the tools they need to avoid getting unnecessarily bogged down in technical tasks is critical.

Organizational Change Management Plan. If the environment or infrastructure—both technical and cultural—do not or will not support the change required to implement and innovative adaptive learning solution, then your program is not going to work. The best way for people to embrace change—both at the customer and technical team levels—is on a personal level. When change management plans are dispersed at a wide and impersonal level, it is easy for individuals to at best lean away from the change, and at worst intentionally thwart it. An adaptive learning solution's organizational change management plan should remain sensitive to the perspectives of both industrial and post-industrial leadership styles, since individuals with either perspective are likely to be a part of your organization. Change is uncomfortable and people are likely to go back to what they have always done unless they *personally* buy-in to change. Creating a culture of innovation that embraces change is a necessity when designing, developing, and implementing adaptive learning solutions. To facilitate this personalized approach to change, having one change champion is a good start, but innovation cannot survive without a network of champions at all levels—investors, leadership, instructors, learners, technical team members, etc. Change is often directed by senior management and embraced by disciplined practitioners, but blocked by the frozen middle. By injecting buy-in at the middle management level—those who are often *not* incentivized to promote change because it is risky and uncomfortable—you empower force-multipliers that are critical to the success of the level of change that comes with transitioning from an Industrial to Information Age infrastructure. An example of how to facilitate and develop this type of change network is to have a high-level leader directing change, but simultaneously creating a middle management layer of change-agents who are empowered by and reporting directly to that high-level leader. This structure created multiple product owners with the autonomy and excitement needed to push the bubble of innovation.

The level of technical change that comes with transitioning to an adaptive learning program also requires a well-planned and well-executed strategy—one that change champions can leverage and that all members of your technical teams embrace. The way SAIC's Learning Next team does this is to hand-pick the high-performers out of varied customer groups to form a well-integrated product team that is aimed at directly exploiting disruptive technologies relevant to adaptive learning techniques.

Simultaneous support to customer-facing efforts and internal research and development efforts, change is fueled by technical team members' know-how, appetite for creativity and innovation, and insatiable curiosity which pushes adaptive learning solutions outside the bounds of even what the most aggressive customers are comfortable with. By custom crafting a culture of innovation, many of the pitfalls associated with transition and change are avoided from the get-go.

Intentional Selection of New Technology. The draw of new technology can be irresistible—something shiny, new, fun, or fancy—but cannot be the sole component around which an adaptive learning solution is designed. There should be a balance between embracing the excitement surrounding a new emerging technology and the intentional and iterative analysis regarding the true usefulness of that technology within the larger adaptive learning solution. Chasing every shiny new piece of technology may seem like the path of innovation, but buyer beware! That exciting new toy may not move the ball forward towards where stakeholders actually want to go. When choosing technologies, subjectivity is important, but a good mix of that with objectivity is better. Technology can be a guide if it is iteratively analyzed against the larger vision and goals of the stakeholders. Iterative, just-in-time training needs analyses enable stable, data-driven changes to program components. This mitigates reactive development and positions practitioners to develop repeatable, scalable learning solutions based on proactive, deliberate agile processes.

Technology in itself is not innovation when the overall intent is to build a cohesive and functioning system for adaptive learning. This biggest challenge faced was finding the appropriate balance technical time, money, and effort between exploring and developing cutting technologies and developing a capability-based Adaptive Learning Framework that allows the technology to be leveraged as an extremely effective instrument for learning. This becomes particularly difficult with multi-modal methods of learning that are served up on a large number of technology platforms. For example, innovative implementation of commercially available, low-cost hardware and software to create fully immersive learning experiences is certainly a technological feat, but without the ability to tie those immersive experiences back into a framework that provides the foundation upon which adaptive learning must occur, then what is the point of developing the innovative technology? Equal effort needs to be spent on developing the backend foundation of the adaptive learning solution. Additionally, SAIC has developed an Adaptive Learning Framework which allows technical teams with the ability to do a rapid performance gap analysis to determine which technologies that will give you the most for your money.

Stakeholder Expectation Management. Stakeholder expectations related to the true scope of technical effort required for adaptive learning (e.g., instructional design, technical interoperability, etc.) must be carefully and frequently managed and communicated. The development of personalized, scalable, and robust adaptive learning does not happen overnight, and chances are high that stakeholders who are not in the technical trenches may not be well versed in the amount of time and effort it takes to blaze a trail in the adaptive learning space. Stakeholders and customers want to see the dazzling game, responsive app, personalized interface, engaging video, individualized learning path, etc. change magically and interactively before their eyes. There is little credit given to the granular metadata tagging, decomposition of curriculum, competency mapping, data feedback loops and metrics that are behind the scenes which make that impressive magic happen. The art of implementing impressive adaptive learning solutions is being able to simultaneously demonstrate functional, visually appealing components that fulfill near-term outcomes, while building the background foundation which makes the entire adaptive learning solution credible and practical. You have to build the arch from both sides, otherwise there will just be a lot of useless disparate parts.

Technical obstacles and roadblocks are a common occurrence that regularly delay and change forward movement. If no care is taken, technical developers can be put in the line of fire and be blamed for issues surrounding the technical modernization changes that are required to support the IT requirements of adaptive learning solutions. For example, if a customer's technical infrastructure cannot currently support a cloud-based, real-time data environment due to an unreliable internet connection within the facility, delays in development timelines might cause frustration for the customer who does not understand the complexity or requirements of transitioning from Industrial to Information Age technologies. They still want that cloud-based solution even though the existing environment cannot technically support it, so having a plan in place to not only minimize these types of technical obstacles but also manage the change as it occurs is critical.

2.3 Keys to Successful Implementation

Based on thorough analysis of the challenges encountered, the team concluded that the key to a successful implementation of an adaptive learning program is an organizational and technical structure that allows for extensibility and reproducibility. These characteristics are supported by the adoption of a well-defined process maturity model and a deliberate instructional systems design framework based in human performance improvement and learning science which ensures the deliberate application of learning technologies. Without these elements, efforts to move traditional training through an innovation phase and come out as adaptive learning solution will fall short, and as a result, the training program as a whole will likely return to its original, suboptimal state. Although we are all working to ultimately seamlessly integrate technology into different learning programs, we must remember that we are working primarily with people – people design the programs, people run the programs, and people participate in the programs. Thus, while technical challenges must be overcome, we must remember to keep people foremost in our minds and have plans and structures to help the people work through these periods of transition and innovation successfully.

3   Repeatable Adaptive Learning Solutions

3.1   Keystone Six

SAIC established Keystone Six, an internal research and development initiative, to document the challenges associated with the implementation of scalable adaptive learning solutions; and to architect repeatable processes, procedures, and solutions to make the transition to data-driven, results-based adaptive learning quicker and easier.

SAIC designed Keystone Six to guide intentional choices of various learning modalities in order to produce personalized learning experiences that are grounded in job-relevant knowledge, skills and performance tasks, all while providing a framework that artificial intelligence (AI) and machine learning (ML) mechanisms can use to design and create systems that will be adaptable now and into the future. Implementation of Keystone Six required research and practice from multidisciplinary fields including adult learning theory, educational psychology, cognitive science, neuroscience, and human performance improvement [9]. Keystone Six demonstrates the shift from traditional curriculum development methodologies to align with the principles of four-dimensional education which emphasizes the development of multi-domain capabilities and allows students to be more effective and adaptable in complex, ambiguous environments [10].

Armed with this new framework, an AI/ML engine can ingest student performance data associated with knowledge, skill, and task proficiency to very precisely track the progress, proficiency, and areas of improvement for each student and the overall student cohort. The AI/ML engine can also provide students with an individualized learning journey based on their proficiency level. This student-focused responsive learning environment engages and motivates learners in individualized ways that traditional training cannot. The system presents the most relevant learning content to the learner based on a variety of characteristics, such as learning style, knowledge level and skill proficiency, while avoiding learning content that includes knowledge the learner has already mastered or learning experiences for which the learner is not ready. This precision-tracking and analytics allows the system to adapt to the learner (instead of the learner adapting to the system). This allows flexibility for the system to adapt to fast and slow learners so that all students reach the required level of knowledge and skill mastery, instead of relying on a curriculum schedule or simply exam scores. For example: it can let fast learners continue to move forward in their training without being held back by a curriculum schedule or other, slower students. Slower learners get the specific attention they need, when they need it to reach knowledge and skill mastery before moving forward in their training. Thus, having a through-put of students that all have an equally high level of mastery [11]. Additionally, any potential issues with a student's overall progress in mastering competencies can be identified and addressed much earlier than in traditional training. When fully implemented, Keystone Six ties together the learner's experience, preferences and proficiencies to the organization's overall objectives.

3.2 Phased Roadmap

To mitigate challenges and ensure quality for future adaptive learning design efforts, SAIC presents a phased roadmap that describes the programmatic structure required for technical success when designing and developing adaptive learning solutions. The actions associated with each phase can be categorized into four areas: processes, people, technology, and governance. Adopting best practices in each of these four areas promotes reliability and consistency in solutions management and delivery capabilities. By adopting this phased approach, SAIC is able to meet targets for current solutions, respond effectively to rapidly changing solutions requirements, and to become a cost-effective, consistent, high-quality training solutions provider that supports critical customer missions worldwide.

Develop the Framework. Phase 1 of the roadmap requires practitioners to create a single, definable, repeatable, and scalable documented framework for recommended best practices in alignment with Government, industry, and organizational strategic standards. Adaptive learning programs are typically quite large in scale and data output compared to traditional computer-based training. Spending time on the front end developing and standardizing a foundational framework of processes, human actions, technology requirements, and governance actions positions adaptive learning programs to mature gracefully. Phase 1 activities support stakeholder concurrence and expectation management by providing references for top-level process definition. During this phase, an organization should support technical stakeholder awareness by creating design and development standards. Additionally, the establishment of a governance process enables an iterative training needs analysis. Governance also promotes cross functional communications standards by clarifying expectations for who communicates with whom, when, about what, and how often (Table 1).

Table 1. Phase 1 – lay the groundwork.

Process	• Develop standardized templates • Adopt and publish an adaptive learning program glossary • Establish governance process for conducting project reviews to assess development efforts and provide recommendations for alignment
Technology	• Establish team collaboration areas • Establish a Configuration Management System (CMS) • Establish Process Asset Library (PAL) - location to publish finalized documents to enable transparency and process maturity • Establish Definitive Media Library (DML) - location to store authoritative versions of SW installs
People	• Obtain executive and other organizational leadership sponsorship • Communicate the need for the change and the desired results of the change • Create a strong Change Champion network with representation from all levels of the organization, customer and other stakeholders • Define and communicate the roles and responsibilities of the stakeholders in charge of governance
Governance	• Publish adaptive learning program strategy • Establish program governance board • Identify and assign required key quality assurance and review personnel, creating new roles as required • Publish strategic and project communications plans • Create policies to ensure that new program purchases are not made without providing added value and conforming to the established governance processes. Note that program purchasing governance is also a check to ensure the technology is not leading the instructional solution

Develop the Framework and Content. Phase 2 involves building on the foundation by maturing the solution toward a higher quality; and ensuring security and capability of the data environment. This is the phase where practitioners continue to flesh out the processes created in Phase 1, ensuring that each stakeholder and technical contributor understands, concurs with, and is trained in their role and responsibilities, including those related to intermural communication. Additionally, Phase 2 is when stakeholder leaders define what success looks like for the program, using understandable metrics. From a technical perspective, design and development of the adaptive learning framework and supporting architectures occurs in Phase 2. Technology is selected to support the performance improvement outcome. The technical and administrative leadership ensure that all stakeholders are aware of and concur with how the selected technical and instructional approaches will affect the release schedule (Table 2).

Table 2. Phase 2 – develop framework and content.

Process	• For each component within the larger adaptive instructional system, create the following supporting guidance:
	  – Solution purpose, scope, and outcomes for each
	  – Activity level details, workflows, and diagrams
	  – Information work products (inputs and outputs)
	  – Roles/Responsibility (RACI)
	  – Metrics (Critical Success Factors (CSFs) supported by Key Performance Indicators (KPIs))

Technology	• Design, develop, test, and deploy functional tools to support each adaptive instructional system component and process • Ensure integration of the adaptive learning program components within delivery platform
People	• Train process owners on their roles and responsibilities • Communicate the desired results of the process
Governance	• Assign adaptive learning solution process owners • Identify required key personnel creating new roles as required • Develop strategic and project communications plans • Publish strategic adaptive learning solution kits (Change, Configuration, Portfolio Management, Cybersecurity, etc.)

Strategy, Design, and Transition. Phase 3 involves further building on previous activities to develop strategy to achieve an overarching adaptive learning program capability and strategies for each component of the adaptive solution. In this phase, practitioners delve deeper into creation of processes and standards to support both the solution development team and the solutions themselves, with artifacts such as Standard Operating Procedures (SOPs) and technical specification documentation. Additionally, ensuring there is an assigned locus of control to own each solution aids in more efficient cross-functional communication and team situational awareness (Table 3).

Table 3. Phase 3 – strategy, design, and transition.

Process	• Develop the SDPs, SOPs, work instructions, and templates necessary to provide/support offered adaptive solutions and applications • Mature the change evaluation, transition planning and support, and release and deployment management processes • Ensure each solution is integrated with adaptive learning program processes in execution • For each solution deliverable, develop and publish all required supporting documentation (User Guides, Technical Specifications, etc.)
Technology	• Design, develop, test, and deploy functional tools to support for each solution process
People	• Train solution managers and product owners • Communicate the desired objectives of the solution
Governance	• Assign service managers and product owners • Ensure process reviews are conducted using established review process • Publish strategic plans (change evaluation, transition planning and support, and release and deployment management, etc.)

Modernize the Program. The final phase is dedicated to ongoing evaluation and maturation of the adaptive learning program or solution portfolio. The process framework from previous phases should enable practitioners to employ a factual approach to decision making about modernization based on analysis of data and information about the organizational impact of learning. It is critical to engage stakeholders in discussions about how and how often programs should be evaluated. Modernization discussions are often centered on whether or not to implement a new instructional modality or media type into the program. Stakeholders should concur on the value of modernization as related to performance improvement outcomes (Table 4).

Table 4. Phase 4 – modernize the program.

Process	• Establish program evaluation and management processes • Develop standardized program assessment templates, priority matrix, and forms • Publish a schedule of key program management activities
Technology	• Design, develop, test, and deploy functional tools to support portfolio management activities
People	• Train solution managers, product owners, and adaptive learning program process owners on the solution management process • Communicate the desired results of the process
Governance	• Publish an Adaptive Solution Management Plan • Identify required key personnel creating new roles as required

4 Conclusion

Development of successful adaptive learning solutions relies not only on a high level of technical expertise, but also effective and efficient processes and process management capabilities to deliver true data-driven, results-based training that provides value to customers.

References

1. Walcutt, J.J., Schatz, S. (eds.): Modernizing Learning: Building the Future Learning Ecosystem. Government Publishing Office, Washington, DC (2019). License: Creative Commons Attribution CC BY 4.0 IGO
2. Bromante, F., Colby, R.: Off the Clock: Moving Education from Time to Competency. Corwin, Thousand Oaks (2012)
3. Doyle, T.: Helping Students Learn in a Learner-Centered Environment: A Guide to Facilitating Learning in Higher Education. Stylus, Sterling (2008)
4. IEEE ICICLE. https://www.ieeeicicle.org/. Accessed 31 Jan 2020
5. Adaptive Instructional Systems (C/LT/AIS) P2247 Working Group. https://site.ieee.org/sagroups-2247-1/. Accessed 31 Jan 2020
6. Pugliese, L.: Adaptive learning systems: surviving the storm. EDUCAUSE Review (2016). https://er.educause.edu/articles/2016/10/adaptive-learning-systems-surviving-the-storm. Accessed 31 Jan 2020
7. Manifesto for Agile Software Development. https://agilemanifesto.org/. Accessed 31 Jan 2020
8. Scaled Agile Framework. https://www.scaledagileframework.com/. Accessed 31 Jan 2020
9. Mayer, R.E.: Applying the Science of Learning. Pearson/Allyn & Bacon, Boston (2011)
10. Fadel, C., Bialik, M., Trilling, B.: Four-Dimensional Education: The Competencies Learners Need to Succeed. The Center for Curriculum Redesign, Boston (2015)
11. Hattie, J., Timperley, H.: The power of feedback. Rev. Educ. Res. **77**(1), 81–112 (2008)

Usability Dimensions of Simulated Detectors for Improvised Explosive Devices

Crystal Maraj[1], Jonathan Hurter[1], Dean Reed[1], Clive Hoayun[1],
Adam Moodie[2], and Latika "Bonnie" Eifert[2(✉)]

[1] Institute for Simulation and Training, University of Central Florida, Orlando,
FL 32826, USA
{cmaraj, jhurter, dreed, choayun}@ist.ucf.edu
[2] US Army Futures Command, CCDC-SC, STTC, Orlando, FL 32826, USA
{adam.b.moodie.mil, latika.k.eifert.civ}@mail.mil

Abstract. Buried explosives, such as Improvised Explosive Devices (IEDs), are a threat to operations in the military. This challenge is compounded by limits in training the military to detect IEDs using a handheld detector called the Minehound. Thus, a call for improved IED detector training is answered through testing Virtual Reality (VR) and Augmented Reality (AR) Minehound trainers: these trainers are subjected to a usability investigation. Further, the VR and AR developments are framed within a Systems Engineering Process Model. Following traditional Minehound instruction, a data collection event occurred over a two-day period, where ten Marines were asked to use the VR and AR Minehound trainers. Following the Marines' interaction with the trainers, the Marines completed a usability questionnaire (i.e., agreement with the usefulness, ease of use, ease of learning, satisfaction, and effectiveness of the trainers; and responses to open-ended questions). Ratings indicated future iterations should not emphasize aspects of ease of use and ease of learning, such as for user interfaces, but emphasize challenging aspects, such as helping users accomplish training tasks. A lower mean score in the usefulness subscale may be linked to breaks in fidelity (e.g., lag issues, weight issues, and a non-standard Marine sweep technique). Primarily, considerations for usefulness, satisfaction, and effectiveness aspects should be highlighted in the future as per an iterative design process. A cost-benefit analysis is given to compare the traditional and experimental forms of training. Limits of the study include experimental, environmental, and technical issues.

Keywords: Training · Virtual Reality · Augmented Reality · Simulation · Usability

1 Introduction

1.1 Problem Space

Buried explosives are a continual threat to military operations. In recent times, the Improvised Explosive Device (IED) has come to reign as a choice form of buried explosives, along with more conventional mines. In 2017, IEDs continued to contribute

R. A. Sottilare and J. Schwarz (Eds.): HCII 2020, LNCS 12214, pp. 130–143, 2020.
https://doi.org/10.1007/978-3-030-50788-6_10

to the death toll in Afghanistan, in part to giving insurgencies what an Afghanistan expert deemed as dominance (Kester and Winter 2017). The use of IED's is related to their accessibility (Secretary-General 2016). Overall, IEDs are categorized as an emplaced munition, and are one method of engagement (Cross et al. 2016). Although IEDs are not necessarily placed in the ground, curbing buried IEDs and mines are the overarching anchor of the present paper. To curb this threat of buried explosives, we focus on one method (out of many possibilities; *Disrupting improvised explosive device* 2008) for reducing IEDs, as well as mines: the use of handheld, human-operated detectors known as VMR2 Minehounds (herein referred to as Minehounds).

1.2 Current Challenges

The problem of reducing the toll of buried explosives using Minehounds is compounded by training issues: the Minehound is fielded in theater without proper training strategies, the Minehound is a complicated system to learn, Warfighter operating skills can perish quickly if regular sustainment training is not conducted, the Minehound has an expensive cost of over $20,000 (Reed et al. 2017), there is a cost of building live training lanes in a specific geographic area, sustainment training costs time and resources, and training is limited by the availability of resources (e.g., equipment, instructors, training environment, and location).

1.3 Related Work

Various systems have been developed that relate to Minehound training. One system is the Counter-Mine Augmented Reality Training System (CMARTS; Maurer et al. 2019). The CMARTS is a modified Minehound with embedded training capabilities and a Head-Mounted Display (HMD) to provide feedback. Area coverage, detected objects, and swing technique were part of feedback. Although the users found the HMD distracting, the authors thought the use of instructor-less training and the non-prepared environments deserve further investigation.

Another detection system is the Mine and IED Detection Augmented by Satellite (MIDAS) system (Maelstrom n.d.). The MIDAS system contains an indoor and an outdoor training system. The indoor training systems uses an HMD to provide training. The outdoor training system contains various sensors, such as for position and height. The goal of the MIDAS system is to provide an alternative detector system with the ability to provide real-time feedback to the trainee.

1.4 Solution Space: Simulation

To address current challenges, simulations are sought as one method of interest. A simulation is defined as "a representation of a real world phenomenon by a computer program that imitates a physical process or object by causing a computer to respond mathematically to data and changing conditions as though it were the process or object itself" (Gee 2008, p. 34). Succinctly, digital simulations can provide a lifelike representation of some aspect of the analogue world. Simulations can be capitalized on for training: by recreating tasks applicable to the true Minehound system, one manages to train through experiential learning (i.e., learning through hands-on activities). Simulations attempt to prepare one for actual situations (e.g., in healthcare; Howard 2018). A simulation's degree of authenticity, or fidelity, may differ between simulations, despite focus on a similar task. Practiceware can be considered a form of high-fidelity training, and minigames a sort of simplified form of practiceware; both are tied to what Aldrich (2009) notes as immersive learning simulations.

Virtual Reality (VR) and Augmented Reality (AR) can be used for simulations. These two ways are variations of virtuality, with VR providing purely synthetic sensory displays, and AR providing a mix of synthetic and real displays: VR and AR lay along a reality-virtuality continuum (Milgram and Colquhoun 1999). In one viewpoint VR and AR are thought to have different applications: "VR is a new reality, AR is about enhancing reality….you are either augmenting or replacing" (Fink 2017). This paper is concerned about the usability of VR and AR Minehound trainers.

1.5   Systems Engineering Design Process

Interdisciplinary teams develop VR and AR simulations for testing and evaluating prototype systems, such as for training. Prototype development goes through an iterative design process: an initial step is identifying the system's requirements, followed by prototype development, and subsequently user testing and evaluation. Formally coined the Systems Engineering Process Model (see Fig. 1), this model provides a comprehensive approach to solving inefficiencies during development (Sotomayor et al. 2017). Through iterative testing and design, the final system results in reduced safety and technical risks, while maintaining reliability and potentially enhancing human performance. There are several variations of the Systems Engineering Process Model applied to different organizations: manufacturing, production and construction. This paper applies the Systems Engineering Process Model to the prototype development of the VR and AR Minehound trainer devices.

Following the requirements analysis, a team of engineers created surrogate VR and AR Minehound devices. Feedback was injected from stakeholders, such as counter-IED/asymmetric warfare trainers and US Army Subject Matter Experts (SMEs). A pilot test was conducted at a Ft. Benning, Georgia annual training event: based on trainee feedback from this Army Expeditionary Warrior Experiment (AEWE), an updated prototype was developed. A usability test of the updated prototype occurred for US Marines at Camp Lejeune, North Carolina. This paper focuses on the usability testing results from the Camp Lejeune event, in relation to the VR and AR Minehound trainers. Before detailing the Camp Lejeune experiment, the authors provide a summary of the updates stemming from AEWE. This is an example of how to apply the Systems Engineering Process Model.

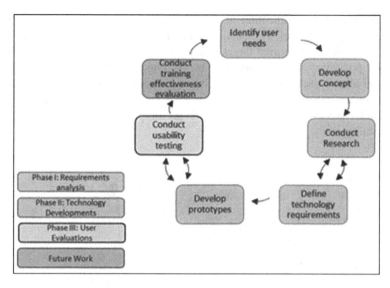

Fig. 1. The systems engineering process model.

At the Ft. Benning AEWE event, ten users evaluated VR and AR Minehound devices. The VR Minehound device contained a virtual representation of the Lawson Army Airfield Minehound training range at Ft. Benning: the engineers matched the exact number, location, and type of buried targets in the VR environment. Nevertheless, user feedback indicated the VR training range simulated too many mines; users noted the density of the targets was too high to be practical. Based on the user feedback, the engineers introduced a menu option to allow a user to customize the density of targets (see Fig. 2).

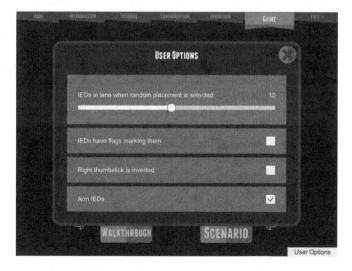

Fig. 2. The Improvised Explosive Device (IED) menu option added after the Army Expeditionary Warrior Experiment (AEWE).

Another requested modification to the VR Minehound system was the ability to dynamically toggle flag markers on and off (see Fig. 3); this capability enables users to render markers above the buried target visible or invisible. Markers allow the user to identify the positions of the buried targets. Adding visibility of exact locations of buried target allows the user to focus on aspects of identification, such as the tonality and sensor return values of the device, instead of locating each target. Following the user feedback from the AEWE event, the VR prototypes were updated in preparation for the usability study.

Fig. 3. An example of target flags off (left) and target flags on (right).

1.6   Paper Scope: Usability Investigation

A usability study was designed to investigate the VR and AR Minehound devices for training. In order to assess the usability of the devices, the Usefulness, Satisfaction, and Ease-of-Use (USE) Questionnaire (Lund 2001) was modified for incorporation into the research study. Thirteen questions were divided into five subscales: Usefulness, Ease of Use, Ease of Learning, Satisfaction, and Effectiveness subscales (see Table 1).

The research is linked to users' response of the USE Questionnaire, and examines the usability of the VR and AR Minehound devices for training. Specifically, are the VR and AR Minehound trainer devices useful, easy to use, easy to learn, satisfactory, and effective? What are the most negative aspects of the Minehound trainer devices? What are the most positive aspects of the Minehound trainer devices? This paper shows how to incorporate a system engineering process into test and evaluation. Further, the recommendations may be considered for other audiences (i.e., non-military users), who may need simulated detector training.

Table 1. Definitions of each Usefulness, Satisfaction, and Ease-of-Use (USE) Questionnaire subscale.

USE subscale	Definition
Usefulness	The device is effective, is useful, and can help accomplish tasks
Ease of use	The device is easy, is user friendly, and can help accomplish tasks in a few steps
Ease of learning	The device is quick to learn and users can recall how to operate the device to accomplish tasks
Satisfaction	The device accomplishes the task based on user directions
Effectiveness	The device can aid the user to perform the task and can be applied to real-world skills and applications

2   Method

2.1   Participants

The inclusion criteria were limited to a military population. As a result, ten US Marines participated in the usability study. All participants were males with an age range from 19 to 35: the mean was 25 and the standard deviation was 6.18. The military ranks ranged from Private 1st Class (E2) to Sergeant (E7), and all Marines identified as Combat Engineers. Regarding handheld detector training using VR or AR simulations, only three participants reported having experience (i.e., using online gaming or live practice with a Minehound). Eight participants reported having counter-IED training. Regarding computer usage, participants reported using the computer at least monthly. Video game experience was recorded at both ends of the spectrum, whereby participants either reported never playing or playing weekly and more. The majority of video games played were first-person shooter games.

2.2   Training Instruments

In terms of the training instrument technology, or VR and AR trainers, various contrasts are evident. For example, the VR scenarios are modeled after real-world training lanes, whereas the AR scenarios use portable mats and Vuforia fiducial tracking for soil; the VR system uses a third-person avatar to automatically exemplify sweep technique, whereas the AR system presents visual arrows for a first-person user's excessive sweep speed; the VR system allows outlining and classifying buried materials through a minigame, whereas the AR system allows marker placement and revealing buried materials; and the AR involves a 3D-printed surrogate. The VR scenario was created in the Unity game engine. For a breakdown of other notable contrasts, see Table 2. Examples of VR and AR tablet scenarios are given in Fig. 4.

Table 2. Contrasts between the Minehound trainer technologies.

Criteria	Augmented Reality	Virtual Reality
User input	User touches user interface, swings device	User touches user interface, uses virtual joystick
Additional tablet mounting	3D-printed shell	None required
External fiducial marker	Required	Not required
Tablet backside camera	On	Off
Built-in walk through tutorial	None	Present
Minimum tablet requirement	ASUS Z-10 or higher	Google Nexus 9 or higher

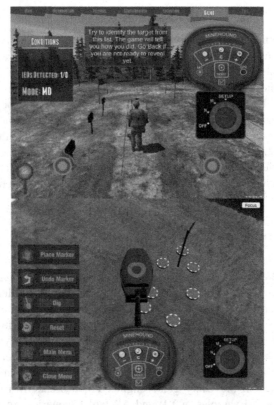

Fig. 4. Examples of a Virtual Reality (VR) scenario (top) and Augmented Reality (AR) scenario (bottom) shown via tablet. Both images from Reed et al. (2019) reprinted with permission.

2.3 Survey Instruments

Two surveys were given: a demographics survey and the modified USE Questionnaire. The demographics survey gathered biographical information, such as military, gaming, and counter-IED-training experience. The USE Questionnaire was modified to include verbiage that focused on the Minehound trainer device. The modified USE Questionnaire contained 13 items rated on a 7-point scale from 1 (strongly disagree) to 7 (strongly agree). The questions were divided into five subscales (i.e., Usefulness, Ease of Use, Ease of Learning, Satisfaction, and Effectiveness subscales) for user evaluation. Additionally, the USE Questionnaire captured open-ended responses regarding the most negative and positive aspects of the Minehound trainer devices.

2.4 Data Collection Procedure

The Marines participated in their traditional 40-h training course required for military service. Following the course, the researchers asked the Marines to participate in the present usability study. Ten Marines agreed to participate. Following a consent process, the participants were provided with a brief introduction to the experimental objectives and research terminology (e.g., empirical research, independent variable, and dependent variable). Following the introductory brief, the participants completed the demographics survey. During the first half of the day, all participants received guidance on the fundamentals and theory of operations for the traditional Minehound device. Following this instruction, the participants interfaced with the VR system. The participants were given approximately 30 min to use the VR system. The experimenters were also present in the event the participants required assistance in setting up or operating the system. During the second half of the day, all participants received instructions for the AR tutorial. The tutorial explained the calibration settings and how to navigate a scenario. The AR Minehound system contained a path viewer feature, which provided after-action-reviews to both the instructor and participant. Participants were given approximately 30-min time to exercise the AR system. The experimenters were also present in the event any technical issues arose.

Following the use of the VR and AR Minehound devices, the participants were asked to complete the USE Questionnaire to assess the perceived usability of the devices. Following the questionnaire, the participant was thanked, debriefed, and dismissed.

3 Results

The data collected from the training event was scored and logged onto an Excel spreadsheet. Table 3 and Fig. 5 report the average scores from the USE Questionnaire statements, and Table 4 reports free responses.

Table 3. Mean Usefulness, Satisfaction, and Ease-of-Use (USE) Questionnaire scores, per statement.

USE questionnaire statement	Mean	Standard deviation
1) The device helps me be more effective	4.4	1.35
2) The device is useful	5.3	1.34
3) The device makes the things I want to accomplish easier to get done	4.8	1.14
4) The device is easy to use	6	0.47
5) The device is user friendly	6.1	0.88
6) The device requires the fewest steps possible to accomplish what I want to do with it	5	1.33
7) I learned to use the device quickly	6.4	0.70
8) I easily remember how to use the device	6.5	0.71
9) I am satisfied with the device	4.9	1.45
10) The device works the way I want it to work	4	1.63
11) The device helped me perform the task	4.5	1.58
12) I could use this device to learn real-world skills	4.9	1.52
13) This device would be beneficial for a broad range of applications	5.3	1.64

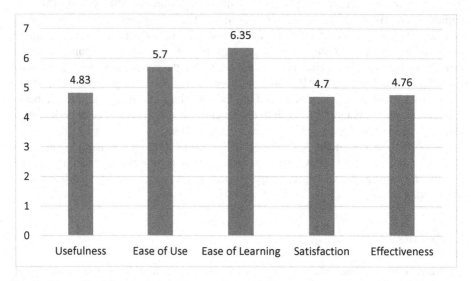

Fig. 5. Mean Usefulness, Satisfaction, and Ease-of-Use (USE) Questionnaire scores, per subscale.

Table 4. Usefulness, Satisfaction, and Ease-of-Use (USE) Questionnaire free responses.

Positive aspects	Negative aspects
Easy to set-up and use	Screen lagging
Good for learning	Weight distribution is off
Tablet is convenient	Could not tell if [one is] reaching or walking forward
Helps learn VMR2 [(i.e., Minehound)]	Height calibration is off
	The Minehound sweep techniques were created for the Army version

4 Discussion

In terms of average usability per subscale, both Ease of Learning and Ease of Use had at least somewhat agreeable scores (i.e., a score of 5); whereas Usefulness, Satisfaction, and Effectiveness scored between a neutral rating (a score of 4) and somewhat agreeable rating (a score of 5). This suggests future iterations should focus on providing the user with a Minehound trainer that helps accomplish training tasks, rather than focus on the interface, or means of interacting with the system. The categorized responses revealed positive and negative aspects about the devices: positive aspects included benefit to learning, ease of use, and convenience of the tablet; negative aspects included screen lag, incorrect weight distribution, and the sweep technique not following the Marine's Standard Operating Procedure (SOP). The free responses, such as the ease of use and convenience, fit with the agreeable score rating for the Ease of Use subscale in the USE Questionnaire. In contrast, the Usefulness subscale score may be linked to breaks in fidelity (e.g., lag issues, weight issues, and a non-standard Marine sweep technique).

4.1 Camp Lejeune Subject Matter Expert and User Feedback: Recommendations and Solutions

Following the data collection event, the researchers compiled a list of modifications based on both the participants feedback and the SME's guidance. Following the Systems Engineering Process Model, the feedback offered was used to improve the systems' design for the next step of the model.

The participants observed that both VR and AR applications render an explosion upon approaching a predetermined IED or buried mine, which forces the application to restart. As a result, the software developers created a user preference that allows the end-user to toggle the explosion behavior.

The SME determined that it was important to have the user complete all initial calibration routines prior to lane target identification activities. To date, the software developers are incorporating a flush puck, deep targets, and shallow calibration targets into the VR and AR scenes on the tablets. The effort will allow the user to perform full calibration before the lane-clearing activity.

Further, the SME requested the inclusion of a non-linear scenario in the VR Minehound system. The current scenario contained a well-defined lane area with pinpointed IEDs or buried mines. A benefit of a non-linear scenario includes IEDs or buried mines in a natural pattern. The addition of hidden targets and new ground disturbances will aid development of a new scenario for Marine training.

The Marine Corps standard procedure for marking explosives differs from the Army procedure. Updates to graphics for a Marine rendering is important to the training cadre. Further, the voice-over components will need to be modified to incorporate "Marine" in lieu of "Soldier." The engineers plan to incorporate a new motion capture effort, using a Marine Corps SME to demonstrate approved sweeping techniques for the avatar in the VR scenario.

4.2   Cost-Benefit Analysis

It is prudent to consider a cost-benefit analysis of how and where this system could be employed in the US Army. An example of a use-case scenario involves a Soldier at a home station. It is assumed that most Soldiers are not located at a site with a premium IED training range. If the unit has a budget for sending Soldiers on travel, or Temporary Duty (TDY), for this type of training, an average trip would cost approximately $926. See Table 5 for an analysis of TDY costs, as well as use cases for multiple trips. In addition to the cost savings, the US Army benefits from training time saved due to environmental considerations (e.g. rain or snow days), and an increase in operational relevance, due to rapid threat response. Specifically, new IED objects can be rapidly modeled in 3D software (e.g., AutoCAD and Autodesk Maya) and presented in the Minehound surrogate software. Finally, the US Army benefits from increased training effectiveness due to the built-in after-action review capabilities, which are unavailable at most live ranges.

Table 5. Use-case scenarios and cost-benefit projections.

Composition of a TDY for traditional training			
Average cost of a TDY		Daily rate	Details
Flight	$500		Round trip/to and from unspecified location
Hotel	$288	$96	Per night/average unspecified location
Per diem	$138	$55	Per full day/$41.25 for first travel
Total	$926		day + $55 for full training day + $41.25 for last day of travel = $138/average for unspecified location
Use case: a single soldier			
	Traditional	Minehound VR/AR training device	Cost Savings to the unit
1 TDY/year	$926	$500	$426
5 TDY/year	$4,628	$500	$4,128
10 TDY/year	$9,255	$500	$8,755
Use case: a unit with ten soldiers that can share a minehound VR/AR training device			
	Traditional	Minehound VR/AR training device	Cost savings to the unit
1 TDY/year each	$9,255	$500	$8,755
5 TDY/year each	$46,275	$500	$45,775
10 TDY/year each	$92,550	$500	$92,050

Note. VR = Virtual Reality; AR = Augmented Reality; TDY = Temporary Duty.

4.3   Limitations

This research effort had several challenges during the data collection process. Challenges that occurred during the data collection activities are divided into experimental, environmental, and technical categories. An experimental challenge with field experimentation is the lack of experimental control. The time frame to start the study was not exact because participants entered the study room at different times. Therefore, the participants may not have received the entire introduction brief. As a result, the participants received inconsistent time on the training systems. The main limit of the study was a pilot-level sample size, reducing the ability to investigate trends with parametric or nonparametric statistical techniques.

The environmental challenge was related to the lack of air-conditioning. The morning training group was comfortable in the room with air-conditioning, whereas the afternoon training group was uncomfortably hot due to the lack of air-conditioning.

The technical challenges focus on the VR and AR Minehound systems. One technical challenge for the AR Minehound system was the perceived user latency during the experiment. The latency issue may be related to the low number of frames-per-second produced in the scene, due to the increased polygon count reaching beyond the video rendering capabilities. Another latency issue may be related to the low update rate of the AR camera. It is possible to have a rendering update rate of over 30 frames per second; but have an asynchronous update rate with the AR pose estimation that is less than 10 Hz. Regarding the VR Minehound system, one technical issue is related to a limited range of motion of the virtual joystick, which may have resulted in the user's lack of fine motor control to navigate the virtual environment on the tablet. A second technical issue is the user's obstructed view of the scene due to the virtual joystick: the current study's virtual joystick system potentially occluded over 7% of the available screen area of the tablet. The challenges listed will follow the Systems Engineering Process Model and undergo revision for the next data collection activity.

5 Conclusion

The results from the usability evaluation may be used to re-design the prototype and inform future experimental design plans for conducting training effectiveness evaluations. The lessons from the pilot study include the benefits of ease of use and ease of learning; and highlight considerations for usefulness, satisfaction, and effectiveness in the iterative design process. Some concerns, which could be improved upon, include the fidelity of the systems. The next step of this research is to update the Minehound trainer, given the lessons learned. Any updated trainers could be evaluated using a larger sample size in a training effectiveness evaluation. This paper showed how to incorporate the Systems Engineering Process Model into test and evaluation. Further, the recommendations found can serve other non-military audiences interested in simulated detector training. Finally, the information learned from the evaluation can be exchanged to improve the design of VR and AR Minehound systems or comparable systems.

Acknowledgments. This research was sponsored by Latika (Bonnie) Eifert of the U.S. Army Futures Command, CCDC-SC, Simulation and Training Technologies Center (STTC) under contract W911NF-15-2-0099. However, the views, findings, and conclusions contained in this presentation are solely those of the authors and should not be interpreted as representing the official policies, either expressed or implied, of the U.S. Government.

References

Aldrich, C.: The Complete Guide to Simulations and Serious Games: How the Most Valuable Content Will Be Created in the age Beyond Gutenberg to Google. Wiley, San Francisco (2009)

Cross, K., Dullum, O., Jenzen-Jones, N.R., Garlasco, M.: Explosive Weapons in Populated Areas: Technical Considerations Relevant to Their Use and Effects. Armament Research Services (ARES), Perth (2016)

National Research Council: Disrupting Improvised Explosive Device Terror Campaigns: Basic Research Opportunities. National Academies Press, Washington, DC (2008)

Fink, C.: War of AR/VR/MR/XR words. Forbes, 20 October 2017. https://www.forbes.com/sites/charliefink/2017/10/20/war-of-arvrmrxr-words/#d613e668d074. Accessed 23 Oct 2019

Gee, J.P.: Getting over the slump: innovation strategies to promote children's learning. The Joan Ganz Cooney Center at Sesame Workshop, New York (2008)

Howard, S.: Increasing fidelity and realism in simulation [Blog post], 19 September 2018. http://nursingeducation.lww.com/blog.entry.html/2018/09/19/increasing_fidelity-zEj0.html

Kester, J., Winter, J.: Pentagon report: IEDs surge in Afghanistan. Foreign Policy, 20 October 2017. http://foreignpolicy.com/2017/10/20/pentagon-report-ied-casualties-surge-in-afghanistan/

Lund, A.M.: Measuring usability with the USE questionnaire. STC Usability SIG Newslett. 8, 2 (2001)

Maelstrom (n.d.): ESA – MIDAS Project. http://maelstrom.com/esa/. Accessed 10 June 2019

Maurer, T., Cook, K., Graybeal, J.: Counter-mine augmented reality training system (CMARTS). In: Detection and Sensing of Mines, Explosive Objects, and Obscured Targets XXIV, vol. 11012. International Society for Optics and Photonics (2019)

Milgram, P., Colquhoun Jr., H.: A taxonomy of real and virtual world display integration. Mixed Real. Merging Real Virtual Worlds 1, 1–26 (1999)

Reed, D., Eifert, L, Reyolds, S., Hillyer, T., Hoayun, C.: U.S. Army mobile augmented and virtual reality training systems for handheld detectors. In; Bruzzone, A.G., De Felice, F., Frydman, C., Longo, Massei, M., Solis, A. (eds.) Proceedings of the International Conference on Modeling and Applied Simulation 2017, pp. 191–196 (2017)

Reed, D., Maraj, C., Hurter, J., Eifert, L.: Simulations to train buried explosives detection: a pilot investigation. In: Proceedings of the Interservice/Industry Training, Simulation, and Education Conference (I/ITSEC) 2019 (2019)

Secretary-General: Countering the threat posed by improvised explosive devices (Report No. A/71/187) (2016). http://www.un.org/ga/search/view_doc.asp?symbol=A/71/187

Sotomayor, T., Maraj, C., Mott, J., Hill, B., Stadler, E.: Humeral head intraosseous access: filling the military training gap. J. Defense Model. Simul. 14(4), 361–369 (2017)

Toward Zero Authoring: Considering How to Maximize Courseware Quality and Affordability Simultaneously

James E. McCarthy[✉] [ID]

Sonalysts, Inc., Fairborn, OH 45324, USA
mccarthy@sonalysts.com

Abstract. The past 60 years has seen tremendous development in adaptive instructional systems such as simulation-based intelligent tutoring systems and media-based adaptive interactive multimedia instruction (IMI). Solid empirical findings have repeatedly demonstrated the power of these technologies. Unfortunately, there are also well-known impediments that prevent the broad adoption of these powerful tools. Among these impediments, the cost and timelines associated with development and sustainment are prominent. To address these impediments, various researchers have worked to develop authoring tools for conventional and adaptive instructional systems. These tools speed the development and maintenance of these systems, reduce the associated costs, and allow less skilled developers to create high-quality courseware. This paper will address the development of authoring tools for adaptive IMI. In it, we will trace the development of these tools over time and explore the mismatch between the current development trajectory and the needs of consumers. Using this discordance as a point of departure, we will explore the possibility of a different approach.

Keywords: Authoring · Adaptive instructional system · Personalized instruction

1 Introduction

Almost as soon as general-purpose computers came to life, researchers began to consider how they could use these powerful machines to improve education and training [22]. These researchers were drawn by the transformative promise of being able to deliver high-quality educational services universally. No longer would the quality of a student's educational experience be limited to their proximity to excellent teachers. Students everywhere could benefit from a state-of-the-art education. Moreover, these electronic teachers would never tire, never lose patience, and never have a bad day.

Soon, however, these researchers began to encounter significant scientific difficulties. They had to wrestle with how best to use this new power to attain educational outcomes. At the same time, the researchers had to develop a language that they could use to communicate their recommendations so that they could be evaluated. These were significant theoretical challenges.

© Springer Nature Switzerland AG 2020
R. A. Sottilare and J. Schwarz (Eds.): HCII 2020, LNCS 12214, pp. 144–163, 2020.
https://doi.org/10.1007/978-3-030-50788-6_11

However, in some ways, the theoretical challenges paled in comparison to the practical ones. Relatively few individuals were competent to develop computer-based courseware. Further, the process of handcrafting this computer-based courseware was frightfully slow. Given the costs and timelines involved, it was impossible for these few pioneers to create a collection of courseware that could meaningfully impact society, or even local enterprises.

Therefore, at the same time that they were developing a "design language" [7] for communicating, testing, and implementing their innovations with respect to computer-based courseware, these early innovators had to address the practical imperatives of developing the courseware faster, cheaper, and with a broader workforce. In the next section, we will review some of these strategies they employed and some of the consequences of those strategies.

2 Cost Reduction Strategies over the Decades

In the early days of computer-assisted instruction (CAI), the load was carried by a few men and women of extraordinary talent. These pioneers needed to be experts in a new and rapidly evolving technology and at the same time master the not-yet developed field of instructional systems design. Much of the early courseware developed in these labs was developed on mini-computers like the DEC PDP-7 or PDP-9 using assembler language (W. Judd, personal communication, December 20, 2019).

Not surprisingly, these early efforts were "exceedingly time consuming and frightfully expensive" (W. Judd, personal communication, December 20, 2019). Almost immediately, the leaders of the field began to look for ways to reduce cost and increase efficiency. More specifically, the hunt was on for approaches that would reduce courseware development timelines and the required expertise. These remain priorities today. Moreover, additional cost drivers that were less important in the early days of the field have come under increased scrutiny. These include reducing the costs associated with media development and hardware procurement and sustainment.

In this section, we will review some of the strategies that they employed and summarize their results.

2.1 The Starting Point: Early Courseware Development Efforts

The first step toward reducing time lines involved switching from assembler languages to higher-order languages such as FORTRAN, COBOL, and others. While these languages reduced programming time, they still required skilled programmers. Further, they often lacked features needed for instructional programming.

Researchers addressed the latter issue by creating extensions of these languages that made them a better fit for CAI. For example, languages like CATO and FOIL were extensions of FORTRAN (W. Judd, personal communication, December 20, 2019). The former issue, however, remained a challenge. By requiring the expertise of skilled programmers, use of these tools limited the pool of potential authors and increased development costs.

To address this limitation, the next step in the evolution of courseware development was the introduction of macros [7]. Macros "rolled-up" more atomic commands into higher-order, easy to remember functions. A less experienced developer could run a macro, provide some arguments, and the system would convert the supplied content to the specific lower-level commands that would be executed to create the learner experience.

2.2 The Rise of Authoring Languages

The need for better tools, the advent of macros, and a few other factors lead to the development of specialized courseware authoring languages. One of the earliest such language was known as TUTOR and it was developed specifically for Programmed Logic for Automatic Teaching Operations (PLATO) system. PLATO used a centralized computer serving a number of "dumb" terminals to present lessons, illustrations, drills, *etc.* to learners [1]. In 1967, Paul Tenczar recognized that a more efficient method of creating PLATO lessons was needed and possible. His efforts led to the development of the TUTOR language [26].

While an advance, TUTOR was still laborious. Sherwood [26] provides a useful example. Imagine that we want to create an exercise that asks the student to name a geometric figure, in this case a triangle. The student will type a response and the system will reply with an indication that the answer is right or wrong. To produce this very simple question, TUTOR (which was unquestionably an advance!) required the series of commands shown in Table 1.

Table 1. Sample TUTOR programming sequence

Command	Tag/Argument	Explanation
unit	geometry	A label for this question
at	1812	A specific screen location; 18 lines down and 12 spaces over
write	What is this figure?	Produces the specified text on the screen at the specified location
draw	510; 1510; 1540; 510	Produces a triangle by drawing from the point five lines down and 10 spaces over, to a point 15 lines down and 10 spaces over, to a point 15 lines down and 40 spaces over, and back to the beginning – five lines down and 10 spaces over
arrow	2015	Indicates where the student should enter his/her response
answer	<it, is, a> (right, rt) triangle	it, is, and a are optional words, right or rt are synonymous important rules that must be present
write	Exactly right!	Feedback to be provided if the student's answer includes the required words
wrong	<it, is, a> square	Specifies a possible wrong answer
write	Count the sides!	Feedback to be provided if the student provides the anticipated wrong answer; all other answers will be met with "no"

While still cumbersome, TUTOR signaled the start of a wave of emerging authoring languages. Frye [6] identified 22 authoring languages. In his analysis, Frye apportioned the languages into the four categories shown in Table 2.

Table 2. Categories of authoring languages

Category	Explanation	Examples
Conventional Programming Languages	General purpose languages that were used to develop CAI, among other things	FORTRAN, Pascal, Algol, LISP
Conventional Languages Enhanced to Support Instruction	Compiler-based languages like FORTRAN that researchers expanded by adding features that make them more suitable for instructional purposes	Mentor, CATO, FOIL
Conventional Languages with Special Abilities	Interpreted languages that were easier to master. They were particularly well suited to environments in which the student used the computer to solve problems. However, they normally did not incorporate features for display, answer processing, and branching that are desirable in a CAI author language	Basic, APL Adept, Joss
Dedicated Authoring Languages	Special purpose languages that included features to facilitate construction and administration of instructional sequences, monitoring of student activities, and collection of performance data. Many of these languages provided the first steps toward adaptive training by supporting decision rules that shape instructional sequences in response to student performance	Coursewriter, CAL, Planit

An argument could be made that Frye could have included at least two more categories in his analysis – table-based systems that separated content and programming logic and question generators (E. Schneider, personal communication, 2020).

These languages made it easier to develop CAI and lowered the barriers to the development task. In doing so, they were a significant first step toward achieving the first two efficiency goals that we introduced above: reducing courseware development timelines and reducing the required level of expertise. However, they were still (unapologetically) programming languages. While they had features that made them well suited to instructional development, they required a level of dedication to learn, use, debug, *etc*. As computers became more sophisticated and the range of input, output, and media options exploded, the barriers to entry and time commitment once again began to increase. However, at the same time, those same capabilities made graphical user interfaces practical and opened the door for the next step in the evolution of authoring tools – the development of authoring systems.

2.3   Continuing Efficiency: The Emergence of Authoring Systems

In some ways, the basis of many authoring systems brings us back to the early days when systems like PLATO were emerging. A contemporary of PLATO, the Time-shared, Interactive, Computer-Controlled Information/Instructional Television (TICCIT) system was designed to test the ability to deliver instruction to homes. TICCIT linked mini-computers to home televisions via coaxial cables [10]. If this wasn't ambitious enough, the TICCIT developers wanted to give learners a significant degree of control over their instructional experience. To achieve their goals, the team had to develop a strategy that would allow instructional experts and software experts to communicate effectively. They also needed a strategy that would make it practical to deliver the content and provide learners with the desired level of control. To meet these challenges, the TICCIT team developed the concept of the "base frame" [10].

For TICCIT, a base frame was a logical unit of instruction. It described a single strategic interaction with the student. Each base frame comprised a series of elements. Within a given frame, some elements remained static; others changed over time in response to the instructional programming or student actions. Not only did this concept provide a foundation for communication and development, it also provided the basis for a range of modern authoring systems such as Authorware, IconAuthor, Quest, *etc.* Developing instruction came to consist of specifying a series of frame types and then describing how to populate the various elements of each frame.

Most authoring tools were essentially "code" generators that hid the programming requirements behind user-friendly interfaces. These tools then produced the detailed computer code that separate "runtime environments" would ingest to create the pro-gramed instructional experiences. Different runtime environments (*e.g.,* computers using different operating systems) would require different programs, so various trans-lators had to be present.

Essentially, these authoring systems provided a more graphical front end on the tried-and-true macros used by earlier developers. Rather than using verbal macros (like a "write" command), these tool used menus, forms, and draggable objects to allow designers to specify their intent and to gather the data needed to populate macros. For this generation of authoring systems, the goal was to hide the complexity of instruc-tional programming behind a graphical user interface. As noted by Gibbons [8], these tools made it easier for non-programmers to outline a series of instructional experience types and then to specify the details of those experiences (including learner-sensitive variations). By eliminating the need for coding (or even pseudo-coding), these tools did a tremendous job of opening the field of instructional development to a much wider range of users. They have significantly reduced the level of expertise required to develop courseware. Further, they have made that development process much faster. However, in doing so, these tools have provided some unintended consequences. We'll discuss these consequences in Sect. 2.5.

2.4 More Recent Trends: Using Standards and Technology to Further Reduce Costs

Earlier developers were not particular concerned with media development or hardware costs. In the former case, the computers of the day did not process and display "media" as we use the term today. As we noted earlier, if a designer wanted a triangle on the screen, he/she did not display a picture of a triangle; rather, the designer used programming tools to *draw* a triangle. Similarly, because fewer computers were involved and their costs, while high, were swamped by development costs, the price of hardware wasn't of much concern.

More recently, these concerns have become more prominent. Just as CAI tools have evolved over the years to reduce "programming" costs, so too have media tools, like Photoshop matured, becoming both more powerful and easier to use. To further reduce costs, customers and producers have become much more interested in reducing cost through re-use. If I want a picture of a triangle, why should I have to hire a graphic artist to create it? Why can't I use one that has already been produced? Similarly, why can't I build one lesson on a topic (*e.g.,* Ohm's Law) and reuse that lesson whenever it is needed. Concerns like these have given rise to various initiatives such as the Sharable Content Object Reference Model (SCORM) and its constituent standards to promote reuse, content portability, and other cost reducing benefits.

Hardware costs have been trending downward on a nearly continuous basis. The concern now isn't so much the concern of the device itself, but rather a concern with maintenance costs. As the number of personal computers and operating systems has proliferated, it has become difficult to manage the software present on each machine. This is especially concerning as cyber security concerns have increased. To reduce maintenance costs while increasing courseware currency, many users are opting for web-based delivery of content. To accommodate this, authoring systems are migrating away from runtime environments and toward plugins, the use of HTML5, and other tools designed to maximize the efficiency of delivery within the available bandwidth.

2.5 The Downside of Efficiency

Let's now return to the notion of unintended consequences that we introduced at the end of Sect. 2.3. Authoring languages and, to a greater extent, authoring systems have made it very simple to create courseware. However, in doing so, they have adopted a specific design language which has arguably, constricted the thinking of would-be designers [7, 9].

Design languages emerge to allow teams of developers, who often come from different communities of practice, to communicate goals and intents effectively. Often, these design languages give rise to tools that embody them. For example, the notion of a base frame in TICCIT that allowed software engineers, instructional designers, and media producers to communicate effectively.

However, this process also works in the other direction. As tools come to embody a certain design language, the tools shape how users come to think about the problem. Those functions that a given tool does not accommodate easily become easier for users to ignore. Those functions that are easiest for tool producers to program and for tool users to employ become preeminent [7]. These effects lead to the narrowing of the range of instructional design.

This becomes increasingly insidious when narrowed design conceptions are coupled with commercial price pressures such as the Government's use of low-price technically acceptable (LPTA) contracts. LPTA contracts mandate that as long as the product meets certain minimal standards, the purchaser must accept the lowest priced offering, even if it does not represent the solution that provides the best values. In these environments, it is easy, perhaps necessary, to adopt the "quick-and-dirty" solutions that authoring systems make very easy to develop. Experience has shown that this leads often to "death by PowerPoint" experiences masquerading as courseware.

3 Imagining a Different Approach

Gibbons and Fairweather [9] noted that when considering authoring tools, users should pick a tool "(1) that allows you to express your powerful ideas in a computer program without compromising them, and (2) allows you to create, read, and maintain the program as easily and efficiently as possible." Experience has shown that these competing goals have been reconciled in ways that are not entirely pleasing.

As we noted in Sect. 2.5, the design language of most tools limits the creativity and power of the designs that they promote. At the same time, customers have repeatedly expressed that the current generation of tools are not easy enough to use. Many customers do not want to pay external developers to produce courses. To save money and to make course maintenance easier, they would prefer that their "in-house" instructors and subject-matter experts build the courses. However, these local personnel generally lack the background and time to use the existing tools.

Gibbons and Fairweather [9] suggested that authoring tools could be described and compared by considering their productivity, ease of use, and power. Productivity refers to the amount of work that an individual can accomplish in a unit of time. For our discussion, this might equate to the length of time required to produce an hour of courseware. The notion of ease of use is fairly easy to understand. Often, researchers expand this to a more general notion of usability as described in Table 3. Power refers to the flexibility of the tool and the number of things that it can be used to accomplish. "A tool has more power than another if it allows the author to accomplish more or if it allows the author to approach and solve a particular problem in more ways" [9].

Table 3. Conventional dimensions of usability

Ease of use dimension	Explanation
Usefulness	The degree to which the product performs a task or function that is valuable to the user
Ease of use	This dimension measures how easy it is to use the product to achieve the user's goals. Measurements along this dimension are often tied to goal statements in the form, X% of users will be able to perform Y (some activity) within Z (some unit of time
Learnability	As its name implies, this dimension measures the user's ability to achieve a certain level of performance after a given period of usage and/or training. Rubin [25] notes that "it can also refer to the ability of infrequent users to relearn the system after periods of inactivity"
Likeability	The likability dimension captures the degree to which positive affect is associated with the product and its usage. Likability ratings can often amplify or clarify problems noted within the other dimensions

Following the general trend in computer engineering, and in keeping with their roots with high-order programming languages, authoring tools have commonly been "general purpose" tools. That is, the designers of these tools have tried to maximize their power. Over the years, ease of use and productivity have been increasingly important and various "shortcuts" have been introduced that gradually reduced or hid the power of these tools.

Our research team is currently exploring the hypothesis that a better approach is possible. Specifically, we want to consider the value of building a collection of highly specialized authoring tools. Each tool would be optimized for a very specific learning task or instructional outcome. Our thought is that by significantly reducing the power of the tool, we can tremendously increase its usability and productivity. The goal is to radically minimize the level of effort that novice developers (*e.g.,* in house instructors or subject matter experts) must expend to achieve a specific learning outcome. Resorting to hyperbole, we refer to this as our "zero authoring goal." In the long term, these very specific zero authoring systems could be federated to create a collection of tools, building up power to the extent needed in a given setting.

We are currently developing the first such system. In the next section, we discuss its foundations.

4   Case Study: Minimal Authoring for Adaptive Rote Learning

The goal of the current effort was to develop the first of a family of hyper-focused "zero authoring" adaptive training systems. To begin this line of research, we wanted to focus on a very basic learning outcome that nonetheless would be amenable to meaningful individual adaptations. Our choice was the rote memorization of facts.

One advantage that our team has is that research on the best way to develop mastery of facts dates back to the very beginning of the study of psychology. For example, one typical application is to learn geography facts [18, 23]. In this application, the instructional system might present learners with an outline of a continent or region and ask the students to identify the shaded country, state, *etc*. Alternatively, the system might present the learners with the name of a country, state, *etc*. and ask them to identify it on a map. Other commonly researched topics are foreign words/phrases [5, 16, 27], math facts [31], history facts [2], and flower types [16].

For these two classes of learning outcomes, the primary instructional manipulation is the intelligent application of the well-documented spacing effect. Dating back to the work of Ebbinghaus in the late nineteenth century, this finding shows that material that is studied across two or more sessions distributed in time is remembered more easily than when an equal amount of time is devoted to studying during a single session (*i.e.*, distributed practice is superior to massed practice). These effects exist for recall over both relatively short periods and relatively long periods. Researchers have postulated several mechanisms for this effect [30], for example:

- The Deficient Processing Hypothesis,
- The Context Variability Hypothesis, and
- The Study-phase Retrieval Hypothesis.

The deficient processing hypothesis holds that when exposure is massed, less processing effort is devoted to a given knowledge item. Because the item is associated with less elaborative processing, its memory trace is weaker and more likely to fade over time. The context variability hypothesis holds that as the time between exposures increases, so does the variability in environmental cues. Associating an increasing number of contextual cues with the knowledge item provides an increasing number of retrieval pathways, thus increasing the likelihood of recall. The study-phase retrieval hypothesis argues that, like exercising a muscle, each time an item is recalled, the original memory trace is strengthened. The more difficult the recall effort, the greater the increase in strength.

At the same time that they have worked to understand the mechanism behind the spacing effect, researchers investigated questions such as:

- What type of exposure is appropriate, and
- By how much should those exposures be separated?

The nature of the exposure that is required is fairly clear – the spacing effect relies on intentional/effortful processing. Manipulations that minimize the effort required to process the information detract from long-term memory [28].

In examining the optimal intervals within the spacing effect, researchers have looked at questions such as whether the spacing should be in fixed or expanding intervals, and whether longer spaces provide a bigger impact on learning.

Experiments comparing fixed and expanding exposure schedules have produced equivocal results [3, 19]. Within the expanding interval model, intervals are short early in the learning process and progressively expand as learning progresses. This contrasts with strategies in which the spacing remains constant. For example, Storm, Bjork, & Storm [29] reported an advantage for an expanding practice interval, but Karpicke &

Roediger [12] reported that equal intervals produced better outcomes. Karpicke & Bauernschmidt [13] reported no difference between the models.

A slightly more consistent pattern of results is seen when examining the effect of the spacing interval. Several studies in the mid-twentieth century seemed to indicate that longer spacing intervals (also known as the interstimulus interval) promoted retention better than shorter intervals (see [3] for a review). However, as Carpenter, *et al.* [3] note, care must be taken to avoid making the spacing interval so long that the content has been forgotten and each exposure approximates a "first exposure."

There is also evidence that the most desirable interstimulus interval (ISI) is dependent on the required retention interval (RI, that is, the gap between the last exposure and some test of memory, also known as the test delay;). In fact, for very short retention intervals, the spacing effect may be reversed, favoring massed practice [28]. Carpenter, *et al.* [3] cited work indicating that the optimal spacing gap was 10%–20% of the retention interval. This effect has been termed the proportionality rule [11]. Mozer and Lindsey [21] described this effect in terms of a power function relationship (see Eq. 1).

$$\text{Optimal Spacing} = 0.097\text{RI}^{0.812} \tag{1}$$

Many of these "timing factors" can be reconciled through the notion of "desirable difficulty." This principle holds that the more difficult it is to retrieve an item during exposure X, the easier it will be to retrieve the item during exposure X+Y [28]. In this way, memory can be likened to weightlifting. Practicing with heavy/difficult weights maximizes gains, as long as those weights are within the capability limits of the performer. Research has indicated that the desirable difficulty might lead to better encoding of the memory trace at each recall opportunity (see [28] for a review).

This is generally consistent with the "retrieval effort hypothesis" [18]. The evidence for this hypothesis holds that the difficulty of a successful retrieval is directly associated with long-term retention of the material. That is, the benefit of practice is maximized when retrievals are difficult, but ultimately successful [12, 14, 24].

Another way of expressing this notion of desirable difficulty is to say that the optimal time to re-expose a learner to an item is just before the learner would otherwise forget that item. This approach would maximize the interstimulus interval while allowing the learner to recall the item successfully. Continuing with the weightlifting metaphor, we want the learner to lift as much as possible without failing. Within this conception, the confusing results regarding fixed or expanding intervals and the optimal interstimulus interval can be seen as consequences of uncontrolled variability – that is, the level of mastery present in a given learner. This level of mastery can be predicted to vary as a function of the individual learner (*e.g.*, differences in aptitude), an individual item (*e.g.*, differences in difficulty), and the interaction between the two. Superior performance might be expected if the exposure schedule (*i.e.*, the interstimulus interval) were adapted to these factors. This is the challenge that we take up in the following section. In doing so, we will move from descriptive to computational models of the spacing effect.

4.1 Describing the Learning Task

The "recipe" for learning facts is well-established [20]:

1. Present the fact to be learned
2. Provide opportunities to recall the fact

Flashcards provide a useful vehicle for this type of instruction. Each flashcard instance represents a combination of a knowledge component/label, a face (picture or text), and a form. A given label might be associated with multiple faces (*e.g.,* multiple pictures of the same thing). Further, the flashcards will assume various forms.

To accomplish the first part of the recipe, students will begin by paging through virtual flashcards delivered via a web browser. The interface, shown in Fig. 1, will show the "face" of the flashcard and present a button with the "label" associated with the card. In this way, a given knowledge component/label might be presented several times, if it is associated with several faces.

Fig. 1. Initial passive presentation of flashcard facts

Thereafter, each student will receive an individualized practice experience comprising various flashcard forms. The various forms will have differing levels of difficulty, allowing the adaptive scheduler (see Sect. 4.2) to make finer-grained decisions. The basic form will present the face of the card and four labeled buttons (see Fig. 2).

Identify this vehicle

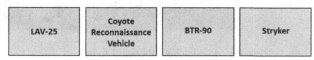

Fig. 2. Label-based flashcard

The second flashcard form will reverse the process. In this form, the system will use a label as the prompt and various faces will serve as clickable options (see Fig. 3).

Which of these vehicles is an LAV-25?
Click on your answer

Fig. 3. Face-based flashcard form

The third option is a "matching" form in which the student must drag four labels to the corresponding faces. This is shown in Fig. 4. For each flashcard form, the student will be given feedback indicating whether his/her answer was correct and, if not, which of the options should have been selected. The student will then click a "next" button and the adaptive scheduler will determine which knowledge component, flashcard, and form to present.

Drag the labels to the images.

Fig. 4. Matching flashcard form

4.2   Calculating the Optimal Spacing Interval

The adaptive scheduler we envision will embody the following design principles.

1. Establish a clear mapping between items and knowledge components.
2. Include a passive learning session prior to active recall attempts.
3. Promote recall from long-term memory.
4. Use recall likelihood to guide item selection.
5. If multiple items are eligible for selection, use cross-item knowledge component estimates to bias selection.
6. Establish a configurable recall likelihood threshold.
7. Consider both individual and item factors when determining the likelihood of recall.
8. Use item difficulty as the primary item factor when determining likelihood of recall.
9. Use knowledge component mastery as the primary individual factor when determining likelihood of recall.
10. Avoid dominating a short session with "failed" attempts.
11. If no items are ready for recall, add new item.
12. If no new items are available, select item with lowest likelihood of recall.
13. Do not retire items.

In keeping with the work of Mozer & Lindsey [21], Choffin, et al. [4] and others, practice items should have a clear association with an identified knowledge component. This mapping could be 1:1, 1:Many, Many:1, or Many:Many.

Mettler, et al. [17] and others have demonstrated that while recall accuracy does not improve with the delivery of passive learning opportunities, recall efficiency does. That is, when the size of the learning gain is divided by the number of trials used, including passive trials actually improves the "learning rate." To take advantage of that effect, RATE will deliver a block of passive trials prior to engaging in active quizzing. Within these passive trials, the object to be learned is presented, together with only the correct answer. After a few seconds (Mettler, *et al.* [17] used four seconds), navigation controls allow the student to advance. After the student has reviewed all knowledge components, active practice begins.

While there is a certain value to massed practice for newly introduced and/or difficult items to build a stable memory trace that the system can then strengthen, this value disappears when students can retrieve information from working memory. To ensure that this does not happen, items pertaining to the same knowledge component should not appear on consecutive trials.

Another stable empirical finding is that systems maximize short- and long-term retention when recall occurs just prior to the point of forgetting. We will incorporate this finding in our approach. However, various research teams have used and/or recommended a wide variety of targeted recall levels, ranging from 33% to 95%. It seems like the optimal value may be the subject of subsequent research and may vary by instructional goals, domains, *etc.* Therefore, we will make this threshold configurable. If the likelihood of recall estimate for several items is below the threshold, the system should select the easiest item associated with the knowledge component with the lowest average likelihood. In this way, the system will attempt to "rescue" the knowledge component most susceptible to forgetting.

Mozer & Lindsey [21] and others demonstrated that (1) there is a high level of variability in both individual factors and item factors that can lead to differences in recall rate, and (2) these factors matter when attempting to derive an optimally individualized practice schedule. Therefore, our system will measure both classes of factors and our scheduler will use these data.

The primary item factor that the system will monitor and employ will be item difficulty. The system will derive its item difficulty estimate from data on accuracy, reaction time, and inter-item confusion. The system will create different difficulty estimates for different forms of a given item (*i.e.,* alternative forms will be considered separate items that are mapped to the same knowledge component).

The primary individual factor that the system will monitor and employ is knowledge component mastery. Calculation of mastery should include aptitude across knowledge items (*i.e.,* taken as a whole, across knowledge components and items does the individual appear to have an aptitude for a given subject-matter domain). The determination should include all available evidence (*e.g.,* the correctness/incorrectness of item types that differ in reliability). The system will assume that different types of evidence have differing reliabilities. Similarly, and in keeping with the various model-based approaches reviewed, the value of this evidence should diminish over time.

Our estimation of the probability of recall will be based on so-called hybrid approaches that merge individual data, group data, and models of learning and forgetting. For example, cognitive models such as ACT-R and the multiscale context model (MCM) provide very accurate and elegant descriptions of memory strength. These models assume that the brain constructs memory traces each time a learner is exposed to an item and that the traces decay at rates dictated by the temporal distribution of past exposures [15]. Unfortunately, these models are not very suitable to real-time adaptation of practice sequences.

To improve the efficiency of the models, Lindsey and his colleagues [15, 21] developed a modeling approach that combined data-driven *machine learning approaches* that use population data to make inferences about individuals and items and *theory-driven* approaches that characterize the temporal dynamics of learning and forgetting. They labeled their model DASH to represent the features to which it is sensitive: Difficulty, Ability, and Study History.

The DASH model has two key components:

1. A representation of study history that can characterize learning and forgetting, and
2. A collaborative filtering approach that can infer latent difficulty and ability factors from incomplete data.

The DASH model begins by modeling forgetting after a student is exposed to material one time. The model does this with a forgetting curve in the form shown by Eq. 2.

$$Pr(R_{si} = 1) = m(1 + ht_{si})^{-f} \tag{2}$$

Where:

R_{si} = the response of student s to item i after retention interval t_{si}.
m = free parameter interpreted as the degree of initial learning ($0 \leq m \geq 1$)
h = a free parameter that acts as a scaling factor time (h > 0)
f = a free parameter that acts as a memory decay exponent (f > 0).

DASH individualizes the decay exponent (*f*) for each student-item using latent traits for student ability and item difficulty. The decay exponent is defined using the formula shown in Eq. 3.

$$f = e^{(\theta_s - b_i)} \tag{3}$$

Where:

θ_s = Student Ability
b_i = Item Difficulty

DASH further individualizes the degree of learning parameter (m) using the formula shown in Eq. 4.

$$m = \frac{1}{1 + e^{-(\theta - b)}} \tag{4}$$

The next step is to include support for an arbitrary study history. That equation takes the form shown in Eq. 5.

$$Pr(R_{sik} = 1 \mid \theta_s, b_i, t_{1:k}, r_{1:k-1}, \phi) = \sigma(\theta_s - b_i + h_\phi(t_{s,1:k}, r_{s,i,1:k-1})) \tag{5}$$

Where:

$Pr(Rsik = 1 \mid \theta_s, b_i, t_{1:k}, r_{1:k-1}, \phi)$ = The probability of student s responding correctly to kth trial of item i, conditioned on that student-item tuple's specific study history.

θ_s = Student Ability
b_i = Item Difficulty
ϕ = is a parameter vector, learned by DASH, that governs the h_ϕ function.
$t_{s,1:k}$ = the times at which trials 1 through k took place
$r_{s,i,1:k-1}$ = the accuracy of each previous trial

As noted above, h_ϕ is a function parameterized by vector ϕ. ϕ is learned by DASH. h_ϕ is the portion of the equation that applies psychological principles of learning and forgetting. Mozer & Lindsey [21] began with a "default" version of this equation (see Eq. 6).

$$h_\phi(t_{s,1:k}, r_{s,i,1:k-1}) = \sum_{W=0}^{W-1} \phi_{2w-1} \log(1 + c_{siw}) + \phi_{2w} \log(1 + n_{siw}) \qquad (6)$$

Where:

w = an index of expanding time windows
c_{siw} = the number of correct outcomes of student s on item i in time window w
n_{siw} = the total number of correct outcomes of student s on item i in time window w

They also created versions of the function that were more closely aligned with the memory dynamics of the more detailed MCM and ACT-R frameworks. The MCM version replaces the time windows with time constants that determine the rate of exponential decay of memory traces. The model assumes that the counts n_{siw} and c_{siw} are incremented at each trial and then decay over time at a timescale specific exponential rate τ_w. Mechanically the c_{siw} and n_{siw} terms in the default versions are redefined to be equal to:

$$c_{siw} = \sum_{\kappa=1}^{k-1} r_{si\kappa} e^{-(t_{sik} - t_{si\kappa})/\tau_w} \qquad n_{siw} = \sum_{\kappa=1}^{k-1} e^{-(t_{sik} - t_{si\kappa})/\tau_w}$$

The ACT-R version of the equation replaces h_ϕ with a function that allows the influence of past trials to continuously decay according to a power law. The redefined h_ϕ is shown in Eq. 7.

$$h_\phi = \phi_1 \log\left(1 + \sum_{\kappa=1}^{k-1} \phi_{3 + r_{si\kappa}}(t_{sik} - t_{si\kappa})^{-\phi_2}\right) \qquad (7)$$

Mozer & Lindsey then tested the ability of the personalized model to schedule content review sessions with middle school students. They compared the ability of six models to predict student performance. Three of the models were variants of the DASH framework that adopted different models of memory dynamics. The other three were a model created in ACT-R, a model based on item-response theory, and a model based on each student's history of accuracy.

All DASH variants outperformed the other models and did not significantly differ among themselves. Mozer & Lindsey [21] also looked at the ability of the adaptive scheduler to improve student performance on exams delivered at the end of a semester and again 28 days later. The researchers compared the performance of the personalized scheduler to a "massed" schedule that concentrated on one unit at a time and a "generic" scheduler that included review of topics from the preceding unit. The personalized scheduler outperformed the alternatives.

To maintain student interest, the system will avoid including several items that have a low likelihood of recall within a given time window. Instead, the system will add new items only when no items in the practice set are below the established threshold. In keeping with previous principles, if there are no new items to add, the system will select the item with the lowest likelihood of recall value. Further, we see no value in retiring items given the temporal fading approach embodied in earlier principles. The system will not remove/retire well-learned items (although students will practice them relatively rarely).

4.3   Authoring the Required Material

As noted earlier, our goal is to minimize the authoring demands associated with the specialized tools that we envision. For this first use case, the authoring task is to create flashcards. All the author needs to do is import a number of "faces" (*i.e.,* images or text passages) and associate them with appropriate labels. The easiest way to accomplish this is to allow the author to pull together all the relevant pictures into a specific folder on the local computer and then import them into the authoring environment all at once. The author would then simply attach a label to each picture. Figure 5 provides an indication of the type of interface that an author might use to complete this task.

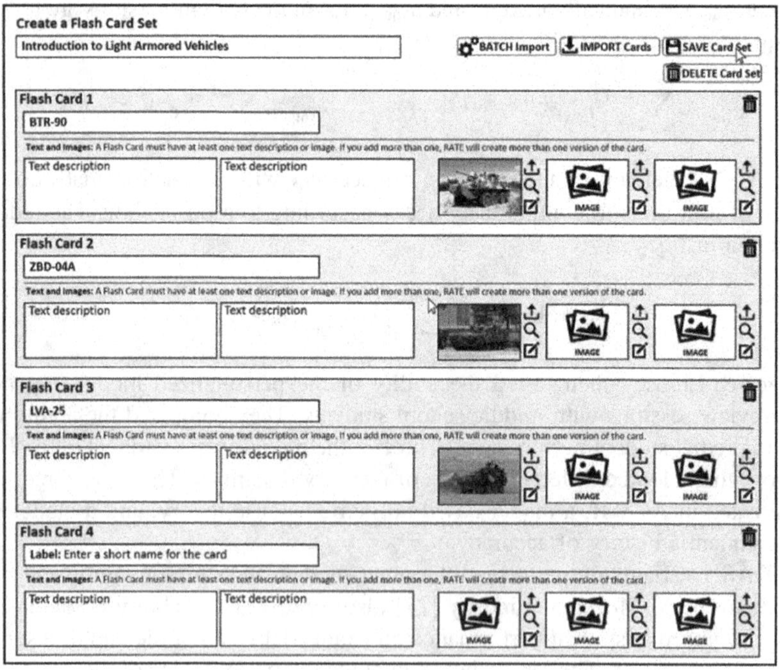

Fig. 5. Labeling flashcards

Figure 5 also hints at other authoring approaches. For example, on the right, it illustrates empty picture slots that can be used to associated additional pictures with a given label. Similarly, along the left, it shows how text-based descriptions, definitions, *etc.* can be associated with each label. The blank row at the bottom indicates that the authoring interface will automatically expand to accept new knowledge components/labels.

5 Conclusion

Over the decades, tremendous progress has been made in techniques to support adaptive training and tools to make the development of training systems more affordable. Nevertheless, although consumers appreciate the gains that adaptive systems bring, they consistently reject the level of effort associated with their development and maintenance.

The current generation of tools seems unlikely to address the challenge of creating powerful learning environments while constraining development timelines. The design language that they employ provides subtle constraints on development while there general purpose focus creates significant development overhead.

To address this issue, our research team is exploring an alternative path. Rather than creating general purpose authoring and delivery tools, we are exploring the viability of creating special purpose tools designed to support specific learning outcomes. Our hypothesis is that by reducing flexibility we can increase usability to the level required by consumers.

The development effort is on-going and we hope to report results in the near future.

Acknowledgements. Portions of the work reported here were performed under Small Business Innovative Research (SBIR) topic N192-132. The author also wishes to express his deep and sincere gratitude to a number of researchers who gave generously of their time to support development of this paper. Special recognition is due to Wilson Judd, Andy Gibbons, Edward Schneider, Susan Chipman, and Dexter Fletcher. Thank you all for sharing your time and expertise.

References

1. Alderman, D.L., Appel, L.R., Murphy, R.T.: PLATO and TICCIT: an evaluation of CAI in the community college. Educ. Technol. **18**(4), 40–45 (1978)
2. Carpenter, S.K., Pashler, H., Cepeda, N.J.: Using tests to enhance 8th grade students' retention of US history facts. Appl. Cogn. Psychol. Official J. Soc. Appl. Res. Mem. Cogn. **23**(6), 760–771 (2009)
3. Carpenter, S.K., Cepeda, N.J., Rohrer, D., Kang, S.H., Pashler, H.: Using spacing to enhance diverse forms of learning: review of recent research and implications for instruction. Educ. Psychol. Rev. **24**(3), 369–378 (2012)
4. Choffin, B., Popineau, F., Bourda, Y., Vie, J.J.: DAS3H: modeling student learning and forgetting for optimally scheduling distributed practice of skills. arXiv preprint arXiv:1905. 06873 (2019)

5. Edge, D., Fitchett, S., Whitney, M., Landay, J.: MemReflex: adaptive flashcards for mobile microlearning. In: Proceedings of the 14th International Conference on Human-Computer Interaction with Mobile Devices and Services, pp. 431–440. ACM, September 2012

6. Frye, C.H.: CAI languages: capabilities and applications. Datamation **14**(9), 34–37 (1968)

7. Gibbons, A.S.: Procedural Authoring Languages (2019, unpublished manuscript)

8. Gibbons, A.S.: Frame Authoring Systems (2019, unpublished manuscript)

9. Gibbons, A.S., Fairweather, P.G.: Computer-Based Instruction: Design and Development. Educational Technology (1998)

10. Gibbons, A., O'Neal, A.: TICCIT: building theory for practical purposes. Int. J. Des. Learn. **5**(2), 1–19 (2014)

11. Glenberg, A.M., Lehmann, T.S.: Spacing repetitions over 1 week. Mem. Cogn. **8**(6), 528–538 (1980)

12. Karpicke, J.D., Roediger III, H.L.: Repeated retrieval during learning is the key to long-term retention. J. Mem. Lang. **57**(2), 151–162 (2007)

13. Karpicke, J.D., Bauernschmidt, A.: Spaced retrieval: absolute spacing enhances learning regardless of relative spacing. J. Exp. Psychol. Learn. Mem. Cogn. **37**(5), 1250 (2011)

14. Landauer, T.K., Bjork, R.A.: Optimum rehearsal patterns and name learning. In: Gruneberg, M.M., Morris, P.E. (eds.) Practical Aspects of Memory, vol. 8, pp. 625-632 (1978)

15. Lindsey, R.V., Shroyer, J.D., Pashler, H., Mozer, M.C.: Improving students' long-term knowledge retention through personalized review. Psychol. Sci. **25**(3), 639–647 (2014)

16. Metzler-Baddeley, C., Baddeley, R.J.: Does adaptive training work? Appl. Cogn. Psychol. Official J. Soc. Appl. Res. Mem. Cogn. **23**(2), 254–266 (2009)

17. Mettler, E., Massey, C.M., Burke, T., Garrigan, P., Kellman, P.J.: Enhancing adaptive learning through strategic scheduling of passive and active learning modes. In: Proceedings of the 40th Annual Conference of the Cognitive Science Society, January 2018

18. Mettler, E., Massey, C.M., Kellman, P.J.: Improving Adaptive Learning Technology through the Use of Response Times. Grantee Submission (2011)

19. Mettler, E., Massey, C.M., Kellman, P.J.: A comparison of adaptive and fixed schedules of practice. J. Exp. Psychol. Gen. **145**(7), 897 (2016)

20. Merrill, M.D.: Component display theory. In: Reigeluth, C.M. (ed.) Instructional-Design Theories and Models: An Overview of their Current Status. Lawrence Erlbaum Associates, Hillsdale (1983)

21. Mozer, M.C., Lindsey, R.V.: Predicting and improving memory retention: psychological theory matters in the big data era. In: Big Data in Cognitive Science, pp. 43–73. Psychology Press (2016)

22. Pagliaro, L.A.: The history and development of CAI: 1926–1981, an overview. Alberta J. Educ. Res. **29**(1), 75–84 (1983)

23. Papousek, J., Pelánek, R., Stanislav, V.: Adaptive practice of facts in domains with varied prior knowledge. In: Educational Data Mining 2014, July 2014

24. Pyc, M.A., Rawson, K.A.: Testing the retrieval effort hypothesis: does greater difficulty correctly recalling information lead to higher levels of memory? J. Mem. Lang. **60**(4), 437–447 (2009)

25. Rubin, J.: Handbook of Usability Testing. How to Plan, Design, and Conduct Effective Tests. Wiley, New York (1994)

26. Sherwood, B.A.: The TUTOR Language (1974)

27. Sobel, H.S., Cepeda, N.J., Kapler, I.V.: Spacing effects in real-world classroom vocabulary learning. Appl. Cogn. Psychol. **25**(5), 763–767 (2011)

28. Son, L.K., Simon, D.A.: Distributed learning: data, metacognition, and educational implications. Educ. Psychol. Rev. **24**(3), 379–399 (2012)

29. Storm, B.C., Bjork, R.A., Storm, J.C.: Optimizing retrieval as a learning event: when and why expanding retrieval practice enhances long-term retention. Mem. Cogn. **38**(2), 244–253 (2010)
30. Walsh, M.M., et al.: Mechanisms underlying the spacing effect in learning: a comparison of three computational models. J. Exp. Psychol. Gen. **147**(9), 1325 (2018)
31. Wang, Y., Heffernan, N.T.: Leveraging First Response Time into the Knowledge Tracing Model. International Educational Data Mining Society (2012)

Agent-Based Methods in Support of Adaptive Instructional Decisions

Robert Sottilare[(⊠)]

Soar Technology, Inc., Orlando, FL 32817, USA
bob.sottilare@soartech.com

Abstract. This paper examines the functionality of artificially-intelligent agents as a methodology for supporting automated decisions in adaptive instructional systems (AISs). AISs are *artificially-intelligent, computer-based systems that guide learning experiences by tailoring instruction and recommendations based on the goals, needs, preferences, and interests of each individual learner or team in the context of domain learning objectives.* AISs are a class of instructional technologies that include intelligent tutoring systems (ITSs), intelligent mentors or recommender systems, and intelligent instructional media. This paper explores various agent-based methods to gauge their impact on four automated decisions within the Learning Effect Model (LEM): 1) determining current and predicting future learner states, 2) making recommendations for new experiences (e.g., courses or problem selection), 3) selecting high level instructional strategies to influence long-term learning, and 4) selecting low level instructional tactics to influence near-term learning.

Keywords: Adaptive instructional system (AIS) · Adaptive models · Agent-based methods · Domain models · Instructional decisions · Interface models · Learner models · Learning Effect Model

1 Introduction

The goal of this paper is to examine artificial intelligence (AI) methodologies to understand their usefulness in supporting the instructional decisions. Specifically, we examined the efficacy of agent-based methods in supporting automated decisions while learners interact with a class of instructional technologies called adaptive instructional systems (AISs). AISs are *artificially-intelligent, computer-based systems that guide learning experiences by tailoring instruction and recommendations based on the goals, needs, preferences, and interests of each individual learner or team in the context of domain learning objectives* [1]. AISs include intelligent tutoring systems (ITSs), intelligent mentors or recommender systems, and intelligent instructional media (Fig. 1). This paper explores various agent-based methods to gauge their impact on four automated decision processes within the Learning Effect Model (LEM) [2–5]: 1) determining current and predicting future learner states, 2) making recommendations for new experiences (e.g., courses or problem selection), 3) selecting high level instructional strategies to influence long-term learning, and 4) selecting low level instructional tactics to influence near-term learning.

© Springer Nature Switzerland AG 2020
R. A. Sottilare and J. Schwarz (Eds.): HCII 2020, LNCS 12214, pp. 164–175, 2020.
https://doi.org/10.1007/978-3-030-50788-6_12

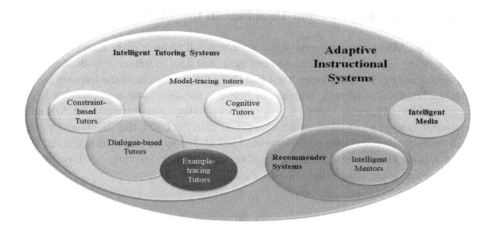

Fig. 1. Categories of Adaptive Instructional Systems

Next, we define AI, compare and contrast adaptability and adaptivity to provide a more comprehensive view of our scope of research. Adapted from van Lent [6], AI (noun) is a *human-produced ability* (as opposed to being produced by nature) to *learn* (acquire knowledge and skill), *apply knowledge to sense* (take in information and judge), *think abstractly and apply skill to favorably manipulate its environment in an effort to achieve its goals*.

In examining adaptivity as a byproduct of the application of AI-based methods, we make a distinction between adaptable and adaptive. In *adaptable systems* flexible control of information or system performance automation resides in the hands of the user [7]. A relevant example of a modern adaptable system is a smartphone which can be changed by the user with settings and applications configured to the specified needs of each individual.

However, *adaptive systems* possess the intellect to change themselves and act on their environment in response to changing conditions and goals/desired outcomes. An adaptive system has adaptation logic to evaluate context in the environment and control parameters to effect changes to itself and act on its environment [8]. This aligns with our goal to examine agent-based methods observe the environment and then act to optimize learning. As part of their role in adaptive instruction, AISs act on the user (individual learner or team) to provide feedback, support or direction, and also act on the environment to adapt scenarios or present new problems to the learner(s) in an effort to optimize learning outcomes.

Last year at Human Computer Interaction International (HCII) 2019, during the affiliated conference for AISs, Bell & Sottilare [9] examined adaptation vectors (opportunities to change and improve instruction) that support both instructionally meaningful (effective) and doctrinally correct (relevant and tactically plausible) actions by the AIS. While that paper focused on recommendations for future AIS research and standards development, this paper provides a next step toward understanding the role of specific artificially-intelligent agents in autonomous instructional decisions.

2   Identifying Instructional Decisions in the LEM

While not all AISs make decisions in the same way, all of them make decisions about the state of the learner, what to recommend next, and how to influence both short and long-term learning. Over the years, the LEM [2–5], originally called the learning effect chain, has evolved to identify interactions between the individual learner and a tutor represented by AIS technologies. It also represents interactions between the AIS and the environment (e.g., problem space, course). Within the LEM, the AIS takes in data about the learner's behaviors, progress toward stated objectives, and evidence about the learner's prior knowledge with the goal of optimizing their learning, but how might they go about determining what is best for each individual learner?

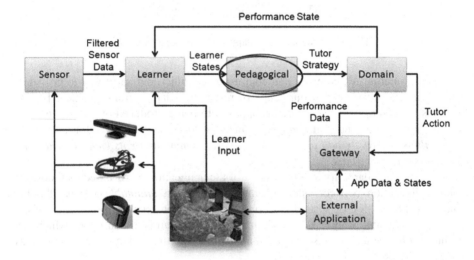

Fig. 2. Representative AIS architecture [9]

While the names may differ slightly, Fig. 2 represents many of the elements found in AISs: a model of the learner, the instruction or pedagogy, the domain, and the human-system interface. These elements are also present in the LEM and include the following instructional decisions: 1) classification/prediction of learner states (e.g., performance, domain proficiency and emotional states), 2) generation of recommendations for next steps or future actions, 3) selection of strategies based on effective methods in the literature (e.g., mastery learning, reflection or worked examples) or experimental results, and 4) selection of actions (e.g., provide feedback, ask questions) that support the strategy and optimize learning outcomes (knowledge and skill acquisition, retention, performance and transfer of learning).

How might the learner assess the effectiveness and credibility of the AIS as an intelligent tutor or mentor? If the AIS' instructional decisions are sound, then the learner's knowledge and skill will increase and the learner will perceive the AIS to be credible. So it all comes back to optimizing learning. How might the AIS weigh these decisions in order to optimize learning outcomes? Agent-based approaches offer a methodology to observe and determine the value of the AIS's feedback, interactions, recommendations, strategy decisions, and other actions. In the next section, we examine agent-based methods, their strengths and their weaknesses.

3 Examining Agent-Based Methods

Intelligent agents are autonomous entities which observe the conditions in their environments through percepts (e.g., sensors) and then act upon the environment using actuators [10]. It might also be characterized as an "an ability to correctly interpret external data, to learn from such data, and to use those learning to achieve specific goals and tasks through flexible adaptation" [11]. Intelligent agents take many different forms.

Simple reflex agents [10] act only in response to the current stimulus or percept while ignoring the rest of their interaction history. These types of agents use condition-action rules to decide on actions. Simple reflex agents have limited intelligence and any change in the environment requires the rules to be updated. These agents tend to be static and may be unresponsive to the learner's needs.

Model-based reflex agents [10] act based on a model that represents its perception history and interprets the current state of the world, how the world has evolved (trends), and the impact of decisions in terms of rewards; uses condition-action rules to determine action selection. A drawback to model-based reflex agents is that they may not have knowledge of the complete environment (e.g., inability to sense learner behaviors that infer particular states – confusion). They may also not know what to do when the environment doesn't specifically imply that an action is required.

Goal-based agents [10] expand on the capabilities of model-based agents by using goal information that describes desirable states. Goal-based agents then use progress toward these goals to determine which action to select next. The issue with goal-based agents is that meeting goals is binary. You either meet the goal or you don't so it is difficult to gauge partial success.

Utility-based agents [10] define a measure of desirability of a particular state called a *utility function*. This maps each state to a measure of the utility. Utility-based agents are an improvement on goal-based agents which can only distinguish between goal states (desirable) and non-goal states (not desirable). The utility-based agent acts to be in states of the highest utility and is considered rational if its utility function matches its environment's performance measure.

Learning agents [10] initially operate in unknown environments and become more competent through additional experience and exploration. Learning agents implement separate processes for *learning* and *performance* which are responsible for improvements and improved action selection respectively. The good news is that they can learn on their own and do not need to be programmed by hand. They have a built in critic that provides performance feedback to the agent's learning process, and can suggest and take innovative actions.

Multi-agent architectures [12] are composed of hierarchies of agents with different functions. Four desirable characteristics for intelligent agents (derived from Russell & Norvig [10]) are behavioral in nature: 1) autonomous – agents are able to act without human direction or intervention to progress toward goals or maximize utility, 2) adaptive and reactive – agents are responsive to changes in their environment and are active in enforcing policies (rules or constraints), 3) proactive and learning – agents take initiative to achieve long-term goals, recognize opportunities to progress toward goals, and learn and adapt to make more effective choices in the future, and 4) social and cooperative – in multi-agent architectures, agents share information and act together to recognize and achieve long-term goals or maximize utility.

4   Reconciling AIS and Agent Environments

As we noted in Sect. 3 of this paper, an agent observes conditions in their environments through percepts (e.g., sensors) and then acts upon their environment using actuators. In AI-based systems (e.g., agent-based systems), the environment may be described as: 1) *fully or partially observable* by the agent's sensors, 2) *deterministic or stochastic* (probabilistic), 3) *episodic or sequential*, 4) *static or dynamic*, 5) *discrete or continuous* and 6) *competitive or collaborative* [10]. These distinctions are important to our application of agents to AIS decisions. In the case of AISs, the agent's environment also includes the learner and the domain (Fig. 3), this makes its understanding of the environment more complex as we discuss below.

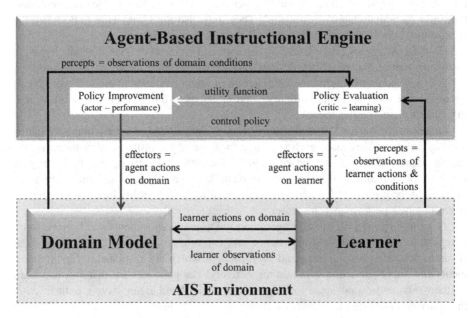

Fig. 3. Learning agent AIS architecture

Prior to describing the alignment between various types of agent-based environments and AIS environments, it is important to note the relationship between agents and their environment, interactions between them, and measures of success. Outcomes (next states) are determined in large part to: 1) the agent's knowledge of the environment, 2) the number and type of available actions, and 3) the measure of performance.

An agent-based system is comprised of an agent, an environment, agent sensors to gather knowledge about the environment, agent actuators or effectors to act on the environment, and some measure that agent uses to gauge progress toward goals. Since sensors provide uncertain information about the agent's environment, the agent must be able to function in the presence of some amount of uncertainty or lack of knowledge. A planning function is needed to visualize future states and make predictions about how their actions might change it in a way that maximizes utility and provides a method of weighing available choices. Russell and Norvig [14] noted that agents may not be as effective in an environment that is partially observable/unknown, stochastic, dynamic, continuous, sequential and multi-agent (collaborative or competitive). Certainly, taking all of these dimensions into account in the design of an agent-based AIS makes for a more difficult challenge for the agent(s) and the designer, but the goal is to guide/support optimal learning for a student. With this in mind, we examine six dimensions of the agent's environment with consideration for how each dimension impacts the agent's performance and its ability to reinforce its learning through new experiences.

4.1   Fully or Partially Observable Environments

In a fully observable environment, the agent's sensors give it access to the complete state of the environment at any point in time. The games checkers and chess are fully observable since all conditions (states) of the game are known. An example of a partially observable environment is a poker game since some states are known and others are not known (e.g., the opponents hand). Sensors may not be the only means for the agent to gather information about its environment. Knowledge may also come in the form of long-term memory which provides information about the laws that govern the environment's behavior (e.g., responses to actions) and the domain proficiency state of the learner. For example, an agent in a chess game should understand the rules of the game (e.g., how each piece moves on the board). If the agent's task was to teach chess, it should also consider the prior knowledge of the learner.

Referring back to Fig. 3, we note that the AIS environment includes both the learner and the domain. While the domain may be largely observable in terms of its possible states, the learner is often not fully observable. For example, the agent may be able to track behaviors (e.g., movements, vocalizations), but it can only infer the learner's cognitive state. Given this limitation, we should design AISs to support scenarios of limited ability to observe the learner and use inferential methods to classify current or predict future states in agent-based AISs.

4.2   Deterministic or Stochastic Environments

A deterministic system is a causal system in which future states of the system are always the same given a set of starting conditions or initial state. In deterministic environments, the next state is determined by the current state and the action selected and executed by the agent. Assuming a fixed set of conditions for the learner and the domain model, the AIS in a deterministic environment would select the same action every time. Given some level of uncertainty about the learner's states, a deterministic approach will not be able to adapt and will fail to optimize utility some portion of the time.

Stochastic/probabilistic systems possess have some inherent randomness in that the same set of initial conditions may lead to different outcomes (states). Examples of a deterministic AIS would one that is either rule-based or decision tree-based. An example of a stochastic AIS would be one that uses a Markov decision process (MDP) to identify outcomes (next states). MDPs are "discrete time stochastic control process" used to model decision making in situations where outcomes are partly random and partly under the control of a decision maker [13]. Since our environment has some uncertainty, it is best to represent that in our decision process by focusing on stochastic methods.

4.3   Static or Dynamic Environments

Static environments remain unchanged while the agent deliberates about its options. Assuming that the number of options is relatively small, this deliberation should be on the order of milliseconds. The learner and the domain should not have changed much in that time so the assumption of a static environment is valid. If, however, the amount of data required to decide on a valid option is large, then the deliberation and classification of a learner's state might be longer and this assumption may not hold up. The other consideration in the design of agent-based AIS is real-time performance. Since AISs are human-in-the-loop systems, the decision processes should be streamlined to support real-time or near real-time interaction. Streamlined processes would reinforce the design of an AIS compatible with a static environment model.

4.4   Discrete or Continuous Environments

Discrete systems have limited number of distinct, clearly defined percepts and effectors (actions) while continuous systems be measured quantitatively to any level of precision. Since real-time interaction is a goal for our agent-based AIS, discrete environments offer smaller number of conditions to define and track. Referring back to Fig. 2, the sensors shown as part of that representation AIS architecture gather continuous streams of data that can be filtered and distilled down into discrete states. While this could be a heavy computational load, much of this processing can be done concurrently to provide a rolling baseline of discrete states to the learner model. For external applications (e.g., serious games), they already track entity location, interactions and other behaviors as discrete states.

4.5   Episodic or Sequential Environments

Episodic environments are a series of occurrences or episodes where only the current or most recent percept is relevant in determining an outcome. Each episode consists of an agent perceiving its environment and then taking a single action. A computer vision agent that examines pictures to determine if tomatoes are present is an episodic event where one picture is unrelated to any other picture being examined. Sequential environments require the system to have memory of past actions to determine the next optimal action. For AISs to determine which content to display for the learner, the AIS needs a history of the learner's prior instructional experiences and domain knowledge. It might also require the AIS to consider more than one action. An agent-based AIS would be most productive in a sequential environment with a history of previous states, but could also operate episodically using Markov processes.

4.6   Collaborative or Competitive Environments

The complexity of the environment rises as we move from individual agents to multiple agents. In a multi-agent environment, the agents could be diversified (perform different functions) or redundant (perform the same or similar functions). Regardless, the ability of agents to work together toward a common goal or set of goals is often desirable, but it may also be useful for the agents to be competitive. Competition enhances and hastens the agent's acquisition of knowledge and skills - learning. While cooperative agents have shared goals, competitive agents have individual goals including maximizing their own utility. "To muddle the waters, competitive systems can show apparent cooperative behavior, and vice versa" [15]. If the goal for an agent-based AIS is to optimize learning outcomes, then it might be feasible to see both collaborative and competitive environments as part of a multi-agent system. Shared goals for collaborative agents could be focused on maximizing the engagement of experiences by selecting content consistent with the learner's proficiency, interests, and learning goals. Competitive agents might find unique solutions to optimize learning. More detailed discussion about applying agents to AIS instructional decision processes follows.

5   Applying Agent-Based Methods to AIS Instructional Decisions

Let's begin our examination of agent-based instructional decisions with an illustrative example of an agent-based AIS: a physics tutor. In our physics tutor, the environment is composed of a set of students. The agent-based physics tutor can act on the students by: displaying a variety of content to the students, providing verbal or text-based feedback, making suggestions or recommendations or prompting the students for more information. The tutor can only observe the students through their input (e.g., answers to questions via a computer keyboard). Now that we have an understanding of our options with respect to agent-based methods and their strengths and weaknesses and how we define our environment, it is time examine how agent-based methods might be applied to AIS instructional decisions.

5.1 Classification and Prediction of Learner States

Referring back to Fig. 3, the agent-based AIS observes learner actions and conditions, evaluates those observations to weight the utility of previous actions. Policies may be created by the designer based on the literature or experimentation, or the policies can be learned by the AIS through experience using learning outcomes as a utility function. Initially, learning though experience will be random and the AIS will often not be useful to human learners. So it would be helpful to have an agent-based student or better yet a diverse set of agent-based students to help train the AIS [16].

How does the designer of the AIS decide what is important to know about the learner and what data is required to infer learner states that infer utility? First, in examining how people learn and the factors that most influence the speed of learning [17–19], five factors were most relevant: 1) the ability or aptitude of the learner, 2) their prior knowledge about the topic of instruction, 3) the quality of the instructor and the content, 4) the learner's motivation and engagement (interest and goals tied to the topic of instruction), and 5) the learner's attention and focus.

Aptitude is the capacity of the learner to acquire a level of proficiency in a domain with a given amount of training. A model of an individual learner's aptitude might be calculated if the resulting learning and total hours of instruction were tracked over time. This information could be available in a long-term learner model and could be used to prime or initialize an agent's knowledge of the learner.

Similarly, *prior knowledge* state could also be calculated based on prior learning experiences, their results, and the time since the instruction took place to account for a decay factor in the knowledge. However, a simple pre-test could also be used to gauge the knowledge of the learner just prior to instruction.

The *quality of the instruction* (instructor and content) could also be evaluated experimentally or determined by the increase in knowledge and skill acquisition of the student population compared to norms or standards.

The learner's *motivation and engagement* states are greatly influenced by ties to their interests and goals. Information in the form of fields in a long-term learner model database could be used by the AIS to recommend courses of interest to the learner. Understanding the learner's motivation will allow the AIS to select appropriate content, make recommendations, and encourage the learner. A short four-question survey with a five-point Likert scale has been effective in gauging motivation just prior to instruction [20] delivered by the Generalized Intelligent Framework for Tutoring (GIFT) [21]:

- Select your level of interest in this course (focus on topical interest)
- Assess your level of enjoyment while learning (focus on emotions associated with the learning process)
- Assess the degree to which you have thought about your learning goals for this course (focus on goal orientation)
- Assess the degree to which you have thought about how you will use knowledge gained in this course (focus on application of knowledge)

The learner's attention and focus comprises information about how long the learner has been engaged in the current learning experience (attention) and longer term data about their ability to sustain focus during a typical instructional session. Agents could be used to determine the attention and focus limits of an individual during any instructional session and intervene to either refocus the learner, call for a break or end the session.

5.2 Generation of Recommendations

Tying back to the discussion of motivation and engagement in 5.1, we expect a large influence in sustaining motivation will be to enable the agent-based AIS to provide relevant recommendations. Recommendations can range from simple suggestions about what content (e.g., problems or scenarios) to engage with in upcoming session to recommendations that time the learner's goals and interests to other learning opportunities. Since it is not just a simple selection from a list of available recommendations, this may be one of the most complex functions within an AIS. It is a complex matching of knowledge about the learner's goals and interests and the learning landscape (wide variety of learning opportunities). Agents are expected to be able to recognize opportunities and it is possible for an agent to search for learning opportunities on the internet based the learner's profile. Near-term recommendations about problem or scenario selection in a current learning experience could be evaluated based on their utility to enhance learning in areas of interest to that individual learner.

5.3 Selection of Instructional Strategies

The important decision of selecting an instructional strategy should be differentiated from learning strategies. Learning strategies are techniques used to help students become more independent, strategic learner by using them effectively to accomplish tasks or meet their goals. Examples of learning strategies include: taking notes, question asking, reflection and journaling, and goal setting. Instructional strategies are domain-independent methods identified in the literature to make a difference in helping students reach their learning goals. Common instructional strategies include: asking questions, requesting the learner to reflect, and prompting the learner for more information. Examples of the most effective instructional strategies include mastery learning, error-sensitive feedback, fading of worked examples and metacognitive prompting [22]. Each of these processes could be managed by an agent to determine when and how the strategy should be implemented. A learning agent will be able to determine the utility of each strategy and employ them based on their effect on learning.

5.4 Selection of Actions

Finally, we discuss the selection of actions with the goal of implementing the strategy selected (see 5.3 of this paper). For example, a mastery learning is a strategy employed by tutors (human and computer-based) as a gate to future learning experiences and is appropriate for domains where prerequisite knowledge is required. Agents will select from available strategies and may require domain-specific information. For example, if the learner is taking an algebra course and the AIS agent classifies the learner's state as confusion, it may elect to ask the learner a question (an instructional strategy), but what question should be asked? Context (where the learner is in the instruction and the proficiency level of the learner) determine that the question to ask is about quadratic equations and should be of moderate difficulty. Questions in a question back may be labeled with metadata to help the AIS select an appropriate question and present it to the learner. The quality of the domain-specific content (question or other media) may be evaluated using the agent's utility function for learning outcomes.

6 Conclusion and Next Steps

Our review of agents and adaptive instructional decisions lead to the conclusion that learning agents are most suitable for implementation in AISs. Learning is a complex process and AISs need to be able to trade off near-term learning objectives for long term learning gains by recognizing opportunities to accelerate learning or by learning through near-term failure to promote long-term gains. Learning agents are able to accommodate the uncertainties associated with human variability and learning. However, the required agent capabilities for adaptive instruction may vary depending on the task being taught, the modes of interaction permitted, and the knowledge required for the agents to make optimal decisions. Interactions for the adaptive instruction of cognitive, psychomotor and collaborative or team tasks will require different modes (e.g., natural language, text, haptics, augmented reality) that agents will require sensory input from in order to reduce uncertainty and make more effective instructional decisions.

Recommended next steps are: 1) to grow a community of interest in adaptive instructional decision support to centralize knowledge and 2) develop a set of common capabilities that can be used to bootstrap developing AIS technologies and products.

Acknowledgments. The author wishes to gratefully acknowledge Benjamin Bell for his contributions to our 2019 paper that formed the basis for this expanded paper. The author also thanks Dr. R. Bowen Loftin, President-Emeritus at Texas A&M University, Dr. J. Dexter Fletcher at the Institute for Defense Analyses, and Dr. Michael van Lent at Soar Technologies, Inc. for their positive influence in shaping the narrative in this paper.

References

1. Sottilare, R., Brawner, K.: Component interaction within the generalized intelligent framework for tutoring (GIFT) as a model for adaptive instructional system standards. In: Proceedings of the 14th International Conference of the Intelligent Tutoring Systems (ITS) Conference, Montreal, Quebec, Canada, June 2018 (2018)
2. Sottilare, R.: Considerations in the development of an ontology for a generalized intelligent framework for tutoring. In: Proceedings of the I3M Conference on International Defense and Homeland Security Simulation Workshop, pp. 19–25, 19 September 2012 (2012)
3. Sottilare, R., Ragusa, C., Hoffman, M., Goldberg, B.: Characterizing an adaptive tutoring learning effect chain for individual and team tutoring. In: Proceedings of the Interservice/Industry Training Simulation and Education Conference, Orlando, Florida, December 2013 (2013)

4. Sottilare, R.: Elements of a learning effect model to support an adaptive instructional framework. In: Generalized Intelligent Framework for Tutoring (GIFT) Users Symposium (GIFTSym4), 31 July 2016, p. 7 (2016)
5. Sottilare, R., Graesser, A., Hu, X., Sinatra, A.: Introduction to tutoring team taskwork. design recommendations for intelligent tutoring systems. Team Tutoring, vol. 6. Army Research Laboratory, Orlando (2018). ISBN 978-0-9977257-4-2
6. van Lent, M.: Artificial intelligence defined. Tech talk on Artificial Intelligence at the 2019 Interservice/Industry Training Systems and Education Conference, Orlando, Florida, Soar Technology, Inc., Ann Arbor (2019)
7. Oppermann, R.: Adaptive User Support: Ergonomic Design of Manually and Automatically Adaptable Software. Routledge, Abingdon (2017)
8. Stober, S., Nürnberger, A.: Adaptive music retrieval – a state of the art. Multimed. Tools Appl. **65**(3), 467–494 (2013). https://doi.org/10.1007/s11042-012-1042-z
9. Bell, B., Sottilare, R.: Adaptation vectors for instructional agents. In: Sottilare, R.A., Schwarz, J. (eds.) HCII 2019. LNCS, vol. 11597, pp. 3–14. Springer, Cham (2019). https://doi.org/10.1007/978-3-030-22341-0_1
10. Russell, S., Norvig, P.: Artificial Intelligent: A Modern Approach. Pearson Education Ltd., Harlow (2003)
11. Kaplan, A., Haenlein, M.: Siri, Siri, in my hand: who's the fairest in the land? On the interpretations, illustrations, and implications of artificial intelligence. Bus. Horiz. **62**(1), 15–25 (2019)
12. Niazi, M., Hussain, A.: Agent-based computing from multi-agent systems to agent-based models: a visual survey. Scientometrics **89**(2), 479–499 (2011). https://doi.org/10.1007/s11192-011-0468-9
13. Bellman, R.: A Markovian decision process. J. Math Mech. **1**, 679–684 (1957)
14. Russell, S., Norvig, S.: Artificial Intelligence: A Modern Approach, 3rd edn. Prentice Hall, Upper Saddle River (2009)
15. Hoen, P.J'., Tuyls, K., Panait, L., Luke, S., La Poutré, J.A.: An overview of cooperative and competitive multiagent learning. In: Tuyls, K., Hoen, P.J., Verbeeck, K., Sen, S. (eds.) LAMAS 2005. LNCS (LNAI), vol. 3898, pp. 1–46. Springer, Heidelberg (2006). https://doi.org/10.1007/11691839_1
16. Rowe, J., Pokorny, B., Goldberg, B., Mott, B., Lester, J.: Toward simulated students for reinforcement learning-driven tutorial planning in GIFT. In: Sottilare, R. (ed.) Proceedings of 5th Annual GIFT Users Symposium, Orlando, FL (2017)
17. Bransford, J.D., Brown, A.L., Cocking, R.R.: How People Learn. National Academy Press, Washington, D.C. (2000)
18. National Research Council: How People Learn: Brain, Mind, Experience, and School: Expanded Edition. National Academies Press, Washington, D.C. (2000)
19. National Research Council, Donovan, S., Bransford, J.: How Students Learn. National Academies Press, Washington, D.C. (2005)
20. Sottilare, R.: Simple Motivation Survey. US Army Research Laboratory, Orlando (2016)
21. Sottilare, R.A., Brawner, K.W., Goldberg, B.S., Holden, H.K.: The Generalized Intelligent Framework For Tutoring (GIFT). US Army Research Laboratory–Human Research and Engineering Directorate (ARL-HRED), Orlando (2012)
22. Durlach, P.J., Ray, J.M.: Designing Adaptive Instructional Environments: Insights from Empirical Evidence. Army Research Institute for the Behavioral and Social Sciences, Orlando (2011)

Representing Functional Relationships of Adaptive Instructional Systems in a Conceptual Model

Robert Sottilare[1(✉)] ⓘD, Anne Knowles[2], and Jim Goodell[3]

[1] Soar Technology, Inc., Orlando, FL 32817, USA
bob.sottilare@soartech.com
[2] Anne Knowles Consulting, San Diego, CA, USA
knowledge.ak@gmail.com
[3] Quality Information Partners, Fairfax, VA, USA
jimgoodell@qi-partners.com

Abstract. This paper examines the relationships of various functional elements within a class of instructional technologies called adaptive instructional systems (AISs) which include intelligent tutoring systems (ITSs), intelligent mentors or recommender systems, and intelligent instructional media. AISs are *artificially-intelligent, computer-based systems that guide learning experiences by tailoring instruction and recommendations based on the goals, needs, and preferences of each individual learner or team in the context of domain learning objectives.* Under Project 2247.1, The Institute for Electrical and Electronic Engineers (IEEE) is developing standards and guidance for the modeling of AIS to characterize what is and is not an AIS. This paper was composed to document recommendations and generate discussion about the four models that have been proposed as core to the concept of AISs: learner models, adaptive models, domain models and interface models.

Keywords: Adaptive instructional system (AIS) · Adaptive models · Domain models · IEEE standards · Interface models · Learner models

1 Introduction

During the last year, the Institute for Electrical and Electronics Engineers (IEEE) working group chartered under Project 2247 has taken on the task of developing standards, guidance, and best practices for adaptive instructional systems (AISs). This IEEE working group will be debating what is and is not an AIS, and what standards and best practices will evolve from the marketplace. To date, the group has identified three potential areas for standardization: 1) a conceptual model for AISs, 2) interoperability standards for AISs, and 3) evaluation best practices for AISs. This paper explores design principles and methods needed to define the standard functional elements of AISs that are defined as: *artificially-intelligent, computer-based systems that guide learning experiences by tailoring instruction and recommendations based on the goals, needs, and preferences of each individual learner or team in the context of domain learning objectives* [1].

R. A. Sottilare and J. Schwarz (Eds.): HCII 2020, LNCS 12214, pp. 176–186, 2020.
https://doi.org/10.1007/978-3-030-50788-6_13

Adaptive instructional systems (AISs) come in many forms and this makes standardization challenging. The most common form of AIS is the intelligent tutoring system (ITS) which is a computer-based system that automatically provides real-time, tailored, and relevant feedback and instruction to learners [2, 3]. Other forms of AISs include intelligent mentors (recommender systems) which promote the social relationship between learners and intelligent agents [4] and web-based intelligent media used for instruction. Today, ITSs are recognized as highly effective learning tools and provide individually-tailored instruction in well-defined, cognitive task domains (e.g., mathematics, physics, or software programming). The adaptations used to tailor instruction may use artificial intelligence (e.g., neural networks) or other methods to select and sequence content, adapt feedback, and guide the learner. The goal of adaptation is to optimize learning (acquisition of knowledge and skill) and performance (application of knowledge and skill) [5]. In his meta-analysis on the effectiveness of ITSs, VanLehn [6] notes that ITSs have evolved to parity with expert human tutors.

A design goal for AISs is to make them effective instructional guides with or without humans-in-the-loop. Meeting this goal would enable the flexibility to apply AIS technologies in traditional classrooms as instructional augmentations to human teachers and as standalone instructional guides in distributed learning contexts. The benefits of AISs as instructional augmentation tools include reduced teacher workload, opportunities to design and deploy AISs to match both the cultural and learning needs of individual students, and the ability to identify and prioritize student issues that require the attention of a human teacher for remediation.

However, the practicality and affordability of using AISs that are not dependent upon human intervention is limited by the robustness of the artificial intelligence within the AIS and the ability to reuse content and components across instructional domains and various AIS architectures. Defining common components and their functions in a standard is a first step toward understanding and designing effective, efficient, and practical AIS solutions.

The goal of the conceptual modeling standard is to define and classify the components and functionality of AISs and to define parameters used to describe AISs. The standard will establish requirements and guidance for the use and measurement of these parameters. The expected outcome of this standardardization project is an AIS conceptual model that describes AIS functions in terms of features. Descriptions of processes and events for individual learners, and ultimately teams of learners may also be included.

The common components of ITSs include a *domain model*, an *individual learner or team model*, an *instructional model*, and an *interface model* [7], but will all AISs have these common components? What is it that makes an AIS and makes other technology not an AIS. The proposed AIS conceptual model describes four functional components that make up an AIS: a *domain model*, an *individual learner model*, and *adaptive model*, and an *interface model*. However, before we proceed with detailed descriptions of the proposed AIS conceptual model, it is important to examine AIS functions in the context of their influence on learning.

2 The Learning Effect Model (LEM)

The learning effect model (LEM) [7–9], a model of interaction between the learner and functional elements of the AIS leading to progress toward learning goals and outcomes (e.g., knowledge, skill acquisition, retention/recall, and transfer of learning/performance) is shown in Fig. 1. The model includes short and long-term representation of the learner, instructional policies, strategies (plans for action) and tactics (actions), and the conditions of the instruction and/or environment in which the learning takes place.

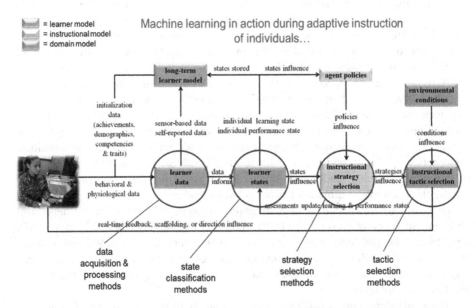

Fig. 1. Learning effect model for individual learners [7]

The LEM also includes methods to assess learning in real-time and update the learner's model of proficiency in the domain being instructed. In self-improving AISs, multiple assessments of learning and learners can be used to influence agent-based policies and improve effectiveness of selected strategies and tactics over time.

Our goal in including the LEM in the discussion of AIS functional components is to have a context in which to discuss the interaction of each component with other functional components and the learner. The inclusion of the LEM aids in considering elements of the AIS design and specifically the information that should be processed and shared by each component. The learning sciences literature describes AISs as being composed of four models: a *domain model*, an *individual learner model*, an *instructional model*, and an *interface model*. The models put forth in this AIS standard differ slightly, but are derived from these common AIS models in the literature and each standard AIS model is discussed in detail in the next section. According to Sottilare et al. [8–10], there are also four primary AI-based processes that are part of the LEM:

- *Learner state inference* – in this process, the AIS uses learner data (e.g., self-reported, assessments, sensory) to infer learner states (e.g., emotions, competency)
- *Recommendation process* – macro-level suggestions about what the learner should do next based on their competency level, goals, preferences, and near-term learning and performance
- *Instructional strategy selection process* – micro-level plans for action based on the current conditions of the learner (e.g., progress toward near-term goals) and the instruction (e.g., situation or problem being worked)
- *Instructional tactic selection process* – near-term actions by the AIS to satisfy the instructional strategy selected and optimize learning outcomes.

3   AIS Functional Components

The following AIS functional components are briefly defined below and shown in simplified form in Fig. 2:

- *domain model* – includes the knowledge model, learning objectives, content, feedback, question banks, and other information relevant to the subject or topical area.
- *individual learner model* – states and traits that describe the critical attitudes, behaviors and cognition of an individual and serve as a basis for adaptation decisions by the AIS
- *adaptation model* – logic that assesses the states and traits of the learner/team and the knowledge from the domain model in order to select content, generate feedback or generate recommendations tailored to that learner; the adaptation model combines features from the instructional model and the recommender to make instructional decisions
- *interface model* – technology (tools or methods) that support learner/team interaction with the other AIS functions

This section defines a set of minimum AIS functional components and discusses their essential functions, salient characteristics, and the type of data exchanged between these functional components, other AIS systems, and external systems (e.g., data repositories, learning management systems).

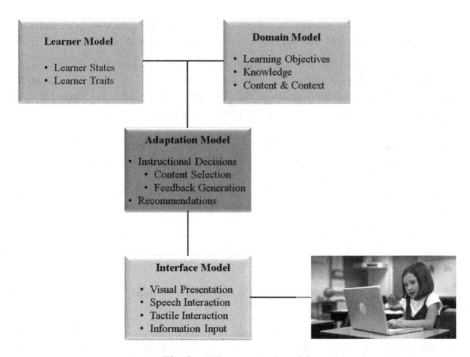

Fig. 2. AIS conceptual model

3.1 Domain Models

The domain model is a fundamental element of an AIS that contains the set of skills, knowledge, and actions available to the AIS for the topic under instruction. It normally contains the ideal learner or expert knowledge model for the domain of instruction along with question banks, common bugs, mal-rules, misconceptions, and content. The knowledge model is a declarative model that includes a set of learning activities, learning objectives, pedagogical frameworks, instructional resources and assessment activities and the relationships between them. (e.g. competency charts, knowledge maps, frameworks/pathways, and instructional models).

A learning activity is a grouping of a single learning objective with one or more instructional resources, and one or more assessment activities. A learning objective is a clear and concise statement of what the learner will be able to do when they successfully complete the associated lesson. In AISs, instructional resources are pieces of digital content associated with a learning objective to help the learner develop mastery of the lesson. They may include videos, text, interactive exercises, hints, worked problems, simulation and games. Assessment activities are pieces of digital content used to measure a learner's mastery of a learning objective and include multiple choice questions, fill in the blank answers, interactive exercises.

The goal of AISs is to recognize opportunities to improve individual learning and adapt to conditions of the both learner and the environment in order to optimize learning. Since recognizing context is a critical step toward effective adaptive instructional strategies, we begin by discussing the function of the domain model which is used by the AIS author/creator to define context.

For example, in ITSs, the domain model describes the set of skills, knowledge, strategies (plans for action), and tactics (actions executed by the ITS) for the topic/domain being instructed [7]. In the case of model tracing tutors, the domain model contains the expert knowledge in the form of an ideal learner model, and also includes assessments to determine progress toward objectives along with methods for detecting bugs, mal-rules, and misconceptions that students periodically exhibit. In the case of constraint-based tutors, the domain model includes constraints that have three data elements [10]:

- Relevance Condition – describes when the constraint is applicable
- Satisfaction Condition – specifies assessments to be applied to ascertain the correctness of the solution
- Feedback Message – communicates with the learner to advise them that their solution is incorrect and why it is incorrect, and provides the learner with corresponding declarative knowledge (e.g., hints, prompts) directly or indirectly

ITSs use the context or constraints found in domain models along with learner states to select optimal instructional strategies. Thinking more broadly about AISs, the domain model includes a knowledge model, learning objectives, content, feedback, question banks, assessments, and other information relevant to the subject or topical area.

It should also be emphasized that the intellectual property in AISs resides primarily within the domain model in the form of content, methods of assessment, and instructional strategies and tactics. This makes it more difficult to generalize or recommend standards or guidance than with other components that may function similarly across domains of instruction. When we examine the interaction of the domain model with other AIS components, we can make the following observations about the domain model's active role within AISs:

- Domain models stimulate and seek to engage the learner by selecting and presenting relevant content to the learner in the form of information, problems, and even representations of physical contexts (e.g., simulated representations of real 3-dimensional environments)
- Domain models should be able to support individual learners in the context of social or collaborative learning
- Domain models influence cognitive load so the content should be germane to the stated learning objectives and not overload the learner with extraneous information
- Domain models may use instructional policies and strategies that have been proven effective across domains (e.g., mastery learning, worked examples and/or reinforcing metacognitive habits that are used to help students understand the way they learn)
- Domain models may use decisions by the adaptive model to narrow the selection of instructional tactics or actions (e.g., provide feedback, ask questions or prompt the learner to reflect)

- Domain models assess progress toward learning objectives through observations and measurement, and update proficiency/competency models within the learner model accordingly

In the next section, we explore another defining AIS component, the learner model as a driver of adaption for AISs.

3.2   Individual Learner Models

For the current standardization effort, the scope of the learner model is a representation of an individual. It is anticipated that a group or team-based learner modeling standard will be developed at a later date. An individual learner model is a structured representation of a learner's knowledge, abilities, dispositions, habits of practice, misconceptions, difficulties, and/or other learner attributes. It may include both facts and inferences about past, current, and predicted future cognitive capabilities and functions.

The proposed standard states that the learner model *shall function as an imperfect "digital twin" of the learner based on behavioral and physiological data.* It is imperfect because the mind of a learner is not directly observable and the scope of data in any system will obviously be limited. However, along with observable event data the learner model may include predictions or assertions about unobservable characteristics of the learner that have been inferred from observable event data.

Learner models may include logs of interaction, transactional performance assessment data and inferred competency assertions derived from that raw data. It may also include physiological attributes (e.g., breathing rates, inter-beat heart rate or electro-dermal activity) as they relate to learning and performance objectives with the domain of instruction. Learner models may also include physiological metrics/abilities/limitations that may be used to assess readiness/lack of readiness, or need for accommodations, scaffolding, or pre-requisite physical conditioning. For example, eye tracking measure may be used to gauge learner engagement.

The learner model may also include both raw transactional data and processed/interpreted data such as a log of a learner's activities, actions, and experiences. This may include data to support spaced learning activities and models of knowledge decay. It may also include various data collected from the learner to indicate learner preferences (e.g., instructional modes), their cultural norms (e.g., processes or behaviors like how they approach problem solving) or other drivers of AIS decision making processes (discussed further in the section describing the adaptation model).

Individual learner models consist of the cognitive, affective, motivational, and other psychological states that evolve during instruction and moderate (enhance or minimize) learning. Since learner performance is primarily tracked in the domain model, the learner model is often viewed as an overlay (subset) of the domain model, which changes over the course of tutoring. For example, "knowledge tracing" tracks the learner's progress from problem to problem and builds a profile of strengths and weaknesses relative to the domain model [5, 7].

While team models are not specifically called out as ITS common components, their focus on the dynamics of team interactions in collaborative learning and collaborative problem solving has placed new emphasis on the design of ITSs for team use

[10, 12–14]. The team model must be able to track progress toward collective task learning objectives for either training or collaborative learning goals. To support team development and enhance collaboration skills, team models are significantly more complex than individual learner models which are primarily focused on the assessment of tasks. Team models also assess teamwork which is the "coordination, cooperation, and communication among individuals to achieve a shared goal" [14].

ITSs use models of individual learners or teams to assess their progress toward defined learning objectives and drive instructional decisions to optimize learning. While some learner attributes are relatively static, most of the attributes in ITS learner models are unique to the task or domain of instruction. Again, this poses a significant challenge to standardizing learner or team models, but standardized data formats could support interoperability by allowing the exchange of information between learner models and other components (i.e., domain, instructional or interface model).

3.3 Adaptation Model

The adaptation model is a fundamental element of an AIS and is defined as *a process model with logic which applies information from the learner model and the knowledge model (part of the domain model) to develop adaptations*. The proposed adaptation model encompasses functions of the ITS instructional model (also known as the pedagogical model or the tutor model) and also includes functions for a recommender system. The proposed standard adaptation model encompasses content selection, feedback generation, and recommendation generation processes. Content selection involves picking the content to present to the learner in a sequence that optimizes the learners experience in terms of the short term learning objectives and long term development. Feedback generation involves the creation of corrective and affirming comments about past attitudes, behavior and recommendations to improve future attitudes, behaviors, and ultimately learning and performance.

Adaptive models are procedural models with the logic which applies information from the learner model and the domain model to select/generate adaptations or recommendations that are tailored to a particular individual learner. Adaptations may include decisions about the learning experience (e.g., feedback, support, selection of different content), learner options, recommendations (e.g., next steps or future learning experiences), interaction with the current lesson, learning objectives, instructional resources, and methods of assessment (e.g., algorithms, gating, machine learning models, etc.).

The AIS adaptive model is both a set of instructional principles or policies (based upon the instructional theory in the literature or through experience via a self-improving mechanism) and a recommender engine to provide options for future actions (e.g., next courses or steps) to learners. The adaptive model may also contribute to the information in the learner model. AISs that offer higher levels of adaptivity generally require more complex and detailed learner models than those that offer lower levels of adaptivity. In the literature, the adaptive model is generally referred to as the instructional or pedagogical model, but the instructional model may or may not include a recommender engine. For this reason, the proposed standard encompasses any and all adaptations used to tailor learner experiences including recommendations.

Adaptation models are often based on some instructional theory that includes strategies to account for how people learn both generally and individually. Pedagogical taxonomies that describe these teaching strategies should be aligned with learning essentials [15] and levels of understanding within the subject domain (e.g., Bloom's cognitive taxonomy) [16]. Strategies are specific plans for near-term action by the AIS. Depending upon design, the tactics (specific actions taken by the AIS and aligned with instructional strategies) may be part of either the adaptation model or the domain model. Like typical ITS instructional models, AIS adaptation models receive input from the domain and learner models and select appropriate tutoring strategies, steps, and actions as part of the decision process for what the AIS should do next in the interaction with the learner. This mode is often described as *tutor-initiated* [17]. In mixed-initiative systems, the learners may also take actions, ask questions, or request help [18, 19], and the AIS still takes initiative with the goal of optimizing learning as determined by the adaptation model, which may be based on known learning or instructional theories and/or techniques which lead to improvement over time based on increased experience.

3.4   Interface Model

The interface model is *a representation of how system components interact with the learner and how the learner interacts with a component of the system*. Interface models may be further classified based on whether the interface represented is between the learner and the system components or between system/software modules. The learner-AIS interface model is a representation of how the learner interacts with a computer program or another device and how the system responds. An Application Programming Interface (API) Model is a representation of how other system components get access to specific information, to trigger special behavior, or to perform some other action in a component of the system (Ref: https://www.w3.org/2008/webapps/).

Interactions between the learner and the AIS interactions depend largely upon the learner's task during instruction. This could include interaction with content, assessments or the process of reflection. The user interface interprets the learner's contributions through various input media (speech, typing, clicking) and produces output in different media (text, diagrams, animations, agents). In addition to the conventional human-computer interface features, some recent systems have integrated natural language interaction [20–22], speech recognition [23], and the sensing of learner emotions [24, 25]. Additional interactions to be considered in the design and standardization of AISs include exchanges with authors, designers, subject matter experts, and AIS evaluators. Next, we explore recommendations for future AIS research and standards.

4   Recommendations for AIS Research and Standards

Establishing AIS standards and guidance opens up new opportunities for research. A few of the many interesting research opportunities include expanding the scope and affordances of AIS models. For example, drawing on a larger population for suggestions regarding novel components that could be added to current iterations of domain, learner, adaptive and interface models. It would be interesting to determine if there are sub-categories of AISs that require additional model(s) and how these new models would interact with the four core models. Real world applications that have expanded the AIS domain to include authoring tools, self-improving functions, and collaborative models are an underrepresented area warranting further work. In addition, further research into determining the learning effectiveness of applying adaptivity at the macro lesson level vs. micro level would provide needed empirical data to help guide the designs of future AIS systems. One final important area to explore is comparing the training efficacy of two similar AIS systems that differ more in design rather than substance, e.g., swapping out one interface model with a different but comparable interface model.

Next steps for AIS standards development are first, to continue with the IEEE process for AIS concept model, system interoperability, and evaluation subgroups seeking international consensus across industry, government and academia. Secondly, standard processes need to be identified within and across each of the four models, as well as standard expected outcomes for these systems. Thirdly, the learner model should be expanded from individual to team for collaborative learning environments. Lastly, additional standards efforts include connecting AIS standards with other computer and AI standards for a more robust and comprehensive systems perspective.

Acknowledgments. The authors wish to gratefully acknowledge all of the contributions of each and every member of the IEEE AIS Working Group under Project 2247. We especially wish to acknowledge the contributions of the members of the AIS Conceptual Modeling Subgroup led by Anne Knowles: Avron Barr, Jeanine DeFalco, Jim Goodell, Vladimir Goodkovsky, Xiangen Hu, Dale Johnson, Bruce Peoples, Ram Rajendran, Khanh-Phuong (KP) Thai.

References

1. Sottilare, R., Brawner, K.: Component interaction within the generalized intelligent framework for tutoring (GIFT) as a model for adaptive instructional system standards. In: Proceedings of the 14th International Conference of the Intelligent Tutoring Systems (ITS) Conference, Montreal, Quebec (2018)
2. Anderson, J.R., Boyle, C.F., Reiser, B.J.: Intelligent tutoring systems. Science **228**(4698), 456–462 (1985)
3. Psotka, J., Sharon, A.M.: Intelligent Tutoring Systems: Lessons Learned. Lawrence Erlbaum Associates (1988). ISBN 978-0-8058-0192-7
4. Baylor, A.: Beyond butlers: intelligent agents as mentors. J. Educ. Comput. Res. **22**(4), 373–382 (2000)
5. Sottilare, R.A.: A comprehensive review of design goals and emerging solutions for adaptive instructional systems. Technol. Instr. Cognition Learn. **11**(1), 5–38 (2018)
6. VanLehn, K.: The relative effectiveness of human tutoring, intelligent tutoring systems, and other tutoring systems. Educ. Psychol. **46**(4), 197–221 (2011)
7. Sottilare, R., et al.: Introduction to team tutoring and GIFT. Des. Recomm. Intell. Tutor. Syst. **6**, 1–15 (2018)
8. Sottilare, R.: Considerations in the development of an ontology for a generalized intelligent framework for tutoring. In: Proceedings of the 13M Conference on International Defense and Homeland Security Simulation Workshop, Vienna (2012)

9. Sottilare, R., Ragusa, C., Hoffman, M., Goldberg, B.: Characterizing an adaptive tutoring learning effect chain for individual and team tutoring. In: Proceedings of the Interservice/Industry Training Simulation and Education Conference, Orlando (2013)

10. Sottilare, R.A., Burke, C.S., Salas, E., Sinatra, A.M., Johnston, J.H., Gilbert, S.B.: Designing adaptive instruction for teams: a meta-analysis. Int. J. Artif. Intell. Educ. (2017). https://doi.org/10.1007/s40593-017-0146-z

11. Mitrovic, A., Martin, B., Suraweera, P.: Intelligent tutors for all: the constraint-based approach. IEEE Intell. Syst. **4**, 38–45 (2007)

12. Sottilare, R., Holden, H., Brawner, K., Goldberg, B.: Challenges and emerging concepts in the development of adaptive, computer-based tutoring systems for team training. In: Proceedings of the Interservice/Industry Training Simulation and Education Conference, Orlando (2011)

13. Johnston, J., et al.: Building Intelligent Tutoring Systems For Teams: What Matters. Emerald Group Publishing, Bingley (2018)

14. Salas, E.: Team Training Essentials: A Research-Based Guide. Routledge, London (2015)

15. Gagné, R.M.: Essentials of Learning for Instruction. Dryden Press, Hinsdale (1975)

16. Krathwohl, D.R.: A revision of bloom's taxonomy: an overview. Theory Into Pract. **41**(4), 212–218 (2002)

17. Sottilare, R.A., Proctor, M.: Passively classifying student mood and performance within intelligent tutors. J. Educ. Technol. Soc. **15**(2), 101–114 (2012)

18. Aleven, V., Mclaren, B., Roll, I., Koedinger, K.: Toward meta-cognitive tutoring: a model of help seeking with a cognitive tutor. Int. J. Artif. Intell. Educ. **16**(2), 101–128 (2006)

19. Rus, V., Graesser, A.C.: The question generation shared task and evaluation challenge. In: Proceedings of the University of Memphis. National Science Foundation (2009)

20. Graesser, A.C.: Conversations with autotutor help students learn. Int. J. Artif. Intell. Educ. **26**(1), 124–132 (2016)

21. Johnson, W.L., Lester, J.C.: Face-to-face interaction with pedagogical agents, twenty years later. Int. J. Artif. Intell. Educ. **26**(1), 25–36 (2016)

22. Nye, B.D., Graesser, A.C., Hu, X.: AutoTutor and family: a review of 17 years of natural language tutoring. Int. J. Artif. Intell. Educ. **24**(4), 427–469 (2014)

23. D'Mello, S.K., Graesser, A., King, B.: Toward spoken human-computer tutorial dialogues. Hum. Comput. Interact. **25**(4), 289–323 (2010)

24. Baker, R.S., D'Mello, S.K., Rodrigo, M.M., Graesser, A.C.: Better to be frustrated than bored: the incidence, persistence, and impact of learners' cognitive–affective states during interactions with three different computer-based learning environments. Int. J. Hum. Comput. Stud. **68**(4), 223–241 (2010)

25. D'Mello, S.K., Graesser, A.: Multimodal semi-automated affect detection from conversational cues, gross body language, and facial features. User Model. User Adap. Interact. **20**(2), 147–187 (2010)

Knowledge-to-Information Translation Training (KITT): An Adaptive Approach to Explainable Artificial Intelligence

Robert Thomson[1(✉)] and Jordan Richard Schoenherr[1,2(✉)]

[1] Army Cyber Institute/Behavioral Science and Leadership Department,
US Military Academy, West Point, USA
{robert.thomson, jordan.schoenherr}@westpoint.edu
[2] Department of Psychology, Institute for Data Science, Carleton University,
Ottawa, Canada

Abstract. Modern *black-box* artificial intelligence algorithms are computationally powerful yet fallible in unpredictable ways. While much research has gone into developing techniques to interpret these algorithms, less have also integrated the requirement to understand the algorithm as a function of their training data. In addition, few have examined the human requirements for explainability, so these interpretations provide the right quantity and quality of information to each user. We argue that Explainable Artificial Intelligence (XAI) frameworks need to account the expertise and goals of the user in order to gain widespread adoptance. We describe the Knowledge-to-Information Translation Training (KITT) framework, an approach to XAI that considers a number of possible explanatory models that can be used to facilitate users' understanding of artificial intelligence. Following a review of algorithms, we provide a taxonomy of explanation types and outline how adaptive instructional systems can facilitate knowledge translation between developers and users. Finally, we describe limitations of our approach and paths for future research opportunities.

Keywords: Explainable AI · Knowledge translation · Adaptive instructional systems

"Be gracious... I think an explanation is well overdue." – Wilton Knight, Knight Rider

1 Introduction

Machine Learning and Artificial Intelligence algorithms (AIs) have revolutionized the speed and complexity at which humans (and our technologies) process information. The last 30 years has seen the rise of computers and increasing automation as complex technologies have become ubiquitous in modern society. With this explosion in computational power, many of the algorithms driving our technology have become so complex that we no longer understand how they process information and make decisions. This lack of interpretability leads to an inability to predict how such algorithms will behave as they approach the edges of their competencies, or even understand what

R. A. Sottilare and J. Schwarz (Eds.): HCII 2020, LNCS 12214, pp. 187–204, 2020.
https://doi.org/10.1007/978-3-030-50788-6_14

their competencies are [1]. As such, there are concerns whether the developers [2], let alone the average user, can reliably interpret the output of modern AIs. Without interpretability, it becomes challenging to trust AIs, especially when their outputs appear to reflect errors [3–5].

Compounding this is the requirement that many of these algorithms require millions of data points for training. These large datasets are themselves so complex that many implicit (or explicit) biases can go undetected [6, 7]. One of the most telling failures of automation was the widely reported case of Google Photos auto-tagging feature that had difficulty accurately classifying the faces of non-Caucasian persons [8, 9]. This was due in part to the fact that their training dataset comprised of substantially more photos of Caucasian faces than non-Caucasian [10]. Detecting and remediating bias in a dataset (i.e., *preprocessing* the data) is a human labor-intensive problem which is generally not well automated for all but the most structured data types (i.e., recently Google has developed AutoML to automatically preprocess text and video input).

Explainable artificial intelligence (XAI) attempts to provide explanations of the structure and operations of AIs in a form that humans can understand. However, explainability alone is not necessarily a solution [11]. In the present study, we consider 1) recent advances in XAI; 2) what kinds of explanations are intelligible to humans; and 3) how adaptive instructional systems (AIS) can be used to facilitate this process. We further differentiate between interpretability, explainability, and believability. We then present the Knowledge-to-Information Translation Training (KITT) framework that acts as an intermediary between humans and non-human learning systems.

2   Explainable AI

XAI has become a buzzword in the information science community. The DARPA XAI Program began in 2016 with a goal to develop novel techniques to create explainable algorithms or induce explainable models from current algorithms [12]. It is based on the assumption that the most computationally complex and opaque algorithms (*black box* algorithms) are the most powerful, and that there is currently a tradeoff between performance and interpretability [13, 14]. That is, most AIs exist on a continuum of interpretability, where the most powerful techniques (e.g., neural networks; reinforcement learning) are the least interpretable. This is increasingly problematic as these black box algorithms are currently supporting key decisions-making processes in the medical, financial, and criminal justice systems, all without being adequately validated. Crucially, there are instances of bias in these systems, such as the apparent racial discrimination in prison sentencing and parole recommendation for minorities accused of non-violent crimes [13, 15].

Interpretability has a number of potential benefits including increased reliability, resilience, and validity of AIs, as well as enhancing trust between AIs and human users. Reliable AIs are those that make unbiased decisions. Bias can be introduced from two sources: the nature of the learning algorithm, and the underlying training data. Assuming the algorithm is valid, interpretable models can aid in the identification of sources of implicit and explicit biases in training data. Similarly, interpretable algorithms let us find the source of bias, whether it be a function of the data or injected by an adversary. By helping to find outlier data points, interpretable AIs increase the resiliency of algorithms. Valid AIs weigh evidence in the manner for which we intended. An example of an invalid AI would be an AI that overweighs the role of zip code (as a proxy for many socioeconomic factors) in parole decisions. Interpretable AIs make it possible to validate their underlying decision-making processes. Finally, humans are more likely to trust an AI's decisions when that AI can provide an explanation, especially when the AI had made an error. In fact, an informative explanation after detecting an error may increase trust in the AI, but only after sufficient trust has been earned [16].

What needs to be explained and how an AI's decisions should be explained are often left ill-defined, reflecting a *squishy* problem [17]. A common theme is to conflate interpretability with an explanation. That is, the ability of the AI to simply describe its decision-making process does not mean that it is intelligible, nor does it mean that such a description can be used to predict the future performance of the model. In fact, these underspecified descriptions can lead to developers having incorrect mental models of the AIs' decisions [18]. Consequently, the believability of an explanation in no way implies that it is valid.

A common requirement of AIs is the provision of why it failed to perform a task as expected. Multiple levels of description are generally available, yet researchers addressing this issue appear to frequently focus on incomplete explanations on only one possible level of analysis. For instance, a technique may break down an AI's decisions to a set of IF-THEN rules (e.g., 'IF probLEFT > probRIGHT THEN turn LEFT') and/or probabilities (e.g., 'I turned LEFT because it was 61% more likely to succeed'). This level of description is generally most relevant to AI developers with a focus on debugging the system. This is generally not the right level of analysis for a typical user, who respond best to causal explanations [5, 19–21].

Following a brief review of core features of AI, we consider a number of approaches to interpretability in XAI research (for a more in-depth review, see [22]).

2.1   What Needs to be Interpreted in Artificial Intelligence Systems

At their core, most AIs can be distilled into a clustering or categorization mechanism. Once provided with a set of inputs, processing occurs, resulting in the selection of an output or set of outputs. Interpretability is required at each of these three stages of processing: the inputs need to have a clear meaning, the processes need to explain how the inputs are transformed, and the outputs need to be meaningful units.

Early approaches to AI were predominantly symbolic and propositional (e.g., a set of IF-THEN rules operating over meaningful primitives). For instance, an early example of XAI, MYCIN, [23, 24] was developed in the context of medical consultation. Following earlier criterion developed for computerized systems, [25] the symbolic processing techniques was adopted "in order to be accepted by physicians, should be able to explain how and why a particular conclusion has been derived".

The challenge for symbolic and propositional systems is that their interpretability does not necessarily scale to more complex problems. As seen in, it can be readily intuited that all irises with petal length greater than 2.45 cm are setosas (i.e., IF petalLength > 2.45 cm THEN setosa[1]). What if there were hundreds of nested decisions? In this case there would need to be some mechanism to distill the most relevant decisions to the user, such as a simplifying model of causation that describes the process. While the model would be considered interpretable since all decisions are available to the user, the model itself is not inherently explainable without additional processing. To be truly explainable, one needs to provide more than the set of primitive decisions. Instead, an explanation requires that a system distills the most relevant criterion that maximize predictability for the particular user's goals [26] (Fig. 1).

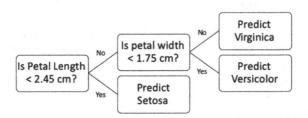

Fig. 1. A Decision Tree representation classifying Irises based on petal length and width. This example was derived from the *sklearn* Python package and visualized using the D3 tree visualization package.

The two approaches of the most productive AIs are *Reinforcement Learners* and *Neural Networks*. Reinforcement learners follow a common theme: there are a set of input states, and a reward associated with every possible action given those states. The *policy* of the learner is the set of learned actions for a given state based on maximizing the reward. In mathematical terms the policy is a map providing the probability of responding when in a given state. Rewards can be immediate or discounted, i.e., based on distal actions. Generally, the space is too vast to capture the set of all possible states and actions. Consequently, there is some sampling or exploration of the space to capture a reasonable set of actions. Similar to the issue of Decision-Trees, classical reinforcement learners are technically interpretable in that each decision is expressed by the policy, but not necessarily explainable at a higher level (e.g., finding hierarchical patterns in states).

Neural networks are loosely inspired by the firing of neurons within the brain. *Deep* neural networks, utilize mathematical inputs (i.e., the input layer vector) which are then processed through distributed layers of 'hidden' states to active the output layer, with these hidden states being updated by some learning signal (see Fig. 2). Supervised networks are trained on labeled data (data with a ground-truth answer) and are generally used for prediction tasks, while unsupervised networks generally cluster data which has no 'correct answer' and are used to cluster data to find potentially meaningful relations. Most neural networks are very data hungry, so finding good labeled

---

[1] Decision trees get more complex when the decisions are probabilistic and become less explainable even though they are still technically interpretable.

data can be a challenge. There are also semi-supervised techniques which utilize substantially less training data. These networks use the limited training data to guide the initial clustering for the larger amount of unlabeled data. The challenge is that these hidden layers are not generally interpretable, take substantial training data, and have hundreds to thousands of manipulable parameters [27].

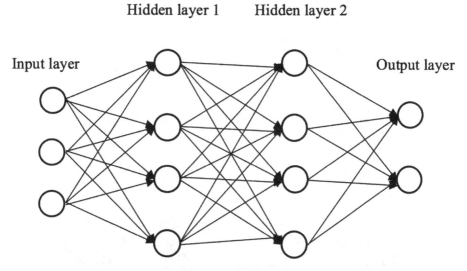

Fig. 2. Deep Neural Network. This example shows an input and output layer as well as two hidden layers. Layers are composed of a set of nodes, each with its own set of connections.

2.2   Approaches to XAI: Models of Interpretability

While there are hundreds of techniques being developed to improve the interpretability of AIs, there are three key approaches which we will discuss: *attention filters, model induction*, and *exemplar presentation*.

Attention Filters
In a comparable manner to theories of human attentional processing, the focus of attentional filter techniques is to highlight a subset of features that have made the most significant contributions to decision or classification process. In images, this typically represents a selection of 'salient' pixels within an image as a sort of heat map (e.g., see Fig. 3). In addition to heatmaps, image data has also been explained by captioning the image with automatic labelling of objects and/or actions, and by producing hierarchical description graphs representing some relationships between the objects and/or actions within the image [26, 28]. While heatmaps provide some information about the underlying focus of an algorithm, they are not interpretable in and of themselves. Instead, they rely on humans to interpret whether the focus is on the relevant labeled object or a potentially spurious correlated feature (e.g., incorrectly *perceiving* a person in a riding outfit sitting on a chair as that person riding a horse due to their outfit being

the most salient feature of the decision). As such, the user is the one generating the explanation (Fig. 3).

Fig. 3. Heatmap of a horse from the HMB-51 dataset using a convolutional neural network

Outside of image data, salient features have been intuited by visualizing salient clusters of high-dimensional representations using t-distributed stochastic neighbor embedding (t-SNE), which is a non-linear dimension-reduction technique. This has been used to discover missing competencies in algorithms in game playing algorithms [29, 30]. These techniques seek to interpret the high-dimensional space of the algorithms' *cognition*[2] in a fashion analogous to using neuroimaging (e.g., fMRI) to intuit human cognitive processes.

Model Induction

Another approach to interpretability reflects an examination of model induction processes. The primary goal of model induction is to train a separate interpretable AI to make the same decisions as the non-interpretable AI, to some level of abstraction [27, 30–32]. These interpretable models include simple linear models, rule lists [33, 34], or decision trees (although see [29] for the use of cognitive models to approximate AI

---

[2] For the sake of analogy, we will refer to the black-box processes and output, such as the hidden layers in a neural network leading to the output layer, as an algorithm's cognition.

decisions). Perhaps the most well-known is LIME (Local Interpretable Model-agnostic Explanations), which samples the decision/classification space of a non-interpretable model and creates an interpretable local representation that approximates the performance of the non-interpretable model [31]. In plainer terms, LIME focuses on interpreting a given prediction as opposed to a perfectly interpretable *global* model. In the case of reinforcement learning, it is possible to decompose the reward signal to better understand the most salient features that impacted the reward by sampling the decision space [35].

The focus of many model induction methods is not to make models inherently more explainable in and of themselves, but instead to make their decisions interpretable to some level of fidelity without guaranteeing that the interpretable model captures any of the actual cognitive processes of the non-interpretable model.

Exemplar Presentation
Similar to attentional techniques, exemplar presentation techniques such as Bayesian Teaching [36] present a subset of data is provided to the user which represent the prototypical exemplar of a given decision. Thus, to understand why a given image was classified as a bird, several training examples most representative of the bird decision are presented to the user. The user should then be able to intuit some of the underlying cognitive processes of the model. This technique is based on being analogous to how children learn in an education setting [37]. At no point is any cognition of the underlying AI model directly interpreted, it is up to the user the intuit the cognition by finding commonalities within the examples.

2.3   Challenges for Existing Approaches

Most existing approaches to AI are not attempting to directly make more interpretable models, instead, they focus on either developing some approximate models which are more interpretable, or they try to expose some salient features which are being used by the model in some capacity, then have the user induce the underlying cognitive processes of the model. Each style has several overlapping limitations. Perhaps the most telling is scale: developing interpretable models is computationally intractable. Each technique generally uses some kind of subsampling or approximation in order to make either the decision-space more understandable (in the case of t-SNE dimensionality reduction), or to simply reduce the computational complexity of the interpretable model so it may be trained in a reasonable amount of time.

Any time one makes an approximation, some amount of information is generally lost. In the case of very complex decision-spaces, it becomes more likely that significant parts of the decision-space will not be explored, and resultingly the interpretable model will be incomplete. Consequently, any attempts to generalize from the current decision might result in an error. In fact, there is evidence that providing limited explanations causes users to overly trust their model and make incorrect predictions of their model's future behavior [18]. Furthermore, attentional and exemplar techniques rely on the user to generate their own mental model of the AI model's cognitive processes. This projects the user's human biases into their perception of the AI model.

Finally, model induction techniques tend to focus on only one level of interpretability, so the provided explanation may not in fact be a proper explanation, and may not be presented at the right level based on the user's goals and expertise. For instance, imagine a very complex model running a nuclear power plant. It is possible to break down this model into a very complex decision-tree consisting of hundreds decisions, however, if the AI initiates an emergency shutdown the kind of explanation might be different based on whether it is the developer, manager, or engineer using the system. To date, most development has focused on the software developer so they may be able to better debug the system [15].

3   Explanations

Bridging the gap between developers who focus on interpretability and users requiring explainability necessitates a consideration of what makes an explanation [38]. In general, explanations consist of two parts: an explanandum (a phenomenon that needs to be explained) and the explanans (the statements purporting to explain the phenomenon). In the context of XAI, explanandum can consist of the algorithm (i.e., an input-output mapping), or any given subset of processes that define an algorithm's function. We will demonstrate that the requirements of explainability are relative to the recipient of the explanation.

3.1   Model Criterion: Interpretability, Explainability, and Believability

Information and computer scientists have considered a number of types of explanations [20, 26, 39–41]. For instance, Marr [39] suggested three independent levels of explanation for understanding systems: the computation level, the algorithmic and representational level, and the implementation level. Importantly, in proposing this distinction, Marr was neither concerned with knowledge translation between information and computer scientists and the general public, nor was he interested in understanding how individuals explain human behaviors to themselves and others, i.e. folk psychology. In contrast to Marr, Samek and Müller [26] consider explanation in terms of recipient, information content, and intentions of the explanation (questions that are answers and how explanation is used). This approach emphasizes the relative nature of explanation.

Doran, Shultz, & Besold [42] provide another approach to classifying XAI systems. They identified two distinct approaches to explaining black box systems (or, *opaque systems*) where input-output mappings are not accessible to the user. *Interpretable systems* reflect systems wherein more technical details are provided to users for them to understand the operations of a system. In their example, Doran et al. contrast regression models wherein outputs and variable weights can be contrasted with deep neural networks that are unlikely to be interpretable. In contrast, *comprehensible systems* symbols such as linguistic markers or images are presented along with the output. They note that users must rely on their "own implicit knowledge and reasoning about them". Doran et al. note that interpretable and comprehensible systems reflect improvements relative to the explainability of opaque systems.

Earlier work by Lipton [1] also highlights the benefits of interpretability. In the context of AI, Lipton notes that "the task of interpretation appears underspecified … [with the] demand for interpretability [arising] when there is a mismatch between the formal objectives of supervised learning (test set predictive performance) and the real-world costs in a deployment setting." Reviewing the literature, Lipton suggests that there are four criteria for interpretability: trust, causality, transferability, informativeness, and fair and ethical decision-making. Each of these criteria, however, is considerably variability in terms of how they are defined and, indeed, interpreted. In this way, these criteria are often externally defined relative to the system due to features of the social environment [19]. Thus, considering the possible explanation that users have access to can help understand their current mental model and promote the development of a more sophisticated understanding of these systems [43].

3.2 Typology of Explanations

Users' needs and goals are crucial to developing effective XAI. Earlier philosophical taxonomies provide insight into what types of explanations are possible. For instance, Aristotle was the first to attempt to systematically differentiate kinds of explanations (i.e., material, formal, efficient cause, and final cause). In that early philosophers relied on their own experience and observations, their formulations of explanation might reflect formalized human intuitions (i.e., folk theories). More recently, Dennett [44] provided a framework that assumes three broad approaches to explanation: the physical stance, design stance, and intentional stance. These stances concern causal/mechanical explanations, functional explanations, and intentional explanations, respectively. For Dennett, explanations are used in order to *predict* the behavior of biological and nonbiological systems through analogical reasoning. Adopting a similar framework, we define three primary explanation types below as well as provide examples of other specific explanation subtypes that demonstrates the inclusivity of this framework.[3]

Causal/Mechanical. The broadest class of explanation is the causal explanation. A casual explanation consists of an appeal to an underlying causal relationship between objects, entities, forces, and events. They take the form X caused Y to do A. For instance, a drone did not find the target after System X failed to classify a target object. Most explanations offered in academic disciplines in the humanities, physical and social science likely fall into this category.

Historical. Historical explanations appeal to past events as causing an event or an entity to engage in an action, e.g., Event X resulted in Event Y. For instance, an algorithm produced a racial bias in an output variable because it was trained on a biased datasets.

Reductive. A reductive explanation appeals to a lower-order property of a system to explain a higher-order property, e.g., Feature A resulted in Action Y. For instance, the autonomous vehicle hit another car because its proximity sensory was not working. In the case of reductive explanations, the explainer selects a subset of features from a total set, ideally, those that are most strongly associated with an outcome.

---

[3] We acknowledge that there is potentially overlap between some explanation types.

Functional/Teleological. A second class of explanation is the functional explanation. Functional explanations appeal to the function, end, or purpose of objects, entities, and events, e.g., X did Y because of Function A. For instance, a surveillance camera feed is flagged because it detected that an individual was potentially carrying a weapon. Here, the function (detect) qualifies why a specific video feed was brought to the user's attention. Functional explanations reflect a more general form of explanation relative to causal or mechanical. Namely, in the detection example, the actual data processing of the detection algorithm is *not* provided as part of the explanation.

Formal or Mathematical. Formal or mathematical explanations can be understood as special cases of functional explanations. Formal explanation appeal to formal principles embedded within an extant logical framework, e.g., X was observed because of Y, where Y is a defined principle. For instance, the program failed to compile because there was an illegal command on Line 5.

Subsumption. Subsumptive explanations appeal to an ontological category of an objects, entities, and events, e.g., X has A because it is a member of Category Y. For instance, a developer noted that an app worked perfectly because it was optimized for the latest release of the Android operating system. In this case, a specific kind of app worked because it was running on a specific kind of operating system.

Macro-to-Micro. A macro-to-micro explanation reflects the application of properties from a macro-level phenomenon to a micro-level phenomenon, e.g., an application failed to work because of a specific line of code that was inserted into the script, like a computer failing to boot because it had the wrong drivers installed. Here, analogical reasoning is used to understand a micro level phenomenon (i.e., insertion of a code) by means of a macro-level phenomenon (i.e., available drivers).

Intentional. The third class of explanation is the intentional explanation. These explanations appeal to the mental states and motivations of an autonomous agent, e.g., X did Y because it wanted or needed A. For instance, an autonomous vehicle swerved away from the patch of icy because it *wanted* to avoid a crash. Here, an analogy is provided based on the user's knowledge of a known domain (i.e., folk psychology) to help understand an unknown domain (i.e., system operations). Intentional explanations reflect the most simplified form of explanation in that they ignore specific causal mechanisms (e.g., software and hardware) as well as the overall function (i.e., what the system was designed to do).

Anthropomorphic Explanations. Often used synonymously with intentional explanations, anthropomorphic explanations emphasize the human-like qualities of a non-human entity. In addition to intentional states, anthropomorphic explanations tend to include affective responses (e.g., happy, sad, mad), behaviours (e.g., 'acting up', 'stubbornness'), or human social bonds (i.e., they're friends, they like one another). For instance, two systems might not like talking one another.

Meta-Explanation. In general, meta-explanations reflect a kind of explanation that is used to understand the failure of lower-order explanations. Meta-explanations appeal to the structure of a scenario, including communication and argumentation between agents, e.g., X believes A while Y believes B, leading them to misunderstand in situations like W. For instance, the team thought that a drone failed to drop its payload because of a software issue. When the team examined the code, they instead realized it was a hardware issue. In that humans are involved in meta-explanations, they frequently reflect a special case of intentional explanations that reflect collective or conjoint intentionality. In this way, XAI might be seen as an effort in meta-explanation, e.g., users do not understand systems failures because they do not understand the operations of the underlying code.

3.3   The Problem of XAI

Having defined the kinds of algorithms the clustering or categorization mechanism that define AI and the explanations types that are intelligible to model developers and users, the problem of XAI becomes one of knowledge translation. Throughout this process, information will be lost, but the essential features and functions of algorithms must be maintained. Two paths are possible: knowledge-to-information translation and information-to-knowledge translation.

Knowledge-to-Information Translation. Knowledge-to-information translation reflects an implementation problem: a developer wants to have a machine perform a given task (knowledge) and they therefore need to create a code that can be used by a system to perform a task given a set of constraints (information). This is the problem faced in information and computer science training and education: developers have a goal-state in mind but need to determine what code satisfies those operations for any given set of functions. This likely reflects the approach to XAI inspired by Marr [39], wherein computational knowledge is translated into an algorithm, or an algorithm is implemented using software and hardware.

When clients or users are considered, the nature of an effective explanation is unclear. Although the client has specific needs (e.g., for a website or software that performs a specific function), they need to communicate this to the developer. Similarly, an application user might want to have software perform a specific task but does not know what command will produce the desired result. In these cases, a client or user without knowledge of information sciences likely has an intentional model of what they want a problem to do, but they do not understand the underlying formal principles. Moreover, if they believe that a system has operated successfully, they will not question the results.

Information-to-Knowledge Translation. In contrast to knowledge-to-information translation, XAI reflects an information-to-knowledge translation problem. Namely, when developers or users are presented with an error, they likely want to understand *why* the output had those properties. However, they might not require or want a comprehensive causal explanation of the phenomenon which would likely require more knowledge of information science. Instead, the user wants to be able to understand the output in a manner that is compatible with their existing knowledge. The "essential" features or functions that can account for satisfaction or violation of goals. For instance, policymakers likely wish to understand how an algorithm functions in order to ensure that the results it provides are not biased (e.g., discriminating based on social categories or socioeconomic status). In this way, the provision of an explanation is part of a learning process.

Finally, explanations are inherently reductive. Explanations are offered as a means to understand a system by simplifying and systematizing its operations. Human information processing follows a similar path. Research suggests that there are shifts from implicit to explicit representations [63] and that conscious processing results in progressively more abstract, simplified representations [64, 65]. By translating information to knowledge, we provide an approach which parallels human cognition.

4   Knowledge-to-Information Translation Training (KITT)

In order to train learners to understand AI, we must account for 1) the objectives of explainability and XAI, 2) what constitutes a good explanation, and 3) the process of learning and communicating information such that it relatable to a learner's knowledge. We refer to this approach as knowledge-to-information translation training, or KITT. Central to this approach is the distinction between interpretability (understanding the output and operations of a system), explainability (using analogical reasoning to predict one system by means of knowledge of another), and believability (acceptance of an analogy but without understanding its basis).

When implemented, the KITT framework assumes that training and learning is mediated through an intelligent tutoring system (ITS; e.g., [45–48]) which can use multiple criteria to monitor and assess expert and non-expert performance. KITT can be implemented in a number of ways, e.g., a standalone training AIS or integrated into an AI used for research, data processing, or consultation. The KITT framework assumes that learners who simply wish to understand an AI would prefer simple explanations (e.g., intentional explanations) but over time, learners will require more in-depth knowledge of the operations of a system. This reflects an adaptive learning process.

4.1   Explanatory Scaffolding Process

Interpretability. Learning has been defined as social scaffolding, wherein an educator assesses a learner's current mental representation of a problem space and identifies what is both relevant and novel to a learner [49, 50]. AISs can address this learning process [43]. In order to accomplish this, the KITT framework assumes that we must first assess the learner's current state of knowledge within the domain of information science (i.e., declarative and procedural knowledge pertaining to the modelling approach being considered) and then provide additional information to extend this knowledge. Unlike other approaches to XAI, KITT assumes that the kind of explanation provided can be quite variable depending on what kind of predictions and level of understanding is desired.

For information science, knowledge-to-information translation will consist of systematically learning core curriculum areas (e.g., programming languages, strategies for debugging, system operations). In these cases, the focus will likely be on causal/mechanistic explanations. Programmers will be taught principles of causation based on the functions of programming languages and the constraints of hardware, i.e., command X results in operation Y, or a PC will crash if program X runs due to insufficient RAM. When debugging a program, they will focus on historical explanations and reductive explanations, i.e., the program failed to run a subroutine due to a failure to close a loop in the code. This makes the learning process comparable to learning neuroscientific principles (e.g., structure of neurons, cell assemblies, fiber tracts).

Explainability and Believability. Developing a bottom-up understanding of programs and systems is not always possible or desirable. For instance, in the case of a typical user, clinician, or policy analyst that wants to verify that an approach is valid, deep descriptive knowledge is not required. Making a similar point, Marr [39] notes that reductive approaches to explanation like "[n]europhysiology and psychophysics have as their business to describe the behavior of cells or of subjects, not to explain such behavior" (p. 15). The KITT framework assumes that interpreting information and translating it into knowledge is facilitated through a process of analogical reasoning using relationships found in known mechanical, functional, and intentional systems. However, in contrast to the relatively simple nature of scaffolding required for developers, KITT requires the selection of an explanation that will be intelligible to the user. It must therefore highlight functional similarities between the operations of an AI and a familiar domain of explanation.

The goals of XAI parallel explanation in psychological science. Namely, psychological phenomena reflect the output of the interactions of neurons. A straightforward means to understand the information-to-knowledge translation processes is to consider how explanations of psychological phenomena are presented to non-experts. Studies of explanations of psychological phenomena have suggest that the addition of mechanistic relationships (e.g., the use of irrelevant neuroscientific evidence in explaining psychological phenomena) can make an explanation more believable [51, 52]. However, Schoenherr, Thomson, & Davies [53] replicated this effect using valid and invalid general mechanistic explanations (i.e., X was drawn to Y by a force) suggesting that neuroscientific explanations themselves might not be the basis for this effect. Instead, mechanistic explanations might appear to be more believable regardless of their validity.

The believability of an explanation does not imply that it facilitates learning. Science educators have considered the utility of certain kinds of explanations [54–58]. For instance, in the context of biology and evolutionary theory, teleological explanations are frequently used, e.g., a feature has adapted *for* survival in an environment [59, 60]. Moreover, evidence suggests that certain kinds of explanations can be used to scaffold learners' understanding. For instance, Tamir and Zohar [57] found that while 10th and 12th graders accepted anthropomorphic formulations (82%), they did not necessarily believe that plants (29%) or animals (62%) actually had intentionality. More recently, studies have replicated these findings noting discrepancies between factors that predict learning and their acceptance and use of these explanations and their associated terms [61, 62]. Thus, following Dennett's [44] proposition, intentional explanations might be more intelligible to learners while learners themselves simultaneously understand the analogical basis for these statements.

In summary, while mechanistic explanations might be more believable, intentional explanations likely provide a more principled means to start a learner's training in understanding AI. Learners might be capable of acquiring superior functional knowledge concerning the operations of a system when framed in intentional turns. Namely, when a non-expert first understands what a system is trying to do (i.e., its intended function), the system can be decomposed into separable, functional units. This is analogous to a student studying cognitive psychology who learners about memory, attention, and decision-making. In the case of some AIs (e.g., deep neural nets), this functional division might not fall neatly along these lines. Rather, functions might reflect a larger number of specific, heterogeneous processes relative to human cognition, e.g., feature identifiers for eyes, image size, luminosity, brow shape. Moreover, different approaches to AI might be more inherently explainable than others, e.g., symbolic and propositional systems relative to deep neural nets. In some cases, functions might be unspecifiable in human terms.

5   Conclusion and Caveats

XAI reflects an approach to AI that allows experts and non-experts to understand and predict the output and operations of artificial systems. Rather than assuming that a single kind or level of analysis is appropriate, we suggest that an effective solution to XAI requires a consideration of the learner's knowledge [19] and that this knowledge and the goals of the user will changes over time. This is not reflected in other frameworks like Marr's [39] that is likely more appropriate when providing explanations to those in information science. Instead, the cognitive science of explanation needs to be used to inform those processes [38]. We have provided a taxonomy based on Dennett [44] that suggest three levels of explanation: causal/mechanistic, functional/teleological, and intentional.

Specifically, while an AI might be interpretable to experts, this does not imply that operations of the systems are accurately understood. Instead, explainability requires the ability to relate information in one domain to another. Simplified explanations can be based on basic features of human intentionality (i.e., wants, desires, goals) or more specific analogies based on human information processing systems (e.g., attention, memory, categorization). The selection of the level that is desirable will depend on the knowledge and goals of the user as well as the nature of the AI.

Knowledge-to-information and information-to-knowledge translation need not be exclusive paths. In a comparable manner to cognitive neuroscience, bottom-up and top-down reasoning can be developed conjointly. Namely, users can have both an ability to interpret a system at a low-level while also having high-level explanations of the function of a system. This process reflects *abductive reasoning* wherein multiple, possible explanations are plausible based on the kinds of explanations that can provide predictive models. In that XAI reflects a squishy problem, we assume that satisficing criteria should be used to judge the abilities of learners wherein a learner's knowledge is assessed in a relative, rather than absolute, manner [43].

Finally, we have described the use of the KITT framework in a manner that is amenable to an AIS. However, like all learning tasks, KITT can be adapted to an empirical approach to do research in XAI. Namely, the accuracy and retention of information concerning an AI being assessed by developers can be used to determine 1) the complexity of explanation that provides a high level of predictive accuracy, as well as 2) the kinds of explanations that are facilitate learning and believability.

Acknowledgements. Research was sponsored by the Army Research Laboratory and was accomplished under the Cooperative Agreement Number W911NF-19-2-0223. The views and conclusions contained in this document are those of the authors and should not be interpreted as representing the official policies, either expressed or implied, of the Army Research Laboratory or the U.S. Government. The U.S. Government is authorized to reproduce and distribute reprints for the Government purposed notwithstanding any copyright notation herein.

References

1. Lipton, Z.C.: The mythos of model interpretability. In: ICML Workshop on Human Interpretability in Machine Learning, New York (2016)
2. Bhatt, U., et al.: Explainable machine learning in deployment. In: Proceedings of the 2020 Conference on Fairness, Accountability and Transparency, pp. 648–657 (2020)
3. Dzindolet, M.T., Peterson, S.A., Pomranky, R.A., Pierce, L.G., Beck, H.P.: The role of trust in automation reliance. Int. J. Hum. Comput. Stud. **58**(6), 697–718 (2003)
4. Andras, P., et al.: Trusting intelligent machines: deepening trust within socio-technical systems. IEEE Technol. Soc. Mag. **37**(4), 76–83 (2018)
5. Rossi, F.: Building trust in artificial intelligence. J. Int. Aff. **72**(1), 127–134 (2019)
6. Caliskan, A.B.J., Narayanan, A.: Semantic derived automatically from language corpora contain human-like biases. Science **6334**(356), 183–186 (2017)
7. Zou, J., Schiebinger, L.: AI can be sexist and racist - it's time to make it fair. Nat. Comments **559**, 324–326 (2018)
8. BCC: Google apologises for photos app's racist blunder. BBC (2015). https://www.bbc.com/news/technology-33347866. Accessed 15 Dec 2019
9. Kasperkevic, J.: Google says sorry for racist auto-tag in photo app. The Guardian (2015). https://www.theguardian.com/technology/2015/jul/01/google-sorry-racist-auto-tag-photo-app. Accessed 14 Dec 2019
10. Hern, A.: Google's solution to accidental algorithmic racism: ban gorillas. The Guardian (2018). https://www.theguardian.com/technology/2018/jan/12/google-racism-ban-gorilla-black-people. Accessed 15 Dec 2019
11. Edwards, L., Veale, M.: Slave to the algorithm: why a right to an explanation is probably not the remedy you are looking for. Duke Law Technol. Rev. **16**, 18–84 (2017)
12. Gunning, D.: DARPA XAI BAA. DARPA (2016). https://www.darpa.mil/attachments/DARPA-BAA-16–53.pdf. Accessed 20 Feb 2020
13. Rudin, C.: Stop explaining black box machine learning models for high stakes decisions, and use interpretable models instead. Nat. Mach. Intell. **1**(5), 206–215 (2019)
14. Arrieta, A.B., et al.: Explainable artificial intelligence (XAI): concepts, taxonomies, opportunities and challenges toward responsible AI. Inf. Fusion **58**, 82–115 (2020)
15. Deeks, A.: The judicial demand for explainable artificial intelligence. Columbia Law Rev. **119**(7), 1829–1850 (2019)

16. Yin, M., Wortman, V., Wallach, H.: Understanding the effect of accuracy on trust in machine learning models. In: Proceedings of the 2019 CHI Conference on Human Factors in Computing Systems, pp. 1–12 (2019)
17. Straunch, R.: Squishy problems and quantitative method. Policy Sci. **6**, 175–184 (1975)
18. Lakkaraju, H., Bastani, O.: "How do I fool you?": manipulating user trust via misleading black box explanations. In: Proceedings of AAAI/ACM Conference on AI, Ethics, and Society (2020)
19. Miller, T.: Artif. Intell. **267**, 1–38 (2019)
20. Hoffman, R., Klein, G., Mueller, S.: Explaining explanation for "Explainable AI". In: Proceedings of the Human Factors and Ergonomics Society Annual Meeting, Los Angeles, pp. 197–201 (2018)
21. Gilpin, L., Bau, D., Yuan, B., Baiwa, A., Specter, M., Kagal, L.: Explaining explanations: an overview of interpretability of machine learning. In: Proceedings of IEEE 5th International Conference on Data Science and Advanced Analytics, pp. 80–89 (2018)
22. Došilović, F., Brčić, M., Hlupić, N.: Explainable artificial intelligence: a survey. In: Proceedings of 2018 41st International Convention on Information and Communication Technology, Electronics and Microelectronics (MIPRO), pp. 210–215 (2018)
23. Fagan, L.M., Shortliffe, E.H., Buchanan, B.G.: Computer-based medical decision making: from MYCIN to VM. Automedica **3**, 97–108 (1980)
24. Shortliffe, E.H.: Computer-Based Medical Consultations: MYCIN. Elsevier/North Holland, New York (1976)
25. Gorry, G.A.: Computer-assisted clinical decision making. Methods Inf. Med. **12**, 45–51 (1973)
26. Samek, W., Müller, K.-R.: Towards explainable artificial intelligence. In: Samek, W., Montavon, G., Vedaldi, A., Hansen, L.K., Müller, K.-R. (eds.) Explainable AI: Interpreting, Explaining and Visualizing Deep Learning. LNCS (LNAI), vol. 11700, pp. 5–22. Springer, Cham (2019). https://doi.org/10.1007/978-3-030-28954-6_1
27. Adadi, A., Berrada, M.: Peeking inside the black-box: a survey on Explainable Artificial Intelligence (XAI). IEEE Access **6**, 52138–52160 (2018)
28. Aditya, S.: Explainable image understanding using vision and reasoning. In: Proceedings of Thirty-First AAAI Conference on Artificial Intelligence (2017)
29. Somers, S., Mtisupoulos, C., Lebiere, C., Thomson, R.: Explaining the decisions of a deep reinforcement learners with a cognitive architecture. In: Proceedings of International Conference on Cognitive Modeling (2018)
30. Somers, S., Mitsopoulos, K., Lebiere, C., Thomson, R.: Cognitive-level salience for explainable artificial intelligence. In: Proceedings of International Conference on Cognitive Modeling, Montreal (2019)
31. Ribeiro, M., Singh, S., Guestrin, C.: "Why should I trust you?" explaining the predictions of any classifier. In: Proceedings of ACM SIGKDD Conference on Knowledge Discovery and Data Mining (KDD) (2016)
32. Ras, G., van Gerven, M., Haselager, P.: Explanation methods in deep learning: users, values, concerns and challenges. In: Escalante, H.J., Escalera, S., Guyon, I., Baró, X., Güçlütürk, Y., Güçlü, U., van Gerven, M. (eds.) Explainable and Interpretable Models in Computer Vision and Machine Learning. TSSCML, pp. 19–36. Springer, Cham (2018). https://doi.org/10.1007/978-3-319-98131-4_2
33. Wang, T., Rudin, C., Doshi-Velez, F., Liu, Y., Klampfl, E., MacNeille, P.: A Bayesian framework for learning rule sets for interpretable classification. J. Mach. Learn. Res. **70**(18), 1–37 (2017)
34. Keneni, B., et al.: Evolving rule-based explainable artificial intelligence for unmanned aerial vehicles. IEEE Access **7**, 17001–17016 (2019)

35. Erwig, M., Fern, A., Murali, M., Koul, A.: Explaining deep adaptive programs via reward decomposition. In: Proceedings of International Joint Conference on Artificial Intelligence - Working on Explainable Artificial Intelligence (2018)
36. Yang, S., Shafto, P.: Explainable artificial intelligence via Bayesian teaching. In: Proceedings of 31st Conference on Neural Information Processing Systems, Long Beach (2017)
37. Shafto, P., Goodman, N., Griffiths, T.: A rational account of pedagogical reasoning: teaching by, and learning from, examples. Cogn. Psychol. **71**, 55–89 (2014)
38. Keil, F.C., Wilson, R.A., Wilson, R.A.: Explanation and Cognition. MIT Press, Cambridge (2000)
39. Marr, D.: Vision: A Computational Approach. Freeman & Co., San Francisco (1982)
40. Biran, O., Cotton, C.: Explanation and justification in machine learning: a survey. In: Proceedings of IJCAI-2017 Workshop on Explainable Artificial Intelligence (XAI) (2017)
41. Park, D.H., Hendricks, L.A., Akata, Z., Schiele, B., Darrell, T., Rohrbach, M.: Attentive explanations: justifying decisions and pointing to the evidence. arXiv preprint arXiv:1612.04757 (2016)
42. Doran, D., Schulz, S. Besold, T.R.: What does explainable AI really mean? A new conceptualization of perspectives. arXiv preprint arXiv:1710.00794 (2017)
43. Schoenherr, J.R.: Adapting the zone of proximal development to the wicked environments of professional practice. In: Proceedings of HCII 2020, Copenhagen, HCI International (2020)
44. Dennett, D.: The Intentional Stance. MIT Press, Cambridge (1987)
45. Anderson, J.R., Gluck, K.: What role do cognitive architectures play in intelligent tutoring systems? In: Klahr, V., Carver, S.M. (eds.) Cognition Instruction: Twenty-Five Years Progress, pp. 227–262. Lawrence Erlbaum Associates, Mahwah (2001)
46. Nwana, H.S.: Intelligent tutoring systems: an overview. Artif. Intell. Rev. **4**, 251–277 (1990)
47. Ohlsson, S.: Some principles of intelligent tutoring. Instr. Sci. **14**, 293–326 (1986)
48. Polson, M.C., Richardson, J.J.: Foundations of Intelligent Tutoring Systems. Psychology Press (2013)
49. Vygotsky, L.S.: Thought and Language. MIT Press, Cambridge (1934/1986)
50. Vygotsky, L.S.: Mind in Society: The Development of Higher Mental Processes. Harvard University Press, Cambridge (1930–1934/1978)
51. Weisberg, D.S., Keil, F.C., Goodstein, J., Rawson, E., Gray, J.R.: The seductive allure of neuroscience explanations. J. Cogn. Neurosci. **20**, 470–477 (2008)
52. Rhodes, R.E., Rodriguez, F., Shah, P.: Explaining the alluring influence of neuroscience information on scientific reasoning. J. Exp. Psychol. Learn. Mem. Cogn. **40**, 1432–1440 (2014)
53. Schoenherr, J.R., Thomson, R., Davies, J.: What makes an explanation believable? Mechanistic and anthropomorphic explanations of natural phenomena. In: Proceedings of the 33rd Annual Meeting of the Cognitive Science Society. Cognitive Science Society, Boston (2011)
54. Bartov, H.: Teaching students to understand the advantages and disadvantages of teleological and anthropomorphic statements in biology. J. Res. Sci. Teach. **18**, 79–86 (1981)
55. Talanquer, V.: Explanations and teleology in chemistry education. Int. J. Sci. Educ. **29**, 853–870 (2007)
56. Talanquer, V.: Exploring dominant types of explanations built by general chemistry students. Int. J. Sci. Educ. **32**, 2393–2412 (2010)
57. Tamir, P., Zohar, A.: Anthropomorphism and teleology in reasoning about biological phenomena. Sci. Educ. **75**, 57–67 (1991)

58. Zohar, A., Ginossar, S.: Lifting the taboo regarding teleology and anthropomorphism in biology education—heretical suggestions. Sci. Educ. **82**, 679–697 (1998)
59. Bardapurkar, A.: Do students see the selection in organic evolution? A critical review of the causal structure of student explanations. Evol. Educ. Outreach **1**(3), 299–305 (2008)
60. Ziegler, D.: The question of purpose. Evol. Educ. Outreach **1**, 44–45 (2008)
61. Barnes, M.E., et al.: Teleological reasoning, not acceptance of evolution, impacts students' ability to learn natural selection. Evol. Educ. Outreach **10**(1), 7 (2017)
62. Thulin, S., Pramling, N.: Anthropomorphically speaking: on communication between teachers and children in early childhood biology education. Int. J. Early Years Educ. **17**, 137–150 (2009)
63. Karmiloff-Smith, A.: Beyond Modularity. MIT Press/Bradford Books, Cambridge (1992)
64. Zeki, S.: The disunity of consciousness. Trends Cogn. Sci. **7**, 214–218 (2003)
65. Dehaene, S., et al.: Conscious, preconscious, and subliminal processing: a testable taxonomy. Trends Cogn. Sci. **10**(5), 204–211 (2006)

User Rights and Adaptive A/IS – From Passive Interaction to Real Empowerment

Ozlem Ulgen(✉)

Birmingham City University, Birmingham, UK
ozlem.ulgen@bcu.ac.uk

Abstract. Adaptive autonomous intelligent systems (A/IS) may satisfy design functionality and user experiential requirements but prior to deployment an assessment must be made of their impact on user rights. A/IS systems may assist rather than replace humans but it is unclear where the line is drawn between supplementing human endeavour and knowledge, on the one hand, and gradual erosion of human cognitive abilities on the other. This paper makes the case for development of ethical standards for user awareness of A/IS in operation, taking account of rights under the EU General Data Protection Regulation (GDPR) and the Council of Europe Modernised Convention for the Protection of Individuals with Regard to Automatic Processing of Personal Data (Convention 108+). It sets out three main user awareness stages (pre-use, during-use, and post-use) along with consideration of commensurate rights. In the pre-use stage potential users will need to be aware that an A/IS is either fully or partially in operation, and consent to such an operation or have the option to opt out. During A/IS use if there is a part of the A/IS operation which involves a "black box" scenario, that is, it is difficult for a human to discern what the system is doing and why, then appropriate risk-based parameters need to be set for the systems use. Post-use requires users to be aware of how their data and information shared with the A/IS will be used by the system and any third parties.

Keywords: User rights · Adaptive autonomous intelligent systems (A/IS) · "Technology-biased approach" (TBA) · "Human-centric approach" (HCA) · GDPR · Convention 108+ · Pre-use, During-use, Post-use awareness and rights stages

1 Rationale for User Awareness and Rights Stages

As technology proceeds at a pace difficult for legislators to keep up with, a corpus of ethical principles has emerged to regulate design, development, and deployment, namely: human agency; human control; privacy and data protection; prevention of harm; fairness; transparency; auditability; accountability; and responsibility. Human agency requires that A/IS designers, developers, and deployers exercise professional and ethical practices, and respect and give effect to the autonomy of A/IS users [1]. This means that humans interacting with A/IS must be able to keep full and effective self-determination over themselves without being subordinated, deceived, manipulated, or coerced by the A/IS. Technology complements rather than replaces human capabilities. Human control

© Springer Nature Switzerland AG 2020
R. A. Sottilare and J. Schwarz (Eds.): HCII 2020, LNCS 12214, pp. 205–217, 2020.
https://doi.org/10.1007/978-3-030-50788-6_15

requires that A/IS designers, developers, and deployers introduce mechanisms to ensure some form of human involvement in the operation of the A/IS or human control over how, when, and where it operates [2]. Privacy and data protection requires that A/IS designers, developers, and deployers have mechanisms in place to safeguard and protect personal data and its use throughout the A/IS lifecycle, respecting users' privacy rights [3]. Prevention of harm requires that A/IS designers, developers, and deployers create and use systems which are not harmful to humans, society, and the environment, and which ensure the well-being of humanity [4]. Fairness requires that A/IS designers, developers, and deployers ensure diversity of personnel involved in assessing risks/problems associated with A/IS, and awareness of different cultural norms in order to ensure non-discrimination in A/IS use [5]. Transparency applies both to the information provided to the user regarding data processing as well as the actual processing and functionality of the A/IS [6]. Auditability requires that A/IS designers, developers, and deployers have auditable mechanisms in place to ensure explainability of A/IS actions, consequences, and responses to risks/problems [7]. Accountability requires that A/IS designers, developers, and deployers account for their actions, respond to user concerns and problems, and provide explanations and justifications for A/IS actions and consequences [8]. Responsibility requires that A/IS designers, developers, and deployers have redress mechanisms in place for errors/complaints/harmful consequences from A/IS, and accept legal responsibility under relevant laws [9].

A/IS technologies may be introduced at various lifecycle stages of a product, service, or system and consideration of lifecycle stages makes it clearer to understand how the technology operates, its intended function, and effects. This can be referred to as the "technology-biased approach" (TBA) which seeks to better understand the capabilities and limitations of the A/IS in order to improve performance, optimise operational efficiency, and identify and rectify any errors or failures. However, given the plethora of ethical principles mentioned above and their focus on the human user, on its own, the TBA creates ethical dissonance by not aligning design, development, and deployment with values protecting the human user. For human-machine interaction, the TBA limits its focus on the system rather than considerations of human wants, needs, and values that can be incorporated into the system lifecycle stages. A "human-centric approach" (HCA) would have such considerations at the forefront of design, development, and deployment. Ultimately, the mergence and integration of TBA and HCA will lead to not only improved functionality and reliance of A/IS, but also to ethically aligned design, development, and deployment to take account of user awareness and rights. The HCA that espouses user awareness and rights is evident in the plethora of international, regional, and national regulatory standards emerging in relation to artificial intelligence, robotics, and emerging technologies more generally [10]. The EU General Data Protection Regulation (GDPR) [11], and the Council of Europe Modernised Convention for the Protection of Individuals with Regard to Automatic Processing of Personal Data (Convention 108+) [12] contain provisions respecting and safeguarding user rights related to A/IS particularly as they relate to data processing and personal data. Lifecycle stages exist as a matter of logical application and purposive interpretation of rights contained in these provisions, even though these are not explicitly mentioned [13]. We can identify and analyse user awareness and rights in three stages: (i) pre-use stage; (ii) during-use stage; and (iii) post-use stage.

2 Pre-use Stage

In the pre-use stage potential A/IS users will need to be aware that an A/IS will be either fully or partially in operation, and consent to such an operation or have the option to opt out. With potential A/IS users being made aware of the existence of an A/IS element in the context of use, they will be empowered to decide for themselves whether they want to interact or engage with such a system or not. Ethically, human agency is exercised through free will and active informed consent in the choice that needs to be made. A number of mechanisms and procedures would need to be in place to enable the user to: (a) have pre-use awareness of the type of A/IS product, service, or system they are interacting with, including whether there is an AI element; (b) opt out of using the product, service, or system; (c) challenge an A/IS decision effectively and efficiently; (d) understand the full terms and conditions that apply to any A/IS interactions; and (e) review at a later date to understand previous A/IS interactions.

2.1 Pre-use Awareness

Potential A/IS users must be able to understand the type of A/IS product, service, or system they are interacting with, including whether there is an AI element and whether the A/IS will be fully or partially in operation. Such information should be conveyed in a manner that is clear, accessible, and provides a real opportunity to exercise human agency prior to any use. This also means making the information easily understandable and accessible without causing undue inconvenience to the user (e.g. avoiding multiple click throughs to get to the relevant information; avoiding non-transparent or hidden locations to display information). The pre-use awareness issues outlined above fall under several provisions of the GDPR, and Convention 108+ (see Table 1).

Table 1. Pre-use stage rights

Right	GDPR provision	Convention 108+ provision
Not to be subject to automated decision-making	Article 22(1)	Article 9(1)(a)
To prior consent	Article 7(1)	Article 5(2)
To be notified of right to withdraw consent prior to giving consent	Article 7(3)	
To be notified of automated decision-making	Articles 13(2)(f), 14(2)(g), 15(1)(h)	Article 9(1)(b)
To access to personal data	Article 15(1)(h)	Articles 8(1), 9(1)(b)
To information on logic in automated decision-making	Articles 13(2)(f), 14(2)(g), 15(1)(h)	Article 9(1)(c)
To information on the significance and envisaged consequences of automated decision-making processing	Articles 13(2)(f), 14(2)(g), 15(1)(h)	
To object to processing of data	Article 21	Article 9(1)(d)

Right Not to be Subject to Automated Decision-Making. Article 22 of the GDPR states:

1. *The data subject shall have the right not to be subject to a decision based solely on automated processing, including profiling, which produces legal effects concerning him or her or similarly significantly affects him or her.*
2. *Paragraph 1 shall not apply if the decision:*

    (a) is necessary for entering into, or performance of, a contract between the data subject and a data controller;
    (b) is authorised by Union or Member State law to which the controller is subject and which also lays down suitable measures to safeguard the data subject's rights and freedoms and legitimate interests; or
    (c) is based on the data subject's explicit consent.

3. *In the cases referred to in points (a) and (c) of paragraph 2, the data controller shall implement suitable measures to safeguard the data subject's rights and freedoms and legitimate interests, at least the right to obtain human intervention on the part of the controller, to express his or her point of view and to contest the decision.*
4. *Decisions referred to in paragraph 2 shall not be based on special categories of personal data referred to in Article 9(1), unless point (a) or (g) of Article 9(2) applies and suitable measures to safeguard the data subject's rights and freedoms and legitimate interests are in place.*

Paragraph 1 makes it clear that a person has the right not to be subject to a decision based solely on automated processing, including profiling [14], which produces legal effects concerning him or her or similarly significantly affects him or her. This represents a general prohibition on such automated decision-making. The negative right formulation also gives rise to exercising human agency prior to any A/IS use (e.g. by requesting confirmation or assurance that such decision-making is not taking place; a person being able to object even if such decision-making is deemed not to have legal effects or similarly significant effects). "Legal effects" refers to affecting a person's legal rights, obligations, or status (e.g. freedom to associate with others; voting in elections; taking legal action; termination or cancellation of a contract; residency or citizenship rights) [15]. "Similarly significant" effects refers to adverse impacts that are similar to legal effects such as affecting the circumstances, behaviour or choices of the individual concerned; having a prolonged or permanent impact on the data subject; or leading to the exclusion or discrimination of individuals [16]. Examples include automatic refusal of online credit applications, e-recruitment without human intervention, automated systems determining access to health and education services.

Paragraph 2 sets out exceptions to the right not to be subject to automated decision-making which include: a) necessity of automated decision-making for entering into or performance of a contract between the data subject and a data controller (contract exception); b) authorisation by EU law or EU Member State law to which the data controller is subject and which also lays down suitable measures to safeguard the data subject's rights and freedoms and legitimate interests; or c) data subject's explicit consent (consent exception). If contract or consent exceptions apply, Paragraph 3 requires the data controller to implement suitable measures to safeguard the data subject's rights and freedoms and legitimate interests, and at least the right to obtain human intervention on the part of the controller, to express his or her point of view, and to contest the decision. These latter user safeguards are relevant to the opt out mentioned below.

Even if an exception applies, under Paragraph 4, the automated decision cannot be based on "special categories of personal data" (i.e. racial or ethnic origin, political opinions, religious or philosophical beliefs, or trade union membership, and the processing of genetic data, biometric data for the purpose of uniquely identifying a natural person, data concerning health or data concerning a natural person's sex life or sexual orientation) [17]. The only exceptions to automated decisions based on "special categories of personal data" is where the data subject has given explicit consent to the processing of such personal data for one or more specified purposes, except where EU law or EU Member State law prevent such consent from overriding the prohibition [18]; or processing of such personal data is necessary for reasons of substantial public interest, on the basis of EU law or EU Member State law which shall be proportionate to the aim pursued, respect the essence of the right to data protection, and provide for suitable and specific measures to safeguard the fundamental rights and the interests of the data subject [19].

In contrast to the GDPR, Article 9(1)(a) of Convention 108+ provides a somewhat weaker right not to be subject to solely automated decisions:

> Every individual shall have a right not to be subject to a decision significantly affecting him or her based solely on an automated processing of data without having his or her views taken into consideration.

If an individual objects to automated decision-making this does not necessarily mean it will not take place. An organisation may show it has "taken into consideration" the individual's objection and justify proceeding with automated decision-making under Article 11 on the grounds that it is provided for by law and constitutes a necessary and proportionate measure in a democratic society for quite wide-ranging purposes including: national defence, national security, public safety, important economic and financial interests of the state, the impartiality and independence of the judiciary or the prevention, investigation and prosecution of criminal offences and the execution of criminal penalties, and other essential objectives of general public interest, protection of the data subject or the rights and fundamental freedoms of others, notably freedom of expression, archiving in the public interest, scientific or historical research purposes or statistical purposes when there is no recognisable risk of infringement of the rights and fundamental freedoms of data subjects.

In any case, Article 5(2) of Convention 108+ contains an implicit right to prior consent to data processing by requiring States Parties to demonstrate that data processing is carried out on the basis of the "free, specific, informed and unambiguous consent of the data subject" or of some other legitimate basis laid down by law. Consent here means the free expression of an intentional choice, given either by statement (in written, electronic, or oral form) or by a clear affirmative action which clearly indicates acceptance of the proposed processing of personal data. Mere silence, inactivity or pre-validated forms or boxes will not constitute consent. Consent should cover all processing activities carried out for the same purpose or purposes. Where there are multiple purposes, consent should be given for each different purpose [20]. Under Article 7(1) of the GDPR there is a general consent provision whereby the data controller must be able to demonstrate that the data subject has consented to the processing of their data. In addition, under Article 7(3) the data controller is required to notify the data subject prior to them giving consent that they have the right to withdraw consent at any time.

Right to be Notified of Automated Decision-Making. Article 13(2)(f) of the GDPR provides that the data controller shall, at the time when personal data are obtained, provide the data subject with information on the existence of automated decision-making, including profiling, referred to in Article 22(1) and (4) and, at least in those cases, meaningful information about the logic involved, as well as the significance and the envisaged consequences of such processing for the data subject. Article 14(2)(g) provides that where personal data have not been obtained from the data subject, the data controller is obliged to provide the data subject with information on the existence of automated decision-making, including profiling, referred to in Article 22(1) and (4) and, at least in those cases, meaningful information about the logic involved, as well as the significance and the envisaged consequences of such processing for the data subject. Article 15(1)(h) provides users with the right of access to personal data along with notification on the existence of automated decision-making, including profiling, referred to in Article 22(1) and (4) and, at least in those cases, meaningful information about the logic involved, as well as the significance and the envisaged consequences of such processing for the data subject.

In contrast to the GDPR, Article 9(1)(b) of Convention 108+ provides a right to:

> obtain, on request, at reasonable intervals and without excessive delay or expense, confirmation of the processing of personal data relating to him or her, the communication in an intelligible form of the data processed, all available information on their origin, on the preservation period as well as any other information that the controller is required to provide in order to ensure the transparency of processing in accordance with Article 8, paragraph 1.

Although this is not expressed in terms of a pre-use right, the reference to "at reasonable intervals" would cover pre, during, and post use stages. This may seem onerous on the organisation using automated decision-making, but the right is exercising by the user requesting such information rather than the organisation being required to disclose prior to use. Under Article 8(1) the organisation has a duty to be transparent in data processing by providing the data subject with information on the legal basis and the purposes of the intended processing, the categories of personal data processed, the recipients or categories of recipients of the personal data, if any, and the means of exercising the rights under Article 9.

Right to Meaningful Information About the Logic Involved in Automated Decision-Making. The reference in Articles 13(2)(f), 14(2)(g), 15(1)(h) of the GDPR to users having the right to "meaningful information about the logic involved" in automated decision-making is intended to enable users to contest, challenge, or dispute the decision. Necessarily the information should be of a type and nature that is comprehensible to the user and that can be used subsequently to challenge any decision.

Recital 58 of the GDPR states that the principle of transparency requires that any information addressed to the public or to the data subject should be "concise, easily accessible and easy to understand, and that clear and plain language and, additionally, where appropriate, visualisation be used." A range of information may fall under this provision including: algorithmic models; datasets; personal data disclosed by the user; previous data about the user held by the organisation; official data sources (e.g. electoral roll; anti-money laundering and fraud detection lists; land registry; births, deaths, and marriages registry); and regulated-industry data sources (e.g. banking; credit reference agencies; insurance; healthcare). Including the algorithmic model upon which the automatic decision-making is based would allow users to challenge the rules that are being applied to assess and reach a decision. Whether or not it is appropriate and necessary to disclose the algorithmic model, their complexity should not be used as an excuse to avoid providing meaningful information. Recital 58 of the GDPR states that the principle of transparency is of "particular relevance in situations where the proliferation of actors and the technological complexity of practice make it difficult for the data subject to know and understand whether, by whom and for what purpose personal data relating to him or her are being collected, such as in the case of online advertising." All other types of information would allow the user to contest the accuracy of the data being used [21].

Article 9(1)(c) of Convention 108+ is similar in providing for a right to obtain, on request, knowledge of the reasoning underlying data processing where the results of such processing are applied to the data subject. This includes knowing the reasoning underlying the processing of data, and the consequences of such a reasoning, which led to any resulting conclusions (e.g. logic of an algorithmic credit scoring system that leads to acceptance or rejection of an application). This right is especially relevant in the context of exercising the right to object and the right to complain under Articles 9 (1)(d) and (f). Article 9(1)(d) contains the right to object at any time to the processing of personal data, unless the data controller demonstrates legitimate grounds for such processing which override the data subject's interests or rights and fundamental freedoms. The right to complain is of relevance at the post-use stage. Although Article 21 of the GDPR provides for a right to object to processing of personal data at any time, some consider this separate and inapplicable to automated decision-making under Article 22 due to the contract and consent exceptions [22]. But such an interpretation would defeat the essence of human agency by not recognising personal autonomy in the decision as to whether to engage with an A/IS. It is also an unrealistic representation of pre-use stage user experience and reactions, and fails to take account of Article 21(5) allowing users to exercise their right to object by automated means.

Right to Meaningful Information About the Significance and the Envisaged Consequences of Automated Decision-Making Processing. The reference in Articles 13(2)(f), 14(2)(g), 15(1)(h) of the GDPR to users having the right to "meaningful information about … the significance and the envisaged consequences of such processing" is a much broader right of explanation which has been interpreted to mean "information must be provided about intended or future processing, and how the automated decision-making might affect the data subject. In order to make this information meaningful and understandable, real, tangible examples of the type of possible effects should be given." [23] Automated decision-making processing that produces legal effects or similarly significantly affects on the data subject falls under this category of A/IS user right to information and disclosure. Overall, this right may require information on the processing system itself, the processing that led to the decision, and the possible consequences to the user. An example of how this right could be operationalised at the pre-use stage is an illustrative, interactive web-based comparator model allowing the user to input varying data to produce different results (e.g. car, home, health insurance premiums based on certain risk factors such as age, dangerous driving habits, year property built, underlying health issues).

Opt Out. Potential A/IS users, who at the pre-use stage identify that the A/IS will be in full or partial operation and do not want to interact with the A/IS, must have the option to opt out of use and for an alternative method of use to be made available. An example where this may be necessary is eligibility assessments and approval decisions for financial products such as mortgages and medical insurance, where the user's particular circumstances and personal details require careful human consideration and evaluation rather than being subjected to algorithmic decision-making. The A/IS must be able to demonstrate the availability of an opt out and alternative methods of use. The opt out may also need to be extended to during-use stage. If through use of the A/IS there is user profiling, this must be clear at the pre-use stage and an opt out for profiling provided. Opting out and using an alternative method should not place the user at a disadvantage in terms of service and user experience. For example, a medical centre deploying an A/IS appointments booking system should ensure that patients who are unable to access the A/IS or do not wish to do so are not placed at a disadvantage in terms of accessing and booking appointments. This may require setting periods of time for human operator availability to deal with telephone or face-to-face bookings, and advertising these times of availability to patients. Another area of concern is potential loss of business for businesses that opt out of using an A/IS appointments booking system, although this may be considered a choice and risk assumed by the business.

3 During-Use Stage

During A/IS use if there is a part of the A/IS operation which involves a "black box" scenario, that is, it is difficult for a human to discern what the system is doing and why, then appropriate risk-based parameters need to be set for the systems use (see Table 2).

Table 2. During-use stage rights

Right	GDPR provision	Convention 108+ provision
To object to processing of data	Article 21	Article 9(1)(d)
To lawful, fair, and transparent processing of data	Articles 5(1)(a) and 6	Article 5(2), (3), (4)
To rectification of inaccurate data	Article 16	Article 9(1)(e)
To withdraw consent	Article 7(3)	Article 5(2)

As already mentioned under pre-use stage, Article 9(1)(d) of Convention 108+ allows the data subject to object at any time to the processing of personal data, including during-use stage. A similar provision exists under Article 21 of the GDPR. However, if consent has already been given for data processing then withdrawal of consent rather than objection to data processing would be most appropriate at the during-use stage [24]. There is a right to lawful, fair, and transparent processing of personal data under Articles 5(1)(a) of the GDPR and Articles 5(2)–(4) of Convention 108+. Article 6(1)(a)–(f) of the GDPR sets out conditions which will make the processing lawful (e.g. data subject's consent; necessary for performance of a contract; compliance with legal obligations; necessary to protect data subject's or another natural person's vital interests; necessary for performance of a public interest task; necessary for pursuing legitimate interests of data controller or third party). During A/IS operation the user may become aware of inaccuracy in the data held or used in relation to them, in which case they must be able to seek rectification of the inaccuracy or error. Article 16 of the GDPR provides the data subject with the right to obtain from the data controller, without undue delay, the rectification of inaccurate personal data, including having incomplete personal data completed. Article 9(1)(e) of Convention 108+ provides for the data subject's right to obtain, on request, free of charge and without excessive delay, rectification or erasure of such data if these *are being* processed contrary to the Convention.

Withdrawal of consent can occur at any time including during-use stage, and Article 7(3) of the GDPR provides a specific right to the data subject to withdraw consent at any time. Although Convention 108+ does not refer to a specific right to withdraw consent, under Article 5(2) it establishes two prerequisites in order to make data processing lawful: either there is consent by the data subject, or there is provision in law for such data processing. As a result, if the data subject consents to data processing they may also withdraw such consent at any time [25]. Whether withdrawing consent under the GDPR or Convention 108+, the lawfulness of data processed prior to the withdrawal will not be affected but continuation of data processing will not be allowed, unless justifiable for some other purpose provided under EU law or EU Member State law, or national law. The key difference between the two instruments is that the GDPR requires a pre-use stage notification to the data subject of their right to withdraw consent.

4   Post-use Stage

Post-use requires users to be aware of how their data and information shared with the A/IS will be used by the system and any third parties, as well as providing redress mechanisms for errors and harm caused. (see Table 3).

Table 3. Post-use stage rights

Right	GDPR provision	Convention 108+ provision
To rectification of inaccurate data	Article 16	Article 9(1)(e)
To an explanation of automated decision	Recital 71	
To obtain human intervention	Article 22(3)	
To express a point of view	Article 22(3)	Article 9(1)(a)
To contest the automated decision	Article 22(3)	Article 9(1)(f)

As with during-use stage, an A/IS user may become aware post-use that there are inaccuracies or errors in the data used in relation to them perhaps leading to an unfair, unlawful, or unreasonable decision. Article 16 of the GDPR provides the data subject with the right to obtain from the data controller, without undue delay, the rectification of inaccurate personal data, including having incomplete personal data completed. Article 9(1)(e) of Convention 108+ provides for the data subject's right to obtain, on request, free of charge and without excessive delay, rectification or erasure of such data if these *have been* processed contrary to the Convention.

A/IS users must have means to contest, challenge, or dispute an A/IS decision or any aspect of interaction with the A/IS. The means of contestation, challenge, or dispute should be readily available and provide a clear complaints procedure that provides all relevant information to a human complaint handler. Recital 71 of the GDPR refers to the right to obtain an explanation of the decision reached after an automated decision-making assessment, and the right to challenge the decision. In the case of contract or consent exceptions to the right not to be subject to automated decision-making, Article 22(3) of the GDPR recognises as minimum safeguards the data subject's rights to obtain human intervention, to express their point of view, and to contest the automated decision. In the context of A/IS users, the right to obtain human intervention can be interpreted as applying at the pre-use and during-use stages (e.g. provision of alternative method of interaction; access to human agent to query or rectify an operational issue). Similar provisions exist under Convention 108+. Article 9(1)(a) contains the right of the data subject to express their view in relation automated decision-making. Article 9(1)(f) provides the right to a remedy where the data subject's rights under the Convention have been violated.

5   Conclusion

It is clear from the GDPR and Convention 108+ provisions that emphasis is on a HCA closely aligned with a TBA that promotes ethical A/IS design, development, and deployment within definable and enforceable rights. Viewed from the perspective of user-system lifecycle stages, these rights can be operationalised and protected. Some differences exist between the GDPR and Convention 108+. At the pre-use stage, only the GDPR contains a user right to be notified prior to their consent that they have the right to withdraw consent at any time; only the GDPR contains a right to information on the significance and envisaged consequences of automated decision-making processing. Regarding the right to object to processing of data, both the GDPR and Convention 108+ contain provisions, although there is some debate as to whether Article 21 of the GDPR applies to automated decision-making. At the during-use stage, the same issue regarding the right to object exists. At the post-use stage, only the GDPR provides for a right to explanation, and a right to obtain human intervention. These differences require further analysis to determine whether they result in material impact on the existence or effect of rights.

References

1. Respect for human autonomy is one of four ethical principles established under the EU AI Guidelines - *Ethics Guidelines for Trustworthy AI*, High-Level Expert Group on Artificial Intelligence (EU AI HLEG), European Commission. https://ec.europa.eu/futurium/en/ai-alliance-consultation/guidelines/2. Accessed 03 Feb 2020, p. 12; cf. Articles 32 (which implicitly predicates the security framework for data processing on guaranteeing the human dignity of natural persons), and 88(2) (which refers to safeguarding the data subject's human dignity in the processing of data for employment purposes) of the European Parliament and Council of the European Union, Regulation (EU) 2016/679 on the protection of natural persons with regard to the processing of personal data and on the free movement of such data, repealing Directive 95/46/EC (General Data Protection Regulation) (GDPR), (OJ L 119, 4.5.2016), 27 April 2016; Preamble of the Council of Europe Modernised Convention for the Protection of Individuals with Regard to Automatic Processing of Personal Data (ETS No. 108+), Amending Protocol to the Convention, adopted by the Committee of Ministers at its 128th Session in Elsinore on 18 May 2018 (Convention 108+) (which refers to securing human dignity and personal autonomy, and predicates the legal framework on safeguarding these)
2. Human agency and oversight represents a key requirement to implement the ethical principle of human autonomy under the EU AI HLEG, pp. 15–16; cf. Principle (d) of the 2019 Guiding Principles on Lethal Autonomous Weapons Systems by the UN Group of Governmental Experts on Lethal Autonomous Weapons Systems (UNGGE Principles). https://undocs.org/en/CCW/GGE.1/2019/3. Accessed 03 Feb 2020, which refers to "the operation of such systems within a responsible chain of human command and control"; Preamble of Convention 108+ (which refers to a person's right to control their personal data and the processing of it)
3. Privacy and data governance represents a key requirement to implement the ethical principle of prevention of harm under the EU AI HLEG, pp. 17; cf. Recital 116, Articles 1(2), 12–18, 20, 21, and 22 GDPR; Preamble and Article 1 of Convention 108+; Principles 1 and 3 of 2019 IEEE Ethically Aligned Design for Autonomous and Intelligent Systems - *The IEEE Global Initiative on Ethics of Autonomous and Intelligent Systems. Ethically Aligned Design: A Vision for Prioritizing Human Well-being with Autonomous and Intelligent Systems* (Final version, 4 April 2019) (IEEE EAD), pp. 19–20, 23–24. https://ethicsinaction.ieee.org. Accessed 03 Feb 2020; IEEE P7002, IEEE Standards Project for Data Privacy Process. https://standards.ieee.org/project/7002.html. Accessed 03 Feb 2020
4. Prevention of harm is the second ethical principle established under the EU AI HLEG, p. 12; generally expressed as violations of privacy and data protection rules under the GDPR; generally expressed as interference with the fundamental rights and freedoms of the individual under Convention 108+

5. Fairness is the third ethical principle established under the EU AI HLEG, p. 12; cf. Recitals 39, 60, and 71, Articles 5(1)(a), 13(2), and 14(2) GDPR; Articles 5(4)(a) and 8(1) of the Council of Europe Modernised Convention for the Protection of Individuals with Regard to Automatic Processing of Personal Data (ETS No. 108+), Amending Protocol to the Convention, adopted by the Committee of Ministers at its 128th Session in Elsinore on 18 May 2018 (Convention 108+)

6. Recitals 39, 58, 60, and 71, Articles 5(1)(a) and 12(1) GDPR; cf. Articles 5(4)(a), 8, and 9(b) Convention 108+; Principle 5 IEEE EAD, pp. 27–28; IEEE P7001, IEEE Standards Project for Transparency of Autonomous Systems. https://standards.ieee.org/project/7001.html. Accessed 03 Feb 2020

7. Explicability, as the fourth ethical principle established under the EU AI HLEG, p. 13, is closely associated with auditability particularly where it concerns "black box" scenarios; cf. GDPR transparency provisions, and safeguarding measures under Article 22; Article 9(1)(c) Convention 108+; generally considered under Principle 5 IEEE EAD

8. Accountability represents a key requirement to implement the ethical principle of fairness under the EU AI HLEG, pp. 19–20; cf Article 5(2) GDPR; Principle 6 IEEE EAD, pp. 29–30

9. Legal responsibility is subsumed in the accountability requirement under the EU AI HLEG, pp. 19–20; Recitals 74 and 79, Article 24 GDPR; Article 15(1) Convention 108+; Principle 6 IEEE EAD

10. 2018 UK House of Lords Select Committee AI Report - *AI in the UK: ready, willing and able?* (16 April 2018). https://publications.parliament.uk/pa/ld201719/ldselect/ldai/100/100. pdf. Accessed 03 Feb 2020; 2018 China's AI Standardisation White Paper - *China's White Paper on Artificial Intelligence Standardisation* (January 2018, Standards Administration of China) - 人工智能标准化白皮书 (白皮书) (2018年1月, 中国标准管理局); 2018 Canada's White Paper on Responsible AI in Government - *Responsible Artificial Intelligence in the Government of Canada* (Digital Disruption White Paper Series, Version 2.0, 2018-04-10); 2019 EU AI Guidelines - *Ethics Guidelines for Trustworthy AI*, High-Level Expert Group on Artificial Intelligence (AI HLEG), European Commission. https://ec.europa.eu/futurium/en/ai-alliance-consultation/guidelines/2. Accessed 03 Feb 2020; 2016 EU Study on Civil Law Rules in Robotics - *European Civil Law Rules in Robotics* (October 2016), PE 571.379. http://www.europarl.europa.eu/RegData/etudes/STUD/2016/571379/IPOL_STU(2016) 571379_EN.pdf. Accessed 03 Feb 2020; 2017 EU Parliament Resolution for further study on the implications of creating legal status for robots - *European Parliament resolution of 16 February 2017 with recommendations to the Commission on Civil Law Rules on Robotics* (2015/2103(INL)); 2019 IEEE Ethically Aligned Design for Autonomous and Intelligent Systems - *The IEEE Global Initiative on Ethics of Autonomous and Intelligent Systems. Ethically Aligned Design: A Vision for Prioritizing Human Well-being with Autonomous and Intelligent Systems* (Final version, 4 April 2019). https://ethicsinaction.ieee.org. Accessed 03 Feb 2020; 2019 Guiding Principles on Lethal Autonomous Weapons Systems by the UN Group of Governmental Experts on Lethal Autonomous Weapons Systems. https://undocs. org/en/CCW/GGE.1/2019/3. Accessed 03 Feb 2020

11. European Parliament and Council of the European Union, Regulation (EU) 2016/679 on the protection of natural persons with regard to the processing of personal data and on the free movement of such data, repealing Directive 95/46/EC (General Data Protection Regulation) (GDPR), (OJ L 119, 4.5.2016), 27 April 2016

12. Council of Europe Modernised Convention for the Protection of Individuals with Regard to Automatic Processing of Personal Data (ETS No. 108+), Amending Protocol to the Convention, adopted by the Committee of Ministers at its 128th Session in Elsinore on 18 May 2018 (Convention 108+)

13. Cf. Wachter, S., Mittelstadt, B., Floridi, L.: Why a right to explanation of automated decision-making does not exist in the General Data Protection Regulation. Int. Data Privacy Law 7(2), 78 (2017); Malgieri, G., Comandé, G.: Why a right to legibility of automated decision-making exists in the General Data Protection Regulation. Int. Data Privacy Law 7 (4), 265 (2017)

14. Under GDPR Article 4(4) "profiling" means "any form of automated processing of personal data consisting of the use of personal data to evaluate certain personal aspects relating to a natural person, in particular to analyse or predict aspects concerning that natural person's performance at work, economic situation, health, personal preferences, interests, reliability, behaviour, location or movements"

15. *Guidelines on Automated individual decision-making and Profiling for the purposes of Regulation 2016/679* ("WP Guidelines"). The WP Guidelines were endorsed by the European Data Protection Board in May 2018, p. 21. https://edpb.europa.eu/node/71. Accessed 31 Jan 2020

16. WP Guidelines, p. 21

17. GDPR Article 9(1)

18. GDPR Article 9(2)(a)

19. GDPR Article 9(2)(g)

20. Convention 108+ Convention for the protection of individuals with regard to the processing of personal data (Council of Europe, June 2018), Explanatory Report (Convention 108+ Explanatory Report), pp. 19–20. https://rm.coe.int/convention-108-convention-for-the-protection-of-individuals-with-regar/16808b36f1. Accessed 31 Jan 2020

21. See examples of practical application of these different interpretations to the information needed: *Automated decision-making on the basis of personal data that has been transferred from the EU to companies certified under the EU-U.S. Privacy Shield Fact-finding and assessment of safeguards provided by U.S. law* (European Commission Final Report, Directorate-General for Justice and Consumers, October 2018), pp. 45–47

22. WP Guidelines, pp. 34–35

23. WP Guidelines, p. 26

24. Convention 108+ Explanatory Report, p. 24

25. Convention 108+ Explanatory Report, p. 20

Supporting Metacognitive Learning Strategies Through an Adaptive Application

Rachel Van Campenhout[(✉)]

Duquesne University, Pittsburgh, PA 15282, USA
vancampenhoutr@duq.edu

Abstract. With constant technological advances, there are new and evolving methods for assisting learners master content. This paper conceptualizes how an adaptive application could deliver metacognitive prompts within an online learning environment to help learners achieve their goals, shift mindsets about learning, and develop motivation to learn. The nature of the adaptive application will be described and literature on the methods for delivery and metacognitive topics reviewed. Combining adaptive technology with metacognitive learning strategies could provide a level of learning support not yet realized in current online learning environments. This paper proposes that this style of prompt-based adaptive application delivering carefully crafted metacognitive prompts on goals, mindsets, and motivation could help foster better learning habits and outcomes.

Keywords: Adaptive learning · Metacognitive prompts · Goal setting · Mindset · Motivation

1 Introduction

Online or digital learning environments provide an opportunity for diverse learners to attempt to master content in countless domains for a variety of reasons. There are online learning environments to support children in primary and secondary school systems, post-secondary education seekers, professional development and training, language learners, and more. While the domains and learners in online learning environments are diverse and have equally diverse needs, there are metacognitive theories which could apply to learners universally. The goal of this paper is to explore possible methods of assisting learners through domain-independent metacognitive strategies, and identify the characteristics of an adaptive application which could be utilized to successfully deploy relevant assistance to the learner.

Each learner is unique in their goals, mindset, and motivation. Gathering information about the learner on each of these topics is critical to understanding the learner and providing further assistance. First, goal theory shows the impact of both purpose goals and target goals on an individual's engagement and success. Learners will have different purpose goals for why they are engaging in a particular learning activity, and these could influence not only their approach to learning, but reaction to intervention. In addition to purpose goals, target goals help learners to stay on track and set achievable milestones. Helping learners align purpose and target goals can make

R. A. Sottilare and J. Schwarz (Eds.): HCII 2020, LNCS 12214, pp. 218–227, 2020.
https://doi.org/10.1007/978-3-030-50788-6_16

learning and mastering content more attainable, improve self-efficacy, and increase persistence. Second, mindset is a well-researched topic with results showing that a learner's mindset can impact their learning outcomes, among other things. Whether it is labeled as growth mindset versus fixed mindset or incremental theory versus entity theory, research has shown that mindset has a large impact on learning. However, mindsets can also be changed. Interventions focused on reinforcement can shift mindsets toward more beneficial ones. These intervention techniques will be explored in relation to adaptive technology options. Third, motivation is another complex aspect which will differ greatly between learners, yet motivation is a key component of why people choose to do activities or learn new things. Some types of motivation are difficult to change because it is related to a person's natural interests. However, it is possible to cultivate a motivation to learn even when doing or learning something may not be particularly enjoyable. Explaining and encouraging motivation to learn has been shown to help increase learning outcomes.

In order for any interventions or treatment to be given to a learner, these characteristics would need to be identified first. This would be done through validated surveys which would assess where the learner falls on a scale or within categories. Adaptive technology could only be applied effectively with the proper understanding of the learner, as interventions and content should not be the same for different characteristics.

This paper will review recent adaptive environment research and approaches which have shown promising results for assisting learners, and research where prompts were utilized to deliver intervention to learners for metacognitive areas. Delivering metacognitive prompts or nudges adaptively could provide a way to deliver intervention techniques for all three learning metrics proposed in this paper. The nature of an adaptive system should be clearly identified based on need. First, the learning characteristics identified for each learner should be used to create a personalized strategy. Second, the learner's actions as they engage with the learning environment should be used to determine when to prompt the learner, and what prompt to deliver. Third, evaluations should be delivered again during the learning process to reassess goals, mindset, and motivation. If shifts begin to occur in these areas for a learner, the system will need to change the strategies selected for that learner.

2 The Nature of the Adaptive Application

2.1 The Learning Environment

The learning theories discussed in this paper would need to be delivered to the learner through a system, which I have conceptualized as an adaptive application. While this specific application does not exist, there are many online environments which fit the basic description for which I envision this application working with. The learning environment is a computer-based intelligent tutoring system (ITS). VanLehn (2011) found that the effect size of intelligent tutoring systems (0.76) were nearly as effective as human tutoring systems (0.79). In this analysis, VanLehn identifies human tutoring specifically as an adult subject matter expert working one-on-one with a student, and an intelligent tutoring system as one which provides students at minimum with practice at a step-based level, with targeted feedback. The learning environment would provide students with content to learn and step-based or substep-based practice and assessment through they prove mastery of that learning content. Practice with immediate targeted feedback would be a requirement for this learning environment, as the adaptive application would monitor student success or failure on practice as well as scored assessments. Other requirements of the learning environment would be a unique login for each student, and real-time data tracking which would feed the adaptive application important information about the learner as they engage with the content and learning environment.

2.2   The Adaptive Application

As Leutner (1995) describes, the system is considered adaptive if it is able to adjust on its own to changing variables or conditions, which is the goal of this application. Today there are a variety of different types of adaptive learning environments in use or in development. With no single standard for what adaptive means or how an environment or content adapts, it is still challenging to identify broad patterns of what is effective or successful in adaptive learning. One proposed adaptive learning environment was recently piloted based on inputs such as prior knowledge, working memory, and learning styles, and resulted in students in the adaptive environment producing better learning outcomes than those who were not (Siddique et al. 2019). Another recent study utilizing an adaptive platform at two different university in multiple disciplines found that the adaptive modality stabilizes learning organization (Dziuban et al. 2018). Early results are promising that adaptive environments will benefit learners. In a study which delivered adaptive remedial instruction for college students, results were mixed, however, researchers noted that time and system flaws could be major contributing factors, indicating how critical careful adaptive environment design is (Liu et al. 2017).

Working within an ITS-model learning environment, I envision an application which would gather information about the learner and adaptively deliver metacognitive support. The adaptive application would require a number of inputs in order to function. First, the application would need to gather information about the learner to generate a profile. Each learner is unique and will have different goals, mindsets, and motivations (each to be discussed in further detail below). The application would need to have the learner respond to validated surveys and questionnaires to determine their unique characteristics for these metacognitive and learning strategies. Only after knowing about the learner could the application make decisions as to what support to deliver.

The application would also require information from the learning environment itself. It would need to gather engagement data about the learner, such as how often and how long the learner logs in, reads/watches content, and completes activities. The application would need to deliver prompts based on what the learner does in the learning environment, in real time.

It is also important for the application to periodically reevaluate the learner. The goal for the application is to assist the learner in accomplishing their set goals, support or shift mindsets, and encourage motivation to learn. If the treatment of metacognitive prompts begins to change a learner's mindset, then the application would better support the learner by shifting the prompt strategy accordingly. Depending on how much content is in the learning environment or how quickly the learner is progressing, the application should reassess the learner at minimum of halfway through to determine if changes to that learner's profile have occurred. A reevaluation at the end of the learning experience should also be completed to determine if the treatment had an effect on mindset or motivation.

2.3 Metacognitive Prompts

The adaptive application's main tool is the delivery of prompts within the learning environment. One advantage to this method of delivery is that the content of the prompts is entirely independent of the content within the learning environment, and therefore would not be delivered in-line with the learning content. The content of the prompts would also be unique to each learner depending on their profile and engagement within the course, and delivered at different times. From a technical perspective it would be more logical to have prompts delivered as notifications within the learning environment.

In a computer-based environment for writing learning protocols, Schwonke et al. (2006) identified that delivering adaptive prompts based on prior assessment strategies were more effective for fostering declarative knowledge and deeper understanding than delivering random prompts, or no prompts at all. Their findings also show that students perceived the adaptive prompts to be considerably more helpful than those who received random prompts. These findings are encouraging for the adaptive application described here, which would deliver adaptive prompts after evaluating the learner, and would do so strategically, not randomly.

Other recent studies have seen promising results using metacognitive prompts, though not in the same adaptive capacity. Colthorpe et al. (2019) studied the ability of pharmacy students to self-regulate their learning. They found that higher achieving students use more self-reflective strategies than low achieving students, and that prompting students to engage in awareness of their own learning could increase learning outcomes. Sonnenberg and Bannert (2015) analyzed two groups of students, one with metacognitive prompt treatment and one without—and found that students who received metacognitive prompts had significantly higher metacognitive activities and higher transfer performance on the task.

There are mixed results in research as to the effectiveness of metacognitive prompts, and more research is needed to better identify types of prompts, frequency, and method for how to best utilize metacognitive prompts (Sonnenberg and Bannert 2015). However, as technologies in learning environments and delivery systems advance, I believe a more robust adaptive system could deliver metacognitive prompts more effectively to learners based on their unique needs.

3   Metacognitive Strategies for Improving Learning

The decision to focus on metacognition was primarily because these learning strategies are content independent; they can be applied to any subject, domain, or environment. The concepts of setting goals and understanding mindset and motivation apply to the learner, and not the content. This allows for improvements to be made in a learner's learning strategies without having to tailor subject matter content, which would be time consuming and costly. Assisting the learner in not just understanding their own mindset and motivation, but how they impact learning and can be changed is beneficial for that individual's long-term learning. Metacognitive strategies can be applied to many areas of learning and cognitive processes, so instructing a learner about their own metacognition can have an impact beyond even the learning process for a content domain.

3.1 Setting Goals

Goal Theory. People set goals routinely as part of everyday life. We set goals to exercise, to eat better, to save money, to travel more, to practice work-life balance. Entire industries market services or products as ways of helping people achieve their goals. Why? Setting goals is effective. Utilizing goal setting can be equally effective in an educational. Bandura (1986) shows the impact of setting goals and the qualities of goals can have on student effort and persistence. He also researched the implications goals and performance standards can have on mindset. Other researchers have set out to create a comprehensive categorization of various goals, such as Ford (1992) who created a taxonomy of 24 goal types. Every learner is complex in their goals and can have multiple goals at the same time. It would be challenging to identify all goals a learner has according to an extensive taxonomy such as Ford's, and less likely to determine actions in a learning environment to help learners with all of their goals.

For the purposes of supporting learners in an online environment, it may be more advantageous to limiting the scope of goal types to two tiers. Bandura described larger future goals as distal goals, which can be obtained through proximal subgoals. He suggested that when students set proximal subgoals to help achieve distal goals, they have increased persistence, self-efficacy, and higher intrinsic enjoyment of learning. In line with this concept, Harackiewicz and Elliot (1998) use the terminology purpose goals and target goals to describe a similar goal relationship. Purpose goals are they reason for doing something, and target goals are how to achieve it. Students who had target goals well aligned to purpose goals had higher intrinsic motivation and found accomplishing target goals increased feelings of competence and encouraged them to continue.

Goal Setting in an Adaptive Application. How can an application use goal setting in an adaptive way to help the learner? First the learner would set goals, identifying both purpose goals (why they are engaging in this learning activity) and target goals (how they plan to achieve their purpose goals). The application would guide learners to set specific target goals, including things like how often they plan on engaging with the content, how much practice they plan to do, and what their target scores would be. This information can then be used to personalize prompts to the learner based on their intended goals. If a learner indicated they hoped to study an hour four days a week, but are only studying for 15 min or once a week, the application could send nudges to remind the learner of their goals. The application would need to respond based on the goals the learner input and the actual engagement the learner has compared to those goals. This would create a unique delivery of prompts adapted to each learner.

In addition to setting purpose and target goals, identifying if a learner operates under performance goals, learning goals, or both could be useful. Those with performance goals seek to display ability, while those with learning goals seek to develop ability (Wentzel and Brophy 2014). Identifying a learner's performance and/or learning goal orientation could help identify if learners with one or both have better engagement and learning outcomes. The application could then provide adaptive prompts to learners based on these findings.

Goal setting can also be advantageous specifically for students with low motivation. Wentzel and Brophy (2014) suggests that goal statements should be phrased using learning accomplishments instead of tasks completed. Goals should be revisited after the tasks are completed and the learner should be asked to review their accomplishments. The application could not only deliver nudges based on the goals set by the learner, but ask the learner to evaluate their progress against them during and after engaging with the learning environment. Reminding learners of their goals and reviewing their effort against them is a metacognitive task in itself which encourages positive engagement behavior as well as self-efficacy.

3.2 Mindsets

Mindset Theories. Mindset is a critical component to learning and is another metacognitive strategy which is entirely independent of content. The power of mindset is engrained in us as a human condition. For example, the phrase "mind over matter" was first used by Sir Charles Lyell in 1863 to describe the importance of the human mind in evolution but is now a common phrase encouraging perseverance over obstacles and using your mind to solve problems. This mind over matter mantra is one I've even said to myself as a way of reminding myself I have the ability to accomplish the challenging task in front of me. Mindset is a powerful social and cultural concept because it—in fact—does make a difference and there is a large body of well-established research on the topic.

Arguably the most well-known mindset concept in recent years is that of growth mindset, pioneered by Carol Dweck (2006). Those with a growth mindset believe their abilities and intelligence can grow, while those with fixed mindset believe their abilities and intelligence are static. The concept of growth mindset is similarly described and studied by motivation theorists as entity theory (ability is a static entity and cannot be controlled) and incremental theory (ability can be changed incrementally with effort). Entity theorists tend to have performance goals rather than learning goals and develop helpless attitudes when confronted with challenges. When entity theorists fail, they often withdraw and seek to repair self-esteem. Incremental theorists set learning goals and persist in attaining them, and when confronted with failure seek to remediate deficiencies (Niiya et al. 2004; Nussbaum and Dweck 2008). Studies of students who are entity or incremental theorists over several years found that entity theorists showed drops in grade point averages and self-esteem, while incremental theorists maintained or increased in those areas (Blackwell et al. 2007; Robins and Pals 2002).

Mindset in an Adaptive Application. How can mindset theory be utilized within an adaptive application? Mindsets can be shifted. Dweck (2008) describes how entity theorists can shift to incremental mindsets through more extensive interventions. In one study, college students were given a treatment of watching a film about how the brain can grow and develop with challenges, and asked to write letters to younger students explaining this concept. At the end of the semester these students had a greater value of academics and a higher grade-point average compared to other college students (Aronson et al. 2002). In another study of elementary students, Blackwell et al. (2007) provided workshops on study skills and one group received lessons on how the brain is malleable and grows with learning activities, and these students put more effort into classroom learning and homework.

The first attempt to assist learners who identify as entity theorists would be to deliver information on these mindsets as treatment. The goal would be to replicate the research findings that informing learners about the brain and how they can expand abilities through effort would transition entity theorists to incremental theorists, and produce better learning outcomes and more beneficial self-attitudes. The second treatment the application could deliver are prompts supporting the shift to incremental mindset. These would require the application to respond to the work learners complete within the learning environment, delivering reinforcement of positive learning outcomes or encouragement after failures. The language used in these prompts should be carefully crafted to attribute success or failure to the effort put forth, and reminding learners that even failure provides a valuable learning opportunity to grow from. Wentzel and Brophy (2014) notes that a learner's effort and persistence are greater when success or failure is attributed to internal causes, and the best motivational patterns are established when students believe success is attributed to their own reasonable effort and sufficient ability.

3.3   Motivation to Learn

Motivation Theory. Motivation is a broad concept with many different theories, models, hierarchies etc. developed in its name. While all may have merits for study, it is necessary to reduce the scope of motivation used here to that which can be impacted within the confines of an adaptive application utilized in an online learning environment. To that end, the focus will be on what is termed *motivation to learn*. Wentzel and Brophy (2014) describes this as follows: "Motivation to learn refers to a student's propensity to value learning activities: to find them meaningful and worthwhile, and to try to get the intended benefits from them. In contrast to intrinsic motivation, which is primarily an affective response to an activity, motivation to learn is primarily a cognitive response involving attempts to make sense of the activity, understand the knowledge that it develops, and master the skills that it promotes." While it is unlikely that a treatment delivered via the adaptive application can change a learner's intrinsic motivations, it is possible to encourage motivation to learn by helping to place value on the learning activity in service of the learner's purpose goals.

Motivation in an Adaptive Application. The adaptive application could support motivation to learn by delivering prompts which enforce the concept that the learning activities themselves are worthwhile. These prompts can ask learners to reflect on what knowledge or skills they are developing, how the activity fits into their larger learning process, and what benefits they are getting from their engagement with the learning environment. Motivation to learn also benefits from goal setting and mindsets. Considering purpose goals and creating target goals to achieve them helps develop motivation to learn. If a learner is prompted to relate the learning activity to their own purpose goals, they could begin to see the value in the activity as a learning tool. Similarly, having or developing an incremental theory mindset encourages learners to appreciate the process of learning, which supports motivation to learn. The benefit of these metacognitive strategies is that they can produce a symbiotic relationship.

4 Summary

The adaptive application conceptualized in this paper is a combination of a particular technical system and thoughtful metacognitive content pulled from an established body of research. The application requires a learning environment designed as an intelligent tutoring system, with a combination of learning content, practice opportunities, and assessment of some type. This learning environment also must be able to feed the application data as the learner engages with it.

The application itself would engage the learner in stages. The first stage would gather information on the learner's goals, mindset, and motivation through validated surveys and questionnaires. This data would generate a unique profile for each learner. The application would base all decisions of which content and prompts to deliver to the learner based on their profile. The second stage would be to deliver information based on this profile to prime the metacognitive prompts to come during the learning process. This content would be tailored to the learner to either confirm positive goals or mindsets the learner already has, or to inform the learner about more beneficial goals or mindsets. It is important to be transparent with the learner, including providing evidence from relevant research in clear language. The third stage is the adaptive delivery of the metacognitive prompts. This requires the application to consider both the learner's profile as well as their real-time engagement within the learning environment. Prompts would need to be carefully worded for each possible metacognitive classification. This would include content-only prompts to reinforce or encourage behaviors or mindsets as well as interactive prompts to have the learner evaluate their own learning. The delivery of prompts should adapt to real-time data as the learner is working in the learning environment in order to deliver the correct type of prompt at the ideal time. The fourth stage is the reevaluation of the learner. This should be done during the learning process to monitor for shifts in the learner's mindset and motivation as they are actively working as well as at the end of the learner's path in the learning environment. This reevaluation would indicate if the treatment of the prompts was successful in helping the learner change their strategies or mindsets.

The combination of metacognitive learning strategies utilized in this adaptive application could have advantages and disadvantages in the analysis. With multiple treatments being delivered for different strategies (goals, mindsets, motivation), how would we determine which were effective? With a large enough sample it might be possible to group learners according to similar states and therefore compare categories. This may prove difficult due to the number of different combination of states in the learner's profile. However, this combination of treatments is still worthwhile. One single strategy may only have a small effect on learning outcomes. This approach provides a more comprehensive strategy, which may yield better results.

Success for this application could come from comparing learning outcomes from a control and experimental group. If one group of students were to work through the learning environment without the adaptive application and one group used the learning environment with the application, learning outcomes could be compared to evaluate the effectiveness of the adaptive component. Another measure of success would be if learners indicated changes in mindset or motivation at the end of their engagement with the adaptive application. Helping the learner to adopt more beneficial learning practices would be an accomplishment itself.

References

Aronson, J., Fried, C., Good, C.: Reducing the effects of stereotype threat on African American college students by shaping theories of intelligence. J. Exp. Soc. Psychol. **38**, 113–125 (2002)

Bandura, A.: Social Foundations of Thought and Action: A Social Cognitive Theory. Prentice-Hall, Englewood Cliffs (1986)

Blackwell, L., Trzesniewski, K., Dweck, C.: Implicit theories of intelligence predict achievement across an adolescent transition: a longitudinal study and an intervention. Child Dev. **78**, 246–263 (2007)

Colthorpe, K., Ogiji, J., Ainscough, L., Zimbardi, K., Anderson, S.: Effect of metacognitive prompts on undergraduate pharmacy students' self-regulated learning behavior. Am. J. Pharm. Educ. **83**(4), 526–536 (2019)

Dweck, C.: Mindset: The New Psychology of Success. Random House, New York (2006)

Dweck, C.: Can personality be changed? The role of beliefs in personality and change. Curr. Dir. Psychol. Sci. **17**, 391–394 (2008)

Dziuban, C., Moskal, P., Parker, L., Campbell, M., Howlin, C., Johnson, C.: Adaptive learning: a stabilizing influence across disciplines and universities. Online Learn. **22**(3), 7–39 (2018)

Ford, M.: Motivating Humans: Goals, Emotions, and Personal Agency Beliefs. Sage, Newbury Park (1992)

Harackiewicz, J., Elliot, A.: The joint effects of target and purpose goals on intrinsic motivation: a mediational analysis. Pers. Soc. Psychol. **24**, 675–689 (1998)

Leutner, D.: Adaptivität und Adaptierbarkeit multimedialer Lehr- und Informationssysteme [Adaptation and Adaptability in multimedia teaching systems and multimedia information systems]. In: Issing, L. (ed.) Information und Lernen mit Multimedia, pp. 139–149. Psychologie Verlags Union, Weinheim, Germany (1995)

Liu, M., McKelroy, E., Corliss, S., Carrigan, J.: Investigating the effect of an adaptive learning intervention on students' learning. Educ. Technol. Res. Dev. **65**(6), 1605–1625 (2017). https://doi-org.authenticate.library.duq.edu/10.1007/s11423-017-9542-1

Nussbaum, A.D., Dweck, C.: Defensiveness versus remediation: Self-theories and modes of self-esteem maintenance. Pers. Soc. Psychol. Bull. **34**, 599–612 (2008)

Niiya, Y., Crocker, J., Bartmess, E.: From vulnerability to resilience: learning orientations buffer contingent self-esteem from failure. Psychol. Sci. **15**, 801–805 (2004)

Robins, R., Pals, J.: Implicit self-theories in the academic domain: Implications for goal orientation, attributions, affect, and self-esteem change. Self Identity **1**, 313–336 (2002)

Schwonke, R., Hauser, S., Nückles, M., Renkl, A.: Enhancing computer-supported writing of learning protocols by adaptive prompts. Comput. Hum. Behav. **22**, 77–92 (2006)

Siddique, A., Durrani, Q.S., Naqvi, H.A.: Developing adaptive e-learning environment using cognitive and noncognitive parameters. J. Educ. Comput. Res. **57**(4), 811–845 (2019)

Sonnenberg, C., Bannert, M.: Discovering the effects of metacognitive prompts on the sequential Structure of SRL-processes using process mining techniques. J. Learn. Anal. **2**(1), 72–100 (2015)

Sonnenberg, C., Bannert, M.: Evaluating the impact of instructional support using data mining and process mining: a micro-level analysis of the effectiveness of metacognitive prompts. JEDM| J. Educ. Data Mining **8**(2), 51–83 (2016)

VanLehn, K.: The relative effectiveness of human tutoring, intelligent tutoring systems, and other tutoring systems. Educ. Psychol. **46**(4), 197–221 (2011)

Wentzel, K.R., Brophy, R.E.: Motivating Students to Learn. Routledge, New York (2014)

Towards Iteration by Design: An Interaction Design Concept for Safety Critical Systems

Thomas E. F. Witte[1]([⊠])(ID), Jonas Hasbach[1], Jessica Schwarz[1], and Verena Nitsch[2]

[1] Fraunhofer FKIE, Fraunhoferstr. 20, 53343 Wachtberg, Germany
{thomas.witte, jonas.hasbach,
jessica.schwarz}@fkie.fraunhofer.de
[2] RWTH Aachen University, Eilfschornsteinstr. 18, 52062 Aachen, Germany
v.nitsch@iaw.rwth-aachen.de

Abstract. Requirements of human-machine systems change over long product lifecycles. Anticipating those changes during the initial design is challenging. Once deployed the changing requirements demands a systematic evaluation of the human-machine system, otherwise inefficiencies and accidents can happen. The interaction design concept *Iteration by Design* introduces a fifth design phase to the user-centred design process of the ISO 9241-210 norm to close the open evaluation loop of safety critical systems with long lifecycles. The implications of *Iteration by Design* are discussed in the context of resilience engineering. A higher order adaptation regulation loop copes with the complexity of the human-machine system interaction design. The resilience principles *drift reaction* and *human in the loop* are utilized to adapt the system to the changing requirements. A design assistance system is proposed to inform a design team about required changes. Finally, adaptive instructional training could be interwoven with the design assistance system to sustain the adaptability of the human-machine system. The value of *Iteration by Design* as an extension for user-centred design is illustrated by the accident of the USS John S. McCain from 2017.

Keywords: *Iteration by Design* · Resilience engineering · Human centered design · Control room design · Console design · Adaptive instructional system

1 Introduction

In 2017, the US Navy destroyer USS John S. McCain had a collision with the tanker Alnic MC, which caused 58 casualties, with ten dead and 48 injured sailors [1]. The costs of damage were estimated to be more than $100 million. In short, the crew of the USS John S. McCain perceived a loss of control of steering, while trying to transfer the control of thrust to another control console. This happened on a highly frequented waterway where consequently the USS John S. McCain crossed the pathway of the Alnic MC, which hit the destroyer with its bulbous bow on the port side. According to the findings of the accident report of the US National Transportation Board (NTSB), there were no technical failures involved in the accident, nor weather conditions.

© Springer Nature Switzerland AG 2020
R. A. Sottilare and J. Schwarz (Eds.): HCII 2020, LNCS 12214, pp. 228–241, 2020.
https://doi.org/10.1007/978-3-030-50788-6_17

Multiple aspects of training, human-system interaction design and operational procedures resulted in the accident [1].

The accident highlights challenges that human factors engineers are confronted with during the design phases of a human-machine system. The incident of the USS John S. McCain provoked discussions on the introduction of interaction devices like touch screens to safety critical areas and the accompanied risks that will be discussed in the following. Bringing in novel technology for human-system interaction, like gesture- or speech-controlled interfaces, can make the design process complex. As a consequence of the accident, the safety of using touchscreens for control consoles on ships was put into question. The U.S. Naval Institute reports that the US Navy will replace the touchscreens with physical throttles on Arleigh Burke class destroyers, a ship class that is in commission since 1991 [2]. Further, the release of assistance systems and artificial intelligence from laboratories into the wild raises the need for multi-agent interaction concepts as well as multi-agent learning [3]. Also, the on-going development of process automation leads to challenges, e.g. those described by Bainbridge's "ironies of automation" [4].

Besides, the demands for interaction design that arise due to scientific and technological developments requirements for a human-machine system can change during the lifecycle. A shift of the context that the system operates in, or an unexpected variation of mission tasks that the system should carry out, can lead to an operation of the system outside of its planned boundaries [5]. For example, the John S McCain's steering system was put into the backup mode, because the crew preferred more control of the ship without the assistance systems. The backup mode was not designed for normal operational use and was therefore in use outside of the planned boundaries of the system. The design of consoles in control rooms should anticipate those changing requirements. In consequence, a human-machine system design that incorporates changes of the design during the lifecycle systematically from the beginning could have ergonomic and safety benefits in comparison to designs that do not, because of a higher resilience [6].

There are three main areas for designers to cope with complexity of human-machine systems: design (e.g. design standards), training (including operational procedures) and automation [7]. Design standards like ISO 11064-1 (ergonomic design of control centers [8]) and ISO 9241-210 (ergonomics of human-system interaction [9]) describe formal phases for the design of human-machine systems. They are providing a framework of factors that could influence the requirements of human-machine systems. Following these standards, mitigates the complexity of the design process. In addition, systematic training of operators of technical systems can lower the likelihood of the occurrence of unforeseen behavior and thereby the likelihood of the occurrence of accidents like the one described above. Also, operational procedures should prevent the use of the system outside of its planned boundaries. Finally yet importantly, automation is often considered for human error prevention. Despite the obvious usefulness and function of norms, training and the introduction of operational procedures, the NTSB has to recommend the revision of training, the incorporation of standards and norms and the reestablishment of operational procedures as safety recommendations to the US Navy [1].

One key principle proposed by the standards is to use iteration. With iteration, the designer can use evolutionary steps to feedback information from different phases and from operational use of the system. *Design by iteration*, is a well-established principle in the human factors domain [9]. We propose to establish *Iteration by Design* for future control rooms and console developments. It extents the common use of iteration, by integrating information gathering, and retrieval for the next iteration into the interaction design of the human–machine system. By evaluating the system systematically during the lifecycle, the chances of preventing accidents like the one of the USS John S. McCain could be higher. In the context of introducing the interaction concept, the usefulness of a design assistance system will be discussed.

2   Towards a Holistic Interaction-Design for Consoles in Safety Critical Areas

To understand the heritage of the proposed extension of iterative interaction design, a short overview of design approaches will be provided in the following. After that, common challenges of described design approached are discussed and highlighted by implications of the accident of the USS John S. McCain.

2.1   A Short History of Control Room and Console Interaction Design

Kontogiannis and Hollnagel [10] describe three main approaches used to design and evaluate human-machine system interactions in the context of control rooms. First, the technology-driven approach was established where "the design was approached from a strictly engineering point of view while human factors considerations were left for the final stage to overcome certain design problems" [6, p. 5]. According to Kontogiannis and Hollnagel, the approach can lead to disadvantages like difficulties to modify the design at a late design stage, low acceptance by users, and challenges in the creation of effective training programs [11, 12].

A second approach is classical ergonomics, which was predominant up to the 1970 s. "Generally speaking the solution advocated by classical ergonomics was to match carefully the interface to known human capacities and limitations" [7, p. 6], especially in the areas of anthropomorphology and biomechanics. The designers attempt to address the limitations by matching the capacity of the technical and the human information processing system and physiological demands. Kontogiannis and Hollnagel conclude that the knowledge and methods of this approach have become widely used, however with the ongoing development of artificial intelligence and automation, technical systems become more and more agents that humans cooperate with, in contrast to a tool that humans use.

From the 1980s onwards, cognitive ergonomics came into focus as a third approach. An example of this approach is cognitive systems engineering. Hollnagel & Woods [13] proposed the joint cognitive systems paradigm. The human operator often lacks complete knowledge of the functions, model and control possibilities of cognitive agents and vice versa. Those agents have their own goals, model of the system and the environment they are a part of, and functions to control the overall human-machine system and/or its environment. Key element of the joint cognitive systems paradigm is to design the interaction of those entities, with a focus on allocation of control, information and goal sharing [10]. An example of an artificial intelligence based agent would be an assistance system on board of a ship to locate and identify radar contacts for a safe navigation.

Two major frameworks for human-systems engineering evolved from the described approaches: (a) system-centred research and development [14], and (b) user-centred research and development [15]. For the purpose of introducing *Iteration by Design,* the concept will be described in the context of user-centred design by integrating principles of resilience engineering. Thereby, a system-centred view will be used to extend user-centred research and development.

2.2 The Open Evaluation Loop of Design by Iteration

User-centred design, described by the ISO norm 9241-210 [9], has four iteratively connected phases (Fig. 1). The stakeholder-centred context and task analysis for a human-machine system leads to system requirements. The designer then tries to match design solutions with the requirements in the design phase. The design solutions will then be evaluated in order to check whether the requirements are met. Once they are met, the design solution will be deployed. This framework can be described as *Design by Iteration*, because the iterative steps lead to a final design.

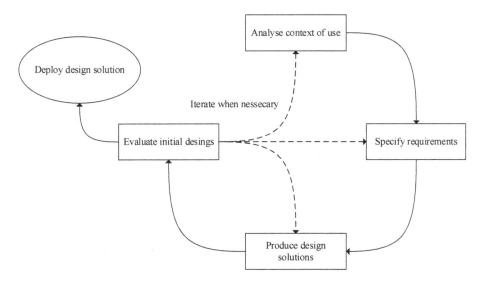

Fig. 1. User-centered design according to ISO 9241-210 [9].

A designer has to predict the use of the system, and variation in human and system performance that can lead to performance issues or catastrophic events, and the implications of the introduction of new technology [16]. Once in operational use, a human-machine system like a console for a frigate often evolves without further systematically following a design framework by designers. Ivergard and Hunt report that "several anecdotes from the maritime domain describe how the placement of a piece of equipment is decided not by standards, rules, or human-factor guidelines but by the length of electric cable available of the installer when needed" [13, p. 231]. Further they report that "it is common that when new equipment is installed, in many cases the older equipment is left where it is" [13, p. 231]. According to Ivergard and Hunt, the described evolution of control rooms during their lifecycle, leads to issues such as "cluttered and non-optimal layout, this also entails extra work, such as finding, choosing, and evaluating which equipment to use." [13, p. 231]. So, while development is common in iterative steps initially, once deployed the next major design overhaul will most likely come with a new project incorporating new technology several years later, especially in safety critical domains, as is demonstrated in Fig. 2. The design team of the frigate class F122 of the German navy had to try to anticipate the use of the system for a lifespan of over 40 years.

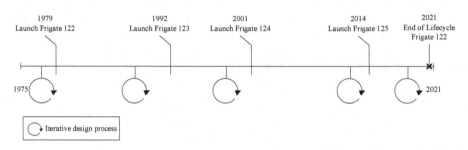

Fig. 2. Simplified overview of design phases for German navy frigates.

An approach to compensate the fragmented design is to standardize systems like control room consoles on a ship, that have a similar purpose. An advantage of a standardized approach is that the consoles can still be fitted to the specific requirements, but have common roots of the design for safety and quality purposes (see Fig. 3). However, the approach cannot encounter the issue of changing requirements during the lifecycle of a specific human-machine system.

In consequence, there is an open evaluation loop with the principle *Design by Iteration* after deployment. Evaluative information from the initial design phase are often not used or relayed for the evolution of the human-machine system during the lifecycle. One consequence among others of the open evaluation loop is a fragmented console and control room design for the different evolutionary design steps of the system.

Controlling the complex design process with an open evaluation loop leads to interaction design challenges, that are further described in the next section.

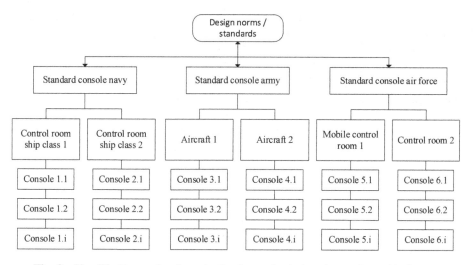

Fig. 3. Simplified example of standardized console designs in a safety critical area.

2.3 Challenges of Interaction Design for Consoles in Safety Critical Areas

One of the main challenges of interaction design in safety critical areas is that different aspects of the interaction design change with a different pace and sometimes in an unexpected way. This is illustrated with the following example. It can be assumed that a ship with a lifecycle of 40 years is in development. Gesture-based interaction is starting to be used in consumer products such as cars. Operators are asking for the new technology, because they think it could be useful. The designer decides to integrate it in the new interaction concept, because it is a user requirement. Gesture technology for ships is not yet fully incorporated into standards and norms, and the interaction effects of the introduction of the technology in multimodal interaction concepts are not sufficiently explored. The designer has to decide to design a console that uses a risky new technology, but is prepared if the technology becomes standard in the next decades; or, to introduce an interaction concept that could be already out of date when it is in operation, but a less risky choice. In this example, as is often the case, the interaction technology progressed faster than the norms and standards. Extrapolating research and norms for a specific system that is in development is time-consuming and sometimes not possible. In conclusion, norms and standards need to be specific for different domains, updated regularly, yet usable for design teams with constraints like time, and human resources, among others [10, 15]. A design assistance system for the design phases could support the design team and mitigate the challenge.

Another challenge is that the requirements of systems can change over a period of several decades as described above. An interaction concept may be suitable for the requirements that are anticipated at present, but may be problematic for requirements that the system has to fulfill in 20 years.

Also, it is demanding that the soft- and hardware architectures of the interaction concept need to be flexible enough to make changes during the lifecycle. With a static console concept, the only option for a major design change is to replace the console with a new one or to place another purpose build console into the control room, which leads to clutter and a fragmented interaction concept.

Individual differences of operators could also lead to challenges [18, 19]. Operators with a high affinity for new technology could be capable of using a specific technology safely; however, other operators could have misconceptions of the technology that could lead to inefficiencies. Operators that use the system twenty years after system launch could also be less familiar with the used technology because it is outdated. To compensate, ongoing training data could be used to prevent a training-technology gap.

Requirements for the next evolution of interaction design concepts coming from the challenges and observations described above are:

(a) Norms and tools for interaction design should be usable to overcome constraints of the designer and the design system.
(b) Norms and tools for interaction design should be dynamic to accommodate the different pace of the development of technology, science, and changing requirements of a specific system [10].
(c) The interaction concept should not only be iteratively developed during the design phase but also systematically during the lifecycle of the system.
(d) Training, the human machine system and operational procedures should adapt to the changing requirements and the changing human-machine system to prevent a training-technology gap.

In the following, the findings of the John S. McCain's accident will be used to illustrate the implications of the aforementioned requirements for a next evolutionary step in interaction design.

2.4   Implications of the USS John S. McCain Accident

Aspects of training, operational procedures and interaction design played a role in the accident according to the findings of the NTSB (see Table 1). Findings one to three are examples of shifted or initially hidden requirements for the system. The crew members did not use the recommended mode that was designed for the situation. They used the backup mode because they wanted more control of the system. The information about that need was not used as feedback to initiate a redesign of the system. As a quick solution, the operators circumvented the assistance system by using the backup mode. The design team did not develop the backup mode for that use. The crewmembers changed the use of the system in a way that the designer did not anticipate [20]. A systematic feedback loop of operational data during the lifecycle of the ship could have led to an iteration of the system where the crewmembers have more control of the system or a better understanding of the functions of the system through training.

Findings four, five, six, and eight demonstrate the interaction of an operator's false mental model of the systems functionality with usability issues of the interaction design. For a design team it is complex to predict these interaction effects. Data of the use of the system could have given information to change the design after the initial launch, likely before the accident. This data could have shown that the ship was navigated in backup mode for uncommonly long periods of time.

Nine of the eleven findings have aspects of training. The NTSB is recommending to "revise the training standards for helmsman, lee helmsman, and boatswain's mate [...] to require demonstrated proficiency in all system functions" [1, p. 40]. In conclusion, operational data can also be valuable for training design to increase the safety of the system by closing training-technology gaps caused by changing or hidden requirements. Therefore, training and operative information should be systematically interwoven to recognize a training-operation gap.

Accidents like the one of the John S. McCain are showing that there could be a need for computer aided assistance systems for the design process. An assistance system could support the human-systems designer to make informed decisions in a complex design process.

Table 1. Summarized findings of John S. McCain's accident report [1].

Finding	Area of interest
1. The control of steering was shifted to another console without notice of the crewmembers	Training, interaction design, situational awareness
2. The unintentional shift of control lead to a perceived loss of control of the ships steering system	Training, interaction design, situational awareness, operational procedures
3. The Crew of USS John S McCain used the backup manual mode for normal operation, because of higher perceived control of the ship compared to the use of assisting systems	Training, interaction design, mental models, situational awareness
4. The crewmembers had false knowledge of the function of the emergency-override-to-manual button of the console. Correct use could have prevented the accident	Training, interaction design, mental models
5. The two propeller were not ganged (connected control for the propeller) when the helmsman followed an order to slow down the ship, which increased unintentionally the turn of the ship	Training, interaction design
6. An input to turn to port to try to regain control of the steering system caused in combination with the unganged propellers the turn of the ship	Training, interaction design
7. There was no high frequency radio announcement to other vessels in the area	Emergency training
8. The interaction design of the touch screen "increased the likelihood of the operator errors that led to the collision" [1, p. 38]	Interaction design
9. The training of the crewmember of the John S McCain were insufficient to perform basic tasks	Training
10. The ships manual was not complete, important functions were not laid out	Manual
11. "The Navy failed to provide effective oversight of the John S Mc Cain in the areas of bridge operating procedures, crew training, and fatigue mitigation." [1, p. 38]	Training, operational procedures, fatigue mitigation

3   Introducing Iteration by Design

Iteration by Design closes systematically the open evaluation loop of *Design by Iteration* through the introduction of a fifth design phase for the user-centered design framework (see Fig. 4). Woods and Hollnagel [16] propose to build a research base of fundamental principles for joint cognitive dynamics and highlight the need to observe the behavior of these systems in their work context. *Iteration by Design* applies this perspective by integrating designers in the lifecycle of human-machine systems as adaptation regulators in order to allow for iterative design shifts also after deployment. Anticipating that the requirements for a human-machine system will change during a long lifecycle and incorporating potential change of the system from the beginning of the design phases has multiple implications for the design process and the design of the human-machine system itself. Those implications are laid out in more details in the following sections.

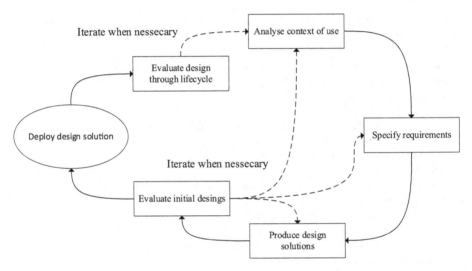

Fig. 4. Iteration by design adds a phase to user-centered design and closes the evaluation loop for the lifecycle of the system.

3.1   Sustained Adaptation

The system-engineering domain tries to use the concept of resilience to prepare a human-machine system for unforeseen events and changing requirements. Resilience can be defined in various ways [21]. Here, we adapt the definition of resilience as "the ability [to] manage/regulate adaptive capacities of systems that are layered networks, and are also part of larger layered networks, so as to produce sustained adaptivity over longer scales" [17, p. 4]. Thus, resilient systems have intrinsic properties that allow for sustained adaptation in the context of their purpose [22]. For example, an observer may attribute the goal of 'staying alive' to biological organisms, and regulative behavior can be the homeostasis of body temperature as well as to flee from predators [23]. As not all behaviors to deal with complexity can be inbuilt, the system must also be adaptive to complexity to deal with unexpected events. In human factors engineering, this relates to the ability to deal with events that were not anticipated during design.

Jackson and Ferris [24] summarized known principles for resilience engineering. One principle is *drift correction*. When a system reaches its boundaries of efficient, safe and satisfying performance a real-time or latent drift correction can encounter a failure of the system. An example of a real-time drift is an online (or real-time) adaptive system that adapts the interactive functions of the technical system to the user state of the operator [25]. The real-time adaptive system introduces flexibility to the system by a dynamic task allocation and can change it to be more resilient. However, a real-time drift system like an adaptive interaction system has boundaries by itself. The real-time adaptive system underlies the same technical, scientific and requirement changes as the human-machine system in its entirety, as it evolves over a long lifecycle. "Latent drift correction pertains to the detection of hidden faults within a system that may result in failure at a later date" [20, p. 7]. Hidden faults could be for example the earlier described ineffective training of crewmembers, unforeseen usage of the system that had no fatal consequence for a long time until the occurrence of an accident, and unknown interactive effects of newly introduced technology. In conclusion, a human machine-system can use real-time and latent drift principles build into the design of the system to sustain adaptation over a long lifecycle especially in safety critical areas.

According to Jackson and Ferris [24] *human in the loop* is another principle of resilience engineering. The principle is "based on the premise that humans are better capable of recognizing and dealing with unprecedented threats than automated systems", [20, p. 6]. For a latent drift of the human-machine system, a human will have more time for decision making than by a real-time drift and is therefore suited for the task. However, it comes with its own challenges. For example, the human must have sufficient information of the actual use of the system. To have numerous bystanders on board of a military ship is impractical because of sparse room on board and high costs of the personnel. Even assuming to have bystanders on board, that information have to be aggregated. Different bystanders could have different subjective perceptions, which could make the aggregated information fragmented and therefore less useful. In addition, operators on board cannot gather the information because this would increase the workload, which should be prevented out of safety and efficiency reasons. Implications of the challenges will be discussed further in the next section.

To conclude, sustained adaptation could be achieved by the evaluation of a human-machine system by a higher order regulator that decides whether system properties must be changed to reach goals given the current constraints (see Fig. 5). The adaptation regulator changes the structure of the human-machine system, the influencing factors of the requirements or the human-machine system - requirements loop in a way to ensure mission success. Human-machine system designers can be seen as adaptation regulators, as they select the structure of the human-machine system with the purpose to optimize the requirements – human-machine system fit. Thus, although we are not yet able to implement sustained adaptive regulators in artificial systems, we can deliberately use humans as regulators for sustained adaptation.

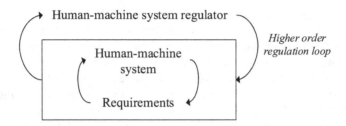

Fig. 5. Human adaptation regulator as decision maker of higher order regulation loop.

3.2   Design Assistant System

Bringing in the proposed fifth design phase to the ISO 9241-210 norm through the application of the described resilience engineering principles requires informed decisions to achieve a benefit in human-machine system design. By *Iteration by Design*, resilience is not exclusively achieved by a fundamental property of the human-machine system itself, but by a higher order adaptation loop consisting of a design team (see Fig. 5).

Consequently, *Iteration by Design* investigates:

(a) How designers can observe and change the human-machine system during the lifecycle, and
(b) How design iteration can be handled during the lifecycle when confronted with operative data and possibilities to adjust the structure of human-machine systems.

Information gathering through human observers during system operation is impractical and cost intensive. Further, finding heuristics and shifting requirements based on operator workshops could lead to false conclusions, because operators are part of the system and could not be aware of hidden requirement shifts or undetected requirements during the initial design phase. To close the information gap, and to tackle the challenges of *Iteration by Design*, a design assistance system can support design decision-making (see Fig. 6). The system should gather information during system operation and prepare them for decision making of the human decision maker. The human-system regulator (design team) evaluates the human-machine system with the support of the design assistance system. The design assistance system informs the regulator, and the regulator makes decisions for offline (latent) drifts of the human-machine system. Implementing the higher order loop in combination with the design assistance system allows to adapt the safety-critical human-machine system to changing requirements during the lifecycle of the system. Therefore, the human-machine system of the higher order regulation loop is a hybrid solution of automation and human in the loop, and can be seen as a system of systems.

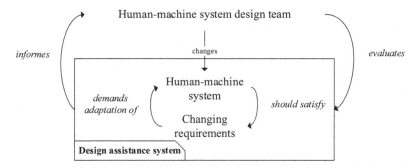

Fig. 6. Iteration by Design: Sustained adaptation for human-machine system during the lifecycle of a safety critical system.

3.3   Reciprocal Interaction Design in Support of Adaptive Instruction

In addition to drift correction and human in the loop as principles for resilience engineering, training as a third component can also contribute to the resilience of the overall human-machine system. Specifically, adaptive training can be regarded as beneficial in several ways in the context of iteration by design: One general advantage of adaptive training compared to common classroom training is that training can be tailored to the specific needs of an individual trainee or a group of trainees [26]. Using on-task measures (e.g. performance, user state), called micro-adaptive training, allows for an online-adaptation during training in order to keep the trainee in an optimal learner state. It is also called zone of proximal development [27], which should make the training more effective and efficient.

In addition to increasing the training effectiveness, adaptive training that collects data on the user's behavior can also be helpful for defining requirements for console design and redesign. For example, if the training of outdated technology takes longer because of unfamiliarity with old technology, the design team could recognize the requirement that an update of the interaction technology is needed. Moreover, collecting this data during training also offers the possibility of offline or macro adaptation of the training. Similar to the proposed continuous evaluation of the console design during the lifecycle, training can be evaluated continuously and can be updated if it is not effective anymore due to changing requirements. In summary, we propose to integrate adaptive training into the iteration by design concept in order to use training data to adapt to the individual operator and to the changing requirements of the system.

4   Irony of the Homunculus Fallacy

A known fallacy for explaining and researching human behavior is the homunculus fallacy [28]. In this case, human behavior and sensation is described as a little man sitting in the human brain and watching on a screen to see what the human is seeing to control the behavior. The problem with the explanation is, who is controlling the little man, and how does he have sensations. Applied to Iteration by Design a potential fallacy of the concept could be that it tries to build a human-machine system that gathers information and controls the behavior of a lower order system. Thus, the problem that arises is that the controlling system by itself needs to be designed and that could be done with a system of system of systems. The irony is that with a hybrid solution proposed by Iteration by Design, containing automation and human in the loop to incorporate resilience, a little human is part of the system that could solve problems a machine alone cannot yet solve. It will be interesting to investigate the implications of the fallacy in the context of *Iteration by Design*.

5   Conclusion and Future Developments

Iteration by Design is a human-machine interaction concept for safety critical systems with long lifecycles. It introduces a fifth design phase for the ISO 9241-210 norm. Implications of the design process are: (a) the requirement that the human-machine system should be evaluated through the lifecycle of the system and (b) the need to adapt the system to changing requirements. The chance of preventing an accident like the one of the USS John S. McCain could be higher by adapting the human-machine system to the demands of changing or initially hidden requirements. The introduced concept *Iteration by Design* leads to research-questions that will be investigated in the future. Future developments will be to investigate the inner workings of the proposed design assistance system and to implement a prototype.

References

1. National Transportation Safety Board: Collision between US Navy Destroyer John S McCain and Tanker Alnic MC., Washington, DC, USA (2019)
2. Eckstein, M.: Navy Reverting DDGs Back to Physical Throttles, After Fleet Rejects Touchscreen Controls. https://news.usni.org/2019/08/09/navy-reverting-ddgs-back-to-physic al-throttles-after-fleet-rejects-touchscreen-controls
3. Tuyls, K., Weiss, G.: Multiagent learning: basics, challenges, and prospects. AI Mag. **33**, 41–52 (2012)
4. Bainbridge, L.: Ironies of automation. Automatica **19**, 775–779 (1983). https://doi.org/10. 1016/0005-1098(83)90046-8
5. Rasmussen, J.: Risk management in a dynamic society: a modelling problem. Saf. Sci. **27**, 183–213 (1997). https://doi.org/10.1016/S0925-7535(97)00052-0
6. Hollnagel, E.: FRAM: The Functional Resonance Analysis Method Modelling Complex Socio-Technical Systems. Ashgate Publishing, Surrey, England (2012)
7. Hollnagel, E.: Coping with complexity: past, present and future. Cogn. Technol. Work **14**, 199–205 (2012). https://doi.org/10.1007/s10111-011-0202-7
8. ISO: Ergonomic design of control centres—Part 1: Principles for the design of control centres (ISO 11064-1), (2000)
9. ISO: Ergonomics of human-system interaction—Part 210: Human-centred design forinteractive systems (ISO 9241-210). http://www.iso.org/iso/catalogue_detail.htm?csnumber=52075, (2010). https://doi.org/10.1039/c0dt90114h
10. Kontogiannis, T., Hollnagel, E.: Application of cognitive ergonomics to the control room design of advanced technologies. Int. J. Cogn. Ergon. **3**, 243–268 (1998)

11. Algera, J.A., Koopman, P.L., Vijlbrief, H.P.J.: Management strategies in introducing computer-based information systems. Appl. Psychol. **38**, 87–103 (1989). https://doi.org/10.1111/j.1464-0597.1989.tb01376.x

12. Bainbridge, L.: Multiplexed VDT display systems: a framework for good practice. In: Weir, G.R.S., Alty, J.L. (eds.) Human-Computer Interaction and Complex Systems. Academic Press, New York (1991)

13. Hollnagel, E., Woods, D.D.: Cognitive systems engineering: new wine in new bottles. Int. J. Hum. Comput. Stud. **51**, 339–356 (1999). https://doi.org/10.1006/ijhc.1982.0313

14. Guastello, S.J.: Human Factors Engineering and Ergonomics: A Systems Approach. CRC Press, Boca Raton (2013). https://doi.org/10.1201/b16191

15. Nitsch, V.: Haptic Human-Machine Interaction in Teleoperation Systems and its Implications for the Design and Effective Use of Haptic Interfaces. Südwestdeutscher Verlag für Hochschulschriften, Saarbrücken, Germany (2012)

16. Woods, D.D., Hollnagel, E.: Joint Cognitive Systems: Patterns in Cognitive Systems Engineering. CRC Press, Boca Raton (2006). https://doi.org/10.1080/00140130701223774

17. Ivergard, T., Hunt, B.: Handbook of Control Room Design and Ergonomics: A Perspective for the Future. CRC Press, Boca Raton (2008)

18. Egan, D.: Individual differences in human-computer interaction. In: Helander, M. (ed.) Handbook of Human Computer Interaction, pp. 543–568. Elsevier Science Publishers, Amsterdam (1988)

19. Schmettow, M., Havinga, J.: Are users more diverse than designs? Testing and extending a 25 years old claim. In: Proceedings of BCS HCI 2013- Internet Things XXVII (2013)

20. Cook, R.I., Woods, D.D.: Adapting to new technology in the operating room. Hum. Factors J. Hum. Factors Ergon. Soc. **38**, 593–613 (1996). https://doi.org/10.1518/001872096778827224

21. Woods, D.D.: Four concepts for resilience and the implications for the future of resilience engineering. Reliab. Eng. Syst. Saf. **141**, 5–9 (2015). https://doi.org/10.1016/j.ress.2015.03.018

22. Woods, D.D.: The theory of graceful extensibility: basic rules that govern adaptive systems. Environ. Syst. Decis. **38**(4), 433–457 (2018). https://doi.org/10.1007/s10669-018-9708-3

23. Ashby, W.R.: An Introduction to Cybernetics. Chapman & Hall Ltd, London (1961)

24. Jackson, S., Ferris, T.L.J.: Resilience principles for engineered systems. Syst. Eng. **16**, 152–164 (2013). https://doi.org/10.1002/sys.21228

25. Schwarz, J., Fuchs, S.: Multidimensional real-time assessment of user state and performance to trigger dynamic system adaptation. In: Schmorrow, D.D., Fidopiastis, C.M. (eds.) AC 2017. LNCS (LNAI), vol. 10284, pp. 383–398. Springer, Cham (2017). https://doi.org/10.1007/978-3-319-58628-1_30

26. Lee, J., Park, O.: Adaptive instructional systems. In: Jonassen, D.H. (ed.) Handbook of Research for Educational Communications and Technology, pp. 651–660. Lawrence Erlbaum Associates, Mahwah (2003)

27. Murray, T., Arroyo, I.: Toward measuring and maintaining the zone of proximal development in adaptive instructional systems. In: Cerri, S.A., Gouardères, G., Paraguaçu, F. (eds.) ITS 2002. LNCS, vol. 2363, pp. 749–758. Springer, Heidelberg (2002). https://doi.org/10.1007/3-540-47987-2_75

28. Kenny, A.J.: The homunculus fallacy. In: Grene, M., Prigogine, I. (eds.) Interpretations of Life and Mind: Essays Around the Problem of Reduction, pp. 155–165. Humanities Press, New York (1971)

Learner Modelling and Methods of Adaptation

Bayesian Student Modeling
in the AC&NL Tutor

Ines Šarić-Grgić[1]([✉]) [ID], Ani Grubišić[1] [ID], Branko Žitko[1] [ID],
Slavomir Stankov[2], Angelina Gašpar[3], Suzana Tomaš[4] [ID],
and Daniel Vasić[5] [ID]

[1] Faculty of Science, University of Split, Split, Croatia
`ines.saric@pmfst.hr`
[2] Split, Croatia
[3] Catholic Faculty of Theology, University of Split, Split, Croatia
[4] Faculty of Humanities and Social Sciences, University of Split, Split, Croatia
[5] Faculty of Science and Education, University of Mostar,
Mostar, Bosnia and Herzegovina

Abstract. The reasoning process about the level of student's knowledge can be challenging even for experienced human tutors. The Bayesian networks are a formalism for reasoning under uncertainty, which has been successfully used for various artificial intelligence applications, including student modeling. While Bayesian networks are a highly flexible graphical and probabilistic modeling framework, its main challenges are related to the structural design and the definition of "a priori" and conditional probabilities. Since the AC&NL Tutor's authoring tool automatically generates tutoring elements of different linguistic complexity, the generated sentences and questions fall into three difficulty levels. Based on these levels, the probability-based Bayesian student model is proposed for mastery-based learning in intelligent tutoring system. The Bayesian network structure is defined by generated questions related to the node representing knowledge in a sentence. Also, there are relations between inverse questions at the same difficulty level. After the structure is defined, the process of assigning "a priori" and conditional probabilities is automated using several heuristic expert-based rules.

Keywords: Intelligent tutoring systems · Student modeling · Bayesian networks

1 Introduction

An important feature of intelligent tutoring is the system's ability to adapt to a student's knowledge and behavior. While the adaptivity in the expert and teacher modules of the general intelligent tutoring system's architecture focuses on what and how to tutor, the adaptivity found in the student module allows conclusions about the learning process. The student module keeps track of this process, and the student model represents a system's beliefs about the learning progress of each student.

There are different student modeling approaches found in the field of intelligent tutoring systems, including the overlay model, stereotypes, perturbation model, student

© Springer Nature Switzerland AG 2020
R. A. Sottilare and J. Schwarz (Eds.): HCII 2020, LNCS 12214, pp. 245–257, 2020.
https://doi.org/10.1007/978-3-030-50788-6_18

models based on machine learning techniques, cognitive theories, constraint-based model, fuzzy student model, Bayesian networks, ontology-based student model, and hybrid approaches that combine some of the previously mentioned models [1]. Regarding the student model's typical applications, there are two groups of models, including the skill modeling group and the models of affect and motivation [2]. Most of the student models deal with skill modeling, and these models should guide the adaptive behavior of intelligent tutoring systems by (i) assigning the current student knowledge level to the skill, (ii) selecting the next tasks of appropriate difficulty level and (iii) deciding whether a student has mastered a skill. Depending on the type of the intelligent tutoring system, the skill corresponds to the topic or *instructional unit*, whereas the task correlates with the testing opportunity or *question*.

The task of shaping a reliable belief of the current level of student's knowledge is characterized by the uncertainty that can be challenging even for experienced human tutors [3]. Two probabilistic student model approaches include the Bayesian-network-based approach and the Logistic-regression-based approach. Although some researchers have compared the Bayesian-network-based and Logistic-regression-based approaches, the results are not conclusive and generalize not the appropriate choice of the modeling approach - in many cases, the researchers pick an approach without providing any rationale for the choice [4]. The Bayesian networks are a formalism for reasoning under uncertainty that has been widely adopted in the field of artificial intelligence [3]. Concerning the type of formalism, student modeling approaches can be based on the static Bayesian networks or more complex Dynamic Bayesian networks.

This research investigates how probabilistic modeling, based on static Bayesian networks, can apply to the environment of the Adaptive Courseware based on Natural Language Processing (AC&NL Tutor) (https://www.acnltutor.net/) [5]. The AC&NL Tutor is a research project, supported by the United States Office of Naval Research (2015–32019) that aims to demonstrate how the effective integration of adaptive courseware and natural language processing enables learning, teaching, and testing processes. Linguistic complexity determines the three difficulty levels of tutoring elements (sentences and questions) in the AC&NL Tutor. The feature of different levels of tutoring elements is used during the process of designing the Bayesian approach in the AC&NL Tutor environment.

The next section focuses on the background literature and an insight into the AC&NL Tutor environment. Then, the elements of the Bayesian network in the AC&NL Tutor environment are determined as well as the structure and network probabilities. The overall probabilities of knowing the text example are simulated for basic learning paths. The conclusion and future research are presented in the last section. It should be noted that the Python language is utilized for conducting all analyses of the proposed model.

2   Research Background

2.1   Bayesian Networks in Student Modeling

The Bayesian networks are a highly flexible graphical and probabilistic modeling framework designed to explicitly represent conditional independence among random variables of interest, and exploit this information to reduce the complexity of probabilistic inference [6]. Formally, Bayesian networks are represented by using a directed non-cyclical graph where variables appear as nodes, and probabilities appear as links between nodes. The conditional independence is seen as a lack of an edge between any pair of nodes. In practice, "a priori" and conditional probabilities are defined using heuristically defined rules by the experts and/or they can be derived from the experimental data. If each node X_i in the network is associated with a conditional probability table that specifies the probability distribution of the associated random variable, given its immediate parent nodes *Parents(Xi)*, then the Bayesian network provides a compact representation of the joint probability distribution over all network variables that are represented by the following equation:

$$P(X_i, \ldots, X_n) = \prod_{i=1}^{n} P(X_i | Parents(X_i))$$

Student models based on static Bayesian networks are used in the case when the probabilities that need to be assessed (e.g. student's knowledge) are not changing as a piece of new evidence (e.g. test results) comes in. Dynamic models allow for changes in the state of variables over time, and in these networks, time is discrete, and a separate network is created for each step. The Bayesian networks are applied in several intelligent tutoring systems [mentioned in 3, 4, 7], and the widely applied approach based on Dynamic Bayesian networks is Bayesian Knowledge Tracing (BKT) [8]. The BKT approach models students' knowledge by observing the correctness of each student's answer. While the basic BKT approach was developed to tutor the same-difficulty-level tasks, the researchers focused on ways to improve upon the base model without losing the simplicity and flexibility that are the core strengths of this model. The advances of the BKT approach include the contextualization of estimates of guessing and slipping parameters [9], the estimates of the probability when the additional help features are used [10], the estimates of the initial probability that the student knows the skill [11], individualization improvements through student-level assessments [12], and introduction of item difficulty to the model [13].

There are several advantages of using Bayesian networks for uncertain student modeling, including (i) compact representation of the joint probability distribution over the knowledge variable, (ii) available algorithms, (iii) the intuitive nature of the graphical representation that helps researchers to focus on identifying the essential dependencies, (iv) the facilitated interpretation of the underlying system behavior based on the results of probabilistic inference, and (v) the facilitated decision-making support regarding the tutorial post-actions [3].

The two most emphasized challenges include the selection of suitable Bayesian network's structure and the calculation of the necessary network's parameters. This research aims to explore how different levels of difficulty in tutoring elements can be used during the design process of the Bayesian student model. The pomegranate Python package [14], which implements fast, efficient, and flexible probabilistic models, such as Bayesian networks, is used.

2.2   The AC&NL Tutor Environment

The AC&NL Tutor environment consists of two components: (i) The Semi-Automatic Authoring Tool (SAAT) that performs knowledge extraction using natural language processing, and (ii) The Tutomat, the intelligent tutoring system that enables adaptive courseware and communication in the controlled natural language.

To enable learning in the Tutomat, a teacher prepares a text using the SAAT. Once the teacher has validated the SAAT output, *tutoring elements* are automatically generated and ready for further use in the Tutomat. The tutoring elements include the sentences and questions of different levels of complexity, along with their visual representations in the form of Domain Knowledge (DK) graphs. The process of learning, in the Tutomat, is realized through so-called *tutoring cycles*. Each tutoring cycle consists of three phases: the learning and teaching phase that is adapted to the current student's knowledge level, the testing phase, and the student model update phase.

There are three difficulty levels of tutoring elements, based on their linguistic complexity. The highest level-1 corresponds to the most complex version of tutoring elements, usually the sentences in their original form, and corresponding questions at the highest linguistic level. The medium level-2 and the lowest level-3 encompass less complicated versions of tutoring elements, including simpler sub-sentences and more focused questions. The current student model in the Tutomat is based on four predefined stereotypes and the overlay approach, as the combination of the mentioned three difficulty levels of tutoring elements (presented in Table 1).

Table 1. Tutoring elements for each stereotype based on linguistic complexity in the Tutomat.

Stereotype	Learning process - sentences		Testing process - questions	
	Textual	DK graph	Textual	DK graph
Beginner	Level-3	Yes, per each sentence	Level-3 questions	No
Intermediate	Level-2	Yes, for complete CE	Level-2 questions	Yes, fill-in
Advanced	Level-1	Yes, for complete CE	Level-1 questions	No
Expert	Level-1	No	Level-1 questions	Yes, find mistakes

Each stereotype has its own set of rules for selection, sequencing, and presentation of a part of domain knowledge aimed for tutoring, which is called a *courseware element (CE)*. The beginner and intermediate stereotypes learn from smaller CE, whereas the advanced and expert stereotypes learn from bigger ones. The tutoring process starts with the beginner stereotype and finishes when a student has reached the highest difficulty level, i.e. knowledge acquisition has been accomplished. The expert stereotype, as the highest difficulty level, includes the most complex tutoring elements without their visual representations (DK graphs).

The student model in the Tutomat is updated using heuristically defined functions over the DK graph elements. The DK graph elements include the number of learned concepts and the number of learned propositions (two concepts connected with an edge). Each student's answer to a specific question is mapped to one or more propositions, and depending on the stereotype, the student can get from 1 to 4 points for each correct proposition. If one concept is part of several propositions, the student must know each proposition to get a maximum score for that concept, so that it can be marked as learned at a certain knowledge level. At the end of each tutoring cycle, the stereotype is updated according to the maximum number of concepts that have the same score, from 1-point concepts (the beginner stereotype) to 4-point concepts (the expert stereotype).

3   The Concept of Bayesian Student Modeling in the AC&NL Tutor Environment

In the following sub-section, the Bayesian student model approach for the AC&NL Tutor environment is proposed. The approach is based on three levels of linguistic complexity of tutoring elements, and the expert-based heuristically defined probabilities.

3.1   Instructional Unit Example

The simple instructional unit, which consists of one complex sentence and DK graph, as its visual representation (Fig. 1), is presented below.

Intelligent tutoring systems are computer-based software packages that apply artificial intelligence techniques to assist in the teaching and learning of some skill.

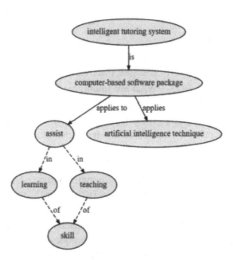

Fig. 1. The DK graph of instructional unit example.

After the processing of the instructional unit within the SAAT, the tutoring elements presented in Table 2 are generated automatically.

Table 2. The automatically generated tutoring elements of the instructional unit example.

Sentence(s)	Question(s)	Answer(s)
The highest difficulty level (level-1)		
$S1_1$ Intelligent tutoring systems **are** computer-based software packages that apply artificial intelligence techniques to assist in the teaching and learning of some skill	$Q1_1$ What are computer-based software packages that apply artificial intelligence techniques to assist in the teaching and learning of some skill?	Intelligent tutoring systems
	$Q1_2$ What are intelligent tutoring systems?	Computer-based software packages that apply artificial intelligence techniques to assist in the teaching and learning of some skill
The medium difficulty level (level-2)		
$S2_1$ Intelligent tutoring systems **are** computer-based software packages	$Q2_1$ What are computer-based software packages?	Intelligent tutoring systems
	$Q2_2$ What are intelligent tutoring systems?	Computer-based software packages
$S2_2$ Computer-based software packages **apply** artificial intelligence techniques to assist in the teaching and learning of some skill	$Q2_3$ What applies artificial intelligence techniques to assist in the teaching and learning of some skill?	Computer-based software packages
	$Q2_4$ What do computer-based software packages apply?	Artificial intelligence techniques to assist in the teaching and learning of some skill
The lowest difficulty level (level-3)		
$S3_1$ Intelligent tutoring systems **are** computer-based software packages	$Q3_1$ What are computer-based software packages?	Intelligent tutoring systems
	$Q3_2$ What are intelligent tutoring systems?	Computer-based software packages
$S3_2$ Computer-based software packages **apply** artificial intelligence techniques to assist in learning of some skill	$Q3_3$ What applies artificial intelligence techniques to assist in learning of some skill?	Computer-based software packages
	$Q3_4$ What do computer-based software packages apply?	Artificial intelligence techniques to assist in learning of some skill
$S3_3$ Computer-based software packages **apply** artificial intelligence techniques to assist in the teaching of some skill	$Q3_5$ What applies artificial intelligence techniques to assist in the teaching of some skill?	Computer-based software packages
	$Q3_6$ What do computer-based software packages apply?	Artificial intelligence techniques to assist in the teaching of some skill

3.2   The Bayesian Network Structure

During the design process of the Bayesian network, it is essential to define (i) *the network structure* and (ii) the network parameters, including the *"a priori" probabilities* for nodes without parents, and *conditional probabilities* for nodes with parents.

Regarding the structure of the Bayesian network in the AC&NL Tutor environment, the network is defined as a set of nodes that represent questions for each sentence, which are related to the node Sentence that represents the knowledge of a complete sentence (Fig. 2). Each question can be followed with its inverse version, so these questions are also associated with an edge. For example, $Q1_1$ (root inverse question) and $Q1_2$ (corresponding inverse question) are inverted questions because their answers are entirely included in the opposite question.

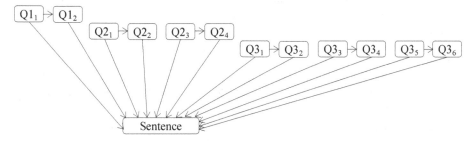

Fig. 2. The Bayesian network structure in the AC&NL Tutor environment.

3.3   "A priori" and Conditional Probabilities

For question nodes without parents (root inverse questions), the "a priori" probabilities include 0.1 for the level-1, 0.2 for the level-2, and 0.3 for the level-3. These probabilities assume that there is 10% of probability that the student would answer the question correctly at the highest level-1 (for $Q1_1$), 20% at the medium level-2 (for $Q2_1$ and $Q2_3$), and 30% at the lowest difficulty level-3 (for $Q3_1$, $Q3_3$, and $Q3_5$). In the background literature, the lucky guess behavior is introduced as the probability of providing a correct answer despite not knowing the answer itself. While the previously set "a priori" probabilities for three question levels can be related to the student's prior knowledge, they can also be the result of the lucky guess behavior.

For question nodes that have another question as a parent (corresponding inverse questions), there are no "a priori" probabilities, but only the conditional probabilities based on the correctness of a root inverse question. If the root inverse question has not been answered yet, the conditional probability is equal to the mentioned "a priori" probabilities for each level (0.1, 0.2, or 0.3). After the root inverse question has been answered correctly, the probability of knowing the corresponding inverse question increases for additional *(1 - "a priori")/(the total number of inverse questions)*. In this case, the calculation of the "a priori" probabilities is calculated as:

- $0.1 + 0.9/2 = 0.55$ (for $Q1_2$),
- $0.2 + 0.8/2 = 0.6$ (for $Q2_2$ and $Q2_4$), and
- $0.3 + 0.7/2 = 0.65$ (for $Q3_2$, $Q3_4$, and $Q3_6$).

Several rules determine the conditional probabilities for the Sentence node:

- If the student answered correctly at least one of the questions at level-1 (the highest difficulty), x_1 is the number of total level-1 questions, and y_1 is the number of correctly answered level-1 questions, there is $(90\%/x_1)*y_1$ of the overall probability that the student knows the complete sentence. At the same time, if the student answered correctly z_1 of the level-2 and level-3 questions, there is an additional 5% $*z_1$ of the overall probability of knowing the complete sentence.
- Else if the student answered correctly at least one of the questions at level-2 (medium difficulty), x_2 is the number of total level-2 questions, and y_2 is the number of correctly answered level-2 questions, there is $(60\%/x_2)*y_2$ of the overall probability that the student knows the complete sentence. At the same time, if the student answered correctly z_2 of the level-3 questions, there is an additional $5\%*z_2$ of the overall probability of knowing the complete sentence.
- Else if the student answered correctly at least one of the questions at level-3 (the lowest difficulty), x_3 is the number of total level-3 questions, and y_3 is the number of correctly answered level-3 questions, there is $(30\%/x_3)*y_3$ of the overall probability that the student knows the complete sentence.
- Else if the student did not answer correctly any of the questions at levels-1, 2, and 3, there is 90% of the overall probability that the student does not know the complete sentence.

The following example describes how the posterior probability of knowing the complete sentence is calculated. If we assume a version of the Bayesian network, which includes only level-1 questions, according to the previously defined rules, the "a priori" and the conditional probabilities are described in Fig. 3.

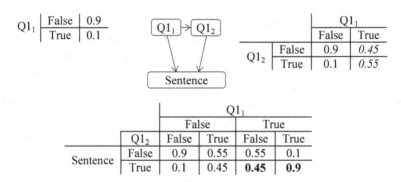

Fig. 3. The calculation of the Bayesian probability of knowing the complete sentence.

In case of having the correct student answer only for the question $Q1_1$, the posterior probability of knowing the sentence is calculated as:

$P(\text{Sent} = T \mid Q1_1 = T) = P(\text{Sent}, Q1_2 = T \mid Q1_1) + P(\text{Sent}, Q1_2 = F \mid Q1_1) =$
$P(\text{Sent} \mid Q1_2 = T, Q1_1) * P(Q1_2 = T \mid Q1_1) + P(\text{Sent} \mid Q1_2 = F, Q1_1) * P(Q1_2 = F \mid Q1_1) =$
$0.9 * 0.55 + 0.45 * 0.45 = 0.6975.$

The posterior probability of knowing the entire sentence covers both cases of knowing $Q1_2$ question (true and false states), and for each of these states, the probability is calculated as a product of the probability of the question node and the conditional probability of the sentence node. So, there is a total of 70% of the posterior probability that the student would know the sentence if the question $Q1_1$ was answered correctly.

3.4 Bayesian Network Probabilities for Basic Learning Paths

Besides the rules that define "a priori" and conditional probabilities, it is essential to define instructional policies, which depend on calculated probabilities. The instructional policies include (i) the rule for detecting mastery of the instructional unit and (ii) the rule for a consequential tutoring instruction – what should be learned next, based on the current level of student's knowledge.

The idea of introducing a probability-based student model implies that the system will adaptively test the student with a minimum number of questions. Therefore, the tutoring process begins at the level-1 and further adapts to the current level of student's knowledge, based on the calculated probability of knowing the complete sentence of the Bayesian network. Regarding the overall probability of knowing the entire sentence, there are heuristically defined thresholds that range from 0 to 1 for the node representing the knowledge of a sentence, including 0.3 as 30% of the probability that the student's knowledge is between the lowest level and the medium level, and 0.6 as 60% of the probability that the student's knowledge is between the medium level and the highest level. So, in case that the probability is below 0.3, the student is tutored using the level-3 sub-sentences and questions. If the probability is between 0.3 and 0.6, the student is tutored using the level-2 sub-sentences and questions; if it is above 0.6, the student is tutored using the most complex tutoring elements. A student has mastered the instructional unit, and the tutoring process is complete when the overall probability of knowing the entire sentence exceeds 0.9 with the assumption that the student knows the observed sentence with 90% of the probability.

The additional assumptions include that the system firstly uses root inverse questions per each level until all inverse pairs have been used in the tutoring process. When there are no more root inverse questions to use, for each root inverse question answered correctly, the system uses the corresponding inverse question. In the case when only one question per level remains as not answered correctly, after each incorrect student performance on that question the tutoring process continues at the one level below the tested one.

For the experimental purposes, the proposed Bayesian network is simulated for basic learning paths, including (i) the first answer incorrect and then all correct answers, (ii) all correct answers, (iii) all incorrect answers, and (iv) the alternating combination of answers starting with incorrect answer (v) the alternating combination of answers starting with correct answer.

In the first example, it is shown how the decrease in the posterior probability impacts the difficulty level of the following tutoring elements (Learning Path 1 in Table 3). The tutoring process begins with the highest level-1 sentence ($S1_1$), but after the first incorrect answer ($Q1_1$), the expected posterior probability of knowing the sentence decreases to 0.29. Since the posterior probability is below 0.3, the student continues to learn at the lowest level-3 ($S3_1$). If the student answers correctly to the level-3 question ($Q3_1$), the posterior probability is equal to 0.33. Since the posterior probability is between 0.3 and 0.6, the student continues to learn at the medium level-2. So, the next sentence to learn is $S2_1$, and the following question to answer is $Q2_1$. In the case of the correct answer to the level-2 question, the posterior probability is equal to 0.49, and the tutoring process continues at the medium level-2. The next sentence to learn is $S2_2$, including the corresponding question $Q2_3$. In the case of the correct answer, the posterior probability is equal to 0.65, which means that the student performed well at the more focused level-2 and level-3 and improved again to level-1. In case of the correct answers to both level-1 questions ($Q1_1$ and $Q1_2$), the student will finish the tutoring process at the highest level.

The second example is the learning path in which the student answered all questions correctly (Learning Path 2 in Table 3). The tutoring process begins, and the student acquires knowledge from the original complex sentence ($S1_1$). The first testing process includes the level-1 question ($Q1_1$), and in the case of the correct answer, the posterior probability is equal to 0.77. Since the posterior probability is above 0.6, the student continues learning at the highest level-1 ($S1_1$). In the second tutoring cycle, the student is tested on the second level-1 question ($Q1_2$) since this is the only remaining level-1 question. In the case of answering the previous question correctly, the posterior probability is equal to 0.9, which is a satisfying result to assume that the student has learned the observed sentence.

Table 3. Learning Paths (LP) described using Question (Q), Student Answer (SA, Incorrect or Correct) and Posterior Probability (PP) of knowing the sentence for a specific tutoring cycle.

	LP 1	LP 2	LP 3	LP 4	LP 5
Q 1	$Q1_1$	$Q1_1$	$Q1_1$	$Q1_1$	$Q1_1$
SA 1	Incorrect	**Correct**	Incorrect	Incorrect	**Correct**
PP 1	0.29	0.77	0.29	0.29	0.77
Q 2	$Q3_1$	$Q1_2$	$Q3_1$	$Q3_1$	$Q1_2$
SA 2	**Correct**	**Correct**	Incorrect	**Correct**	Incorrect
PP 2	0.33	0.9	0.27	0.33	0.6
Q 3	$Q2_1$	–	$Q3_3$	$Q2_1$	$Q2_1$
SA 3	**Correct**		Incorrect	Incorrect	**Correct**
PP 3	0.49		0.26	0.29	0.66
Q 4	$Q2_3$	–	$Q3_5$	$Q3_3$	$Q1_2$
SA 4	**Correct**		Incorrect	**Correct**	Incorrect
PP 4	0.65		0.24	0.34	0.66
Q 5	$Q1_1$	–	$Q3_1$	$Q2_3$	$Q2_3$
SA 5	**Correct**		Incorrect	Incorrect	**Correct**
PP 5	0.84		0.24	0.30	0.72
Q 6	$Q1_2$	–	$Q3_3$	$Q2_1$	$Q1_2$
SA 6	**Correct**		Incorrect	**Correct**	Incorrect
PP 6	0.9		0.24	0.50	0.72
Q 7	–	–	$Q3_5$	$Q2_3$	$Q2_2$
SA 7			Incorrect	Incorrect	**Correct**
PP 7			0.24	0.50	0.74

If we assume that after the incorrect student's answer to the first level-1 question, the student continues to perform incorrectly at the lowest level-3 (Learning Path 3 in Table 3), the posterior probability will not increase to the medium level-2. In this case, a student should be offered additional help or hint.

In case of having the alternate combination of answers starting with the incorrect answer to level-1 question ($Q1_1$), a posterior probability changes between the lowest level-3 and the medium level-2 (Learning Path 4 in Table 3).

In addition to the previous example, in case of starting with the correct answer to level-1 question ($Q1_1$), a posterior probability changes between the medium level-2 and the highest level-1 (Learning Path 5 in Table 3).

4   Conclusions and Future Research

The reasoning process about the student's knowledge level can be challenging even for experienced human tutors. The Bayesian network is the formalism for reasoning under uncertainty that has been successfully used for different artificial intelligence applications, as it has been extensively used in user modeling, specifically student modeling. While the Bayesian networks are a highly flexible graphical and probabilistic modeling framework, their main challenges are related to the structural design and the definition of "a priori" and conditional probabilities.

Since the AC&NL Tutor's authoring tool automatically generates tutoring elements with different linguistic complexity, the sentences and questions are grouped into three difficulty levels. In the case of mastery-based intelligent tutoring with questions of different complexity, we proposed the probability-based student model based on the Bayesian network. Generated questions define the structure of the network as nodes linked to the node that represents the knowledge of a complete sentence. Besides the previous edges, there are edges between inverse questions on the same difficulty level. The process of assigning the "a priori" and conditional probabilities in the network relies on several heuristically defined and expert-based rules. To finish the tutoring process, it is expected that the student answers all the questions correctly at the highest difficulty level. In the case of difficulties during the tutoring process, the medium and the lowest levels are used for adaptive tutoring.

In future research, the expert-based parameters should be compared to the probability parameters derived from the experimental data. Regarding additional edges in the Bayesian network, the relations between tutoring elements at different difficulty levels should be investigated, as well as the probabilities between different sentences in the text. Besides the Bayesian networks, the other techniques should also be tested, such as Dynamic Bayesian networks and Logistic-regression-based approaches.

Acknowledgments. This paper is part of the Adaptive Courseware & Natural Language Tutor project (N00014-15-1-2789) and the Enhancing Adaptive Courseware based on Natural Language Processing project (N00014-20-1-2066) that are supported by the United States Office of Naval Research Grant.

References

1. Chrysafiadi, K., Virvou, M.: Student modeling approaches: a literature review for the last decade. Exp. Syst. Appl. **40**, 4715–4729 (2013). https://doi.org/10.1016/j.eswa.2013.02.007
2. Pelánek, R.: Metrics for evaluation of student models. JEDM J. Educ. Data Mining **7**, 1–19 (2015). https://doi.org/10.5281/zenodo.3554665
3. Conati, C.: Bayesian student modeling. In: Nkambou, R., Bourdeau, J., Mizoguchi, R. (eds.) Advances in Intelligent Tutoring Systems. Studies in Computational Intelligence, vol. 308. Springer, Heidelberg (2010). https://doi.org/10.1007/978-3-642-14363-2_14
4. Pelánek, R.: Bayesian knowledge tracing, logistic models, and beyond: an overview of learner modeling techniques. User Model. User-Adapt. Interact. **27**, 313–350 (2017). https://doi.org/10.1007/s11257-017-9193-2
5. Grubišić, A., Stankov, S., Žitko, B.: Adaptive Courseware based on Natural Language Processing (AC & NL Tutor), United States Office of Naval Research grant (N00014-15-1-2789) (2015)
6. Pearl, J.: Probabilistic Reasoning in Intelligent Systems. Elsevier, Amsterdam (1988). https://doi.org/10.1016/C2009-0-27609-4
7. Millán, E., Loboda, T., Pérez-de-la-Cruz, J.L.: Bayesian networks for student model engineering. Comput. Educ. **55**, 1663–1683 (2010). https://doi.org/10.1016/j.compedu.2010.07.010
8. Corbett, A.T., Anderson, J.R.: Knowledge tracing: modeling the acquisition of procedural knowledge. User Model. User-Adapt. Interact. **4**, 253–278 (1994)

9. Baker, R.S.J.d., Corbett, A.T., Aleven, V.: More accurate student modeling through contextual estimation of slip and guess probabilities in Bayesian Knowledge tracing. In: Woolf, B.P., Aïmeur, E., Nkambou, R., Lajoie, S. (eds.) ITS 2008. LNCS, vol. 5091, pp. 406–415. Springer, Heidelberg (2008). https://doi.org/10.1007/978-3-540-69132-7_44

10. Beck, J.E., Chang, K., Mostow, J., Corbett, A.: Does help help? Introducing the Bayesian evaluation and assessment methodology. In: Woolf, B.P., Aïmeur, E., Nkambou, R., Lajoie, S. (eds.) Intelligent Tutoring Systems, pp. 383–394. Springer, Heidelberg (2008). https://doi.org/10.1007/978-3-540-69132-7_42

11. Pardos, Z.A., Heffernan, N.T.: Navigating the parameter space of Bayesian knowledge tracing models: visualizations of the convergence of the expectation maximization algorithm. In: EDM (2010)

12. Pardos, Z.A., Heffernan, N.T.: Modeling individualization in a Bayesian networks implementation of knowledge tracing. In: De Bra, P., Kobsa, A., Chin, D. (eds.) UMAP 2010. LNCS, vol. 6075, pp. 255–266. Springer, Heidelberg (2010). https://doi.org/10.1007/978-3-642-13470-8_24

13. Pardos, Z.A., Heffernan, N.T.: KT-IDEM: introducing item difficulty to the knowledge tracing model. In: Konstan, J.A., Conejo, R., Marzo, J.L., Oliver, N. (eds.) UMAP 2011. LNCS, vol. 6787, pp. 243–254. Springer, Heidelberg (2011). https://doi.org/10.1007/978-3-642-22362-4_21

14. Schreiber, J.: Pomegranate: fast and flexible probabilistic modeling in python. J. Mach. Learn. Res. **18**(164), 1–6 (2018)

Nature at Your Service - Nature Inspired Representations Combined with Eye-gaze Features to Infer User Attention and Provide Contextualized Support

Carla Barreiros[1,2](✉) ⓘ, Nelson Silva[1,2](✉) ⓘ,
Viktoria Pammer-Schindler[1,2](✉) ⓘ, and Eduardo Veas[1,2](✉) ⓘ

[1] Graz University of Technology, Graz, Austria
[2] Know Center, Graz, Austria
{cbarreiros,nsilva,vpammer,eveas}@Know-center.at

Abstract. Internet of Things (IoT) enables the creation of sensing and computing machines to enhance the level of continuous adaptation and support provided by intelligent systems to humans. Nevertheless, these systems still depend on human intervention, for example, in maintenance and (re)configuration tasks. To this measure, the development of an Adaptive Instructional System (AIS) in the context of IoT allows for the creation of new, improved learning and training environments. One can test new approaches to improve the training and perception efficiency of humans. Examples are the use of virtual and augmented reality, the inclusion of nature inspired metaphors based on biophilic design and calm computing principles and the design of technology that aims at changing the users' behaviour through persuasion and social influence. In this work, we specifically propose a nature inspired visual representation concept, BioIoT, to communicate sensor information. Our results show that this new representation contributes to the users' well-being and performance while remaining as easy to understand as traditional data representations (based on an experiment with twelve participants over two weeks). We present a use case under which we apply the BioIoT concept. It serves the purpose of demonstrating the BioIoT benefits in a AR setting, when applied in households and workplaces scenarios. Furthermore, by leveraging our previous experience in the development of adaptive and supportive systems based on eye-tracking, we discuss the application of this new sensing technology to the support of users in machine intervention by using the user attention, i.e., eye-gaze, on different machine parts as a way to infer the user's needs and adapt the system accordingly. In this way, a new level of continuous support can be provided to the users depending on their skill level and individual needs in the form of contextualized instructions and action recommendations based on user attention.

Keywords: IoT · BioIoT · Augmented reality · Eye-tracking · Attention · Recommendation · Support

© Springer Nature Switzerland AG 2020
R. A. Sottilare and J. Schwarz (Eds.): HCII 2020, LNCS 12214, pp. 258–270, 2020.
https://doi.org/10.1007/978-3-030-50788-6_19

1   Introduction

In the last decades, technology advancements shaped our daily life, changing how we communicate, how we learn and work, and how we live in today's modern society. Examples of impactful technologies are the Internet of Things (IoT), artificial intelligence, sensors, networking, embedded systems, and automation. IoT encompasses multiple technologies and connected devices to communicate, analyze sensor data and ultimately act based on information. Supposedly these devices are intended to be mostly self-sufficient. However, people still interact with these devices to perform tasks such as installation, monitoring, maintenance, and (re)configuration. The complexity commonly inherent to such tasks, and the fast-pace changes lead to the need for continuous learning and support accordingly to the users' personal needs. To this measure, the development of an Adaptive Instructional System (AIS) in the context of IoT allows for the creation of new, improved learning and training environments. In this work, we propose the use of augmented reality and the inclusion of new nature inspired metaphors based on biophilic design and calm computing principles. These proved to improve the users well-being and productivity [8–11,18] and the design of technology that aims at changing the users' behaviour through persuasion and social influence [3,12,15,16], as well as, to the use of eye-tracking on the development of adaptive and supportive systems [30–33].

In the present work, we describe a new AR system concept where we combine nature inspired representations (BioIoT) [2] with eye-gaze features to continuously infer the users' attention and provide contextualized support and guidance. We present the results of a two weeks comparison study to verify the augmented reality (AR) BioIoT representations against a standard dashboard like representations. In this study, 12 participants interacted with an IoT coffee machine enhanced with an AR interface, i.e., using either a tree representation or a dashboard-representation. The study aimed to verify the understandability of the AR tree representation when compared with a dashboard representation and to study the effects of the tree representation on the affect (emotion) and maintenance behaviour. Finally, we discuss the opportunities and challenges associated with the development of such a system.

2   Related Work

2.1   Augmented Reality Applications

Augmented reality technologies allow users to observe the real world enhanced with virtual objects, which can be superimposed or combined with the real world [1]. Latest technological advancements created new opportunities to apply AR in diverse domains, such as industry, medical, and education [4,5]. The users' perception and interaction with the world change because the virtual objects can display additional information and help users to perform real-world tasks. AR can provide cognitive support for difficult tasks [6], e.g. driver training [36], practising complex surgical procedures [35], learning how to change a filter on a space station [36], aiding field workers of utility companies while performing maintenance, planning and monitoring underground infrastructure [37]. In classrooms AR can increase student motivation [38], contribute to student learning outcomes [39,40]. AR also affects students' learning attitudes positively and facilitates the application of learned content to real-life situation [39].

2.2 Making Use of Nature Representations to Communicate Data

Data can be communicated through plants and nature representations, e.g. lights, bird sounds, water, and humans can interpret it easily [13,14]. Also, it can affect users' behaviour, as reported in a study intended to promote green transportation. Fourteen participants used a mobile application for three weeks, which displayed self-reported transported behaviour using natural themes, i.e. a garden and a polar scene. Findings showed that participants adopted more conscious behaviours and felt motivated and engaged [17].

Several studies showed that humans tend to perceive machines as being conscious and intelligent, especially if the machines have anthropomorphic characteristics. As reported by [12,15] machines can be seen as social actors and social rules are applicable in this context. For example, participants in a study with a cat robot were instructed to kill the robot after playing a game with it. Participants that played with a helpful and intelligent cat took almost three times longer to turn it off than the participants that interacted with a not so helpful cat [16]. Another field study evaluated the maintenance behaviour of twelve participants during two weeks, comparing a two-dimension nature inspired representation, i.e. 2D virtual tree, with an icon-based dashboard, which was used to communicate the state of a coffee machine. Results showed that the participants' affect (emotion) and behaviour was affected positively by the tree representation. Participants reported an emotional engagement with the machine and performed significantly more non-compulsory maintenance tasks when interacting with the tree representation [3].

2.3 Eye-Tracking Applied to Guidance and Recommender Systems

Today's eye-tracking technology allows us to determine where a person is looking at [Just and Carpenter 1980]. Affordable eye-tracking devices are reliable and can be used to record and analyze visual behaviour unobtrusively. Eye-tracking found its way into research, and it is already used in the evaluation of visualization systems [19,20]. Emerging topics such as guidance systems [21,22] and recommender systems can be used to support the users, e.g., by guiding the user to relevant visual objects, or by suggesting interesting data. Guidance is an essential component in support of users when exploring large datasets in visualization systems. It can also be applied to the guidance of users to valuable visual items. Renner and Pfeiffer [23] used eye-tracking for attention guiding in the context of assistance through augmented reality. Also, Blattergerste et al. compared selection mechanisms in VR, which included eye-gaze. Recommender systems support users in identifying relevant items and is applied to different domains, e.g., e-commerce and information retrieval [7]. Felfernig et al. [24] suggested improvements to the development of recommender systems such as the use of pervasive techniques (e.g., eye tracking) in new recommendation applications. Example recommender systems that integrate eye-tracking (using pre-processed data to build an offline model) were developed to help and guide people in the selection of products [25–27], support reading, browse images, and select videos [28]. New recommendation models were developed to continually adapt the user interface and the data displayed to the current users' interests by taking advantage of continuous analysis of eye-tracking data, and in providing active support to the users [30–33]. Advantages and pitfalls of using eye-movement data in adaptive systems were also previously discussed by Bednarik [29]. In this way, eye-tracking offers a new and vital channel through which applications can adapt to the users' interests.

3   Nature Inspired Representations Combined with Eye-gaze Features

The new proposed AR concept system enhances the BioIoT concept [2] by combining nature inspired representations with eye-gaze features in order to support and guide the users while interacting with IoT devices. The new concept targets the following objectives: i) the design of systems that positively influence well-being by displaying nature inspired representations, accordingly with several studies, have a positive effect on human well-being and productivity; ii) the efficient communication of the current IoT devices' status and to positively influence the maintenance behaviour of the users; iii) contextualized support and guidance through human behaviour sensing, i.e., using eye-gaze and attention.

As depicted in Fig. 1, the system is composed of five main components. First, an IoT device which generates sensory data which reflects the device's state. Second, a backend application responsible for communication and encoding the sensory data using the nature inspired language, and to adapt the user interface accordingly with the user model and user's sensing data relevant to provide support. Third, the user interface e.g. augmented reality visualization. Fourth, nature inspired language used to encode the IoT data, which can include, for example, visual, sound, and scent elements, e.g. tree representation. Fifth, a user model and user sensing data, e.g. user's preferences, user's expertise level, eye-gaze and context data.

Next, we describe our approach using the interaction with an IoT Coffee machine as an example use case (also considered in the study presented in Sect. 4). The system allows the user to easily monitor the general state of the IoT coffee machine, based only on the observation of the AR tree representation. The status of the machine is encoded in the tree properties, e.g. leaves colour, foliage density. In this way, if the machine presents abnormal temperature, the tree will present red leaves. In this case, the user is alerted about an issue with the machine, i.e., abnormal temperature, and that it relates to a cooling component. However, when the user approaches the problematic machine,

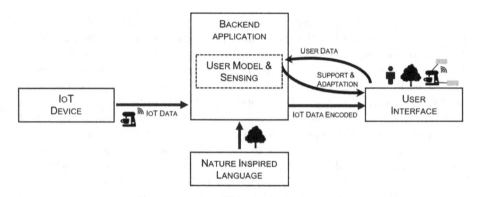

Fig. 1. The enhanced BioIoT concept combines with eye-gaze features. Adapted from Barreiros et al. [2].

the information needs are altered. The system is therefore required to adapt the level of detail (LOD) of the information. This adaptation depends on the distance and attention of the user to the target machine parts. Our proposed system makes use of eye-tracking data to provide contextualized user support and adaptation. To illustrate our system, we provide three examples: 1) the user's eye-gaze areas-of-interest (AOIs) can be used to detect to which machine part the user is looking at, enabling the system to provide additional information about the part, e.g. showing in-context information about the cooling fluid level and machine temperature; 2) the use of eye-tracking data, i.e., a sequence of fixated AOIs (machine parts) and fixation time on those areas, can be used to distinguish the expertise level of the user as suggested by [34]. For example, for a novice user the system can guide the attention of the user to the parts that need maintenance and consequently provide step by step instructions on how to refill the cooling fluid; 3) Depending on the machine status and focused parts, the system can recommend other potentially relevant check-ups or maintenance procedures. For example, whenever the temperature of the machine raises to a certain level, due to low fluid levels, the filter x is likely to have residues. Therefore the system can recommend an immediate check-up and guide the attention of the user to the relevant machine part, i.e., filter part.

4   Study - IoT Coffee Machine

The field study aims to validate the AR nature inspired representation concerning three dimensions, understandability, affect, and maintenance behaviour. We investigated the participants' responses to the machine's states encoded in two visual representations: an AR tree representation (AR-Bio) and an AR dashboard representation (AR-Dash). This study followed the overall design presented by Barreiros et al. [3], with the addition of using augmented reality to present the machine's states.

The research questions considered are:

- RQ1 - Understandability: Can AR-Bio be understood as easily as AR-Dash?
- RQ2 - Affect: Does AR-Bio evoke affect and empathy towards the machine?
- RQ3 - Behaviour: To what measure does AR-Bio influences the user's maintenance behaviour?

4.1 AR Tree Representation and AR Dashboard Representation of a Coffee Machine's States

The IoT coffee machine prototype is connected to one Arduino Uno and one Ethernet board. These boards collect real-time data from several sensors and transfer it to an MQTT server (Message Queue Telemetry Transport). The general state of the machine is a result of the combination of three types of sensors: an ultra-sonic sensor HC-SR04, two force-sensitive resistors, and a temperature sensor LM35. The coffee machine has five possible general states: non-operational, operational with warnings, operational without warnings, optimal and maintenance. The inferred general state of the machine is communicated to the participant. This communication is done by displaying the AR tree or the dashboard visual representations as an AR hologram next to the coffee machine. Figure 2 depicts the optimal state of the coffee machine when encoded using the tree representation. The different characteristics of the tree encode multiple sensor data: temperature is encoded in the leaves' colour; the water level is encoded in the foliage density, the maintenance status is encoded in the size of the flowers. Also, the presence of the coffee capsule is encoded by an animation of the sunlight.

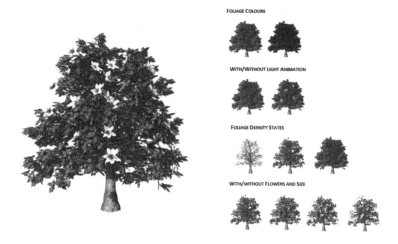

Fig. 2. Left: A tree representing the "optimal" state of a IoT machine. Right: Showcase of the encoding schema of the sensor data using the tree characteristics.

Figure 3 depicts the "operational with warnings" state of the coffee machine in the dashboard, because the water level is low. The sensors data is showed individually (A, B, C, D, E panels) and combined (F and G panels).

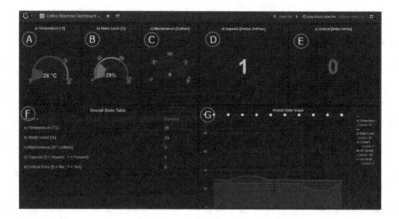

Fig. 3. Top: Dashboard showing the optimal state of the coffee machine. Bottom: Showcase of the encoding schema of the sensor data using the dashboard.

4.2   Procedure

The field study took place in a kitchen like setting in our lab and had a duration of two weeks. During this period participants were able to interact freely with the coffee machine. In the first session of the study, the participants received training regarding the coffee machine use and maintenance, as well as information about the encoding of the machines states in AR-Bio representation and AR-Dash representation. Also, the participants were instructed on the use of the head-mounted display during the interaction with the machine. After, participants were invited to wear the MS Hololens and brew their own coffee, giving them the chance to interact with the coffee machine. Questions and doubts were clarified during this initial session. Participants received instructions on how to proceed each time they brewed a coffee. The instructions were: 1) Wear the MS Hololens during the task; 2) Before starting, register the current state of the machine in a questionnaire; 3) Interact with the coffee machine (e.g. brewing a coffee, performing maintenance, refilling water, removing old capsule); 4) After, register the current state of the machine in a questionnaire.

After the training session, the participants were asked to prepare ten coffees (for two weeks at their convenience). Every time a participant arrived in the room, the researchers configured the MS Hololens to show the assigned visualization. Then the researchers observed the participant interactions with the coffee machine, filling an observation grid (e.g. room conditions, system performance, participants comments, and ground truth regarding the machine state). Participants were randomly split into two groups over the two conditions. Group 1 started with the AR-Bio condition and after five interactions changed to AR-Dash. Group 2, started with the AR-Dash condition and changed after five interactions to AR-Bio. After completing the ten interactions, each participant filled a post-questionnaire to evaluate the system usability and answered a closing interview. The states of the machine were semi-controlled by the researcher, who randomly introduced abnormal temperature values, added to the number of coffees brewed and created critical errors by altering the sensors readings.

4.3 Participants

Twelve participants ($7M$, $5F$) took part in the study, four aged between 20 and 29, six between 30 and 39, and two between 40 and 49. All participants were volunteers and recruited via an invitation email in our company.

4.4 Apparatus

The IoT coffee machine prototype was used in combination with one of the two immersive visualizations, AR-Bio and AR-Dash. Each visualization was available as a hologram through the head mounted display, i.e. MS Hololens. Figure 4-right depicts a participant wearing the head-mounted display while interacting with the coffee machine. On the top left one can see the coffee machine with the tree hologram next to it, and on the bottom left the dashboard hologram. The ingredients and equipment were ready for participants to brew their own coffee, and all was placed in a kitchen-like setting in the laboratory.

Fig. 4. Left: The participant wearing the Ms Hololens was able to see an hologram of the tree representation or the dashboard representation. Right: Participant interacting with the BioIoT coffee machine.

4.5 Results

RQ1-Understandability. In the AR-Bio condition, participants interpreted correctly 90 out of 120 general machine states. The median of correct general states per participant is 8.5 (range between 2 and 10). In the AR-Dash condition, the participants interpreted correctly 81 out of 120 general machine states. The median of correct general states per participant is 7 (range between 1 and 10). We summed the errors for the overall state per participant and condition. Paired-sample t-tests revealed significant differences in accumulated errors $t(11) = 2.35, p < .05$. Participants made less errors with AR-Bio ($M = 0.92$) than with AR-Dash ($M = 1.92$). In perceiving the general condition of the machine, participants performed more accurately in AR-Bio than in AR-Dash. In the AR-Bio condition participants correctly interpreted the detailed sensory information for the temperature, the presence/absence of the capsule, and the critical error without any errors. We averaged errors and right answers per participant and condition. A paired-samples t-test revealed a significant difference in the mean accumulated error $t(11) = -1.065, p < .01$. The mean accumulated error in AR-Dash ($M = 4.08$) was significantly larger than in AR-Bio($M = 1.83$). A paired samples t-test revealed a significant difference in right answers, $t(11) = 3.45, p < .01$. Participants gave more correct answers in AR-Bio ($M = 23.17$) than in AR-Dash ($M = 20.92$).

RQ2-Affect. All twelve participants considered the interaction with AR-Bio appealing ($4P$ Agree, $8P$ Strongly Agree). Participants revealed a more neutral opinion regarding the appeal of AR-Dash ($1P$ Disagree, $6P$ Neither Agree or Disagree, $5P$ Agree). Moreover, the participants considered the BioIoT tree metaphor representation of the machine states aesthetically pleasant ($4P$ Agree, $8P$ Strongly Agree). Regarding the dashboard interface, the participants had more diverse opinions ($3P$ Disagree, $3P$ Neither Agree or Disagree, $6P$ Agree).

RQ3-Behaviour. While using AR-Bio, participants stated to feel strongly compelled to take care of the machine ($2P$ Agree, $10P$ Strongly Agree). In the AR-Dash condition, participants gave a more distributed answer ($1P$ Strongly Disagree, $2P$ Disagree, $4P$ Neither Agree or Disagree, $4P$ Agree, $1P$ Strongly Agree). Beyond the subjective response, we intended to clarify whether they engaged in predictive maintenance in any condition. We verified that participants took better care of the machine looking into two points: i) Was the water refilled?; ii) was maintenance performed? *RQ3-Behaviour-i).* The water level varied according to the participants' actions, e.g. brewing a coffee, and refilling water. Participants refilled the water 68 times out 240 interactions. In the AR-Bio condition, participants refilled the water 43 times ($63, 2\%$), while in the AR-Dash condition participants refilled the water 25 times ($36, 8\%$). *RQ3-Behaviour-ii).* For us, it was interesting to analyze how participants behaved when the maintenance state was identified as "soon required" and "eventually required" because the maintenance task was optional. The participants identified 41 "eventually required" states and performed maintenance in the AR-Bio $= 7\%$, and in the AR-Dash $= 4\%$. For the 48 interpreted as "soon required", participants performed maintenance 29% in AR-Bio and 26% in AR-Dash.

5   Discussion

Our results confirm that the BioIoT nature metaphor is an appropriate and innovative way to communicate real-time sensor information. The results with regards to RQ1-Understandability reveal that BioIoT is at least well understood as conventional visual representations of sensor data. Participants made fewer mistakes interpreting the general status of the machine with the tree representation than with the dashboard. Also, results underline the effectiveness of this metaphor. The error rates interpreting the exact condition of each sensor was lower with BioIoT than with the dashboard. It implies that this metaphor can be used as an alternative to traditional dashboard-like visual representations. Beyond being effective, we intended to promote a positive bonding effect towards the machine through the BioIoT metaphor. Responses for RQ2-Affect indicate that the metaphor is appealing and more *likeable* than the conventional dashboard visualization. In looking into whether the metaphor leads people to care for the machine RQ3-Behaviour, we found that participants maintenance behaviour was positively affected by the tree representation, confirming previous results with 2D tree representations [3]. We recognize the complexity of human behaviour research field, and that identifying what leads people to behave in a certain way is not easy. However, even considering these limitations, our findings confirm that nature inspired representations positively influence users' interaction with the IoT device and the maintenance behaviour through persuasion and social influence.

Future studies will focus on the integration of eye-tracking technology, responsible for providing adaptive contextualized support and guidance. By combining the BioIoT concept with the eye-tracking technology, we expect to improved training environments, as well as learning at the workplace by changing the interaction paradigm with the device itself and providing contextualized support and guidance.

6   Limitations and Further Research

We intended to have an ecological validation of the BioIoT metaphor. Therefore, instead of running a fully controlled study in one session, we chose a relaxed format resembling the real operation of the device. Nevertheless, to fully understand the effects of the BioIoT concept, the experiment should run for an extended period and in a completely unsupervised setting. To be fair with the comparison between the different visual representations, we decided to use immersive displays in both conditions. However, traditional dashboards are usually presented in a monitor. The holographic display of the dashboard may have introduced undesired effects, such as disturbances in the field of view. Also, future studies will focus on the integration of eye-tracking technology as a sensing modality to permit the continuous adaptation and support to the users' needs.

Acknowledgements. This work was funded by the LiTech K-project and by Know Center GmbH. Both funded by the Austrian Competence Centers for Excellent

Technologies (COMET) program, under the auspices of the Austrian Federal Ministry of Transport, Innovation, and Technology; the Austrian Federal Ministry of Economy, Family, and Youth; and the Austrian state of Styria. COMET is managed by the Austrian Research Promotion Agency FFG.

References

1. Azuma, R.T.: A survey of augmented reality. Presence: Teleoperators Virtual Environ. **6**(4), 355–385 (1997). https://doi.org/10.1162/pres.1997.6.4.355
2. Barreiros, C., Veas, E., Pammer, V.: Bringing nature into our lives. In: Kurosu, M. (ed.) HCI 2018. LNCS, vol. 10902, pp. 99–109. Springer, Cham (2018). https://doi.org/10.1007/978-3-319-91244-8_9
3. Barreiros, C., Pammer-Schindler, V., Veas, E.: Planting the seed of positive human-IoT interaction. Int. J. Hum.-Comput. Interact. **36**(4), 355–372 (2020). https://doi.org/10.1080/10447318.2019.1642674
4. Barreiros, C., et al.: What if factories looked like forests? Redesigning the manufacturing industry 4.0 workplaces with an augmented reality inspired nature metaphor. In: CEUR - Workshop Proceedings i-know 2017, vol. 2025, pp. 4 (2017)
5. Mekni, M., Lemieux, A.: Augmented reality: applications, challenges and future trends. In: Proceedings of the 13th International Conference on Applied Computer and Computation Sciences (ACACOS 2014). pp. 205–215. WSEAS Press (2014)
6. Bower, M., Howe, C., McCredie, N., Robinson, A., Grover, D.: Augmented reality in education—cases, places, and potentials. In: 2013 IEEE 63rd Annual Conference International Council for Education Media (ICEM), pp. 1–11 (2013). https://doi.org/10.1109/CICEM.2013.6820176
7. Ricci, F., Rokach, L., Shapira, B., Kantor, P.B. (eds.): Recommender Systems Handbook. Springer, Boston (2011). https://doi.org/10.1007/978-0-387-85820-3
8. Ulrich, R., Simons, R., Losito, B., Fiorito, E., Miles, M., Zelson, M.: Stress recovery during exposure to natural and urban environments. J. Environ. Psychol. **11**(3), 201–230 (1991). https://doi.org/10.1016/S0272-4944(05)80184-7
9. Kahn, P., Severson, R., Ruckert, J.: The human relation with nature and technological nature. Curr. Direc. Psychol. Sci. **18**(1), 37–42 (2009). https://doi.org/10.1111/j.1467-8721.2009.01602.x
10. Parsons, R.J.: Environmental psychophysiology. In: Cacioppo, J.T., et al. (eds.) Handbook of Psychophysiology, pp. 752–786. Cambridge University Press, Cambridge (2007)
11. Largo-Wight, E., Chen, W., Dodd, V., Weiler, R.: Healthy workplaces: the effects of nature contact at work on employee stress and health. Publ. Health Rep. **126**(1 suppl), 124–130 (2011). https://doi.org/10.1177/00333549111260S116
12. Nass, C., Yen, C.: The Man Who Lied to His Laptop: What We Can Learn About Ourselves from Our Machines. Penguin Publishing Group, New York City (2010)
13. Chien, J., Guimbretière, F., Rahman, T., Gay, G., Matthews, M.: Biogotchi!: an exploration of plant-based information displays. In: Proceedings of the 33rd Annual ACM Conference Extended Abstracts on Human Factors in Computing Systems, pp. 1139–1144 ACM, New York (2015). https://doi.org/10.1145/2702613.2732770
14. Eggen, B., Van Mensvoort, K.: Making sense of what is going on 'Around': designing environmental awareness information displays. In: Markopoulos, P., et al. (eds.) Awareness Systems: Advances in Theory, Methodology and Design, pp. 99–124. Springer, London (2009). https://doi.org/10.1007/978-1-84882-477-5_4

15. Fogg, B., Nass, C.: How users reciprocate to computers: an experiment that demonstrates behavior change. In: CHI 1997 Extended Abstracts on Human Factors in Computing Systems, pp. 331–332. ACM, New York (1997). https://doi.org/10.1145/1120212.1120419

16. Bartneck, C., Hoek, M., Mubin, O., Mahmud, A.: "Daisy, Daisy, Give Me Your Answer Do!" switching off a robot. In: 2007 2nd ACM/IEEE International Conference on Human-Robot Interaction (HRI), pp. 217–222 (2007)

17. Froehlich, J., et al.: UbiGreen: investigating a mobile tool for tracking and supporting green transportation habits. In: Proceedings of the SIGCHI Conference on Human Factors in Computing Systems, pp. 1043–1052. ACM, New York (2009). https://doi.org/10.1145/1518701.1518861

18. Browning, B., Garvin, C., Fox, B., Cook, R.: The Economics of Biophilia. Terrapin Bright Green, New Yor (2012)

19. Andrienko, G., Andrienko, N.V., Burch, M., Weiskopf, D.: Visual analytics methodology for eye movement studies. IEEE Trans. Vis. Comput. Graph. **18**(12), 2889–2898 (2012). https://doi.org/10.1109/tvcg.2012.276

20. Kurzhals, K., Fisher, B., Burch, M., Weiskopf, D.: Evaluating visual analytics with eye tracking. In: Proceedings of the BELIV Workshop: Beyond (2014). https://doi.org/10.1145/2669557.2669560

21. Collins, C., et al.: Guidance in the human-machine analytics process. Visual Inform. **2**(3), 166–180 (2018). https://doi.org/10.1016/j.visinf.2018.09.003

22. Ceneda, D., et al.: Characterizing guidance in visual analytics. IEEE Trans. Visual. Comput. Graph. **23**(1), 111–120 (2017)

23. Renner, P., Pfeiffer, T.: Attention guiding techniques using peripheral vision and eye tracking for feedback in augmented-reality-based assistance systems. In: Proceedings of the Symposium on 3D User Interfaces, pp. 186–194 (2017). https://doi.org/10.1109/3dui.2017.7893338

24. Felfernig, A., Jeran, M., Ninaus, G., Reinfrank, F., Reiterer, S.: Toward the next generation of recommender systems: applications and research challenges. In: Multimedia Services in Intelligent Environments, pp. 81–98. Springer (2013). https://doi.org/10.1007/978-3-319-00372-6_5

25. Castagnos, S., et al.: Eye-tracking product recommenders' usage. In: Proceedings of the ACM Conference on Recommender systems, pp. 29–36. ACM (2010). https://doi.org/10.1145/1864708.1864717

26. Castagnos, S., Pu, P.: Consumer decision patterns through eye gaze analysis. In: Proceedings of the Workshop on Eye Gaze in Intelligent Human Machine. ACM (2010). https://doi.org/10.1145/2002333.2002346

27. Chen, L., Pu, P.: Users' eye gaze pattern in organization-based recommender interfaces. In: Proceedings of the 16th International Conference on Intelligent User Interfaces, pp. 311–314. ACM (2011). https://doi.org/10.1145/1943403.1943453

28. Xu, S., Jiang, H., Lau, F.: Personalized online document, image and video recommendation via commodity eye-tracking. In: Proceedings of the 2008 ACM conference on Recommender systems, pp. 83–90 ACM (2008). https://doi.org/10.1145/1454008.1454023

29. Bednarik, R.: Potentials of eye-movement tracking in adaptive systems. In: Proceedings of the 4th Workshop on Empirical Evaluation of Adaptive Systems, pp. 1–8 (2005)

30. Shao, L., Silva, N., Eggeling, E., Schreck, T.: Visual exploration of large scatter plot matrices by pattern recommendation based on eye tracking. In: Proceedings of the 2017 ACM Workshop on Exploratory Search and Interactive Data Analytics, pp. 9–16. ACM (2017)

31. Silva, N., Settgast, V., Eggeling, E., Ullrich, T., Schreck, T., Fellner, D.: Increasing fault tolerance in operational centres using human sensing technologies: approach and initial results. In: European Project Space on Computer Vision, Graphics, Optics and Photonics, p. 25. SCITEPRESS (2015)

32. Silva, N., et al.: Sense.Me - open source framework for the exploration and visualization of eye tracking data. In: Proceedings of the 2016 IEEE Conference on Information Visualization. IEEE (2016)

33. Silva, N., Schreck, T., Veas, E., Sabol, V., Eggeling, E., Fellner, D.: Leveraging eye-gaze and time-series features to predict user interests and build a recommendation model for visual analysis. In: Proceedings of the 2018 ACM Symposium on Eye Tracking. Research and Applications, vol. 13. ACM (2018). https://doi.org/10.1145/3204493.3204546

34. Gegenfurtner, A., et al.: Expertise differences in the comprehension of visualizations: a meta-analysis of eye-tracking research in professional domains. Educ. Psychol. Rev. **23**(4), 523–552 (2011). https://doi.org/10.1007/s10648-011-9174-7

35. Cristancho, S., Moussa, F., Dubrowski, A.: A framework-based approach to designing simulation-augmented surgical education and training programs. Am. J. Surg. **202**(3), 344–351 (2011). https://doi.org/10.1016/j.amjsurg.2011.02.011

36. Regenbrecht, H., Baratoff, G., Wilke, W.: Augmented reality projects in the automotive and aerospace industries. IEEE Comput. Graph. Appl. **25**(6), 48–56 (2005). https://doi.org/10.1109/MCG.2005.124

37. Schall, G., et al.: Handheld Augmented Reality for underground infrastructure visualization. Pers. Ubiquit. Comput. **13**(4), 281–291 (2009). https://doi.org/10.1007/s00779-008-0204-5

38. Billinghurst, M., Duenser, A.: Augmented reality in the classroom. Computer **45**(7), 56–63 (2012). https://doi.org/10.1109/MC.2012.111

39. Jerry, T., Aaron, C.: The impact of augmented reality software with inquiry-based learning on students' learning of kinematics graph. In: 2010 2nd International Conference on Education Technology and Computer, pp. V2-1–V2-5 (2010). https://doi.org/10.1109/ICETC.2010.5529447

40. Lee, K.: Augmented reality in education and training. Techtrends Tech Trends **56**(2), 13–21 (2012). https://doi.org/10.1007/s11528-012-0559-3

Adapting Instruction by Measuring Engagement with Machine Learning in Virtual Reality Training

Benjamin Bell[1]([✉]), Elaine Kelsey[1], Benjamin Nye[2],
and Winston ("Wink") Bennett[3]

[1] Eduworks Corporation, Corvallis, OR, USA
{benjamin.bell,elaine.kelsey}@eduworks.com
[2] USC Institute for Creative Technologies, Playa Vista, CA, USA
nye@ict.usc.edu
[3] Warfighter Readiness Research Division, 711 HPW/RHA,
Wright-Patterson AFB, OH, USA
winston.bennett@us.af.mil

Abstract. The USAF has established a new approach to Specialized Under-graduate Pilot Training (SUPT) called Pilot Training Next (PTN) that integrates traditional flying sorties with VR-enabled ground-based training devices and data-driven proficiency tracking to achieve training efficiencies, improve readiness, and increase throughput. Eduworks and USC's Institute for Creative Technologies are developing machine learning (ML) models that can measure user engagement during any computer-mediated training (simulation, course-ware) and offer recommendations for restoring lapses in engagement. We are currently developing and testing this approach, called the Observational Motivation and Engagement Generalized Appliance (OMEGA) in a PTN context. Two factors motivate this work. First, one goal of PTN is for an instructor pilot (IP) to simultaneously monitor multiple simulator rides. Being alerted to distraction, attention and engagement can help an IP manage multiple students at the same time, with recommendations for restoring engagement providing further instructional support. Second, the virtual environment provides a rich source of raw data that machine learning models can use to associate user activity with user engagement. We have created a testbed for data capture in order to construct the ML models, based on theoretical foundations we developed previously. We are running pilots through multiple PTN scenarios and collecting formative data from instructors to evaluate the utility of the recommendations OMEGA generates regarding how lapsed engagement can be restored. We anticipate findings that validate the use of ML models for learning to detect engagement from the rich data sources characteristic of virtual environments. These findings will be applicable across a broad range of conventional and VR training applications.

Keywords: Adaptive training · Machine learning · Virtual reality

R. A. Sottilare and J. Schwarz (Eds.): HCII 2020, LNCS 12214, pp. 271–282, 2020.
https://doi.org/10.1007/978-3-030-50788-6_20

1   Introduction

1.1   Problem Summary

To support a complex array of current and envisioned missions, the U.S. Air Force trains and educates a large uniformed workforce across diverse Air Force Specialty Codes (AFSCs). Early-stage training in many AFSCs presents Airmen and officer trainees with large corpora of foundational knowledge to master, delivered through a variety of modalities. This content is taught at technical training or flight schools in courses lasting up to several months. Because motivation is a necessary element for learning retention and force readiness, Air Force education and training stakeholders continue to look for ways to engage their constituencies, through gamified interactive learning, simulation, and the use of mixed-reality immersive environments.

To maintain an engaged, motivated cadre of Airmen, OMEGA, via a service-oriented, general-purpose appliance operating in concert with the learning environment, will recommend interventions when end-users are showing signs of a lapse in engagement. These services will be accessible to any AF instructional system, which can automatically or through a human instructor locally effect OMEGA's recommendations. OMEGA will enable AF and DoD learning environments to identify and adapt to detected lapses in engagement, promoting greater motivation, retention, and readiness.

1.2   Project Context: Pilot Training Next

The test case for OMEGA, selected by the Air Force, is Pilot Training Next (PTN). PTN, now training its third iteration of pilots, aims to the reduce the time and cost of undergraduate pilot training (UPT) by leveraging virtual and augmented reality, biometrics, AI, and data analytics. While PTN student pilots fly the same hours and sorties in the T-6 as do their legacy pilot training counterparts, the ground-based training is done using an immersive PC-based flight simulator (Lockheed Martin's Prepar3D®), VR headset (HTC's VIVE™ Pro), stick, throttle and rudder pedals, and a syllabus of PTN-specific scenarios (Fig. 1).

Fig. 1. PTN station: VR headset, controls, displays. (U.S. Air Force photo by Sean M. Worrell)

PTN has maintained a heavy emphasis on data collection and analysis. Reliable and predictive metrics are needed not only to assure instructors and higher command that student pilots are achieving the same skills as their legacy training counterparts, but also because PTN students qualify for graduation on the basis of achievements rather than on calendar time. This fundamental change in how students progress requires an abundance of data that supplement instructor evaluations to ensure skill mastery.

During scenarios flown in the simulator, objective data is readily captured for every time interval, such as aircraft state (position, attitude, airspeed) and configuration (aileron, rudder and elevator deflections; flap and gear positions). Instructors can also monitor how the scenario is progressing overall and can provide verbal feedback in real-time.

Some important metrics though are less directly observable or measurable. Student engagement is widely accepted as a critical mediating factor in both learning retention [1] and learning outcomes [2]. The importance of engagement is not lost on instructors (though labels like attention and focus are more common in pilot training), and is often the basis for, or at least an element of, scoring situational awareness (SA).

Two additional factors make engagement even more salient for PTN. First, instructors have less visibility into student engagement (due to the VR headset) than in conventional simulators. Second, a vision for PTN is for one instructor to be monitoring multiple students simultaneously. Indirectly-observable measures such as engagement will thus require some level of automation support to cue instructors when lapses are detected.

2 Modelling Engagement

2.1 Conceptual Model of Engagement

In training sorties flown in the aircraft or in conventional simulators, an instructor pilot (IP) monitors the student pilot's performance. Maneuvers are evaluated by observing air speed, vertical speed, attitude, angle of attack, and so on. Instructors are also interested in situational awareness (SA), which they can assess by observing the student's ability to "stay ahead of the airplane": anticipating upcoming changes in heading, airspeed, or altitude; applying smooth control inputs to adjust bank angle, pitch and power; and maintaining proper scan of the flight instruments.

Several theoretical frameworks for characterizing engagement informed our model of engagement. We created an inventory of nine relevant engagement and disengagement models from the literature that emphasize behavioral indicators (e.g., data from log files or from direct queries to the user) [3]. These included Intrinsic vs. Extrinsic [4]; Two Factor Hygiene-Motivator Theory [5]; Motivators from Maslow's Hierarchy (Ibid); Achievement Goal Theory [6]; D'Mello & Graesser's Engagement model [7]; and Baker's indicators of passive vs. active disengagement [8]. From this we synthesized a multi-timescale engagement and motivation model [9].

More recently, we refined the model to reflect the aviation focus of this project, preferring metrics associated with *event response* tasks (e.g., maneuvering to avoid a new hazard) and *monitoring* tasks (e.g., maintaining straight and level attitude). We incorporated significant research conducted to identify indicators of distraction and disengagement for accidents attributed to loss of control and airplane state awareness [10, 11]. A subset of these states is relevant to flight tasks performed in simulated environments:

- Attention vs. Distraction: Situational awareness was particularly reduced by the induction of diverted attention. Channelized attention or attentional tunneling also indicated loss of situational awareness [10];
- Boredom and Distraction: Distraction can be characterized by any time without interaction with the system; engaged pilots interacted with the system to optimize performance, even when this was not required to meet performance requirements [12];
- Attentional Tunneling: Attentional tunneling is indicated by lack of interaction with one or more system elements, coupled with strong interaction with another element [11];
- Vigilance: Diligence, distraction and daydreaming all lead to failures in practical monitoring tasks [13].

Composite Measure of Engagement: Inverse weighted average of Performance, Efficiency, and Responsiveness			
Weight	Category	Metric	Calculation
15%	Performance (Over/Under)	Metric 1: Conf(Expected)	Conf(Expected) * % Tasks Missed (z-score) / Expected (z-score)
		Metric 2: % Tasks Missed (z-score)	
		Metric 3: % Expected (z-score)	
35%	Efficiency	Metric 4: Deviation from an ideal path (max(0, |z-score| -1) of closest distance	Normalized, weighted composite
		Metric 5: Time to complete each segment (z-score)	
		Metric 6: % Resources (Fuel) Remaining (z-score)	
50%	Responsiveness (Reaction Time)	Metric 7: Reaction Time: How long after an 'event' does a detectable change occur? - Normalized by expertise level (% Expected) - Rapid response discounted (if incorrect)	Normalized, weighted composite
		Metric 8: Corrections - How long to correct after going off-course	

Fig. 2. Engagement model

The model resulting from this additional analysis is shown in Fig. 2. The resulting expert model is based on eight input metrics, used to compute three mid-level features: Performance, Efficiency, and Responsiveness. An overall composite measure of current engagement within a given data window is derived from these mid-level features. The relative weights and derivation methods shown in Fig. 2 represent the initial trial conditions. We anticipate that these will be refined through additional testing.

2.2 Engagement Metrics and Virtual Reality

A desktop flight simulator generates a rich set of data, including aircraft position, attitude and configuration. From such data, objective performance metrics can be calculated with some reliability. For instance, detecting when a student pilot lowers the gear while the airspeed exceeds the maximum gear-down speed is straightforward. To monitor engagement, however, requires aggregating observable measures to generate an indirect estimate of engagement. Our model, for instance, specifies eight such indirect measures.

The addition of a VR head-mounted display (HMD) adds additional data points that could be incorporated as part of a suite of metrics to monitor engagement levels. Typical VR headset and sensors can capture head position and movement; higher-end devices, such as the VIVE Pro Eye, can capture eye tracking data. The VR environment thus adds to the already rich data stream available from the simulator. This apparent abundance of data, however, does not solve the problem of developing reliable measures of engagement. Several challenges for interpreting the data remain, including, non-exhaustively:

1. Understanding which data points are relevant to engagement;
2. Setting proper coefficients representing how each data point should be weighted;
3. Distinguishing between and properly applying a single data point x observed at time t compared with a trend of how x behaves over some interval (*e.g.*, from $t - 5$ s to $t + 5$ s).
4. Incorporating the velocity of the change in a data point, for instance, how abrupt an aileron deflection or throttle movement the student applied.

A principal emphasis of this work is to explore the role that machine learning models could play in interpreting simulator and VR device data in order to develop measures to drive our conceptual model of engagement. This machine learning approach is summarized in the next section.

3 Machine Learning Approach

3.1 Machine Learning Model

We employ machine learning to allow OMEGA to develop more accurate predictive associations between raw data inputs and higher-level aggregated engagement metrics. This section describes the techniques and architecture of the OMEGA machine learning component. Our design leverages the underlying data streams available from Prepar3D to provide better predictive power in situations where there is limited access to interpreted data (e.g. when interpreted metrics of event occurrence, event success/failure, and efficiency are not available). To achieve this, we employ three methods in combination:

1. We use **standard machine learning** techniques to attempt to accurately predict engagement and disengagement in input metric sequences. These approaches are attractive because they enjoy fast estimation methods with low run-time, and therefore can provide near-instant feedback to instructors. Based on the features and

data available in Prepar3D, we have selected Support Vector Machine (SVM) and Binomial Regression as the most applicable approaches. These techniques are most powerful in cases where sequence classification is not strongly context-dependent. For OMEGA, however, we expect some context-dependence in the data. For example, rapid adjustments of heading, altitude and airspeed may represent recovery from a period of inattention if these maneuvers occur between waypoints, but may represent an attentive reaction if observed during an event requiring active response (e.g. a heading change when passing a waypoint). To mitigate this risk and to improve the model, we deploy two additional "deep learning" layers of machine learning that are more robust to sequence classification in context-dependent data.

2. We use a form of deep learning called **bidirectional long short term memory (BD-LSTM),** a type of recurrent neural network, to produce improved results in sequence classification problems that are heavily context-dependent. In this case, determining whether a given sequence of composite low-level metric readings represents disengagement is likely to be highly context-dependent, for instance a climb at full power versus a climb at normal cruise speed. We us bidirectional LSTMs, which consider the 'context' of both the preceding and following time slice data when predicting disengagement, to reduce the incidence of false-positive detection of disengagement in this environment. The tradeoff for improved disengagement and inattention detection is the high resource and time cost of maintaining bidirectional LSTM in OMEGA. Recurrent Neural Networks (RNNs) like LSTM are can be difficult to train due to memory-bandwidth-bound computation limitations. For this reason, we have selected a second deep learning approach in case the performance requirements present too much risk.

3. We use an alternative deep learning approach called **Attention-based Modeling** as the third layer in OMEGA's machine learning stack. Attention-based models are sequence-to-sequence models designed to improve performance of RNN-based approaches. This third layer provides an alternative mechanism in cases where bidirectional LSTM is too resource-intensive to be effective in real-time.

3.2   Training the Model

Data for training the machine learning components derives from experimental subjects who fly a pre-selected set of PTN scenarios in a data collection station that mirrors most of a PTN simulator, namely, the simulation software, stick and throttle, and VIVE Pro HMD and sensors. The data collection station also includes a dedicated application for the experimenter to monitor each scenario, interact with the subject, and time-stamp relevant events. Figure 3 shows an experimenter and subject during a data collection session.

Fig. 3. Data collection (background), experimenter (foreground) stations. Photo by the authors.

For purposes of creating training data for the machine learning models, experimenters are trained in a protocol to (1) time-stamp lower-intensity and higher-intensity segments of a scenario, to help the models account for workload in processing measures of user activity; and (2) engage the subject in conversation at specific points during a scenario. Conversing with the subject acts as a surrogate for disengagement. We posit that loss of attention, or distraction, will be statistically detectable in the simulation log files. Specifically, we anticipate three possible types of deviations:

1) Response Time: Most dominantly, we anticipate that subjects' time to respond to changes in the environment will be slower and/or less precise when engaging in conversation. Specifically, we anticipate a longer duration with no response after an event that requires a maneuver (*e.g.* heading change), followed in some cases by an initial control input that is more abrupt, more prone to overcorrect, or may even be in the wrong direction.
2) Performance: We anticipate more likely failure to accomplish scenario goals (e.g., missing required waypoints).
3) Efficiency: We anticipate that periods of distraction will tend to be less efficient, due to the above issues and due to less precise control over the aircraft (e.g., slower damping of over-correcting heading changes).

Subjects were recruited from flying clubs in the Corvallis, OR and Los Angeles regions. Subjects qualified for the study through meeting either flying hour criteria or flight simulator experience criteria. Each subject was given a practice period with the PTN station and then asked to complete six PTN scenarios. The collected data are being used to train the machine learning model, comparing both the predictive power and the latency and resource requirements for each of our deep learning modeling techniques.

4   Adaptive Instruction

4.1   Adaptive Recommendations Model

OMEGA processes detect engagement levels to generate adaptive recommendations to help an instructor restore lapsed engagement. During a scenario, based on combinations of different state signals, OMEGA will generate a set of intermediate inferences. These inferences include, for example, whether poor performance is due to consistently bad results versus irregular behavior or inconsistency (e.g., carelessness). The model employs both the basic state model and the aggregated inferences as inputs to calculate a scoring ranking for different adaptive interventions.

Our model considers three levels of outcomes: performance, responsiveness, and efficiency, each representing a distinct dimension of quality. Performance represents the basic ability to complete the assigned tasks, based on the performance criteria for those tasks (e.g., following a set of waypoints). Responsiveness represents the speed and effectiveness for a learner to adjust to new tasks or requirements (e.g., if a waypoint is moved, how quickly does the user adjust heading). Efficiency represents lean and strategic use of resources to complete a scenario (e.g., faster completion times).

These quality criteria can each be thought of as building upon each other: a learner must adjust heading to a new waypoint or else there is no way to determine responsiveness. Likewise, efficiency is impossible if the user is not responsive enough to stay on course. This means that only some factors should be addressed with certain types of learners (e.g., high vs. low expertise). For example, if a user is failing to master proper take-off procedures, critiquing fuel efficiency would add no training value. On the other hand, an otherwise high-performing student pilot who is drifting off-course or leaving assigned altitudes may benefit from noting a need for improved in-flight checks.

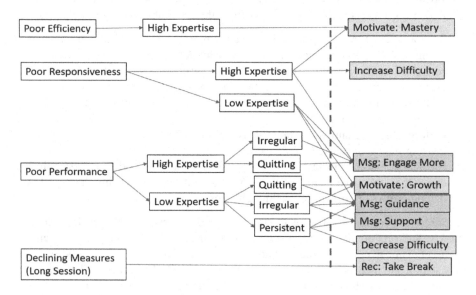

Fig. 4. High-Level policy for adaptive interventions in PTN

The policy for adaptive interventions is depicted schematically in Fig. 4. The right-hand side of Fig. 4 shows the interventions proposed for PTN. These include three distinct types of interventions: Messaging (Information about the task), Motivation (Context about the task and learning goals), and Recommendations (Suggestions on different tasks or breaks to improve learning). The left-hand side of Fig. 4 outlines a high-level policy for when specific interventions are expected to be appropriate for users with different skill levels and in different states. These connections between intervention types and student states do not represent the actual model. Instead, they represent key dynamics that the model will produce. However, since the actual state space to calculate an effective intervention policy is too large to easily convert into a short graph, this model captures the key behaviors that the intervention model will be tested against, to ensure it behaves reasonably versus what would align to theoretical frameworks for engagement and responding to disengagement. The intervention types are outlined in Table 1.

Table 1. Intervention types for PTN

Category	Type	Description
Messaging	Engage more	A suggestion or warning that signs of decreased engagement were noticed, with a suggestion on how to improve
	Guidance	A useful hint about how to do better on the specific scenario or skills
	Support	Affective feedback to help a learner who is struggling
Motivate	Mastery	Information about how better training can improve later real-life performance
	Growth mindset	Feedback about how sustained effort leads to improved skills and outcomes
Recommend	Increase difficulty	Suggest that the user might need more challenging scenarios to engage with
	Decrease difficulty	Suggest user might benefit from trying some easier scenarios before this one
	Take break	Suggest that user returns after taking a break, due to decreasing performance

4.2 Generating Adaptive Recommendations

We propose two distinct methods for generating adaptation recommendations based on the internal state of the models used to measure engagement. The first approach is much less computationally-intensive and will produce recommendations with lower latency. However, given the highly contextualized nature of the input data, we expect the second approach to produce more accurate results. Work is currently in-progress for testing the trade-offs between timeliness and quality under different simulation conditions.

In the first approach, we use the calculated values from the engagement model (performance, efficiency, and responsiveness) as inputs to a machine learning classification model. Using the labeled data set produced during the data collection trials discussed above, we apply several traditional machine learning modeling techniques to the classification task, where the outputs are the available set of adaptations available in the PTN training environment. We use both Naive Bayes and Support Vector Machine (SVM) approaches. Since the input metrics include variables that are highly interdependent, we expect that SVM will yield superior results. SVMs have been demonstrated to predict the likelihood of learner withdrawal from online courses, for example [14]. These techniques do not account for the contextual nature of the data, instead analyzing each time slice as a separate case. As was the case for detecting engagement levels, the determination of an appropriate adaptation will depend on the context in which the disengagement event occurs, as well as on the environmental conditions being simulated.

We define *context* as the data stream of pilot behaviors and actions preceding and following a time slice, and *environment* as the set of conditions that obtain for that particular segment of the simulation (e.g. aircraft attitude, airspeed, status of systems). In order to fully account for the contextual nature of both disengagement detection and the recommendation of an appropriate adaptation, we are developing a second, more powerful model for capturing temporal information and learning high-level representations hidden in the metric data stream based on Artificial Neural Networks (ANN).

Much of the research in applying ANN to the interpretation of sensor data streams has been focused on traditional neural network approaches, such as feed-forward neural networks (FFNN) and deep convolutional neural networks (CNN). Al-Shabandar, *et al.* [15] employed a range of machine learning models including ANNs to investigate factors driving student motivation in massively-online open courses (MOOCs). Recent success of recurrent neural networks (RNN) with long short-term memory (LSTM) in other applications has led to promising trials of this approach in using sensor data to predict highly contextual operational states. RNNs have been used for, among other applications, associating student engagement with outcomes in MOOCs [16].

Variations of this approach have recently explored incorporating operational conditions into the predictive model. These approaches use several BD-LSTM models and a final FFNN layer to integrate both the contextual information encoded in the data stream (representing the sensor data) and the available operating context and environmental data. The model we have designed adapts this approach to the interpretation of Prepar3D data for (1) predicting pilot engagement and detecting disengagement; and (2) using context about the nature of the disengagement to predict the most effective adaptation to recommend to the human instructor in the context of PTN training.

The model is composed of several stacked layers of ANNs. The first BD-LSTM network extracts latent features from the multiple metric data streams describing pilot behavior. The second BD-LSTM network extracts latent features from the metric data stream describing aircraft movement, and the third BD-LSTM network extracts higher level features describing the operational environment. These layers are stacked with a final neural network layer to predict pilot disengagement level and events, depicted schematically in Fig. 5. The states of the internal layers of these BD-LSTM networks are then used as the input into a separate recommendation model to predict the most appropriate adaptation in a given context. The recommendation model layer is a CNN network, which will be trained using the labeled data set from the pilot trials.

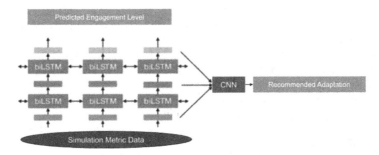

Fig. 5. Adaptation recommendation stacked neural network architecture

5   Conclusions

We have concluded data collection and will present our results from the machine learning model development during the conference. A formative evaluation using Air Force instructor pilots to provide feedback to OMEGA's recommendations will immediately follow the model development. Simulations enhanced with VR provides immersive training that promises to advance learning outcomes and retention. A key factor in achieving positive results is learner engagement, which is more challenging to assess than directly observable or objectively measurable factors. In some instances, the VR environment itself can obscure cues relevant to learning engagement from instructor view. OMEGA addresses this gap by using machine learning models to develop predictive associations between simulation events and learner actions on the one hand, and learner engagement on the other. OMEGA also incorporates a model of adaptive interventions to remedy engagement lapses, and employs machine learning to develop associations between the context and environment of the engagement lapse and the optimal intervention to recommend.

Our results will provide concept validation to establish more general-purpose, service-oriented appliance that client learning applications can employ for detecting lapses in engagement and motivation, and for recommending adaptive interventions. OMEGA can thus address a need, across the service branches, to ensure that simulation-based training, and training incorporating VR, results in engaged and motivated warriors, using adaptive instruction and providing data to help training managers track the efficacy of new technologies and paradigms.

References

1. Hu, P.J.H., Hui, W.: Examining the role of learning engagement in technology-mediated learning and its effects on learning effectiveness and satisfaction. Decis. Support Syst. **53**(4), 782–792 (2012)
2. Chi, M.T., Wylie, R.: The ICAP framework: linking cognitive engagement to active learning outcomes. Educ. Psychol. **49**(4), 219–243 (2014)

3. Core, M.G., Georgila, K., Nye, B.D., Auerbach, D., Liu, Z.F., DiNinni, R.: Learning, adaptive support, student traits, and engagement in scenario-based learning. In: I/ITSEC, 2016 (2016)
4. Porter, L.W., Lawler, E.E.: Managerial attitudes and performance (1968)
5. Gawel, J.E.: Herzberg's theory of motivation and Maslow's hierarchy of needs. Pract. Assess. Res. Eval. 5(11), 3 (1997)
6. Pintrich, P.R.: Multiple goals, multiple pathways: the role of goal orientation in learning & achievement. J. Educ. Psychol. 92(3), 544 (2000)
7. D'Mello, S., Graesser, A.: Dynamics of affective states during complex learning. Learn. Instruct. 22(2), 145–157 (2012)
8. Baker, R.S., Corbett, A.T., Roll, I., Koedinger, K.R.: Developing a generalizable detector of when students game the system. User Model. User-Adap. Interact. 18(3), 287–314 (2008)
9. Bell, B., Kelsey, E., Nye, B.: Monitoring engagement and motivation across learning environments. In: Proceedings of the 2019 MODSIM World Conference, Norfolk, VA (2019)
10. Harrivel, A.R., et al.: Prediction of cognitive states during flight simulation using multimodal psychophysiological sensing. In: AIAA Information Systems-AIAA Infotech, p. 1135 (2017)
11. Wickens, C.D.: Attentional tunneling and task management. In: 2005 International Symposium on Aviation Psychology, p. 812 (2005)
12. Cummings, M.L., Mastracchio, C., Thornburg, K.M., Mkrtchyan, A.: Boredom and distraction in multiple unmanned vehicle supervisory control. Interact. Comput. 25(1), 34–47 (2013)
13. Casner, S.M., Schooler, J.W.: Vigilance impossible: diligence, distraction, and daydreaming all lead to failures in a practical monitoring task. Conscious. Cogn. 35, 33–41 (2015)
14. Kloft, M., Stiehler, F., Zheng, Z., Pinkwart, N.: Predicting MOOC dropout over weeks using machine learning methods. In: Proceedings of EMNLP 2014 Workshop on Analysis of Large Scale Social Interaction in MOOCs, pp. 60–65 (2014)
15. Al-Shabandar, R., Hussain, A.J., Liatsis, P., Keight, R.: Analyzing learners behavior in MOOCs: an examination of performance and motivation using a data-driven approach. IEEE Access 6, 73669–73685 (2018)
16. Piech, C., et al.: Deep knowledge tracing. In: Advances in Neural Information Processing Systems, pp. 505–513 (2015)

Realizing the Promise of AI-Powered, Adaptive, Automated, Instant Feedback on Writing for Students in Grade 3-8 with an IEP

Paul Edelblut[(✉)]

Vantage Labs, New Hope, PA 18938, USA
pedlelblut@vantage.com

Abstract. After more than two decades of large scale use of the IntelliMetric™ Artificial Intelligence for automated marking, research into the application of AI has begun to take on a decidedly different focus. Inquiry into IntelliMetric now centers on questions of how to leverage the highly reliable and immediately available information provided by IntelliMetric into an adaptive learning environment creating a customized learning pathway. IntelliMetric's feedback engine, MY Tutor™, provides a patented process of selective writing feedback, specific to the individual needs of the user. MY Tutor feedback incorporates comments and prompts provided to the user which are generated in response to assessment of the student's written text. Skill level and developmentally appropriate comments on various genre specific domains are provided in real-time and on-demand modalities as selected by the user.

Through the data presented in this paper we demonstrate the positive impact of providing adaptive, machine generated, instant feedback in a quantifiable manner for students in grades 3 through 8. We take a deeper dive into the adaptive feedback created by MY Tutor and discuss the analysis conducted by IntelliMetric needed to feed the MY Tutor feedback.

Keywords: Artificial Intelligence · Adaptive learning · Automated essay scoring

1 Introduction

1.1 Background and Overview

With the evolution of and ubiquity of technology, we face the challenges of producing better writing more frequently than ever. Compared to 30 years ago when the sole method of written communication was the handwritten (or typed) letter, we write e-mails, send text messages, and chat online almost every day. The importance of strong writing skills continues to grow. We tend to write more frequently these days and speak less during initial engagement at schools, at workplaces, and even at home. This new paradigm has raised the question of "how should we prepare for an era where the importance of writing will become more pronounced every day?"

© Springer Nature Switzerland AG 2020
R. A. Sottilare and J. Schwarz (Eds.): HCII 2020, LNCS 12214, pp. 283–292, 2020.
https://doi.org/10.1007/978-3-030-50788-6_21

Writing instruction can be thought of as a symbiotic interaction between two equally important participants, the teacher and the student. To be successful in the standard paradigm of writing instruction both participants, the teacher and student, need to put forth substantial effort in a timely manner with a complex set of interdependent variables. In the traditional classroom the nexus of those two participants and the many variables intersecting is extremely low and the teachable moment is often lost before the teacher ever realizes. As part of a technologically driven adaptive learning environment, with computer generated feedback, the very moment a student begins to write the essential elements are brought together in a dynamic, on-demand, adaptive learning environment.

The complexity and difficulty of the writing process is something that many take for granted and most never consider. In total, the process of writing requires a larger amalgam of basic skills than nearly any other activity and exposes the subjects' ultimate understanding of language. This complexity is compounded for educators working in classrooms where approximately 20% of the student population has some form of language based learning disability, undiagnosed in nearly 12%. This research investigates the impact of providing instantaneous, machine generated feedback for this sub-population.

Beginning with the earliest handwriting exercises and continuing through keyboarding where children are expressing their understanding of the English language they must combine complex physical and cognitive processes to render or select letters precisely and fluidly. As writing tasks become more difficult, students must call on an increasingly wide range of skills to not only write legibly, logically, and in an organized way but also to invoke rules of grammar and syntax. This combination of requirements makes writing the most complex and difficult use of the English language.

Students as young as first graders validate their progress with English by writing nearly every day and are asked to do more with this skill than with any other except reading. Writing requirements—from homework assignments and class work to note taking and tests appear to be increasing across the curriculum. Admissions tests and high-stakes assessments for state or Common Core standards have added a variety of writing tasks. The result of the added quantity of writing is a greater emphasis for teachers to teach all students with a heavier emphasis on writing. Yet, many of these students, nearly 1 in 5, have an underlying disability interfering with their ability to maximize the instruction provided. Additionally, many teachers chose not to emphasize writing in their classrooms due to the time and expertise required.

A language based learning disability can have devastating impacts on an individual child's progress and on a teacher's ability to support that child. In most other school subjects there are reasonably well accepted ways of both quantifying and supporting learning disabilities. School requirements demand a high level of writing proficiency, and a child who struggles with an unrecognized writing disability will find it increasingly difficult to express his knowledge on many subjects, as the writing process itself will stand firmly in the way of academic performance.

The solution to this challenge may lie in the provision of evaluation and immediate, adaptive feedback provided by IntelliMetric an advanced Artificial Intelligence system that scores writing at or above reliability rates of humans and the MY Tutor patented feedback mechanism it employs. When used in conjunction with the MY Tutor engine that provides prescriptive instruction customized to the scoring completed by IntelliMetric the dream of B.F Skinner demonstrated in 1954 with his "teaching machine" may have been fully realized (Bonaiuti and Skinner 2004).

As IntelliMetric approaches its nineteenth birthday, research into its use has begun to take on a decidedly different focus. Whether or not open-ended assessments can be scored using computers is no longer the key question. Rather, inquiry into IntelliMetric centers on questions of how to leverage the highly reliable information provided by IntelliMetric into an adaptive learning environment that creates a customized learning pathway for every student. In short, the focus has turned to adaptive learning as a way to transform the educational process.

MY Tutor™ is a patented process of selective writing assessment with tutoring, specific to the individual needs of the user. MY Tutor™ feedback incorporates comments and prompts provided to the user which are generated in response to assessment of the written text. Skill level and developmental level comments, remarks and prompts on various genre specific domains areas are provided in real-time and on-demand modalities as selected by the user. The data presented within this paper provides a valid argument for using MY Tutor™ with IntelliMetric scoring for students who have a language based learning disability.

Through the statistics presented below we demonstrate the positive impact of providing machine generated, instant feedback in a quantifiable manner for students in grades 3 through 8.

Before turning to the study, it may be useful to review what IntelliMetric and MY Tutor are and what each does. The next section provides an introduction to IntelliMetric, the feature structure used in evaluation of responses and the links to the MY Tutor feedback, and a summary of the findings.

1.2   Understanding IntelliMetric AI Scoring

IntelliMetric has been shown to be an effective tool for scoring constructed response questions across K-12, higher education and professional training environments as well as within a variety of content areas and assessment purposes.

IntelliMetric is an intelligent scoring system that emulates the process carried out by human scorers and is theoretically grounded in the traditions of Cognitive Processing, Computational Linguistics, Natural Language Understanding, and Classification. The system must be "trained" with a set of previously scored responses containing "known score" marker papers for each score point allowing for greater reliability in analytic features. These papers are used as a basis for the system to infer the rubric and the pooled judgments of the human scorers. Relying on Vantage Learning's proprietary CogniSearch™ and Quantum Reasoning™ Technologies, the IntelliMetric system internalizes the characteristics of the responses associated with each score point and applies this intelligence in subsequent scoring. The approach is consistent with the procedure underlying holistic scoring.

IntelliMetric creates a unique solution for each stimulus or prompt. This is conceptually similar to prompt-specific training for human scorers. For this reason, IntelliMetric is able to achieve both high correlations with the scores of human readers and matching percentages with scores awarded by humans.

IntelliMetric is based on a blend of artificial intelligence, natural language processing and statistical technologies. It is essentially a learning engine that internalizes the characteristics of the score scale through an iterative learning process. In essence, IntelliMetric internalizes the pooled wisdom of many expert scorers. It is important to note that AI is widely believed to better handle "noisy" data and develop a more sophisticated internalization of complex relationships among features. IntelliMetric was first commercially released in January 1998 and was the first AI based essay-scoring tool made available to and used successfully by educational agencies.

IntelliMetric uses a multi-stage process to evaluate responses. First, IntelliMetric is exposed to a subset of responses with known scores from which it derives knowledge of the characteristics of each score point. Second, the model reflecting the knowledge derived is tested against a smaller set of responses with known scores to validate the model developed and confirm IntelliMetric's ability to accurately and reliably score responses to that prompt. Third, once generalizability is confirmed, the model is applied to score novel responses with unknown scores. Using Vantage Learning's proprietary Legitimatch™ technology, responses that are anomalous either based on the expectations established by the set of essays used in initial training or with respect to expectations for edited American English are identified as part of the process.

Features

- IntelliMetric analyzes more than ninety semantic, syntactic and discourse level features. These features fall into five major categories.
- Focus and Unity – Features pointing towards cohesiveness and consistency in purpose and main idea.
- Development and Elaboration – Features of text looking at the breadth of content and the support for concepts advanced.
- Organization and Structure – Features targeted at the logic of discourse including transitional fluidity and relationships among parts of the response.
- Sentence Structure – Features targeted at sentence complexity and variety.
- Mechanics and Conventions – Features examining conformance to conventions of edited American English.

This model is illustrated in the diagram below.

IntelliMetric Feature Model

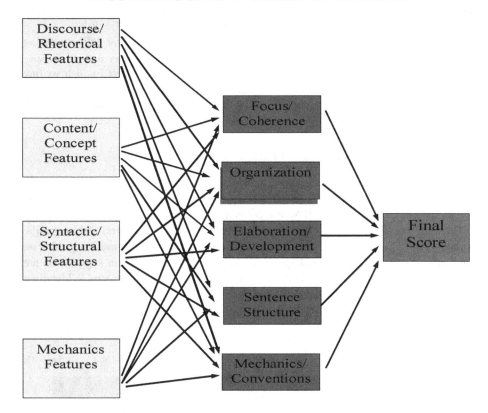

1.3   Understanding MY Tutor

When students submit their writing, IntelliMetric provides immediate scores so that they can begin the process of revision at once. Prompts trained to be evaluated through our IntelliMetric scoring system with MY Tutor (TM), provide students with even more feedback than a comprehensive holistic score, breaking down their submission into each of the standard domains of writing and MY Tutor provides goals and examples to help students focus their revision activities through immediate, detailed and developmentally appropriate prescriptive feedback. For each domain, Focus and Meaning, Content and Development, Organization, Language Use, Voice and Style, and Mechanics and Conventions students have a narrative learning pathway that adjusts to their changes.

Additionally the MY Editor tool, a subset of the MY Tutor functionality, helps students in identifying potential errors and recommends corrections in grammar, style, mechanics, and usage. MY Editor identifies the level of writing a student has provided and provides feedback specific to the errors identified and at the most developmentally appropriate level based on the writing, without consideration for the formal grade-level of the student. Levels including Developing, Proficient and Advanced Proficient. As the writing improves the levels become more aggressive in the application and interpretation of the rules of edited American English or edited British English.

These robust tools provide text and audio support in multi-lingual delivery during the process of composition, giving students with a learning disability a multi-sensory environment and ELL/ESL students the opportunity to improve their English writing proficiency by receiving feedback in their native languages.

Students are guided through the recursive writing process based on the feedback they receive along with the various available resources within the system.

1.4   Delivery in the MY Access! Platform

MyAccess! is a web-based instructional writing tool that fully blends IntelliMetric AES technology with feedback from MY Tutor. In addition to score feedback (Fig. 1) on holistic and domain scores IntelliMetric provides, MyAccess! provides text feedbacks to allow the users to learn why they have received the scores in general and in specific domains (Fig. 2). MyAccess! text feedback also encompasses the revision guides on how users can improve their writings. Specific feedback and revision suggestions are offered to users in essential five domains. These domains consist of Focus & Meaning, Content Development, Organization, language Use, Voice & Style, and Mechanics & Conventions. The content within each domain that MyAccess! analyzes and judges the scores upon are described (Fig. 3):

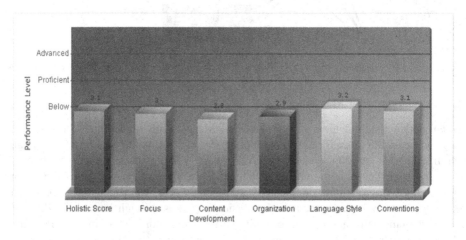

Fig. 1. MyAccess! score feedbacks on holistic and domain levels

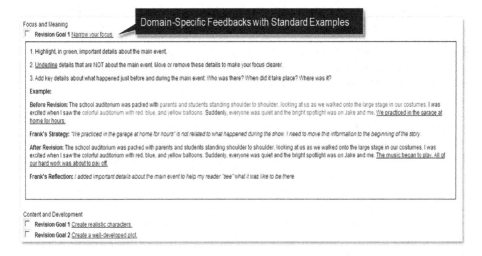

Fig. 2. MY tutor text feedback on domains

Fig. 3. MyEditor-text feedback on grammar, mechanics, spelling and style

Focus and Meaning (Focus): The extent to which the response establishes and maintains a controlling idea (or central idea), an understanding of purpose and audience, and completion of the task.

Content Development (Content): The extent to which the response develops ideas fully and artfully using extensive, specific, accurate, and relevant details. (facts, examples, anecdotes, details, opinions, statistics, reasons, and/or explanations).

Organization: The extent to which the response demonstrates a unified structure, direction, and unity, paragraphing and transitional devices.

Language Use, Voice and Style (Language): The extent the response demonstrates control of conventions, including paragraphing, grammar, punctuation, and spelling.

Mechanics and Conventions (Conventions): The extent to which response demonstrates an awareness of audience and purpose through effective sentence structure, sentence variety, and word choice that creates tone and voice.

2 Research Findings

The research question addressed by this study seeks to determine the efficacy of an AI driven system that immediately scores and provides adaptive feedback to the students. Specifically we chose to do a post-hoc analysis of data on K-12 students using the MY Access! platform powered by IntelliMetric with feedback by MY Tutor.

The data is comprised of nearly 18,400 student essay responses from and initial cohort of more than 7,600 students in 42 different states. Students responded to persuasive writing tasks appropriate for the proximal grade level. Students were identified by their school administration as having an Individual Educational Plan or IEP and had the MY Tutor functionality turned on for all writing assignments.

Papers were scored on both 6 point holistic and 6 point analytic rubrics. IntelliMetric scores and MY Tutor™ narrative feedback were provided both summatively as well as during the drafting process. Narrative feedback was provided on Focus, Content, Organization, Language Use and Style and Mechanics. MY Editor feedback was provided both summatively as well as during the drafting process.

As shown below in Table 1, we initially extracted 18,431 student writing samples meeting the parameter; having an IEP for Specific Learning Disability and having written to a persuasive prompt within MY Access during the previous 24 months. A two year cycle was used initially to ensure we would have a sufficient number of submissions and less than 24 months might have led to seasonality in the selection of papers. Students ranged in US grade levels of 3 to 12. No students in the sample were identified by their schools as being in grade 4.

Table 1. Total cases

Initial data	Cases					
	Included		Excluded		Total	
	N	Percent	N	Percent	N	Percent
Avg holistic score * submission number	18389	99.8%	42	.2%	18431	100.0%

A review of the mean holistic score across five submissions showed a steady and relatively consistent increase with each successive submission. This increase over time of just over 16%, is consistent with the findings of an earlier analysis for non-IEP students indicating similar improvement over 2.75 uses of the system. (Han 2009) and for a higher-ed version of the same design (Elliot and Mikulas 2014) (Table 2).

Table 2. Average holistic score by submission

Avg holistic number	Report of average holistic score by submission						
Submission number	Mean	N	Std. Deviation	Kurtosis	Skewness	Minimum	Maximum
1	3.344019	7633	1.1616373	−.358	.187	1.0000	6.0000
2	3.551508	4277	1.1449967	−.500	.074	1.0000	6.0000
3	3.650378	2833	1.1223732	−.444	.085	1.0000	6.0000
4	3.759976	2072	1.0649335	−.400	.010	1.0000	6.0000
5	3.882579	1574	1.0288661	−.353	−.023	1.0000	6.0000
Total	3.532442	18389	1.1447850	−.432	.079	1.0000	6.0000

Furthermore, since the number of student who re-submitted declined as the re-submissions grew, the smaller group continued to see incremental improvements suggesting continued benefit from the process or revision-feedback-revision provided by MY Tutor despite the decreasing sample size. See Table 3 below for the frequency of submissions over time.

Table 3. Number of submissions at subsequent attempts

Submission number		Frequency	Percent	Valid percent	Cumulative percent
Valid	1	7661	41.6	41.6	41.6
	2	4286	23.3	23.3	64.8
	3	2836	15.4	15.4	80.2
	4	2073	11.2	11.2	91.5
	5	1575	8.5	8.5	100.0
	Total	18431	100.0	100.0	

3   Conclusion and Discussion

Students identified on an IEP as having a Specific Learning Difference using an instructional tool with Artificial Intelligence based scoring and feedback mechanism improved their writing scores substantially. The delivery of immediate, adaptive, machine-generated feedback during the drafting process in parallel with similar feedback on a summative reports led to strong gains despite limited use of the services. These findings are in-line with previous research on a general population.

We continue to review the data to further identify what elements of the feedback, if any had a more significant impact. We are also beginning to design a follow-on study utilizing fNIRS technology to gather data on the oxygenation levels in the brain. We have two hypotheses we wish to test. The first we would like to evaluate is whether the temporal proximity of the feedback is leveraging increased oxygenation and "open" connections in the brain. The second hypothesis we are looking to evaluate is whether the machine generated feedback is merely stimulating the long-term memory in the parietal lobe or if the pre-frontal cortex is activated and the student is comprehending and applying the learnings from the feedback.

References

Bonaiuti, G., Skinner, B.F.: Teaching machine and programmed learning (2004). https://www.youtube.com/watch?v=jTH3ob1IRFo

Han, S.: Scientific Proof and Case Studies: The Effect of Frequent Writing on One's Writing Skills (2009)

Elliot, S., Mikulas, C.: A Quasi Experimental Study of the Effectiveness of Instructional Applications Employing Automated Essay Scoring (AES), AERA (2014)

Declarative Knowledge Extraction in the AC&NL Tutor

Ani Grubišić[1]([✉]) [ID], Slavomir Stankov[1] [ID], Branko Žitko[1] [ID],
Ines Šarić-Grgić[1] [ID], Angelina Gašpar[2], Suzana Tomaš[3] [ID],
Emil Brajković[4] [ID], and Daniel Vasić[4] [ID]

[1] Faculty of Science, University of Split, Split, Croatia
ani.grubisic@pmfst.hr
[2] Catholic Faculty of Theology, University of Split, Split, Croatia
[3] Faculty of Humanities and Social Sciences, University of Split, Split, Croatia
[4] Faculty of Science and Education, University of Mostar, Mostar,
Bosnia and Herzegovina

Abstract. Automatic knowledge acquisition is a rather complex and challenging task. This paper focuses on the description and evaluation of a semi-automatic authoring tool (SAAT) that has been developed as a part of the Adaptive Courseware based on Natural Language AC&NL Tutor project. The SAAT analyzes a natural language text and, as a result of the declarative knowledge extraction process, it generates domain knowledge that is presented in a form of natural language sentences, questions and domain knowledge graphs. Generated domain knowledge presents expert knowledge in the intelligent tutoring system Tutomat. The natural language processing techniques are applied and the tool's functionalities are thoroughly explained. This tool is, to our knowledge, the only one that enables natural language question and sentence generation of different levels of complexity. Using an unstructured and unprocessed Wikipedia text in computer science, evaluation of domain knowledge extraction algorithm, i.e. the correctness of extraction outcomes and the effectiveness of extraction methods, was performed. The SAAT outputs were compared with the gold standard, manually developed by two experts. The results showed that 68.7% of detected errors referred to the performance of the integrated linguistic resources, such as CoreNLP, Senna, WordNet, whereas 31.3% of errors referred to the proposed extraction algorithms.

Keywords: Natural language processing · Knowledge extraction · Automatic question generation · Question answering evaluation · Gold standard evaluation · Intelligent tutoring systems

1 Introduction

Because the development of intelligent tutoring systems (ITSs) is a complex and time-consuming process, their cost-effectiveness has been given a great deal of consideration. Acquisition of domain knowledge is one of the key issues in ITSs. It is not a viable solution to rely only on domain knowledge expert who would build it from scratch. The ability to automatically extract domain knowledge from documents will

© Springer Nature Switzerland AG 2020
R. A. Sottilare and J. Schwarz (Eds.): HCII 2020, LNCS 12214, pp. 293–310, 2020.
https://doi.org/10.1007/978-3-030-50788-6_22

help overcome this obstacle. For years, artificial intelligence researchers have been focusing on an automatic process of knowledge extraction based on natural language processing. Undoubtedly, natural language processing is the driving force for many applications, including intelligent tutoring systems, but due to the dynamic nature of the English language, it can also be a bottleneck. In this paper, we present how natural language processing techniques were used to extract declarative domain knowledge and demonstrate how the generated knowledge structures could support an intelligent tutoring system.

An Adaptive Courseware and Natural Language Tutor (the AC&NL Tutor) has been developed since 2015 [1]. The AC&NL Tutor is a learning environment, based on adaptive content and natural language communication, which provides personalized online learning, teaching, and testing adaptive to the learner's knowledge level. In this single environment, the knowledge extraction and generation of domain knowledge graphs, as well as natural language sentences and questions of various complexities, occur. The AC&NL Tutor (Fig. 1) consists of a semi-automatic authoring tool (SAAT) and an ITS, called Tutomat. Whereas a domain knowledge expert, acting as an instructional designer or teacher, and a language expert (linguist) are involved in the SAAT to design/redesign natural language text representing domain knowledge, the sole users of the intelligent tutoring system are learners in charge of their own learning, knowledge acquisition, and progress. The SAAT enables the extraction of declarative domain knowledge that is further used for the learning and teaching process in the Tutomat.

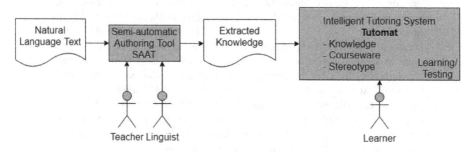

Fig. 1. The AC&NL Tutor's structure

Developing any knowledge extraction tool is a demanding task. Therefore, our intention was to develop a tool that would enable teachers to easily generate sentences and questions of different complexity level, along with their visual representations in a form of domain knowledge graphs, that can be further used in intelligent tutoring system Tutomat, or independently for some other learning and teaching purposes.

In the next section, we consider various approaches to automatic knowledge extraction based on natural language processing. Furthermore, we describe our approach to declarative domain knowledge extraction and how it was implemented in the SAAT. At last, the conclusion and final remarks are given.

2   Research Background

Over the last several decades, research in the field of artificial intelligence (AI) in education has been marked by the development and application of authoring tools that have supported the design of ITS for non-programming authors [2, 3]. These authoring tools reduce costs, increase efficiency and enable a wide range of intelligent tutoring systems capabilities. Research challenges mainly refer to the alignment between intelligent tutoring systems and natural language processing [4], which allows domain knowledge design that does not involve knowledge represented with the appropriate formalism.

The field of natural language processing has long been in the focus of researchers dealing with the computational processing and understanding of human language [5]. Natural language processing is a process that enables natural language communication with the computer [6].

Knowledge extraction is a process of obtaining domain knowledge from natural language sentences, using customized rules and aided by lexical resources such as WordNet. Natural language text is a sequence of sentences, each sentence being a string of words. The natural language understanding process uses syntactic and semantic analysis to extract knowledge from natural language text. Annotation of natural language text denotes syntactic and semantic labeling. Syntactic labeling refers to words tagged by their lemma (Lemmatizer), part-of-speech (POS Tagger),named entity (NE Recognizer), word dependencies in sentences (Dependency Parser) defining them as well as coreferences where word or string of words in a phrase may be co-referred to some word or string of words in the samo or previous sentence (Coreference Resolver). Semantic role labeling refers to word sense disambiguation (WSD) and the identification of predicates and words, or string of words as their semantic roles (SR Labeler). Some words or the string of words in a phrase may be co-referred to some word or string of words in the same or previous sentence (Coreference Resolver) during semantic role labeling. The Stanford CoreNLP 3.8 (stanfordnlp.github. io/CoreNLP/index.html) is used for lemmatization, part-of-speech tagging, named entity recognition (the task of identifying named entities like a person, location, organization, drug, time, clinical procedure, biological protein, etc. [7]), parsing processes and coreference resolution. Senna SRL 3.0 [8] and WordNet 3.1 [9] tools are used for semantic role labeling and coreference resolution, and a word sense disambiguation, respectively. Coreference resolution is the task of determining linguistic expressions that refer to the same real-world entity in natural language [10]. Unlike the work of Panaite et al. [11], in which the ReaderBench framework utilizes all of the above-mentioned NLP processes, but dependency parsing, co-reference resolution and named entity recognition were found redundant, and thus removed to reduce the processing time.

An automatic knowledge extraction process based on natural language processing has been a focus of artificial intelligence researchers for years. Several groups of authors have addressed this issue. The Controlled Language-Based Tutor (CoLaB Tutor), developed for the Croatian language [12], is based on teacher-learner communication in controlled natural language. Another system, the AutoTutor, supports conversation in natural language based on latent semantic analysis [13]. Inspired by the AutoTutor, Olney [14] developed GnuTutor, an open-source intelligent tutoring system. The Sharable Knowledge Object, a web-based version of AutoTutor, uses a tutorial dialogue [15]. Recently, a fully integrated ElectronixTutor was developed that included several intelligent learning resources as well as texts and videos [16]. The CIRCSIM-Tutor was developed to enhance students' problem-solving skills in cardiovascular physiology based on the conversation in natural language [17]. The Why2-Atlas interacts with a student through dialogue intended to remedy the missing or misconceived students' beliefs about physics [18].

Certainly, a huge repository of knowledge is required and considered a prerequisite for the success of intelligent tutoring systems. According to [19], knowledge acquisition has always been the major bottleneck for knowledge-based systems. The existing ITS with natural language typically support only short answer questions; at most, they can analyze student essays but then revert to pre-authored short answer dialogues if remediation is necessary [20].

3 A Semi-automatic Authoring Tool for Knowledge Extraction

The SAAT is a semi-automatic authoring tool because sentences in academic or technical discourse are seldom simple in nature (having a subject and a predicate), which can be often easily processed by the tool. However, a single sentence can convey multiple ideas due to the complex nature of the sentences. Processing, splitting, and converting complex sentences into independent ones risk the separation of thoughts the author intended to convey and a lack of text coherence (a semantic property) and cohesion (cohesive linguistic devices such as conjunction, reference, etc. that indicate relations between sentences). The quality of the knowledge extraction process is affected by a teacher's knowledge and writing skills [21]. Therefore, both teacher and linguist are involved in the process of preparing natural language text. Human intervention is required to assure that teaching material is semantically and grammatically correct and, after processing in the SAAT, it can be transferred to the Tutomat for teaching, learning and testing. Since the language is the medium through which teaching material is learned, it should be easily understood, concise and accurate, allowing learners to engage more with the content (what is being taught) than with the structure of the language. Linguistic knowledge includes grammatical structures, stylistic features and domain-specific terminology. The role of the linguist is to support the teacher in designing content-based instruction.

In our approach, an analogy "disassemble to reassemble" defined by [22] is used to describe a process where a text is disassembled until its structure is clear and then reassembled as domain knowledge graphs, sentences and questions. Building domain knowledge from natural language text in the SAAT, as shown in Fig. 2, includes the following steps:

1. A teacher and a linguist prepare natural language text (design phase)
2. The SAAT generates and extracts layered knowledge (disassemble phase)

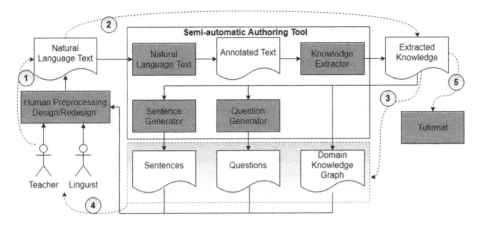

Fig. 2. The SAAT structure

3. The SAAT generates sentences, questions and domain knowledge graphs from extracted knowledge (reassemble phase)
4. The output quality affects two experts' decision-making on the next step:
   a. rewrite natural language text and go to Step 1 (redesign phase)
   b. accept generated layered knowledge and continue to Step 5
5. Domain knowledge is ready to be imported into the Tutomat.

The main advantages of the SAAT approach are semi-automatic domain knowledge graph mining (the result of natural language understanding process) and automatic generation of domain knowledge graph and different levels of natural language sentences and questions (the result of natural language generation process). Each of them will be described in more details further.

3.1 Natural Language Text Disassembling

Natural language text is a sequence of sentences, each sentence being a string of words. The SAAT converts natural language text into various types of data structures. Disassembling results with very fine grains of knowledge so-called knowledge propositions, which allow for the generation of different levels of sentences and questions.

Knowledge extracted from each natural language sentence is presented using three different layers presented as graphs: *language knowledge* - annotated sentences are transformed into language knowledge graphs, *foreground knowledge* - language knowledge is presented as a graph of key terms and their synonyms, and *domain knowledge* - foreground knowledge is transformed into the domain knowledge graph.

Language Knowledge
Language knowledge is presented as a combination of tagged phrase tree (Part-of-Speech Tagging, Lemmatization, Named Entity Recognition), semantic role graph (Semantic Role Labeling), dependency graph (Dependency Parsing) and coreference graph. Tagged phrases can be a noun phrase, verb phrase, adjective phrase, adverbial

phrase, wh-phrase (what, which, ...), prepositional phrase (of, for, to, ...), or a phrase with coordinating conjunction (and, or, ...).

We define language knowledge as a set of *language triples* that form a graph whose vertices are language nodes and the arcs are labeled language relations. More specifically, a language triple is a pair of language nodes connected with language relations. The first language node in a triple is the *governor* and the second one is the *dependent*.

Each *language node* is a tagged phrase with a headword (other words being its constituents) selected as the vertex after the Word Sense Disambiguation process (using WordNet 3.1). The *predicate language node* is a language node whose headword is a verb or other verbal structure. Each language node has an identifier that defines its position in an observed natural language sentence.

Each *language relation* contains information about dependency and semantic roles. Dependencies can be nominal subject (nsubj), passive nominal subject (nsubj-pass), direct object (dobj), indirect object (iobj), adjectival clause (acl), adverbial modifier (advmod), nominal modifier (nmod), etc. [23]. The direction of the relationship determines its dependent. Semantic role labeling refers to identification of predicates and words, or the string of words, as their semantic roles (SR Labeler). During semantic role labeling, some words or the string of words in a sentence can be co-referred to some word or the string of words in the same or previous sentence (Coreference Resolver). Semantic roles can be verb (V), subject and/or object of a verb (A0, A1, A2, A3, A4, A5) and their continuation prefix C- (C-A0, C-A1, C-A2, C-A3, C-A4, C-A5), manner (AM-MNR), temporal (AM-TMP), locational (AM-LOC), adverbial (AM-ADV), etc. [24].

Figure 3 shows a language knowledge of the natural language sentence "*Intelligent tutoring systems are computer-based software packages that apply artificial intelligence techniques to assist in the teaching and learning of some subject matter or skill.*"

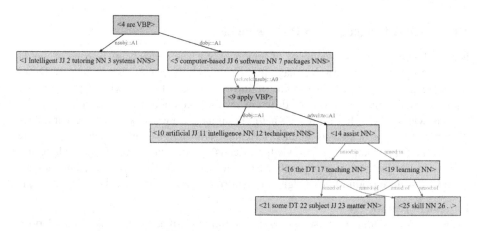

Fig. 3. Language knowledge

Foreground Knowledge

Foreground knowledge is a set of *foreground triples*, each one containing a pair of language nodes that have a concept identifier from the WordNet and a foreground relation. Each language knowledge node (i.e. computer-based software packages, apply) is mapped to its concept identifier from the WordNet (i.e. `software.n.01`, `use.v.01`) creating a *foreground language node*. During this mapping phase, function words in the phrase are omitted. If a concept is not found in the WordNet (i.e. concept Intelligent tutoring systems), its identifier is `00` (the number of synsets - a set of synonyms). Figure 4 shows a foreground knowledge for an example sentence.

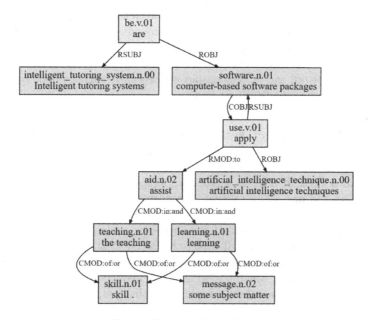

Fig. 4. Foreground knowledge

The process of building foreground knowledge starts with the identification of governor language nodes, whose outgoing language relations have semantic roles, and their dependent language nodes.

There are two types of *foreground relations* used to connect governor and dependent language nodes in a foreground knowledge triple: relational and conceptual. The *relational foreground relation* is determined by a governor language node having a verb as headword (the *predicate foreground node*). If there is no subject relation with a dependent language node left from the predicate, then the subject foreground relation

RSUBJ (or RSUBJPASS for passive clause) is created. Moreover, if there is no object relation with the dependent language node right from the predicate, then the object foreground relation ROBJ (or RIOBJ for the indirect object) is created. All other relations are mapped to the relation modifier RMOD if there is any subject related with dependent language node left from the predicate and any object related with dependent language node right from the predicate.

After building relational foreground knowledge from predicates and their dependents in language knowledge, conceptual foreground knowledge is generated using the remaining triples from language knowledge. The *conceptual foreground relation* is built between two related language nodes having a noun as the headword. The CEQ relation is made if two language nodes are in apposition or coreference relation or language nodes are mutual noun modifiers using 'like' or 'such as' to create a relationship between them. The CPOSS relation is made if one language node contains (possesses) another language node. The CMOD relation corresponds to creating RMOD relations in relational foreground knowledge. The COBJ relation is created if one language node has a gerund or infinitive as a headword and its relationship with another language node (in language knowledge) is based on the DOBJ relation.

Domain Knowledge

Domain knowledge is a set of *domain knowledge triples* represented in a form of a graph consisting of two vertices (language nodes) and an arc (predicate language node) between them. Each domain knowledge triple, i.e. *knowledge proposition* has a parent, a relation and a child. If there is a predicate foreground node that has at least one RSUBJ relation and one ROBJ relation, dependents of these relations (or more precisely their mapped correspondents from language knowledge) are parent and child respectively, and predicate foreground node becomes a relation.

In domain knowledge graph, all triplets based on CMOD foreground knowledge relation are presented with dashed arrow lines. The CMOD:of relation is mapped to domain knowledge relation which has no language node, but has preposition *of* taken from the CMOD:of relation. All other triples are visually represented with solid arrow lines.

If the predicate foreground node (i.e. use.v.01) has the modifier foreground relation RMOD (i.e. RMOD:to) with some foreground node (i.e. aid.n.02) and the subject foreground relation RSUBJ with some other foreground node (i.e. software.n.01), dependent of the subject foreground relation becomes parent (i.e. computer-based software packages), the dependent of the modifier foreground relation becomes child (i.e. assist), and the predicate foreground node becomes relation (i.e. applies to). The relation includes foreground language node (or more precisely its mapped correspondent from language knowledge) and function words from foreground knowledge relation. Figure 5 shows domain knowledge for the example sentence.

intelligent tutoring system
is
computer-based software package
applies to
applies
assist
artificial intelligence technique
in
in
learning
teaching
of
of
of
of
skill
subject matter

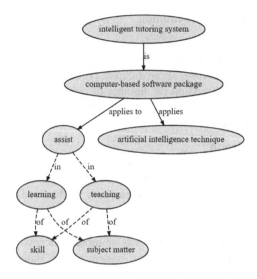

Fig. 5. Domain knowledge

A Customized Set of Rules for Error Detection and Correction

We incorporated different lexical resources into our approach and enhanced them with the customized set of rules that improve their quality and accuracy and reduce irregularities and errors. The main objective of error detection is to recognize incorrectly interpreted sentences that need correction and to alert and guide the teacher and linguist to the problematic part of the sentence. Errors can be found in virtually every knowledge layer. If an error occurs during the extraction of language knowledge, it is likely to result in the error propagation in all knowledge layers.

One type of errors can have a more serious effect than the other, so its significance levels may be either low or high. Low errors (or warnings) refer to the changes made by the SAAT in order to avoid possible high errors and to provide teacher and linguist information about their significance. High errors usually require the intervention of teacher and linguist, i.e. sentence restructuring. Figure 6 shows errors detected and corrected by the SAAT during knowledge extraction process for an example sentence (high errors marked in red).

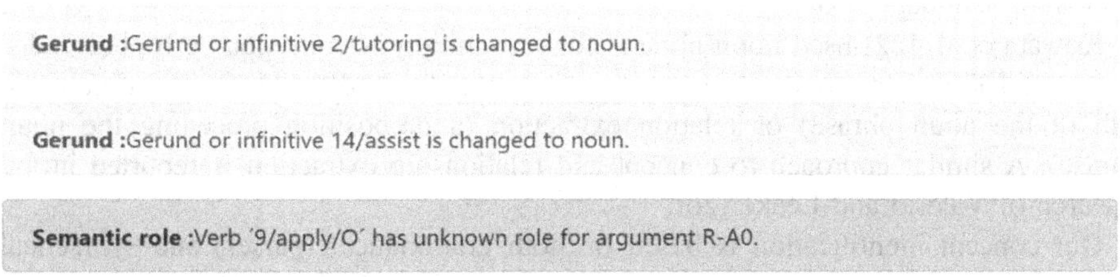

Gerund :Gerund or infinitive 2/tutoring is changed to noun.
Gerund :Gerund or infinitive 14/assist is changed to noun.
Semantic role :Verb '9/apply/O' has unknown role for argument R-A0.

Fig. 6. Errors reported by the SAAT for an example sentence (Color figure online)

3.2   Domain Knowledge Reassembling

The natural language generation process converts data structures obtained through knowledge extraction (disassembling) and generates domain knowledge graph, sentences and questions (reassemble). Three different types of sentences and questions can be generated in the SAAT based on the number of predicates and conjunctions in the original natural language text. Each of the generated structures is thoroughly described in the following subsections.

Domain Knowledge Graph

In our approach, the development of the domain knowledge layer has consequently resulted in a visual representation that can be described as a combination of a knowledge graph and a concept map. Researchers in the field of concept mapping generally refer to Novak and Cañas [25] who claim that "Concept maps are tools for organizing and representing knowledge that include concepts and named relationships between concepts. Propositions contain two or more concepts connected with relationships that form a meaningful statement." According to Valerio and Leake [26], a proposition is not inherently a full sentence suggesting that high granularity may be required when parsing the text. This approach corresponds to our knowledge propositions. A typical knowledge graph has a similar structure; it is a directed graph with vertices corresponding to entities, and arcs corresponding to relations between these entities [27]. Novak's approach to concept map includes topology that our domain knowledge graph lacks, so we decided to combine previously mentioned knowledge structures into one and make the best out of both approaches, similar to [28] and [22].

Our approach to domain knowledge graph building has the following features: concepts are usually represented as single words or multi-word expressions and they are directly extracted from the natural language text.

According to the simplicity and semi-formality criteria proposed by Villalon and Calvo [21], in our approach, synonyms are identified in foreground knowledge and all language nodes from language knowledge are used in order to minimize the loss of information, while the domain knowledge graph is a true visual representation of the natural language sentence. It represents the same words used in natural language text which simplifies the task of retrieving information.

The research findings on the semi-automatic generation of concept maps intended for further human refinement were proposed by Valerio and Leake [26], Zouaq et al. [29], and others. Our approach is also semi-automatic due to the quality of generated knowledge extraction output which requires the teacher and/or the linguist to redesign the natural language text.

Kowata et al. [22] used noun phrases for recognition of concepts, verb phrases for concept relation extraction and prepositional phrases for both concept recognition (the pith of the noun phrase) or relation extraction (a preposition preceding the noun phrase). A similar approach to concept and relationship extraction is reported in the research of Valerio and Leake [26].

Our concept identification is based on both grammatical (parser) and syntactical information (punctuation, conjunctions and prepositions). A high degree of granularity in our knowledge extraction process makes the generated domain knowledge graph connected with no isolated concepts. The syntactical and dependency information are used to identify semantic relationships between words. Also, the relationships are generated from the text itself, which enables our approach to be applied in any domain. In addition, our algorithm produces concepts based on word phrases rather than on individual words, making the concept labels more complete.

Sentence Segmentation

Extracted language knowledge and foreground knowledge is used to generate natural language sentences and questions. The preparation phase refers to a sentence segmentation that is realized using SRL arguments of language knowledge relations. Sentence segmentation is a way of "splitting" a natural language sentence into sentence segments (sub - sentences) that have a subject-predicate-object (S P O) structure. Each element (subject, predicate and object) in a sentence segment is made of a language node (called root), its semantic role and a list of language nodes that belong to a subgraph of the language knowledge graph whose root is the selected language node.

The sentence segmentation process depends on the number of predicate language nodes and conjunctions that connect or separate the language nodes. In the first type of sentence segmentation, for each predicate language node, one sentence segment of the original sentence is defined. The first predicate language node defines the main sentence segment. Further, predicate language nodes split the original sentence into sub-sentence segments. Other type of sentence segmentation depends on conjunction. The idea is to create a sub-sentence segment for each language node connected or separated by a conjunction.

Generating Natural Language Sentences

Based on the described approach to sentence segmentation, it is possible to generate natural language sentences of three different levels of lexical and semantical complexity. Since elements in sentence segments are ordered, their ordering makes sub-sentences.

The structure of natural language sentence levels depends on the number of predicate language nodes and the number of conjunctions (it depends on the number of sentence segments). The 1st level usually contains only one, the most complex natural language sentence, generated according to the main sentence segment. If original sentence is compound sentence (containing 2 or more independent clauses), than 1st level can have 2 or more sentences. The 2nd level contains as many sub-sentences as there are predicate language nodes. These sub-sentences are generated according to sub-sentence segments that are defined by each predicate language node. The 3rd level contains as many sub-sentences as there are predicate language nodes and conjunctions. The first column of Table 1 presents three levels of sentences generated for the example natural language sentence.

Table 1. Generated sentences and questions for an example natural language sentence.

Sentences	Questions
Level 1	
Intelligent tutoring systems are computer-based software packages that apply artificial intelligence techniques to assist in the teaching and learning of some subject matter or skill	QUE What are computer-based software packages that apply artificial intelligence techniques to assist in the teaching and learning of some subject matter or skill? *ANS Intelligent tutoring systems*
	QUE What are intelligent tutoring systems? *ANS Computer-based software packages that apply artificial intelligence techniques to assist in the teaching and learning of some subject matter or skill*
Level 2	
Intelligent tutoring systems are computer-based software packages	QUE What are computer-based software packages? *ANS Intelligent tutoring systems*
	QUE What are intelligent tutoring systems? *ANS Computer-based software packages*
Computer-based software packages apply artificial intelligence techniques to assist in the teaching and learning of some subject matter or skill	QUE What applies artificial intelligence techniques to assist in the teaching and learning of some subject matter or skill? *ANS Computer-based software packages*
	QUE What do computer-based software packages apply? *ANS Artificial intelligence techniques to assist in the teaching and learning of some subject matter or skill*
Level 3	
Intelligent tutoring systems are computer-based software packages	QUE What are computer-based software packages? *ANS Intelligent tutoring systems*
	QUE What are intelligent tutoring systems? *ANS Computer-based software packages*
Computer-based software packages apply artificial intelligence techniques to assist in the teaching of some subject matter	QUE What applies artificial intelligence techniques to assist in the teaching of some subject matter? *ANS Computer-based software packages*
	QUE What do computer-based software packages apply? *ANS Artificial intelligence techniques to assist in the teaching of some subject matter*
Computer-based software packages apply artificial intelligence techniques to assist in the teaching of skill	QUE What applies artificial intelligence techniques to assist in the teaching of skill? *ANS Computer-based software packages*

(*continued*)

Table 1. (*continued*)

Sentences	Questions
	QUE What do computer-based software packages apply? *ANS Artificial intelligence techniques to assist in the teaching of skill*
Computer-based software packages apply artificial intelligence techniques to assist in <u>learning</u> of some <u>subject matter</u>	QUE What applies artificial intelligence techniques to assist in learning of some subject matter? *ANS Computer-based software packages*
	QUE What do computer-based software packages apply? *ANS Artificial intelligence techniques to assist in learning of some subject matter*
Computer-based software packages apply artificial intelligence techniques to assist in <u>learning</u> of <u>skill</u>	QUE What applies artificial intelligence techniques to assist in learning of skill? *ANS Computer-based software packages*
	QUE What do computer-based software packages apply? *ANS Artificial intelligence techniques to assist in learning of skill*

Our approach is, to our knowledge, the only one that enables different levels of complexity of natural language sentence generation. In this way, we have enabled three different types of presentation for each natural language sentence, based on the number of its predicates and conjunctions.

Generating Natural Language Questions

Natural language questions are generated from sentence segments by selecting one SRL argument (except argument labeled with V) which is to be replaced with a question word (who, what, where etc.). Replacement of SRL argument with a question word depends on the type of argument as well as POS, NER and/or animacy of the root node's headword, and it is done according to the following set of rules (Table 2).

Position of the root nodes of the numeric arguments A0, A1, A2, A3, A4 and A5 in regard to the predicate, has an important role in natural language question generation. Node A is left or right from node B if the node identifier of A is less or greater than the node identifier of B. According to this position, there are several types of questions:

- subject question: if the numeric argument root node is left from the predicate node,
- object question: if the numeric argument root node is right from the predicate node,
- modifier question: if the argument is a modifier such as AM-TMP, AM-MNR, AM-LOC, etc.

Natural language questions are generated separately for each sub-sentence previously generated. Therefore, there are also three levels of questions that correspond to

Table 2. Rules for generating questions

Rule	SRL argument	Additional condition	Question word
1	numerical	POS is NNP, NNPS or PRP or NER is PERSON or ORGANISATION or animacy is ANIMATED	Who
2	numerical	condition from Rule 1 is not satisfied	What
3	AM-MNR		How
4	AM-LOC		Where
5	AM-TMP	NER is DURATION	For how long
6	AM-TMP	condition from Rule 5 is not satisfied	When
7	AM-PNC or AM-CAU		Why
8	AM-ADV	the first node of argument nodes has headword whose POS is "to" or "in"	"what" and prepositions "to" or "in" occur as the last words in the sentence
9	AM-ADV	condition from Rule 8 is not satisfied	How
10		if all conditions from rules above are not satisfied	What

the levels of sentences. Our approach is, to our knowledge, the only one that enables different levels of complexity in natural language question generation. In this way, we have enabled three different types of question generation for each sub-sentence, based on the number of its predicates and conjunctions.

Sometimes, there is no numeric argument left or right from the predicate node. In that case, if there is a modifier argument left or right from predicate node, that argument would become question word, and form a subject or an object question. However, if there are more than one modifier arguments left or right from predicate node, one of them is chosen according to their priority as follows: AM-MNR, AM-PNC, AM-CAU, AM-LOC, AM-TMP, then all others.

Simple replacement of the argument's node with question word is done for subject questions and modifier questions. However, a simple replacement is not recommended for object questions, which will result in grammatically incorrect question. In object questions, a question word and other words related to the argument of an object are spread across the sentence. Therefore, general rules for object questions are:

1. insert the question word at the beginning of the main sentence segment
2. find auxiliary, negation and/or modal verbs and insert them after question words
3. move the predicate node's headword to the final position the main sentence segment.

Complex verb always has the main verb which is moved to the final position in the main sentence segment. Other words in a complex verb are ordered after question word. The second column of Table 1 presents three levels of questions generated for the example natural language sentence.

3.3   Evaluation

A subset of the unstructured, not preprocessed text from Wikipedia article in computer science was used for analysis (https://en.wikipedia.org/wiki/Computer, from May 2018), precisely the first 160 sentences. For each sentence, two experts manually checked correctness of the following output generated by the SAAT: tokens (word, part-of-speech tag POS, named entity relation NER), dependency (governor, relation, dependent), coreferences (type, sentence and word that it refers to), sentences (sentence level, predicate, sentence text), questions (question level, type, predicate, question text) and domain knowledge graph (type, parent, relation, child).

The experts improved the quality of the output by correcting erroneous data and providing solutions – a false negative (FN). If the output of the tool lacked some data, the experts inserted it – a false positive (FP). Data that were correctly pre-filled were – a true positive (TP).

Afterwards, for each sentence and for each feature observed (word, POS, NER, dependency, coreference, sentence, question, proposition, concept, relation – 10 features in total), we have calculated a total number of true positives TP (contained in both SAAT output and experts analysis), false negatives FN (contained only in SAAT output) and false positives FP (contained only in experts analysis). In total, there were 30 variables we have analyzed (10 features multiplied by three calculated values – TP, FN and FP).

For each sentence, we have compared the annotation, extraction and generation processes performed by the SAAT and experts. Therefore, for each sentence, we have calculated well-known measures from information retrieval and information extraction systems such as Precision P, Recall R and F1 (the harmonic mean of P and R) for each of the observed features [30, 31].

Results indicate that the SAAT performs very well in tasks related to linguistic annotation of natural language text – the values calculated for word, POS, NER and dependency are over 96% (these are results gained for CoreNLP enhanced by the rules implemented in the SAAT). High precision and high recall suggest that linguistic annotations are almost completely accurate. The results are not so good for domain knowledge graph. The lowest results are obtained for natural language sentence and question generation. These results suggest that we should enhance the algorithm for natural language sentence and question generation.

To conclude: (i) the highest number of correct outcomes is for concept (78.9%) and relation (71.7%) extraction, (ii) the highest number of incorrect outcomes is for sentence (41.1%) and question (35.4%) generation, (iii) the highest number of errors related to CoreNLP is for proposition (77.6%) and sentence (73.2%) generation, and (iv) the highest number of errors related to our extraction algorithm is for relation extraction (42.9%) and question generation (37.3%). It is obvious that we have to improve our algorithms related to relation extraction and question generation. Improvements in proposition and question generation depend on changes that will be implemented in CoreNLP in the future.

4   Conclusion

To develop an effective tool for knowledge extraction is a demanding task because the extracted knowledge could be incomplete or ambiguous. This motivated us to develop a tool that will allow teachers to easily generate sentences and questions of different levels of complexity, along with their visual representation in a form of the domain knowledge graph, that can be further used in the intelligent tutoring system, or independently for some other learning and teaching purposes.

The presented features of the SAAT reflect its twofold nature, the automatic one relying on the integrated resources and their performance, and the human one referring to knowledge, skill, and adaptive strategies applied by the teacher and the linguist.

Our approach is, to our knowledge, the only one that enables natural language sentence, question and domain knowledge graph generation in a single environment. Therefore, we can only compare our results with the research findings that refer to at least one of the mentioned outcomes. Further research aims to improve the accuracy of knowledge extraction because the extracted knowledge, delivered to the intelligent tutoring system, affects its performance. To do so, further evaluation methods will be used to identify the strengths and weaknesses of the tool.

Acknowledgments. The presented results are the outcome of the research projects "Adaptive Courseware based on Natural Language Processing (AC & NL Tutor)" and "Enhancing Adaptive Courseware based on Natural Language Processing" undertaken with the support of the United States Office of Naval Research Grants N00014-15-1-2789 and N00014-20-1-2066.

References

1. Grubišić, A., Stankov, S., Žitko, B.: Adaptive courseware based on natural language processing (AC & NL Tutor), United States Office of Naval Research grant (N00014-15-1-2789) (2015). www.acnltutor.net
2. Dermeval, D., Paiva, R., Bittencourt, I.I., Vassileva, J., Borges, D.: Authoring tools for designing intelligent tutoring systems: a systematic review of the literature. J. Artif. Intell. Educ. **28**, 336–384 (2018). https://doi.org/10.1007/s40593-017-0157-9
3. Frasson, C., Gauthier, G., Lesgold, A.M. (eds.): Intelligent Tutoring Systems, Third International Conference, ITS 1996, Montréal, Canada, 12–14 June 1996 (1996)
4. Rickel, J.W.: Intelligent computer-aided instruction: a survey organized around system components. IEEE Trans. Syst. Man Cybern. **19**, 40–57 (1989)
5. Otter, D.W., Medina, J.R., Kalita, J.K.: A Survey of the Usages of Deep Learning in Natural Language Processing (2018). CoRR abs/1807.10854
6. Khurana, D., Koli, A., Khatter, K., Singh, S.: Natural language processing: state of the art, current trends and challenges. CoRR (2017). arXiv:1708.05148
7. Yadav, V., Bethard, S.: A survey on recent advances in named entity recognition from deep learning models. In: Proceedings of the 27th International Conference on Computational Linguistics, COLING 2018, Santa Fe, New Mexico, USA, 20–26 August 2018, pp. 2145–2158 (2018)
8. Collobert, R., Weston, J., Bottou, L., Karlen, M., Kavukcuoglu, K., Kuksa, P.: Natural language processing (almost) from scratch. J. Mach. Learn. Res. **12**, 2493–2537 (2011)

9. Fellbaum, C.: WordNet: an electronic lexical database. Libr. Q. **69**, 406–408 (1999)
10. Zheng, J., Chapman, W.W., Crowley, R.S., Savova, G.K.: Coreference resolution: a review of general methodologies and applications in the clinical domain. J. Biomed. In-form. **44**, 1113–1122 (2011). https://doi.org/10.1016/j.jbi.2011.08.006
11. Panaite, M., et al.: Bring it on! Challenges encountered while building a comprehensive tutoring system using readerbench. In: Artificial Intelligence in Education - 19th International Conference, AIED 2018, London, UK, 27–30 June 2018, Proceedings, Part I, pp. 409–419 (2018). https://doi.org/10.1007/978-3-319-93843-1_30
12. Žitko, B.: Model of intelligent tutoring system based on processing of controlled language over ontology. Ph.D. thesis, University of Zagreb, Faculty of Electrical Engineering and Computing, Croatia (2010)
13. Graesser, A.C., VanLehn, K., Rosé, C.P., Jordan, P.W., Harter, D.: Intelligent tutoring systems with conversational dialogue. AI Mag. **22**, 39–51 (2001)
14. Olney, A.: GnuTutor: an open source intelligent tutoring system based on autotutor. In: AAAI Fall Symposium Series, Cognitive and Metacognitive Educational Systems, pp. 70–75 (2009)
15. Wolfe, C., Widmer, C.L., Weil, A.M., Cedillos-Whynott, E.M.: Working with pedagogical agents: understanding the "back end" of an intelligent tutoring system. J. Excell. Coll. Teach. **26**, 145–164 (2015)
16. Graesser, A.C., et al.: ElectronixTutor: an intelligent tutoring system with multiple learning resources for electronics. Int. J. STEM Educ. **5**, 15 (2018)
17. Evens, M.W., Chang, R.-C., Lee, Y.H., Shim, L.S., Woo, C.W., Zbang, Y.: CIRCSIM-Tutor: an intelligent tutoring system using natural language dialogue. In: Fifth Conference on Applied Natural Language Processing: Descriptions of System Demonstrations and Videos, pp. 13–14. Association for Computational Linguistics, Washington, DC, USA (1997). https://doi.org/10.3115/974281.974289
18. VanLehn, K., et al.: The architecture of Why2-Atlas: a coach for qualitative physics essay writing. In: Cerri, S.A., Gouardères, G., Paraguaçu, F. (eds.) ITS 2002. LNCS, vol. 2363, pp. 158–167. Springer, Heidelberg (2002). https://doi.org/10.1007/3-540-47987-2_20
19. Zouaq, A., Nkambou, R., Frasson, C.: The knowledge puzzle: an integrated approach of intelligent tutoring systems and knowledge management. In: Proceedings of the 18th IEEE International Conference on Tools with Artificial Intelligence, Washington, DC, USA, pp. 575–582. IEEE Computer Society (2006). https://doi.org/10.1109/ICTAI.2006.111
20. Dzikovska, M.O., Moore, J.D., Steinhauser, N., Campbell, G., Farrow, E., Callaway, C.B.: BEETLE II: a system for tutoring and computational linguistics experimentation. In: Proceedings of the ACL 2010 System Demonstrations, Stroudsburg, PA, USA, pp. 13–18. Association for Computational Linguistics (2010)
21. Villalon, J.J., Calvo, R.A.: Concept map mining: a definition and a framework for its evaluation. In: Proceedings of the 2008 IEEE/WIC/ACM International Conference on Web Intelligence and Intelligent Agent Technology, Sydney, Australia, vol. 03, pp. 357–360. IEEE Computer Society (2008). https://doi.org/10.1109/WIIAT.2008.387
22. Kowata, J.H., Cury, D., Claudia, M., Bocres, S.: Concept maps core elements candidates recognition from text. In: Proceedings of the Fourth International Conference on Concept Mapping, Viña del Mar, Chile, pp. 120–127 (2010)
23. de Marneffe, M.-C., et al.: Universal stanford dependencies: a cross-linguistic typology. LREC. **14**, 4585–4592 (2014)
24. Carreras, X., Màrquez, L.: Introduction to the CoNLL-2004 shared task: semantic role labeling. In: HLT-NAACL 2004 Workshop: Eighth Conference on Computational Natural Language Learning (CoNLL-2004), Boston, Massachusetts, USA, pp. 89–97. Association for Computational Linguistics (2004)

25. Novak, J.D., Cañas, A.J.: The theory underlying concept maps and how to construct and use them. Technical report IHMC CmapTools 2006-1. Florida Institute for Human and Machine Cognition, Pensacola. http://cmap.ihmc.us/Publications/ResearchPapers/Theory UnderlyingConceptMaps.pdf. Accessed 10 June 2020
26. Valerio, A., Leake, D.: Jump-starting concept map construction with knowledge extracted from documents. In: Proceedings of the Second International Conference on Concept Mapping, pp. 296–303, San José, Costa Rica (2006)
27. Han, X., Liu, Z., Sun, M.: Joint representation learning of text and knowledge for knowledge graph completion. arXiv Preprint. arXiv:161104125 (2016)
28. Gaines, B., Shaw, M.L.G.: Using knowledge acquisition and representation tools to support scientific communities. In: Proceedings of the Twelfth National Conference on Artificial Intelligence, pp. 707–714. AAAI Press/MIT Press, Menlo Park (1994)
29. Zouaq, A., Nkambou, R., Frasson, C.: Building domain ontologies from text for educational purposes. In: Duval, E., Klamma, R., Wolpers, M. (eds.) Creating New Learning Experiences on a Global Scale, pp. 393–407. Springer, Heidelberg (2007)
30. Manning, C.D., Schütze, H.: Foundations of Statistical Natural Language Processing. MIT Press, Cambridge (1999)
31. Jia, Y., Qi, Y., Shang, H., Jiang, R., Li, A.: A practical approach to constructing a knowledge graph for cybersecurity. Engineering **4**, 53–60 (2018)

On the Importance of Adaptive Operator Training in Human-Swarm Interaction

Jonas D. Hasbach[1,2(✉)], Thomas E. F. Witte[1], and Maren Bennewitz[2]

[1] Human-Machine-Systems, Fraunhofer Institute for Communication,
Information Processing and Ergonomics FKIE, Wachtberg, Germany
{jonas.hasbach,thomas.witte}@fkie.fraunhofer.de
[2] Humanoid Robots Lab, University of Bonn, Bonn, Germany
maren@cs.uni-bonn.de

Abstract. Human-swarm interaction (HSI) as a research discipline can be seen as a combination of swarm robotics and human factors engineering. In this work, we combine perspectives from cognitive systems engineering and systems science to discuss the importance of operator training in HSI and how training of swarm dynamics may be implemented. The concept of neglect benevolence, i.e. temporal sensitivity in swarm control, is described as a case example for operator training in HSI. We propose the application of adaptive instructional systems to (1) optimize mission performance, (2) increase understanding of swarm dynamics and (3) allocate mental workload to different work demands over a variety of complexities. Future empirical investigations must show the utility of the proposed concepts.

Keywords: Human-swarm interaction · Swarm robotics · Human factors · Joint cognitive systems · Complex systems · Resilience · Adaptive training · Neglect benevolence

1 Introduction

Swarm robotics (SR) seeks to develop flexible, scalable and robust multi-robot systems consisting of rather simple agents which operate by decentralized mechanisms, often by drawing inspiration from biological swarms like bird flocks, fish schools or ant colonies [1–4]. SR has been called a grand challenge of modern robotics [5]. Artificial swarms are expected to be beneficial in scenarios such as search and rescue, military operations, ocean cleaning or sea and space exploration [1–4].

However, real world swarm deployment requires human operators to be included in the control loop. Similar to other human-machine loops, reasons are the inability of the swarm to capture or react to all relevant mission variables (i.e. inadequate models [6]), the allocation of tasks to operators for the benefit of system performance (i.e. human out-of-loop issues [7]) or because of ethical concerns.

© Springer Nature Switzerland AG 2020
R. A. Sottilare and J. Schwarz (Eds.): HCII 2020, LNCS 12214, pp. 311–329, 2020.
https://doi.org/10.1007/978-3-030-50788-6_23

Human-swarm interaction (HSI) as a research field investigates methods for the regulation and communication between human operators and robotic swarms. HSI can be seen as a subfield of SR [1] and human factors engineering [8]. The challenge of HSI is to join the decentralized nature of swarms with the centralized control and information demands of operators. For example, in remote HSI an operator could either convey input signals to subsets of a swarm [9,10] or bias the swarm behaviour via environmental manipulation [11]. In proximal HSI, the GUARDIANS project demonstrated how the operator could be treated as a special swarm member where the swarm adjusted its behaviour based on the human state [12,13].

Kolling et al. [3] published a survey on HSI where they described HSI in terms of human-machine interaction. In our paper, we build on the work of Kolling et al. by formulating a cognitive systems engineering (CSE) perspective on HSI, which treats HSI as part of a larger socio-technical system. In particular, we focus on efficient operator training in HSI, as this, to our best knowledge, has been fairly neglected in the literature so far.

In Sect. 2, we argue for the optimization of mission performance rather than isolated HSI which highlights the importance of operator training as well as distributing mental workload (MWL) between mission demands. Section 3 describes what makes swarm dynamics particular hard to understand from the point of view of system science. How operator training may be implemented by adaptive training implementing bottom up exploration over a variety of complexities to enhance mission performance, understanding of SR and allocation of MWL is presented in Sect. 4. Section 5 presents a conclusion.

2   Operator Dynamics in HSI

CSE [14–16] takes a cybernetic perspective on human factors engineering. From a CSE point of view, scientific investigations in HSI should focus on how the operator and the swarm can regulate the mission variables as a joint system. Thus, the focus is on how the mission system components (humans, machines and their interactions) in particular contexts can act together to enhance mission performance (Fig. 1) rather than how an operator can interact with a swarm as an isolated problem.

From this perspective, the mental models (MM) [17–19] of operators are an explicit part of the human-machine loop [15, pp. 19–21]. Figure 1 shows the role of the operator in an abstracted human-swarm loop from a CSE perspective which defines two challenges for HSI. First, the operator's MM about swarm dynamics change as a result of the human-swarm loop [15, pp. 19–21] which in turn may change mission behaviour (Sect. 2.1). Second, swarm control and other mission tasks the operator has to face require operator workload (Sect. 2.2).

2.1   Mental Models About Swarm Dynamics

Considering human behaviour as part of the system loop can be demanding. As experienced in daily life, our MM of specific aspects of the world are not

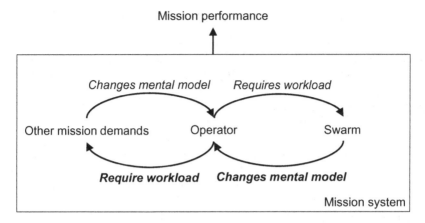

Fig. 1. Human-swarm loop from a CSE perspective stressing mission performance, changes of MM and distribution of MWL

static but change with experience, and this may influence how we act upon the world [17–19]. Thus, human-swarm behaviour can change as a result of the operator's learning about swarm control demands (Fig. 1). This implicates that the cognitive complexity of swarm control [3] is not static but depends on the MM of the operator [15, p. 73] [23, p. 40] [24, pp. 17–19], highlighting operator training as one opportunity to decrease cognitive complexity. During the learning process, the operator may explore different strategies to optimize goal achievement, while the chosen strategies can differ between individuals [25].

Given human adaptation to work demands [16, pp. 17–21], we propose that the evolution of MM of swarm dynamics (i.e. the progress of training) should be explicitly considered when designing and evaluating HSI. First, like all control systems, operators require a good MM of the swarm in order to effectively regulate it [6]. Understanding the evolution and current fit of the MM is therefore fundamental. Second, the way humans adapt to systems can provide valuable information about the underlying demands [16, pp. 37–41]. For example, when choosing between two swarm algorithms for HSI, one of the two algorithms might be easier to adapt to (i.e. being less demanding) and therefore may be preferred. Differences between the algorithms can uncover demanding properties in the context of the situation. Valuable information about HSI can also be drawn from observations about which strategies the operators come up with, as has been demonstrated by Walker and Kolling [25]. This information can then be used for HSI design iteration and theory building. For example, provided that control strategy A results into better control of a swarm algorithm compared to control strategy B, the designer could improve the training or user support for control strategy A.

In sum, operator adaptation in HSI is argued to be an important part of the system loop and therefore should be considered during the design process.

2.2   Mental Workload Demands in Missions

From an overall missions perspective, swarms supervision can be challenging to implement. First, automation in socio-technical systems may not always decrease demands, but only shift them [7,15,16]. Although SR are expected to be beneficial, swarm supervision also induces new control demands on mission staff which can change mission system dynamics. Second, human operators can not always focus on swarm regulation alone as they may have other tasks at hand but only limited mental resources and time (Fig. 1). For example, a swarm operator would need to coordinate swarm goals with overall mission goals and let the team members know where targets have been identified. In an extreme case, human resources are so rare that there is even less time to focus on swarm coordination, because the operator must, for example, also supervise the overall overview of the situation (i.e. supervise other deployments as well). Even in cases where expert swarm operators have been defined with no other tasks at hand, allowing for flexibility of task allocation between team members can turn out beneficial [26].

While MWL is a well known framework for understanding operator limitations in human-factors engineering [20–22], the multiple resource theory suggests that human processing of tasks depends on the task demand, human resource structure and the allocation of resources [27,28]. Unfortunately, the processing of tasks in multitask scenarios interact with each other. One must therefore focus on overall mission demands because HSI developed in isolation may not perform as expected when being part of an overall mission system where demands interact with each other. This results in the need to check each task combination in order to understand which multitask scenarios are sustainable and which are not.

In sum, understanding the mission system should be a sine qua non in order to design HSI. Individual MWL should be reasonable allocated between relevant mission tasks in a way that promotes socio-technical resilience (see Hollnagel [29] and Woods [30] for definitions of resilience). However, this should not be misunderstood as minimizing MWL for swarm supervision as both overload and underload may lead to undesired effects [20]. Instead, the goal should be to hold MWL in a reasonable interval for all possible combinations of demands.

3   Understanding Swarm Dynamics

As natural and artificial swarms can be seen as complex systems [1, p. 2], we discuss in the following how complex systems can be understood (Sect. 3.1). In Sect. 3.2, neglect benevolence (NB) is described as a challenge for operator training in HSI.

3.1   Coping with Complex Systems

Model Exploration. Describing swarms as complex systems stresses that swarms are made of a large number of components with often complicated (i.e.

non-linear) dynamics and interactions. Scalability of swarms poses a particular challenge for understanding SR, as the number of agents is not static but may vary during deployment which leads to reorganisations of the network. Developing methods for understanding complex systems is an open challenge in science [31]. Different agent-based modelling frameworks exist for modelling and teaching the dynamics of complex systems, with NetLogo [32] and RePast [33] being examples for agent-based modelling software packages. The frameworks allow both investigators and students alike to build models, adjust model parameters and observe the emerging model dynamics.

Bottom-Up Understanding. SR engineers design and test swarms from bottom up, i.e. building macrolevel swarm dynamics out of microlevel interaction rules. In turn, an operator is commonly confronted with the assembled macrolevel system. Without prior exposure or explanations, the assembled swarm will be a black box for her/him, meaning that she/he has no representative MM of the swarm dynamics. However, top down understanding, or analysis, of complex systems that present a black box for the observer is much harder than invention, as Braitenberg postulated with his 'law of uphill analysis and downhill invention' [34, p. 20]. If this rule is applied to training in HSI, in which swarm dynamics also pose a black box phenomenon for the operator, SR may be best trained by first teaching robot behaviours and then moving to interactions between robots which form the swarm, rather than starting with the swarm and taking it apart for explaining SR.

Embracing Complexity. From a CSE perspective, the trend to simplify complexities by hiding information in human-machine interaction is treated with caution [15, pp. 82–91]. Instead, complexity should be embraced when the process in focus is complex, as hiding information can lead to system failures by promoting human out-of-loop situations. Thus, operators of the human-swarm loop should be given enough time for training in the complexities of the swarm, so they are able to identify different situations and selecting the correct response during deployment. Embracing complexity should however not be confused with overwhelming the operator with unnecessary information. Rather, complex phenomena may be abstracted without loosing information about the process in focus.

Ironically, as complexity of the system is defined by the observer rather than by the system of concern itself [15, p. 73] [23, p. 40] [24, pp. 17–19], training the operator in the complexity of SR can reduce the complexity for the operator when the MM becomes sophisticated enough to allow for the identification of abstract patterns [18].

Taken together, understanding swarm dynamics is challenging but may benefit from model exploration in a bottom up approach while embracing complexity.

3.2   Neglect Benevolence in HSI

A concept formulated in HSI is neglect benevolence; the counterintuitive phenomenon that it may be beneficial to observe swarm behaviour for a certain time interval before issuing the control signal [25,35–37]. The performance of SR therefore can be sensitive not only to the issued command itself but also to temporal shifts of the command. In order to robustly control the swarm, the operator must be aware of how his input effects the present and future swarm state. In the following, we will shortly review work done on NB as it poses a particular challenge to HSI.

Walker and Kolling [25] demonstrated NB in a task where operators had to balance between the application of heading commands and flocking constraints. The authors observed two different kinds of strategies adapted by the operators. One group preferred to maximize control of swarm heading while the other preferred to cover a larger area with the drawback of less heading control. There was no difference in performance in the particular foraging task.

Nagavalli et al. [35] defined NB formally and showed how the input interval for optimal task performance could be determined in a formation convergence task. They thereby provided the foundations for an objective measure of optimal input timing as well as user support systems. The optimal temporal length of operator input was investigated in a computational model as well [37]. In [36] it was shown that human operators are able to approximate the optimal timing via training. The training consisted of a passive phase, were the impact of shifts in input timing on performance was demonstrated, followed by an active phase, were the operator could explore the dynamics and was provided corrective feedback. During the testing phase, performance improved for a condition without user support, whereas performance was stable with user support.

Taken together, work on temporal input sensitivity in HSI suggests that operators can adapt to optimal input timings for swarm regulation.

4   Adaptive Training in HSI

The operator's MM was argued to be an important part of the human-swarm loop. To summarize the preceding sections, training solutions in HSI should deal with the following requirements:

1. The training system should allow for the analysis of training progress (Sect. 2).
2. The training system should aim at increasing mission performance, MM correctness and allocation of MWL between tasks (Sect. 2).
3. The training system should allow for swarm model exploration (Sect. 3).
4. The training system should allow for bottom up SR training (Sect. 3).
5. The training system should embrace complexity (Sect. 3).

Requirement 1 allows to check the correctness of the MM and deduce information for HSI design based on the adaptation of the operators. The goal of the training is formulated by requirement 2; to enhance mission performance, optimize the correctness of the MM and distribute MWL between tasks. Requirement 3, 4 and 5 translate how swarm dynamics may be trained efficiently; by swarm model exploration in a bottom up approach over a range of complexities.

Based on these requirements, we propose the application of adaptive training (AT), or adaptive instructional systems (AIS), for operator training in HSI. An AIS is a technical system which observes relevant learning variables, makes a decision on how the learning should be adjusted to optimize learning performance and executes this adjustment. Thus, an AIS is a closed-loop feedback system which adjusts properties of the task based on learning performance (Fig. 2) [38,39]. An AIS can thereby compensate for differences of individual MM progression.

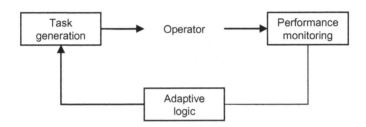

Fig. 2. Closed-loop feedback in adaptive training (adapted from [38])

AT (i.e. a closed-loop feedback) can also be implemented by a teacher who observes how the student is progressing and adapts task difficulty or supports the student. When studying complex systems, the investigator her/himself implements the closed loop, as she/he will monitor if the system is understood and adapts behaviours in turn. In contrast, a static learning task is an open-loop system which does not allow for individual tracking and adjusment of the task. In the domain of complex systems the former is to be preferred, given that complex systems are hard to understand and can result in individual control strategies [25].

In the following, we describe each AIS component (Fig. 2) in the context of HSI. Section 4.1 presents the adaptation space and Sect. 4.2 the measurement space. The adaptive logic is discussed in Sect. 4.3. Finally, Sect. 4.4 describes how optimal input timing could be trained adaptively.

4.1 Task Adaptation Space

AT requires a definition of the adaptation space that influences the operator's learning (Fig. 3). We define two dimensions in the adaptation space. The first dimension is the complexity dimension, which is common to AIS and makes the learning task easier or harder by training simple or complex training tasks. This dimension relates to requirement 5 in that it allows for an exploration of different complexity situations. The second dimension is deducted from requirement 4 and is specific to the training of complex systems: the emergence dimension. The emergence dimension ranges from microlevel (human-robot interaction, HRI) to macrolevel (HSI).

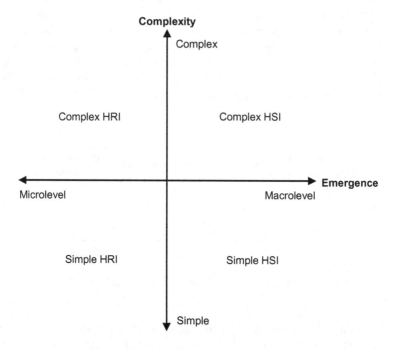

Fig. 3. Adaptation space for AT in HSI

Complexity Dimension. Here we group the complexity dimension into components of the human-machine loop (excluding the operator as she/he is the training target): (1) mission task complexity, (2) swarm complexity, (3) human-swarm interface complexity, (4) environmental complexity and (5) simulation complexity. See Kelley [38] for an alternative grouping. Note that the complexities are formulated from an operators perspective. Table 1 gives an overview of the complexity dimension.

(1) Mission task complexity. Each single mission task can vary in parameter difficulty. For example, a single mission task can be made more difficult by decreasing the time limit to mission failure or by increasing the size of a target area. Adding conditions for a single task or increasing the number of parallel tasks can also increase difficulty. An additional condition might be that particular regions are now to be avoided while locating targets. Additional tasks may be swarm control tasks (e.g. locate targets and control formation) or other mission tasks (e.g. provide sitreps or coordinate non-swarm deployments as well).

Table 1. Complexity dimension of the adaptation space

Components	Complexity ranges (simple - complex)
(1) Mission	• Easy task - Difficult task
	• Single task - Multiple tasks
(2) Swarm	• Single robot - Multiple robots
	• Offline scalable - Online scalable
	• Simple behaviour - Complex behaviour
	• Single behaviour - Multiple behaviours
(3) Interface	• Low user support - High user support
	• Low transmission delay - High transmission delay
(4) Environment	• Empty environment - Full environment
	• Homogeneous environment - Heterogeneous environment
	• Static environment - Dynamic environment
	• Friendly environment - Hostile environment
	• Easy mission targets - Difficult mission targets
(5) Simulation	• Low speed - High speed

(2) Swarm complexity. Scalability complexity can be varied on two dimensions; swarm size and deployment flexibility. The swarm size can vary from three robots to many [1, pp. 4–5]. The deployment scalability can either be offline, meaning that the swarm size is varied between sessions, or online, meaning that swarm size is adjusted during the task. The latter poses increased complexity for the operator as swarm networks will self-organize after the number of nodes have been adjusted. A possible scenario could be the convergence of two swarms into one or the loss of robots in harsh environments.

The behaviour of single robots as well as the emerging swarm dynamics can either be simple or complex in nature. The dynamics of a single robot which depends only on one stimulus (e.g. light) is easier to understand and predict than the dynamics which depend on multiple stimuli modalities [34]. The same logic may be applied to swarm behaviour. Other behavioural complexities can be the size of the behavioural possibilities, how behaviours interact and the determinism of the behaviour. Also, some behaviours may be easier to understand than others; robot movements in path following in general seem easier to comprehend than environmental exploration. Finally, as with mission tasks, robot and swarm behaviour can be single or multiple; a path following swarm can be increased in complexity by following the path only in the presence of a certain stimulus.

(3) Human-swarm interface complexity. Interfaces may be able to provide a range of user support. Providing estimations of the future swarm state [3] or providing the optimal temporal interval for user input [36] can be seen as increases in user support. From an operator point of view, user support is

placed on the simple range of the complexity axis whereas no user support is more complex. This relation becomes inverted when taking a technical point of view, as providing user support is more challenging to implement. Transmission delay is also an important factor in HSI. No transmission delays lie on the simple spectrum, whereas increased delays can result in complexities [25].

(4) Environmental complexity. The mission environment, i.e. the environment in which the swarm and in some cases also the human operator are placed, can vary in complexity. The control environment (i.e. the environment for the operator) can however differ from the mission environment in remote interaction. The environment can be an open field (empty environment) or have many obstacles (full environment) [11] which block the path to a target, complicate communications between agents or complicate operation of the operator and the swarm. Environmental homogeneity and dynamics in terms of terrain, obstacles and other agents are additional factors. An urban environment with reoccurring structures can be high in homogeneity (lower complexity), but at the same time agents like citizens are highly heterogeneous and dynamic (higher complexity). In addition, the mission and control environment can vary in swarm and human hostility. The conditions for a fire fighter unit, like a dark room filled with smoke, are relatively hostile for swarm and operator [13] and therefore more likely to lead to robot, human or interaction failures.

Kelley [38] gives g-force, vibration, oxygen pressure and drugs as examples for work space adaptation. G-force can be an important consideration in HSI; the future combat air system is a concept of a modern fighter jet which is accompanied by multiple drones. Vibration also seems important for scenarios where drones are controlled from mobile platforms such as helicopters [40]. Finally, where and how mission targets are placed also influences complexity; a single accessible high value target is easier to exploit than multiple elusive medium valued targets.

(5) Simulation complexity. In the particular case of training in a simulation, the speed may be adjusted with low speed providing more time for the operator, resulting in lower complexity.

Emergence Dimension. The emergence dimension ranges from HRI at the microlevel to how the swarm solves a particular task (HSI, macrolevel) that is more than summed up single robot behaviours (emergence). Thus, emergence depends on the local interactions between individual robots. For example, based on the behaviour of local interaction rules (microlevel), the robot collective forms flocks (macrolevel) [41]. Path selection in ants, a form of decision making, is another example where the choice is made by the colony (i.e. interacting agents, macrolevel) rather than by individual ants [42]. See Camazine [43] and Bonabeau [44] for more examples.

Thus, the emergence dimension relates individual robot behaviours to swarm behaviour while considering operator influence. Moving from microlevel to macrolevel is overlapping with a variation in swarm size on the complexity dimension. However, they are conceptually different in that the emergence dimension relates to emergence behaviour of a swarm whereas the complexity dimension relates to complexity variation.

4.2   Learning Performance Measurement Space

AT requires estimations of the learning process as input. From a cybernetic perspective, the measurement variables are the ones optimized during training, as these are the learning outputs which trigger a change in task complexity to which the operator adapts. As a result of the preceding discussion, we focus on the measurement of mission performance, correctness of the MM and MWL (requirement 2). Here we treat mission performance as a whole mission systems measurement and MM correctness as well as optimal ranges of MWL as an operator measurement. While at least mission performance and MWL [20] as well as mission performance and MM fit [17] are expected to correlate, accessing all three variables should provide more valid data of the training progress.

Mission Performance. Measurement of mission performance is defined by the mission objectives. In a search and rescue scenario, the mission objective may be to find and report victims. One performance measurement could then be the area covered or the number of correctly identified targets over a given time period [25]. The number of identified victims and locations must also be reported by the system, which should be reflected in the training scenario and the performance measurement (i.e. correctly reported targets in addition to correctly identified targets). Alternatively, the mission objective may be to build an overview of the situation. Here the system is additionally required to group and rate the importance of victim locations and communicate these findings. Taken together, the performance measurements should reflect the mission goals and the associated demands for the human-swarm loop in a holistic fashion covering mission demands, rather than single HSI measures like accuracy of target identification in isolation.

Mental Model Correctness. MM are normally accessed via knowledge elicitation methods [18]. For example, participants are asked to implement the phenomenon in focus in a fuzzy-cognitive-map [45]. These methods seem in general not easily usable in AIS. Alternatively, questionnaires can be presented in which the operator is tested for understanding. In addition, measurement of situational awareness [46] may be used to quantify MM fitness as both cognitive concepts depend on each other [47].

As MM are about concepts and their interactions [18], issued questions in closed form should also focus on the interaction between concepts. Thus, the questions should take the form of 'if inputs/conditions, then what outputs/states are the result?'. For example, it may be asked how a robot or swarm reacts to the presence of a certain stimulus (combination).

Mental Workload. Several reviews on MWL measurement exist [20–22]. The methods for determining MWL are normally grouped into three categories: primary and secondary task performance, introspection (subjective ratings) and physiological measurement. Given that we discuss AT as a technical system, task performance and physiological measures are to be preferred. Task performance was here already treated as part of mission performance.

MWL should be distributed over mission tasks. Here we define MWL as the mental resources the operator has at disposal and engages in particular environments in order to keep the task performance in an acceptable range [20, 21]. Importantly, if in a particular environment mental resources are directed to a task from the currently available mental resources which depend on the current operator state (skill, vigilance etc.), less capacity is free to attend to other mission tasks, although the free resources would depend on the particular task combination [28]. This definition of MWL is pragmatic as we are interested in the overall exhaustion of the operator without the need to separate the effects of tasks, cognitive constructs and environment from another. Thus, by observing an increased mental stress of the operator, one can infer that the situation has placed increased MWL demands on the operator.

For example, increased heart rate in combination with decreased heart rate variability can be an indicator for MWL [20], provided that the operator is not engaged in any physical tasks. This is an important drawback of using physiological measures; MWL estimations cannot be differentiated from physical work load. In environments where the operator also has to do physical work (like in fire fighting [13]) MWL estimations by physiological methods is challenging. In such situations, introspection methods could be used as an alternative input to the AIS. Alternatively, one applies physiological workload measurement nonetheless and makes the assumption that high physical workload will also decrease the availability of mental resources. This assumption can be made as we are not interested in the load of a particular task, but in the capacity to cope with mission tasks in general. For an overview of other physiological MWL measures (i.e. respiration, ocular behaviour, skin conductance, blood pressure and neurodynamics) we refer the reader to Cain [21], Charles and Nixon [22] and Wickens et al. [48].

4.3   Adaptive Logic: From Learning Progress to Task Adaptation

The adaptive logic defines the mapping between the estimates of learning performance and task adaptation. The logic may be build by the designer, as Durlach [49] described when pointing out that there is still much art in the design of AIS. The mapping can be implemented by traditional or fuzzy logic, with fuzzy-cognitive-mapping [45] being a candidate for the latter. The application of machine learning in AIS has been discussed as well [50]. A further choice must be made between different kinds of adaptations to performance [38].

The AIS should maximize mission performance as well as MM fit while being in a reasonable MWL interval over a range of complexities. We see a good MM of the emergence domain as a precondition [17] (horizontal axis in Fig. 3) that should be satisfied before optimizing mission performance and MWL allocation (vertical axis in Fig. 3).

Emergence Adaptation via MM Fit Measurement. We propose to first allow for bottom-up (i.e. starting with the microlevel at low complexity, left bottom corner in Fig. 3) guided exploration of the microlevel-macrolevel axis (requirement 3). Closed-loop exploration could be implemented by the operator or by a technical AIS. Preferably, the operator is first allowed to manually explore the dynamics of the microlevel, implementing the closed-loop learning her/himself. As the microlevel-macrolevel dimension is about understanding the underlying principles of swarm dynamics (i.e. opening the black box), mission performance and MWL may not be validate indicators of understanding in their own right, whereas the operator can check by introspection if her/his MM fits her/his observations. The operator may additionally be tested for understanding of the microlevel afterwards by promoting questions in the form of 'how does a robot react to stimulus x?'. If successful, the guided exploration moves to the macrolevel (right bottom corner in Fig. 3), which focuses on the robot assembly as a swarm. After guided but manual exploration, the MM of the operator is again tested for correctness of the microlevel-macrolevel mapping by questions like 'Why does the swarm change its movements often when the robots are spread in the environment?'. It may be necessary to repeat microlevel training in order to open the black box again if understanding of the macrolevel was not sufficient. The easiness of understanding the microlevel-macrolevel axis can be a first indicator of the demands that the operator is exposed to by the swarm algorithm (requirement 1).

Complexity Adaptation via Mission Performance and MWL Measurement. After confirmation that a fundamental MM about the particular swarm dynamics has been established, AIS training includes the measurement of mission performance and MWL. This is the domain of AT [38] where the task complexity (vertical axis in Fig. 3) is varied so to increase learning performance, while the emergence axis MM building can be seen as the pre-training to establish fundamental understanding. Depending on the mission task and the complexity variable that is varied, the complexity level may be varied at the swarm level alone (right side in Fig. 3). Alternatively, with each complexity level variation, a new manual exploration of the emergence axis is allowed, resulting in vertical and horizontal variation in Fig. 3 over the whole training session.

In any case, mission performance and MWL measurement trigger a change in task complexity. Whereas mission performance criteria are formulated objectively, the correct interval of reasonable MWL needs to be identified for each individual participant before training. If either mission performance or MWL fall outside the predefined ranges, complexity is increased or decreased. The reader is referred to Kelly [38] for fundamentals on how to adapt training and to Durlach [49] for model building. For example, adaptation should not be implemented directly after performance or MWL fall outside the tolerance, as this would lead to oscillating task adaptations. The evolution of task adaptation can be used by the designer to identify demanding situations (requirement 1). For example, a certain swarm algorithm might be easy to cope with in empty mission environments but demanding in full mission environments. A solution could then be to switch between swarm algorithms based on the number of obstacles in mission environments.

AIS Dynamics Summarized. Taken together, we suggest the operator should first be trained in the emergence dimension of Fig. 3 where AT is either implemented by a human, an AIS which checks understanding by prompting questions or a combination of the two. Afterwards, training continues in the complexity dimension of Fig. 3 based on mission performance and MWL deviations either at the macrolevel or with microlevel-macrolevel variations. Whereas training on the emergence axis can be seen as building a fundamental MM about swarm dynamics, variations on the complexity axis extend the fundamental MM over a variety of situations and should therefore further enhance understanding.

4.4 Training Optimal Input Timing

In the HSI foraging task of Walker and Kolling [25], the operators had to explore the environment by balancing between network density and alignment consensus. When a heading command from the operator is induced in the swarm with an error for each robot, the robots communicate their headings with their local neighbours to reach consensus. At the same time, the operator has to supervise the network density in order to preserve local robot communications while allowing for movement space between robots. Importantly, the performance depended on the input timing and frequency of the operator commands. Thus, this particular implementation of HSI requires the operator to develop a MM of correct input timing. In the following, we discuss a possible training of this particular implementation for approximating the optimal input timing in the context of search and rescue.

Note that providing user support for optimal input timing intervals [35] does not exclude training the operator in optimal input timing intervals, as the dynamics of swarms should be understood by the operator for resilient performance in unexpected situations. In other words, providing user aids without training the operator in the underlying dynamics reinforces the role of the operator as a compensator for technical limitations instead of reinforcing human adaptivity to increase resilience.

The optimal input timing interval could be trained by an AIS. The training could be implemented in the following order

1. Providing instructions for single robot behaviour
2. Robot dynamic exploration at low complexity
3. Providing instructions for swarm behaviour
4. Swarm dynamic exploration with increasing swarm size complexity
5. Varying task complexity

(a) Mission complexity: identifying targets - plus reporting targets - plus fusing multiple sensor data
(b) Interface complexity: low transmission delays - high transmission delays
(c) Environmental complexity: empty environment - full environment

Providing HRI Instructions. In step 1, the operator is instructed in the capabilities of single robot behaviours. Singe robots in the experiment of Walker and Kolling [25] would move straight forward if allowed to and stop or change direction as a result of human input. Although not part of the particular task implementation by Walker and Kolling, increasingly realistic scenarios would feature additional robot behaviours such as obstacle avoidance [11]. For example, the operator could be provided with an explanation about the change of heading when a robot senses an obstacle in front of it.

Exploration of HRI Dynamics. Afterwards, in step 2, the operator is asked to explore the model (left bottom corner of Fig. 3). For example, she/he could first manually explore the dynamics of the robot followed by a task in which she/he must guide the robot into a goal area. In this particular task, it could make sense to vary in the environment complexity dimension to increase the number of obstacles (variation at the left side in Fig. 3). Task performance (e.g. number of commands and time to reach goal area) may be used as a measurement on when to adapt the number of obstacles. However, this may only be done after the operator was allowed to manually explore dynamics without any time constrains. Step 2 is completed with testing the operator's MM with questions of the sort of 'What does happen if the movement path of the robot is blocked by an obstacle?'. The microlevel exploration may be repeated if the test of the MM was not successful.

Providing HSI Instructions. Step 3 provides instructions for the swarm behaviour which build on the microlevel behaviour. The robots exchange their heading with their local neighbours to reach consensus. The operator may now also apply flocking constraints, which lead to higher area coverage while preserving local neighbour communications. The explanations provided describe the swarm as an entity.

Exploration of HSI Dynamics. Similarly to step 2, step 4 starts with manual exploration at low complexity (right bottom corner of Fig. 3) without time constrains where the closed-loop training is implemented by the operator. After manual exploration, the operator has to steer the swarm through the empty environment in a foraging task, where she/he must approximate the optimal input timing for enhanced performance. Before the complexity is adapted based on task performance, the operator is tested for understanding of the swarm dynamics by questions like 'What influence has your input timing on the performance of the foraging task?'. Different operator strategies [25] may already be identifiable at this point.

Variations in Task Complexity. After successful training of macrolevel dynamics at low complexity, complexities can be adapted (right side in Fig. 3). Step 5 is arguably the most important step of the training, as MWL intervals and mission performance are optimized while expanding the MM over different complexity situations. Thus, the operator should build an intuition of optimal temporal input intervals given the current situations.

In the discussed fictive scenario, mission complexity is increased by adding additional mission tasks to swarm control (e.g. reporting identified targets to a higher mission command level). In addition, data from other sensors are provided to the operator via a map layer that would allow her/him to increase his view of the environment but which needs to be coordinated. For example, what should the operator do if confronted with conflicting results between the swarm and another sensor system? This decision requires additional understanding of the capabilities of the different sensors as well as the environment.

Transmission delays pose additional complexity on the system [25]. Starting with none or low transmission delays, the delays may be varied to the point where the adaptation capabilities of the operator fail to optimize MWL or mission performance. Similarly, the number of obstacles of the environment is increased until swarm regulation fails. The complexities may be either adapted in succession or in nested combinations. The objective however should be to cover all combinations of complexities, as the MWL induced by task combinations do not simply add up.

Importantly, varying the different complexities provides the designer with a first estimation of expected bounds of the implemented human-swarm design choice as part of a mission over a range of situations.

5   Conclusion and Future Work

In this work, we have discussed the role of operators in human-swarm interaction (HSI) from a cognitive systems engineering perspective. Training was argued to be an important facet of the human-swarm loop that can additionally be used to identify hidden demands the operators have adapted to. During deployment, mental workload must be distributed over a variation of mission tasks in which supervising a swarm can be one of many tasks. This has to be considered during design. In addition, training swarm robotics may benefit from bottom up exploration of swarm dynamics while embracing complexity to promote representative mental model building over a variety of situations.

The application of adaptive instructional systems was formulated as a possible solution for effective training in HSI. The discussed AIS proposal allows for the tracking of training progress and considers mission performance, mental model fit and mental workload to be optimized during training by utilizing the respective variables as triggers for task adaptation. A combination of manual and guided swarm dynamics exploration in a bottom up fashion was proposed in order to facilitate a fundamental understanding of swarm dynamics. The operator is then exposed to a variety of complex situations where the training is tuned to achieve a balance of mental workload over tasks and an increase in mission performance.

The presented concepts are theoretical in nature. Future empirical work has to explore the usefulness of adaptive instructional systems in the domain of HSI. In addition, other possibilities for operator training may also be explored. For example, we are developing a gamification approach for teaching swarm intelligence with a board game where players influence the behaviours of ants via placing pheromones (Fig. 4). Importantly, operator dynamics should be seen as an important system function of the human-swarm loop, where the adaptive behaviours of humans are investigated to identify swarm control demands. In general, human adaptivity should be supported by design to facilitate resilient performance of the overall mission system.

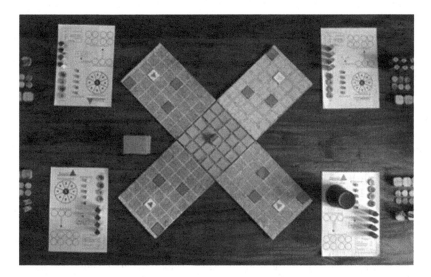

Fig. 4. Board game for gamified teaching of swarm intelligence

References

1. Hamann, H.: Swarm Robotics: A Formal Approach. Springer, Cham (2018). https://doi.org/10.1007/978-3-319-74528-2
2. Brambilla, M., Ferrante, E., Birattari, M., Dorigo, M.: Swarm robotics: a review from the swarm engineering perspective. Swarm Intell. **7**(1), 1–41 (2013)
3. Kolling, A., Walker, P., Chakraborty, N., Sycara, K., Lewis, M.: Human interaction with robot swarms: a survey. IEEE Trans. Hum.-Mach. Syst. **46**(1), 9–26 (2016)
4. Barca, J.C., Sekercioglu, Y.A.: Swarm robotics reviewed. Robotica **31**(3), 345–359 (2013)
5. Yang, G.Z., et al.: The grand challenges of science robotics. Sci. Robot. **3**(14) (2018)
6. Conant, R.C., Ross Ashby, W.: Every good regulator of a system must be a model of that system. Int. J. Syst. Sci. **1**, 89–97 (1970)
7. Bainbridge, L.: Ironies of automation. Automatica (1983)
8. Guastello, S.J.: Human Factors Engineering and Ergonomics: A Systems Approach. CRC Press (2013)

9. Pendleton, B., Goodrich, M.: Scalable human interaction with robotic swarms. In: AIAA Infotech@Aerospace (I@A) Conference, pp. 1–13 (2013)
10. Brown, D.S., Kerman, S.C., Goodrich, M.A.: Human-swarm interactions based on managing attractors. Proceedings of the 2014 ACM/IEEE International Conference on Human-Robot Interaction - HRI 2014, pp. 90–97 (2014)
11. Kolling, A., Sycara, K., Nunnally, S., Lewis, M.: Human swarm interaction: an experimental study of two types of interaction with foraging swarms. J. Hum.-Robot Interact. **2**(2), 104–129 (2013)
12. Alboul, L., Joan, S.P., Penders, J.: Mixed human-robot team navigation in the GUARDIANS project. In: Proceedings of the 2008 IEEE International Workshop on Safety, Security and Rescue Robotics, SSRR 2008, pp. 95–101 (2008)
13. Penders, J., et al.: A robot swarm assisting a human fire-fighter. Adv. Robot. **25**(1–2), 93–117 (2011)
14. Hollnagel, E., Woods, D.D.: Cognitive systems engineering: new wine in new bottles. Int. J. Man-Mach. Stud. **18**, 583–600 (1983)
15. Hollnagel, E., Woods, D.D.: Joint Cognitive Systems. Foundations of Cognitive Systems Engineering (2005)
16. Woods, D.D., Hollnagel, E.: Joint Cognitive Systems: Patterns in Cognitive Systems Engineering (2006)
17. Staggers, N., Norcio, A.F.: Mental models: concepts for human-computer interaction research. Int. J. Man-Mach. Stud. **38**, 587–605 (1993)
18. Jones, N.A., Ross, H., Lynam, T., Perez, P., Leitch, A.: Mental models: an interdisciplinary synthesis of theory and methods. Ecol. Soc. **16**(1) (2011)
19. Johnson-Laird, P.N.: Mental models and human reasoning. Proc. Natl. Acad. Sci. **107**(43), 18243–18250 (2010)
20. Young, M.S., Brookhuis, K.A., Wickens, C.D., Hancock, P.A.: State of science: mental workload in ergonomics (2015)
21. Cain, B.: A review of the mental workload literature. Defence research and development Toronto (Canada), pp. 4-1–4-34 (1998) (2007)
22. Charles, R.L., Nixon, J.: Measuring mental workload using physiological measures: a systematic review. Appl. Ergon. **74**(January), 221–232 (2019)
23. Ashby, W.R.: An Introduction to Cybernetics. Chapman & Hall Ltd. (1961)
24. Casti, J.: Alternate Realities: Mathematical Models of Nature and Man. Wiley, New York (1989)
25. Walker, P., Nunnally, S., Lewis, M., Kolling, A., Chakraborty, N., Sycara, K.: Neglect benevolence in human control of swarms in the presence of latency. In: Conference Proceedings - IEEE International Conference on Systems, Man and Cybernetics, pp. 3009–3014 (2012)
26. Naikar, N., Elix, B.: Designing for self-organisation in sociotechnical systems: resilience engineering, cognitive work analysis, and the diagram of work organisation possibilities. Cogn. Technol. Work (0123456789) (2019). https://doi.org/10.1007/s10111-019-00595-y
27. Navon, D., Gopher, D.: On the economy of the human-processing system. Psychol. Rev. **86**(3), 214–255 (1979)
28. Wickens, C.D.: Multiple resources and mental workload. Hum. Fact. **50**(3), 449–455 (2008)
29. Hollnagel, E.: Resilience Engineering in Practice: A Guidebook. Ashgate Publishing, Ltd. (2013)
30. Woods, D.D.: Four concepts for resilience and the implications for the future of resilience engineering. Reliab. Eng. Syst. Saf. **141**, 5–9 (2015)

31. Holland, J.H.: Studying complex adaptive systems. J. Syst. Sci. Complexity **19**, 1–8 (2006)
32. Wilensky, U.: NetLogo. Center for Connected Learning and Computer Based Modeling Northwestern University Evanston IL (1999). http://ccl.northwestern.edu/netlogo/
33. North, M.J., et al.: Complex adaptive systems modeling with Repast Simphony. Complex Adap. Syst. Model. **1**, 3 (2013)
34. Braitenberg, V.: Vehicles: Experiments in Synthetic Psychology. MIT Press (1986)
35. Nagavalli, S., Luo, L., Chakraborty, N., Sycara, K.: Neglect benevolence in human control of robotic swarms. In: Proceedings - IEEE International Conference on Robotics and Automation, pp. 6047–6053 (2014)
36. Nagavalli, S., Chien, S.Y., Lewis, M., Chakraborty, N., Sycara, K.: Bounds of neglect benevolence in input timing for human interaction with robotic swarms. In: 2015 ACM/IEEE International Conference on Human-Robot Interaction, pp. 197–204, March 2015
37. Ma, J., Lai, E.M., Ren, J.: On the timing of operator commands for the navigation of a robot swarm. In: 2018 15th International Conference on Control, Automation, Robotics and Vision, ICARCV 2018 (2018)
38. Kelley, C.R.: What is adaptive training? Hum. Fact.: J. Hum. Fact. Ergon. Soc. **11**(6), 547–556 (1969)
39. Gaines, B.R.: The learning of perceptual-motor skills by men and machines and its relationship to training. Instr. Sci. **1**, 263–312 (1972)
40. Frey, M.A., Schulte, A.: Tactical decision support for UAV deployment in MUM-T Helicopter missions: problem analysis and system requirements. In: Proceedings - 2018 IEEE International Conference on Cognitive and Computational Aspects of Situation Management, CogSIMA 2018 (2018)
41. Reynolds, C.W.: Flocks, herds, and schools: a distributed behavioral model. In: Proceedings of the 14th Annual Conference on Computer Graphics and Interactive Techniques, SIGGRAPH 1987 (1987)
42. Deneubourg, J.L., Aron, S., Goss, S., Pasteels, J.M.: The self-organizing exploratory pattern of the argentine ant. J. Insect Behav. **3**(2), 159–168 (1990)
43. Camazine, S., Deneubourg, J.L., Franks, N.R., Sneyd, J., Theraulaz, G., Bonabeau, E.: Self-organisation in biological systems (2003)
44. Bonabeau, E., Dorigo, M., Theraulaz, G.: From natural to artificial swarm intelligence (1999)
45. Kosko, B.: Fuzzy cognitive maps (1986)
46. Meireles, L., Alves, L., Cruz, J.: Conceptualization and measurement of individual situation awareness (SA) in expert populations across operational domains: a systematic review of the literature with a practical purpose on our minds. Proc. Hum. Fact. Ergon. Soc. **2**, 1093–1097 (2018)
47. Endsley, M.R.: Situation awareness misconceptions and misunderstandings. J. Cogn. Eng. Decis. Making **9**(1), 4–32 (2015)
48. Wickens, C.D., Hollands, J.G., Banbury, S., Parasuraman, R.: Engineering Psychology and Human Performance. Psychology Press (2015)
49. Durlach, P.J.: Fundamentals, flavors, and foibles of adaptive instructional systems. In: Sottilare, R.A., Schwarz, J. (eds.) HCII 2019. LNCS, vol. 11597, pp. 76–95. Springer, Cham (2019). https://doi.org/10.1007/978-3-030-22341-0_7
50. Roessingh, J.J., Poppinga, G., van Oijen, J., Toubman, A.: Application of artificial intelligence to adaptive instruction - combining the concepts. In: Sottilare, R.A., Schwarz, J. (eds.) HCII 2019. LNCS, vol. 11597, pp. 542–556. Springer, Cham (2019). https://doi.org/10.1007/978-3-030-22341-0_43

The Mental Machine: Classifying Mental Workload State from Unobtrusive Heart Rate-Measures Using Machine Learning

Roderic H. L. Hillege[1,2]([✉]), Julia C. Lo[1,3], Christian P. Janssen[4], and Nico Romeijn[4]

[1] ProRail B.V., Utrecht, The Netherlands
[2] Ordina N.V., Nieuwegein, The Netherlands
roderic.hillege@gmail.com
[3] Faculty of Technology, Policy and Management,
Delft University of Technology, Delft, The Netherlands
[4] Experimental Psychology & Helmholtz Institute, Utrecht University,
Utrecht, The Netherlands

Abstract. This paper investigates whether mental workload can be classified in an operator setting using unobtrusive psychophysiological measures. Having reliable predictions of workload using unobtrusive sensors can be useful for adaptive instructional systems, as knowledge of a trainee's workload can then be used to provide appropriate training level (not too hard, not too easy). Previous work has investigated automatic mental workload prediction using biophysical measures and machine learning, however less attention has been given to the level of physical obtrusiveness of the used measures. We therefore explore the use of color-, and infrared-spectrum cameras for remote photoplethysmography (rPPG) as physically unobtrusive measures. Sixteen expert train traffic operators participated in a railway human-in-the-loop simulator. We used two machine learning models (AdaBoost and Random Forests) to predict low-, medium- and high-mental workload levels based on heart rate features in a leave-one-out cross-validated design. Results show above chance classification for low- and high-mental workload states. Based on infrared-spectrum rPPG derived features, the AdaBoost machine learning model yielded the highest classification performance.

Keywords: Mental workload classification · Machine learning · Remote photoplethysmography · Adaptive Instructional Systems

1 Introduction

The concept of mental workload is recognized as a critical component in the management of operational work. It is also one of the most widely used concepts within the field of cognitive engineering, human factors & ergonomics next to situation awareness (e.g. [1,2]). Besides the development of various measurement

© Springer Nature Switzerland AG 2020
R. A. Sottilare and J. Schwarz (Eds.): HCII 2020, LNCS 12214, pp. 330–349, 2020.
https://doi.org/10.1007/978-3-030-50788-6_24

tools to identify the mental workload of operators, researchers have focused on the application of adaptive automation for the management of operator workload [3–5]. More recent developments also focus on the support of novice operators by providing individual tailored feedback through Adaptive Instructional Systems (AIS) dynamically [6, 7]. These systems aim to adapt the environment or problem difficulty based on the capacity of a student in real-time [8].

The use of psychophysiological measures in adaptive automation and AIS has proven useful, particularly by their ability to present continuous data and potential real-time assessment of mental workload [9]. Previous research has explored various psychophysiological measurement instruments, such as Electro-EncephaloGraphy (EEG), electrocardiogram (ECG) and functional Near InfraRed spectroscopy (fNIRS) [10–12].

An open question is whether other metrics can also successfully detect the mental workload of operators. In particular, can these measures help to reliably differentiate low and high mental workload conditions? Moreover, can this be detected through sensors that are less obtrusive to wear compared to typical clinical research instruments? Having less obtrusive, yet reliable sensors available would be valuable, as it would allow for measurement in more mobile and social settings.

Given these objectives, we explore the use of a psychophysiological measure using remote photo-plethysmography (PPG) in the color-, and infrared-spectrum, based on camera data. Mental workload measures are obtained in a railway traffic human-in-the-loop simulator, in which 16 professional expert train traffic controllers participated. Within the scenarios train traffic controllers operate under low-, medium-, and high-workload conditions, as identified by training experts. The question is then whether unobtrusive, objective, psychophysiological measures can also detect these three workload levels. To find patterns in the measures that can separate the mental workload levels, a machine learning model will be used. Machine learning is chosen due to its flexibility in finding relations in high dimensional spaces compared to statistical modeling, yet offering some degree of explainability compared to (deep) neural nets, which inner workings are a blackbox [13]. Furthermore, machine learning has been successfully used in previous work where mental workload was classified using multimodal input [14–17]. By looking at the features that contribute to the performance of the model, more can be learned about the underlying mechanisms that underlie mental workload.

1.1 Mental Workload

A universal definition of mental workload has not been agreed upon. Various definitions can be found in the literature where some recurring components can be deduced, for example, external task demand, internal competence, and the internal capacity to deal with the task [2, 18, 19]. Since internal capacity has substantial impact on task performance [20], having a better grasp of its state could significantly boost the prediction of task performance.

Current methods for measuring mental workload include self-reports like the NASA-TLX [21], expert observations, and physiological measurements (i.e. EEG, ECG and so on). A detailed overview of measures (and their obtrusiveness) to capture mental workload can be found in Alberdi, et al. [22]. We will summarize a couple of the key metrics below.

Self-report questionnaires require the subject at set intervals to report on their mental state, while performing a task. However, a disadvantage is that such reporting is hard to do fully in parallel with task performance, thereby impacting performance and clouding the workload measure [23]. Expert observations require manual classification of mental workload, which makes it expensive and not scalable to actual work settings such as that of train traffic controllers. Heart rate features, among others, are often used as physiological signals. Other physiological means are for example EEG, and functional magnetic resonance imaging (fMRI). The traditional apparatus to obtain these measures are obtrusive, requiring static task-, or controlled (lab-) environments [24]. Advances in wearable sensors reduce this obtrusiveness; however, true unobtrusiveness and data quality remain a challenge [25–27].

In summary, the traditional measures lack practical applicability outside of lab environments since they interrupt the workflow, physically limit or restrict the freedom of movement due to attached sensors, are expensive, require expert judgments, or have a combination of these factors. However, the new trend of the quantified self brings opportunities for physically less- or even unobtrusive psychophysiological mental workload measures [28]. An example is camera-based remote photo-plethysmography (rPPG), which can detect heart features [29–31] and requires no physical contact. This metric in turn can be used to determine the inter-beat-interval or heart rate variability, which can be used to classify mental workload [2, 32].

The aforementioned metrics can be used in experiments, to post-hoc test whether different levels of workload can be detected. However, for real-time use in an actual operator work context, ad-hoc workload assessment is of added value. Current ad-hoc workload classification models based on automated and high-frequency sampled metrics have already been developed e.g., Martinez, et al. [16], Gosh, et al. [17], and Lopez et al. [14]. These studies reported on models that utilize unobtrusive features to classify mental workload. All three studies used skin conductance- and heart rate-features measured at the wrist, in conjunction with machine learning models, and were able to classify various levels of mental workload states. Van Gent et al., [15] conducted a multilevel mental workload classification experiment in a driving simulator. Using heart rate features extracted from a finger-worn photo-plethysmography-sensor and machine learning, a multi-level mental workload classifier was built. It achieved a group generalized classification score of 46% correct if miss-classification-by-one-level was allowed.

These studies show the potential of automated and timely fine granular mental workload classification models using sensors that should be physically worn and could be perceived as obtrusive. It is currently unknown if non-invasive measures, complemented by other machine learning models can improve classification and practicality in daily use. The current study builds further upon previous mental workload classification studies, and contributes by exploring the use of cameras as an unobtrusive measure to develop a mental workload prediction model in a railway traffic control setting.

2   Methods

2.1   Experiment Setup

We used a human-in-the-loop simulator to collect a dataset of psychophysiological responses by expert train operators that worked on a scenario with varying levels of mental workload. The study was conducted in a Dutch regional railway traffic control center in Amsterdam. This data was collected to train and test three machine learning algorithms to classify mental workload levels.

2.2   Participants

Sixteen ProRail train traffic controller operators (four female, $M = 13.44$, $SD = 10.00$ years of working experience) were recruited to voluntarily participate in the study. The setup of the study followed the guidelines set out in the Declaration of Helsinki. All participants were informed about the goal of the study beforehand and provided written informed consent.

2.3   Experimental Design

A within-subjects design that manipulated workload as being low, medium, or high was used. The workload scenarios were part of one larger scenario developed by five subject matter experts (see Fig. 1 for a schematic overview). The task of the operator was to execute their regular job: manage the train traffic while adhering to the correct safety protocols. The events in the scenario started at set times; however, the duration of each scenario varied depending on the chosen strategy and efficiency applied by the operator. Overlap of tasks from one scenario to the next was minimized due to the largely serial nature of the workflow (e.g., the fire department is not involved until they are called by the operator, in which case the operator needs to wait for clearance from the fire department before continuing their work).

Mental workload was manipulated through the complexity and number of activities the operator had to act on. In the lowest workload condition, train traffic operated according to plan and only passive monitoring was required from the operator. In the medium workload condition, monitoring and occasional input were required (e.g., removing obstructions, setting permissions for trains to move – but no bi-directional communication with other parties). In the high workload condition, an emergency call was received requiring direct input-, communication-, and decision-making from the operator (e.g., gather information regarding the event, make a decision on what protocol is applicable, and execute the actions associated with the applicable protocol).

Four possible scenarios were drafted in which each scenario consisted of a slight variation in the emergency event that occurred. Due to time constraints, each operator conducted two scenarios, pseudo-randomly chosen. The scenarios were validated by five subject matter experts to be comparable in expected mental workload. The duration of a session varied between 15 and 35 min, dependent on the execution and efficiency of the plan deployed by the operator.

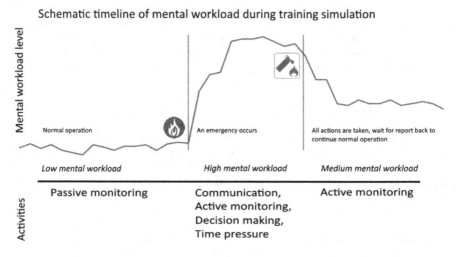

Fig. 1. A schematic timeline of the mental workload scenarios. The first third of the scenario starts with all traffic according to plan. The second third a fire alarm is given: communication and actions are required. The last third, all necessary input from the operator is done and active monitoring for updates is required.

2.4   Aparatus

Heart rate features were recorded from the color- and infrared spectrum using remote camera-based photoplethysmography.

The participants were recorded in the color spectrum with a GoPro Hero Black 7 (GoPro Inc., San Mateo, CA, USA; see Fig. 2B) with a resolution of 1280×720 at 59.94 frames per second, and in the infrared spectrum with a Basler acA640-120gm (Basler AG, An der Strusbek, Ahrensburg, Germany) with a 8 mm $f/1.4$ varifocal lens with a resolution of 659×494 at 24 frames per second (see Fig. 2C). Many factors influence the quality of rPPG [33,34]. In the next section, measures related to the quality of the frame recording taken to this end are discussed. Prior to data storage, the image streams were compressed.

Fig. 2. The following components were used: (A.) The LED light with a CRI rating of 95+ (B.) GoPro Hero 7 Black mounted on a tripod. (C.) Basler acA640-120gm Infrared camera and (D) four 24 in. HP monitors with a resolution of 1920× 1080 at 60 Hz, displaying the railway simulator.

Image stream compression reduces the amount of data per time unit, which is favorable for the storage and throughput of an image stream. However, this negatively affects rPPG quality, which relies on color fluctuation between frames. With heavy compression, these fluctuations are lost. For an optimal result, raw or very lightly-compressed image streams (at least $4.3*10^4$ kb/s for random motion) are needed [34]. The GoPro supported a maximum image stream compression of $4 * 10^4$. The proprietary Basler "Pylon Viewer 5.2.0" package supports either raw $200 * 10^5$ kb/s, or compressed MPEG-4 image streams at $1.9 * 10^3$ kb/s. Due to storage-, and video container-limitations handling the uncompressed frame stream, the compressed stream was used.

Since the GoPro image sensor can only capture light that is reflected from a surface, a LED lamp with a color temperature of 3000 K and a Color Rating Index (CRI) of 95% was used to illuminate the left front of the operator (see Fig. 2A). The infrared spectrum was lighted with an integrated two watt infrared flasher from Smart-Eye, which was synchronized with the shutter speed of the sensor to provide optimal lighting.

After the completion of simulation sessions, an informal survey was recorded. The expert operators were asked to rate their subjective experienced mental workload during the simulation. "On a scale from 1 to 7, with 7 being the highest possible score, what grade would you give the workload you experienced during the experiment?"

3   Data Analysis and Model Construction

All data processing was done using Python 3.7 [35] and the Scikit-learn package [36]. Figure 3 summarizes the data processing steps. There were three main steps that are described next: (1) pre-processing, (2) feature extraction, and (3) model construction.

Pre-processing. The first step was to detect the face on each frame. To this end, on each frame from the color- and infrared-spectrum recordings of the operator, a deep neural net face detector was applied to extract 68 facial landmarks, see the red dots in Fig. 4A for an example [37,38].

We then identified a patch of skin on the forehead, and extracted the mean color intensity from it as input for the rPPG algorithm [39]. This forehead region of interest spanned the space between the facial landmarks 20, 21, 24, and 25. The horizontal distance between 21 and 24 was used to vertically shift 21 and 24 upwards, creating a patch on the forehead between those points (see the black patch in Fig. 4A). The forehead was chosen as region of interest because, compared to the cheeks, the lighting was more evenly distributed and under vertical head movements, it remained in-frame for a larger proportion of the time [40].

For each frame where facial landmarks could be detected, the averaged pixel values from the region of interest of the three color channels (red-, green-, blue) and the one infrared channel were calculated. The results from a sequence of frames formed a time series.

To filter noise sources from the color time series the amplitude selective filtering algorithm developed by Wang et al. [41] was used and rewritten for python implementation. The amplitude selective filtering algorithm uses the known reflective properties of the skin to assess signal change frequency, and to remove frequencies that are outside the expected heart rate frequency band (e.g., head movement, reflections of light) from the color channels. These filtered color channels were then used as input for the rPPG plane orthogonal skin response algorithm, developed by Wang et al. [42]. This resulted in a one dimensional PPG signal which was then band-pass filtered between 0.9 Hz and 2.5 Hz, corresponding to a minimum and maximum heart rate of 54 and 150 beats per minute.

To remove noise from the infrared signal, visual inspection was used. This was done due to the one-dimensional nature of the infrared signal which the amplitude selective filtering algorithm can not process. The amplitude selective filtering requires three color channels to remove noise. The obtained filter after visual inspection was a high-pass filter at 0.9 Hz and low-pass filter at 2.5 Hz. Visually, this resulted in a PPG-like signal, however containing more amplitude variations than the amplitude selective filtered color signal.

The preprocessed rPPG data was split into temporal windows (see Fig. 4B). Each window overlaps with the previous one with a specific overlap factor, where the size of the overlap was equal between the rPPG measures (color-

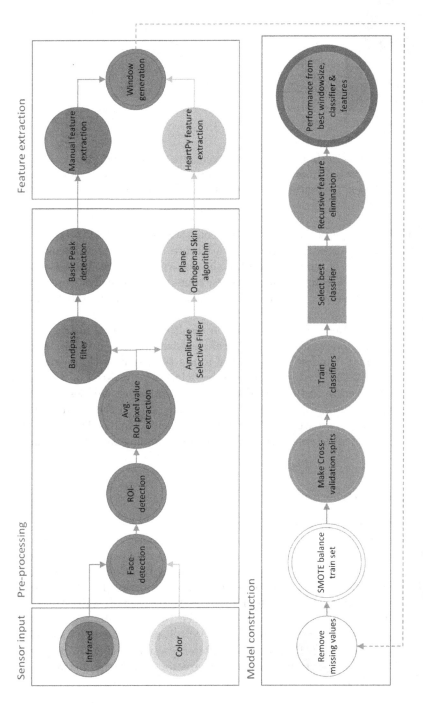

Fig. 3. An overview of the data pre-processing, feature extraction, and model construction.

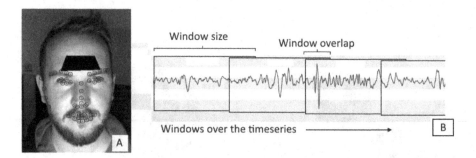

Fig. 4. A) An example of the facial landmark points (red dots) and the region of interest (black square) extracted from it. (B) A schematic overview of the sliding window approach for rPPG-derived heart rate calculation. (Color figure online)

and infrared). The temporal-step size between a window and its succeeding window was equal for all sensors. Heart rate feature calculations are sensitive to the temporal length of windows and the shared overlap between windows they are calculated over. For heart rate features, time-domain features were reliably found from 20-s windows, and frequency domain features from 120-s windows [43, 44].

To explore the effect of window sizes on resulting calculated heart rate, two sets with varying window-sizes but identical step sizes were created for the rPPG sources. The "small window" consisted of a 45 s time span with an overlap of 95% resulting in 2.25 s step sizes. The "large window" consisted of a 60 s time span with 95% overlap, resulting in 3 s step sizes. Missing samples in a heart rate window that did not exceed two seconds were, due to the gradual change over time of heart rate features [45], interpolated using Pandas 24.0 interpolate function [46]. In all other cases, windows containing missing values were removed from the dataset.

3.1   Feature Extraction

Heart rate features were calculated over each window. The filtered infrared signal was analyzed for heart rate features, using the basic 'find peaks'-function from the scipy signal package [47]. The filtered color signal was analyzed for heart rate features using the 'find peaks'-scipy signal function (marked in Fig. 5 and Table 2 as "basic"') in addition to the HeartPy toolbox [15]. The following features were extracted from both signals: Beats per minute (BPM)[1,2], Inter beat interval (IBI)[1,2], Mean absolute difference (MAD)[1], Standard deviation of intervals between adjacent beats (SDNN)[1,2], Standard deviation of successive differences (SDSD)[1,2], Proportion of differences greater than 20 ms between beats (pNN20)[1,2], Proportion of differences greater than 50 ms between beats (pNN50)[1,2] ([15][1], [48][2]).

3.2   Machine Learning Datasets

Based on the part of the scenario that participants were performing, mental workload levels could be assigned to each time frame and its associated features. This labelled data set could then be used for a supervised machine learning model that aims to classify workload level based on feature observations.

Data Bias. Absolute heart rate characteristics can identify individuals, especially given the small sample size in our dataset. To avoid model overfitting on absolute heart rate values, and since the heart rate features rely on relative changes over time, the heart rate values were normalized within participant [62]. Overfitting on the training-data caused by unbalanced within-participant proportions of the workload levels was reduced by applying the synthetic minority over-sampling technique (SMOTE) on the training set [49,50]. SMOTE was used because, compared to random oversampling, it preserves some of the variances in the oversampled instances. Auto-correlation is an inherent risk in human physiological data [15]. To avoid such leaking of information, leave one out cross-validation was used. The data of two participants was withheld from the training set and used as the test set. The test- (and resulting training-) set composition were used as input for the model to iteratively run over all possible unique combinations (k) of one and two, from the total number (n) of nine participants $\frac{n!}{(k!(n-k)!)}$ for a total of 28 cross-validation train-test sets.

To create a performance baseline, and test for data bias, the classifiers were run with randomly shuffled train-set labels.

3.3   Models and Classifiers

Out of all the options for machine learning models we used two types of classifiers, random forest (100 trees) and AdaBoost- (60 estimators). Random Forest was chosen as it is frequently used in similar mental workload classification studies [14–17]. AdaBoost falls under the same ensemble learner family as Random Forest, and shares a lot of similarities - however, depending on the data it performs better in some cases [51–55]. The feature importance was determined using Scikit-learn's cross-validated recursive feature elimination ranking [56]. Using the identified best features, a new model was built with only these features. Scikit-learn's "ROC-AUC-CURVE" performance evaluation [36], for the average area under the receiver-operator-characteristic curve of all cross-validated models was used to evaluate the performance [57]. Each workload condition was evaluated in a one- vs. other-mental workload classification manner, resulting in three mean cross-validated AUC-ROC curves.

4   Results

In this results section, a brief description of the empirical data is given first. This is followed by the perceived mental workload, performance of the classifiers and the feature importances. Finally the AUC-ROCs results obtained from using the best performing classifier, window size and features are given.

Sample Selection. From the sixteen participants, data of only nine participants could be used for analysis purposes. Six participants were excluded due to data logging problems, another participant was excluded as the data preprocessing left less than 40 usable samples in both the low- and medium mental workload condition, which is too few to train a classifier on.

For an overview of the samples per workload condition after removing missing values, see Table 1.

Table 1. Number of samples per sensor, before-, and after-SMOTE oversampling.

	Workload level	Color		Infrared		Color and infrared	
Small window:							
Raw	Low		3300		3169		3064
	Medium		2946		2896		2740
	High		2205		2111		1971
SMOTE	Low	+26%	4153	+30%	4106	+27%	3890
	Medium	+41%	4153	+42%	4106	+42%	3890
	High	+88%	4153	+95%	4106	+97%	3890
Large window:							
Raw	Low		2450		2327		2231
	Medium		2191		2126		2012
	High		1630		1513		1413
SMOTE	Low	+26%	3090	+29%	3012	+28%	2861
	Medium	+41%	3090	+42%	3012	+42%	2861
	High	+90%	3090	+99%	3012	+102%	2861

Perceived Mental Workload. The perceived difficulty score recorded from the survey was $M = 3.75$, $SD = 1.13$ for the first-, and $M = 4.00$, $SD = 1.67$ for the second-scenario. The ROC-AUC curves from a model trained on randomly shuffled labels returned chance level performance for all mental workload levels (low $M = .50$, $SD = 0.07$, medium $M = .50$, $SD = 0.05$ and high $M = .51$, $SD = 0.04$). Confirming that there is no data bias that the model could exploit in its classification process and a baseline performance at chance level.

Performance. Considering both window sizes, per-mental workload level AdaBoost outperformed Random Forest for low- ($M = .64$, $SD = 0.09$) and medium- ($M = .54$, $SD = 0.05$) mental workload (see Table 2, bold scores). Random forest scored best for high mental workload ($M = .61$, $SD = 0.09$). See Table 2 for an overview.

Table 2. Model performance for AdaBoost & RandomForest classifier, small & large windows, color-, infrared- and color & infrared data. Italic marking the best scores per classifier & window combination. Bold scores marking the overall best score per workload level.

Workload level	Sensor	Small window		Large window	
		AdaBoost	Random forest	AdaBoost	Random forest
		AUC-ROC (*SD*)	AUC-ROC (*SD*)	AUC-ROC (*SD*)	AUC-ROC (*SD*)
Low	Color	0.54 (0.06)	0.54 (0.05)	0.54 (0.05)	0.54 (0.04)
	Infrared	0.62 (0.09)	*0.61 (0.08)*	**0.64 (0.09)**	*0.62 (0.08)*
	Color and infrared	*0.63 (0.08)*	0.61 (0.08)	0.63 (0.09)	0.62 (0.09)
Medium	Color	0.52 (0.01)	0.52 (0.03)	0.51 (0.03)	0.52 (0.03)
	Infrared	**0.54 (0.05)**	*0.54 (0.06)*	0.52 (0.07)	*0.54 (0.07)*
	Color and Infrared	0.52 (0.03)	*0.54 (0.06)*	*0.52 (0.06)*	0.53 (0.06)
High	Color	0.54 (0.04)	0.54 (0.03)	0.53 (0.04)	0.53 (0.03)
	Infrared	*0.57 (0.06)*	*0.56 (0.06)*	*0.58 (0.08)*	**0.61 (0.10)**
	Color and infrared	*0.57 (0.06)*	*0.56 (0.06)*	0.58 (0.08)	0.61 (0.08)
Average best sensor per classifier		0.58 (0.06)	0.57 (0.07)	0.58 (0.08)	0.59 (0.08)

The recursive-cross-validated feature elimination of one vs. other mental workload states using the AdaBoost classifier and AUC-ROC performance scoring, found that: (1) the best performing low-mental workload window size is large, (2) the best performing medium-mental workload window is small, and (3) the best performing high-mental workload window size is large (see Table 2, values in bold).

Feature Elimination. Recursive feature elimination was used to inspect the relative feature-performance contribution. The used window sizes were large, small, large for respectively low-, medium- and high-mental workload. For an overview of the best features after recursive feature elimination, see Table 3. For an overview of the cumulative contribution of the best features to the AUC-ROC score for respective best workload level-window size combination, see Fig. 5.

Using the AdaBoost classifier three models were created, one for each mental workload condition containing the best performing features (Table 3) and window size (Table 2). AUC-ROC scores of low- ($M = .67$, $SD = 0.07$ AUC-ROC), medium- ($M = .55$, $SD = 0.05$ AUC-ROC) and high- ($M = .57$, $SD = 0.08$ AUC-ROC) were found. See Fig. 6 for the resulting AUC-ROC plots. As the AUC-ROC score is a continuum of the true-positive (y-axis) vs. false-positive (x-axis) rate, the standard deviation (grey are) represents the variation in classification performance given different train- and test sets. Since the test sets are comprised of two individuals, the mean variation should be taken as an indicator for model performance, where standard deviation crossing chance does not invalidate the results as is the case in statistical modelling.

Table 3. Feature importance obtained from Scikit learn's cross-validated recursive feature elimination, given the best window size per mental workload level & using the AdaBoost classifier.

Infrared features:	Mental workload levels		
	Low	Medium	High
Inter beat interval (IBI)	0.58	0.33	0.20
Std. dev. of intervals between adjacent beats (SDNN)	0.42	0.27	0.13
Proportion of diff. greater than 20 ms between beats (pNN20)		0.40	0.10
Std. dev. of successive differences (SDSD)			0.20
Beats per minute (BPM)			0.10
Color features:			
Mean Abs. difference (MAD)			0.08
Std. dev. of intervals between adjacent beats (SDNN)			0.05
Inter beat interval (IBI)			0.05
Beats per minute (BPM)			0.03
Proportion of diff. greater than 50 ms between beats (pNN50)			0.03
Std. dev. of intervals between adjacent beats (SDNN)			0.02

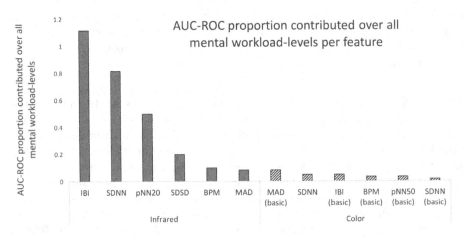

Fig. 5. The cumulative contribution of each feature towards classification performance for all mental workload levels, using the best window size per workload level. The "basic" label indicates use of basic scipy signal peak detection & filtering during (pre-) processing. The features are: Inter beat interval (IBI), Standard deviation of intervals between adjacent beats (SDNN), Proportion of differences greater than 20 ms between beats (pNN20), Standard deviation of successive differences (SDSD), Mean absolute difference (MAD), Proportion of differences greater than 50 ms between beats (pNN50). (basic) denotes basic Scipy 'find peak' filtering

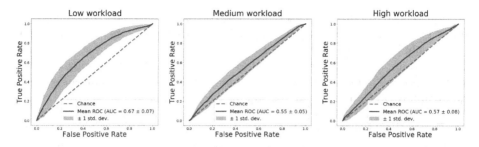

Fig. 6. The AdaBoost cross-validated AUC-ROC curves of the best features and best window size per workload vs. others classification. The red line indicates chance performance, the blue line the mean and the grey the standard deviation received from the cross validations. A large standard deviation indicates large classification variance between different train- and test-sets. The standard deviation is an indicator of the generalizability of the classification. (Color figure online)

5 Discussion

The main objective of this research was to determine to what extent cameras, based on data from the color-, and infrared-spectrum, can differentiate mental workload levels in a human-in-the-loop simulator setting. The measures were taken using remote photoplethysmography, which can be used to detect heart rate. We used an AdaBoost and a Random Forest machine learning model to train a mental workload classifier. We found that low- and high mental workload could be classified above chance. For both low- and high mental workload, classification was best using a large window (i.e., 60 s timespan), regardless of classifier and (combination of) color spectrum (see Table 2). We found the performance of AdaBoost to be on par with RandomForest. Where AdaBoost achieved the best classification score for the low- and medium mental workload levels, Random Forest achieved the best classification score for the high mental workload level.

Looking at the color and infrared spectra and the combination of both, infrared was found to achieve the best classification performance. When decomposing what features the model uses to achieve its performance, the inter beat interval (IBI), standard deviation of intervals between adjacent beats (SDNN) and the proportion of differences greater than 20 ms between beats (pNN20) contribute significantly across classification of the three mental workload levels (cf. [15,48]).

6 Limitations and Future Work

Our scenarios were developed by subject matters experts, with the goal to reflect low, medium and high workload in the expert operators. However, perceived mental workload survey outcomes and debriefing indicated that participants experienced at most moderate workload. Therefore, subjective experience might not have aligned with intended workload. A major factor of this subjective overall low experienced workload was ascribed by participants to the lack of communication (e.g. with train operators, fire departments) that they otherwise encounter in their job. The communication in this experiment was fewer-, less varied- and serial in nature because the experiment leader was limited in simulating communication from all different stakeholders by him/herself. These limitations suggest workload levels found in the field might be even more pronounced.

Furthermore, the transition between levels of mental workload was modeled as instantaneous. During the labeling of the data, the trigger of an event resulted in an immediate mental workload change (e.g., from low to high). However, the psychophysical mental workload change is typically more gradual [58]. Because of this more gradual psychophysiological change, data sections spanning these transitions are of ambiguous mental workload state. To combat this mixing of states, a solution could be finer grained levels of mental workload to capture the mental workload transition states as was done by Van Gent et al. [15]. Furthermore, it would be interesting to see informed data selection around an event, as is typical for EEG event-related research [59].

Further improvements can be made during the processing and classification of the data. The preprocessing, feature extraction, and workload state labeling can contribute to a better model. Better performance of the 60 s window size compared to the 45 s window size was observed in this study. Heart rate features have been reliably extracted from segments spanning this temporal size in earlier studies [43,44], thus perhaps the quality of the rPPG required longer spanning windows to pick up on a pattern - or find a reliable pattern. Other research that uses heart rate features for mental workload detection has even used windows of up to five minutes [26]. Thus it is interesting to explore the use of larger window sizes and its effect on classification.

Combining the infrared and color channel, and using this merged signal as input for the amplitude selective filter algorithm, could be another improvement. This would effectively allow one to make use of both the infrared- and color channels, similar to what Trumpp et al. [39] have done. The color channels can be used to remove non-heart rate related frequencies, and the infrared for the heart rate related frequency. To sustain temporal synchronization one would need to control for the facial landmark tracking, time synchronization, and the horizontal camera vantage point between the infrared- and color-spectrum recording.

As the rPPG algorithm relies on color changes from artery reflections, improving the frame capture is expected to yield a stronger rPPG signal. The quality of the rPPG signal can be improved on three fronts; (1) by the used hardware, (2) the used lighting, and (3) recording compression-settings.

From the literature the low performance of the color spectrum was not expected, as green light (around 550 nm wavelength) reflects on the arteries [42,60]. When looking at the setup used, some pointers for the observed performance difference between color and infrared can be theorized. The infrared camera came with a dedicated light-source, where for the color spectrum, a CRI95+ rated LED light was used. Furthermore, whilst head-on lighting was possible for the infrared camera, head-on lighting for color camera was not possible without obtrusively blinding the participants due to the intensity of the LED lamp. The direct versus orthogonal lighting resulted in a better illuminated infrared image stream compared to the color image stream. Furthermore, the default wide-angle lense on the color camera is suboptimal for focusing the light reflected from the expert operator. The 8 mm f/1.4 lense of the infrared camera was much better equipped for this purpose of focusing the light reflecting from the expert operator on the image sensor. Given the comparatively lower performance of the color spectrum, these differences in illumination (head-on dedicated vs from the side) and camera setup warrant further research. We suggest recording the color spectrum using a camera with a dedicated lens for indoor use, to produce more detailed frames.

The compression of the image stream can also be improved. Due to the restraints of the proprietary Basler software, the recordings we used were moderate- to strongly compressed. McDuff et al. [34] show that using raw, uncompressed recordings yields a much cleaner PPG signal with a significantly higher signal-to-noise ratio. Preliminary testing on sub-two minute recordings using the same infrared Basler camera, confirmed this finding of very clean rPPG signal.

For practical and technical reasons, the images in this study were recorded and analyzed for features post-hoc. However, should future studies incorporate (industrial) cameras that allow direct access to their raw image stream, preprocessing could be done on-line, which removes the need to encode, store, decode, and then separately process the images. Given powerful enough hardware, processing and classification of mental workload state could possibly be done on-line, thereby enabling real time access to the mental workload state.

7 Conclusion

Ideally this mental workload model can be used as a tool for real-time mental workload feedback of novice operators during their education program. This insight can be used to provide novice operators and/or instructors feedback in terms of their mental workload development in relation to conducted tasks. Many other domains have the potential to use such knowledge as well. In particular, over the last decades there has been a rise of settings and domains in which humans interact with automation, including use by non-professional users [61]. This includes for example monitoring semi-automated vehicles, drones, and health applications. These domains require novel models of attention management [61]. Our work can contribute to this, by providing methods to automatically detect human workload (and potentially underload and overload).

Acknowledgments. We would like to thank J. Mug & E. Sehic, for their feedback on the experimental design, W. L. Tielman & T. Kootstra for their contribution to the data analysis and from the ProRail Amsterdam train traffic control center the train traffic controllers that participated in this study. This work was supported by ProRail.

References

1. Parasuraman, R., Sheridan, T.B., Wickens, C.D.: Situation awareness, mental workload, and trust in automation: viable, empirically supported cognitive engineering constructs. J. Cogn. Eng. Decis. Making **2**(2), 140–160 (2008)
2. Young, M.S., Brookhuis, K.A., Wickens, C.D., Hancock, P.A.: State of science: mental workload in ergonomics. Ergonomics **58**(1), 1–17 (2015)
3. Brookhuis, K.A., Waard, D.D.: On the assessment of (mental) workload and other subjective qualifications. Ergonomics **45**(14), 1026–1030 (2002)
4. Kaber, D.B., Endsley, M.R.: The effects of level of automation and adaptive automation on human performance, situation awareness and workload in a dynamic control task. Theor. Issues Ergon. Sci. **5**(2), 113–153 (2004)
5. Parasuraman, R.: Adaptive automation for human-robot teaming in future command and control systems. Int. C2 J. **1**(2), 43–68 (2007)
6. Park, O., Lee, J.: Adaptive instructional systems. In: Jonassen, D.H. (ed.) Handbook of Research on Educational Communications and Technology. Simon & Schuster, New York (1996)
7. Bruder, A., Schwarz, J.: Evaluation of diagnostic rules for real-time assessment of mental workload within a dynamic adaptation framework. In: Sottilare, R.A., Schwarz, J. (eds.) HCII 2019. LNCS, vol. 11597, pp. 391–404. Springer, Cham (2019). https://doi.org/10.1007/978-3-030-22341-0_31
8. Lane, H.C., D'Mello, S.K.: Uses of physiological monitoring in intelligent learning environments: a review of research, evidence, and technologies. In: Parsons, T.D., Lin, L., Cockerham, D. (eds.) Mind, Brain and Technology. ECTII, pp. 67–86. Springer, Cham (2019). https://doi.org/10.1007/978-3-030-02631-8_5
9. Byrne, E.A., Parasuraman, R.: Psychophysiology and adaptive automation. Biol. Psychol. **42**(3), 249–268 (1996)
10. Ayaz, H., Shewokis, P.A., Bunce, S., Izzetoglu, K., Willems, B., Onaral, B.: Optical brain monitoring for operator training and mental workload assessment. Neuroimage **59**(1), 36–47 (2012)
11. Prinzel III, L.J., Freeman, F.G., Scerbo, M.W., Mikulka, P.J., Pope, A.T.: Effects of a psychophysiological system for adaptive automation on performance, workload, and the event-related potential P300 component. Hum. Fact. **45**(4), 601–614 (2003)
12. Taylor, G., Reinerman-Jones, L., Cosenzo, K., Nicholson, D.: Comparison of multiple physiological sensors to classify operator state in adaptive automation systems. In: Proceedings of the Human Factors and Ergonomics Society Annual Meeting, vol. 54, no. 3, pp. 195–199 (2010)
13. Goebel, R., et al.: Explainable AI: the new 42? In: Holzinger, A., Kieseberg, P., Tjoa, A.M., Weippl, E. (eds.) CD-MAKE 2018. LNCS, vol. 11015, pp. 295–303. Springer, Cham (2018). https://doi.org/10.1007/978-3-319-99740-7_21
14. Suni Lopez, F., Condori-Fernandez, N., Catala, A.: Towards real-time automatic stress detection for office workplaces. In: Lossio-Ventura, J.A., Muñante, D., Alatrista-Salas, H. (eds.) SIMBig 2018. CCIS, vol. 898, pp. 273–288. Springer, Cham (2019). https://doi.org/10.1007/978-3-030-11680-4_27
15. Van Gent, P., Melman, T., Farah, H., van Nes, N., van Arem, B.: Multi-level driver workload prediction using machine learning and off-the-shelf sensors. Transp. Res. Rec. **2672**(37), 141–152 (2018)
16. Martinez, R., Irigoyen, E., Arruti, A., Martín, J.I., Muguerza, J.: A real-time stress classification system based on arousal analysis of the nervous system by an F-state machine. Comput. Methods Programs Biomed. **148**, 81–90 (2017)

17. Ghosh, A., Danieli, M., Riccardi, G.: Annotation and prediction of stress and workload from physiological and inertial signals. In: 2015 37th Annual International Conference of the IEEE Engineering in Medicine and Biology Society (EMBC), pp. 1621–1624. IEEE, August 2015
18. Gaillard, A.W.K.: Comparing the concepts of mental load and stress. Ergonomics **36**(9), 991–1005 (1993)
19. Welford, A.T.: Mental work-load as a function of demand, capacity, strategy and skill. Ergonomics **21**(3), 151–167 (1978)
20. Staal, M.A.: Stress, cognition, and human performance: a literature review and conceptual framework (2004)
21. Hart, S.G., Staveland, L.E.: Development of NASA-TLX (Task Load Index): results of empirical and theoretical research. In: Advances in Psychology, vol. 52, pp. 139–183, North-Holland (1988)
22. Alberdi, A., Aztiria, A., Basarab, A.: Towards an automatic early stress recognition system for office environments based on multimodal measurements: a review. J. Biomed. Inform. **59**, 49–75 (2016)
23. Mitchell, J.P., Macrae, C.N., Gilchrist, I.D.: Working memory and the suppression of reflexive saccades. J. Cogn. Neurosci. **14**(1), 95–103 (2002)
24. Hogervorst, M.A., Brouwer, A.M., Van Erp, J.B.: Combining and comparing EEG, peripheral physiology and eye-related measures for the assessment of mental workload. Front. Neurosci. **8**, 322 (2014)
25. Yu, H., Cang, S., Wang, Y.: A review of sensor selection, sensor devices and sensor deployment for wearable sensor-based human activity recognition systems. In: 2016 10th International Conference on Software, Knowledge, Information Management & Applications (SKIMA), pp. 250–257. IEEE, December 2016
26. Lo, J.C., Sehic, E., Meijer, S.A.: Measuring mental workload with low-cost and wearable sensors: insights into the accuracy, obtrusiveness, and research usability of three instruments. J. Cogn. Eng. Decis. Making **11**(4), 323–336 (2017)
27. Lux, E., Adam, M.T., Dorner, V., Helming, S., Knierim, M.T., Weinhardt, C.: Live biofeedback as a user interface design element: a review of the literature. Commun. Assoc. Inf. Syst. **43**(1), 257–296 (2018)
28. Swan, M.: Sensor mania! the Internet of Things, wearable computing, objective metrics, and the quantified self 2.0. J. Sens. Actuator Netw. **1**(3), 217–253 (2012)
29. Verkruysse, W., Svaasand, L.O., Nelson, J.S.: Remote plethysmographic imaging using ambient light. Opt. Express **16**(26), 21434–21445 (2008)
30. Takano, C., Ohta, Y.: Heart rate measurement based on a time-lapse image. Med. Eng. Phys. **29**(8), 853–857 (2007)
31. Huelsbusch, M., Blazek, V.: Contactless mapping of rhythmical phenomena in tissue perfusion using PPGI. In: Medical Imaging 2002: Physiology and Function from Multidimensional Images, vol. 4683, pp. 110–117. International Society for Optics and Photonics, April 2002
32. Charles, R.L., Nixon, J.: Measuring mental workload using physiological measures: a systematic review. Appl. Ergon. **74**, 221–232 (2019)
33. Zaunseder, S., Trumpp, A., Wedekind, D., Malberg, H.: Cardiovascular assessment by imaging photoplethysmography - a review. Biomedical Engineering/Biomedizinische Technik **63**(5), 617–634 (2018)
34. McDuff, D.J., Blackford, E.B., Estepp, J.R.: The impact of video compression on remote cardiac pulse measurement using imaging photoplethysmography. In: 2017 12th IEEE International Conference on Automatic Face & Gesture Recognition (FG 2017), pp. 63–70. IEEE, May 2017

35. Van Rossum, G.: Python tutorial, Technical Report CS-R9526, Centrum voor Wiskunde en Informatica (CWI), Amsterdam (1995)
36. Pedregosa, F., et al.: Scikit-learn: machine learning in Python. J. Mach. Learn. Res. **12**(Oct), 2825–2830 (2011)
37. Bulat, A., Tzimiropoulos, G.: How far are we from solving the 2D & 3D face alignment problem? (and a dataset of 230,000 3D facial landmarks). In: Proceedings of the IEEE International Conference on Computer Vision, pp. 1021–1030 (2017)
38. King, D.E.: Dlib-ml: a machine learning toolkit. J. Mach. Learn. Res. **10**(Jul), 1755–1758 (2009)
39. Trumpp, A., et al.: Camera-based photoplethysmography in an intraoperative setting. Biomed. Eng. Online **17**(1), 33 (2018)
40. Lempe, G., Zaunseder, S., Wirthgen, T., Zipser, S., Malberg, H.: ROI selection for remote photoplethysmography. In: Meinzer, H.P., Deserno, T., Handels, H., Tolxdorff, T. (eds.) Bildverarbeitung für die Medizin, pp. 99–103. Springer, Heidelberg (2013). https://doi.org/10.1007/978-3-642-36480-8_19
41. Wang, W., den Brinker, A.C., Stuijk, S., de Haan, G.: Amplitude-selective filtering for remote-PPG. Biomed. Opt. Express **8**(3), 1965–1980 (2017)
42. Wang, W., den Brinker, A.C., Stuijk, S., de Haan, G.: Algorithmic principles of remote PPG. IEEE Trans. Biomed. Eng. **64**(7), 1479–1491 (2016)
43. Salahuddin, L., Cho, J., Jeong, M.G., Kim, D.: Ultra short term analysis of heart rate variability for monitoring mental stress in mobile settings. In: 2007 29th Annual International Conference of the IEEE Engineering in Medicine and Biology Society, pp. 4656–4659. IEEE (2007)
44. McNames, J., Aboy, M.: Reliability and accuracy of heart rate variability metrics versus ECG segment duration. Med. Biol. Eng. Compuy. **44**(9), 747–756 (2006)
45. Borst, C., Wieling, W., Van Brederode, J.F., Hond, A., De Rijk, L.G., Dunning, A.J.: Mechanisms of initial heart rate response to postural change. Am. J. Physiol.-Heart Circulatory Physiol. **243**(5), H676–H681 (1982)
46. McKinney, W.: Data structures for statistical computing in python. In: Proceedings of the 9th Python in Science Conference, vol. 445, pp. 51–56, June 2010
47. Jones, E., Oliphant, T., Peterson, P.: SciPy: Open source scientific tools for Python, 2001 (2016)
48. Heart rate variability: standards of measurement, physiological interpretation, and clinical use. In: Task Force of the European Society of Cardiology and the North American Society of Pacing and Electrophysiology. Circulation, vol. 93, pp. 1043–1065 (1996)
49. Cawley, G.C., Talbot, N.L.: On over-fitting in model selection and subsequent selection bias in performance evaluation. J. Mach. Learn. Res. **11**(Jul), 2079–2107 (2010)
50. Chawla, N.V., Bowyer, K.W., Hall, L.O., Kegelmeyer, W.P.: SMOTE: synthetic minority over-sampling technique. J. Artif. Intell. Res. **16**, 321–357 (2002)
51. Wyner, A.J., Olson, M., Bleich, J., Mease, D.: Explaining the success of adaboost and random forests as interpolating classifiers. J. Mach. Learn. Res. **18**(1), 1558–1590 (2017)
52. Scikit-learn: scikit-learn.org. Choosing the right estimator. https://scikit-learn.org/stable/tutorial/machine_learning_map/index.html. Accessed 2 Oct 2019
53. Head, T., et al.: scikit-optimize/scikit-optimize: v0.5.2 (Version v0.5.2). Zenodo. https://doi.org/10.5281/zenodo.1207017
54. Breiman, L.: Random forests. Mach. Learn. **45**(1), 5–32 (2001)
55. Freund, Y., Schapire, R., Abe, N.: A short introduction to boosting. J.-Jpn. Soc. Artif. Intell. **14**(771–780), 1612 (1999)

56. Guyon, I., Weston, J., Barnhill, S., Vapnik, V.: Gene selection for cancer classification using support vector machines. Mach. Learn. **46**(1–3), 389–422 (2002)

57. Huang, J., Ling, C.X.: Using AUC and accuracy in evaluating learning algorithms. IEEE Trans. Knowl. Data Eng. **17**(3), 299–310 (2005)

58. Kim, H.G., Cheon, E.J., Bai, D.S., Lee, Y.H., Koo, B.H.: Stress and heart rate variability: a meta-analysis and review of the literature. Psychiatry Invest. **15**(3), 235 (2018)

59. Luck, S.J.: An Introduction to the Event-related Potential Technique. MIT Press (2014)

60. van Gastel, M., Stuijk, S., de Haan, G.: Motion robust remote-PPG in infrared. IEEE Trans. Biomed. Eng. **62**(5), 1425–1433 (2015)

61. Janssen, C.P., Donker, S.F., Brumby, D.P., Kun, A.L.: History and future of human-automation interaction. Int. J. Hum Comput Stud. **131**, 99–107 (2019)

62. Dietterich, T.G., Kong, E.B.: Machine learning bias, statistical bias, and statistical variance of decision tree algorithms. Technical report, Department of Computer Science, Oregon State University (1995)

Production Implementation of Recurrent Neural Networks in Adaptive Instructional Systems

David R. King[✉]

ACT Inc., Iowa City, IA 52243, USA
david.king@act.org

Abstract. This paper reviews current research on deep knowledge tracing (DKT) and discusses the benefits of using DKT in adaptive instructional systems (AIS). Namely, DKT allows for accurate measurement of ability levels across a set of attributes in a content domain and this information can be leveraged to deliver personalized content to the learner. DKT uses a recurrent neural network with long short-term memory units (RNN-LSTM), which is difficult to interpret, although provides higher prediction accuracy than Bayesian knowledge tracing (BKT) or item response theory (IRT) measurement approaches. This makes DKT ideal for learner-focused or formative assessment systems, in which the measurement of attribute proficiencies and the delivery of relevant content to promote learning is valued above the understanding of the measurement process itself. The paper focuses on practical considerations for preparing and deploying an RNN-LSTM in a production system. Namely, data demands for training the network are explored through an analysis on real data from an adaptive tutoring program, and novel methods for training the network when no data are available and for measuring learning trajectories are proposed. Finally, strategies around monitoring production prediction services are discussed, as well as tips for approaching latency, stability, and security issues in production environments. These discussions are meant to provide a researcher or data scientist with enough information to effectively collaborate with technical teams on the production implementation of RNNs, with the goal of making cutting-edge advances in DKT available to real learners.

Keywords: AIS · RNN · LSTM · Applied research · Production

1 Introduction

This paper discusses the advantages of employing recurrent neural networks (RNN) for predicting learner outcomes in adaptive instructional systems (AIS). The focus is on the application of state-of-the-art research in deep knowledge tracing (DKT) in production systems, including practical solutions for deploying and maintaining RNN prediction services. The target audience is researchers or data scientists working closely with software development teams to productionize prediction algorithms. This paper aims to

© Springer Nature Switzerland AG 2020
R. A. Sottilare and J. Schwarz (Eds.): HCII 2020, LNCS 12214, pp. 350–361, 2020.
https://doi.org/10.1007/978-3-030-50788-6_25

streamline the process by which learners can benefit from research advances in adaptive instruction.

1.1 AIS and Personalized Learning

Adaptive instructional systems (AIS) are self-improving, computer-based assessment systems that involve a human learner and an artificial tutoring agent [1]. They are self-improving because performance of the tutoring agent is monitored and tutoring policies are automatically updated over time to improve performance across learners in the system (i.e., a reinforcement learning system). AIS measure learner competencies across a set of attributes (or knowledge components) and deliver personalized content to the learner based on learner or system goals (e.g., improve competency on a given attribute, increase engagement with study tools, etc.). The personalized delivery of content allows the same AIS to be used by learners of varying competency levels and learning styles.

The objective in traditional adaptive measurement approaches has been to reduce assessment time or improve measurement precision by delivering content that captures the most information about the learner's ability levels. This approach works well for measuring learner ability at a single time point, although is not ideal for adaptive learning systems that need to measure changes in ability levels (i.e., learning) across days or months. In these systems, the purpose of measurement is typically not focused on reporting achievement, but on identifying opportunities to help the learner achieve course goals.

1.2 Problems with Traditional Measurement Approaches

Two popular approaches for measuring attribute-level mastery are Bayesian knowledge tracing (BKT) [2] and item response theory (IRT) [3]. BKT models the learner's response as a function of four probabilities: initial learning, acquisition, guess, and slip. The probabilities are combined with an observed response from the learner on an attribute to determine the learner's mastery of the attribute. The original formulation of BKT assumed that mastery does not decrease after an attribute is mastered and that exercises measuring the same attribute are equivalent in difficulty. Further, attribute masteries are modeled independently, and information about one attribute proficiency level does not provide information about another attribute proficiency level, even if the attributes are closely related in the content domain.

IRT models an item response as a function of both item and learner characteristics. Models parameterize item characteristics such as difficulty and complexity, and learner characteristics such as ability and motivation. Because these characteristics are parameters, they must be estimated following the collection of initial calibration data. A subset of models that directly measure attribute proficiency levels are diagnostic classification models [4].

Complex sources of information about the learner's interactions with an assessment environment such as eye tracking or clickstream data cannot be directly incorporated into BKT or IRT models. Further, these models assume measurement of a single time point (or fixed set of time points in some multidimensional models), but do not model the time-series data collected across a course semester or extended learning session.

1.3 Recurrent Neural Networks for Deep Knowledge Tracing

Recurrent neural networks (RNN) are deep learning techniques that identify complex non-linear relationships between a set of inputs and associated outputs. Namely, the inputs are time-series data such as learner scores or response times on assessment content, and the outputs are predictions such as the probability a learner will request a learning aid or respond correctly to the next assessment item. This deep learning approach applied to knowledge tracing is called deep knowledge tracing (DKT).

RNNs provide highly accurate predictions for outcomes involving time series data such as speech recognition [5]. For measuring learner ability levels across a set of attributes (i.e., knowledge tracing), RNNs (namely the long short-term memory variant or LSTM) have outperformed IRT-based methods, Bayesian knowledge tracing methods, and other dynamic probability-based methods [6].

A diagram of an RNN is shown in Fig. 1. A vector of inputs at time t, x_t, is transformed through a hidden layer to produce a set of probabilities at time t, A_t, one for each attribute in the domain. The network is recurrent because the same network recurs at each time point, with some information carried over from the previous time point.

A problem with basic RNNs is referred to as the *vanishing gradient* problem and occurs because information carried over from a previous time point is multiplied by a small gradient value. After this process repeats across several time points, this product approaches zero and the information is lost.

Hochreiter & Schmidhuber [7] proposed a solution to the vanishing gradient problem by including LSTM units in the hidden layer. Each LSTM unit includes a forget gate (?), an input gate (+), and an output gate (=). The forget gate determines how much information from the previous time point should be forgotten. The input gate determines how much information from the current time point should be kept. The output gate takes a linear combination of the forget gate and input gate products and passes the information to the network at the next time point.

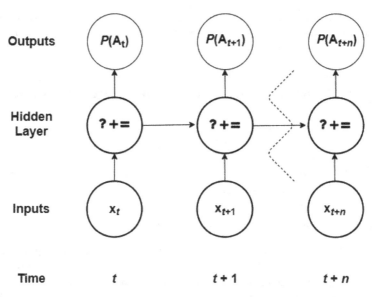

Fig. 1. A representation of a recurrent neural network with long short-term memory units for the hidden layer. $P(A_t)$ is the probability of mastery for each knowledge component at time t. $\mathbf{x_t}$ is the input vector at time t. **?** represents the forget gate, **+** represents the input gate, **& =** represents the output gate.

1.4 Limitations of DKT

The high accuracy of DKT over BKT and IRT approaches has generally been corroborated, although the limitations of the approach have been discussed as it has gained popularity. Mao, Lin, and Chi [8] found that DKT was better than BKT at predicting learning gains, although performed worse when predicting post-test scores.

Ding and Larson [9] noted that DKT performed better than BKT and performance factor analysis (PFA; a logistic regression approach). Although they found that parameter tuning appeared to have little affect on the performance of DKT, with a tuned network showing similar performance as an untuned network. They also found that DKT appeared to be measuring a general ability factor, with improvements on one attribute contributing to improvements on other attributes. Finally, they highlighted the lack of interpretability of DKT, a criticism that is commonly applied to deep neural networks.

The high accuracy of DKT might be the result of the flexibility of the model [10]. There are a high number of free parameters to estimate for DKT, whereas there are a limited number for BKT. Further, DKT is a data driven approach, whereas BKT incorporates a strong theory of learning.

Lastly, Wilson, Karklin, Han, and Ekanadham [11] found that hierarchical IRT (i.e., models multilevel structures such as groups of items) and temporal IRT (i.e., models ability as changing over time) approaches outperformed DKT. However, these authors did not use the same information for training the IRT models as they did for training the DKT network. Namely, the authors used exercise tag in addition to attribute tag for training the IRT models, whereas they only used attribute tag for training the DKT network.

2   Practical Considerations When Training DKT Networks

Several practical concerns arise when prediction algorithms are used to estimate ability levels or deliver personalized content to customers. Three covered in this paper are (a) initializing the DKT network with no data, (b) delivering measurements that are consistent with the observed data, (c) determining the amount of data needed to train the network, and (d) measuring learning trajectories.

2.1   Initializing the DKT Network with no Data

When launching a new AIS, the prediction service will likely be required to make predictions before data are collected. This might occur during the pre-release stage (in alpha or beta testing) of the new product or service. In these stages of development, it's important to verify that each of the services is working as expected and the full user flow can be tested.

For example, in a basic DKT network, the input data are item scores (i.e. item-level or step-level scores) and attribute tags. Rather than hard-coding predictions during the testing phase or sampling predictions from $U(0, 1)$, a more thorough approach is to simulate learner scores for training the DKT network. This allows for end-to-end testing of the service. In this approach, learner scores are generated to be as representative of the expected observed data as possible, given the information available.

In generating the data, the researcher can fix known quantities and make assumptions about other quantities. Suppose the researcher knows that there are 120 attributes in the measured domain. The researcher might examine data from previous AIS and determine that learners respond to between two and 130 items. The researcher could then sample each item score from $B(1, 0.5)$ to get random learner responses with randomly assigned attribute tags. This allows for the DKT to be trained, although the resulting predictions are meaningless.

A better approach is to incorporate more information into the data simulation to make the resulting predictions meaningful. One piece of information that can be leveraged is the ordering of the attributes in the domain. This information is valuable to the extent that attributes are mapped to a directed domain graph, with a clear path from foundational attributes to more advanced attributes that build on previous attributes. For example, pre-algebra is a subject area where foundational skills (e.g., addition, subtraction) act as prerequisites to more advanced skills (e.g., addition/subtraction of fractions). If a domain graph is not available, attribute ordering might be derived from a course textbook. Although many decision rules could be used to determine the attribute ordering from a course textbook, one is: *order the attributes according to the first occurrence of each attribute in the table of content*Given the attribute ordering, the following equation could be used to determine the binomial probabilities for simulating learner scores:

$$\text{logistic}(\theta_s - A_k + e_{sk}) \tag{1}$$

where the higher-order ability level for learner s is $\theta_s \sim N(0, \sigma^2)$, the standardized location (i.e. ordering) for attribute k is A_k, and the error term for learner s on attribute k is $e_{sk} \sim N(0, \tau^2)$. Note that this formulation is equivalent to the two-parameter logistic IRT model, albeit with an error term added to prevent overfitting of the network to the data.

This approach assumes that a learner will have a higher probability of correctly responding to items measuring earlier attributes in the domain graph, and a lower probability of correctly responding to items measuring later attributes.

2.2 Delivering Measurements that Are Consistent with the Observed Data

Previous research on DKT has focused on overall prediction accuracy, although in a production setting, predictions need to be accurate for each user. Namely, it's not enough for a prediction algorithm to work well for most users and not work well for a minority of users. Yeung and Yeung [12] found two issues with DKT predictions: (a) a correct response on an attribute did not always lead to an increase in the estimated probability of mastery for the attribute (and vice versa), and (b) attribute mastery probabilities sometimes fluctuated substantially across time points. Yeung and Yeung provided regularization terms to add to the loss function that significantly reduce the occurrence of these issues.

In a production setting, these issues would contribute to a negative user experience and confusion around attribute proficiencies. Heuristics might need to be implemented to ensure that a user doesn't observe attribute masteries decrsing after a correct response or attribute masteries fluctuating between mastered and non-mastered states.

2.3 Determining the Amount of Data Needed to Train the Network

With neural networks, prediction accuracy tends to increase as a function of the amount of data used to train the network. A company may want to achieve a certain level of prediction accuracy before using a service for high-stakes assessment or before releasing a product or service to paying customers.

To determine general data demand trends, DKT networks were trained using two popular datasets from an online adaptive tutoring program called ASSISTments. These datasets were used in a majority of the DKT analyses reviewed in this paper, although previous research has not explored prediction accuracy as a function of number of learners in the training set. The first, ASSISTment 2009[1] (ASSIST2009) contains 4,151

---

[1] https://sites.google.com/site/assistmentsdata/home/assistment-2009-2010-data/skill-builder-data-2009-2010.

learners, with each responding to approximately 70 items. The second, ASSISTment 2015[2] (ASSIST2015) contains 19,917 learners, with each responding to approximately 34 items.

To examine prediction accuracy as a function of both number of learners and average number of item responses, 3500 learners were randomly sampled from both ASSIST2009 and ASSIST2015. For each dataset, 2500 learners were assigned to the training sample and 1000 learners were assigned to the test sample. Performance was assessed using *AUC* for sample sizes of 500, 1000, 1500, 2000, and 2500 learners. The DKT networks were retrained at each sample size increment, similar to how the networks would be retrained in a production environment as new data becomes available.

For consistency with past DKT analyses on these datasets [e.g., 6], the networks were specified with a single hidden layer with 200 nodes and a mini-batch size of 100. Additionally, the regularization terms discussed in Sect. 2.2 were used to improve the consistency of the predictions, an important consideration when communicating attribute proficiencies to learners in a production setting. Results of the analysis are presented in Fig. 2.

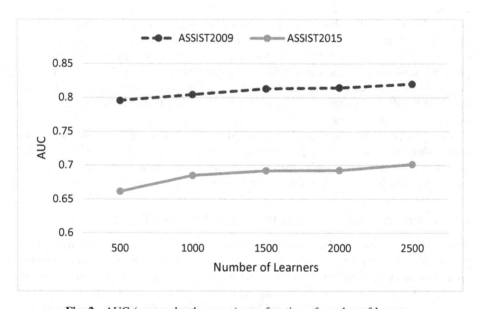

Fig. 2. AUC (area under the curve) as a function of number of learners.

For both ASSIST2009 and ASSIST2015, prediction accuracy increased monotonically as the number of learners increased. For the network trained from 2500 learners in the ASSIST2009 dataset, the AUC of 0.8199 approached the AUC reported in [12] of 0.8212 from using the full dataset. In contrast, for the network trained from

---

[2] https://sites.google.com/site/assistmentsdata/home/2015-assistments-skill-builder-data.

2500 learners in the ASSIST2015 dataset, the AUC of 0.7013 was substantially lower than the AUC reported in [12] of 0.7365 from using the full dataset. However, the current analysis only used 2500 of the 19,917 learners from the full ASSIST2015 dataset, so this discrepancy was expected.

Of particular note is the increased prediction accuracy of the ASSIST2009 network over the ASSIST2015 network. The number of learners was held constant for this study, which indicates that the average number of item responses per learner (70 for ASSIST2009 vs 34 for ASSIST2015) likely contributed to the substantially higher prediction accuracy. Also, worth noting is that for the smallest sample size (500 learners with an average of 34 item responses per learner), the AUC of 0.6615 is high enough to provide useful predictions early in the lifecycle of an AIS.

2.4 Measuring Learning Trajectories

The output from the RNN-LSTM provides an estimate on a [0, 1] scale for each attribute in the content domain indicating the learner's proficiency on the attribute (or the probability that the learner would correctly respond to an item or item-step measuring the attribute). This point estimate captures current ability information, although doesn't provide the learner with information about the rate at which an attribute is changing. A potential approach for representing this information to the learner is to calculate the slope for the previous n point estimates for attribute k. The slope can be calculated by regressing the point estimates on time for each attribute. Future time points can be included in the calculation by simulating learner responses and using these data as inputs to the network at future time points. This information might be leveraged to communicate to the user the number of successful exercises needed to reach an attribute proficiency level.

3 Production Implementation of DKT Network

After the network is trained, a typical outcome for a research project is a research or paper presentation. If the researcher is working at an educational testing company, he or she may hand off the research code to a software development team to implement in a production system. However, this paper argues that the production implementation of the neural network is more effective if the researcher(s) works closely with the software development team to ensure that the prediction service is correctly implemented and monitored in the system.

Figure 3 shows an example of system architecture for an AIS. After the network is deployed to (1), the process is cyclical, with personalized content recommendations resulting in new user data, which in turn updates and improves the prediction service.

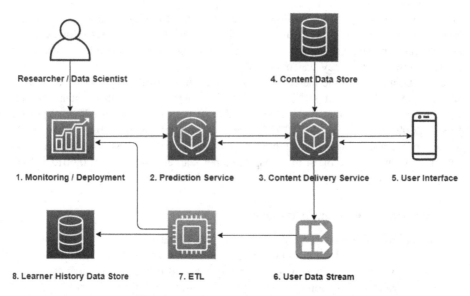

Fig. 3. System architecture for an AIS.

3.1 Real-Time Monitoring of Prediction Performance

A dashboard can be used to monitor performance of prediction algorithms in real-time. The dashboard can provide metrics for both deployed prediction algorithms, as well as for candidate algorithms. This is helpful for identifying issues with deployed classifiers, monitoring performance across subgroups (e.g., DIF analyses), and understanding app usage. This entry point to the system can also serve as a command post for promoting new models or retiring old models.

For the DKT application, if the trained network was deployed to (2), then metrics such as AUC and r^2 could be monitored for the DKT network, as well as for BKT and IRT models. If one of the candidate models outperformed the DKT network, then it could be deployed to (2) and the DKT network could be retired.

Customized dashboards can be developed using modern web frameworks such as Angular (JavaScript), Django (Python), or Shiny (R). There are also managed solutions that are easy to setup, including JupyterLab, Databricks, or AWS Sagemaker.

3.2 Retraining the Network

Neural networks tend to perform better as more data are acquired for training. The system can provide a more personalized experience for the end user (i.e., the user interacting with the app at (5)) to the extent that the network can be quickly retrained as new data flow through the system. Neural networks are computationally expensive to retrain in comparison to other simpler models such as logistic regression. For more computationally expensive prediction algorithms, a job can be specified to retrain the model on a fixed schedule (e.g., once every night). Although the computational resources required to train neural networks are high, the actual computations required are basic. These computations can be processed in parallel using GPU processing through deep learning frameworks such as HorovodRunner [13] for substantial reductions in training runtime.

Tools such as Jenkins and Databricks Jobs can be used to schedule the model training work, and tools such as TensorFlow Serving or Databricks MLFlow can be used to seamlessly deploy the updated models without interrupting the end user experience. Although even with these tools it is worthwhile to run the candidate model through a series of automated test cases to confirm that desired response times are met, and that the model can provide correct responses for a variety of requests.

3.3   Other Production Considerations: Latency, Stability, Security

When moving a prediction service from a researcher's local machine to a production system, there are several additional considerations around latency, stability, and security.

Latency is the time it takes for services in the system to communicate. This can be reduced by reducing the amount of information sent over the network. For example, the prediction service may be used to determine the optimal content to deliver to the user based on the user's goals and ability profile. Instead of passing the content (e.g., a video file) across the network, an identifier can be sent to the user's device to signal the presentation of pre-loaded content. Latency can also be reduced by hosting services on always-on compute resources. Many cloud service providers allow for autoscaling of compute resources to minimize costs, which means that additional compute resources will be added when the system experiences high usage (i.e., load).

Stability refers to the robustness of the system to external events (e.g., a thunder storm), internal events (e.g., a high number of concurrent users), and the extent to which the user experience is impacted from these events. The stability of the system can be increased through stress testing, in which the maximum expected number of users are simulated to identify (and fix) bottlenecks in the system. Further, a stable prediction service should be able to handle bad requests sent from the user (i.e., missing or unexpected information in the request).

Security refers to the protection of learner information, as well as protection of the system itself. AIS may require the learner to set up a username and password to use the app and this information is passed in an HTTP header when communicating with the production services to authenticate the user and access the user's sensitive information. Additionally, access to the system should be restricted as well, and only users that need to monitor, deploy, or maintain the services or databases should have access. As a precautionary measure, user data can be de-identified to not include any personally identifiable information. User data such as first name, last name, username, and password might be saved in a separate database from ability level information, with the records linked through a universally unique identifier (UUID).

4 Discussion and Future Directions

This paper reviewed current research on DKT and discussed the benefits of using DKT in an AIS. Namely, DKT allows for accurate measurement of ability levels across a set of attributes in a content domain and this information can be leveraged to deliver personalized content to the learner. DKT uses an RNN-LSTM, which is difficult to interpret, although provides higher prediction accuracy than BKT or IRT measurement approaches. This makes DKT ideal for learning-focused or formative assessment systems, in which the measurement of attribute proficiencies and the delivery of relevant content to promote learning is valued above the understanding of how the attribute proficiencies were measured.

Although this paper focused on the RNN-LSTM approach, the use of RNNs for knowledge tracing is a rapidly evolving area of research and other approaches are worth further investigation. For example, Pandey and Karypis [14] found that a self-attentive RNN better handled sparse learner data than an RNN-LSTM, and Ai et al. [15] found that incorporating concept-level information into a modified Dynamic Key-Value Memory Network improved performance over RNN-LSTMs.

Finally, the focus in DKT has been on measuring attribute proficiency levels using item score data. RNN-LSTMs allow for myriad data sources and might be used to predict other outcomes of interest such as learner motivation or future engagement with AIS. Zhang [16] found increased prediction accuracy from using multiple input sources including response times and the use of instructional aids such as hints. The challenge with using multiple input sources is that the dimensional space of the one-hot encoded inputs substantially increases as features are added. Zhang found success by using an autoencoder to reduce the dimensionality of the feature space. This area of research warrants future investigation as multiple input data sources are readily available from device interactions such as clickstream and affect data.

References

1. Sottilare, R.A.: A comprehensive review of design goals and emerging solutions for adaptive instructional systems. Tech. Inst. Cogn. Learn. **11**, 5–38 (2018)
2. Corbett, A.T., Anderson, J.R.: Knowledge tracing: modeling the acquisition of procedural knowledge. User Model. User-Adap. Inter. **4**(4), 253–278 (1994)
3. Birnbaum, A.: Some latent trait models and their use in inferring an examinee's ability. In: Lord, F.M., Novick, M.R. (eds.) Statistical Theories of Mental Test Scores, pp. 395–479. Addison-Wesley, Reading (1968)
4. Rupp, A.A., Templin, J.L.: Unique characteristics of diagnostic classification models: a comprehensive review of the current state-of-the-art. Measurement **6**(4), 219–262 (2008)
5. Graves, A., Mohamed, A.R., Hinton, G.: Speech recognition with deep recurrent neural networks. In: Acoustics, Speech, and Signal Processing (ICASSP), pp. 6645–6649 (2013)
6. Piech, C., et al.: Deep knowledge tracing. In: NIPS Conference Proceedings, pp. 1–12 (2015)
7. Hochreiter, S., Schmidhuber, J.: Long short-term memory. Neural Comput. **9**, 1735–1780 (1997)

8. Mao, Y., Lin, C., Chi, M.: Deep learning vs. Bayesian knowledge tracing: student models for interventions. J. Educ. Data Mining **10**, 28–54 (2018)
9. Ding, X., Larson, E.: Why deep knowledge tracing has less depth than anticipated. Paper Presented at the 12th International Conference on Educational Data Mining, pp. 282–287 (2019)
10. Montero, S., Arora, A., Kelly, S., Milne, B., Mozer, M.: Does deep knowledge tracing model interactions among skills? Paper Presented at the 11th International Conference on Educational Data Mining, pp. 462–466 (2018)
11. Wilson, K.H., Karklin, Y., Han, B., Ekanadham, C.: Back to the basics: Bayesian extensions of IRT outperform neural networks for proficiency estimation. Paper Presented at the 9th International Conference on Educational Data Mining, pp. 539–544 (2016)
12. Yeung, C.K., Yeung, D.Y.: Addressing two problems in deep knowledge tracing via prediction-consistent regularization (2018)
13. HorovodRunner: Distributed Deep Learning with Horovod. https://docs.databricks.com/applications/deep-learning/distributed-training/horovod-runner.html. Accessed 02 Mar 2020
14. Pandey, S., Karypis, G.: A self-attentive model for knowledge tracing. Paper Presented at the 12th International Conference on Educational Data Mining (2019)
15. Ai, F., Chen, Y., Guo, Y., Zhao, Y., Wang, Z., Fu, G.: Concept-Aware deep knowledge tracing and exercise recommendation in an online learning system. Paper Presented at the 12th International Conference on Educational Data Mining (2019)
16. Zhang, L.: Incorporating rich features into deep knowledge tracing. Masters thesis, Worcester Polytechnic Institute (2017)

Pilot State Monitoring for Cursus Recommendation

Maëlle Kopf[(✉)], Daniel Lafond, and Jean-François Gagnon

Thales Digital Solutions Inc., Québec, Canada
`maelle.kopf@thalesgroup.com`

Abstract. The training curriculum of air force cadets is currently identical for all, not taking trainees' individual differences in skill acquisition into account. A model of physiological arousal conceptualized as "ease in flight" is proposed as an objective metric for individualization. Considering that a significant part of air force cadets training takes place on a flight simulator, the metrics used to provide cursus recommendation should be valid both in flight and in a simulator. This work concerns the validation of "ease in flight" as a metric for training individualization in a simulated task environment. Eight participants performed two consecutive flights on a low fidelity aircraft simulator, whilst wearing a chest strap to measure the electrical activity of the heart and respiratory activity. Results show that declared ease in flight and declared stress are strongly negatively correlated. In addition, measured ease in flight increased significantly from first to second flight. Together, these results suggest that the ease in flight model previously defined using data from experts in-flight generalizes to simulated flight, both from a perceived and objective point of view. Finally, the potential of the model for providing adaptive cursus recommendation through the individualized analysis of measured ease in flight across different required skills is discussed.

Keywords: Training · Adaptation · Wearable · Sensors · Cognitive · Readiness · Trainee functional state

1 Introduction

When learning to fly a fighter plane, trainees' individual differences have a strong impact on their respective learning curves. If we consider the inverted-U shaped relationship between arousal and performance [1], we can argue that optimal training performance (i.e., where skill acquisition is at its highest) is associated with a specific level of arousal at every stage in the training process. Based on this premise, it should be possible to (1) infer training performance by monitoring individual arousal, and (2) identify the optimal timing to add or remove cursus elements to the training. By identifying the precise moment to inject complexity in training scenarios, trainers now have the capability to induce optimal levels of arousal with respect to performance and learning efficiency. Here, we assume that "performance" of the trainee does not relate to absolute task performance (e.g., performing a specific maneuver) but rather to being cognitively and physiologically disposed for skills acquisition. Indeed past research has linked physiological predictors with pilot performance and cognitive readiness [2, 3].

From an operational standpoint, pilots in training typically refer to their subjective "ease in flight" when describing their level of physiological arousal during flight.

© Springer Nature Switzerland AG 2020
R. A. Sottilare and J. Schwarz (Eds.): HCII 2020, LNCS 12214, pp. 362–371, 2020.
https://doi.org/10.1007/978-3-030-50788-6_26

Previous work [4] showed that a physiological model of ease in flight was able to discriminate between experts and non-experts when performing similar flights. This can be explained by the dual process theory according to which experienced pilots are more likely to rely predominantly on automated processes (System 1) whereas less experienced pilots rely predominantly on controlled processes (System 2). System 1 is fast, automatic and effortless, driven by intuition, recognition and experience. System 2 is based on slower, more analytical and consciously monitored processes [5].

Whilst the "ease in flight" model appears to be an efficient tool for monitoring pilots' in-flight skills acquisition, most if not all training programs include simulators as one of the tools used in conjunction with in-flight training. When measured during two similar flights, psychophysiological parameters such as heart rate, and heart rate variability follow a similar pattern, but at different levels between a real flight and a simulated one [6]. Thus, demonstrating the generalization of the model to a simulated environment would therefore potentially lead to a single metric to assess skill acquisition across environments.

The experiment presented in this paper is a first step towards cursus recommendation for air force cadets based on this model. More precisely, it shows the integration of the ease in flight model in a new (simulated) environment, testing its generalizability, and demonstrating how ease in flight assessments can be linked to contextual information such as maneuvers performed to highlight specific learning challenges in order to adapt and individualize the trainees' curriculum.

The general objective of the paper is to demonstrate the usefulness of the ease in flight model as a potential tool for adaptive cursus recommendation in the training of aircraft pilots. Two specific objectives are addressed in the current effort:

Objective #1. Test if the ease in flight model is able to generalize to simulated flights.

> *H1a.* Self-reported ease in flight is negatively associated with self-reported level of stress.
> *H1b.* The output of the ease in flight physiological model is positively associated with an increase in piloting experience as manipulated by two equivalent consecutive flights.

Objective #2. Test if the model is a good candidate to provide adaptive and individual cursus recommendation, through the individualized analysis of an objective ease in flight measure for the corresponding skills and abilities during the execution of specific exercises.

> *H2.* Patterns of measured ease in flight (using the model) will vary across participants and flights phases, but will remain coherent within trainees.

2   Method

2.1   Participants and Procedure

Eight participants aged 28 to 45 (mean = 37.3, sd = 6.5, 3 females) took part in the experiment. They volunteered and were remunerated for their time. The experiment lasted around 2 to 4 h per participant, depending on the amount of practice performed in the initial familiarization. Each participant performed three flights on a low fidelity flight simulator: one familiarization flight, followed by two experimental flights during which data were collected. All pilots were novices, and did not have a pilot license.

2.2 Familiarization

Prior to the experiment, participants read a description of the maneuvers they would be asked to perform, as well as a simplified user guide on how to use basic flight instruments (Altimeter, airspeed indicator, artificial horizon, anemometer, directional gyro) and the fundamentals of aircraft controls (throttle control, rudder pedals, yoke, flaps). Participants practiced the maneuvers during the familiarization flight. If needed, they were shown how to perform the different maneuvers, and could ask questions. The objective of this flight was to ensure that participants understood the basics of flight and simulator controls.

2.3 Experimental Flights

Two experimental flights were executed after the familiarization flight. Participants had a memory aid for aircraft commands and maneuver execution during the two experimental flights.

Two scenarios were defined for testing purposes. The sequence was counterbalanced across participants. The structure of the two flights was identical; participants performed maneuvers when they were asked to, indicating when the maneuver started and when it ended. The differences between the two flights were the location, and the fact that the experimenter triggered an engine failure during final approach of landing for one the two flights (flight B).

The maneuvers performed during the flights were (1) Takeoff, (2) Wing over, (3) Nose up recovery, (4) Nose down recovery, (5) Clover leaf, and (6) Landing. These maneuvers were chosen amongst the firsts maneuvers taught during the initial training of air force cadets.

2.4 Material

Simulator. The flights were performed with the X-plane 11 simulator (Laminar Research), including all tools and accessories required for initial training of cadets (rudder pedals, yoke, throttle Quadrant). The cockpit view was displayed through three HD screens, as recommended by the provider. The flights were performed on a Grob Tutor 115E, which is similar to the aircrafts used for initial flight training.

Sensors. During their two flights, participants were equipped with the Zephyr Bio Harness 3.0 chest strap, measuring the electrical activity of the heart, and respiration rate. The Sensor Hub [7] application was used on an android mobile phone to synchronize and process collected physiological data from the belt, as well as contextual data from the simulator (speed, altitude, global positioning system coordinates etc.).

2.5   Self-report

Participants were asked to fill one questionnaire before each of the two flights, where they indicated their fatigue and overall stress level on a scale from 1 to 10. At the end of the flight and before the debriefing, they completed a NASA TLX questionnaire relative to the whole flight, and declared, on a scale from 1 to 10, their stress level and ease in flight level during the execution of each maneuver type.

3   Results

3.1   Hypothesis 1a

Repeated measures correlation was carried out using declarations made by the participants during each of their flights, and for each maneuver. Correlations were computed with the rmcor package in R [8]. The correlation coefficient between "declared ease in flight" and "declared stress" is $rrm(20) = -0.83$, $p < 0.005$, 95% CI = $(-0.93, -0.61)$. The value distribution is given in Fig. 1. As perceived stress decreases, perceived ease in flight increases. We previously associated high ease in flight with automatic processes, and lower mental effort [4]. The results obtained here support this hypothesis.

In addition, a paired t-test showed that declared ease in flight was significantly higher in the second flight (mean = 7.8, sd = 1.24) than for the first flight (mean = 6.3, sd = 1.29) $(t(3) = 2.7815$, $p < 0.05)$. Due to technical issues, only the declarations of four participants were complete. The occurrence of the engine failure did not have a significant effect on the declared ease in flight for the landing phase.

Results showed no significant changes in NASA TLX scores from one flight to another.

3.2   Hypothesis 1b

Physiological Changes Measured
Results show that there was a significant decrease in heart rate between the first (mean = 78.9, sd = 9.37) and the second flight (mean = 75.7, sd = 8.83) $(t(7) = 6.0712$, $p < 0.005)$, but there was no significant difference between the two flights for respiration rate and heart rate variability. Also, the standard deviation of heart rate significantly decreased $(t(7) = -6.14$, $p < 0.005)$ from the first flight (mean = 39.40, sd = 4.67) to the second flight (mean = 37.85, sd = 4.39).

Ease in Flight Values Measured and Declared
Results show that there was a statistically significant increase of the ease in flight value (as measured by the model) from Flight 1 (mean = 0.73, sd = 0.21) to Flight 2 (mean = 0.79, sd = 0.20), $t(7) = 3.5084$, $p < .005$ (Fig. 2). The only participant for whom the ease in flight in the second flight is not higher than the first flight (Participant 9 in Fig. 2) is also the only participant whose perceived performance was lower in

Flight 2 compared to Flight 1. This very participant orally reported dreading the second flight, since no engine failure had occurred in their first flight.

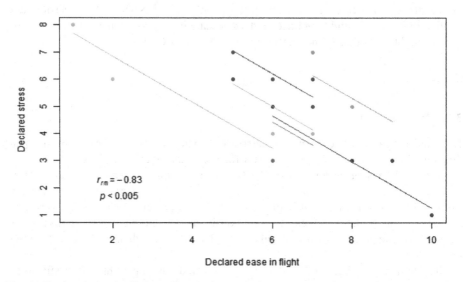

Fig. 1. Declared ease in flight and stress for each maneuver type for each flight. Each color represents a participant (Color figure online)

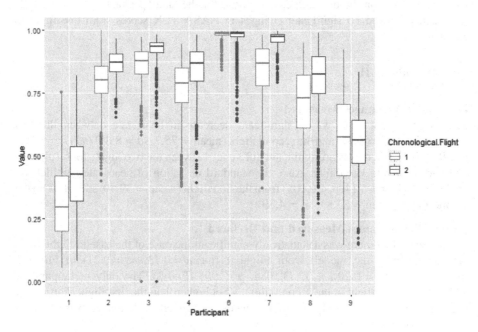

Fig. 2. Ease in flight between participants

Results showed no statistically significant differences between the measured ease in flight during the landing - with or without engine failure ($p > 0.05$).

3.3 Hypothesis 2

Contextualized data was used to categorize each moment of the flight into four different phases; ground (at the beginning and the end of the flight), take off, flight and landing. This automatic labeling was made using two logistic regressions ("glm" model of the "caret" package in R) relying only on speed and altitude features, and whose organization and coefficients is given in Fig. 3. The first step of the process was to identify whether the considered data is either "Ground", or "Flight". To do so, two logistic regressions ("glm" model of the "caret" package in R) were performed to identify the data as "Ground" or "Flight" (one regression per phase). The classification thresholds were set to 0.5 to classify a flight segment as ground or flight: if the probability of being in this phase is equal or higher than 0.5, this phase was assigned to the segment.

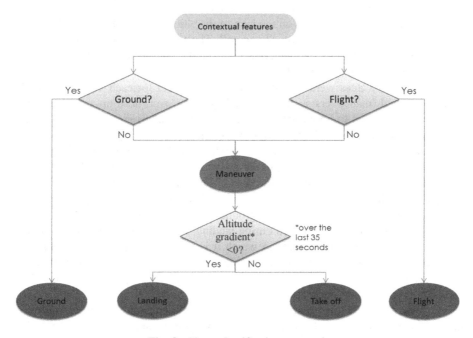

Fig. 3. Phase classification approach

The different features used to predict the phase and resulting coefficients are given in Table 1.

Table 1. Coefficients for the two linear regression models and the associated features: Ground identification and in flight

Coefficients		
Feature	Ground identification	In flight identification
Intercept	2.47	−7.30
Speed in meter per second	−0.19	0.15
Speed gradient (30 s)	−0.80	−0.05
Altitude (from starting point)	0	0.002
Altitude gradient (30 s)	0	−0.02

The second processing step occurred when the data was neither "Ground" nor "Flight". In this case, the data was either "Take off" or "Landing". The discrimination between the latter two was based on the sign of the altitude gradient over the last 35 s: if positive, "Take off", if negative, "Landing". The two models were trained with a leave-one-flight-out method, on data collected in flight, and manually labelled. Overall the two models combined reached an accuracy of 90.4%.

Ease in flight values were considered individually and for each of the four flight phases identified (maneuvers such as clover leaf, wing over, nose up and nose down recovery are expected to be classified as "flight"). The values are displayed for each participant, and each chronological flight in Fig. 4.

The measured ease in flight values varied across participants without following a recurrent pattern. None of the four phases was constantly associated with a higher or lower ease in flight. For example, in the case of Participant 4, the maneuver for which the ease in flight values are the highest is the take off and the lowest values are measured during the flight and on the ground, whereas for Participant 9 the lowest values clearly appear to be measured during landing, with or without an engine failure. Notably, if we consider the context in which it is applied, the model seems to have captured the beginning of a "learning" pattern which is specific to each participant (Fig. 4). To quantitatively assess this coherence pattern, we proposed a metric calculating the proportion of intrapersonal coherence as opposed to inter-participant variability. For each participant and phase, the ratio between intra-variability from one flight to another and overall variability (inter-variability and intra-variability) was computed, as a coherence metric, from 0 to 100. All participants and phases combined, the average coherence value observed was 77% (with a range of 64% to 93% across participants).

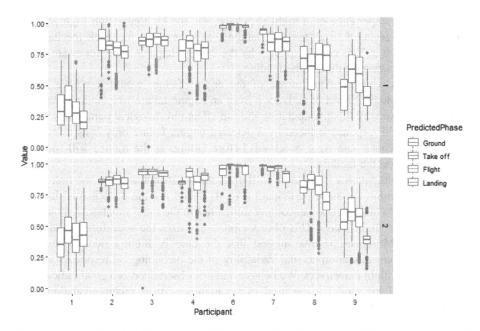

Fig. 4. Ease in flight and flight phases. "Flight" includes all maneuvers different from Take off and Landing

In this context, one specific phase being associated with the lowest "ease in flight" in both flights could be targeted by the instructor and their trainee in the adaptation of the training, as it appears to be harder to acquire these specific skills for the trainee.

4   Discussion

The subjective measures collected in this experiment showed that the perception of "ease in flight" by potential trainees was associated with perceived stress, and thus activation. This conceptual framework was also supported by the changes (physiological and perceived) measured throughout the experiment, where a significant decrease in heart rate was detected, as well as measured and declared ease in flight, across the two training scenarios. These observations support the validity of the "ease in flight" notion and support the first hypothesis, i.e. the generalization capacity of the ease in flight model, and its sensitivity to physiological changes occurring between two flights. It is however important to keep in mind that due to technical issues, subjective data was only available for the two flights for four of the participants. Data relative to one flight were available for two other participants, but without the possibility of comparing them with the other flight.

Results did not show an effect of the engine failure appearance on neither the physiological response nor the declaration. The lack of increased perceived stress could be explained by the lack of experience of the trainees. Indeed, all of the participants had few or no prior experience on a flight simulator, and the familiarization flight did not allow them to get used to a "normal" landing, and the usual feedback mechanisms which come with it. This could explain why the first participants were not aware of the engine failure occurring during the landing.

Participants who were not aware of the engine failure would not have had a different physiological level of activation from an engine failure free landing. Another explanation as to why this manipulation did not affect physiological parameters is that the physiological response induced by a detected engine failure only lasts a few seconds (peaks in heart rate were observed) before fading, as the trainee will focus its attention back on the landing.

The recurrent patterns in the ease in flight values distribution from the first to the second flight within the same participant (Fig. 4) underlines the participants' individuality, as they do not necessary encounter difficulties in the same situations; in our case during the same flight phase. This observation emphasizes the need for training individualization. Moreover, results suggest that the ease in flight model is sensitive enough to capture this interpersonal variability of the physiological responses associated to specific flight maneuvers. We believe that this observation is a good indicator of the potential of the model to be used as an adaptive cursus recommendation tool. Indeed, recurrent differences in the ease in flight values between maneuvers can be associated to the corresponding levels of attentional resources deployed described by [9], and supposedly this can be an indicator for quantifying skills and abilities acquisition. The observation of recurrent patterns of measured ease in flight within the same individuals supports the assumption that using individualized baselines for each trainee could increase the model's relevance. For instance, after a trainee's first flight, the absolute "raw" ease in flight values could be adjusted according to the instructor's perception or some other type of initial "calibration" procedure.

A limitation of the study however is the restricted number of participants. Tendencies were highlighted by the analysis on eight participants, but additional experimentations are required to confirm the generalization capacity of the model. Supplementary scenarios will also be considered in further experimentations.

Participants who took part in the experiment had the same experience in terms of piloting an aircraft. Hence, the analyses made on the data collected only concerned early stages of the training of air force cadets (basic commands and maneuvers). A metric used for cursus recommendation must prove its relevance at every stage of the training process, which is why additional experimentation is all the more needed to establish the potential of the ease in flight model at every stage of the curriculum.

The ease in flight model measures variations in physiological parameters associated with effort. This effort can be influenced by several factors, one of them being the experience. Indeed, for an equivalent performance, we consider a simplified scheme where the activation level is affected by three factor types: (1) Expertise, (2) Task difficulty and (3) Tools. In previous work which led to the development of the ease in flight model [4], task difficulty and tools were kept identical between experts and novices, as the flights were performed in tandems. In the experiment presented here, the use of a simulator also made it possible to freeze "task difficulty" as well as "tools" amongst participants. Therefore we associate the physiological changes measured from one flight to another with expertise and skill acquisition, thus supporting the second hypothesis given above. The approach of skill mapping presented here is promising as it will be used to ensure a longitudinal tracking of the progression of the trainees. Collecting and contextualizing data from several flights for the same individual will also reduce noise and highlight the specificities of each trainee individually. In this case, variations in task difficulty and tools such as weather, mission type and aircraft will be documented and could be integrated in the evaluation of the ease in flight to reduce bias.

Besides the analysis of physiological information, the process suggested here to provide cursus recommendations relies on an independent contextualization of the data. In our case, contextual information is provided through automated detection of flights elements (phases and/or maneuvers). Building trust in the process of element detection is equally important as trust in the physiological modeling, in order to provide appropriate cursus adaptation. Figure 4 presents a flight segmentation made with automatically detected flight phases (ground, take off, flight, landing) rather than performed maneuvers (take off, wing over, nose up recovery, nose down recovery, clover leaf, and landing). Flight segmentation based on maneuvers would provide finer grained contextualization and will be validated in future efforts.

Finally, future work will consist in testing the cursus recommendation tool with more diversified scenarios and stages in the training, in order to demonstrate its efficiency in the context of pilot training.

References

1. Yerkes, R.M., Dodson, J.D.: The relation of strength of stimulus to rapidity of habit-formation. J. Comp. Neurol. Psychol. **18**(5), 459–482 (1908)
2. Johnston, P.J., Catano, V.M.: Investigating the validity of previous flying experience, both actual and simulated, in predicting initial and advanced military pilot training performance. Int. J. Aviat. Psychol. **23**(3), 227–244 (2013)
3. Martinussen, M.: Psychological measures as predictors of pilot performance: a meta-analysis. Int. J. Aviat. Psychol. **6**(1), 1–20 (1996)
4. Ferrari, V., Gagnon, J.-F., Camachon, C., Kopf, M.: Psycho-physiological evaluation of the pilot: a study conducted with pilots of the French air force. In: Harris, D. (ed.) EPCE 2018. LNCS (LNAI), vol. 10906, pp. 285–295. Springer, Cham (2018). https://doi.org/10.1007/978-3-319-91122-9_24
5. Kahneman, D.: Maps of bounded rationality: psychology for behavioral economics. Am. Econ. Rev. **93**(5), 1449–1475 (2003)
6. Magnusson, S.: Similarities and differences in psychophysiological reactions between simulated and real air-to-ground missions. Int. J. Aviat. Psychol. **12**(1), 49–61 (2002). https://doi.org/10.1207/S15327108IJAP1201_5
7. Gagnon, J.F., Lafond, D., Rivest, M., Couderc, F. Tremblay, S.: Sensor-Hub: a real-time data integration and processing nexus for adaptive C2 systems. In Proceedings of the Sixth International Conference on Adaptive and Self-Adaptive Systems and Applications, pp. 63–67 (2014)
8. Bakdash, J.Z., Marusich, L.R.: Repeated measures correlation. Front. Psychol. **8**, 456 (2017)
9. Wickens, C.D.: Processing resources and attention. Multiple-Task Perform. **1991**, 3–34 (1991)

Experimental Evaluation of Heart-Based Workload Measures as Related to Their Suitability for Real-Time Applications

Dennis Mund[(⊠)] and Axel Schulte

University of the Bundeswehr, Werner-Heisenberg-Weg 39,
85579 Neubiberg, Germany
{dennis.mund, axel.schulte}@unibw.de

Abstract. We conducted an experiment to evaluate the viability of using heart rate parameters for real-time adaptation of applications to the mental state of human operators. The experiment consisted of a fast-jet flying task with secondary tasks in our simulator. We created five mission segments to induce differing levels of workload. During the experiment, heart rate data and subjective workload ratings were collected. The subjective workload ratings show different workload levels for each mission segment. However, from the considered heart rate parameters, we were only able to reproduce two of the known correlations from the literature; namely, average heart rate and high frequency activity of the heart rate variability. Additionally, we encountered the opposite of the expected relationships for the RMSSD of the heart rate as well as the standard deviation across the principal axis of the Poincaré plot. We suppose that the short time-frame, which we deemed necessary for real-time applications, is a possible explanation for our surprising results. Finally, we conclude that heart rate variability parameters may not be robust enough for real-time applications, especially as each measured parameter had participants who showed converse reactions to the average.

Keywords: Heart rate · Mental workload · Adaptive assistance

1 Introduction

Human mental workload (MWL) is a construct that describes the individual psychological reaction to the work that a human has to master in order to fulfil their given set of tasks [1]. Various studies have shown a relationship between MWL and performance in different domains [2–4]. Extreme workload conditions can cause severe human performance decrements, especially in high-risk environments. Therefore, it is valuable to maintain manageable MWL levels, which can often be achieved through the addition of automated functions. However, too much automation comes with another set of issues, such as complacency and confirmation bias [5–7]. Thus, finding the right amount of automation remains a challenging problem that depends on the assessment of MWL. This assessment cannot be done through any direct measure, but there are various indirect measures that have been linked to MWL.

R. A. Sottilare and J. Schwarz (Eds.): HCII 2020, LNCS 12214, pp. 372–382, 2020.
https://doi.org/10.1007/978-3-030-50788-6_27

Additionally, assessing MWL in real time allows for on-line customizations of human machine interfaces to adapt to the mental states of the human operators. Such an adaptive system has been employed successfully in the military helicopter domain to recover human errors and mitigate critical situations on the basis of an extensive model of the domain tasks [8]. On the contrary, as we argued in [9], there are limits to what model-based approaches can assess on their own. Another approach for MWL assessment is the use of ECG-data. Various studies have shown correlations between heart rate, heart rate variability, and cognitive workload. [10] and [11] have shown that the mean heart rate increases with a rise in cognitive workload. In [4] and [12], higher operator workload (due to the participants' inexperience or to a more challenging task, respectively), is associated with a decrease in the square root of the mean squared differences (RMSSD) between successive RR intervals. [13] found a negative correlation between workload and the HRV-Triangular Index (RRTri), i.e. the integral of the histogram of RR-peaks divided by its height. In the frequency analysis of the heart rate variability data, as well as in non-linear analysis methods such as the Poincaré plot analysis there are additional parameters that were connected to workload. The high frequency band (0.15–0.4 Hz) of the heart rate variability, as obtained through a Fast Fourier transformation, presents a lower activity with higher cognitive workload [14]. Finally, the standard deviation along the principal axis (SD2) of a Poincaré plot decreases with rising workload levels [15]. Table 1 presents these parameters, along with the effect from the literature.

Table 1. Changes of physiological parameters with an increase in MWL

Measure	Unit	Description	Expected change	Source
Avg. HR	1/min	The average rate of heartbeats	Increase	[10, 11]
RMSSD	ms	Square root of the mean squared differences between successive RR intervals	Decrease	[4, 12]
RRTri	–	Integral of the RR interval histogram divided by its height	Decrease	[13]
HF normalized	–	The normalized high frequency (0.15–0.4 Hz) component of HRV	Decrease	[14]
Poincaré SD2	ms	Standard deviation along the principal axis in the Poincaré analysis	Decrease	[15]

These measures can be detected in near real-time and are therefore suited for use in adaptive assistance. However, according to [16], the analysis of the heart rate variability to detect cardiovascular diseases is unreliable, if the analysed timeframe is below five minutes. This raises the question of whether workload estimation shares this drawback and thus cannot be used for real-time applications.

Therefore, we conducted an experiment in our flight simulator in order to assess the possibility of using heart rate variability measures to correctly infer mental workload, despite having a small time-frame of about two minutes or less. The experiment contained two different aviation tasks, combined with two cognitive tasks, in five separated mission segments. Each mission segment is designed to induce a different workload level. We then compared the resulting heart data with the designed difficulty for each mission segment, as well as subjective workload ratings, using the NASA-TLX questionnaire [17].

2 Experiment

2.1 Participants

Data from 10 volunteer aerospace engineering students was collected. The participants were all male in the age range of 21 to 24. Before the experiment, written consent was obtained from each participant.

2.2 Study Design

The data was collected in a manned-unmanned teaming experiment in our fast-jet research simulator. The participants had to perform three tasks: manual flying (Aviate/Terrain Following), commanding several UAV (Delegation), and performing mental arithmetic tasks. These tasks were separated into five phases of varying difficulty (as shown in Table 2).

Table 2. Phases of the experiment with the performed tasks

Phase	Tasks
Difficulty I	Aviate
Difficulty II	Aviate, delegation
Difficulty III	Aviate, mental arithmetic
Difficulty IV	Aviate, delegation, mental arithmetic
Difficulty V	Terrain following, delegation, mental arithmetic

The Different Tasks
In the "Aviate" task, the participants had to manually fly their own jet along a pre-defined route at a constant speed of 500 kts and at a constant altitude of 5000 ft MSL. To maintain a constant difficulty between the different phases, the route for every phase consisted of two route legs of similar length with a 110° turn in between.

For the "Delegation" task, multiple scenario elements were displayed in a tactical map. The existing elements were buildings, waypoints, surface-to-air missile sites (SAM-sites), and radars. The participants had to tap the element using touch input, choose an appropriate task for the respective element in a popup-menu, and delegate the task to one UAV in a timeline display. For buildings, the correct task was "Investigate;" for waypoints, the task was "Fly-Over;" for SAM-Sites, "Suppress;" and there was no task for radars. Each phase with a delegation task had two instances of each scenario element. Additionally, it was required that each of the three UAV not get the same type of task twice. Figure 1 shows the four different scenario elements, as well as the timeline display.

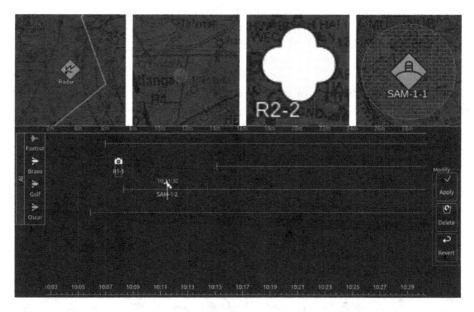

Fig. 1. (Top) Images of the four possible scenario elements in the tactical map. From left to right: radar, waypoint, building, SAM-site. (Bottom) The timeline display used for delegating tasks to the UAV

The "Mental Arithmetic" task had simple arithmetic exercises; for example "The square root of 49 divided by 7 plus 4". These exercises were dictated to the participants until they gave the correct answer. Once they answered correctly, the next exercise was given.

The final task, "Terrain Following," is also a manual flight task along a predefined route. However, in contrast to the aviate task, the given altitude constraint was changed from a barometric altitude to an altitude of 500 ft above ground. This increases the difficulty, as the altitude is now dependent on the terrain and therefore is harder to maintain.

Additional Experiment Design Constraints
Since our participants were students, not trained pilots, we expected training effects to be an issue. To counteract these effects, the study was split into two groups with different orderings of the above-mentioned phases, as shown in Table 3.

Table 3. Ordering of difficulties per group

Phase	Group 1	Group 2
1	Difficulty I	Difficulty II
2	Difficulty V	Difficulty III
3	Difficulty III	Difficulty I
4	Difficulty IV	Difficulty V
5	Difficulty II	Difficulty IV

Additionally, the difficulty of terrain following tasks is strongly dependent on the terrain along the route. In order to maintain a comparable difficulty level for the terrain following task between the two groups, the route for this task was the same in both configurations. The two different mission designs that were created under the given requirements are presented in Fig. 2.

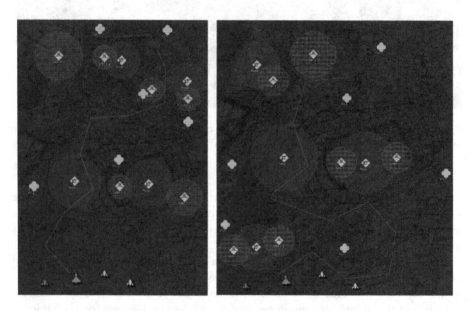

Fig. 2. The two different mission designs

2.3   Procedure

Initially, each participant received an introduction to our simulator along with an explanation on how to fly the aircraft. Afterwards, each participant had a training flight to get comfortable with flying the aircraft, as well as to perform the additional tasks.

After the training, the participants received a short presentation about the order of the different phases, as well as the route they would be flying, and the measured part of the experiment began. During the flight, the ECG-data were collected using the BioPac

Bionomadix sensors [18]. After each phase, the simulation was paused, and the subjective workload was assessed through the NASA-TLX questionnaire without the individualized weights. Afterwards, the participant was informed again about the tasks in the next phase, and the simulation was resumed. Due to route and speed requirements each phase took about three minutes.

After the experiment, the heart data was processed with an implementation of the Pan-Tompkins-QRS-detector [19], and the resulting RR-intervals were analysed with Kubios-HRV [20]. Due to our intention to use this algorithm in a closed-loop application, we refrained from manual corrections of noisy data. The analysed data was taken from a time-frame beginning 30 s after the start and ending at the 2-min mark of each phase. The first 30 s were cut off to make sure the participants were re-immersed in the workload situation after the simulation freeze and were able to correct deviations from the required altitude. Additionally, the end of each phase was removed because some participants managed to process the "Delegation" task before the end of the phase and therefore did not have the additional task-load in that time-frame.

The performance of the participants was assessed through the square root of the sum of squared distances to the given altitude requirement, as well as the number of correctly answered mental math questions. The final performance metric was the number of correctly delegated tasks to the UAVs.

3   Results

3.1   Treatment of Data

The electrocardial activity data of the first participant was lost due to logging issues. Therefore, the analysis of the heart rate parameters was conducted on the remaining nine participants. Additionally, the high T-waves of participant three caused the Pan-Tompkins QRS-detection to detect many false positives and was thus replaced by a custom peak detection algorithm. Due to a lack of baseline measurements, the parameters were normalized using the highest and lowest value per participant. Finally, the data from participant six in *Difficulty II* and from participant ten in *Difficulty I* were discarded because they were too noisy.

For the performance evaluation, there is no data for the first two participants from the additional tasks (Delegation and Mental Arithmetic), and therefore the analysis of these tasks is based on the remaining eight participants.

3.2   Analysis

Subjective Workload Ratings
The responses from the NASA-TLX questionnaire shows significant increases in subjective difficulty ratings from each phase to the next ($t(10) = -5.1$, $p < 0.001$ for I and II; $t(10) = -2.3$, $p = 0.048$ for II and III; $t(10) = -4.5$ $p = 0.001$ for III and IV; $t(10) = -2.5$, $p = 0.03$ for IV and V). Figure 3 shows a boxplot of the average workload ratings per difficulty.

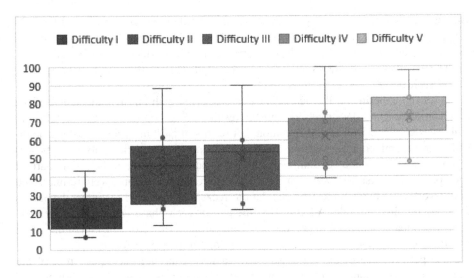

Fig. 3. NASA-TLX responses for the five different phases

Performance
Figure 4 shows boxplots of the participants' flight performances.

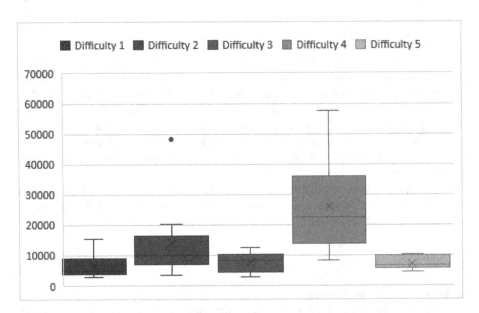

Fig. 4. Flight performance in the five different phases

In the analyzed timeframes, the overall performance decreases with an increase in difficulty. For the adherence to the altitude requirement there is an increase from *Difficulty I* (Median: 4640 ft, MAD: 1362 ft) to the next two difficulties, which are about equal (*Difficulty II* Median: 9981, MAD: 3426 and *Difficulty III* Median: 8468, MAD: 2950). Additionally, there is an increase to *Difficulty IV* (Median: 22597 ft, MAD: 9606 ft). However, the performance in *Difficulty V* (Median: 6705 ft, MAD: 1400 ft) is better than in *II, III, and IV*.

For the "Mental Arithmetic" task, the performance decreased from *Difficulty III* (Median: 18.5, MAD: 5.5) to the remaining two, and was similar for those (*Difficulty IV* Median: 10, MAD: 4 and *Difficulty V* Median: 11.5, MAD: 4.5). In the "Delegation" task there was only one missing task delegation in *Difficulties II* and *IV,* and the number of missing task delegations increased in *Difficulty V* to four out of the overall 48 necessary delegations in each difficulty.

Measurements

For an analysis of the heart rate data, we used the NASA-TLX averages for the different phases as workload references. Therefore, we searched for correlations between the heart rate parameters and these subjective workload ratings. Table 4 shows these correlations per participant, as well as the resulting average correlation.

Table 4. Correlation of the heart rate parameters with the average NASA-TLX scores

Participant	Avg. HR	RMSSD	RR tri	HF	SD2
2	0.98	0.93	0.75	0.02	0.74
3	0.72	−0.25	0.30	−0.93	0.72
4	−0.19	−0.15	0.96	−0.86	0.94
5	0.98	0.63	0.64	0.44	0.08
6	−0.37	0.58	−0.56	0.16	0.62
7	0.96	−0.16	0.42	−0.88	0.59
8	0.49	0.67	0.24	−0.17	0.82
9	0.72	0.33	0.52	−0.33	0.32
10	0.42	−0.64	0.57	−0.15	−0.25
Avg	0.52	0.22	0.42	−0.30	0.51

For the strongest two correlation averages (normalized heart rate and SD2, we computed dependent t-tests to determine which changes are significant. For the normalized heart rate there was no significant change between two adjacent difficulties. However, there was a significant change from *Difficulty II* to *Difficulty IV* ($t(9) = -2.65$, $p = 0.03$), as well as to *Difficulty V* ($t(9) = -2.93$, $p = 0.02$). Similarly, the increases from *Difficulty I* to *Difficulty IV* ($t(9) = -4.60$, $p = 0.001$) and to *Difficulty V* ($t(9) = -2.71$, $p = 0.03$) are also significant.

The significance analysis of the SD2 of the Poincare plot shows a significant change from *Difficulty I* to *Difficulty III* ($t(9) = -2.89$, $p = 0.02$), as well as to *Difficulty IV* ($t(9) = -2.81$, $p = 0.02$), and from *Difficulty II* to *Difficulty IV* ($t(9) = -3.49$, $p = 0.008$). Figure 5 shows a visualization of these two heart parameters.

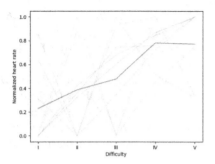 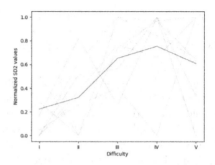

Fig. 5. Normalized Heart rate(left) and SD2 values(right) over the five mission segments. The opaque line shows the average over all participants, while the semi-transparent lines represent the individual participants

While the data average over all participants (shown with the opaque line) conforms with the expected results from the literature, the per-participant development varies. This can also be seen in the correlation of the physiological measures with the subjective workload; for example, there is a strong correlation between heart rate and NASA-TLX for participant five, while participant six in fact shows a negative correlation.

4 Discussion

In general, our experiment shows a correlation between the expected difficulty of our mission design, the performance of the participants, their subjective workload ratings, and common heart rate parameters in the literature.

However, the expected difficulty increase of switching from flying at a constant altitude to a low-level flight task did not result in an increased workload, indicated by the physiological parameters (despite getting increased subjective workload ratings in the NASA-TLX questionnaire). Additionally, the median flight performance in the low-level flight section is better than in all other sections (except for *Difficulty I*). Therefore, we assume that terrain following might be an easier task than constant altitude flight in a multitask situation, because the visual feedback of the terrain is a lot more prominent than the altitude in the interface. In contrast, the threat of crashing is higher in the low-level flying task, which might increase the subjective ratings.

For the ECG-data, we can reproduce the relationships between the average heart rate and workload, as well as the high frequency band activation and workload, with varying effect intensities. We could not reproduce the decrease of the RMSSD that was reported in [4] and [12]. Furthermore, for the SD2 and the HRV-Triangular index, we encountered results converse of the literature. Although we found strong correlations using the average reaction of the participants, the characteristics of the individual curves show different behaviours. Thus, larger sample sizes may be well suited for a distinction of workload in differing conditions; however, the parameters do not seem robust enough to allow for individual workload analyses. A possible explanation for these individual discrepancies is a difference in the mean workload levels. This would mean that, for example, the heart rate is a good indicator for a workload increase at medium workload levels, while it stops increasing at a high workload level and then another parameter becomes more relevant.

5 Conclusion

This study investigated the relationship between subjectively perceived mental workload and various heart rate parameters using shorter time-frames of about 90 s. We could reproduce an increase in the average heart rate, the RMSSD, and the SD2/SD1 ratio of the Poincaré plot analysis, as well as a decrease in the normalized power of the high frequency band of the RR intervals, with an increase in mental workload. Additionally, we found that for each of these parameters, there were participants that did not show the expected effect. We therefore conclude that we could not find a single robust measure for a real-time mental workload estimation based on ECG-data. However, there might be a combined measure similar to the Baevsky-stress index [21] for physical workload. Such a metric could remedy individual differences and deserves further research in a study with a bigger sample size.

References

1. Young, M.S., Brookhuis, K.A., Wickens, C.D., Peter, A.: State of science: mental workload in ergonomics. Ergonomics **58**(1), 1–17 (2015)
2. Acker, C.E.: Higher mental workload is associated with poorer laparoscopic performance as measured by the NASA-TLX tool. Simul. Healthc. **5**(5), 267–271 (2010)
3. Svensson, E., Sjöberg, L., Olsson, S.: Information complexity-mental workload and performance in combat aircraft. Ergonomics **40**, 0139 (2010)
4. Lyu, N., Xie, L., Wu, C., Fu, Q., Deng, C.: Driver's cognitive workload and driving performance under traffic sign information exposure in complex environments: a case study of the highways in China, pp. 1–25 (2017)
5. Sarter, N.B., Woods, D.D., Billings, C.E.: "Automation Surprises", Human Factors. Cognitive Systems Engineering Laboratory The Ohio State University, pp. 1–25 (1997)
6. Bainbridget, L.: Ironies of automation, vol. 19, no. 6 (1983)
7. Parasuraman, R., Riley, V.: Humans and automation: use, misuse, disuse, abuse. Hum. Fact. **39**(2), 230–253 (1997)
8. Brand, Y., Schulte, A.: Design and evaluation of a workload-adaptive associate system for cockpit crews task-based operationalization of the mental state as precursor of adaptive assistance (2018)
9. Mund, D., Pavlidis, E., Masters, M., Schulte, A.: A Conceptual augmentation of a pilot assistant system with physiological measures existing workload-estimation through task determination (2020)
10. Vuksanović, V., Gal, V.: Heart rate variability in mental stress aloud. Med. Eng. Phys. **29**(3), 344–349 (2007)
11. Roscoe, A.H.: Heart rate as a psychophysiological measure for in-flight workload assessment. Ergonomics **36**(9), 1055–1062 (1993)

12. Mehler, B., Reimer, B., Wang, Y.: A comparison of heart rate and heart rate variability indices in distinguishing single-task driving and driving under secondary cognitive workload, pp. 590–597 (2011)
13. Sereke, F.: Research Collection: Theses (2012)
14. Cinaz, B., La Marca, R., Arnrich, B., Tröster, G.: Monitoring of mental workload levels monitoring of mental workload levels, pp. 189–193 (2010)
15. Mukherjee, S., Yadav, R., Yung, I., Zajdel, D.P., Oken, B.S.: Sensitivity to mental effort and test-retest reliability of heart rate variability measures in healthy seniors. Clin. Neurophysiol. **122**(10), 2059–2066 (2011)
16. Li, K., Rüdiger, H., Ziemssen, T.: Spectral analysis of heart rate variability: time window matters. Front. Neurol. **10**(MAY), 1–12 (2019)
17. Hart, S.G.: NASA-task load index (NASA-TLX); 20 years later. In: Proceedings of Human Factors on Ergonomics Soceity, pp. 904–908 (2006)
18. "Biopac." www.biopac.com
19. Pan, J., Tompkins, W.J.: A real-time QRS detection algorithm. IEEE Trans. Biomed. Eng. **1**(3), 230–236 (1985)
20. Tarvainen, M.P., Niskanen, J.-P., Lipponen, J.A., Ranta-Aho, P.O., Karjalainen, P.A.: Kubios HRV–heart rate variability analysis software. Comput. Methods Programs Biomed. **113**(1), 210–220 (2014)
21. Baevsky, R.M., Chernikova, A.G.: Heart rate variability analysis: physiological foundations and main methods (2017)

EEG Covariance-Based Estimation of Cooperative States in Teammates

Raphaëlle N. Roy$^{(\boxtimes)}$, Kevin J. Verdière, and Frédéric Dehais

ISAE-SUPAERO, Université de Toulouse, Toulouse, France
{raphaelle.roy,kevin.verdiere,frederic.dehais}@isae.fr

Abstract. In real life settings, human operators work in cooperation to optimize both safety and performance. The goal of this study is to assess teammates' cooperation level using cerebral measures and machine learning techniques. We designed an experimental protocol with a modified version of the NASA MATB-II that was performed in 8 five-minute blocks. Each participant was either Pilot Flying (PF) or Pilot Monitoring (PM) with specific sub-tasks to attend to. In half the blocks they were instructed to cooperate by helping the other with one of his/her subtasks. Five teams of two healthy volunteers were recruited among the students of the ISAE-SUPAERO engineering school. In addition to behavioral data, their electroencephalogram (EEG) was recorded. The cooperation level of the participants was estimated using a brain-computer interface pipeline with a classification step applied on basic connectivity features, i.e. covariance matrices computed between participants' EEG sensors. Behavioral results revealed a significant impact of cooperative instructions. Also, the implemented estimation pipeline allowed to estimate cooperative states using covariance matrices with an average accuracy of 66.6% using the signal filtered in the theta band, 64.5% for the alpha band and 65.3% for the low beta band. These preliminary estimation results are above the adjusted chance level and pave the way towards adaptive training tools based on hyperscanning for aeronautical settings.

Keywords: Cooperation · EEG · Hyperscanning · Mental state monitoring · Covariance

1 Introduction

Although mental states such as fatigue and workload are quite extensively studied in the mental state monitoring literature and in neuroergonomics, most of the time these states are assessed at the single operator level. As human operators work in cooperation to optimize safety and performance in real life settings, there is yet to develop the study of mental state monitoring on operator dyads, or teammates. This is particularly the case in aviation whereby crews are composed of a pilot flying and a pilot monitoring. The scientific field of study that answers this need for teammate mental state assessment mostly originated from

© Springer Nature Switzerland AG 2020
R. A. Sottilare and J. Schwarz (Eds.): HCII 2020, LNCS 12214, pp. 383–393, 2020.
https://doi.org/10.1007/978-3-030-50788-6_28

Social Neuroscience. When approached from the autonomous system perspective it is often called 'interpersonal physiology' or 'physiological synchrony' [1], while it is usually referred to as 'hyperscanning' when based on cerebral measures [2,3]. Cerebral measures allow for a more subtle characterization of mental states than autonomous system based measures (e.g. cardiac activity) that only permit assessing the level of arousal. Thanks to cerebral measures, mental states such as mental workload, fatigue and attentional engagement can be assessed at the single participant level [4–8], or at the team level [9,10].

Mental state monitoring can be performed through classical ergonomic tools such as questionnaires (i.e. subjective measures) and behavioral metrics (e.g. response times and accuracy - objective measures). But a new means that allows for continuous monitoring during training or working is physiological computing [11], that enables to build neuroadaptive technology, a.k.a. passive brain-computer interfaces (BCI) [12,13], that perform biocybernetic adaptation [14]. The main idea is to perform an implicit system adaptation based on neurophysiological measures on which machine learning methods are applied.

Regarding the features that can be used for mental state estimation, although Stevens and collaborators [15] developed the assessment of team's cognitive state assessment based on what they called 'neurophysiologic synchronies', they simply used metrics to assess workload at an individual level and then identify the teammates that exhibit similar workload level for instance. Indeed, one should note that hyperscanning literally means *scanning several operators* and does not necessarily mean that these operators are synchronized or even cooperating in any way. When considering mental states other than cooperation, their assessment can be performed both independently and jointly at the subject/team level (i.e. using physiological features extracted from only one teammate or the whole team). Hence, Verdière and collaborators have compared workload estimated from teammates and from the whole team using EEG spectral features [16]. Regarding cooperation, the same authors have estimated it using spectral features, with a significantly higher than chance yet low estimation accuracy (60%).

Only recently did EEG connectivity metric-based cooperation estimation raise some focus in the research community, with the work of Toppi and collaborators who first assessed cooperative states based on interbrain connectivity in an ecological setting [17]. Hence, there is still very little literature on hyperscanning for cognitive state monitoring, and what's more, the authors mostly remain at the characterization level and do not try and estimate this cooperation state using machine learning tools. Therefore, there is a need for more studies to improve cooperation assessment accuracy. Promising venues include using connectivity metrics and machine learning techniques such as the ones based on Riemannan geometry recently applied to active BCI applications [18].

To address this lack in the literature, the goal of this study is to assess teammates' cooperation level using cerebral measures extracted from the EEG signal and dedicated machine learning techniques. This is only the first step towards adaptive systems. Indeed, the ultimate goal is to develop training systems that make use of the detected mental states to enhance trainees' performance and safety, be it offline as a tool to analyze the training session, or online as a tool to feed a neuroadaptive system that would, for instance, modify the instructions and information given to the trainees.

2 Materials and Methods

Fig. 1. Experimental setup with the two teammates equipped with a 64 electrode EEG system and performing a modified version of the MATB.

2.1 Participants

Ten healthy volunteers, i.e. five teams of two participants, were recruited among the students of the ISAE-SUPAERO engineering school, Toulouse, France (5 females; 24.9 ± 3.1 age in average). All had normal or corrected-to-normal vision and audition, and no history of neurological or psychiatric disorders. The study was approved by the local ethic committee (IRB number: IRB00011835-2019-05-28-129) and all participants gave their informed written consent.

2.2 Experimental Protocol

An experimental protocol based on a modified version of the Multi-Attribute Task Battery (MATBII) was implemented. The MATBII was initially developed by NASA [19], and its original version is freely available on the NASA website [20]. It is composed of 4 sub-tasks:

- SYSMON sub-task: a system/alarm monitoring task that requires the participants to respond as quickly as possible to lights and scale fluctuations via keystrokes (F1 to F6);

- TRACK sub-task: a tracking task that requires the participants to keep a circle as close to the center as possible using a joystick;

- RESMAN sub-task: a fuel/resource management task that required them to keep tanks' levels as close to 2500 as possible via managing 8 pumps with the keyboard or the mouse;

- COMM sub-task: a communication task that requires them to only answer broadcast messages that correspond to their call name by indicating the heard radio and number.

The task was modified to allow for implementing a cockpit-like task allocation with the "pilot flying" on the left side in charge of the 2 upper tasks namely the SYSMON and TRACK tasks, and the "pilot monitoring" on the right side in charge of the two lower tasks namely the RESMAN and COMM tasks. The task difficulty for the pilot flying and pilot monitoring were modulated independently by changing the difficulty of the TRACK and RESMAN tasks. The number of alarms (SYSMON) and communications (COMM) during each scenario remained the same. Two levels of difficulty were implemented: EASY and HARD. As the difficulty of the task was modulated independently for each teammate, it gave rise to 4 different difficulty conditions: EASY-EASY, EASY-HARD, HARD-EASY and HARD-HARD.

Moreover, in order to induce cooperation between the teammates, they had to cross-monitor their partner's one of their partners' sub-tasks in half the experimental blocks (COOP condition; the SYSMON and the RESMAN sub-tasks) in order to improve the team's overall performance. In the other half of the experimental blocks they did not have to perform this cross-monitoring, they just had to perform their own sub-tasks. These blocks correspond to the control condition, i.e. the DONTCOOP condition. Also, a dependency between the TRACK and RESMAN tasks was implemented in all scenarios in order to make the two participants' environment dependent and therefore more realistic [21].

This MATB task was performed in 8 five-minute blocks (i.e. 4 difficulty configurations * 2 cooperation v. no cooperation conditions), each presented once in a random order. The participants were randomly attributed one role: either pilot flying or pilot monitoring. Upon arrival, they were seated approximately one meter from each other, as in a cockpit, in front of duplicated screens. After having given their consent and been seated they performed a short tutorial to learn how to perform each sub-task separately. Next, before performing the 8 scenarios they trained during four 2.5 min sessions of the control condition (i.e. DONTCOOP).

2.3   Data Acquisition

Both behavioral and physiological objective data were recorded from the participants. Regarding their behavioral data, their performance to the MATB task was rated out of 400 for each scenario (100 per sub-task) as computed in the following manner:

- SYSMON score: average response time, 0 for 7 s and 100 for 0.5 s;
- TRACK score: average distance from the center, 0 for the border and 100 the center;
- RESMAN score: average distance from 2500 units, 0 for 1000 and 100 for 0;
- COMM score: number of good answers: 10 for 100 and 0 for 0.

In addition to this performance index, cooperation was evaluated via participants' keystrokes. The pilot flying was considered to be cooperating when he/she helped the pilot monitoring by modulating the activity in the RESMAN task i.e. activating or deactivating a pump (by pressing a number from 1 to 8). As for the pilot monitoring, he/she was considered to be cooperating when he/she responded to alarms of the SYSMON task (i.e. pressing a number from F1 to F6 when needed). Then, a percentage that represents the number of keystrokes performed by the helper over the total number of keystrokes per sub-task was computed.

Also, another objective measure was the electroencephalogram (EEG) of the participants. It was recorded at 256 Hz with two BioSemi ActiveTwo EEG systems composed of 64 Ag/AgCl active electrodes positioned according to the 10–20 system (see setup on Fig. 1).

2.4   Cooperation Estimation Pipeline

The cooperation level of the participants was estimated in an intra-subject manner and independently from the workload (i.e. across difficulty configurations) using a traditional passive brain-computer interface pipeline that includes a preprocessing step, a feature extraction step and a classification step [22]. Each stage is detailed in Fig. 2 and in the following:

- **Preprocessing:** The preprocessing step was composed of an epoching step for extracting 2 s windows, then a downsampling to reduce the number of samples by going down to 256 Hz, and lastly a denoising step using the Artifact Subspace Reconstruction (ASR) technique [23].

- **Feature extraction:** Then, the feature extraction step mostly consisted in filtering the signal in 3 bands: theta (4 8 Hz), alpha (8 12 Hz) and low beta (12 16 Hz) using a FIR (Finite Impulse Response) filter of order 150, and computing the covariance matrices for each of this band, each epoch and each couple between all available EEG sensors. Only 12 electrodes per participant were kept to reduce the dimension of the matrices: Fp1, Fp2, Fz, C3, C4, Cz, T7, T8, P3, P4, Pz and Oz. Hence, the covariances matrices were of 24 by 24 dimension.

- **Mental State Estimation:** Lastly, the mental state estimation step consisted in first projecting the matrices onto the Riemannian tangent space and then applying a classifier on this projected data, a Linear Discriminant Analysis (LDA), following the work of Barachant and collaborators [18] who

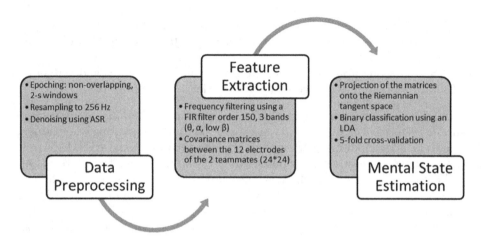

Fig. 2. Cooperation state estimation pipeline. ASR: Artifact Subspace Reconstruction; FIR filter: Finite Impulse Response filter; LDA: Linear Discriminant Analysis.

worked on active BCI applications, and using their publicly available code [24]. In order to determine the accuracy of this mental state estimation, a 5-fold cross-validation procedure was used, and the chance level was adjusted following the recommendations of Combrisson and Jerbi [25].

3   Results

Behavioral results revealed a significant impact of cooperative instructions and difficulty levels. There was a significant impact of the difficulty configuration on the performance index (i.e. score summed over the four sub-tasks; $F(3, 12) = 3.51$, partial $\eta^2 = 0.47$, $p < 0.05$). Indeed, the overall score decreased almost linearly from the BOTH EASY condition to the BOTH HARD one (linear polynomial $p = 0.08$, quadratic and cubic ones n.s.; Fig. 3). Also, there was a trend for an impact of the cooperative condition on the performance index ($F(3, 12) = 0.23$, partial $\eta^2 = 0.06$, $p = 0.08$) with a lower performance in the cooperate condition than in the don't cooperate one (Fig. 3).

As regards cross-monitoring, when analyzing the percentage of helping actions (cross-clicks) in the cooperative conditions, it can be seen that both teammates helped more their partner in their EASY condition than in their HARD one, although the effect of the difficulty configuration was not significant (Fig. 4).

As for the mental state estimation results, the implemented estimation pipeline allowed to estimate cooperative states using covariance metrics with an average accuracy of 66.55% using the signal filtered in the theta band, 64.52%

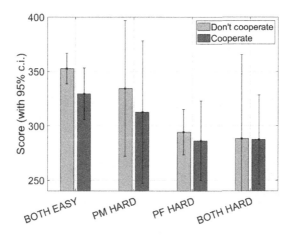

Fig. 3. Team performance over the whole MATB task depending on the cooperative and the difficulty conditions. Bars indicate 95% confidence interval.

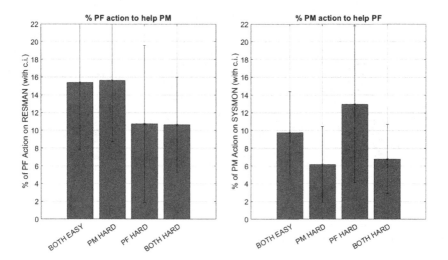

Fig. 4. Cross-monitoring during the cooperative scenarios depending on the task difficulty configuration and the participant's role. Bars indicate 95% confidence interval.

for the alpha band and 65.34% for the low beta band (Figs. 5 and 6). These estimations are above the adjusted chance level and are higher than those obtained by Verdière and collaborators using the power in these frequency bands [16].

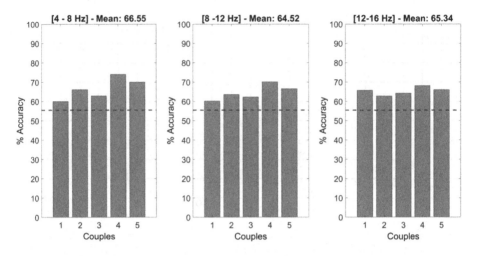

Fig. 5. Cooperation classification results based on covariance matrices extracted for each of the three following frequency band: theta (4–8 Hz), alpha (8–12 Hz) and low beta (12–16 Hz) for each of the 5 considered dyads. In red: adjusted chance level.

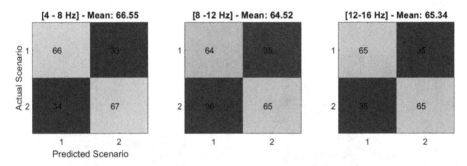

Fig. 6. Confusion matrices for the cooperation estimation results, per frequency band: theta (4–8 Hz), alpha (8–12 Hz) and low beta (12–16 Hz). Scenario 1 corresponds to the non cooperative one, and 2 to the cooperative one.

4   Discussion and Conclusion

The goal of this study was to evaluate the feasibility of assessing teammates' cooperation level using cerebral measures extracted from the EEG signal. The participants had to perform the MATB task originally developed by NASA [20] but modified so as to allow for task allocation between teammates to create the roles of pilot flying and pilot monitoring, as well as to allow for cross-monitoring in specific blocks and disable it in others. Hence, the teammates where instructed to cooperate with their partner in half the experimental blocks, and not to cooperate in the other half. As expected, the cooperative instructions as well as the level of difficulty of the task impacted their behavioral performance, thus validating the protocol.

Moreover, thanks to a processing pipeline based on that developed by Barachant and collaborators for active BCI applications [18], the cooperative and non cooperative conditions were estimated using EEG covariance matrices with an accuracy above the adjusted chance level. The best performance reached 66.6% using the signal filtered in the theta band. These results are above the ones obtained in the study of Verdière and collaborators [16] that only reached 60% at the highest, using the EEG power of the theta, alpha and low beta bands and a shrinkage LDA. Although state-of-the-art, these results have yet to be improved for instance by applying electrode selection algorithms before the classification step, and by using several additional physiological activities such as cardiac and ocular ones. Also, a higher number of participants has to be considered to evaluate the performance of such a mental state estimation pipeline more thoroughly. A limit to this study is also the notion of cooperation as measured in these tasks. Indeed, one could rather consider that what is measured is more akin to a higher workload level due to the multitasking that results from helping one's partner with an additional task. Yet it seems unclear whether one could cooperate without increasing one's workload.

Nevertheless, these preliminary results are quite promising and they pave the way towards adaptive training tools based on hyperscanning. Hence, interfaces/tasks that take into account the whole team's mental states, such as workload, fatigue or cooperation, could enhance their training and subsequent task performance. These systems could be used in an offline manner, that is to say that they would allow for analyzing the training session and give recommendations for the next session or the actual task performance. They could also be used in an online manner by implementing an adaptive interface. Such neuroadaptive technology has been recently investigated in the educational domain for instance for adapting instructional material for arithmetic learning [26]. To our knowledge, however, this technology has not yet been developed for teamwork. Given that EEG features can be used to assess teams' cooperation level, adaptive interfaces that are modified accordingly could either promote higher levels of cooperation or lower ones with the goal to enhance teamwork performance and safety.

References

1. Palumbo, R.V., et al.: Interpersonal autonomic physiology: a systematic review of the literature. Pers. Soc. Psychol. Rev. **21**(2), 99–141 (2017)
2. Montague, P.R., et al.: Hyperscanning: simultaneous fMRI during linked social interactions. NeuroImage **16**, 1159–1164 (2002)
3. Babiloni, F., Astolfi, L.: Social neuroscience and hyperscanning techniques: past, present and future. Neurosci. Biobehav. Rev. **44**, 76–93 (2014)
4. Brouwer, A.M., Hogervorst, M.A., Van Erp, J.B., Heffelaar, T., Zimmerman, P.H., Oostenveld, R.: Estimating workload using EEG spectral power and ERPs in the n-back task. J. Neural Eng. **9**(4), 045008 (2012)
5. Roy, R.N., Charbonnier, S., Bonnet, S.: Detection of mental fatigue using an active BCI inspired signal processing chain. IFAC Proc. Volumes **47**(3), 2963–2968 (2014)

6. Roy, R.N., Charbonnier, S., Campagne, A., Bonnet, S.: Efficient mental workload estimation using task-independent EEG features. J. Neural Eng. **13**(2), 026019 (2016)

7. Charbonnier, S., Roy, R.N., Bonnet, S., Campagne, A.: EEG index for control operators' mental fatigue monitoring using interactions between brain regions. Expert Syst. Appl. **52**, 91–98 (2016)

8. Dehais, F., Roy, R.N., Scannella, S.: Inattentional deafness to auditory alarms: inter-individual differences, electrophysiological signature and single trial classification. Behav. Brain Res. **360**, 51–59 (2019)

9. Stevens, R.H., Galloway, T.L., Willemsen-Dunlap, A.: Neuroergonomics: quantitative modeling of individual, shared, and team neurodynamic information. Hum. Fact. **60**(7), 1022–1034 (2018)

10. Stevens, R.H., Galloway, T., Berka, C., Behneman, A.: A neurophysiologic approach for studying team cognition. In: Interservice/Industry Training Simulation and Education Conference (I/ITSEC), paper no. 10135 (2010)

11. Fairclough, S.H.: Fundamentals of physiological computing. Interact. Comput. **21**(1–2), 133–145 (2009)

12. Zander, T.O., Kothe, C., Jatzev, S., Gaertner, M.: Enhancing human-computer interaction with input from active and passive brain-computer interfaces. In: Tan, D., Nijholt, A. (eds.) Brain-Computer Interfaces, pp. 181–199. Springer, London (2010). https://doi.org/10.1007/978-1-84996-272-8_11

13. George, L., Lécuyer, A.: An overview of research on "passive" brain-computer interfaces for implicit human-computer interaction. In: International Conference on Applied Bionics and Biomechanics - Workshop W1 Brain-Computer Interfacing and Virtual Reality (2010)

14. Stephens, C., et al.: Biocybernetic adaptation strategies: machine awareness of human engagement for improved operational performance. In: Schmorrow, D.D., Fidopiastis, C.M. (eds.) AC 2018. LNCS (LNAI), vol. 10915, pp. 89–98. Springer, Cham (2018). https://doi.org/10.1007/978-3-319-91470-1_9

15. Stevens, R.H., Galloway, T., Berka, C., Sprang, M.: Can neurophysiologic synchronies provide a platform for adapting team performance? In: Schmorrow, D.D., Estabrooke, I.V., Grootjen, M. (eds.) FAC 2009. LNCS (LNAI), vol. 5638, pp. 658–667. Springer, Heidelberg (2009). https://doi.org/10.1007/978-3-642-02812-0_75

16. Verdiére, K.J., Dehais, F., Roy, R.N.: Spectral EEG-based classification for operator dyads' workload and cooperation level estimation. In: IEEE, Systems, Man and Cybernetics Conference, pp. 3919–3924 (2019)

17. Toppi, J., et al.: Investigating cooperative behavior in ecological settings: an EEG hyperscanning study. In: PloS one **11**(4), e0154236 (2016)

18. Barachant, A., Bonnet, S., Congedo, M., Jutten, C.: Multiclass brain-computer interface classification by Riemannian geometry. IEEE Trans. Biomed. Eng. **59**(4), 920–928 (2011)

19. Santiago-Espada, Y., Myer, R.R., Latorella, K. A., Comstock Jr., J. R.: The multi-attribute task battery II (MATB-II) software for human performance and workload research: a user's guide (2011)

20. NASA: MATB-II: Revised multi-attribute task battery (2019). https://matb.larc.nasa.gov/

21. Liu, T., Pelowski, M.: Clarifying the interaction types in two-person neuroscience research. Front. Hum. Neurosci. **8**, 276 (2014)

22. Lotte, F., Roy, R.N.: Brain–computer interface contributions to neuroergonomics. In: Neuroergonomics, pp. 43–48. Academic Press (2019)

23. Mullen, T., et al.: Real-time modeling and 3D visualization of source dynamics and connectivity using wearable EEG. In: 35th Annual International Conference of the IEEE Engineering in Medicine and Biology Society (EMBC), pp. 2184–2187 (2013)
24. Barachant, A.: Covariance toolbox (2013). https://github.com/alexandrebaracha nt/covariancetoolbox
25. Combrisson, E., Jerbi, K.: Exceeding chance level by chance: the caveat of theoretical chance levels in brain signal classification and statistical assessment of decoding accuracy. J. Neurosci. Methods **250**, 126–136 (2015)
26. Gerjets, P., Walter, C., Rosenstiel, W., Bogdan, M., Zander, T.O.: Cognitive state monitoring and the design of adaptive instruction in digital environments: lessons learned from cognitive workload assessment using a passive brain-computer interface approach. Front. Neurosci. **8**, 385 (2014)

Adapting the Zone of Proximal Development to the Wicked Environments of Professional Practice

Jordan Richard Schoenherr[1,2](✉)

[1] Department of Psychology, Institute for Data Science, Carleton University,
Ottawa, Canada
`jordan.schoenherr@carleton.ca`
[2] Army Cyber Institute, Behavioral Science and Leadership Department, US
Military Academy, West Point, USA

Abstract. Many real-world questions that professionals face occur in complex, dynamic environments where information is often sparse, e.g., clinical decision-making, cyber security, stock market prediction. In many cases, problems are open-ended without a single or optimal solution. Providing effective training in these ill-defined environments presents an important challenge for educators. Using the healthcare professions as a case study, this chapter outlines a framework for knowledge acquisition in the professions. It argues that dynamic, adaptive criteria must be identified based on educational theory, psychometric techniques, and properties of expert performance. From this approach, educators must develop assessment criteria that satisfice, framing problems in terms of an order of difficulty relative to the learner's current level of comprehension. This reflects a quantitative approach to the zone-of-proximal development (ZPD), that removes the upper-bound for knowledge acquisition. In health professions education, this approach can be used to create a competency profile. Finally, given that professional practices often focus on the efficient use of resources, I argue that measures of the speed-accuracy trade-off should be used to assess expert performance.

Keywords: Adaptive instructional system · Zone of proximal development · Wicked environments · Squishy problems

1 Introduction

"[there are] two kinds of things the nature of which it would be quite wonderful to grasp by means of a systematic art...

the first consists in seeing together things that are scattered about everywhere and collecting them into one kind, so that by defining each thing we can make clear the subject of any instruction we wish to give...
[the second], in turn, is to be able to cut up each kind according to its species along its natural joints, and to try not to splinter any part..."

-Plato, *Phaedo*

© Springer Nature Switzerland AG 2020
R. A. Sottilare and J. Schwarz (Eds.): HCII 2020, LNCS 12214, pp. 394–410, 2020.
https://doi.org/10.1007/978-3-030-50788-6_29

As our scientific knowledge, technological and social environments expand, the task of an educator becomes increasingly complex. Many real-world questions that professionals face are often ill-defined, reflecting limited knowledge of complex environments, e.g., clinical decision-making, stock market prediction, cyber security, risk assessment. Initially, all environments present learners with a "blooming, buzzing confusion." With the acquisition of knowledge and skills, learners can navigate their environment more effectively. In the case of professional practice where practitioners are presented with novel multifactorial or multidimensional problems, even the most advanced knowledge in a field might be insufficient to provide optimal solutions. Consequently, typical instruction methods might be inadequate in the development of these competencies beyond early stages of training. Moreover, professionals often have limited resources to engage in educational practices. Developing adaptive instructional systems (AIS) to address these needs provides one such solution.

In what follows, I outline a theoretical framework for knowledge acquisitions in professional practice that can be implemented in an AIS. First, features of education in the healthcare professions are defined to illustrate shifts from passive, time-based approaches in education to an active, competency-based approach which identifies and monitors development of specific knowledge and skills. Second, professional education is considered in terms of 'squishy problems' that are nonreductive and open-ended and 'wicked environments' that reflect the complex, dynamical nature of professional practice.

In order to accommodate the demands of learning responses to these problems, an approach based on satisficing is developed. It assumes that the concept of the zone of proximal development (ZPD; [1, 2]) can be operationalized for use in AIS [3, 4]. Extending this idea, the ZPD can then be used to create a competency profile for each learner. In that expert performance is defined by both fast and accurate responses to problems, an efficiency criterion is described that considers the relative balance between speed and accuracy, [5] i.e., the Speed-Accuracy Trade-off (SAT; [6]). Given the demands of learning in complex environments of professional practice and the requirements of computing SAT, the potential for an AIS in healthcare professions education is discussed.

2   Professional Education: Learning in Wicked Environments

Regardless of the knowledge domain, professions have a number of consistent social and cognitive features. At a social level, professions represent groups with high levels of social cohesion and a system of norms and conventions [7, 8]. Monitoring and regulations mechanisms are typically developed to ensure that professionals conform to ethical norms, as well as standards of declarative and procedural knowledge, i.e., expertise [9]. As the number of professionals within a group increases, the greater the demands will be for regulatory mechanisms in order to ensure that any given member of a profession meets the standards of practice. For instance, the healthcare professions in North America have a number of organizations along these lines (the Royal College of Physicians and Surgeons Canada (RCPSC) and the Accreditation Council for Graduate Medical Education in the United States) which have parallels and precedence elsewhere (e.g., Royal College of Physicians and Royal College of Surgeons in England in the United Kingdom). Rather than assuming that candidates will acquire knowledge over time (i.e., a time-based model of education) or merely through close interaction with other group members (i.e., an apprenticeship model), contemporary approaches to education in the healthcare professions have considered specific competencies that practitioners should have to navigate their physical and social environments [10]. For instance, the RCPSC has identified a number of 'roles' clinicians must assume over the course of their career including communicator, collaborator, leader, health advocate, scholar, professional, and medical expert which integrates the other roles (i.e., CanMEDS; [11]).

Competency-based education frameworks assume that there are specific cognitive representations (i.e., knowledge) and procedures (e.g., skills) that professionals can be identified, assessed, and developed. In most professional domains, problems and solutions are not necessarily clearly understood even by the professionals themselves, requiring constant reexamination and redefinition, i.e., continuing professional education and development. In the healthcare professions, this persistent uncertainty is evidenced in a number of studies that have examined expert performance. For instance, in a study of diagnostic radiology, Drew et al. [12] found that 83% of experienced radiologist missed an abnormal non-pathological stimulus embedded in images they were evaluating and only 55% successfully identified a pathology. Millington et al. [13] observed similar results in their study of lung point-of-care ultrasound. Using six different diagnostic categories for pathologies, they found significant difference in the amount of agreement between experts, which varied from 21% to 60%. Moreover, despite the low diagnostic agreement, post-decisional confidence reports exceeded agreement (i.e., 72% to 82%), suggesting an overall overconfidence bias. Given the prevalence of human medical errors in the healthcare professions [14] and the reluctance of clinicians to assign low grades to learners, [15] objective assessment methods must be developed to maintain professional standards.

3 Psychometrics and Squishy Problems

How a problem is defined will affect the kinds of solutions that are offered [16]. A 'squishy' problem is a problem that is not defined, ill-defined, or can be readily redefined. Strauch [17] initially proposed this concept as a means to discuss the inherently problematic nature of applying quantitative methods within certain domains. When attempting to understand a problem, an individual develops a mental model of the domain. Mental models consist of relevant features, their associations, functions, and structure [18]. For simple problems, there can be a high degree of correspondence between a mental model and the state of the world. For Strauch, squishy problems are complex problems that exceed the representational capacity of simple models, which he believes, are inherently too reductive. Consequently, he claims that mathematical or rational models are 'perspective' or 'surrogate' for the substantive problem a decision-maker is faced with.

In healthcare professions education, Strauch's concerns are echoed in debates over the nature and importance of simulator 'fidelity' in training [19]. These training methods assume that educators have a target domain in which they want to develop a learner's skills (e.g., laparoscopic surgery, hip replacement, critical care medicine, neonatology, oncology). Due to both ethical and practical concerns, it is not possible to practice on live patients (i.e., the target domain). Moreover, even if a pool of live patients were available a learner cannot explore the total problem space represented by all possible factors (e.g., 'complications', interprofessional communication problems). For instance, variable training tasks have been suggested as a means to address this [20, 21]. Thus, simulation exercises reflect formal problems of a substantive domain according to Straunch's approach. However, it is equally important to note that the fidelity of a model is not important. Rather, ensuring that learners and educators share similar mental models will determine the efficacy of training [19].

3.1 Applicability of Quantitative Methods

While Strauch's discussion raises important concerns about the nature and the number of assumptions that are required to ground a complex domain into one that statistical models can be applied to, this reflects an ongoing discussion in psychometrics. In contrast to how the outputs of psychometricians are viewed outside of the discipline, they reflect ongoing challenges and debates within the disciplinary communities [22]. For this reason, assessment instruments are never 'validated', rather studies provide validity evidence that supports their use within a specific domain and context. Moreover, advances in machine learning and artificial intelligence have the potential to render formally squishy problems interpretable and explainable [23].

An alternative approach for understanding the problems faced by educators in complex domains is Hogarth's [24] notion of 'wicked environments' wherein information and environmental feedback is presented in an irregular manner. For any given period of time, a subset of variables relevant to learning and decision-making (e.g., $\alpha = \{a, b,$ and $c\}$) might be held constant. Yet, during a different interval, they might vary while other variables remain constant (e.g., $\varepsilon = \{d, e,$ and $f\}$). Thus, while a specifiable set of factors determines a correct solution over all time scales (i.e., $\omega = \{a, ..., n\}$), this might not be clear to a learner – or an educator. For instance, in the context of either epidemiology or cybersecurity, viruses might exploit new vulnerabilities in immune systems or network security, respectively. Solutions can eventually be identified; however, additional information and experience is required.

When confronted with squishy problems or wicked environments, criteria adopted in traditional approaches to learning and decision-making are likely inappropriate. As Simon [25] observed in the context of organizational decision-making, optimization criteria are neither desirable nor practical when time and information are limited. In complex domains, even if all possible factors required to make an optimal decision could be identified, the time requirements might be far too great to make a decision in practice. Yet, decisions *must* be made in these environments in timely and accurate manner.

To address the needs of decision-making in complex environments, Simon suggest that we adopt *satisficing* criteria–using solutions that are satisfactory given the resource limitations e.g., time, knowledge, money. By identifying a subset of features that result in acceptable outcomes, decisions can be made in information and time-limited environments. Models of decision-making provide support for the comparative efficiency of satisficing when compared to optimization algorithms [26, 27]. Education and training programs in the professions must adopt similar approaches [28]. Rather than approaching professional education in a haphazard manner, theoretically informed assessment criteria must be developed to accommodate learning in these environments.

4   Learning in the Zone of Proximal Development

In contrast, to the assumption that cognitive development represents an automatic, inviolable sequence (stage-based theory; [29, 30]), Vygotsky [1, 2] suggested that the social environment, and language in particular, provided a means to acquire knowledge. Instructors provide a social scaffolding[1] to aid in the development of a higher level of performance in learners. This approach assumes that new knowledge and skills vary in their proximity relative to the learner's current abilities. Vygotsky [1, 2] assumed that instructional methods would then aid in the development of associations between a learner's current knowledge and new information that is closely associated with existing knowledge, i.e., within a zone of proximal development (ZPD). This idea gains support from studies that suggest that prior knowledge appears to be the best predictor of subsequent learning [31–33].

Suggestions for an Adaptive ZPD. Despite the frequent reference to Vygotsky's concept, quantifiable operationalization of the ZPD has not been seriously considered. Those that have attempted to develop the concept in the context of AIS have generally offered theoretical extensions. For instance, educators have focused on the socially-mediated nature of learning [34, 35]. In this tradition, Chaiklin [36] has emphasized the importance of social dynamics of the learning environment and selection of appropriate instructional interventions. Luckin and du Boulay [37–39] sought to further specify the ZPD in social-cognitive terms. They assumed that the resources available to the learner within the instructional environment need to be accounted for, thereby creating a Zone of Available Assistance (ZAA). Of these resources, a subset will be congruent with a learner's needs, reflecting a Zone of Proximal Adjustment (ZPA; i.e., ZPA $\in$ ZAA). Presumably, both of these measures are quantifiable with additional assumptions concerning what constitutes a resource.

In order to adapt the ZPD to AIS, criteria are required to quantify learner performance. A few attempts are noteworthy [3, 4]. For instance, Murray and Arroyo [4] provide a simple computation implementation of the ZPD for intelligent tutoring systems (ITS). In light of the social context of learning, Murray and Arroyo assume that a specific ZPD (SZPD) can be understood in terms of the number of hints that are required to assist the learner is acquiring new information. The SZPD is defined by

---

[1] Vygotsky did not use this term himself.

three parameters: H, the desired number of hints required to complete each problem set; ΔH, the variation that defines the ZPD; and, P, the minimum number of problems the student will see during a training phase. The SZPD is given by H ± ΔH. From this they derived a measure of a learner's performance, Z, as: $Z = H^* - H$. Where H^* reflects the number of hints that a training system provided to a learner. With Z specified, they note that zones of confusion (Z > ΔH) and boredom (Z < ΔH) can be defined. However, they note that "[i]t is left to the instructional designer to specify the default SZPD parameters for a particular system, and how the system will respond to the learner being in the bored or confused zone." (p. 4).

The attempt to create quantitative measure of a ZPD is both a useful and necessary step to advance educational theory and practice. However, in the case of Murray and Arroyo [4], the SZPD is still somewhat unclear. For instance, the nature of what constitute an effective 'hint' is left to the instructor, it is not defined in terms of the objective properties of the task. Hints themselves might not be clearly defined. For instance, in the case of a simple mathematical problem (e.g., $y = mx + b$), a hint in terms of the order of operations might be clearly specified (e.g., 'BEDMAS' or 'PEDMAS' would remind the learner to multiply first). In other domains, this is not as clear. For instance, experts tend to classify problems in terms of the kinds of causal forces used (e.g., resistance, gravity), whereas novice focus on surface similarity (e.g., both questions involve a pendulum; [40]). Similarly, studies of analogical reasoning also suggest that what constitutes a hint depends on prior knowledge that is culturally-situated [41] and domain similarity [42]. Thus, the nature of hints might be organized hierarchically in terms of classification structure used in an expert domain or heter-archically in terms of multiple classification structures. To that end, determining the desired number of hints (H), is underspecified. In fact, Murray and Arroyo suggest that the parameters should be empirically determined. Consequently, this approach appears to present a somewhat circular method to understanding learning.

Normalized ZPD for Dynamic Assessment. While a ZPD should be operationalized and empirical derived as Murray and Arroyo have suggested, a measure of ZPD should be embedded firmly within measurement and information theory. In contrast to the underspecified notion of a 'hint', learner's knowledge should simply be examined in terms of their performance. What reflects a strong hint (or, response cue), can be identified based on performance, i.e., the greater the increase in performance, the better the 'hint'. Thus, these cues can be located *in* a ZPD and reflect a learner's knowledge, rather than simply being used to facilitate knowledge acquisition. Moreover, cues might also be associated with individual differences.

To understand this, classical test theory [43, 44] assumes that the object of assessment is a hypothetical "true score" (T), i.e., what the learner actually knows. In contrast, the observed score (O) is based on the responses that a learner provides but deviates from the true score. A major source of discrepancy between the true score and the observed score is error (e). In addition to unsystematic error, later formulations of measurement theory assume that bias (β) reflects systematic response biases of the learner. Thus, the general relationship between O and T is given by the equation:

$$O = T + (e + \beta)$$

In the context of AIS or any other assessment method, we require a reliable assessment of a learner's knowledge (T) within a domain but must use the learner's actual performance (O) as a substitute. In this context, the kinds of social factors considered in the Vygotskian approach would be reflected in the bias score component, β. Namely, learners might use study, recall, or response strategies (e.g., regulatory focus) that will be congruent or incongruent depending on specific environment cues and teaching strategies. In this case, 'hints' as described by Murray and Arroyo [4] would be reflected in this bias if they are associated with a specific response strategy.

In order to gain a closer approximation to T, repeated testing is used. For the accuracy of responses to any given set of questions, a learner's responses can be described by a normal distribution with mean, $\bar{x}$, and a standard deviation, σ. Depending on assumptions about competency, a ZPD can be represented by $\sigma = 1$, i.e., performance that is one standard deviation away from the average level of performance[2]. Thus, even if multiple learners have different levels of a given competency relative to a desired level for a population of professionals, the ZPD can be identified in each case without the need to identify what constitutes a hint. Moreover, while the Vygotskian approach emphasizes the social aspects of learning, social learning only requires that the educator and learner attempt to understand each other's mental models (the operationalization of this process is described below).

Complementing the measurement theory approach, the ZPD can also be understood in terms of Information Theory. For instance, Shannon's [45] definition of information focus on the reduction of uncertainty. In this way, the ZPD can be defined as new knowledge or skills that reduces a learner's uncertainty in their performance within a given environment. If information (i) provided by an instructor to the learner is too advanced for the learner ($i > \sigma$) they will have a low-probability of acquiring this new information. The further the new information is away from the current state of a learner's knowledge (e.g., $i \gg \sigma$), the less likely a learner will acquire it in that it is outside the ZPD. Conversely, if the information provided from the instructor is not new ($i < \bar{x}$), the learner will not acquire new information. While information is under-specified in Shannon's theory, in terms of cognitive theory, it can be understood as *distinctive*, i.e., a feature is novel relative to the exemplars stored in memory [46]. For instance, in Millington et al.'s [13] study of lung ultrasound, despite the inherent difficulty of the task, performance can be normalized relative to mean expert performance in each diagnostic category, with learners receiving a score relative to this criterion. Thus, Murray and Arroyo's [4] zone of confusion and boredom, merely reflect regions that significantly deviate from $\bar{x}$.

4.1 Adapting the ZPD to Complex Learning Domains

Identifying a quantitative variant of the ZPD represents the first step in developing a framework for professional education and training programs using AIS [4]. In that the

---

[2] In terms of σ, the value is likely bound within a range, i.e., it should be outside a learner's skill level. The value 1 is used here for convenience.

learning objectives of these programs are to develop and extend expertise, a consideration of expert knowledge and skills is required before considering how an AIS can assist in expert performance development.

The Focus of Expertise. Measuring expert performance has been a persistent focus of research [47]. The development of expertise in the healthcare professions provides a useful model for understanding education and training in wicked environments more generally. For instance, professional education is believed to consist of the identification of milestones, the development of assessment instruments to accurate identify a learner's current level of performance, and the provision of instructional interventions to develop a learner's competencies.

Healthcare professionals acquire knowledge [48, 49] in a manner that is consistent with expertise more generally [50]. For instance, studies of category learner have observed that, over time, attention shifts from the total set of features presented in an array to a subset of diagnostic features [51]. Similar results have been observed in medical expertise development with comparatively inexperienced medical students requiring more time to examine a display in order to produce a diagnosis relative to clinicians with greater levels of expertise. [52, 53] Similar observations can be made at a procedural level. For instance, Klein [54] has noted that expert decision-making is defined by decision points, i.e., location in a decision-making process that provide experts with alternative responses. In studies of surgical decision-making, Moulton et al. [55, 56] has noted that experienced experts can identify times in a procedure when they should 'stop and think'. Thus, the ZPD for expertise development represents the fast and accurate identification of diagnostic features and social dynamics, decision points within a procedure, and response selection.

By keeping the definition of ZPD relatively simple, multidimensional representations of a learner's abilities can be readily obtained. For instance, the RCPSC framework for physician competencies (CanMEDS) requires that clinicians have competencies in performing seven specific roles, i.e., professional, communicator, scholar, collaborator, health advocate, leader, and the integrative role of medical expert. Once a representative sample of assessments has been performed, a competency profile for a learner can be created for their expected performance relative to specific milestones. Figure 1 provides a polar plot wherein performance has been normalized with an upper bound of 1. Learner's that fall below a given level can be identified and educational interventions can be provided for remediation that fall within the ZPD for a specific skill. More specific skills can also be represented in this manner. For instance, competencies within an area of specialization such as clinical ultrasound can be decomposed into knowledge and skills such as attentional capacity, visuospatial reasoning ability, and declarative knowledge of relevant physiology, anatomy, and pathologies. Each of these can be represented quantitatively based on individual assessment instruments [22].

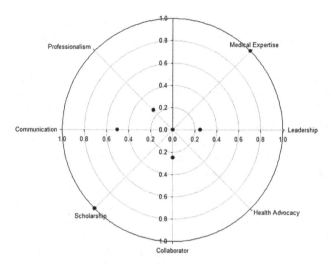

Fig. 1. Hypothetical competency profile based on the RCPSC CanMEDS roles. Each competency is represented in on axis without regard for orthogonality of the underlying assessment dimensions.

Instruction as Joint Attention Process. At the core of the Vygotskian approach is the requirement of the social construction of knowledge. In that an AIS can be considered a partner, replacing a human educator in a dyad, elements of the social learning process can be preserved. For instance, in the context of simulation training, Schoenherr and Hamstra [19] have conceptualized learning as a joint attentional process wherein instruction is focused on shifting a learner's attention to the relevant affordances of the professional environment, e.g., diagnostic features of a pathology, vulnerabilities in interprofessional communication. Namely, in an environment defined by n features, a learner's attention is focused on one set of feature (e.g., α, where $\alpha \leq \omega$, and $\alpha \in \omega$) whereas an instructor's attention is focused on another set of features (e.g., ε, where $\varepsilon \leq n$ and $\varepsilon \in \omega$). If an instructor observes overt behaviour that they construe as suggesting that the affordance that they observe are not the focus of a learner's attention ($\alpha \neq \varepsilon$), they can identify the discrepancies ($\alpha \Delta \varepsilon$), and can then attempt to engage in a joint attentional process to shift learners attention to the relevant features until their mental models shared the same features (i.e., $\alpha = \varepsilon$).

In that joint attention requires monitoring on the part of the educator and learner, the ZPD reflects the extension of which the learner has allocated their attention to the appropriate features. For instance, the relative discrepancy between expert and learner eye gaze [52] would suggest the extent to which learners have identified the appropriate diagnostic features. The extent to which learners can discriminate diagnostic from nondiagnostic features (e.g., location, colour, morphology) or the relevant decision points in an operative procedure, can then be used to identify the ZPD: inaccurate responses can be further categorized based on what kinds of unsystematic (i.e., random response selection) and systematic errors are observed.

The Role for AIS in Competency Assessment. At least for the foreseeable future, AIS will not have the ability to understand intentionality, i.e., what the learner believes (for attempts to achieve this with an ITS, see [57–60]. Like a joint attentional process, the correct and incorrect responses produced by learners can be used by an AIS to gain a better understanding of whether 1) learners have identified the diagnostic features, 2) whether their errors reflect systematic responses, and 3) if the errors are systematic, the learner's mental model of the problem space. For instance, ITS have been used to monitor the mental states of learners during highly constrained tasks, e.g. mathematics. [61]. Using a computer-interface, these systems provide learners with instruction, provide assistants when requested by the learner, and flag errors during problem-solving. However, other methods have been considered such as using fMRI to monitor and predict the stage of problem-solving [62]. In line with the notion of joint attention, researchers have examined gaze patterns during learning [63]. In a study by Belenky et al. [64], an ITS was used to facilitate collaboration between students. They found that high-scoring pairs of students were more likely to look at the same regions of a display presenting a problem than low-scoring pairs of students. Thus, by incorporating eye gazing patterns and response selection, AIS can develop mental models of learners' knowledge. Indeed, gaze patterns defined expert performance [51, 52].

At the simplest level of implementation, an AIS can use similarity-based metrics of errors to determine the relative proximity of a learner's performance, thereby identifying distance from correct response ($\sigma = 0$) or whether it is within ($1 > \sigma > 0$) or outside the learner's ZPD ($1 \gg \sigma$). Consequently, provided features of a problem are classified in terms of their similarity to diagnostic features, they can be used to better adapt to a learner's current level of knowledge. If response alternatives have been developed to include elements of the correct response, error commission can additionally be assessed to determine the nature and extent of the deviation from the correct response. When available, eye-tracking data can be used to supplement this response with the additional possibility of providing learners with preemptive feedback prior to response selection.

At a more complex level of implementation, with a sufficiently large sample of questions from a problem space, feature associations can be derived from learner responses. In a comparable manner to multidimensional scaling, learner's location in a problem space can also be identified. Importantly, depending on the complexity of the task, an AIS might be better suited to measuring the multidimensional nature of the problem space than a human instructor. While multidimensional category structures can be learned by humans, [65] representations of this knowledge tend to be inaccessible to experts. Consequently, an AIS can provide a more transparent means to assess a learner's mental model of normal health, pathologies, and clinical situations that healthcare professionals will encounter. Thus, the task of assessing the competencies necessary for professional practice does not necessarily reflect a squishy problem. Methods such as AIS might be more effective at training learners to engage in decision-making in wicked environments.

4.2   Efficiency and Speed-Accuracy Tradeoffs: An Alternative Metric for Expertise Assessment

The potential for AIS enhancing professional development and education is not limited to monitoring sets of stimulus association. Other multi-criterion assessment strategies should be considered. While expertise requires accurately identifying responses to a class of stimuli and situations, it is also associated with faster responses. Consequently, the extent to which leaners can both rapidly and accurately activate knowledge can be used to assess learner competency [5].

Efficiency in Professional Practice. When both decision time and accuracy are considered in the context of clinical decision-making, the discussion tends be associated with 'efficiency'. Discussions of efficiency in healthcare delivery focus on high-level procedures for the allocation of resources and treatment [66]. In the context of decision-making in the healthcare professions, efficiency is frequently invoked as a desirable criterion but left underspecified. For instance, in a study by Braddock et al. [67] they sought to identify "informed decision-making that were highly effective yet reasonably time-efficient" (p. 1831). Mauksch et al. [68] defined efficiency as "making the best use of available time" (p. 1388). Efficiency is also used to refer to features of an education program such as the number of learners that can be trained, i.e., doubling the number of learners in the same training session; Wulf et al. [69]. Thus, efficiency must be operationalized in order to be used as an assessment of evaluation criterion.

Speed-Accuracy Trade-Off. A straightforward means to operationalize efficiency in learner assessment is to consider the trade-off between the speed of a learner's response and their response accuracy, referred to as the Speed-Accuracy Trade-Off (SAT; [6]). An SAT is evidenced when a learner's speed is inversely related to their accuracy: the faster a learner responds, the greater the reduction in the accuracy of their decisions. In a critical care environment, a clinician must consider a subset of all possible symptoms and treatment options in a rapid manner in order. The clinician's ability to respond both quickly and accurately (i.e., the clinician's SAT) will be a major determinant of a patient's survival. While in clinical settings that are defined by reduced time constraints, a speeded response might not be as critical for treatment, the nature of expertise nevertheless suggests SAT will be evidenced. Thus, approaches to adaptive learning should considered both speed and accuracy of responses [5].

While expert decisions are typically faster, they will also demonstrate a range of variability. This reflects their location along a SAT function. For instance, when attempting to treat a patient, Clinician 1 believes that she needs to stabilize the patient quickly to stop a cardiac arrest. She quickly decides to administer blood thinners. Shortly after this treatment, she realizes that she could have operated to repair the ventricles instead. She could have performed the procedure more effectively (Fig. 2, point [1]). With additional experience, Clinician 1 might understand the immediate needs to stabilize a patient and reconsider the administration of blood thinners. However, taking time to reflect on other procedures, she realizes that if she administers blood thinners, she might not be able to repair the damaged ventricles. Thus, her increased decision time resulted in high-accuracy but a slower overall response (Fig. 2,

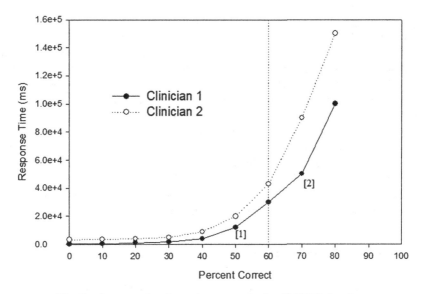

Fig. 2. An example of speed-accuracy trade-off (SAT) function.

point [2]). Taken together, the difference between [1] and [2] reflects a speed-accuracy tradeoff. However, overall response strategies are evidenced by examining SAT functions. For instance, as Fig. 2 demonstrates, Clinician 1's and Clinician 2's performance differs: despite the same level of accuracy, Clinician 1 is generally faster than Clinician 2. This suggests that while her colleague might take longer to make a decision, his judgments are no more accurate than her judgments. Equally important, the SAT functions presented in Fig. 2 suggests that a performance asymptote exists: after a certain point, additional time is not projected to assist in decision-making. Namely, performance here is no greater than correct diagnosis of 80% of cases. Consequently, if a clinician knows their SAT function in a given domain, they can make more efficient use of their time by reallocating their efforts once an upper bound has been reached. The development of such a metacognitive strategy can be facilitated by an AIS.

Slow and Fast Guessing. Crucially, adopting the SAT as an assessment criterion also introduces another means to assess learner competencies: categorizing their overall decision strategy. In other words, while SATs might be evidenced, variability within a SAT function will reflect strategies that suggest how much information will be accumulated or how long a practitioner will spend on a problem, i.e., the SAT for Clinician 1. In most cases, clinicians might not be concerned with the properties of correct decisions, they might instead be concerned with the properties of errors or what happens when they must guess.

Using the notion of SAT, Petrusic (1992) introduced Slow-and-Fast Guessing Theory (SFGT). In addition to overall SATs, Petrusic additionally assumed that learners adopt response strategies. These strategies are most readily identified by examining the mistakes produced by learners when they attempt to answer a question.

For ease of assessment, individual decision-making strategies can be classified as slow guessing and fast guessing depending on the amount of information they attempt to gather from a situation. Clinicians and other professionals likely implicitly consider these strategies throughout the course of their daily practice. This might be influenced by individual differences (e.g., regulatory focus, conscientiousness). By identifying slow and fast guessers, educators can provide more specific feedback. If errors are made due to fast guessing, providing learners with metacognitive strategies to slow their decision process will likely improve performance [55]. If errors are made due to slow guessing, this instead means that relevant knowledge was not available to the learner. In this case, the learner will likely need to be provided with more domain-specific knowledge to alter the focus of their attention not different affordances in order to improve their performance. An AIS can thus classify learners based on these overall patterns of performance to provide more effective feedback.

5   Conclusions: AIS in Professional Education

As the above review indicates, expert performance is embedded within a social learning process. Professional societies must define competencies, which must in turn be further decomposed into social, cognitive, and motor responses [21]. Competency development must be monitored in a manner that ensure that learners can acquire significant practice and that specific feedback is provided in order for them to identify and correct errors or ineffective satisficing strategies [25]. This could be as simple as emphasizing decision points [54] where learners should stop and reflect [55].

At a granular level, learners must reach specific educational milestones that are defined by a profession [8]. Given the complexity of the healthcare professions, multi-criterion assessment instruments are required. For an instructor, this approach might be too demanding, leading to the provision of low-quality feedback and reluctance to fail learners. Indeed, when developing education and assessment instruments, the context of the learning environment must also be considered in order to implement a task, i.e., implementation validity [28]. Consequently, the introduction of an AIS can provide parallel opportunities for training and education while keeping clinical educators involved in the process.

Squishy or Wicked Healthcare? Healthcare professions education is likely defined by wicked environments wherein only a limited set of factors are available to consider at any given time [24]. Learners will require years of experience solving common and uncommon problems in order to understand the affordances of clinical practice. Whether these problems are truly open-ended is less certain. Healthcare has continued to progress in a manner that repeatedly answers what initially appeared to be intractable "squishy" problems. In that many of these questions have not turned out to be open-ended, it is not clear that they reflect Strauch's [17] notion of a squishy problem.

Identifying the Zone-of-Proximal Development. Based on performance criteria and milestones, a learner's performance can be compared to others and monitored over time. With sufficient training, an average level of expected performance can be defined. Assuming that the knowledge and skill that define competencies reflect a normal distribution, inference can be made concerning the ZPD by selecting an appropriate measure and establishing how performance deviates. The use of competency profile can facilitate this assessment and comparison process. Competency profiles can be created for overall competencies or specific kinds of knowledge and skills, e.g., cardiac or thoracic ultrasound; empathy and communication skills [19]. Similarly, provided with sufficiently powerful computing technology, response selection and eye gaze information can be used to infer a learner's mental model of a problem space. More refined feedback targeting the ZPD can be provided to facilitate the identification of affordances by considering the nature and extent of the deviation from the mental model.

Facilitating Multi-criterion Assessment. A single criterion based on total scores (e.g., proportion correct) assumes that regardless of question format (e.g., true-or-false, multiple choice, short answer or essay questions) what matters most is the learner's overall score. The speed of a learner's responses is often ignored [5]. This presents a significant problem for professional education, especially in the healthcare professions. In that expert performance is defined by fast and accurate responses in critical care settings, greater consideration needs to be given to composite measures such as the speed-accuracy tradeoff. This reflects a more general concern to expert domains that often require rapid responses to problems, e.g., network security, policing and military. Simply invoking the notion of 'efficiency' is not enough without qualification and operationalization. The speed-accuracy trade-off [6] presents a straightforward means to assess expert performance. AIS can monitor both the speed and accuracy of responses of learner responses, identify SATs, and provide learners with feedback in a manner that is likely outside the resources that many educators have at their disposal.

Acknowledgments. Research was sponsored by the Army Research Laboratory and was accomplished under the Cooperative Agreement Number W911NF-19-2-0223. The views and conclusions contained in this document are those of the authors and should not be interpreted as representing the official policies, either expressed or implied, of the Army Research Laboratory or the U.S. Government. The U.S. Government is authorized to reproduce and distribute reprints for the Government purposed notwithstanding any copyright notation herein.

References

1. Vygotsky, L.S.: Mind in Society: The Development of Higher Mental Processes, pp. 1930–1934. Harvard University Press, Cambridge (1978)
2. Vygotsky, L.S.: Thought and Language. MIT Press, Cambridge 1934/1986
3. Shabani, K., Khatib, M., Ebadi, S.: Vygotsky's zone of proximal development: instructional implications and teachers' professional development. Engl. Lang. Teach. **3**, 237–248 (2010)
4. Murray, T., Arroyo, I.: Toward measuring and maintaining the zone of proximal development in adaptive instructional systems. In: Cerri, S.A., Gouardères, G., Paraguaçu, F. (eds.) ITS 2002. LNCS, vol. 2363, pp. 749–758. Springer, Heidelberg (2002). https://doi.org/10.1007/3-540-47987-2_75
5. Kellman, P.J.: Adaptive and perceptual learning technologies in medical education and training. Mil. Med. **178**, 98–106 (2013)

6. Wickelgren, W.A.: Speed-accuracy tradeoff and information processing dynamics. Acta Psychol. **41**, 67–85 (1977)
7. Andrew, A.: The System of Professions: an Essay on the Division of Expert Labour. University of Chicago Press, Chicago (1988)
8. Elliot, F.: Professionalism, The Third Logic: On the Practice of Knowledge. University of Chicago, Chicago (2001)
9. Schoenherr, J.: Moral economies and codes of conduct: the social organization of Canadian experimental psychology. Sci. Can. **41**, 31–54 (2019)
10. Carraccio, C., Wolfsthal, S.D., Englander, R., Ferentz, K., Martin, C.: Shifting paradigms: from flexner to competencies. Acad. Med. **77**, 361–367 (2002)
11. Royal College of Physicians and Surgeons of Canada: CanMEDS: Better standards, better physicians, better care (2020). http://www.royalcollege.ca/rcsite/canmeds/canmeds-framework-e. Accessed 14 Feb 2020
12. Drew, T., Võ, M.L.-H., Wolfe, J.M.: The invisible gorilla strikes again: sustained in attentional blindness in expert observers. Psychol. Sci. **24**, 1848–1853 (2013)
13. Millington, S.J., et al.: Expert agreement in the interpretation of lung ultrasound studies performed on mechanically ventilated patients. J. Ultrasound Med. **37**, 2659–2665 (2018)
14. Kohn, L.T., Corrigan, J., Donaldson, M.S.: To Err is Human: Building a Safer Health System. National Academy Press, Washington (2000)
15. Dudek, N.L., Marks, M.B., Regehr, G.: Failure to fail: the perspectives of clinical supervisors. Acad. Med. **80**, S84–S87 (2005)
16. Getzels, J.W.: Problem finding: a theoretical note. Cogn. Sci. **3**, 167–172 (1979)
17. Strauch, R.E.: "Squishy" problems and quantitative methods. Pol. Sci. **6**, 175–184 (1975)
18. Gentner, D., Stevens, A.: Mental Models, pp. 299–324. Erlbaum, New Jersey (1983)
19. Schoenherr, J.R., Hamstra, S.J.: Beyond fidelity: deconstructing the seductive simplicity of fidelity in simulator-based education in the health care professions. Simul. Healthcare **12**, 117–123 (2017)
20. Elliott, D., Hansen, S., Grierson, L.E., Lyons, J., Bennett, S.J., Hayes, S.J.: Goal-directed aiming: two components but multiple processes. Psychol. Bull. **136**, 1023–1044 (2010)
21. Grierson, L.E.: Information processing, specificity of practice, and the transfer of learning: considerations for reconsidering fidelity. Adv. Health Sci. Educ. Theory Pract. **19**, 281–289 (2014)
22. Schoenherr, J.R., Hamstra, S.J.: Psychometrics and its discontents: an historical perspective on the discourse of the measurement tradition. Adv. Health Sci. Educ. **21**, 719–729 (2016)
23. Thomson, R., Schoenherr, J.R.: Knowledge-to-information translation training (KITT): an adaptive approach to explainable artifical intelligence. In: Proceedings of HCII 2020, HCI International, Copenhagen (2020)
24. Hogarth, R.M.: Educating Intuition. University of Chicago Press, Chicago (2001)
25. Simon, H.A.: Administrative Behavior Organization: a Study of Decision-Making Processes in Administrative Organization. Free Press, New York (1947)
26. Thorngate, W.: Efficient decision heuristics. Behav. Sci. **25**, 219–225 (1980)
27. Gigerenzer, G., Selten, R.: Bounded Rationality: The Adaptive Toolbox. MIT Press, Cambridge (2002)
28. Schoenherr, J.R., Hamstra, S.J.: Situating simulation: a program evaluation framework for healthcare professions education. In: Simulation in Healthcare (accepted)
29. Piaget, J.: The Construction of Reality in the Child (M. Cook, trans.). Basic Books, New York, 1937/1954
30. Fischer, K.W.: A theory of cognitive development: the control and construction of hierarchies of skills. Psychol. Rev. **87**, 477–531 (1980)
31. Alexander, P.A., Judy, J.E.: The interaction of domain-specific and strategic knowledge in academic performance. Rev. Educ. Res. **58**, 375–404 (1988)

32. Glaser, R.: Education and thinking: the role of knowledge. Am. Psychol. **39**, 93–104 (1984)
33. Tobias, S.: Interest, prior knowledge, and learning. Rev. Educ. Res. **64**, 37–54 (1994)
34. Wertsch, J.V., Tulviste, P.: LS Vygotsky and contemporary psychology of development. Dev. Psychol. **22**, 81–89 (1992)
35. De Valenzuela, J.: Sociocultural Views of Learning. SAGE, Thousand Oaks (2006)
36. Chaiklin, S.: The zone of proximal development in Vygotsky's analysis of learning and instruction. In: Kozulin, A., Gindis, B., Ageyev, V., Miller, S., (eds.) Vygotsky's Educational Theory and Practice in Cultural Context. Cambridge, Cambridge University Press (2003)
37. Luckin, R., du Boulay, B.: Ecolab: the development and evaluation of a Vygotskian design framework. Int. J. Artif. Intell. Educ. **10**, 198–220 (1999)
38. Luckin, R., du Boulay, B.: Reflections on the ecolab and the zone of proximal development. Int. J. Artif. Intell. Educ. **26**, 416–430 (2016)
39. Luckin, R.: Ecolab': Explorations in the zone of proximal development. Unpublished D.Phil. Thesis (1998)
40. Chi, M.T., Feltovich, P.J., Glaser, R.: Categorization and representation of physics problems by experts and novices. Cogn. Sci. **5**, 121–152 (1981)
41. Chen, Z., Mo, L., Honomichl, R.: Having the memory of an elephant: long-term retrieval and the use of analogues in problem solving. J. Exp. Psychol. Gen. **133**, 415–433 (2004)
42. Chen, Z., Klahr, D.: Remote transfer of scientific-reasoning and problem-solving strategies in children. In: Advances in Child Development and Behavior, JAI, vol. 36, pp. 419–470 (2008)
43. Gregory, R.J.: Psychological Testing: History, Principles, and Applications. Allyn, Needham Heights (1992)
44. Traub, R.: Classical test theory in historical perspective. Educ. Meas.: Issues Pract. **16**, 8–14 (1997)
45. Shannon, C.E.: A mathematical theory of communication. Bell Syst. Tech. J. **27**, 379–423 (1948)
46. Hunt, R.R., Worthen, J.B.: Distinctiveness and Memory. Oxford University Press, New York (2006)
47. Ericsson, K.A.: Developmenf of Professional Expertise: Toward Measurement of Expert Performance and Design of Optimal Learning Environments. Cambridge University Press, Cambridge (2009)
48. Ericsson, K.A.: Acquisition and maintenance of medical expertise: a perspective from the expert-performance approach with deliberate practice. Acad. Me. **90**, 1471–1486 (2015)
49. Norman, G.R., Grierson, L.E.M., Sherbino, J., Hamstra, S.J., Schmidt, H.G., Mamede, S.: Expertise in medicine and surgery. In: The Cambridge Handbook of Expertise and Expert Performance, pp. 331–355. Cambridge University Press, Cambridge (2018)
50. Ericsson, K.A., Hoffman, R.R., Kozbelt, A.: The Cambridge Handbook of Expertise and Expert Performance. Cambridge University Press, Cambridge (2018)
51. Meier, K., Blair, M.: Beyond probability gain: information access strategies in category learning. In: Proceedings of the Annual Meeting of the Cognitive Science Society, Cognitive Science Society, pp. 1394–1399 (2011)
52. Krupinski, E.A., et al.: Eye-movement study and human performance using telepathology virtual slides. Implications for medical education and differences with experience. Hum. Pathol. **7**, 1543–1556 (2006)
53. Sonmez, D., Altun, A., Mazman, S.G.: How prior knowledge and colour contrast interfere visual search processes in novice learners: an eye tracking study. international association for development of the information society. In: IADIS International Conference on Cognition and Exploratory Learning in Digital Age (CELDA 2012), vol. IADIS International

Conference on Cognition and Exploratory Learning in Digital Age (CELDA 2012). International Association for Development of the Information Society, pp. 42–49 (2012)

54. Klein, G.A.: Sources of Power: How People Make Decisions. MIT press, Cambridge (2017)
55. Moulton, C.A., Regehr, G., Lingard, L., Merritt, C., MacRae, H.: 'Slowing down when you should': initiators and influences of the transition from the routine to the effortful. J. Gastrointest. Surg. **14**, 1019–1026 (2010)
56. Carol-anne, E.M., Regehr, G., Mylopoulos, M., MacRae, H.M.: Slowing down when you should: a new model of expert judgment. Acad. Med. **82**, S109–S116 (2007)
57. Bloom, C.P., Bell, B.R., Linton, J.F.N., Haines, M.H., Norton, E.H.: US West Advanced Technologies Inc., assignee. Intelligent tutoring method and system. United States patent US 5,597,312, 28 January 1997
58. Nwana, H.S.: Intelligent tutoring systems: an overview. Artif. Intell. Rev. **4**, 251–277 (1990)
59. Ohlsson, S.: Some principles of intelligent tutoring. Instruct. Sci. **14**, 293–326 (1986)
60. Polson, M.C., Richardson, J.J.: Foundations of Intelligent Tutoring Systems. Psychology Press, London (2013)
61. Anderson, J.R.: Cognitive psychology and intelligent tutoring. In: Proceedings of the Sixth Annual Cognitive Science Meetings, pp. 37–43 (1984)
62. Anderson, J.R., Betts, S., Ferris, J.L., Fincham, J.M.: Neural imaging to track mental states while using an intelligent tutoring system. Proc. Nat. Acad. Sci. **107**, 7018–7023 (2010)
63. Conati, C., Aleven, V., Mitrovic, A.: Eye-tracking for student modelling in intelligent tutoring systems. Des. Recommendations Intell. Tutor. Syst. **1**, 227–236 (2013)
64. Belenky, D.M., Schalk, L.: The effects of idealized and grounded materials on learning, transfer, and interest: an organizing framework for categorizing external knowledge representations. Educ. Psychol. Rev. **26**, 27–50 (2014)
65. Ashby, F.G., Valentin, V.V.: Multiple systems of perceptual category learning: theory and cognitive tests. In: Handbook of Categorization in Cognitive Science, pp. 157–188. Elsevier (2017)
66. Cochrane, A.L.: Effectiveness and Efficiency: Random Reflections on Health Services, vol. 900574178. Nuffield Provincial Hospitals Trust, London (1972)
67. Braddock, I.C., Hudak, P.L., Feldman, J.J., Bereknyei, S., Frankel, R.M., Levinson, W.: Surgery is certainly one good option": quality and time-efficiency of informed decision-making in surgery. J. Bone Joint Surg. **90**, 1830–1838 (2008)
68. Mauksch, L.B., Dugdale, D.C., Dodson, S., Epstein, R.: Relationship, communication, and efficiency in the medical encounter: creating a clinical model from a literature review. Arch. Internal Med. **168**, 1387–1395 (2008)
69. Wulf, G., Shea, C., Lewthwaite, R.: Motor skill learning and performance: a review of influential factors. Med. Educ. **44**, 75–84 (2010)
70. Schoenherr, J.R., Waechter, J., Millington, S.J.: Subjective awareness of ultrasound expertise development: individual experience as a determinant of overconfidence. Adv. Health Sci. Educ. **23**, 749–765 (2018)
71. Schoenherr, J.R., Hamstra, S.J.: Psychometrics and its discontents: An historical perspective on the discourse of the measurement tradition. Adv. Health Care Educ. **21**, 719–729 (2016)
72. Wainer, H.: Computerized Adaptive Testing: A Primer, 2nd edn. E Lawrence Erlbaum Associates, Mahwah (2000)

An Adaptive Instructional System for the Retention of Complex Skills

Jelke van der Pal and Armon Toubman[(✉)]

Royal Netherlands Aerospace Centre, Amsterdam, The Netherlands
{Jelke.van.der.Pal,Armon.Toubman}@nlr.nl

Abstract. Many professional operations require employees with complex skills. Once these skills have been taught, it is important that the skills are (a) retained, and (b) retrained when the skills start to decay. The ability to determine the precise moment when a skill needs to be retrained will have a positive effect on the productivity of the individual, and therefore also on the cost-effectiveness of scheduled training courses. However, modelling the retention of complex skills remains challenging as it is difficult to gather enough data. In this paper, we present an online adaptive instructional system that serves two purposes: (1) to gather performance data on a complex video game called *Space Fortress*, so that the skill retention can be modelled, and (2) to apply the newly built model directly to the participants, so that its effectiveness can be analysed. We expect that the lessons learned by building and applying the model in the context of *Space Fortress* will transfer to complex real-world skills.

Keywords: Adaptive instructional systems · Complex skills · Skill retention · Skill decay · Machine learning

1 Introduction

Newly developed performance monitoring systems have enabled a gradual shift from rigid training curricula to performance-based training (PBT). PBT promises (a) optimal training and cost effectiveness, and (b) enhanced personnel satisfaction. PBT is especially relevant in the military domain, where (b) may also lead to (c) increased willingness among trained specialists to remain in service.

One possible improvement is the personalised scheduling or refresher training. Immediately after an initial qualification, any level of refresher training may appear redundant. However, any other moment may be far too late, when serious loss of proficiency may have already taken place. A *personalised model of skill retention* may predict the optimal moment for refresher training for a specific person, i.e., the moment in time when the refresher training will return the performance of the person to the level of the initial qualification. This paper describes a new adaptive instructional system (AIS) that we built to (1) collect performance data on a complex task, upon which a personalised model of skill retention will be built, and (2) apply the model to the same complex task.

The paper is structured as follows. We introduce the paper (Sect. 1), and then provide a brief overview on earlier research on the retention of complex skills (Sect. 2).

© Springer Nature Switzerland AG 2020
R. A. Sottilare and J. Schwarz (Eds.): HCII 2020, LNCS 12214, pp. 411–421, 2020.
https://doi.org/10.1007/978-3-030-50788-6_30

Next, we introduce the *Space Fortress* game, which has a long history in human factors research, and discuss its suitability for skill retention research (Sect. 3). In the remainder of the paper we describe the AIS that we built around *Space Fortress*, and how we use the AIS to collect data for a skill retention model (Sect. 4). Next, we discuss the use of machine learning to model skill retention (Sect. 5). We conclude the paper by a discussion of our research (Sect. 6).

2 The Retention of Complex Skills

Skills have the inhabitable quality to fade if it not used. The issue may not appear urgent unless realizing that in many professions vital skills are seldomly applied until in moments of truth. We all have an interest in proficient professionals that can deal with our aircraft in a stall, provide surgery on a rare disease, bring the bank system online again after a software hack, and that can defend our homeland when facing a bomber or terrorist attack. These situations do not occur daily but they do require serious and recurrent training to be prepared. In any currency and in hundreds of professions, billions are spent to ensure that this is the case. And yet, there is relatively little knowledge in optimizing effectiveness and costs of this enormous investment in our safety and security.

This seems to be in stark contrast to the thousands of studies that have been published for more than a century on the topic of retention, also known as skill decay or skill fading, terms that highlight a specific aspect of the same topic. Indeed, much is known about the decay of the kind of knowledge of skill that can be trained easily and quickly under stringent laboratory conditions. Overall, the studies reveal a ubiquitous power law curve, often of a depressing nature; our newly learned knowledge or skill deteriorates in such a high pace that the initial training almost seems useless. Gladly, repeated training does help. Performance gradually decays less fast after repeated practice. Great effort has been made to unravel the factors that cause or influence this decay process. With success, a great many factors were identified. We do know quite well what kind of task, training, situation, personal capability, or trait leads to a steeper or shallower power law curve. A series of excellent reviews of these studies are provided by [1–3].

These reviews all indicate certain omissions in the knowledge base on retention. In particular there is a lack of knowledge about longer term decay on the more complex skillsets. Most research has been done with elementary knowledge or skills that are quick to learn. Retention was often measured within the week after the learning took place. For that reason, the first author took part in a new systematic literature review focusing on empirical, longitudinal studies of complex skills retention of the last 10 years [4]. This review confirmed earlier findings but also found indications that expertise may not only slow down the decay function: expertise building may imply structural change in the mechanics of decay, gradually changing from a power law into an S-curve function. This recent review confirms there is still a great need for a well-controlled longitudinal study of complex skills. This paper describes the preparations for this undertaking by using an online game that is available for many participants and for a long period of time.

3   The Space Fortress Game

Space Fortress (SF) is a video game in which the player controls a spaceship in a small area of space. The goal of the game is to use the ship to destroy the hostile fortress in the center of the screen. SF was originally presented by Mané and Donchin "as an experimental task for the study of complex skill and its acquisition" [5]. Although the goal of the game is straightforward, it requires complex skills to achieve.

Since its inception as a task for skill acquisition research, SF remains to be a useful research tool. Most notably, it was found that player skill in SF predicts real-world flight performance scores [6]. SF has also been used as the main task in studies on optimal training instructions [7, 8]. The combination of multiple game elements enables the creation of many part-tasks (or "subgames"). This allows SF to be used in studies on the transfer of skills between part-tasks and the whole task [9–11]. Furthermore, the complex skills required to play SF make it a very interesting testbed for machine learning algorithms [12, 13].

Below, we review the gameplay of SF (Subsect. 3.1). Next, we discuss the complex skills required to play SF (Subsect. 3.2) and how we measure the skills in SF (Subsect. 3.3).

3.1   Gameplay

As stated above, the goal of SF is to destroy the fortress in the center of the screen. The player controls a ship and must fire missiles as the fortress in order to destroy it. While firing at the fortress, the player needs to protect their ship from multiple threats. The game ends when the fortress is destroyed a preset number of times, or when the ship has been hit four times by a threat (see shells and mines, below).

The fortress can only be destroyed by following the correct procedure. The player needs to fire ten missiles at the fortress, with at least 250 ms between each missile. Next, the player needs to fire to missiles at the fortress with less than 250 ms between the two missiles. Only then is the fortress destroyed. If the timing of the player is off, the procedure is reset and the player must start from the beginning. The ship only has a finite number of missiles, so the player must take care to aim and time their shots.

While the player is attacking the fortress, the fortress will try to defend itself by slowly rotating towards the player and firing shells at the player. The player has to evade the shells by maneuvering the ship in the space around the fortress. Additionally, the ship will be attacked by mines. The mines chase the ship and detonate upon impact with the ship. There are two types of mines, 'friend' and 'foe' mines. Friend mines are energized when they are hit by a missile, meaning that they will count as a missile hit on the fortress and will no longer damage the ship. Foe mines are invulnerable against missiles unless they are correctly identified. The player can identify foe mines by means of a letter that is displayed on the screen when a mine is active. If the letter matches on of the three letters that are shown to the player at the beginning of the game, the mine is a foe mine. In this case, the player must press a button twice with an interval of 250–400 ms to identify the mine and make it vulnerable to missiles. After identifying the foe mine, the player still must fire a missile at it to neutralize the threat.

The player earns points for their behaviour in the game. For example, points can be earned for:

- Hitting the fortress with a missile;
- Hitting a mine with a missile;
- Destroying the fortress;
- Identifying a foe mine;
- Not maneuvering the ship too fast or too slow.

Points can also be subtracted, for example when the ship is hit by a shell or a mine, or when the ship wraps the screen (i.e., when the ship flies through the edge of the screen, and is respawned on the opposite edge).

Apart from the ship and the fortress trying to destroy each other, there is a bonus system by which the player can earn extra points and missiles. Random symbols are shown (one at a time) in the corner of the screen for a limited amount of time. If the dollar sign ('$') is shown two times consecutively, the player can press a button to earn extra points, or another button for extra missiles. The choice for points or missiles depends on how many missiles the ship has remaining, since the ship can only carry a limited amount of missiles.

3.2 Complex Skills in SF

Playing SF requires (a) perceptual skills, (b) cognitive skills, (c) motor control skills, and (d) procedural knowledge.

Perceptual skills are needed to observe many pieces of information on the game screen: e.g., the presence of a mine, the number of missiles that the ship has remaining, and the orientation of the ship and the fortress.

Cognitive skills are needed to process the information on the screen for decision making: e.g., remembering and applying the letters that identify foe mines, detecting whether a bonus can be collected, and determining whether the bonus should be collected as points or as missiles.

Motor control skills are needed to operate the ship: e.g., maneuvering the ship, evading shells and mines, and firing at the fortress with the correct intervals.

Procedural knowledge is needed to survive and win the game: e.g., the methods to dispose of friend and foe mines, and the intervals between the missiles necessary to destroy the fortress.

3.3 Player Measurements

The complexity of SF provides many opportunities for measurements of the player's behavior. Values such as the score obtained in the game, or the number of missiles fired by the player, are simple to record. However, in terms of skill retention, such values are meaningless if they are not linked to a particular skill. Therefore, we have attempted to identify the skills necessary for SF, and then define the measurable values that can be used as a proxy for measuring the skill. Below, we list three skills that we identified.

1. Perceptual skills, i.e., the ability to perceive and understand information that is presented infrequently and possibly in different locations. We measure perceptual skills as: (a) the *speed* subscore which indicates how fast the player deals with mines, (b) the number of failed attempts at destroying the fortress with correctly timed shots, and (c) the number of times the player attempts to fire a missile when the player has no missiles left.
2. Cognitive skills with respect to multitasking, i.e., the ability to perform two or more tasks in the same period of time. We measure multitasking skills in SF as: (a) the number of times the player obtained a bonus while a mine was active (more often is better), and (b) the number of times the ship was hit by the fortress while a mine was active (less often is better).
3. Motor control skills, i.e., systematic regulation of voluntary (intended) movement by integrating sensory information and use of muscles. We measure motor control skills in SF as: (a) the number of times the ship wraps around the screen (flies out one side and appears on the opposite site of the visible section of space), (b) the *velocity* subscore that is awarded for flying not too fast nor too slow, and (c) the *control* subscore that is awarded for flying not too far nor too near the fortress.
4. Procedural knowledge, i.e., remembering and performing actions in the correct sequence. Important procedures in SF are the procedures for destroying the fortress and disposing of mines. However, it is difficult to purely measure procedural knowledge as (a) the procedure may be remembered, but not performed correctly due to various factors (e.g., lacking motor control), or (b) the player can opt to forego certain procedures (e.g., evading a mine instead of disposing of it). We are able to count the number of times the player destroys the fortress and disposes of mines, but because of (a) and (b), these are only weak indicators of the procedural knowledge.

4 The Space Fortress Adaptive Instructional System

We have built a custom AIS to facilitate our skill retention study. We refer to the AIS the Space Fortress Adaptive Instructional System (SF-AIS). The SF-AIS is an interactive website where participants learn to play SF. To this end, several types of tasks can be (automatically) assigned to participants (see Subsect. 4.1). The participants perform an initial training, reaching a personal level of achievement (personal baseline), and then start a time interval without play (the retention interval). After this interval, the participants are invited to return to the website and play a game of SF, so that their skill retention can be measured. If loss of skill is measured, the participant will follow a refresher training to improve the retained skills until the personal baseline is reached again (see Subsect. 4.2).

The skill retention measurements are the basis for a predictive model of skill retention. This model will assign retention intervals to participants, so that only a short refresher training after the interval will be required to regain the personal baseline level (i.e., the level after the initial training). Ideally, this would mean that the model is capable of predicting the optimal moment for refresher training. That is, the moment when the participant's skill has decayed to such a level that a refresher training will be beneficial, but only a short training is enough to boost the skill back to the personal baseline.

4.1   Features

The SF-AIS allows the definition of several types of tasks that can be assigned to participants. These are:

- Didactical actions, i.e., pages with study material that can be concluded with a press on one of a set of configurable buttons. For example, for a particular didactical action, we can define a button "Continue" by which the page is closed. For another didactical action, we can define the buttons "I understand" and "I do not understand". Each button press is saved in the database and may later be used in an analysis.
- Questionnaires.
- SF games with varying configurations.
- Waiting tasks that force the participant to wait for a certain time before starting the next task. An email notification is sent when the waiting time has passed.
- Analyses. The SF-AIS can store and execute R-scripts to automatically analyse (a) the results of didactical actions, (b) the results of questionnaires, (c) the performance in SF, (d) and the results of previous analyses. Based on the results of the analyses, new tasks can instantly be assigned to participants.
- Learning paths, i.e., sequences of tasks that can be assigned to participants as a whole.

Participants are directed to the next task by their personal dashboard. The dashboard also displays a graph of the scores that were obtained in SF over time.

4.2   Workflow of the Participants

In this subsection we describe the workflow of the participants using the SF-AIS. The workflow is presented graphically in Fig. 1. Upon registration, the SF-AIS prepares the initial training (see below) for each participant, so that the can immediately begin their study of SF.

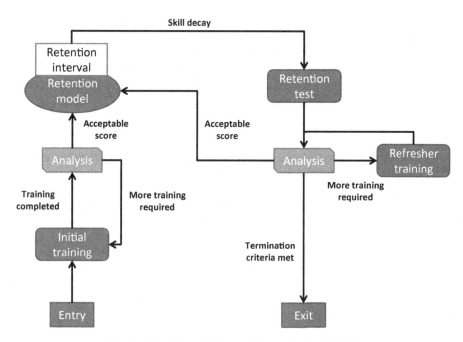

Fig. 1. Workflow of the participants in the SF-AIS.

Initial Training. Upon entry to the SF-AIS, the participant is given a brief training to get acquainted with the various game elements. Using didactical actions (see Subsect. 4.1), the game elements are described and small learning objectives are provided for a series of games. Initially, the games are configured to be easier than the full game, by, e.g., disabling the shell-firing capability of the fortress. At the end of the initial training, a series of full games is presented to the participant to measure the participant's personal baseline game score. The baseline game score is analysed (see *Analysis*) to determine whether the participant has reached a minimally required score. If this is so, the participant may continue to the first retention phase. Participants that reveal a strong positive learning curve in the last practice session may continue practicing as they apparently have not reached their personal ceiling. Participants with a negative learning curve may be subject to fatigue or distractions, and are asked to take a pause after which another practice session follows.

Retention Model. The retention phase starts by application of the retention model. The retention model takes as input the latest game scores achieved by the participant, and outputs a time period that the participant has to wait in order to continue to the retention test (i.e., the retention interval). Ideally, the retention model is able to produce the optimal time period for each participant. Data from the first retention test will be used to collect data for calibrating the model. The first period is randomly selected between 1 and 52 weeks.

Retention Test. After the retention interval has passed, the player is invited via email to perform the retention test. The retention test is a single game of SF to measure the skill decay of the participant. If the score on the retention test is acceptable (i.e., near or above the level that was achieved after the initial training), the participant may immediately start the next retention interval. However, if the score is not acceptable, the participant starts a refresher training.

Refresher Training. The refresher training consists of a series of games to bring the performance of the participant back to the level that was achieved after the initial training. The performance after the refresher training is analysed to determine whether the participant needs additional training, or if a new retention interval can be started. However, if one of the following termination criteria is met, the study terminates for this participant: (a) if the participant cannot regain to his personal baseline after repeated refresher training, or (b) if the next retention interval would end after the conclusion of the project, the participant exits the study at this point.

Ideally, participants perform as many retention interval-test loops as possible. This would make it possible to study any effects of diminishing returns after repeated refresher training. However, we consider a participant as making a contribution to the study if they complete at least one retention interval, one retention test, and possibly the following refresher training.

4.3   Target Audience

Registration in the SF-AIS is open to the general public at https://spacefortress.nlr.nl. However, we are restricting participation to people aged 18 years or older. Participation is rewarded with a chance to win a travel voucher.

5   Modelling Skill Retention by Means of Machine Learning

Machine learning techniques are known for their pattern recognition abilities [14]. Especially in highly dimensional data, machine learning techniques are able to discover patterns where humans only see noise. A famous example is the ability of machine learning to detect cancerous regions in x-ray photos with very high accuracy [15]. The data that we collect in the SF-AIS is also highly dimensional, as we measure gameplay data of different nature (e.g., scores and game events) as well as characteristics of the participant (e.g., age, previous gaming experience, and motivation level after a game session).

Recently, machine learning has been discovered as a powerful tool for modeling skill retention. As an example, we discuss the competing models for the *second language acquisition modeling* task [16].

Settles et al. [16] released a dataset of language learners labeling words. The data was collected in the language-learning app Duolingo. The modeling task was to predict future labeling errors by the learners. Fifteen teams participated in a challenge to produce the most accurate predictive model. Two of the top three teams used recurrent neural networks (RNNs) to model the learner behaviour. RNNs are function approximators that incorporate, by design, the dimension of time (see, e.g., [17]). This makes them highly suitable for predicting the future performance of a learner based on the past performance. Furthermore, this property is thought to make RNNs sensitive to the *spacing* of tasks, such as the retention intervals, including the practice sessions, present in our SF data. However, Sense et al. [18] state that although RNNs may be powerful function approximators, they do not aid in understanding the cognitive processes that are being approximated. To aid the understanding, Sense et al. propose combining the RNNs with predictions made by explicit models of cognitive processes.

An alternative approach to RNNs may be the use of genetic programming. Genetic programming is a branch of evolutionary algorithms in which computer programs are automatically constructed. Similar to RNNs, the genetic programs would attempt to predict skill retention based on observations of the participants' scores and characteristics. However, unlike RNNs, genetic programs can be built in such a way that the programs remain accessible and readable to some extent. This way, genetic programs may provide insight into cognitive processes in a way that RNNs cannot. Furthermore, the complexity of the programs can be controlled, by providing an evolutionary advantage to programs that make the most accurate predictions relative to the number of operations that they need to reach the predictions. Examples of genetic programming in time series prediction are [19, 20].

Different types of machine learning models can also be developed and used for predictions in parallel. The so-called ensemble methods allow multiple models to contribute to a prediction, and have in some cases shown improved accuracy over single-model predictions (see, e.g., [21]).

6   Discussion

Our construction of a predictive model for the retention process in general and in particular for SF is ongoing and in this process we are facing a range of challenges. Building a predictive model for the retention of complex skills is a complex task. The construction of the model requires data, which first has to be gathered. By packaging our skill measurements into an online game, we are able to reach a wide audience, and thus a wide selection of potential participants. Ensuring sufficient numbers of participants register and keep playing for a long time require considerable attention and effort.

Using an online game has considerable advantages, but also disadvantages. Participants cannot be controlled as well as in laboratory conditions. A number of measures were taken to ensure that participants have certain limitations, such as the input device. Only a keyboard can be used to play the game, but in general, we have sacrificed control over the play environment in order to reach as many potential participants as possible and (after the compulsory pauses) let them play at times of their own choice.

On a technical note, our data collection process requires the selection of retention intervals for participants, so that we can measure the performance of participants after periods of no-play. Ideally, the retention intervals are selected by the predictive model. Since we do not have the predictive model yet, we have had to manually construct a simple replacement model. Currently, for the first retention interval of each participant, a period between 1 and 52 weeks is randomly selected. For each following retention interval, a retention interval is selected based on the predictive model which is fed by range of measures.

Although machine learning offers powerful tools for modeling, the tools operate using the *garbage in, garbage out* principle, i.e., the concept that nonsense input data will produce nonsense output data. The success of modeling the retention of the skills necessary to play SF will rely greatly on (a) the quality of the data, but also (b) the amount of available data, and (c) the selection of features in the data. We expect the gameplay data to have a relatively large variance, as there are many ways to play the game. A large amount of data should help smooth the variance, but collecting a large amount of data depends on the willingness of the participants to play. The factor that we have the most control over is the feature selection. As noted in Sect. 5, the data that we collect is highly dimensional. We have made a preliminary mapping between the skills that are necessary to play SF and the measurements that we can make in the game to measure these skills (see Subsect. 3.2 and 3.3), but whether this mapping holds any truth in the data that we collect remains to be seen. Feature selection methods (see, e.g., [22]) may aid in reducing the dimensionality of the data. However, the high dimensionality of our data also offers opportunities, such as studying the feasibility of building a predictive model per identified skill, rather than treating the playing of SF as a single complex skill.

Our study and optimization of the predictive retention model will last for two years (end of 2021) in which period we hope to have gained insight from the data of hundreds of participants and even more optimization iterations.

References

1. Farr, M.J.: The Long-Term Retention of Knowledge and Skills: A Cognitive and Instructional Perspective. Springer, New York (1987). https://doi.org/10.1007/978-1-4612-1062-7
2. Arthur Jr., W., Bennett Jr., W., Stanush, P.L., McNelly, T.L.: Factors that influence skill decay and retention: a quantitative review and analysis. Hum. Perform. 11(1), 57–101 (1998). https://doi.org/10.1207/s15327043hup1101_3
3. Arthur Jr., W., Day, E.A.: A look from 'aFarr' (1987): the past, present, and future of applied skill decay research. In: Individual and Team Skill Decay: The Science and Implications for Practice, pp. 405–427. Routledge/Taylor & Francis Group, New York (2013)
4. Vlasblom, J.I.D., Pennings, H.J.M., Van der Pal, J., Oprins, E.A.P.B.: Competence retention in safety-critical professions: a systematic literature review. Educ. Res. Rev. 30 (2020). https://doi.org/10.1016/j.edurev.2020.100330
5. Mané, A., Donchin, E.: The space fortress game. Acta Physiol. 71(1–3), 17–22 (1989)
6. Gopher, D., Well, M., Bareket, T.: Transfer of skill from a computer game trainer to flight. Hum. Factors 36(3), 387–405 (1994)
7. Day, E.A., Arthur Jr., W., Gettman, D.: Knowledge structures and the acquisition of a complex skill. J. Appl. Psychol. 86(5), 1022 (2001)
8. Regian, J., Goettl, B.M., Ashworth III, A., deBoom, D., Anthony, M.: Training Research in Automated Instruction (TRAIN). Galaxy Scientific Corp, Egg Harbor Township, NJ (2003)
9. Roessingh, J., Hilburn, B.: The Power Law of Practice in adaptive training applications. National Aerospace Laboratory NLR (2000)

10. Roessingh, J., Kappers, A., Koenderink, J.: Transfer between training of part-tasks in complex skill training. National Aerospace Laboratory NLR (2002)
11. Anderson, J.R., Bothell, D., Fincham, J.M., Anderson, A.R., Poole, B., Qin, Y.: Brain regions engaged by part-and whole-task performance in a video game: a model-based test of the decomposition hypothesis. J. Cogn. Neurosci. **23**(12), 3983–3997 (2011)
12. van Oijen, J., Poppinga, G., Brouwer, O., Aliko, A., Roessingh, J.J.: Towards modeling the learning process of aviators using deep reinforcement learning. In: 2017 IEEE International Conference on Systems, Man, and Cybernetics (SMC), pp. 3439–3444 (2017)
13. Agarwal, A., Sycara, K.: Learning time-sensitive strategies in space fortress, arXiv preprint arXiv:1805.06824 (2018)
14. Jordan, M.I., Mitchell, T.M.: Machine learning: trends, perspectives, and prospects. Science **349**(6245), 255–260 (2015). https://doi.org/10.1126/science.aaa8415
15. Shen, L., Margolies, L.R., Rothstein, J.H., Fluder, E., McBride, R., Sieh, W.: Deep learning to improve breast cancer detection on screening mammography. Sci Rep. **9**(1), 1–12 (2019). https://doi.org/10.1038/s41598-019-48995-4
16. Settles, B., Brust, C., Gustafson, E., Hagiwara, M., Madnani, N.: Second language acquisition modeling. In: Proceedings of the Thirteenth Workshop on Innovative Use of NLP for Building Educational Applications, New Orleans, Louisiana, pp. 56–65 (2018). https://doi.org/10.18653/v1/w18-0506
17. Che, Z., Purushotham, S., Cho, K., Sontag, D., Liu, Y.: Recurrent neural networks for multivariate time series with missing values. Sci. Rep. **8**(1), 1–12 (2018). https://doi.org/10.1038/s41598-018-24271-9
18. Sense, F., Jastrzembski, T., Mozer, M.C., Krusmark, M., van Rijn, H.: Perspectives on computational models of learning and forgetting. In: Proceedings of the 17th International Conference on Cognitive Modeling, Montreal, Canada (2019)
19. Graff, M., Escalante, H.J., Ornelas-Tellez, F., Tellez, E.S.: Time series forecasting with genetic programming. Nat. Comput. **16**(1), 165–174 (2017). https://doi.org/10.1007/s11047-015-9536-z
20. Moskowitz, D.: Implementing the template method pattern in genetic programming for improved time series prediction. Genet. Program Evolvable Mach. **19**(1), 271–299 (2018). https://doi.org/10.1007/s10710-018-9320-9
21. Ribeiro, M.H.D.M., dos Santos Coelho, L.: Ensemble approach based on bagging, boosting and stacking for short-term prediction in agribusiness time series. Appl. Soft Comput. **86**, 105837 (2020). https://doi.org/10.1016/j.asoc.2019.105837
22. Li, J., et al.: Feature selection: a data perspective. ACM Comput. Surv. **50**(6), 94:1–94:45 (2017). https://doi.org/10.1145/3136625

Learner Modeling in the Context
of Caring Assessments

Diego Zapata-Rivera[✉], Blair Lehman, and Jesse R. Sparks

Educational Testing Service, Princeton, NJ 08541, USA
{dzapata,blehman,jsparks}@ets.org

Abstract. Learner models maintain representations of students' cognitive, metacognitive, affective, personality, social and perceptual skills. This information can be used to adapt the adaptive instructional system's interactions with the student. Our work on caring assessments has provided us with an opportunity to explore learner modelling issues applied to assessment. This paper elaborates on issues such as the nature of the learner model, types of student emotions in assessment and opportunities for adaptations, and the role of individual differences in student characteristics that could inform an expanded learner model to support fine-tuned adjustments to assessment tasks. Other issues discussed include using cognitive and affective information to implement adaptations, as well as implications for reporting systems and open learner models, supporting student access to these systems, and data privacy and data security challenges.

Keywords: Caring assessments · Learner modeling · Emotions · Individual differences

1 Introduction

Keeping students engaged in task related behavior is a challenge shared by Adaptive Instructional Systems (AISs) and assessment systems. Learner models are representations of students' cognitive, metacognitive, affective, personality, social and perceptual skills that AISs have maintained and used to adapt the system's interactions (e.g., type and amount of feedback, content presented, interaction type, question difficulty, and access to additional content and related materials) to the characteristics of the student [1]. A variety of techniques have been used to implement learner models in AISs (e.g., probabilistic models, cognitive models, machine learning models, constraint-based models, agent-based models, stereotype models, and overlay models) [1–3].

We describe issues related to learner modeling in the context of caring assessments that take into account a broad view of the learner as well as information about the learning context to create engaging assessment situations that can be used to collect valid assessment information about what the student knows or can do [4]. Work in this area includes exploring student interaction with technology-rich, conversation-based assessments that make use of traditional item types and dynamic conversations with

© Springer Nature Switzerland AG 2020
R. A. Sottilare and J. Schwarz (Eds.): HCII 2020, LNCS 12214, pp. 422–431, 2020.
https://doi.org/10.1007/978-3-030-50788-6_31

artificial agents to assess skills such as science inquiry, collaboration, and argumentation [5]; identifying and dealing with unexpected responses [6]; exploring emotions [7]; evaluating the impact of source credibility and question format on the quality of student responses [8]; examining student-level individual differences relevant to assessment performance that could be incorporated into an expanded conception of a learner model [9]; and opportunities for adaptive interactions [10].

Topics discussed in this paper include: (a) what types of background variables, individual differences, cognitive and affective variables have potential to be included in the learner model; (b) what types of adaptations can be implemented to support student engagement while keeping in mind considerations of fairness, validity and reliability of the assessment system; (c) how cognitive and affective information can be used to improve adaptive processes (e.g., recommendations for next activities and feedback); (d) considerations for reporting learning model information to particular stakeholders (e.g. open learner models; [11]); (e) what types of supports should be available to ensure that students, especially those from underserved groups, can access the assessment environment and consider it an appropriate way to demonstrate their knowledge and skills [12, 13]; and (f) data privacy and data security challenges regarding the procurement and handling of learner model information required to implement this approach. Implications for future research in the area of learner modeling for caring assessments, and for AISs in general, will be discussed.

2 Learner Modeling in Caring Assessments

Assessment methodologies such as Evidence-Centered Design (ECD) [14] are used to design assessments that rely on assessment arguments showing how tasks are designed to provide the evidence needed to measure the intended construct (i.e., knowledge, skills, and abilities being measured). The assessment design structure (usually represented as the student, evidence and task models) can be thought as components of a learner model [15].

Caring assessments broaden the scope of the learner model to include aspects such as students' motivation, metacognition, and affect; consider information about the learning context; and support different levels of caring (see Fig. 1).

Two possible use cases include (a) providing an unmotivated student with information aimed at making the task relevant to the student (e.g., how the data will be used) [16], offering other alternatives to demonstrate his/her knowledge [17], or considering the student's motivational state when making inferences about the student's knowledge, skills or ability levels [18]; and (b) offering just-in-time instructional materials (e.g., on-line content or AISs, if available) to students who have not previously had the opportunity to learn about a particular topic or taking into account the student's knowledge level/exposure level when making inferences. In general, caring assessment can keep track of information about the learner and the learning context to improve the student's assessment experience without negatively affecting the technical properties of the assessment.

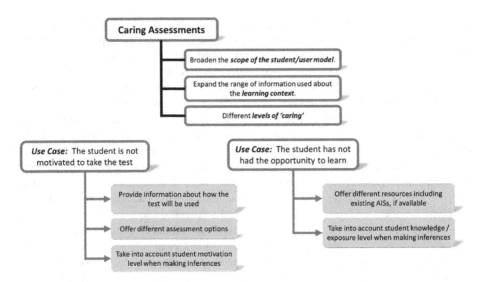

Fig. 1. Caring assessments and two example use cases. © Educational Testing Service 2020. All Rights Reserved.

Several challenges to the realization of this vision include gathering information about the learner and the learning context; improving communication channels among teachers, parents and students and assessment providers; and improving processes for collecting, maintaining, sharing and protecting learner model information (e.g., who controls what type of information?) [4].

An approach to identifying possible assessment design, student motivation issues, and the types of variables that should be monitored and kept as part of the learner model involves exploring the presence of unexpected responses in assessments that require students to explain or defend their ideas via open-ended response items. We have explored unexpected responses in the context of conversation-based assessments [5]. In this approach, we reviewed existing log file data [6, 19] to identify unexpected responses, created a list of possible categories, designed possible solutions or ways to deal with these situations, and gathered feedback from expert teachers. Categories explored include the following:

- Confused: the response makes little sense or lacks an explanation.
- Frustrated: The student seems annoyed by his or her interaction with the characters (e.g., "I already said that").
- Repetitive: The student repeats the same answers to slightly different questions across multiple turns of the conversation.
- Unmotivated: The student does not care to answer or provides short answers due to lack of motivation (e.g., "no," "idk," "sure," "yep").
- Irrelevant: The student does not answer the right question, or the answer is off topic.
- Asking for help: The student asks characters for additional information (e.g., please repeat the question or show additional materials).

- Gaming the system: The student tries to test the capabilities of the system (e.g., by entering profanity).
- Attempting to communicate: The student does not answer the question (e.g., "I answered a similar question before").
- Using different languages: The student answers the question in a language other than English.
- Giving up: The student expresses a wish to quit.

Results of this work suggest that detectors can be developed to deal with many of these issues. Approaches to deal with these issues can be used to inform the development of caring assessment systems that can take in a variety of inputs from the user and respond appropriately. How the system may react depends on several aspects including the purpose of the assessment, information about the learning context, resources available and learner characteristics.

The proposed unexpected response categories suggest that students' emotional states should be incorporated as part of the learner model, which has been done in AISs (see [20] for a review). The following section presents work on identifying the types of emotions students experience as part of an assessment.

3   Exploring Emotions in Caring Assessments

The impact of a variety of emotions on learning outcomes in AISs has been investigated for over 20 years (see [21] for a review) and during the last ten years has focused on how student emotions can be augmented during learning to improve outcomes [20]. However, research on the role of emotions during assessments has been more limited. Originally the focus of this area of research was limited to the impact of test anxiety [22], but a wider range of emotions was identified as impacting assessment outcomes [23]. Research on how to augment student emotions during assessments has been very limited (see [16] for an exception).

Recent research has established that efforts to provide emotion-sensitive support during assessments should move beyond targeting only test anxiety [7, 23], but exactly what states should be targeted is still an open question. For example, research on both the achievement emotions [24] and learning-centered emotions [21] promote the identification and tracking of individual emotions and have been explored in assessments, but the two sets of emotions differ. Recent research has also suggested that emotion intensity should be considered along with the nature of the individual emotion detected [7]. It is also possible that the identification of individual emotions is not necessary for adaptations and that in order to provide effective interventions, assessment systems simply need to track states that deviate from an engaged learning experience [16].

Despite the difficulties of determining what states to detect and the technological difficulties of detecting those states, there is evidence that emotion-sensitive support could be helpful during the completion of assessments [7, 16, 17]. However, this leads to the next open question of how best to provide support during assessments. Currently, the only emotion-sensitive support that is adaptively deployed during assessments occurs in effort-monitoring computer-based tests [16]. This support is intended to increase test-taking motivation by providing on-screen messages that highlight the importance of the low-stakes test to either the student or their institution. These on-screen messages have proven effective in terms of reducing unmotivated responses and increasing test reliability. Additional research is needed to understand how these messages can be designed to further facilitate emotion regulation.

Emotion-sensitive support during assessments could potentially go beyond on-screen messages. Alterations to the assessment task (e.g., framing, format) are another potential method to facilitate emotion regulation. Task framing modifications could be used to increase engagement by selecting the task context based on student interests (e.g., basketball game vs. painting) [25]. Tasks could also be modified by adaptively presenting them in different formats (e.g., game-based assessment, multiple-choice items) to provide each student with the best opportunity to show their knowledge, skills, and abilities [17].

Research on emotion-sensitive support during assessments is still in its infancy and thus there are many potential issues that must be addressed before this type of adaptivity can be incorporated into assessment systems. As mentioned previously, reliable emotion detection is still an ongoing area of research [26]. It is critical that assessment systems are confident in the emotion or state that has been detected before deploying support; otherwise, the support deployed could be distracting or negatively impact engagement with the assessment. Another issue related to the effectiveness of emotional interventions is the degree to which they should be tailored to the individual student [27]. To deploy the most effective interventions, it may be necessary to also consider student characteristics, as described in the next section. Lastly, while the deployment of emotion-sensitive support during assessments has the goal of creating a more egalitarian opportunity for all students and resulting in a more valid assessment outcome, research is needed to ensure there are no unintended negative side effects on the fairness and validity of the assessment. Despite the need for further research, the incorporation of student emotions into learner models for assessments holds great promise for allowing assessments to care.

4 Leveraging Individual Differences in Caring Assessments

In addition to their attention to momentary affective states, caring assessments have the potential to consider a broader set of student-level characteristics as learner model variables. Metacognitive or motivational characteristics have been considered part of the space of student-level variables that are routinely tracked and used for decision-making and adaptation in the domain of intelligent tutoring systems [28, 29]. These include such variables as learner effort or degree of persistence, self-reported confidence, help seeking, which may be mediated by the domain or the task design, or relatively stable characteristics such as Big-Five personality constructs like neuroticism and openness to experience. A system that tracks these learner characteristics has the potential to deliver more fine-grained, precise adaptations to tasks and situations that can take these characteristics into account [29].

Attention to student-level characteristics during assessments has often been considered from a summative perspective; consider research examining student-level demographic or contextual variables that meaningfully relate to assessment performance, exemplified by reports using data from the National Assessment of Educational Progress (NAEP; [30, 31]). Based on these analyses, we know that student demographics, home environment, and exposure to high-quality instructional practices are key factors that contribute to student performance on achievement tests [31]. Thus, for example, a caring assessment could take into account whether or not students have been exposed to relevant instructional strategies (e.g., doing hands-on activities, working in small groups) by providing additional instructional materials or alternative resources for the student to engage with before they are ready to tackle the expected challenge of the assessment (see Fig. 1).

Beyond these variables for which there is empirical evidence demonstrating links to achievement test scores, there has been increasing attention to other student-level characteristics that can impact academic outcomes, but which have been little studied in the realm of assessment – characteristics such as grit [32], growth mindset [33], and self-efficacy beliefs [34, 35], to name a few. Research with middle school students has found that these student-level individual differences (in addition to cognitive flexibility) as measured by student self-report significantly predicted performance on an interactive conversation-based assessment of science inquiry skills [9]. Thus, a caring assessment could incorporate such "non-cognitive" characteristics as elements within a learner model that could be used to adapt an assessment task. For example, for students identified as having a fixed mindset, messages could be implemented at the beginning of the assessment to encourage a growth mindset prior to the task (see [36] for a review of potential interventions).

In addition to these individualized interventions based on levels of particular variables, multiple measures could be meaningfully combined into user profiles, which could streamline interventions for subgroups of students. Using such student-level variables as inputs to a hierarchical cluster analysis, we were able to identify four distinct subgroups of students with similar profiles [37]; these subgroup designations could provide a means to target certain student subgroups with a particular intervention, without the need to develop fully individualized interventions tuned to all the known characteristics of a specific individual. We are currently examining whether these same profiles or patterns are apparent in the context of an interactive conversation-based assessment of mathematical argumentation skills. As with the affective interventions described previously, additional research is required to investigate the impact of proposed interventions, whether targeted toward specific characteristics or combinations thereof, in order to determine whether the desired impact on performance is obtained, and whether unintended consequences can be minimized. Ultimately, the aim is to detect (combinations of) student characteristics, and to deliver to each student a tailored assessment version that maximizes engagement and opportunity to perform to the best of their ability [4, 10, 27].

5 Discussion

In this section we discuss how our work on caring assessments informs learner modeling research and future work.

- *Learner model variables.* Cognitive, social and emotional aspects of the learner can influence levels of engagement and performance on assessments. Regarding the types of variables that should form the learner model, research shows that malleable variables that when supported have potential to improve student learning (e.g., cognitive abilities, metacognitive skills, affective states) may be good candidates to include [1, 9]. However, additional information about learners and the learning context can prove valuable in dealing with the cold start problem and making appropriate instructional recommendations [38].

- *Types of adaptations.* The types of adaptations that are appropriate for assessment systems include making changes to the graphical interface for accessibility purposes [12], providing adaptive feedback and sequencing of tasks, engaging students in conversations with artificial agents perhaps with different characteristics or knowledge levels [8, 9], granting additional time and opportunities to make revisions, and recommending additional activities or learning materials. Some types of adaptations may be more appropriate than others depending on the purpose of the assessment. Adaptations should consider fairness, validity and reliability aspects of the assessment [27].

- *Making recommendations based on cognitive and motivational aspects of the learner model.* AISs can make recommendations based on both cognitive and motivational aspects of the learner. For example, additional activities or support messages can be triggered based on motivation and knowledge levels (e.g., assigning additional tasks to motivated students and providing unmotivated students with supporting messages). By monitoring both cognitive and emotional aspects of the learner it is possible to keep students engaged for longer periods of time.

- *Reporting systems and open learner models.* Learner model information can be used to support students', teachers', and administrators' decision making [11, 39, 40]. Work on designing and evaluating reporting systems for innovative assessments highlights the importance of (1) following an iterative, audience-centered approach, (2) using student response and process data to support stakeholder's decisions, and (3) evaluating both comprehension and preference aspects of the visual representations [39, 40]. Also, principles for effective visualizations from areas such as cognitive science and information visualizations can inform the development of effective reporting systems and open learner modeling interfaces [41].

- *Supporting student access to AISs.* Accessibility features [12], as well as strategies to support student interaction with AISs can be informed by the information maintained in the learner model. Adaptations to the delivery system (e.g., additional supporting messages) as well as to administration conditions (e.g., providing additional time) can be put in place to support cognitive bandwidth recovery strategies so students can be in better conditions to demonstrate what they know or can do [13].

- *Data privacy and data security.* Learner model information should be protected, and users should have control over what information is being kept and how it is used [42]. Appropriate mechanisms should be in place to ensure the safety of learner model information.

6 Future Work

Future work in this area includes continued exploration of the potential of caring assessment to improve the current state of assessments. This work involves the design, implementation and evaluation of adaptive features in digital assessments. Results will inform both the development of new caring assessments and AISs.

References

1. Shute, V.J., Zapata-Rivera, D.: Adaptive educational systems. In: Durlach, P. (ed.) Adaptive Technologies for Training and Education, pp. 7–27. Cambridge University Press, New York (2012)
2. Abyaa, A., Khalidi Idrissi, M., Bennani, S.: Learner modelling: systematic review of the literature from the last 5 years. Educ. Technol. Res. Dev. **67**(5), 1105–1143 (2019). https://doi.org/10.1007/s11423-018-09644-1
3. Chrysafiadi, K., Virvou, M.: Student modeling approaches: a literature review for the last decade. Expert Syst. Appl. **40**(11), 4715–4729 (2013)
4. Zapata-Rivera, D.: Toward caring assessment systems. In: Tkalcic, M., Thakker, D., Germanakos, P., Yacef, K., Paris, C., Santos, O. (eds.) Proceedings of Adjunct User Modeling, Adaptation and Personalization Conference, New York, pp. 97–100 (2017)
5. Zapata-Rivera, D., Jackson, T., Katz, I.R.: Authoring conversation-based assessment scenarios. Des. Recomm. Intell. Tutor. Syst. **3**, 169–178 (2015)
6. Zapata-Rivera, D., Lehman, B., Sparks, J.R., Por, H.-H., James, K.: Identifying and addressing unexpected responses in conversation-based assessments (Research Memorandum No. RM-18-13). Educational Testing Service, Princeton (2018)
7. Lehman, B., Zapata-Rivera, D.: Student emotions in conversation-based assessments. IEEE Trans. Learn. Technol. **11**(1), 1–13 (2018)
8. Sparks, R., Zapata-Rivera, D., Lehman, B., James, K., Steinberg, J.: Simulated dialogues with virtual agents: effects of agent features in conversation-based assessments. In: Penstein Rosé, C., et al. (eds.) AIED 2018. LNCS (LNAI), vol. 10948, pp. 469–474. Springer, Cham (2018). https://doi.org/10.1007/978-3-319-93846-2_88
9. Sparks, J.R., Peters, S., Steinberg, J., James, K., Lehman, B.A., Zapata-Rivera, D.: Individual difference measures that predict performance on conversation-based assessments of science inquiry skills. Paper presented at the Annual Meeting of the American Educational Research Association, Toronto, Canada (2019)
10. Zapata-Rivera, D., Vassileva, J.: Exploring opportunities for caring assessments. In: Guin, N., Kumar, A. (eds.) Exploring Opportunities for Caring Assessments Workshop at the Intelligent Tutoring Systems Conference, pp. 81–84 (2018)
11. Bull, S., Kay, J.: Open learner models. In: Nkambou, R., Bourdeau, J., Mizoguchi, R. (eds.) Advances In Intelligent Tutoring Systems. Studies in computational intelligence, vol. 308, pp. 301–322. Springer, Berlin (2010). https://doi.org/10.1007/978-3-642-14363-2_15

12. Hansen, H.G., Zapata-Rivera, D., White, J.: Framework for the design of accessible intelligent tutoring systems. In: Craig, S.D. (ed.) Tutoring and Intelligent Tutoring Systems, pp. 69–101. Nova Science Publishers, New York (2018)

13. Verschelden, C.: Bandwidth Recovery: Helping Students Reclaim Cognitive Resources Lost To Poverty, Racism, and Social Marginalization. Stylus, Sterling (2017)

14. Mislevy, R.J., et al.: On the structure of educational assessments. Measur.: Interdisc. Res. Perspect. **1**(1), 3–62 (2003)

15. Zapata-Rivera, D., Hansen, E., Shute, V.J., Underwood, J.S., Bauer, M.: Evidence-based approach to interacting with open student models. Int. J. Artif. Intell. Educ. **17**(3), 273–303 (2007)

16. Wise, S.L., et al.: Taking the time to improve the validity of low-stakes Tests: the effort-monitoring CBT. Educ. Meas.: Issues Pract. **25**(2), 21–30 (2006)

17. Lehman, B., Jackson, G.T., Forsyth, C.: A (mis)match analysis: examining the alignment between test-taker performance in conventional and game-based assessments. J. Appl. Test. Technol. **20**, 17–34 (2019)

18. Wise, S.L., DeMars, C.E.: An application of item response time: the effort-moderated IRT model. J. Educ. Meas. **43**(1), 19–38 (2006)

19. Zapata-Rivera, D., Liu, L., Chen, L., Hao, J., von Davier, A.A.: Assessing science inquiry skills in an immersive, conversation-based scenario. In: Kei Daniel, B. (ed.) Big Data and Learning Analytics in Higher Education, pp. 237–252. Springer, Cham (2017). https://doi.org/10.1007/978-3-319-06520-5_14

20. Malekzadeh, M., Mustafa, M.B., Lahsasna, A.: A review of emotion regulation in intelligent tutoring systems. Educ. Technol. Soc. **18**(4), 435–445 (2015)

21. D'Mello, S.: A selective meta-analysis on the relative incidence of discrete affective states during learning with technology. J. Educ. Psychol. **105**(4), 1082–1099 (2013)

22. Zeidner, M.: Test Anxiety: the State of the Art. Plenum Press, New York (1998)

23. Pekrun, R., Goetz, T., Perry, R.P., Kramer, K., Hochstadt, M., Molfenter, S.: Beyond test anxiety: development and validation of the test emotions questionnaire (TEQ). Anxiety Stress Coping **17**(3), 287–316 (2004)

24. Pekrun, R.: The control-value theory of achievement emotions: assumptions, corollaries, and implications for educational research and practice. Educ. Psychol. Rev. **18**, 315–341 (2006). https://doi.org/10.1007/s10648-006-9029-9

25. Lehman, B., Kinsey, D.M., Finn, B.: How do test-takers perceive leveling in scenario-based tasks? An initial exploration. In: The Annual Meeting of the American Educational Research Association, San Francisco, CA (2020, accepted)

26. Aghaei Pour, P., Hussain, M.S., AlZoubi, O., D'Mello, S., Calvo, R.A.: The impact of system feedback on learners' affective and physiological states. In: Aleven, V., Kay, J., Mostow, J. (eds.) ITS 2010. LNCS, vol. 6094, pp. 264–273. Springer, Heidelberg (2010). https://doi.org/10.1007/978-3-642-13388-6_31

27. Lehman, B., Sparks, J.R., Zapata-Rivera, D.: When should adaptive assessments care? In: Guin, N., Kumar, A. (eds.) Exploring Opportunities for Caring Assessments Workshop at the Intelligent Tutoring Systems Conference, pp. 87–94 (2018)

28. Du Bolay, B., Avramides, K., Luckin, R., Martínez-Mirón, E., Méndez, G.R., Carr, A.: Towards systems that care: a conceptual framework based on motivation, metacognition, and affect. Int. J. Artif. Intell. Educ. **20**(3), 197–229 (2010)

29. Self, J.: The defining characteristics of intelligent tutoring systems research: ITSs care, precisely. Int. J. Artif. Intell. Educ. **10**, 350–364 (1999)

30. Anthony, J., Qureshi, F., Horvath, S., Bertling, J.P.: Key contextual factors for science achievement [Internal Memorandum]. Educational Testing Service, Princeton (2016)

31. Braun, H., Coley, R., Jia, Y., Trapani, C.: Exploring what works in science instruction: a look at the eighth-grade science classroom. ETS Policy Information Report. ETS, Princeton (2009)
32. Duckworth, A.L., Peterson, C., Matthews, M.D., Kelly, D.R.: Grit: perseverance and passion for long-term goals. J. Pers. Soc. Psychol. **92**(6), 1087–1101 (2007)
33. Dweck, C.S.: Mindset: The New Psychology of Success. Ballantine Books, New York (2006)
34. Richardson, M., Abraham, C., Bond, R.: Psychological correlates of university students' academic performance: a systematic review and meta-analysis. Psychol. Bull. **138**, 353–387 (2012)
35. Schneider, M., Preckel, F.: Variables associated with achievement in higher education: a systematic review of meta-analyses. Psychol. Bull. **143**(6), 565–600 (2017)
36. Yaeger, D.S., et al.: Using design thinking to improve psychological interventions: the case of the growth mindset during the transition to high school. J. Educ. Psychol. **108**(3), 374–391 (2016)
37. Sparks, J.R., Steinberg, J., Castellano, K., Lehman, B., Zapata-Rivera, D.: Generating individual difference profiles via cluster analysis: toward caring assessments for science. Paper to be presented at the Annual Meeting of the National Council for Measurement in Education, San Francisco, CA (2020)
38. Denaux, R., Dimitrova, V., Aroyo, L.: Integrating open user modeling and learning content management for the semantic web. In: Ardissono, L., Brna, P., Mitrovic, A. (eds.) UM 2005. LNCS (LNAI), vol. 3538, pp. 9–18. Springer, Heidelberg (2005). https://doi.org/10.1007/11527886_4
39. Zapata-Rivera, J.D., Katz, I.R.: Keeping your audience in mind: applying audience analysis to the design of interactive score reports. Assess. Educ. Princ. Policy Pract. **21**, 442–463 (2014)
40. Zapata-Rivera, D., et al.: Designing and evaluating reporting systems in the context of new assessments. In: Schmorrow, D.D., Fidopiastis, C.M. (eds.) AC 2018. LNCS (LNAI), vol. 10916, pp. 143–153. Springer, Cham (2018). https://doi.org/10.1007/978-3-319-91467-1_12
41. Hegarty, M.: Advances in cognitive science and information visualization. In: Zapata-Rivera, D. (ed.) Score Reporting Research and Applications. Routledge, New York (2018)
42. General Data Protection Regulation. Art. 22 GDPR. Automated individual decision-making, including profiling. https://gdpr-info.eu/art-22-gdpr/. Accessed 15 Jan 2020

Evaluating the Effectiveness of Adaptive Instructional Systems

The Evolving Assessment Landscape and Adaptive Instructional Systems - Moving Beyond Good Intentions

Michelle D. Barrett$^{(\boxtimes)}$ (iD)

ACT, Iowa City, IA 52243, USA
michelle.barrett@act.org
http://www.act.org

Abstract. Adaptive instructional systems (AIS) hold great promise for improving the efficiency and availability of quality learning experiences for lifelong learners. Some have speculated that the rich, authentic, and personalized evidence available from AIS in support of a learner's competency may indeed become so good that the need for summative assessment will diminish. This paper suggests that to prepare for this eventuality, a number of actions may be taken to move from good intent to well understood and research best practices. Specifically, this paper examines aspects of fairness, equity of access, and security as they relate to the use of AIS evidence for eventual summative decision-making. It makes a case for minimally instrumenting AIS to allow for collection of contextual metadata in addition to learning evidence in support of robust research agendas in these areas and in preparation for proper evaluation of suitability of purpose of individual data elements during formative and summative decision-making processes.

Keywords: Summative assessment · Standardized assessment · Adaptive instructional system

1 Introduction

Adaptive instructional systems (AIS), defined as

> ... artificially-intelligent, computer-based systems that guide learning experiences by tailoring instruction and recommendations based on the goals, needs, and preferences of each individual learner or team in the context of domain learning objectives [1]

hold great promise for improving the efficiency and availability of quality learning experiences for lifelong learners. Interestingly, as AIS become more widely available and adopted, potential uses beyond tailored instruction and recommendation, or at least uses of the data they collect, have entered the dialogue. One such proposed use is as a replacement to standardized and summative assessment. For example, Marten Roorda, CEO of ACT, recently commented,

© Springer Nature Switzerland AG 2020
R. A. Sottilare and J. Schwarz (Eds.): HCII 2020, LNCS 12214, pp. 435–446, 2020.
https://doi.org/10.1007/978-3-030-50788-6_32

And then at some point in time, the learning systems will become so good, they will be used continuously every day, and we should be able to minimize summative testing, to a point where it only validates the learning process. Over time, the role of summative [assessment] will diminish, and formative [assessment] will take over [2].

The future learning ecosystem [3] is envisioned to be life-long and learner-focused, a dynamic system of interacting elements with linked formal and informal learning experiences that transcend time, space, medium, and format [4]. It will value competency over seat time, social learning alongside and integrated with domain learning, and personalization and self-agency. Research from the learning sciences and learning engineering practices will be used to optimize learning experiences [5]. Individuals will have universal learner profiles that will compile information about competency across learning experiences and systems.

AIS are positioned to become important components within this ecosystem, collecting rich multi-modal data which is analyzed and used for the formative purposes of personalization and recommendation to improve learning outcomes toward a learner's specified goals. This is well within the existing definition of an AIS and many implementations of AIS to date achieve this end.

As the focus turns to demonstrated competency from AIS, possibly through stackable credentials and micro-credentials added to universal learner profiles, however, an increased focus on using evidence collected by the system for summative purposes may also be required. As those credentials become part of mainstream decision-making influencing life trajectories for individuals, stakes increase, and a higher degree of scrutiny is likely to be given to the validity and reliability of them. In addition, AIS are likely to encounter more buyer demand for proven efficacy and efficiency over time as their developers work to differentiate them in a crowded and price-sensitive market.

While the hope is that AIS may provide more authentic experiences for learners and collect a richer array of data points from which to model competency and 21st century skills than a traditional large-scale standardized and summative assessment, lessons learned from answering and addressing concerns from stakeholders about validity and reliability of standardized and summative assessment results can be informative for building robust and transferable evidence of competency into the systems. We have to understand what would make an AIS "so good" it can diminish summative assessment in order to move beyond good intent into implementation.

To this end, it's of pragmatic importance to consider the problems the prescriptive methods used in standardized and summative assessment were meant to solve as the exercise illuminates gaps that exist in methodology, infrastructure, policy, and governance to be addressed before the ubiquitous use of AIS can finally diminish the role of summative assessment or even tip the balance to favor formative over standardized assessment. By understanding the problems to be solved, and directly addressing identified issues with novel solutions, the change from standardized and summative to the future learning ecosystem may be accelerated from a gradual natural evolution fueled by good intent to a series of thoughtful and well-researched best practices.

We conclude our introduction with some definitions, as it is useful to understand the distinctions between standardized assessment, summative assessment, and formative assessment for the later conversation. As this paper bridges two existing disciplines (AIS and psychometrics), and there is an extensive body of literature debating these terms and their relationships with one another, simple and reasonably common working definitions are presented for the purposes of this paper. It is not the intent of this paper to add to the debate on terminology but to use these working definitions as a basis for understanding the relationship of AIS to assessment use and interpretation.

1.1 Standardized Assessment

As defined by the AERA/APA/NCME Standards for Educational and Psychological Testing, an assessment is standardized when the "directions, testing conditions, and scoring follow the same detailed procedures for all test takers" [6]. As further outlined in these standards, standardization is implemented to increase accuracy and comparability, ensure all test takers have the same opportunity to demonstrate competency, and to remove unfair advantages, e.g., due to test security breaches. Standardization is meant to allow comparability both within and across test administrations. The rigor of standardization typically increases with the stakes of the assessment. This is why standardized assessment is sometimes conflated with summative assessment, although they are not technically the same and are not always simultaneously present.

1.2 Summative Assessment

Summative assessment is often referred to as "assessment of learning". The notion behind summative assessment is that evidence is collected following instruction, examined, and then used to reflect a learning outcome. The term is sometimes used to represent quizzes, tests, and papers [3] that impact final grades in an instructional course (or the final grade itself), but the term is more often used to reflect a test with high-stakes for an individual in education or workplace settings (e.g., post-secondary or other admissions decisions, hiring, promotion, or firing decisions) or the educational setting itself (e.g., accountability for schools, districts, or other educational entities). These assessments are sometimes criticized for not providing actionable feedback to individual learners or their teachers.

1.3 Formative Assessment

Formative assessment is often referred to as "assessment for learning". The notion behind formative assessment is that evidence is collected, examined in terms of learning needs, and then used to adjust curriculum or pedagogy to improve learning outcomes for one or more students, creating a feedback loop of continuous improvement. Note that this working definition has less to do with a specific format (e.g., quiz, test, paper) than it has to do with the intended use of the assessment results. It has also been argued that the time-scale for this feedback loop (e.g., within a lesson, between lessons, or in between units) and the individual implementing the feedback loop (e.g., teacher, curriculum advisor, intelligent tutor) are not distinguishing factors when determining whether an assessment is formative [7].

2   Considerations for Use of Adaptive Instructional System Evidence for Summative Purposes

Much consideration is warranted as we look to AIS to minimize and even diminish the need for summative assessment as we currently recognize it and the breadth and width of topics for a comprehensive treatment of the subject is quite large. This paper will explore two key issues: fairness and equity of access and security. These are both closely related to validity of the use of test evidence for intended purposes and threats thereof, and are both areas within AIS research which stand to greatly benefit from an active research agenda. Note that this paper explicitly does not attempt to serve as a primer in construct validity; while critically important, we assume basic understanding of evidence-centered design [8], familiarity with on-going work to extend evidence-centered design for learning and assessment applications [9], and familiarity with a number of threats to validity of interpretation when using data from learning platforms as evidence [10].

Finally, our assumption as we explore the premise that the AIS will minimize and diminish the need for summative assessment is that the AIS is not simply adding a standardized summative assessment at the end of the course of instruction (e.g., an end of chapter or end of course assessment administered under standardized conditions) to provide a certificate or credential; rather, that it is using evidence gathered during the course of instruction to eliminate the need for what one might consider a more traditional summative assessment.

2.1   Fairness and Equity of Access

As the discipline of measuring psychological or cognitive traits has matured over the last hundred years, an increased focus on fairness has become a driver for many of the policies, procedures, and professional standards which govern assessments in which summative decisions will be made. Eager to develop and administer assessments that do not cause inequity, even if and sometimes because they reflect societal inequities in their results, and in response to stakeholder concerns in relation to equity and fairness, international and national professional testing standards each have sections that focus on the rights of test-takers and issues of fairness [6, 11, 12]. In 2011, the International Organization for Standardization published ISO 10776, a standard for assessment in work and organizational settings based largely on the International Test Commission guidelines, which was reviewed and confirmed again in 2017 [13].

It is worth noting that most of these standards provide relatively broad views of what qualifies as an assessment, with the International Test Commission Guidelines on Test Use explicitly describing the relevance of their guidelines

> ...for any assessment procedure that is used in situations where the assessment of people has a serious and meaningful intent and which, if misused, may result in personal loss or psychological distress (for example, job selection interviews, job performance appraisals, diagnostic assessment of learning support needs) [14].

This interpretation is adopted by other standards [12,13]. The reader will recognize that some AIS may already come close to falling within this interpretation, although there tends to be an assumed view of day-to-day diagnoses and recommendation as low-stakes and not resulting in outcomes within the category of "serious and meaningful intent." If the formative evidence collected over time is used to make summative decisions, however, the assumption that AIS engine decisions are low-stakes is challenged.

Interpretations of what it means to be fair are nuanced and it is well beyond the scope of this article to expound upon them; we'll use a helpful framework the AERA/APA/NCME Standards on Educational and Psychological Testing [6] propose for considering fairness in testing as we look at the problems of fairness AIS may need to solve. These standards describe fairness from four different perspectives: 1) fairness in treatment during the testing process, 2) fairness as a lack of measurement bias, 3) fairness in access to the construct(s) being measured, and 4) fairness as validity of individual test score interpretations for the intended uses, each of which is described as defined by the Standards in more detail below. Underlying each of these perspectives is the understanding that variance irrelevant to the construct being measured can have a real impact on test scores, and it may differently impact subgroups of individuals.

Fairness in Treatment During the Testing Process. This view of fairness proposes that a fair testing process maximizes the opportunity for examinees to demonstrate their knowledge, skills, and ability on the construct the test is intended to measure. It is from this definition that many of the practices in standardized testing arise, such that differences in administration conditions do not influence the performance of some examinees relative to others. For example, in a technology-administered assessment setting, differences in bandwidth may cause delays in rendering of content for some examinees more than others, or differences in equipment may cause media to appear with different levels of clarity. In a typical large-scale setting, proctors are typically available to ensure all examinees have the same access to ancillary materials, that examinees are producing their own work, and that the setting is free of disruptive noise or other distractions.

Fairness as a Lack of Measurement Bias. This view of fairness recognizes that there may be characteristics of a test unrelated to construct being measured, or that there may be a use of the test scores, that result in different meanings of scores for different subgroups. It is a common practice, therefore, to conduct studies of differential item functioning, differential test functioning, and predictive bias on high-stakes assessments, especially when linguistically and culturally diverse populations, populations including examinees with disabilities and neuro-divergence, populations including examinees from a wide range of socio-economic conditions, and other diverse populations are being tested.

Fairness in Access to the Construct(s) Being Measured. This interpretation of fairness requires that barriers an individual may have to demonstrating their knowledge, skills, and abilities on the construct being measures be removed to the extent possible. Barriers of this sort may arise from disability, age, language, and such. As a simple example, an individual with sight impairment may need a braille or large-print format in order to access the content and demonstrate their ability. Over time in the context of summative testing, robust testing accommodations procedures have been developed and implemented to provide examinees with supports that improve access without changing the construct being measured, and at least in the United States, individuals have a right to accommodations under Section 504 of the Rehabilitation Act of 1973, a civil rights law preventing discrimination on the basis of disability [15]. Test delivery platforms are often required by stakeholders to meet web content accessibility (WGAC) guidelines [16] and many testing organizations practice universal design [17] in their assessment design and development frameworks so that accessibility is considered from the start. The International Test Commission guidelines for linguistically and culturally diverse populations outline several best practices for ensuring access to the construct of interest [18]. Additional access issues of relevance outside of specific test presentation and response interactions described above include access to bandwidth both within and outside of educational settings for sufficient practice and familiarity, cost of the assessment, and other limitations for examinees in demonstrating performance on the construct of interest. Examples of progress in addressing these access issues include efforts to expand bandwidth [19] and offers of fee wavers by testing organizations, as in [20].

Fairness as Validity of Individual Test Score Interpretations for the Intended Uses. This fourth perception of fairness recognizes that individual difference exists within subgroups used in higher-level aggregate evaluations of fairness, and that it is important to consider individual characteristics of the examinee in interpreting test scores for that examinee, or in considering whether standardized procedures or conditions are appropriate for the individual.

Fairness and Equity of Access in AIS. The promised personalization of AIS may indeed allow us to solve issues of fairness and access in novel ways.

Indeed, as indicated at the start of this article, core to the definition of AIS is the inclusion of functionality to adapt to the goals, needs, and preferences of each individual learner, and as such, one might assume that it will be inherently better at addressing complexities of fairness and equity than traditional methods of instruction and large-scale assessment. The prospect is exciting and the basic architectural components are now well articulated [21]. In addition, extended from their roots in intelligent tutoring systems, which were typically closed and domain-specific, AIS have an additional goal of being inter-operable platforms which augment other forms of formal and informal learning [21] and may therefore be capable of capturing important contextual variables.

Yet, personalization algorithms are likely to suffer from bias as well. To date there is little published research to date examining dimensions of fairness and access in these systems, let alone proposing mitigating functionality and practice such as those outlined in standards for assessment. There is important work to do. At a minimum and as a start, contextual data related to each of the four aspects of fairness and access described above should be included in AIS instrumentation. For example: as the IEEE Adaptive Instructional Systems (C/LT/AIS) P2247 Working Group defines a standard conceptual model for AIS [22], due attention should be paid to detection and representation of learner states influenced by membership in a number of underrepresented classes; AIS literature does not yet present models for content, adaptive drivers, and learning pathways that may be most appropriate for culturally and linguistically diverse, neuro-divergent, geographically diverse, and socio-economically diverse populations; AIS interaction models may not use universal design or other design methods intended to limit construct-irrelevant variance; statistical methodologies to detect when content, instructional decisions, or interaction models limit the ability of an individual to demonstrate their competence on the construct of interest due to construct-irrelevant factors have not yet been developed (or extended from existing psychometric methods, as appropriate); and evidence collected may not yet have enough contextual metadata or means to interpret this metadata to ensure suitability of the use of this evidence for subsequent decision-making.

In addition, it is also possible that AIS could magnify fairness issues, especially those around measurement bias and access, due to an extended timeline of system use and complex interactions required of authentic experiences. If ongoing algorithmic use of invalid learner evidence occurs, the impact may even compound. As an example, one can imagine loss of time and opportunity to learn as a potential outcome. If a learner is provided with repetitive inner loops unnecessarily because the evidence collected is muddied with construct-irrelevant variance, they may remain in a non-mastery state for longer than necessary, falling further and further behind same-ability peers. If the evidence within or the outcome of the AIS is then used for summative means (e.g., course completion or promotion, certificate) it is possible the system will begin to become a cause of inequity, especially as in the future learning ecosystem, the importance of competency-based credentials for admissions, hiring and promotion is expected to increase.

Therefore, it is of critical importance that research on AIS fairness and equity issues, updates to AIS conceptual models, and resulting best practices, be prioritized prior to summative use of AIS evidence. In fact, the potential impact of lack of fairness and access indicates that an active research agenda should be actively pursued even within the current assumption that evidence collected within AIS serve a formative purpose only.

2.2   Security and Impact of Security Breaches

As might be expected, the higher the personal stakes associated with an assessment, the higher the incentive to achieve desired outcomes at all costs. As with fairness and equity issues, cheating is another way in which the validity of using collected evidence for a summative decision may be threatened. Unfortunately, large-scale summative assessment has considerable experience in this area, with scandals such as teachers changing responses provided by students for better school accountability metrics [23] and parents paying bribes to inflate college admissions test scores to gain entrance for their students into highly competitive colleges [24]. In response, test users and testing organizations carefully proctor test administration sites for cheating, take extensive measures to confirm an examinee's identity, monitor global exposure of test questions, and complete sophisticated statistical analyses following assessments to identify exam attempts that indicate a high probability of cheating. In addition, to reduce opportunities for systematic cheating by those with conflicts of interest, the International Test Commission guidelines state that "Proctors and/or test administrators should not also serve as instructors, subject matter experts, trainers, or in other roles that provide access to content assessed by the test or in other ways present possible conflicts of interest that may impact a test taker's performance" [25]. Some of the most common ways in which cheating occurs include: use of proxy, use of unapproved ancillary materials and item pre-knowledge.

Security in AIS. If evidence collected in an AIS will be used for eventual summative decisions such as admissions, hiring, or accountability, it is likely attempts to game the AIS will occur. This is a rich area of future study for the AIS community, as existing literature on detection of cheating within an AIS is minimal and requires extension (e.g., [26]). For the most part to date, AIS learner models operate on the assumption that the learner is interacting with the system in good faith.

It can be argued that cheating will be much more difficult in an AIS due to ongoing longitudinal data collection and algorithm sophistication. Over time, each learner should develop a digital "fingerprint" for learning. Yet, this presumes two things: (1) The learner is either using the same AIS over an extended period of time or different AIS a learner encounters can share the "fingerprint" with one other, and (2) AIS are prepared with the instrumentation, contextual metadata and the statistical and algorithmic methodology to detect anomalies in the "fingerprint." Neither of these hold true today.

Use of Proxies. A simple example of a security incident that changes the suitability of evidence for decision-making may be that of use of a proxy during un-proctored use of the system. One might imagine a parent or teacher completing work in the system for a learner, or a learner engaging a higher-ability proxy to complete work, if the actual or perceived stakes associated with the outcome or speed of achieving that outcome are high (e.g., a higher course grade, entry to a higher level tracked course, a certificate required for a job). Technologies are improving for identity verification. While it may not be necessary to verify identity for every interaction that happens within and AIS, it may be sufficient at the outset to simply tag atomic AIS evidence as "verified identity" or "unverified identity" so that suitability of use of that evidence for different purposes may be evaluated. This would also allow for the study and modeling of potential anomalies.

Access to Ancillary Material and Support. The amount of ancillary information an individual has access to while working in an AIS will also influence the interpretation of results. Many standardized and summative tests tightly control access to ancillary information so as to improve comparability of results across individuals. For example, during standardized tests, locked-down browsers and highly specified formula sheets are standard fare. A quick google search on "how can I cheat on a test" can reveal a great deal of effort expended by cheating test-takers to conceal "cheat sheets" and explains the rigorous rules and procedures employed as examinees enter test centers. In a learning situation, it is likely undesirable to limit an individual's access to external material at all times, but knowing what the learner accessed when interacting with the AIS may be critical context for proper interpretation of results. Therefore, an AIS should consider how to capture and store data indicating use of ancillary materials or other support with each interaction.

Item Pre-Knowledge. Item pre-knowledge occurs when a student has access to test questions and their answers prior to a test. For high-stakes summative assessments, item harvesters, who interact with an assessment for the sole purpose of memorizing a subset of assessment items which are then sold to incoming examinees, can cause significant threats to the validity of the examination results. There are a number of practices used in response to these challenges: large item banks or automated item generation on the fly, adaptive testing (which doesn't change the item itself but changes the order of or the set of items an examinee encounters), and statistical methods to detect unusual response times on items. Given the expense of creating authentic learning experiences within AIS, and the memorability of authentic learning experiences, item harvesting would certainly be possible. Yet, it isn't clear it would be probable. Regardless, existing methods related to response time and some of the measures of engagement used in AIS may provide a foundation work for detection of item pre-knowledge if it occurs. An AIS should also be able to provide indications of number of attempts on any given content an individual student has had as metadata to collected evidence.

Other Gaming. In some cases, methods of gaming the system may be counter to expectations yet could influence a summative decision. It may not be identifiable as cheating. For example, in a system on which this author worked that was never released beyond a beta stage, students purposefully did not answer items correctly so that they would be placed with a human instructor more quickly. While not detrimental to their learning outcome, but slowing their pace, this practice rendered use of the evidence gathered inappropriate for summative decision-making about the students' ability. Another example of unexpected use may be a teacher providing prompting or scaffolding outside of the system. As the learner then enters what look like independent responses in the system, it may limit the use of those results for subsequent summative use as they would cause an overestimate of the learner's independent ability on the construct. In both of these cases, contextual metadata would be important to evaluating the evidence for suitability of use for different types of decisions.

3   Discussion

This paper examined two aspects of standardized and summative testing as they may relate to the use of evidence from an AIS for summative decision-making, those of fairness and equity of access and of security. At this point it should be recognized that an understanding of the potential uses of evidence from the AIS should be explicated and become a basis for system design to maximize viability of the solution for any summative purposes in addition to the formative purposes around which the AIS is built.

As a first step, an analysis of contextual variables that will allow for the study and elaboration of methods to address fairness, equity of access, and security should be completed. AIS should be instrumented to minimally collect this metadata with each interaction event. As the body of research expands and methods evolve, interoperability standards such as Caliper or xAPI should be updated with specifications for contextual information such that individual data elements may be judged for suitability of use for various types of decision-making.

At the same time, new technologies in areas such as identity recognition, low bandwidth sensors, and edge computing are likely to expand the realm of possibility for understanding the ways in which learners are interacting with AIS, which may in turn allow for novel solutions to the problems originally addressed by standardized assessment conditions for all learners.

Fairness, equity of access, and security are some of the key reasons that standardized and summative assessment evolved to the state it is today, and as such are critical topics to explore as we consider a world in which authentic experiences in learning via AIS are captured in evidence that can be eventually be used for summative decision-making. This paper has attempted to outline a few suggestions to move our understanding and technology in these areas beyond good intent.

That said, they are not the only issues to be considered. Data privacy will continue to dominate discussions and will have different implications for different segments of the life-long learning journey and for citizens of different nationalities. As learners will have interaction with AIS of varying origin, interoperability standards become critical to the ability to understand the context, temporal aspects and granularity of data from multiple AIS and being able and to make sense of it to truly understand the learner's amalgamated learning experience. Grading, micro-credential, and certification policies and procedures that employ AIS evidence, including thoughtful consideration of the impact of those policies on learner willingness to make mistakes within the AIS and the relative weight to afford different pieces of evidence, will need to be examined and adjusted. Nuances of collecting evidence on learner progress while at the same time collecting evidence on system efficacy, modeling learning content, and tuning algorithms may introduce additional contextual metadata needs. Costs of delivering AIS at scale may be challenged, especially for authentic interactions that require human interpretations of evidence presented for learners. Communication to learners about the potential future use of their learning evidence will be important to develop and the result of that communication may influence teacher, learner, and parent or other stakeholder behavior in the AIS systems. Finally, it remains to be studied how bias or errors in diagnosis and recommendations over time in a low-stakes environment accumulate and impact decisions that are made with serious and meaningful intent.

At this cross-roads between formative and summative, personalized and standardized, researchers, psychometricians, and technologists have a golden opportunity to ensure AIS of the future collect rich evidence that serves as a conduit, rather than a hurdle, to a learner's destinations.

Acknowledgements. The author is grateful to Dr. Alina von Davier and Dr. Robert Sottilare for their thoughtful review and comments during the preparation of this paper.

References

1. Bell, B., Sottilare, R.: Adaptation vectors for instructional agents. In: Sottilare, R.A., Schwarz, J. (eds.) HCII 2019. LNCS, vol. 11597, pp. 3–14. Springer, Cham (2019). https://doi.org/10.1007/978-3-030-22341-0_1
2. Cavanagh, S.: No Longer Just a Testing Company: Inside ACT's Transformation. EdWeek Market Brief, 15 August 2019
3. Walcutt, J.J., Schatz, S. (eds.): Modernizing Learning: Building the Future Learning Ecosystem. Government Publishing Office, Washington, D.C. (2019)
4. Bannon, B., Dabbagh, N., Walcutt, J.J.: Instructional strategies for the future. In: Walcutt, J.J., Schatz, S. (eds.) Modernizing Learning: Building the Future Learning Ecosystem. Government Publishing Office, Washington, D.C. (2019)
5. IEEE IC Industry Consortium on Learning Engineering Homepage. https://www.ieeeicicle.org/. Accessed 15 Jan 2020
6. American Educational Research Association, American Psychological Association, and National Council of Measurement in Education: Standards for Educational and Psychological Testing. American Educational Research Association, Washington, D.C. (2014)
7. William, D.: Formative assessment: getting the focus right. Edu. Assess. **11**(3), 283–289 (2006)
8. Mislevy, R.J., Steinberg, L.S., Almond, R.G.: On the structure of educational assessments. Measur.: Interdisc. Res. Perspect. **1**, 3–67 (2003)

9. Arieli-Attali, M., Ward, S., Thomas, J., Deonovic, B., von Davier, A.A.: The expanded evidence-centered design (e-ECD) for learning and assessment systems: a framework for incorporating learning goals and processes within assessment design. Front. Psychol. **10**, 853 (2019)

10. Huggins-Manley, A.C., et al.: A commentary on construct validity when using operational virtual learning environment data in effectiveness studies. J. Res. Educ. Eff. **12**(4), 750–759 (2019)

11. International Test Commission. https://www.intestcom.org. Accessed 15 Jan 2020

12. European Federation of Psychologists' Associations and European Association of Work and Organizational Psychologists: European Test User Standards for test use in Work and Organizational settings. http://www.eawop.org/uploads/datas/10/original/European-test-user-standards-v1-92.pdf?1297020028. Accessed 18 Jan 2020

13. ISO 10667–1:2011 Assessment service delivery – Procedures and methods to assess people in work and organizational settings – Part 1: Requirements for the client. https://www.iso.org/standard/56441.html. Accessed 18 Jan 2020

14. International Test Commission: International Guidelines on Test use. https://www.intestcom.org/files/guideline_test_use.pdf. Accessed 17 Jan 2020

15. United States. Section 504 of the Rehabilitation Act of 1973: Handicapped Persons Rights under Federal Law. Department of Health, Education, and Welfare, Office of the Secretary, Office for Civil Rights, Washington, D.C. (1978)

16. Web Content Accessibility Guidelines (WCAG) 2.0. https://www.w3.org/TR/WCAG20/. Accessed 18 Jan 2020

17. Meyer, A., Rose, D.H., Gordon, D.: Universal Design for Learning: Theory and Practice. CAST, Wakefield (2014)

18. International Test Commission, International Guidelines for the Large-Scale Assessment of Linguistically and Culturally Diverse Populations. https://www.intestcom.org/files/guideline_diverse_populations.pdf. Accessed 12 Jan 2020

19. Jones, R., Fox, C.: Navigating the Digital Shift 2018: Equitable Opportunities for All Learners. State Educational Technology Directors Association (SETDA), Washington, D.C. (2018)

20. ACT, Inc.: Fee Waiver Eligibility Requirements 2019–2020. https://www.act.org/content/dam/act/unsecured/documents/FeeWaiver.pdf. Accessed 18 Jan 2020

21. Sottilare, R.A.: A comprehensive review of design goals and emerging solutions for adaptive instructional systems. Technol. Inst. Cogn. Learn. **11**, 5–38 (2018)

22. Adaptive Instructional Systems (C/LT/AIS) P2247.1. https://site.ieee.org/sagroups-2247-1/. Accessed 10 Jan 2020

23. Blinder, A.: Atlanta educators convicted in school cheating scandal. New York Times (2015). https://www.nytimes.com/2015/04/02/us/verdict-reached-in-atlanta-school-testing-trial.html

24. Burke, M.: Former SAT/ACT test administrator pleads guilty in college admissions scandal. NBC News (2015). https://www.nbcnews.com/news/us-news/former-sat-act-test-administrator-pleads-guilty-college-admissions-scandal-n1081196

25. International Test Commission: International Guidelines on the Security of Tests, Examinations, and Other Assessments. https://www.intestcom.org/files/guideline$_$test$_$security.pdf. Accessed 12 Jan 2020

26. Yang, J., Oh, K., Lee, S.: A design of learning management system using adaptive recommendation method. In: Proceeding of the 6th International Seminar on Industrial Engineering and Management (2013). https://isiem.net/wp-content/uploads/2015/06/DSS-p9-13.2013.pdf

Contextual Barriers to Validity in Adaptive Instruction and Assessment

Karen Barton[✉]

Moyock, NC 27958, USA
karenbarton77@yahoo.com

Abstract. The value and validity within highly personalized programs can either be strengthened or diminished by variability in implementation, environment, and interpretation. Developers of adaptive programs have an opportunity – a responsibility – to provide transparency and insights on how variation plays a part in the value and validity of the program. This paper describes the impact variability can have on value perceptions and the resulting degradation of trust in results from an adaptive assessment used as part of an instructional program. Described is the process used to redesign score reports that considers the context of the administration and resulting interpretations. The paper then presents a theoretical challenge to the adaptive nature of instructionally situated assessments intended to reflect ultimate use.

Keywords: Validity · Adaptive assessment · Assessment administration

1 Introduction

Adaptive learning and assessment systems are intended to meet individual needs and support timely and targeted instruction with flexibility and individualization. The value and validity within highly personalized programs can either be strengthened or diminished by variability in implementation, environment, and interpretation. Research on the effectiveness of educational programs and assessments indicates that contextual factors in the instructional environment and characters therein (i.e., teachers, administrators, students) play a major role. Environmentally, the likelihood of a program to positively impact student success greatly depends on the implementation in terms of fidelity, quality, and acceptability (Albers et al. 2017). Those involved in the program also have an impact. Expectations of individual and groups of teachers can have a collective impact on student achievement (Eells 2011), as can students' expectations. Hattie's (2009) meta-analysis found that students' own expectations for success have a very large effect (effect size of 1.44) on student achievement. The relationship and interactions between teachers and students are also important (effect size of 0.72). Context and characters can also impact the validity of assessments. Messick (1998), known for extensive writings on psychometric validity along with Cronbach (1971) and others, posited that assessment validity was just as much about the context, interpretations, actions taken from results as the test itself.

© Springer Nature Switzerland AG 2020
R. A. Sottilare and J. Schwarz (Eds.): HCII 2020, LNCS 12214, pp. 447–457, 2020.
https://doi.org/10.1007/978-3-030-50788-6_33

There will always be diverse learning environments and infinite variability in relationships, perspectives, and expectations. While attending to fidelity in implementation is a start, developers of adaptive programs have an opportunity – a responsibility – to provide transparency and insights on how variation plays a part in the value and validity of the program. Program designs should directly consider and account for diverse uses and contexts, much like that of design thinking approaches. That is, by attending to the end user and the purposes for which they are likely to use a product and supporting users with clarity and caution as they use a product can contextualize expectations and maximize the promised value. In so doing variability relative to purpose (validity) and value (including use) can come into balance.

This paper describes the impact variability can have on value perceptions and the resulting degradation of trust in results from an adaptive assessment used as part of an instructional program. Described is the process used to redesign score reports that considers the context of the administration and resulting interpretations. The paper then presents a theoretical challenge to the adaptive nature of instructionally situated assessments intended to reflect ultimate use.

2   Classroom Scenario

Consider a middle school teacher of mathematics responsible for 30 sixth to eighth grade students in each of four classes. The teacher is accountable for ensuring each of the 120 students of mixed abilities is instructed according to the district scope and sequence for each grade, with material aligned to and reflective of the grade-level state standards. The teacher is also responsible for providing evidence that students show growth. The teacher's annual performance review will consider how much students grow in terms of score increases on the assessment.

The district purchases personalized instruction and assessment program for teachers to use. Administrators receive aggregated reports across classes, grades, and schools. Results of the assessments are sometimes used to placed students in instructional programs or classes, and district policy requires the scores serves as the primary metric in evaluating the teacher. Individual student and class level reports provide scale scores, score confidence intervals, normative scores, domain and skill level scores, and growth as a difference in scores from one administration to the next.

Because the assessment is designed to provide a personalized testing experience and resulting instruction, the assessment adapts to each student's ability by administering items that can be on, above, or below the grade of the student (i.e., "grade agnostic"). The adaptive engine continues testing each student until ability estimates reach a minimum threshold of precision (standard error of measure) or when the student reaches a maximum number of items allowed. There are also algorithmic constraints on content coverage (minimum number of items) to determine where in a content domain a student should begin their learning activities.

The adaptive assessment is given at the beginning of the school year and again closer to the end of year, just before the spring administration of the state's summative assessment. The testing windows for the adaptive assessment are about 8 to 10 weeks long, and teachers can administer the assessment anytime during those weeks, earlier or later as they see fit. Guidance for administering the assessment, provided by the developers of the program, suggests ways to minimize distractions and ensure administrations are comparable. In reality, few teachers take the time to read the guidance document. And, given various logistical challenges (for example, access to computers or devices for testing) and precious little instructional time, teachers often direct students to start and continuing working on the assessment at various points during class, across class periods, and as time permits. As a result, students in a class complete their assessments at different times and in as many test sessions as they need and have time to finish, even across days or weeks within the test window.

3   Designing Value and Validity in Reporting

Assuming programs are developed defensibly, validity is most at stake when the stakeholder or end user receives and interprets reports. If the reports convey accurate data in such a way that is misinterpreted, validity is at risk. Recall that Messick (1998) explained that validity is not only a characteristic of the test, but also of the interpretations. Where and with whom does the responsibility for validity in interpretations lie?

The Standards (2014) deem valid and accurate reporting is ultimately the developer responsibility and interpretation is the test user responsibility. However, the Standards also note that interpretive materials should be provided by the developer to minimize misinterpretation and resulting negative consequences. These may include indications of score precision, administration guidelines, and interpretive guidance.

Developers should understand and design for the realities of how the program is used, how assessments are administered, and what decisions will be made from the results. Then, information should be made readily available to provide end users with insights about how the program is designed to work and how administrative context may have an impact.

Building reports that increase transparency and understanding about how a program is intended to work and to be used builds trust and usefulness – validity. For example, teachers tend to be very curious (even suspicious) about how adaptive assessments really work. Generic illustrations like Fig. 1 are often provided in training or support materials to explain how adaptive assessments work. The actual path of a student's adaptive test administration is not provided as part of any score reporting. By seeing how the test works, teachers, students and parents can gain understanding and trust in the adaptive test.

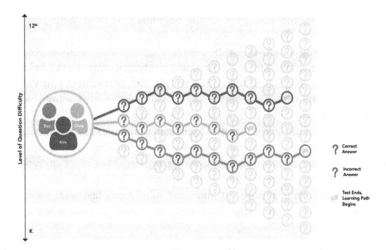

Fig. 1. Illustration to describe how an adaptive assessment adapts. *Courtesy of Edmentum*

Teachers are also interested in seeing the actual items students receive on assessments. After all, their jobs may depend upon their students' performance on those items. And, with item level reports for a class, teachers can see what items students struggle or do well so as to group students and help with instructional planning. On adaptive assessments, developers do not typically show the actual items students were administered for various reasons. These include protecting the depth of item pools and for ease of interpretation given students likely receive little if any of the same items on an adaptive test, making it difficult to aggregate and providing limited instructional value.

3.1   Variability in Context

Assume the after fall and winter test administrations, the middle school math teacher reviews the results from each class. The growth scores show unexpected score drops for some students and large increases for others. The teacher is confident the results do not reflect what students know and have demonstrated during class, or how they are really growing. However, there is nothing in the reports to indicate any reason for the differences in scores from one administration to the next other than actual student performance. It is assumed that the scores are all valid and accurate.

Even though the teacher disagrees with the results, what evidence does the teacher have to confirm or challenge their accuracy? Is there any information provided to the teacher that might indicate any differences in the administration conditions between the fall or winter tests? Perhaps students were simply distracted or unmotivated in the second assessment and showed significant decrease in scores, or negative growth. The opposite may also be true: students could have been very unmotivated or distracted during the first assessment compared to the second, such that the magnitude of positive growth is welcomed albeit unexpected. What responsibility does a vendor have in supporting the teacher with greater contextual information to better explain the differences and for valid interpretations?

3.2 A Practical and Transparent Solution

The teacher in this scenario could benefit from some additional transparency into the testing experience. By taking into consideration what happened during the administrations, the interpretations and subsequence decisions could be made with greater confidence. Showing the teacher contextualized information would presumably lead to more valid interpretations.

Developers are encouraged to "conduct research to help verify that reports and materials can be interpreted as intended" (Standards 2014, p. 119). In complement and extension of early research on score reporting by Zenisky and Hambleton (2012) and principled report design provided by Lewis (2019), Barton and Kosh (2019) developed a process for score report design and validation intended to illuminate and bring greater understanding of the adaptive nature of assessments and potential variability in administrations on a student level. The inspiration for the work stemmed from concerns expressed by teachers about how long the test seemed to take and the perceived inaccuracy of the growth scores reported. The researchers conducted extensive investigations and validated the algorithm and the scores were working as designed. They found that actual testing times were not any longer than one might expect and an in many cases shorter. The scores and psychometric characteristics were validated by a technical advisory board and independently verified.

Curious as to the culprit of the negative perceptions, observations in classrooms using the program and administering the assessment were informally conducted. It became clear that the contributing factor could be non-standard administration practices and the informal nature of the teachers' directions for taking the assessment (for example, treating the assessment as an assignment to be completed when time permitted).

To bring greater transparency in the reports, Barton and Kosh (2019) worked with report designers to develop score reports that show each assessment experience in full. The reports, an example of which is provided in Fig. 2, focus on providing as much information as possible about the administration conditions, student effort, and the way in which the adaptive algorithm adjusts based on student response accuracy. The reports can be viewed with respect to administration, student effort, and student performance.

Administrative Contexts. To illuminate administrative conditions and contexts, the report displays the date on which the student first started taking the assessment and the last day the assessment was finished. This provides a sense of the span of days the student may have had to start and restart, signally to teachers how a long testing window can impact student effort, motivation, performance and comparability from one test to the next. Within those days are test sessions, reported so that it is easy to see if a student had one or two sessions over a couple of days, or 7 sessions over 20 days. The reports provide the total duration of the assessment in terms of time by summing the minutes a student was actually in the system. These key metrics help teachers discern whether their perception of a "long test" has to do with actual test time or span of days or frequency of sessions.

Part of the perception of a test being too long was also related to the assumption that the test has too many items. Most adaptive assessments don't report exactly how many items each student received, save for technical documentation of stopping rules driven by a maximum number of items. By not showing the information directly, teachers naturally become more curious, suspicious, and frustrated, especially when they are accustomed to receiving information about the total points and items in non-adaptive assessments.

Experience. To help provide insights into the student test experience, the researchers worked to develop an "experience" view report similar to illustrations of how a test adapts. An item-by-item, bubble view of student performance (correct/incorrect) for each administration or test experience helps convey how the algorithm works and the number of items students were administered (see Fig. 2). Each item bubble can be interactively explored to see the skill each item measured. This can help teachers dig into the skills students may need to review. (Student performance on specific content domains are also provided to support instruction.)

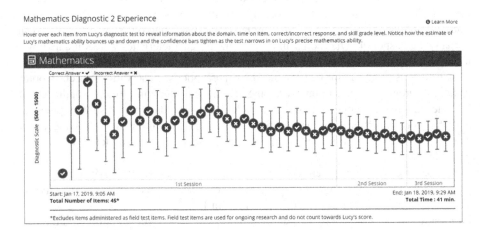

Fig. 2. Adaptive assessment report to illuminate variability in assessment administration and ensure comparability of scores. *Courtesy of Edmentum*

Effort. Student effort can undermine the validity and value of reports. When students spend too little time on an item, it may be a lack of motivation or guessing behaviors for students unable to provide a considered response. Providing some information about student effort is a first step. Wise (2017) has conducted extensive research in the area of rapid-guessing on items in adaptive assessments and how scores might be presented in the context of rapid-guessing data. Why might a student provide a rapid-guess? What else is going on in the administration context that demotivates a student, encourages rapid guessing, or generally sheds light on the scores reported? Are scores even comparable? Do they reflect inconsistencies in administration or motivation, rather than actual performance?

Wise (2019) suggests ways to determine response time thresholds and subsequent score adjustments. While the scores in the program described here are not adjusted for lack of effort, descriptive information is provided in the reports for teachers to consider, contextually. Each of the interactive item bubbles also shows how much time the student spent on each item. This can help teachers determine the items on which students spend more or less time. When a student is spending a long time on a single item, the teacher can consider the skill associated with the item and if there is some expected challenge for the student; or where in the progress of testing the student may have had a long response time that might indicate distractions in the classroom. For example, the researchers observed administrations where students were asked to stay on the first item until the teacher permitted them to move to the next item. In many classrooms, students took the tests only as time permitted, such as in the last few moments of class, or while lots of other activities were going on. All the information can help a teacher consider and interpret the results based on conditions of testing, distractions, motivation, and potential skill-related challenges.

3.3   Validity Testing

By addressing end-user concerns and misunderstandings about the assessments directly and with transparency in the reports, perceptions in this example moved from "what's wrong with your test" to helping teachers understand what they can do to ensure trustworthy results. Training teachers on the importance of comparable test administrations, less distracting test-taking environments, and the impact on the results can greatly increase the validity, value, and trust of the scores. To be sure, taking steps to validate interpretability of reports, and providing supports for increasing literacy, the validity of the reports and ultimately the efficacy of the program can be greatly improved.

A user experience or usability study is helpful for ensuring the features and aesthetics of reports are agreeable. Taking the time to also validate interpretations is a critical additional step. Barton and Kosh (2019) conducted a validation study with virtual, interactive focus groups with teachers, asking open ended questions to gauge understanding and interpretations of the information presented. In addition to asking questions like "do you like this new feature? Would you use this button? Or can you find this link?" asking open ended questions forces participants to consider how they might actually interpret and use the information provided in reports.

In their validation study of reports provided for a computer adaptive assessment, Barton and Kosh (2019) found teachers misinterpreted the meaning of scores and of aesthetics. For example, in the first version of a report that shows the student experience through the computer adaptive assessment, item bubbles were colored to show the domain to which each item was aligned. Teachers misinterpreted the colors to mean that the assessment was adapting within domain, rather than at the overall ability estimate. As a result of the study, reports were adjusted to bring clarity to the reports and improve the validity of user interpretation.

Prior assessment literacy also plays a role in score interpretations. Barton and Kosh (2019) found that teachers struggled to understand the meaning of national percentiles and standard errors of measurement, among other key metrics useful to valid interpretation. As it is the developer's responsibility to minimize misinterpretations, opportunities to increase assessment literacy, made readily available such as through videos and concise explanations of assessment concepts, would seem especially helpful. (See Fig. 3 example of reports with embedded literacy links.)

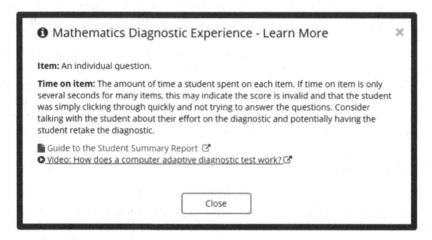

Fig. 3. Adaptive assessment report to illuminate variability in assessment administration and ensure comparability of scores. *Courtesy of Edmentum*

4   Contextual Considerations – A Challenge to Broad Adaptivity

Part of assessment literacy is the level of literacy of the designers and developers of educational programs. Assessments used in instructional programs as well as for accountability (i.e., growth and predictability to state assessment performance) should reflect at least some understanding by the teams in development, user experience, and the like, of the context, purpose, and ultimately the decisions to be made from the assessment results. As exampled in this paper, such understanding should drive design of reports. It should also drive the design for how the program or assessment adapts.

An important benefit of computer adaptive assessments is the efficiency with which information about student ability can be provided (Wise and Kingsbury 2000). By attending to minimum error thresholds, ability for each student can be estimated with higher reliability and typically with fewer items than non-adaptive assessments. Reliability is a necessary condition for the validity of an assessment, though it is not the only important consideration ("necessary but not sufficient"). A measure should be both reliable and valid. The heart of validity is the usefulness - how a measure and results align with the purpose, intention, and decisions to be made. Leucht et al. (1998)

go on to note that, while there is a strong advantage of efficiency and precision in computer adaptive assessments, there are disadvantages in terms of content validity if content expectations are ignored, or in contrast when content is over emphasized. The key is to determine very clearly what is the purpose - and end use - of the results from the test.

Consider personalized adaptive assessments as an example. Computer adaptive assessments are often given to provide, not only highly efficient testing, but a personalized testing experience. When students take an adaptive assessment, different students will likely receive different items, different numbers of items, and finish the assessment at different times. The administration is considered personalized, finding just where each student is "ready to learn." Personalized instruction and personalized assessment are popular phrases with varied interpretations. Peruse any assessment vendor's websites and one can find claims about personalized programs, such as: *Results are personalized and show educators just where students are ready to learn, regardless of grade level.*

According to the Office of Educational Technology (2017), "(p)ersonalized learning refers to instruction in which the pace of learning and the instructional approach are optimized for the needs of each learner." (p. 9) The definition conveys two key points: 1) that students are allowed to learn at their own pace, 2) that instruction matches the needs of each student or learner. To provide the personalized results about the learner and inform pace and instruction, some assessments adapt items across grades; that is students may receive items that are aligned to grades above or below their class grade. Adapting instruction or assessments based on material that may be above or below a student's grade is believed to be the best way to target just what a student is or is not ready to learn.

Personalization through adaptivity that is unconstrained by grade level is not without its practical challenges. Assume that in the middle school scenario, results show students have a wide range of grade-level ability and needs. For some students, the program recommends that instruction begin as far back as third grade. Other students are ready for advanced eighth grade material. However, students are typically assigned to a grade level and receive instruction in said grade level by a teacher who is trained in and required to provide instruction against the grade-level standards. Teachers in the US are also accountable for providing students the opportunity to learn the grade-level standards and ensure students show growth in learning against those grade-level standards during the academic year. Further, the teacher is responsible for teaching all students the on-grade standards according to the pre-defined, required instructional calendar for the district (i.e., scope and sequence).

To make use of the results and personalize instruction, the teacher will need to find time to provide instruction to those students not working on grade according to the assessment reports, all while ensuring the on-grade material is covered adequately as required by the district. While the program provides personalized content and recommendations, there can be additional challenges. The teacher may not be accustomed to covering material or have access to material far outside the on-grade material needed to supplement the content provided within the program. The reality is, with a limited number of hours and days for instruction, the teacher is likely to prioritize on-grade material, thus minimizing the potential benefits of the personalization.

What the teacher needs is information about what the learner is ready to learn based on content that is on or very near the grade-level standards s/he is required to teach. What across-grade assessments assume is that there is a shallowness to content within grade, such that only by adapting across grades can the assessment really show personalized performance and needs. Such an assumption fully ignores content depth and complexity. Plus, adaptive assessments are limited to machine-scored items, further limiting items with greater complexity and depth of knowledge. By accepting such a limitation at face value, the assessments' validity in terms of trust and usefulness and perceived value falls short for the teacher's context.

5   Discussion

When assessments are situated in the context of learning, such as in an instructional program, there is often greater flexibility and less standardization in assessment administration conditions. The variability in administration is usually welcomed as it provides flexibility around what may otherwise be logistical burdens for students and teachers, burdens such as limited access to technology or constraints on class schedules limiting dedicated administration time.

Unfortunately, even in adaptive assessments for learning, extensive variability in administration procedures can have a negative impact on the score comparability from assessment to assessment and student to student, as described in the classroom scenario. Measurement errors can be inflated when an assessment is given in non-standard administration. In assessments, variability or noise in data can be attributable to and estimated quantitatively in terms of measurement error, often reported as confidence intervals around scores. The Standards for Educational and Psychological Assessment [or Standards; AERA, APA, NCME 2014] require assessment developers to work to not only report but reduce the noise (measurement error) and to ensure scores reflect comparable outcomes by building assessments with comparable content. Standardizing assessment administrations in terms of timing, environment, mode, schedule, and so forth, can also help to minimize systematic measurement errors (See Standard 3.4).

Classrooms can be wonderfully noisy – in decibels and in the variability of data. Teachers and students are diverse, from different backgrounds and experiences. Classroom structures and instructional methods, school culture, implementation, can all be quite different, even within the same school and teacher across different classes of students. The challenge is to balance standardization to maximize trust in the results with the promised flexibility in instructional programs.

Validity is directly tied to the purpose, intention, interpretations, and decisions made from the results. Considering context in throughout report development and confirming with validation studies is but one step - a necessary but not sufficient condition. Considering the context of use and interpretation – the purpose – of an adaptive assessment, and then attending to what gets measured and the way in which an assessment adapts is also important to validity.

Developers should understand and then design for the realities of how the program is used, how assessments are administered, and what decisions will be made from the results. They should validate the interpretations of the results. They should provide information to the end users about how the program is designed to work and how administrative context may have an impact. By considering the context in which the assessment will be used could present a balance to reliability and validity, to efficacy and perception, to the ultimate trust and usefulness of the results.

References

American Educational Research Association, American Psychological Association, National Council on Measurement in Education, Joint Committee on Standards for Educational and Psychological Assessment (U.S.): Standards for Educational and Psychological Assessment. AERA, Washington, DC (2014)

Albers, B., Pattuwage, L., Vaughan, T.: Summary of key findings of a scoping review of Implementation in Education. Melbourne: Evidence for Learning (2017). https://www.evidenceforlearning.org.au/assets/Collateral/Albers-and-Pattuwage-2017-Implementation-in-Education.pdf. Accessed 20 Jan 2020

Barton, K., Kosh, A.: Designing score reports to maximize validity and instructional usefulness. In: Invited Presentation at the Maryland Assessment Research Center Conference, University of Maryland, College, Park, MD (2019)

Cronbach, L.J.: Test validation. In: Thorndike, R.L. (ed.) Educational Measurement, 2nd edn, pp. 443–507. American Council on Education, Washington, DC (1971)

Curriculum Associates: i-Ready Diagnostic and Personalized Learning. https://www.casamples.com/downloads/iready-diagnostic-and-personalized-learning-whitepaper-2017.pdf. Accessed 20 Jan 2020

Eells, R.J.: Meta-analysis of the relationship between collective teacher efficacy and student achievement, dissertation, Loyola University of Chicago (2011). https://ecommons.luc.edu/luc_diss/133. Accessed 20 Jan 2020

Hattie, J.: Visible Learning: A Synthesis of Over 800 Meta-analyses Relating to Achievement. Routledge, Milton Park, UK (2009)

Lewis, D.: A principled approach to score reporting in support of user's needs and values. Paper presented at the Annual Meeting of the National Council on Measurement in Education, Toronto, CA (2019)

Leucht, R.M., de Champlain, A., Nungester, R.J.: Maintaining content validity in computerized adaptive testing. Adv. Health Sci. Educ. 3, 29–41 (1998). https://doi.org/10.1023/A:100978931401

Messick, S.: Validity of psychological assessment: Validation of Inferences from Persons' Responses and Performances as Scientific Inquiry into Score Meaning. Research Report RR-95-45. Educational Testing Service, Princeton (1998)

US Department of Education, Office of Educational Technology: Reimagining the role of technology in education: 2017 national education technology plan update, Washington, DC (2017)

Zenisky, A.L., Hambleton, R.K.: Developing assessment score reports that work: the process and best practices for effective communication. Educ. Measur.: Issues Pract. 31(2), 21–26 (2012)

Wise, S.L.: An information-based approach to identifying rapid-guessing thresholds. Appl. Measur. Educ. 32(4), 325–336 (2019)

Wise, S.L.: Rapid-guessing behavior: Its identification, interpretation, and implications. Educ. Measur.: Issues Pract. 36(4), 52–61 (2017)

Wise, S.L., Kingsbury, G.: Practical issues in developing and maintaining a computerized adaptive testing program. Psicológica 21, 135–155 (2000)

Does Time Matter in Learning? A Computer Simulation of Carroll's Model of Learning

Alfred Essa[1]($\boxtimes$) and Shirin Mojarad[2]($\boxtimes$)

[1] Simon Institute, Carnegie Mellon University, Pittsburgh, USA
`alfred.essa@gmail.com`
[2] Apple Inc., Cupertino, USA
`shirin.mojarad@gmail.com`

Abstract. This paper is an exploratory theoretical study of the role of *time* in *learning*. We present a computer simulation based on Carroll's model of school learning. Our aim is to probe some key theoretical questions in educational research: Can all students learn well? If so, under what conditions? What is time's role in learning achievement? How does time relate to other instructional variables such as student aptitude, student perseverance, and quality of instruction? In our approach we regard learning as a *causal system* in which a few variables predict and explain different levels of learning. While the simulation is not a causal analysis in the strict sense, it lays some of the groundwork for a fuller causal approach. Our main result confirms the *Carroll-Bloom hypothesis* that time, as *opportunity to learn*, is a central variable in learning achievement and also key to closing the *achievement gap*. We also demonstrate that time, as learner *perseverance*, accelerates achievement, especially for less prepared students. However, perseverance becomes effective only when the instructional environment surpasses a *basic quality threshold*. We conclude by considering some implications for designing alternative learning environments, particularly adaptive instructional systems.

Keywords: Time on task · Adaptive instructional systems · Mastery learning · Computer simulation

1 Introduction

The systematic interest in time as a *central variable* in instruction originates with John Carroll's model of school learning [1]. Subsequent research has followed at least two major threads. The first thread has aimed at strategies for measuring *time on task* and validating it as an important predictor for *how much* students learn. The pace of these efforts has picked up considerably with the advent of online learning systems and the abundant opportunities they offer to analyze trace data. The second thread has focused on designing *alternative instructional environments*. Among these the most significant are pedagogical environments

© Springer Nature Switzerland AG 2020
R. A. Sottilare and J. Schwarz (Eds.): HCII 2020, LNCS 12214, pp. 458–474, 2020.
https://doi.org/10.1007/978-3-030-50788-6_34

based on Bloom's concept of mastery learning [2]. Benjamin Bloom credits Carroll's model of learning as both the inspiration and theoretical foundation of mastery learning [3,4]. It is believed that in mastery learning environments *most students* are capable of achieving a *high degree of learning* given *sufficient time*.

The maturity of a scientific domain can be gauged by the strength, variety and interconnection of its formal models. A formal model tries to describe, explain, and predict some phenomenon in terms of a small set of basic variables and constants. The relationship among the variables and constants is expressed mathematically. It is often the case, however, that the model's implications are not obvious from its mathematical expression. In such cases, simulations can clarify the model's structure by revealing how changes in one or more variables influence other variables, an important prelude for causal analysis [5].

Our goal in this paper is theoretical. We seek to investigate three fundamental questions in educational research:

Q1: What factors explain *variation* in learning achievement?
Q2: Is time a factor?
Q3: What other factors play an explanatory role and how are they related to time?

Our simulation reconstructs a formal model described by Carroll at a 1961 symposium on the uses of digital computers. Although Carroll's accompanying computer program is now lost, he provides sufficient detail of the model to make a modern reconstruction possible [6]. Our simulation is written in Python and the code is publicly available in github for review, comment, and modification.

1.1   Learning Time and Academic Performance

It takes time to learn. It takes more time to learn well. Both are truisms. Researchers, however, have consistently found a weak or unreliable relationship between *elapsed time* and achievement [7–11]. An extensive study of the issue concludes, for example, that "there is at best only a very small relationship between amount of studying and grades" [12].

Attempts to link *quality time* or time-on-task to achievement seem more promising. Most studies report a positive correlation [13,14]. The positive relationship is thought to hold also in online environments, including adaptive instructional systems [15].

Time has multiple meanings in learning and has been studied from a variety of perspectives. In an important recent paper Rushkin and colleagues demonstrate the benefits of "user slowness" in online environments: "Users who, according to this model, tend to take longer on submits are more likely to complete the course, have a higher level of engagement, and have a higher grade" [16]. A study of procrastination suggests that "*habitually* delaying learning tasks lead to adverse outcomes to the point of catastrophe" [17]. Ericsson and colleagues have demonstrated that time, considered as deliberative practice, can improve academic performance [7]. Finally, the benefits of spaced practice, or time as distributed time, are well known [18,19].

While these studies continue to advance our understanding of the role of time in learning achievement, measuring time remains a complex and challenging task [20]. Karwin and Slavin have also pointed out that differences in operational definitions of time on task, different sample sizes, and different observation intervals all lead to significant inconsistencies in interpreting results [21].

In summary, a persuasive body of research evidence supports the notion that time, particularly time on task, plays an important role in increasing achievement. Despite these advances, however, the nature of the connection between time and achievement remains murky.

1.2   Carroll-Bloom Hypothesis

In this section we state the *Carroll-Bloom Hypothesis* (CB Hypothesis). It will serve as an important guidepost for our investigation because it defines operationally what is meant by the claim that "most students are capable of high achievement given sufficient time".

Both Carroll and Bloom share the thesis that nearly all students are capable of high achievement. Therefore, in their view a paramount goal of educational research should be to design learning environments in which all students, not just a few, can achieve a high degree of learning.

We state two versions of the *Carroll-Bloom Hypothesis*. The general version makes no mention of time. The specific version incorporates time as a key variable.

Carroll-Bloom Hypothesis (General). An optimal learning environment is achievable. In an *optimal* learning environment at least 80% of students can reach the criterion level of attainment attained by 20% of the students in a *conventional* learning environment.

The general version of the *CB Hypothesis* is stated most famously in Bloom's paper describing the *2 Sigma Problem*. In the paper Bloom contrasts three modes of instruction: conventional, mastery learning, and 1–1 tutorial. Bloom reports that variation of student achievement in the three environments is such that "about 90% of the tutored students and 70% of the mastery learning students attained the level of summative achievement reached by only the highest 20% of the students under conventional instructional conditions" [22].

Bloom's *2 Sigma* paper can be read in two ways. First, it advocates mastery learning as the pedagogical approach for designing an optimal learning environment. Bloom claims that under mastery learning conditions it is possible to achieve an effect size gain of one *sigma* and beyond compared to conventional instruction. Second, Bloom advocates the *search* for learning environments and pedagogical strategies where outcomes can reach one *sigma* and beyond.

Carroll and Bloom also shared the thesis that large effect sizes in education would be made possible only by incorporating time as a key variable. We can now state the time-specific version of the *CB Hypothesis*.

Carroll-Bloom Hypothesis (Time Specific). An optimal learning is achievable. In an optimal learning environment (i.e. effect size of one σ or greater), time is a key variable.

Figure 1 contrasts the final achievement distribution of conventional learning environments (green) with optimal learning environments (purple). In an optimal leaving environment more than 80% of students get "Bs" and "As" compared to only about 20% of students in a conventional environment.

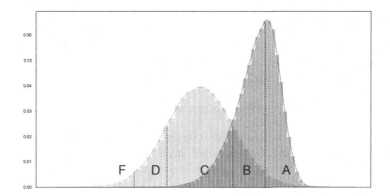

Fig. 1. Final achievement distribution: conventional vs optimal

2   Formal Model and Computer Simulation

In this section we describe Carroll's model of learning as a formal model. We then apply the model as the basis of our simulation.

The essence of Carroll's model of learning is captured in a basic ratio. Both the numerator and denominator of the ratio are time variables. Henceforth, we will refer to the ratio as the *Carroll Ratio*.

Degree of Learning = Time Spent / Time Needed

Intuitively, the *Carroll Ratio* states that if a learner is given the amount of time she *needs* to learn and if she perseveres for that amount of time, she will reach the target or criterion level of achievement. In the ideal case the ratio is 1. However, in most cases the learner is either not afforded the time they need to learn, or they don't spend the amount of time needed, or both. The student's degree of learning then is the ratio of actual time spent over time needed. It is understood that in the context of the model, time spent is time-on-task and not elapsed time.

The degree c_i to which an individual i learns a task, unit of instruction, or program of study, therefore, is a direct function of time spent to time needed:

$$c_i = f\left(\frac{t_{spent}}{t_{needed}}\right) \tag{1}$$

The quantity c_i ranges from 0 to 1. The model does not allow for overlearning. Because the numerator and denominator are both temporal variables, c_i is unitless.

2.1 Basic Variables

The two temporal variables in the *Carroll Ratio* are calculated from five basic variables: o, p, g_i, a_i, and m_i. We can express degree of learning c_i, therefore, as a function of the five basic variables:

$$c_i = f(o, p, g_i, a_i, m_i) \tag{2}$$

The five basic variables fall into two classes: instructional environment variables, and learner variables. Instructional environment variables are *external* to the learner while learner variables are *internal* states or abilities of the learner (Fig. 2).

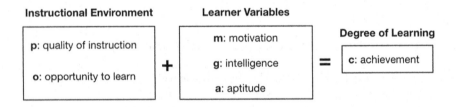

Fig. 2. Basic variables in Carroll's model of learning

2.1.1 Instructional Environment Variables

- The variable 'o' represents *opportunity to learn* and is the time allowed for learning the task, measured in units of time.
- The variable 'p' represents *quality of instruction* and is the adequacy with which the learning task is presented or taught. To the extent that p is less than optimal, the time needed for learning increases.

2.1.2 Learner Variables

- The variable 'g_i' represents *general intelligence*. It is a relatively stable characteristic of the learner and determines her ability to understand the material. The higher the intelligence the less time it should take to learn the task.

- The variable 'a_i' represents *aptitude* and is the time required by the learner to learn the task to a specified criterion of learning. Aptitude can be interpreted partially as prior knowledge. Those with more aptitude come in with a higher degree of prior knowledge. Those with higher aptitude have a lower value for a_i.
- The variable 'm_i' represents *motivation* and is the maximum time a learner is willing to expend in learning the task. Carroll, as do we, uses the term motivation and perseverance equivalently.

We note that the learner variables are indexed, where the index i represents an individual learner. The instructional environment variables (o and p) in the model are the same for each learner. However, in the simulation we vary both variables to trace their influence on achievement.

2.2 Derived Variables

In addition to the five basic variables, we derive three additional variables: u_i, a_i', t_i

- The variable 'u_i' represents *understanding* of the task requirements of learning. It is a function of general intelligence g_i and quality of instruction p.

$$u_i = f_1(g_i, p) \tag{3}$$

  The function f_1 is set so that $u_i = f_1[p/A(g_i)]$, where $A(g_i)$ is normal-curve area above the value of g_i. Also, $u_i = 1$ for all cases in which $p > A(g_i)$.
  As the quality of instruction (p in the numerator) increases, so does each student's understanding. Understanding is also a function of general intelligence in the denominator. Instead of using 'g' directly we map it to the corresponding area of the normal-curve above the value of g_i. The higher the value for intelligence, the smaller the value for $A(g_i)$ in the denominator.
- The variable 'a_i'' is the time actually needed by individual i to learn a task. It is computed as:

$$a_i' = \frac{a_i}{u_i} \tag{4}$$

  In the case that $u_i = 1$ (perfect understanding), $a_i' = a_i$. If the learner has difficulty in understanding the material (i.e. $u_i < 1$), the individual will require more time to learn.
- The variable 't_i' represents the time *actually* spent by the learner. It is a function of a_i', m_i, and o. In fact, it is the smallest or minimum of the three values.

$$t_i = \min(a_i', m_i, o) \tag{5}$$

2.3 Carroll Ratio

Given the basic and derived variables, we can readily calculate the *Carroll Ratio* as:

$$c_i = \frac{t_i}{a_i'} \tag{6}$$

2.4   Populating the Variables

For the simulation we populate the five basic variables as follows:

- The variable p, adequacy or *quality of instruction*, is measured on a scale from 0 (completely inadequate) to 1 (perfectly adequate). During different rounds of the simulation we will allow p to vary from 0 to 1 in increments of .1.
- The variable o, *opportunity to learn*, is measured in units of time. It falls in the range from 1 to 10. During different rounds of the simulation we allow o to vary from 1 to 10 in increments of 1.
- The variable m_i, motivation for a learner i, is drawn randomly from a normal distribution with a mean $\bar{m} = 5.0$ and standard deviation $\sigma = 1.0$.
- The variable a_i, aptitude for a learner i, is also drawn randomly from a normal distribution with a mean $\bar{a} = 5.0$ and standard deviation $\sigma = 1.0$. As stated previously, a_i specifies a criterion for learner under the assumption of perfect understanding (i.e $u_i = 1$). The true aptitude a_i' is calculated as a function of u_i and a_i.
- The variable g_i, general intelligence, is drawn from a normal distribution with mean $\bar{g} = 0$ and $\sigma = 1$.

In the model, the values for intelligence, aptitude, and motivation are randomly and independently assigned to each learner.

2.5   Simulation Rounds

The simulation is performed in rounds. We arbitrarily chose $n = 10,000$ students, but n can be set at any number in the model and in the computer code. We confirmed that the simulation results are the same to a small approximation for any sufficiently large n (e.g. $n > 100$).

Each round $\rho_{j,k}$ of the simulation is an ordered pair (o_j, p_k). For example, in the round $\rho = (2, .2)$ both opportunity to learn $o = 2$ and quality of instruction $p = .2$ are low. By contrast, in the round with $\rho = (8, .8)$ both opportunity to learn $(o = 8)$ and quality of instruction $(p = .8)$ are high.

The sum of the rounds is a set R, which is the cartesian product of *opportunity to learn* and *quality of instruction*:

$$R = O \times P = \{(o, p) \mid o \in O, p \in P\} \tag{7}$$

Again, the values for o range from 1 to 10 and the values for p range from .1 to 1.0. However, during the simulation we set the lower and upper boundaries at $(2, 9)$ for o and $(.2, .9)$ for $.p$. Therefore, the total number of rounds for the simulation (cardinality of R) was 64.

$$|R| = |O| \times |P| \tag{8}$$

3   Results

We analyze the simulation with three principal questions in mind:

Q1. How does degree of learning (c) vary as we vary the instructional environment (o, p)?
Q2. How does degree of learning (c) vary as we vary learner characteristics (g, a, m)?
Q3. Can the achievement gap be closed? In other words, can learners with low aptitude (a) achieve a high degree of learning?

As noted previously, the simulation contains $n = 10,000$ students with 64 rounds. Each round consists of a different combination of o and p.

3.1   Performance

First, we analyze performance of the 10,000 learners. Performance is analyzed in terms of pass rates and performance distributions in each round.

Pass rates for different combinations of opportunity to learn (o) and quality of instruction (p) are displayed in Fig. 3. Although we set the criterion for pass at ($c >= .65$), the observed pattern holds for nearby thresholds.

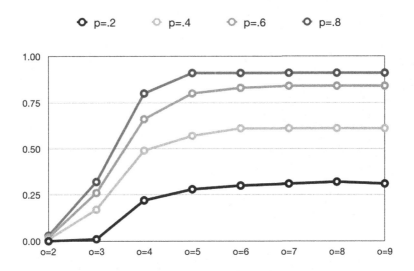

Fig. 3. Pass Rates: Different Combinations of **o** and **p**

First, we see that when instructional quality is very low (i.e. $p \le .2$), there is little benefit in increasing time as opportunity to learn (o). Pass rate remains well below 50%. Everyone suffers in a low quality instructional environment.

However, once instructional quality increases to ($p = .4$) or above we see a significant rise in pass rates as opportunity to learn (o) increases from ($o = 3$)

to $(o = 4)$. Working in tandem, opportunity to learn and quality of instruction work fuel a sharp rise in achievement. The optimal area is where $(o = 5, p = .6)$. Performance begins to plateau after $(o = 5)$ and there is only a marginal improvement in pass rates beyond $(p = .6)$.

Next, we examine performance distributions instead of pass rates. In analyzing performance distributions we set the environment $(o = 3, p = .4)$ as the *baseline* instructional environment for comparison. Why? Because in the baseline environment 20% of students achieve a criterion of .8 or above (i.e. equivalent to an "A" or a "B"). This matches our discussion of the Carroll-Bloom hypothesis where we stated that in a conventional learning environment approximately 20% students achieve a high degree of learning.

Table 1. High achievement rates

Environment	Percentage
Baseline (o = 3, p = .4)	16.7%
(o = 6, p = .4)	44.1%
(o = 8, p= .8)	76.1%

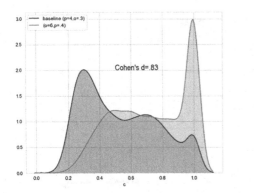 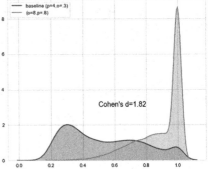

Fig. 4. Performance distributions: baseline vs optimal

Figure 4 shows performance distributions of baseline environment $(o = 3, p = .4)$ compared to two optimal environments, $(o = 6, p = .4)$ and $(o = 8, p = .8)$. The first optimal environment $(o = 6, p = .4)$ shows an effect size gain of approximately one standard deviation, while the second $(o = 8, p = .8)$ shows an effect size gain of approximately two standard deviations.

Table 1 summarizes percentage of learners who achieve high degree of learning $(c \geq .8)$ in the three environments. By high degree of learning we mean the percentage of students who achieved criterion level of .8 or above in those environments.

The simulation results show convincingly that both time, as opportunity to learn, and quality of instruction significantly affect performance. We also confirm, at least theoretically, that the time specific version of the Carroll-Bloom hypothesis.

3.2   Pearson Correlations

Next, we analyze the results of the simulation by examining how Pearson correlations r between degree of learning (c) varies as we vary, on the hand, intelligence (g), aptitude (a) and motivation (m), and, on the other hand, quality of instruction (p) and opportunity for learning (o).

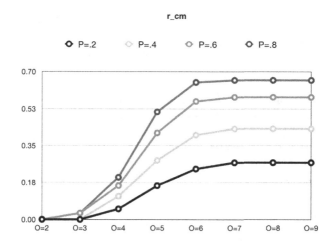

Fig. 5. Pearson correlations: degree of learning vs motivation

Figure 5 displays the Pearson correlations $(y\text{-}axis)$ between motivation (m) and degree of learning (c) for different combinations of p and o. Similarly, Fig. 6 displays the correlations between aptitude (a) and degree of learning for different combinations of p and o. Finally, Fig. 7 displays the correlations between intelligence (g) and degree of learning for different combinations of p and o.

As we might expect, environments in which the opportunity to learn (o) is low (in the range of 2–4) the correlation of motivation to achievement (Fig. 5) is low. *This remains the case even as we vary the quality of instruction.* We interpret this to mean that below a certain threshold $(o \leq 4)$, motivation or perseverance by itself is not sufficient to overcome environmental handicaps.

However, having crossed a certain threshold in opportunity to learn $(o = 4)$ we see a sharp increase in achievement. The slope of the increase also increases with an increase in the quality of instruction as p increases from .2 to .4 and higher. We also observe that benefits begin to plateau all around once opportunity to learn crosses the threshold $(o = 6)$. This suggests that as we design instructional environments we need to consider tradeoffs between cost and benefit.

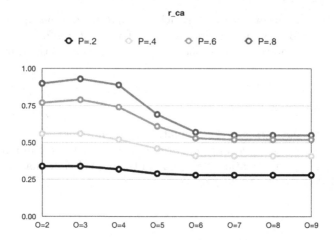

Fig. 6. Pearson correlations: degree of learning vs aptitude

What is the role of aptitude (e.g. prior knowledge) in achievement? If we vary o, the amount of time given for learning, we would expect that less apt students will have less and less chance to catch up with more apt students if there is less opportunity given. As o decreases, we would expect that the correlation between aptitude ($-a_i$, that is, the amount of time needed by the individual, measured in reverse) and success in learning to increase. And this is what we see in Fig. 6.

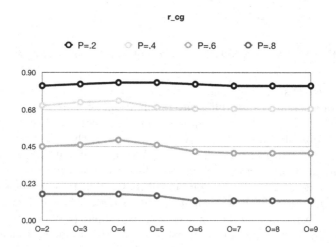

Fig. 7. Pearson correlations: degree of learning vs intelligence

What do we see when we examine the correlations between degree of learning and intelligence? In general all students suffer from poor quality of instruction. However, students with high intelligence (g) are able to better withstand poor learning quality environments. Figure 7 shows that the correlation of achievement to intelligence is highest when quality of instruction is lowest. As quality of instruction increases, however, the correlation of intelligence to achievement decreases. We also see that correlation of intelligence to achievement stays relatively constant as opportunity to learn varies.

3.3   Multiple Regression

Next, we ran separate multiple regressions for each of the 64 rounds of the simulation.

A multiple linear regression model with k predictor variables $X_1, X_2, \ldots, X_k$ and a response Y, can be written as:

$$y = \beta_0 + \beta_1 x_1 + \beta_2 x_1 + \ldots + \beta_k x_k + \epsilon. \tag{9}$$

Applying it to the Carroll model, the predictor variables are g, a, and m. The target or response variable is c.

$$c = \beta_0 + \beta_g \times g + \beta_a \times a + \ldots + \beta_m \times m + \epsilon. \tag{10}$$

Figure 8 displays the relative importance of the three coefficients of the regression for the 64 rounds. We display the combinations only for $(p = .2, .4, .6, .8)$.

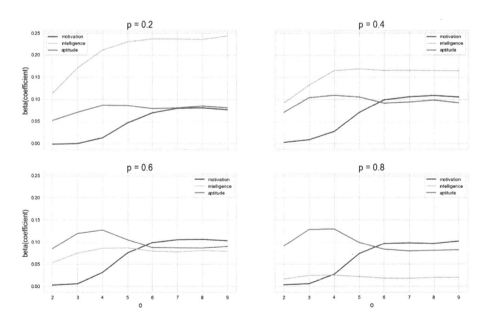

Fig. 8. Multiple regression coefficients

When quality of instruction is very low $(p = .2)$, intelligence dominates. The importance of motivation begins to rise as opportunity to learn increases. It eventually catches up with aptitude. However, both aptitude and motivation remain well below intelligence.

When quality of instruction is very high ($p = .8$), aptitude dominates at the beginning. But as opportunity to learn increases, motivation or perseverance begins to rise sharply and overtakes aptitude at ($o = 6$). General intelligence remains relatively flat throughout.

In the middle where quality of instruction is moderate to high (i.e. $p = .4$ to $p = .6$), aptitude plays a stronger role when opportunity to learn is low. However, motivation rises sharply and overtakes aptitude in importance as opportunity to learn increases. Intelligence diminishes in importance as both opportunity to learn and quality of instruction rise.

3.4   Closing the Achievement Gap

We have already seen that increasing time in the sense of opportunity of learn (variable "o") and improving the quality of instruction (variable "p"), benefits everyone. In this section we shine the spotlight on the achievement gap. How do less prepared students fare? Is there sufficient opportunity to close the achievement gap?

We define less prepared students as students whose aptitude is one or more standard deviations below the mean. Because in our model aptitude is normally distributed, 16% of the students fall in this category.

Figure 9 show performance of low aptitude students with a high motivation in two environments: ($o = 5, p.5$) and ($o = 6, p = .6$). Their performance is compared against all students in the baseline environment of ($o = 3, p = .4$). In the first environment, the low-aptitude and high motivation effect size is approximately Cohen's d $= 1.0$. In the second environment, the effect size is approximately Cohen's d $= 2.0$.

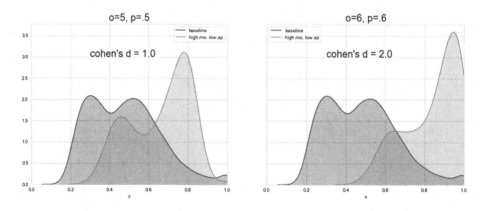

Fig. 9. Performance distributions: high motivation, low aptitude

Figure 10 shows bivariate distributions of motivation vs achievement for low aptitude students in three environments. The distribution in ($o = 4, p = .4$) is

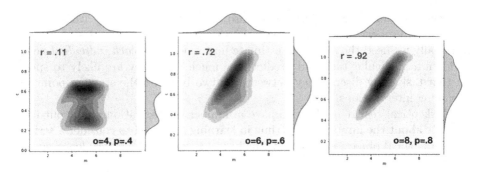

Fig. 10. Low aptitude students: bivariate distribution (degree of learning vs motivation)

bimodal with a correlation of $r = .11$. As the learning environment provides greater support with opportunity to learn and improved quality of instruction, achievement increases and so does the correlation of motivation to achievement.

In summary, three factors play significant roles in closing the achievement gap: time as opportunity to learn, quality of instruction, and high motivation.

4 Discussion

Explaining variation in learning achievement is a perennial problem in education research. Most research studies take a single shot strategy. By convention we a set of explanatory variables are isolated for study. Then the study results report their relationship to an outcome variable such as achievement. The relationship typically takes the form of statistical significance, correlation or regression. We have put forward an alternative approach where a **theoretical model** generates a *range of possible outcomes* along with their probabilities. Much like a Monte Carlo simulation, the formal model allows us to treat outcomes as probability distributions.

We have seen that a modeling approach unmasks potential flaws of single shot studies. The regression analysis demonstrated, for example, that the regression coefficients can vary wildly depending on the instructional environment, i.e. the specific values of instructional quality (p) and time as opportunity to learn (o).

A formal model provides other benefits. The simulation reveals not only *that* the coefficients vary, but *how* they vary. We saw, for example, that perseverance matters. But it matters and is effective only when the instructional environment exceeds a certain threshold. In this case, theory can inform experiment and practice. If grit, for example, contributes to achievement, it is important to understand the background conditions and context in which it is effective.

We confirmed the *Carroll-Bloom hypothesis* that time, as opportunity to learn, matters in learning. As a result, instructional environments that aim to improve learning must seriously take into account time as a key variable. For online environments and adaptive instructional systems, a clear lesson is that minimally we need the ability to estimate how much time *each individual* needs to learn a particular task and predict how much time they are likely to spend on that task. Any discrepancy between the two becomes the starting point for designing interventions.

A skeptical reader is likely to have a number of reservation about our conclusions about the importance of time in learning. We need to consider a serious methodological objection raised by Slavin in his review of mastery learning:

> In an extreme form, the central contentions of mastery learning theory are almost tautologically true. If we establish a reasonable set of learning objectives and demand that every subject achieve them at a high level regardless of how long that takes, then it is virtually certain that all students will ultimately achieve that criterion.
>
> If we establish a reasonable set of learning objectives and demand that every student achieve them at a high level *regardless of how long that takes*, then it is virtually certain that all students will ultimately achieve that criterion [23].

Slavin's objection is that if we allow an infinite amount of time for any learner to achieve a learning criterion, then it will be trivially true that all learners will eventually achieve the criterion. The objection, though valid, can be met with a rejoinder. The theoretical model does not allow for an infinite time to reach the criterion, but is constructed so that the opportunity to learn occurs stepwise and in stages. Having said that, it is the task of experiment and empirical evidence to discover precisely the difference the stages. The model states a difference between $o = 4$ and $o = 5$. It is also the work of experiment to discover the effect size differences between the two levels.

In his review of mastery learning Slavin posed another important objection about the significance of time in achievement. Slavin's second objection is practical.

> If some students take much longer to learn a particular objective, then one of two things must happen. Either corrective instruction must be given outside of regular class time, or students who achieve mastery early on will have to spend considerable amounts of time waiting for their classmates to catch up. The first option, extra time, is expensive and difficult to arrange, as it requires that teachers be available outside of class time to work with the nonmasters and that some spend a great deal more time on any particular subject than they do ordinarily [23].

Slavin's assumption that time allocation is a zero-sum exercise is valid only in a traditional classroom model. Slavin reasons correctly that human instructors have a fixed amount of time that they can devote to all students in their class. If some students need additional time for learning, surely it will come at the expense of other students.

But an important promise of educational technology is that instructor time and allocation need not be a zero-sum game. Slavin's objection provides the pathway of opportunity for introducing adaptive instructional systems. If additional time is needed by students to learn and learn well, adaptive systems can serve as intelligent coaches. Human instructor time is finite. Computer instructor time is infinite. Human instructors working in concert with intelligent computer instructor assistants can work in tandem to deliver optimal instructional environments.

5 Conclusion

A prevailing view in education is that there are good learners and there are poor learners. Achievement then is largely a function of intelligence and other relatively stable characteristics of the learner. Many school systems and instructional environments continue to be organized on this basis. During the early 1960s Carroll challenged this assumption with his model of school learning. Our enactment of his model in the form of a computer simulation lends theoretical support to the Carroll-Bloom hypothesis that most learners are capable of high achievement given sufficient time. We also highlight the importance of theoretical models in designing learning environments.

References

1. Carroll, J.B.: A model of school learning. Teach. Coll. Rec. **64**, 723–733 (1963)
2. Guskey, T.R.: Closing achievement gaps: revisiting Benjamin S. Bloom's 'Learning for Mastery'. J. Adv. Acad. **19**(1), 8–31 (2007)
3. Bloom, B.S.: Time and learning. Am. Psychol. **29**(9), 682 (1974)
4. Bloom, B.S.: Learning for mastery. Instruction and curriculum. Regional education laboratory for the Carolinas and Virginia, topical papers and reprints, number 1. Eval. Comment **1**(2), n2 (1968)
5. Durán, J.M.: Computer Simulations in Science and Engineering: Concepts–Practices–Perspectives. TFC. Springer, Cham (2018). https://doi.org/10.1007/978-3-319-90882-3
6. Carroll, J.B.: Computer applications in the investigation of models in educational research. In: Proceedings of a Harvard Symposium on Digital Computers and Their Applications, 3–6 April 1961 (1962)
7. Plant, E.A., Ericsson, K.A., Hill, L., Asberg, K.: Why study time does not predict grade point average across college students: Implications of deliberate practice for academic performance. Contemp. Educ. Psychol. **30**(1), 96–116 (2005)
8. Beer, J., Beer, J.: Classroom and home study times and grades while at college using a single-subject design. Psychol. Rep. **71**(1), 233–234 (1992)
9. Gortner Lahmers, A., Zulauf, C.R.: Factors associated with academic time use and academic performance of college students: a recursive approach. J. Coll. Stud. Dev. (2000)
10. Masui, C., Broeckmans, J., Doumen, S., Groenen, A., Molenberghs, G.: Do diligent students perform better? Complex relations between student and course characteristics, study time, and academic performance in higher education. Stud. High. Educ. **39**(4), 621–643 (2014)

11. Doumen, S., Broeckmans, J., Masui, C.: The role of self-study time in freshmen's achievement. Educ. Psychol. **34**(3), 385–402 (2014)
12. Schuman, H., Walsh, E., Olson, C., Etheridge, B.: Effort and reward: the assumption that college grades are affected by quantity of study. Soc. Forces **63**(4), 945–966 (1985)
13. Romero, M., Barbera, E.: Quality of e-learners' time and learning performance beyond quantitative time-on-task. Int. Rev. Res. Open Distrib. Learn. **12**(5), 125–137 (2011)
14. Wagner, P., Schober, B., Spiel, C.: Time students spend working at home for school. Learn. Instr. **18**(4), 309–320 (2008)
15. Baker, R.S.J.: Modeling and understanding students' off-task behavior in intelligent tutoring systems. In: Proceedings of the SIGCHI Conference on Human Factors in Computing Systems, pp. 1059–1068 (2007)
16. Rushkin, I., Chuang, I., Tingley, D.: Modelling and using response times in MOOCs (2017)
17. Essa, A., Agnihotri, L.: Measuring Procrastination and Associated Probabilities for Student Success, Unpublished Manuscript (2018)
18. Caple, C.: The Effects of Spaced Practice and Spaced Review on Recall and Retention Using Computer Assisted Instruction (1996)
19. Rohrer, D., Pashler, H.: Increasing retention without increasing study time. Curr. Dir. Psychol. Sci. **16**(4), 183–186 (2007)
20. Kovanović, V., Gašević, D., Dawson, S., Joksimović, S., Baker, R.S., Hatala, M.: Penetrating the black box of time-on-task estimation. In: Proceedings of the Fifth International Conference on Learning Analytics and Knowledge, pp. 184–193 (2015)
21. Karweit, N., Slavin, R.E.: Time-on-task: Issues of timing, sampling, and definition. J. Educ. Psychol. **74**(6), 844 (1982)
22. Bloom, B.S.: The 2 sigma problem: the search for methods of group instruction as effective as one-to-one tutoring. Educ. Res. **13**(6), 4–16 (1984)
23. Slavin, R.E.: Mastery learning reconsidered. Rev. Educ. Res. **57**(2), 175–213 (1987)

Competency Development Through Experiential Training: Mapping Scenarios with Assessments

Benjamin Goldberg[1($\boxtimes$)], Michael Hoffman[2], Chris Meyer[3], and Mike Kalaf[3]

[1] U.S. Army Combat Capability Development Command – Soldier Center, Orlando, FL 32826, USA
benjamin.s.goldberg.civ@mail.mil
[2] Dignitas Technologies, Orlando, FL 32817, USA
mhoffman@dignitastech.com
[3] Synaptic Sparks, Inc., Orlando, FL 32832, USA
{chris,mike}@synapticsparks.org

Abstract. A training ecosystem leverages multiple complementary instructional resources to target competency and skill development. In this paper, we introduce work that is integrating assessment functions in the Generalized Intelligent Framework for Tutoring (GIFT) with core components in the Total Learning Architecture (TLA) to support persistent performance tracking and reporting in dynamic simulation-based environments. This capability creates a data strategy to translate multi-modal raw data into contextualized statements of performance for use in a long-term readiness monitoring strategy. In this paper we discuss the integration activities, what this new extended architecture supports, and provide a high-level use case associated with infantry squad level competency sets.

Keywords: Adaptive training · Real-time assessment · Competency tracking · GIFT · Total Learning Architecture · Competency and Skill System

1 Introduction

The U.S. Army is modernizing the way it employs simulation-based technologies to train today's Soldier. The program, called the Synthetic Training Environment (STE), aims to leverage recent advancements in gaming, virtual, and augmented reality tools and methods to build immersive and engaging interactions that promote team development and collective readiness. Part of the STE are a set of Training Management Tools (TMT) that assist in the Planning, Preparation, Execution and Assessment of all scenarios and interactions supported within. Part of that capability set includes the provision of adaptive instructional system (AIS) functions at two levels of interaction. The first, aims to optimize the learning gains within a single training exercise by establishing data-derived performance assessments, using those assessments to drive real-time coaching and exercise control, and facilitating in depth After Action Reviews (AAR) in the absence of expert trainers. The second level of interaction is focused on

This is a U.S. government work and not under copyright protection in the U.S.;
foreign copyright protection may apply 2020
R. A. Sottilare and J. Schwarz (Eds.): HCII 2020, LNCS 12214, pp. 475–492, 2020.
https://doi.org/10.1007/978-3-030-50788-6_35

skill acquisition tracking and establishing persistent representations of performance over time. Through this capability requirement, STE will specify performance data to be captured and stored across all interactions and environments.

What does persistent performance tracking provide? Under a persistent context, skills are built to establish higher-level transferable competencies that associate with measurable requirements for solving a problem or completing a task. To support both AIS interaction levels in STE, two primary challenges need to be addressed; establishing a framework of both individual and team-level competency models across appropriate echelon structures and team configurations, and establishing a workflow for converting raw data captured in a training scenario into meaningful measures of performance and effectiveness that not only drive real-time coaching and exercise control, but also map to the competencies of interest. This supports an evidence-centered design strategy for persistently tracking performance through data-driven methods, but requires careful consideration on authoring AIS functions for a specific scenario and configuring it with a long-term competency framework.

In this paper, we describe on-going work to extend the Generalized Intelligent Framework for Tutoring (GIFT [1]) to fit within a competency development strategy that utilizes an ecosystem of training resources [2]. This involves integrating GIFT's assessment and pedagogical models with persistent learner modeling functions and building authoring workflows to map scenario level performance with a competency framework tracking a long-term knowledge and skill development progression. To support this experiential tracking requirement, GIFT is integrating with functional components from the Advanced Distributed Learning (ADL) Initiative's Total Learning Architecture (TLA [2]) that enable longitudinal performance tracking across a set of specified competency models. For our purposes, these baseline components are being extended to enable tracking of team-level attributes correlated with performance outcomes and mastery determinations.

To contextualize the discussion, we will present a low-level use case based on measurement of infantry squad competencies, and how training strategies can apply data-driven methods to track progression toward a state of readiness across disparate training interventions/environments (e.g., game-based, immersive simulation, live, etc.). Using this example, we will define the extended architecture and inherent data dependencies created by integrating GIFT and the TLA. We will then review the flow of data between architectural components that link trainee(s) interaction to real-time assessments in GIFT, the translation of those assessments into granular and aggregated measures of performance and measures of effectiveness, and how tracked measures map to an infantry squad competency model that tracks both individual and team level performance. Based on this data strategy, an authoring and configuration workflow will be considered that addresses each level of data inference.

1.1 Competency Development Training Strategy

A competency-driven training strategy is based on carefully designed pedagogical and andragogical experiences that target a set of specified Knowledge, Skills, Abilities, Attitudes (KSAAs [21]). When developing a training strategy to target specific job roles and functions, these KSAA representations are carefully established within a defined "competency object". In this instance, a job role or educational topic is comprised of a competency model (i.e., multiple inter-related competency objects) that associates with KSAAs to support domain understanding and ability to perform domain functions. Within this context, the operational definition for each category is as follows:

- Knowledge: an understanding of the declarative, procedural and conceptual components of a topic or job function.
- Skill: context-driven behaviors that can be learned and improved over time.
- Ability: underlying natural or inbuilt behaviors that are transferrable and can be honed and improved upon to some extent (e.g., speed, strength, intelligence, etc.).
- Attitude: affective and emotional control functions driven by task characteristics/demands and common job/role functions.

When considering the interplay between competency dimensions, the common rule is that ability and knowledge combine to create usable skills [3]. Knowing how to do something, and having the cognitive and physical attributes to apply that knowledge under realistic task conditions is the foundation skill builds from. Through this formalization, competency models establish these KSAA inter-dependencies. And training strategies establish a crawl, walk, run approach to development [4, 23], and design a program of instruction based on the established competency model relational dependencies. When knowledge and ability combine to create skill, the trainee requires multiple opportunities of replication under realistic conditions, with supporting scaffolds to guide mental model development and deliberate feedback to correct errors and reinforce proper technique [5]. The goal of a competency-based strategy is to achieve a specified level of mastery across the KSAAs [6], so that their application is seamless and accurate when required during operation.

For complex job roles and across military occupational specialties, it is recognized that the development of knowledge and skill is not contained within a single environment or interaction. An ecosystem, like the TLA, establishes a library of resources that are mapped across a set of competency objects. The overall competency model establishes a high-level abstracted view of measurable data fields across KSAAs that are independent of any deliverable training or educational experience within that ecosystem. This abstracted view of competency objects is then mapped to the available resources, and can then ultimately be used to prescribe training and track progress towards expert role standards. The objective is to create a path through the resources (i.e., training aids, devices, simulations and simulators) that build the KSAAs, and then provide ample opportunities to apply of those skills under novel contexts. The dependency to implement a strategy of this nature is access to data from the training resources a model of this nature would subscribe to.

The challenge is properly contextualizing the data cross multiple sources and variables. The assumption is a training or educational experience is designed with problems/events/scenarios that target the application of specific competency objects. Within this paradigm, the scenario context defines the competencies required to meet task objectives, along with context-oriented assessments to inform performance and derive evidence [24]. GIFT's real-time assessment tools provide the ability to code those context oriented assessments in its domain-agnostic task model, providing a translation layer and converting raw multi-modal data into key measures of performance and effectiveness. Tracking this recorded evidence over time across a large number of assessment opportunities provides a reinforcement update function for adjusting competency assertions and building a competency profile of high confidence. What's critical is establishing profiles that track team competencies and developing models to measure readiness as a means of experience applying core competencies over time and under required conditions determined by leadership.

1.2 Team Competencies and Accelerating Readiness

In the arena of military operations, it is well understood that most occupational specialties are not performed in an isolated fashion. Majority of individuals are trained to serve a role within a team structure, where skill sets are combined to support complex mission types with often multiple associated objectives. As such, from an organizational perspective, it is critical to not only track an individual's ability to apply a set of skills within a unique set of contexts (i.e., can they perform their role functions?), but it is also vital to monitor the impact of that function on overarching team performance and outcomes (i.e., can they serve as an optimal teammate while satisfying their role?). In examining the literature, team-level attributes are critical when determining what makes an expert team [7]. Building unit-level competency objects and tracking performance dimensions that correlate with team outcomes is a critical component the research looks to support (see Fig. 1 [8]). Building out these competencies into their constituent KSAAs and establishing assessments techniques to track progress against them, programs of instruction can use these data points to better guide follow-on training events that target weak points recognized. To that point, there is a need for training resources that focus on team development techniques, and applying proven sports psychology coaching methods to establish policy-driven andragogical models that focus on experiential learning events. Using GIFT to support a training strategy of this nature is an objective we are designing towards. Specifically, authoring and configuration specifications are required to map assessments captured in a scenario to models tracking long-range performance.

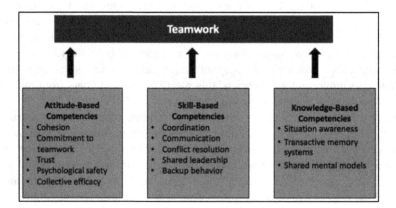

Fig. 1. Team competencies: attitudes, behaviors, and cognitions. This figure provides a subset of evidence-based team competencies [8].

2 Architecture

To support a data-driven competency-based training strategy using AIS applications, an architecture is required to enable data capture across multiple training experiences. In this instance, data capture associates with experiential measures of performance derived from a training environment that are contextualized around a task and an associated competency model. Ultimately, the framework will convert raw data generated during execution of a scenario or problem into meaningful evidence statements, where evidence is used to drive updates to a persistent model that tracks levels of mastery. As described above, a training intervention or exercise is selected based on the foundational assumption that the content is linked against specific competencies, and that measures generated are realistic and sensitive to the context they are derived within, and that the measures provide discriminatory evidence against defined standards and criteria for successful application [9].

To support this vision through a proof of concept prototype, we are integrating three technology baselines: (1) the Generalized Intelligent Framework for Tutoring (GIFT) to provide data contextualization through its real-time assessment functions, (2) the Learner Record Store (LRS) with xAPI statements to provide a performance reporting data standard to enable warehousing of performance records across multiple environments, and (3) the Competency and Skill System (CaSS) to provide a data-defined competency model standard that consumes LRS data to build competency profiles based on available evidence. In the following subsections, each technology baseline within the architecture is described. This section is then followed up by a use case highlighting the competency-based training strategy applied within the domain of infantry squad development and implemented within the persistent AIS framework.

2.1 Generalized Intelligent Framework for Tutoring (GIFT)

The Generalized Intelligent Framework for Tutoring (GIFT [10, 11]) is an open-source, domain-independent, modular, service-oriented architecture used to make computer-based tutoring systems. The careful design of GIFT provides levels of reusability across domains, training applications and technologies. It has also been proven to be a backbone for the integration of automated and observed real time assessments across the Live, Virtual and Constructive (LVC) training system landscape. One unique feature of GIFT is the ability to easily define assessment and pedagogical/andragogical models for individual or team training by creating a Domain Knowledge File (DKF).

A DKF is used by the GIFT architecture (see Fig. 2) to continuously evaluate the learner against scenario specific measures while executing tasks in the training environment. The structure of the DKF provides a configurable schema to define the measures that are important for contextualizing various streams of raw data for higher level meaning. GIFT can utilize state information produced by the training environment (e.g. entity locations), physical sensors (e.g. breathing waveform), biographical information, affective state (e.g. excitement) and historical data to determine learner state across performance, cognitive and affective categories. In order to make sense of the continuous real time assessments being calculated, DKF authors organize measures as evidence of performance for each concept being evaluated.

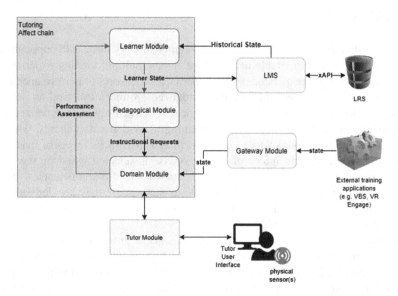

Fig. 2. GIFT real-time assessment components that contextualize data in evidence based performance statements.

Concepts are user defined labels given performance assessment values which can be used by GIFT for updating learner state during training. These learner state updates (e.g., trainee performance transitioned from at-expectation to below-expectation after observed error) are used to trigger real-time adaptations, and populate After Action Reviews (AARs), as part of historical records. The same concepts can then be reused across DKFs for persistent tracking of learner state, the concepts are elevated to course concepts. Course concepts can be used in other parts of the course beyond training applications such as surveys/quizzes/tests, tagging of content with metadata, identification of which concepts should be taught in a specific portion of a course, and the specific concepts that need remediation to be delivered.

During a GIFT course, learner state information is continuously being evaluated, updated and shared between various components of the GIFT architecture. This information can be delivered to external, long term learner record stores (LRS) for use in future training experiences by GIFT and other applications. In order to facilitate this collaboration among disconnected systems there needs to be an agreed upon standard by which records can be defined and understood. A widely used standard that provides this shared format for both the receiving and sending of data is the eXperience Application Program Interface (xAPI [12, 13]). The GIFT application currently produces and consumes xAPI statements from a Learner Record Store (LRS).

2.2   eXperience Application Programming Interface (xAPI) and Learner Record Stores (LRS)

GIFT consumes, analyzes and interprets various forms of raw data such as training environment state information and historic events. By routing selected information like learner state to the LMS module in GIFT, xAPI statements can be written to a Learner Record Store (LRS) for long term storage and reuse later. LRSs are useful for receiving, storing and returning information about learning events created by one or more systems in which the event happened or was documented in. These events can be anything from high level experiences (e.g. Alice scored an 89 on the Algebra test) to low level training environment details (e.g. GPS location of Bravo team). This same LRS can easily be updated or read from by other systems the learner may interact with in order to provide a hub for a learning ecosystem (see Fig. 3 for anxAPI data flow strategy [2]).

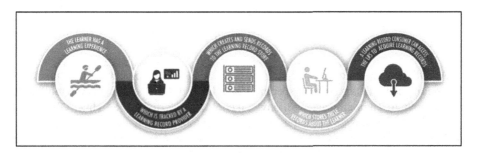

Fig. 3. The Advanced Distributed Learning Initiative xAPI Data Flow (Experience API, 2020)

To support interoperability across platforms that utilize LRSs in their reporting functions, xAPI is being applied in this use case. The Advanced Distributed Learning (ADL) Initiative xAPI effort was created in order to meet a need to track overall learning experiences. While xAPI is a vast and growing technical specification [14], one basic building block of xAPI relevant to GIFT is the "Statement" object. A Statement in consists of syntactical subcomponents, namely Actors, Verbs, Objects, Results, and Contexts (see Fig. 4 for an example).

These subcomponents, being bound together by additional syntax rules, provide the specification necessary to create well-formed Statements. When implemented correctly, these well-formed Statements allow disparate systems to communicate about learning experiences and outcomes in a common language. Thus GIFT, being both a consumer and producer of xAPI statements, is able to participate in learner ecosystems.

```
{
        "actor" : {
                "objectType": "Agent",
                "mbox":"mailto:test@example.com"
        },
        "verb" : {
                "id":"http://example.com/commented",
                "display": {
                        "en-US":"commented"
                }
        },
        "object" : {
                "objectType":"StatementRef",
                "id":"8f87ccde-bb56-4c2e-ab83-44982ef22df0"
        },
        "result" : {
                "response" : "Wow, nice work!"
        }
}
```

Fig. 4. An Example xAPI Statement [13]

As GIFT is an ongoing open-source research and development project, the team does not mandate the use of any specific LMS. Instead, GIFT offers a compatible API with options to communicate with any stakeholder preferred LMS. Thus, GIFT provides a direct AIS subcomponent as either a standalone learning experience with basic LRS options, or as part of a larger instructional system framework such as the Total Learning Architecture (Total Learning Architecture [15]).

It is worth noting GIFT's utilization of the xAPI specification has been architected in strict compliance with the official xAPI standards in order to both produce and consume data. The open nature of GIFT's API has allowed for compatibility with the learning community at large, and allowed GIFT to be integrated with other systems architected in similar fashion. The next section will describe one such framework with which GIFT has been integrated, the Competency and Skill System (CaSS).

2.3   Competency and Skill System (CaSS)

The CaSS is a project that began in 2016 under ADL [16]. Like GIFT, the CaSS consists of open source code and was created in an effort to satisfy similar high-level goals of being able to improve the sharing of information concerning learners and learning resources. In this section we present a brief introduction to CaSS, the services that CaSS provides, and the relevant integrations with GIFT.

The reader is welcome to visit the CaSS Homepage at the link above for a full explanation of CaSS, but for the purposes of this paper, please reference the CaSS Overview Document [17]. Directly quoted; CaSS provides the following two services:

- (1) "Define, store, manage, and access objects called competencies that are organized into structured collections called frameworks. Competencies can represent competencies, skills, knowledge, abilities, traits, learning objectives, learning outcomes, and other similar constructs that define performance, mastery, attainment, or capabilities. Frameworks are associated with a knowledge domain, a domain of endeavor, a job, or a task with structure defined by relations among the competencies they (or other frameworks) contain."
- (2) "Store assertions about the competencies held by an individual (or team), and compile assertions and other data into profiles that describe a learner's current state. CaSS is designed to respond to queries from other applications that, for instance, ask whether an individual X holds a competency Y (at performance level Z). CaSS will answer yes or no and might include a number indicating its confidence in the answer, a link to evidence, and an expiry date. In addition, CaSS can collect assertions and other data from multiple sources and apply relations and rules to formulate a response to a query."

At this time, GIFT software developers are in the process of formally integrating GIFT capabilities with the first CaSS service revolving primarily around the storage and access of competencies. To support mission readiness analysis in the future, a second CaSS service will be integrated to make assertions across individual and team competency structures. As referenced in the introduction, the concept and implementation of a system in support of KSAAs can be directly related to combining software suites like GIFT and CaSS.

Competency Models in CaSS. CaSS, through a database of Subject Matter Expert (SME)-defined competencies, acts first as a store of expert knowledge concerning KSAAs that are necessary to meet job/role requirements. Every Competency Object in a CaSS database can be accessed not only as an individual object, but also contains relationships to other objects in that CaSS instance. The competency relationships consist of links such as "requires," "narrows," or "is the same as" to name just a few. Integrated with a fully defined CaSS competency network, other software frameworks such as GIFT can gain historical performance records previously inaccessible concerning learner qualifications across the user base.

As referenced above, GIFT contains information in the DKF that is used to analyze learner performance throughout a course. Utilizing knowledge about a learner gained through course/DKF analysis, GIFT is able to contrast that information against competencies defined in a CaSS database. The end result is an aggregated training tool that, combined with xAPI and an LRS, constitutes an AIS capable of real-time performance analysis, tracking and gauging learner skills over time, and mission readiness analysis for both individuals and teams. For a visual representation of the technological components of a GIFT-to-CaSS integration, please see Fig. 5.

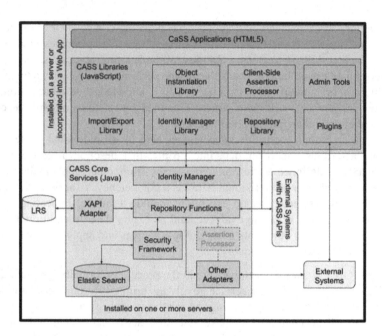

Fig. 5. CaSS Components adapted from CaSS Developer Guide [17]

The second CaSS service relating to assertions about learner qualifications was less integrated with GIFT at the time of this writing, but is being designed to support a proof of concept implementation in the area of squad infantry tactical competencies. After all new GIFT capabilities relating to xAPI, LRS/LMS operations, and integration with a CaSS framework reach technological maturity, the GIFT software suite will be able to utilize an assertion system in conjunction with the DKF to allow authorized stakeholders to query on topics such as mission readiness on a learner database. This capability requires careful consideration on the configuration and mapping workflows, which will be conceptually introduced below in the use case example.

With KSAAs, GIFT's DKF, xAPI, LRS, and CaSS components discussed, it should be evident how training content metadata combined from these disparate systems can help create an adaptive training plan for a learner utilizing an AIS assessment function resident in GIFT. Furthermore, as a learner consumes more training content in a configured ecosystem, the learner's performance is tracked and cataloged over time creating a robust learner profile from which to gauge past performance, current readiness, and future training recommendations related to both individual and mission goals.

3   Infantry Squad Use Case: From Individual to Unit

To drive the discussion from concept to application, in this section we present a high-level use case focused on unit competencies associated with an Army infantry squad, and a proposed data strategy to manage performance tracking across a training cycle. This involves establishing KSAAs at the role level, and development of cohesion and expertise at the unit level. From a performance and tactical perspective, an infantry squad must be well trained across a group of Mission Essential Tasks (METs). Among these are a set of commonly encountered situations called Battle Drills (BDs).

BDs are defined as "a collective action rapidly executed without applying a deliberate decision-making process [18]". Mastering these competency sets requires training cycles that focus on instilling an automated response to mission situations that require this set of common collective actions. Focusing on specific BD level competencies that target individual and unit KSAA constructs is serving as the first use case to support data strategy development and prototyping, in this instance Moving Under Direct Fire. The below subsections will discuss the utility of an ecosystem of resources to support unit mastery of a specific BD, and then discuss the system level requirements to build evidence across the resources using the architecture components described above.

3.1   An Ecosystem of Training Experiences

A strategy leveraging an ecosystem of training resources that combine didactic pedagogical instruction with experiential andragogic interactions can be used to guide unit development. This might involve common courseware to introduce the fundamentals of the BDs (e.g., multi-media, classroom lecture, worked example walkthroughs, etc.), exposing cognitive decision making points and assessing tactical understanding through semi-immersive gaming environments, providing fully immersive mixed-reality environments that combine the cognitive and physical task characteristics, and then evaluating application in a live environment with full task fidelity under realistic operational constraints. An approach of this nature was examined under the Squad Overmatch program, which focused on a program of instruction leveraging simulation-based techniques to target the crawl and walk portions of skill development [19]. This research builds off the success of that program, and examines data analytic techniques that help refine the utility of training resources based on the needs of a given unit. In addition, the data strategy proposed is designed to scale across team structures and operational domains.

When instituting a training ecosystem, it will initially apply existing Training Aids, Devices, Simulators and Simulations (TADSS [20]) available to the command. For an approach of this nature to meet its intended application, an assumption is the TADSS at play are enabled to meet data reporting specifications required to track KSAA development. Thus, an ecosystem is only realized when systems at play are able to share data. It is important to covey here that GIFT is not required to support the data strategy at the system of system level of resources; however, each TADSS must adhere to the performance reporting requirement through the production of xAPI Statements that are used as assertions against the defined squad level competency model. Following an interaction, a set of experience statements (via xAPI) are required to contextualize the resource completed and evidence of observed performance. In the following sub-section, we walk through the data flow where GIFT is utilized to translate data into performance metrics, and mapping those metrics to a competency model established in CaSS.

3.2 Proposed Data Strategy

Below is a set of data inference procedures that specify the data strategy being implemented through the GIFT and CaSS integration at the learning resource level. The flow represents the required analytic processes to contextualize data, regardless of the environment, and defines the data flow for single instance of training executed in a multi-modal dynamic training environment. Following, we examine the role GIFT and CaSS have in the data strategy.

1. Training environment PRODUCES multi-modal Raw Data (e.g., STE Training Simulation Software) comprised of simulation events, behavioral sensors, physiological sensors, verbal and non-verbal communication, etc.
2. Raw data is CONSUMED by Training Management Tools (e.g., GIFT) and PRODUCES Metrics (e.g., task performance, team performance, model features) and States (e.g., fatigue, workload, team work, etc.).
   a. NOTE: These metrics and states are delivered to the GIFT LMS module for long term storage.
3. GIFT LMS GENERATESxAPI (experiential statements on specified data context).
   a. NOTE: The GIFT LMS module, connected to an LRS, translates performance and state information into xAPI statements.
4. xAPIROUTED TOLRS/DataLakes for storage
5. LRS/DataLakesACCESSED BY Competency and Skills System (CaSS)
6. CaSSUPDATES Squad Lethality Competency Profile based on data assertions captured during training interaction.
7. FUTURE: Recommender engines linked to CaSSTARGET solider development opportunities and GUIDE and/or AUTOMATE plan/prepare scenario generation activities across subsequent training resources.

Building Evidence with GIFT. In this subsection, we highlight the functions of GIFT that translate data generated during a training exercise into contextualized measures of performance and effectiveness. Specifically within the DKF, GIFT has been architected according to Data Encapsulation Design Patterns. These design patterns, represented at conditional classes, are mapped against a designated task model built using GIFT's DKF authoring environment (see Fig. 6 for example of DKF interface with BD task model established within).

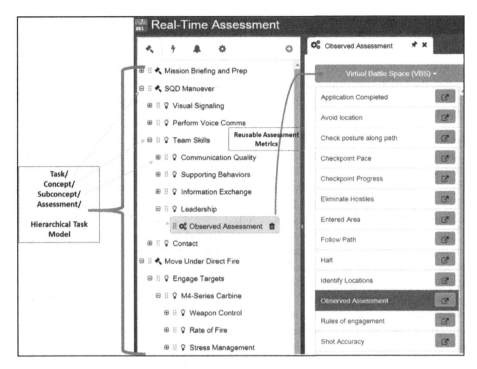

Fig. 6. Real-Time Assessment Domain Knowledge File task and concept representation for squad level battle drill.

As described in the architecture section above, the DKF allows an author to build a customized task model for use within a specified training environment. For a squad level exercise, the DKF is structured around the tasks a unit can experience within a specified scenario storyboard. In this instance, as seen in Fig. 5, there are three tasks represented in the Virtual Battle Space 3 (VBS3) training environment, each with established performance concepts represented within. Each concept can be graded using data-driven processes supported across the reusable metrics, or they can specify a human observer to provide the assessment state based on their subjective expertise. From a skill development standpoint, understanding the limitations of VBS3 is critical when linking the experience to a competency-based training ecosystem. There needs to be a way to distinguish similar task models applied in environments of varying fidelity (e.g., semi-immersive vs. fully-immersive). Essentially, an instructional designer should ask, "what are the learning objectives of a training resource and how do they support operational performance?"

At run-time, the data produced during interaction is consumed within GIFT's gateway and passed to the domain module for assessment. There are currently a set of pre-existing domain independent condition classes that can be applied to drive concept performance state determination (see Fig. 6 for list supported in VBS3). Through this mechanism, the DKF task structure creates a scalable and traceable data schema to build performance context within a simulated training environment. Each inferred state (e.g., concept 1 is at-expectation) and transition between states (e.g., concept 1 changed from at-expectation to below-expectation) is reported to the LMS module for long-term storage. Additionally, there are scoring rules to establish a skill state (e.g., novice, journeyman, expert) based on all observed performance states. Fundamentally, the DKF is the GIFT representation of a superset of data, and the evaluation on the actual learning experience is what is translated into xAPI statements and broadcast out to other interested systems.

Establishing Persistence with xAPI, and CaSS. The concept of data persistence combines all topics discussed in this paper up to this point. The evidence created by GIFT described in the previous section forms the initial data element for the perspective analysis. Considering the GIFT software suite as part of a larger system, the complex relationships between all parts of the system and how those relationships affect data permanence is what needs to be considered.

First, it is important to understand internal GIFT data representations may not necessarily be exposed to outside systems 100% of the time, namely the DKF. It is beyond the scope of this paper to fully describe all internal GIFT processes, so the reader should simply note that internal GIFT data along with the DKF and associated processes are constantly being created and referred to by GIFT during authoring and tutoring user experiences. A complete DKF contains real time assessment metrics as well as overall assessment rules that would define overall pass/fail grading on selected concepts. When the DKF is completed those selected concepts are graded based on the events that unfolded. The grades are then sent to the LMS module where they are converted into CaSS compatible xAPI statements and stored in the LRS connected to GIFT.

At the time of this writing, CaSS uses xAPI statements strictly for its assertion processing logic. The Assertion logic is the part of CaSS responsible for comparing learner performance (gleaned through xAPI messages) to the internal framework of CaSS competencies, and then returning assessments of readiness/mastery. CaSS can either directly receive xAPI statements or poll an existing xAPI endpoint. It's worth noting, CaSS stores any data received about learners through xAPI statements until purged. A good, simple example that explains competency acquisition can be found here [16].

CaSS can then use the information gained from xAPI messages (for instance, Learner "X" "Scored" "At-Expectation" on "Concept 1" in "Course Y") and then respond to queries as to the qualifications of the learners in question. This could be useful in the short-term as learners gain competencies throughout a GIFT course piping out xAPI statements that other systems in an architecture, say such as the TLA or STE, may be interested in. Or, over the long term, GIFT or Instructor Dashboards or LMSs, for instance, will be able to ping the CaSS Server against Learner Profiles to be able to quickly assert which learners possess which competencies, so as to personalize current training content. That long-term store of learner information, combined with the Subject Matter Expert-created CaSS database, combined with GIFT course content tagged against that CaSS database, will allow us to analyze which content is most appropriate to deliver to the learner through GIFT to maximize readiness and track individual/squad readiness over time.

Linking GIFT to CaSS. Linking DKF configurations with CaSS frameworks is an important authoring consideration that needs to be addressed. Current development is underway to connect the two modeling components. Ultimately, we envision two potential paths. The first is where authors can start from scratch and explore existing CaSS frameworks, hopefully with some text searching capabilities to make it easier to find what a developer is looking for based on key terms. If a framework is found that relates to what will be taught than authors are able to select specific concepts under that framework that will be assessed during the GIFT course. This approach provides a quick templated format to authoring a specific domain as well as providing a possible indirect link to other training assets that can be referenced/imported into the training ecosystem. For example, if the M249 Machine Gun concept in a CaSS Framework had assertions or references to a PDF, VBS training content/scenarios or even other GIFT courses could re-apply that material in instructional or remedial capacities.

The other approach is to start adding the concepts you want to teach and then link each concept to a concept in one or more CaSS frameworks. If CaSS didn't have a relevant entry it wouldn't prevent GIFT authors from continuing to build out the course and the GIFT assessments. GIFT could continue to store overall assessments in a long-term learner model with the hope that other systems like CaSS would one day be another consumer besides GIFT. There could even be some post processing logic we would run on the GIFT LRS to help link xAPI statements to newly created or discovered CaSS frameworks and concepts.

Also communicating with an LMS System could be the integrated CaSS Framework, primarily to satisfy the CaSS Assertion capability. GIFT tracks all previously mentioned course, learner, and assessment data. CaSS, contrarily, is a database storing only competencies, relationships between competency frameworks, and performing logic on capability readiness assertions. GIFT stores and reads information revolving around course metadata, learner profiles, and learner assessments. CaSS stores information relating to competencies, and then queries other systems for learner performance data to assert positive or negative qualification status. Together, both GIFT and CaSS are architected in such a way to encourage communication with a permanent learner data store such as LRS/LMS systems. This architecture, as visually represented below in Fig. 7, allows each system to perform its specialized function, communicate necessary information in a common xAPI syntax, and reach higher effective levels of training, assessment, and recommendation through centralized competency profile systems that are a result of all software suites working together in the same network.

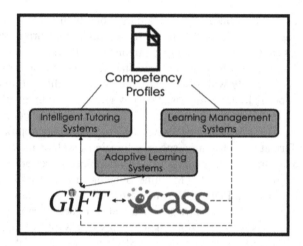

Fig. 7. Centralized Competency Profile as a Persistent Model

4 Future Work and Conclusions

In this paper, we introduced on-going work that enables GIFT to support competency tracking in a training ecosystem model of skill development. GIFT was integrated with the TLA and CaSS through the xAPI data standard. This integration enables complex skill tracking in dynamic multi-modal data environments, and supports andragogic experiential training. Yet, future work is required.

Establishing granular representations of experience is critical to support the experiential training approach being described in this paper. Generally speaking, at what level in the DKF concept structure do we report performance for competency tracking? We believe the level is something that goes back to when GIFT course concepts are authored. For example, the author would create a course concept 'move under direct fire' mapped to an entry in the CaSS framework with a similar meaning, name and ID XXX.XX.XXXX. The author can then continue to define the course concepts as they see fit. Perhaps they don't author M249 Machine Gun as a course concept even though it's in the CaSS framework because the training environment doesn't support that weapon system. Maybe the author adds a photon torpedo as a course concepts because they are assessing a space force training environment but CaSS framework doesn't have an entry for that yet.

Future work is also establishing a "headless" version of GIFT that allows other environments to leverage the DKF run-time assessment capabilities without linking it directly to a GIFT course. In this instance, an external system is leveraging the DKF to consume and contextualize data, but does not associate with a course concept structure that is built at the course level. As a result, headless GIFT essentially means that some other logic like an API needs to provide similar information to GIFT that would normally come from things like a course.xml. In one implementation, the external system initializing a GIFT configuration could provide the course concepts object via an API in the Gateway module. The structure of that object could be the same structure that GIFT stores in the course.xml so that two data models aren't being managed.

References

1. Sottilare, R., Goldberg, B.: Designing adaptive computer-based tutoring systems to accelerate learning and facilitate retention. Cogn. Technol. **17**(1), 19–33 (2012)
2. Walcutt, J.J., Schatz, S. (eds.): Modernizing Learning: Building the Future Learning Ecosystem. Government Publishing Office, Washington, D.C. (2019)
3. Day, E., Arthur, W., Gettman, D.: Knowledge structures and the acquisition of a complex skill. J. Appl. Psychol. **86**(5), 1022 (2001)
4. Goldberg, B., Davis, F., Riley, J.M., Boyce, M.W.: Adaptive training across simulations in support of a crawl-walk-run model of interaction. In: Schmorrow, D.D., Fidopiastis, C.M. (eds.) AC 2017. LNCS (LNAI), vol. 10285, pp. 116–130. Springer, Cham (2017). https:// doi.org/10.1007/978-3-319-58625-0_8
5. Ericsson, A.: Deliberate practice and acquisition of expert performance: a general overview. Acad. Emerg. Med. **15**(11), 988–994 (2008)
6. Stafford, M.: Competency-based learning. In: Walcutt, J.J., Schatz, S. (eds.) Modernizing Learning. ADL, Alexandira (2019)
7. Sottilare, R., Burke, S., Salas, E., Sinatra, A., Johnston, J., Gilbert, S.: Designing adaptive instruction for teams: a meta-analysis. Int. J. Artif. Intell. Educ. **28**(2), 225–264 (2018). https://doi.org/10.1007/s40593-017-0146-z
8. Lacerenza, C., Marlow, S., Tannenbaum, S., Salas, E.: Team development interventions: evidence-based approaches for improving teamwork. Am. Psychol. **73**(4), 517 (2018)
9. Tuxworth, E.: Competence-based education: background and origins. In: Burke, J. (ed.) Competence-Based Education and Training. Routledge, London (1989)
10. Sottilare, R.A., Brawner, K.W., Goldberg, B., Holden, H.K.: The generalized intelligent framework for tutoring (GIFT). US Army Research Laboratory–Human Research & Engineering Directorate (ARL-HRED), Aberdeen Proving Grounds, MD (2012)
11. Sottilare, R.A., Brawner, K.W., Sinatra, A.M., Johnston, J.H.: An updated concept for a Generalized Intelligent Framework for Tutoring (GIFT). US Army Research Laboratory–Human Research & Engineering Directorate (ARL-HRED), Aberdeen Proving Grounds, MD (2017)
12. Kevan, J.M., Ryan, P.R.: Experience API: flexible, decentralized and activity-centric data collection. Technol. Knowl. Learn. **21**(1), 143–149 (2016). https://doi.org/10.1007/s10758-015-9260-x
13. Advanced Distributed Learning (ADL) Initiative Experience API (xAPI) Webpage. https:// github.com/adlnet/xAPI-Spec/blob/master/xAPI-About.md#partone. Accessed 20 Feb 2020
14. Blake-Plock (managing ed.): xAPI: a guide for technical implementers. Prepared by: IEEE Learning Technology Standards Committee Technical Advisory Group on xAPI (2018)
15. Advanced Distributed Learning (ADL) Initiative Total Learning Architecture Webpage. https://adlnet.gov/projects/tla/. Accessed 20 Feb 2020
16. Eduworks Competency and Skills System (CaSS) Webpage. https://www.cassproject.org. Accessed 20 Feb 2020
17. CaSS Developer Guide Webpage. https://devs.cassproject.org/index.html. Accessed 20 Feb 2020
18. Department of Army: Infantry rifle platoon and squad. Field Manual (FM) 3-21.8, Washington, DC (2007)

19. Johnston, J.H., Napier, S., Ross, W.A.: Adapting immersive training environments to develop squad resilience skills. In: Schmorrow, D.D., Fidopiastis, C.M. (eds.) AC 2015. LNCS (LNAI), vol. 9183, pp. 616–627. Springer, Cham (2015). https://doi.org/10.1007/978-3-319-20816-9_59
20. Army Training Support Center Training Aids, Devices, Simulators, and Simulations Product Line Webpage. https://www.atsc.army.mil/tss/TADSS.asp. Accessed 14 Feb 2020
21. Ford, R., Meyer, R.: Competency-based Education 101. TiER1 Performance Solutions, Covington (2015)
22. Smith, B., Gordon, J., Hernandez, M.: Competency-Based Learning in 2018. U.S. Advanced Distributed Learning (ADL) Initiative W900KK-17-D-0004, Orlando, FL (2018)
23. Poltrack, J., Robson, R.: Using competencies to map performance across multiple activities. In: Interservice/Industry Training, Simulation, and Education Conference (I/ITSEC), Orlando, FL (2017)
24. Robson, R.: Assessing competency instead of learning outcomes. In: International Conference on Artificial Intelligence in Adaptive Education (AIED), Beijing, China (2019)

Does Gamification Work? Analyzing Effects of Game Features on Learning in an Adaptive Scenario-Based Trainer

Cheryl I. Johnson[1]([⊠]), Shannon K. T. Bailey[2],
and Alyssa D. Mercado[1]

[1] Naval Air Warfare Center Training Systems Division,
Orlando, FL 32826, USA
{cheryl.i.johnson,alyssa.mercado}@navy.mil
[2] Immertec (Immersive Technology Inc.), Tampa, FL 33602, USA
shannon@immertec.com

Abstract. Although many praise the positive benefits of game-based training to increase learner engagement and performance, there has been little empirical research to support these claims. The goal of this experiment was to establish whether adding game features has a positive impact on performance during training and leads to better learning outcomes. Specifically, we explored whether the presence of game features (i.e., performance gauges) and competition features (i.e., leaderboard) affected motivation and learning outcomes within the Periscope Operator Adaptive Trainer (POAT). We conducted an experiment with 49 Submarine Officer Basic Course students who were assigned randomly to either training with a version of POAT with game features (Game Features condition) or one without game features (Control condition). Analyses revealed no differences between the two conditions on learning gains or reported motivation. The results did show that students in both conditions improved significantly on the accuracy (i.e., angle on the bow and range) and timeliness of their periscope calls from pre-test to post-test, providing additional support for the benefits of adaptive training but not game features.

Keywords: Gamification · Adaptive training · Motivation · Game-based training · Competition · Reward

1 Introduction

In an effort to modernize training to make it more effective and learner-centered, the U.S. Navy is exploring emerging technologies to provide quality training at the point of need to the fleet. Currently, gamification is a popular topic among researchers and training providers; however, there is little empirical evidence to support its use in training systems to improve training outcomes. The term "gamification" is used to describe the inclusion of game features (e.g., competition and rewards) in training and educational tasks, such as training systems. Although many theorize that gamification will increase learners' interest and motivation to complete educational content,

R. A. Sottilare and J. Schwarz (Eds.): HCII 2020, LNCS 12214, pp. 493–504, 2020.
https://doi.org/10.1007/978-3-030-50788-6_36

resulting in better learning outcomes and performance, the research on such benefits is mixed (e.g., Cagiltay et al. 2015; Hays 2005; Mayer 2019; O'Neil and Perez 2008; Sitzmann 2011; Wouters et al. 2013). A potential reason for the disparity in training effectiveness findings is due to a lack of systematic research investigating what games are beneficial for training, for which learning objectives, and for which kinds of learners, which has been pointed out in a number of reviews (Bedwell et al. 2012; Lister and College 2015; Mayer 2019; Mayer and Johnson 2010; O'Neil and Perez 2008; Plass et al. 2015). Therefore, the goal of this experiment was to establish whether adding game features has a positive impact on performance during training and leads to better learning outcomes. Specifically, we explored whether the presence of game features (i.e., performance gauges and score) and competition features (i.e., leaderboard) affected motivation and learning outcomes within the Periscope Operator Adaptive Trainer (POAT).

1.1 Game Features

Games can include a number of different features such as points, leaderboards, ranking, badges, trophies, time pressure, and levels, among many others (Lister and College 2015; Plass et al. 2015). In this experiment, we chose to explore rewards and competition, because they both have been cited as a reason games may increase learning outcomes through motivation in previous studies (Cagiltay et al. 2015; Cameron et al. 2005; Hawlitschek and Joeckel 2017; Lister and College 2015; Plass et al. 2013).

Rewards are game features such as points, score, stars, badges, trophies, etc. that are given for meeting performance or achievement standards (Wang and Sun 2011). Reward features are thought to increase a learner's engagement, leading to higher motivation on a task (Shute et al. 2013). Higher motivation is theorized to improve learning outcomes, because learners are motivated to spend more time actively processing the learning material (Hawlitschek and Joeckel 2017). For example, Cameron and colleagues (2015) conducted an experiment that gave monetary rewards for performance achievements on a puzzle-solving task. The researchers found that the monetary rewards increased interest on the puzzle-solving task and also increased time on task after performance was no longer rewarded. Additionally, Cameron et al. found that rewards did not distract from the problem-solving task.

In the context of computer-based educational games, "competition" is defined as, "the activity of students comparing their own performances with the performance of a virtual opponent," with either a computer or other student as the virtual opponent (Vandercruysse et al. 2013, p. 929). This social comparison can take the form of game features such as a leaderboard that presents a score or ranking of an individual or team compared to that of the virtual opponent(s). Competition is hypothesized to increase motivation on a task by increasing attention to the material, fostering a sense of challenge, or by creating a "unidirectional drive upward" social comparison (Cagiltay, Ozcelik, and Ozcelik; Garcia et al. 2006). For example, an experiment by Cagiltay and colleagues (2015), compared two versions of an educational computer game for learning database modeling concepts: one version included a leaderboard that updated in real-time with the learner's performance score and rank compared to their peers, and the non-game version did not present a leaderboard. They found that the competition group scored higher on the post-test on conceptual knowledge and higher on motivational measures compared to the non-competition group.

1.2 Theory

From a theoretical perspective, adding game features could have positive effects on learners. Cognitive Load Theory (van Merriënboer and Sweller 2005) posits that learners have a limited capacity of working memory resources and that instruction should be designed to limit the amount of cognitive load imposed on the learner. There are three different types of cognitive load. (1) Extraneous load arises from poor instructional design, such as using a poor interface or including unnecessary information in the training. (2) Intrinsic load stems from the instructional content itself, such as the number of elements learners must hold in their working memory at one time. (3) Germane load is the level of mental effort the learner exerts in order to understand the material; this load is productive and could include the learner relating learned material to prior knowledge. The three types of cognitive load are traditionally thought of as additive, such that once an individual has reached their capacity (this is referred to as cognitive overload), learning and performance suffers.

Proponents of gamification have cited the motivational power of games for training (Driskell et al. 2002; Gee 2003; Prensky 2001). They argue that games are intrinsically motivating, and learners will want to continue playing to improve their performance. According these researchers, motivation evokes productive cognitive processing (i.e., germane load), which increases the player's potential for learning (van Merriënboer and Sweller 2005). That is, game features serve to increase motivation to play, and therefore, free up additional cognitive resources that can be directed to learning the content and improving learning outcomes.

1.3 Present Experiment

The purpose of this experiment was to compare the value-added of game features in a scenario-based trainer on learners' performance outcomes and motivation. In this experiment, we utilized the Periscope Operator Adaptive Trainer (POAT) as our training testbed. An adaptive trainer provides instruction that is tailored to an individual learner's strengths and weaknesses (Landsberg et al. 2012). POAT simulates a periscope operator's task in which the trainee observes a contact (e.g., a ship) in a periscope view and must determine the contact's angle on the bow (AOB) and range within one minute. AOB is the side (e.g., port or starboard) and direction (e.g., angle between 0–180°) a contact is heading relative to the viewer's line of sight. Range is the distance to the contact from the viewer's ownship, which requires a mental math calculation based on the size of the contact in the periscope's reticle. After each periscope call,

POAT provides adaptive feedback to the trainee based on the accuracy of his or her performance. The amount of detail provided in the feedback varies based on the accuracy of the participant's response; when the periscope call is more accurate, students receive less feedback. If the call is inaccurate, students receive detailed process information to improve their calls. In addition, the scenario difficulty was also adapted based on trainee performance during training, such that students who were performing well received more difficult scenarios and those performing poorly received easier scenarios. These difficulty adaptations occurred after a set of 15 scenarios, or a "testlet." POAT includes scenarios of beginner, intermediate, and advanced difficulty.

The Game Features condition featured performance gauges to display how well students were performing during training. These indicators included stars that filled up with more accurate and timely periscope calls, a score that was displayed based on performance points that were additive with each scenario, and a difficulty meter that showed the current level of difficulty of the scenario (see Fig. 1). In addition, students in the Game Features condition also received a leaderboard after each testlet that displayed the student's score relative to 23 other players (see Fig. 2). The other players and scores were the same for all students in this condition, but where students were ranked on the leaderboard was dependent upon their individual performance. A colored arrow also was displayed on the leaderboard screen to indicate whether a student's ranking went up, down, or stayed the same relative to the previous testlet's leaderboard. For example, if Student A was ranked #12 after the first testlet and ranked #10 on the second testlet, then Student A would see a green arrow next to their ranking on the second testlet's leaderboard to indicate their ranking improved over the previous testlet.

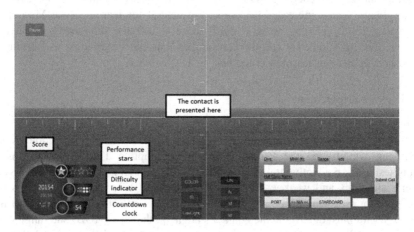

Fig. 1. Screenshot of Game Features condition in which trainees are shown a contact and input their periscope call (including AOB and range). Specific features are explained in callout boxes.

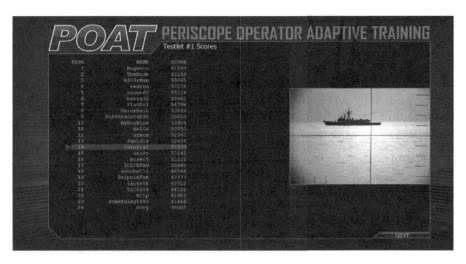

Fig. 2. Screenshot of Game Features condition's leaderboard. In this case, username "tutorial" was ranked 14th.

Participants in the Control condition did not receive performance indicators, scores, or leaderboards. Figure 3 displays a screenshot of an example scenario from the Control condition.

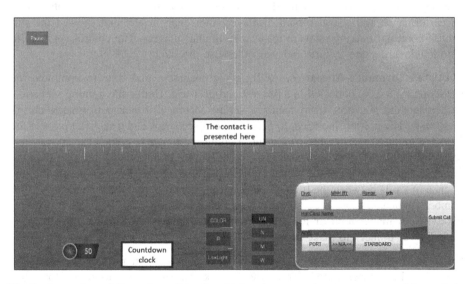

Fig. 3. Screenshot of Control condition in which trainees are shown a contact and input their periscope call (including AOB and range). Specific features are explained in callout boxes.

Consistent with Cognitive Load Theory and based on findings from previous gamification studies using competition and rewards, we predicted that the Game Features condition would show higher learning gains on AOB and range than the Control condition from pre- to post-test. We also predicted that having game features during training would encourage faster periscope call times on the post-test. Furthermore, we predicted that individuals in the Game Features condition would report higher motivation than those in the Control condition.

2   Method

2.1   Participants and Design

Fifty-six students from the Submarine Officer Basic Course were assigned to a condition using a randomized block design. Six students were removed from analyses due a fire alarm interruption during the experiment, and one was removed due to experimenter error. Therefore, a total of 49 students (45 males, 4 females) were included in the analyses with 25 students in the Game Features condition and 24 students in the Control condition. The students' average age was 23.94 years ($SD = 0.93$) with a range of 22-26 years.

2.2   Materials

Testbed. The two versions of POAT described above were used in this experiment. The Game Features version included scores, stars, and a difficulty level indicator based on performance and a leaderboard displayed after every testlet that showed the student's score and ranking relevant to other (artificial) players. The control version did not include any game features but was otherwise the same.

POAT Performance Measures. AOB, range accuracy, and time to complete the periscope calls were collected in a pre-test and post-test. Unlike the training scenarios, participants did not receive any feedback on the accuracy of their performance during these tests. The pre-test included 20 periscope call scenarios and was given prior to the POAT training scenarios. Following the training, participants completed 20 post-test scenarios. AOB accuracy is measured as the difference in degrees (0–180) between the trainee's called AOB and the actual AOB of the contact. Range accuracy is the difference in yards between the trainee's call and the actual range of the contact. Smaller numbers indicated more accurate calls (i.e., better performance) for AOB and range. Likewise, a smaller number for call time indicated better performance, because it is desirable for trainees to make faster calls.

Intrinsic Motivation Inventory (IMI). The IMI included 23 items and measured how motivated the trainees were to complete the task (i.e., state motivation) on four subscales: 1. Interest/Enjoyment, 2. Perceived Competence, 3. Effort/Importance, and 4. Pressure/Tension (Ryan and Deci 2000). An example item from the Effort/Importance subscale is, "It is important for me to do well at this task." Participants responded to each question on a scale from 1 ("Not at all true") to 7 ("Very true"). Each subscale was averaged to indicate motivation in each factor. High scores on all of the subscales except Pressure/Tension correspond with higher motivation during the task.

Participant Characteristics

Demographics. Participants completed a demographic questionnaire that included questions about their age, sex, highest level of education, time in the military, and experiences with periscope training.

Spatial Ability. The Paper Folding Test (PFT) is a timed measure of spatial visualization in which participants answer 10 items within three minutes (Ekstrom et al. 1976). For each item, participants must match an image of a folded piece of paper with a hole punched through to an image of how the paper would look when it is unfolded. Participants select one of five answer choices for each item. Previous research with the POAT testbed has found spatial ability to be a critical individual difference variable for predicting performance (Van Buskirk et al. 2014).

Achievement Motivation Scale (AMS). The AMS asked participants 14 questions related to their overall motivation prior to the task (i.e., trait motivation; Ray 1979). An example item is "Are you satisfied to be no better than most other people at your job?" Participants indicated their agreement with each question on a three-point scale, from 1 ("No") to 3 ("Yes"). The sum of items was calculated to determine overall achievement motivation, with higher scores corresponding with more motivation.

2.3   Procedure

Students participated in groups of four to six, and the experiment took approximately two hours to complete. Upon consenting to participate, students were assigned using a randomized block design to either the Game Features or Control conditions, completed a demographics questionnaire, and the Achievement Motivation Scale. Prior to using POAT, all students completed a tutorial that provided basic information on how to make a periscope call (e.g., defining port and starboard) and how to use the POAT interface. Students then completed a 13-item knowledge quiz to ensure they understood the material in the tutorial before they began the training. If students missed any questions on the knowledge quiz, a researcher went over the correct answer before moving on. Next, all students completed the pre-test, followed by training in POAT that varied by condition. Altogether, students completed five testlets during training, or a total of 75 training scenarios. In the Game Features condition, students received scores and gauges depicting their level of performance for each trial, and a leaderboard was presented after each testlet during training. In the Control condition, students used POAT, but they did not receive any of the game features during training. After the training, participants completed a post-test and the Intrinsic Motivation Inventory to measure state motivation. Finally, participants were thanked and debriefed.

3 Results

3.1 Participant Variables

Initial analyses were performed to determine whether the groups differed by potentially-influential characteristics, including spatial ability and trait motivation. Means, standard deviations (*SDs*), and results from the *t*-tests are presented in Table 1. First, Paper Folding Test scores, which were used as a measure of spatial ability, did not differ significantly between groups. Second, we used the Achievement Motivation Scale (AMS) as a measure of trait motivation. AMS scores also did not differ by training condition. The scores of both groups were around the midpoint of the scale (*midpoint* = 21), suggesting that participants were moderately motivated individuals overall.

Table 1. Participant variables means and SDs by condition

	Game Features		Control		T-test results	
	M	SD	M	SD	t	p
Paper Folding Test	7.25	2.51	7.36	1.76	0.196	.845
Achievement Motivation	18.60	3.07	19.79	3.67	0.963	.341

Note. *df* = 47

3.2 AOB Performance

AOB scores on the pre- and post-tests[1] were calculated by using the median absolute difference in degrees (0–180) between the called and actual AOB by scenario for each test. Next, a gain score was computed for AOB for each participant. Gain scores were used to determine the extent to which participants' performance improved after taking into account how much they could have improved from pre- to post-test. The gain score data are presented in the top row of Table 2. Based on a *t*-test, there were no significant differences on AOB range scores by condition.

---

[1] The data were also submitted to a repeated measures ANOVA with training condition as the between-subjects variable and test type (pre- and post-test scores) as the within-subjects variable. The results indicated that AOB accuracy improved for both groups between the pre- and post-test [$F(1,47) = 11.456$, $p = .001$, $\eta p2 = .196$], but there was no difference between training groups [$F(1,47) = 0.192$, $p = .663$, $\eta p2 = .004$], nor was there an interaction between variables [$F(1,47) = 1.573$, $p = .216$, $\eta p2 = .032$]. Overall, adaptive training increased AOB accuracies by approximately 50%.

Table 2. AOB and range gain scores by condition

	Game Features		Control		T-test Results	
	M	SD	M	SD	t	p
AOB gain	.254	.250	.124	.352	1.495	.141
Range gain	.290	.375	.377	.274	−0.929	.145

Note. $df = 47$

3.3 Range Performance

Similar to AOB score calculations, range scores[2] for each test were calculated using the median difference in called and actual range in yards. Then, a gain score was computed by determining the difference in pre- and post-test scores and dividing by the absolute value of the pre-test score. Range scores by condition are presented in the second row of Table 2. Based on a t-test, there was no difference found between the two conditions on range gain scores.

3.4 Call Time Performance

Since reporting accurate periscope calls as quickly as possible is a desirable skill in this domain, we also explored the potential benefits of adding game features during training on call time performance. A repeated measures ANOVA was conducted on pre- and post-test call times. Means and SDs for call times by test are presented in Table 3. There was a main effect of test, such that time to make a periscope call decreased from pre- to post-test, [$F(1,47) = 141.643$, $p < .001$, $\eta p2 = .751$]. However, the training groups did not differ on call time [$F(1,47) = 0.762$, $p = .387$, $\eta p2 = .016$], nor was there an interaction [$F(1,47) = 0.376$, $p = .543$, $\eta p2 = .008$]. This indicates that students made faster periscope calls after adaptive training, regardless of game features condition.

Table 3. Periscope call time means and SDs by test and condition

	Game Features		Control	
	M	SD	M	SD
Call time pre-test	48.55	4.53	49.31	5.23
Call time post-test	37.82	5.59	39.63	7.92

Note. $df = 47$

---

[2] A second repeated measures ANOVA was conducted on pre- and post-test range scores. As with AOB, the accuracy for range scores also improved after adaptive training [$F(1,47) = 20.846$, $p < .001$, $\eta p2 = .307$]. Again, the training groups did not differ on range accuracy [$F(1,47) = 0.052$, $p = .821$, $\eta p2 = .001$], nor was there an interaction [$F(1,47) = 0.257$, $p = .615$, $\eta p2 = .005$].

3.5   State Motivation

The IMI measured motivation on the task (i.e., state motivation) in four subscales: 1. Interest/Enjoyment, 2. Perceived Competence, 3. Effort/Importance, and 4. Pressure/Tension. As shown in Table 4, motivation on the task as measured by the IMI did not differ depending on whether participants received game features during training.

Table 4. State motivation means and *SD*s by condition

	Training condition				Difference in conditions	
	Game Features		Control			
IMI Subscale	*M*	*SD*	*M*	*SD*	*t*	*p*
Interest/Enjoyment	4.43	0.86	4.46	0.90	−0.096	.924
Perceived Competence	3.89	1.15	3.96	0.97	−0.213	.832
Effort/Importance	4.91	0.92	4.92	0.93	−0.025	.980
Pressure/Tension*	2.99	1.31	2.88	1.07	0.337	.738

Note: *Pressure/Tension is reverse scored, such that higher scores indicate lower motivation; $df = 47$

4   Discussion

The goal of this experiment was to examine the impacts of adding game features to a scenario-based training system on performance outcomes and motivation. In particular, we explored game features that we intended to provide rewards for good performance through the use of performance gauges (i.e., scores, stars, and difficulty level indicators) and foster competition through the use of leaderboards. Overall, we found that performance results showed that adaptive training was successful at increasing AOB and range accuracy; these results were not surprising given that adaptive training techniques have been found to lead to higher learning outcomes in several different domains, including this one (Landsberg et al. 2012; Marraffino et al. 2019; Van Buskirk et al. 2019). However, contrary to our hypotheses, we did not find evidence that game features led to higher learning gains on AOB or range from pre- to post-test over a control condition with no such features. Furthermore, there is no evidence that including game features led to faster periscope call times relative to the control. The results suggest that when trainees receive adaptive training, game features may not add value to the training because they do not increase performance or motivation more than the control condition.

Participants' trait motivation was measured prior to training to determine how generally motivated the students were before beginning the task. In general, both groups were around the midpoint on the motivation scale. Following the training, motivation on the task was assessed in both groups to understand how the different training conditions affected state motivation of the participants. On all four different factors of state motivation, including engagement, effort, competence, and pressure, the two training groups did not differ significantly from each other. There was no evidence that including game features during training increased motivation or engagement on the task compared to the control group that did not receive game features. Therefore, counter to our prediction, we found no evidence that game features such as performance gauges and leaderboards increased feelings of engagement, competence, or effort toward the task.

It is possible that the way these game features were implemented in the testbed were not rich enough to increase motivation to improve learning outcomes. For example, the leaderboards contained artificial scores and rankings, and perhaps a sense of competition would be heightened if students were aware that they were competing directly with their peers. Likewise, it is possible that one exposure to the training was not enough to foster motivation, and perhaps repeated exposures to the training are necessary to drive the impacts of the game features on learning. That is, in this experiment, participants were not given the opportunity to decide to play again, and future research should explore the impacts of game features on trainees' willingness to continue to train, which would be a richer assessment of motivation than a self-report questionnaire.

From a practical perspective, although game features did not lead to measurable improvements in performance and motivation relative to a control condition in this case, including game features did not lead to significant decrements in performance either. More research is needed to determine the conditions under which gamification serves to improve learning and increase motivation to inform the training and education communities on when and how to invest in these technologies.

Acknowledgments. We gratefully acknowledge Dr. James Sheehy who sponsored this work through the Section 219 Naval Innovative Science and Engineering Basic and Applied Research program. We would also like to thank Derek Tolley developing the versions of POAT used in the experiment. Presentation of this material does not constitute or imply its endorsement, recommendation, or favoring by the U.S. Navy or Department of Defense (DoD). The opinions of the authors expressed herein do not necessarily state or reflect those of the U.S. Navy or DoD.

References

Bedwell, W.L., Pavlas, D., Heyne, K., Lazzara, E.H., Salas, E.: Toward a taxonomy linking game attributes to learning: An empirical study. Simul. Gaming **43**(6), 729–760 (2012)

Cagiltay, N.E., Ozcelik, E., Ozcelik, N.S.: The effect of competition on learning in games. Comput. Educ. **87**, 35–41 (2015)

Cameron, J., Pierce, W.D., Banko, K.M., Gear, A.: Achievement-based rewards and intrinsic motivation: a test of cognitive mediators. J. Educ. Psychol. **97**(4), 641–655 (2005)

Ekstrom, R.B., French, J.W., Harman, H.H.: Manual for Kit of Factor-Referenced Cognitive Tests. Educational Testing Service, Princeton (1976)

Garcia, S.M., Tor, A., Gonzalez, R.: Ranks and rivals: a theory of competition. Pers. Soc. Psychol. Bull. **32**(7), 970–982 (2006)

Garris, R., Ahlers, R., Driskell, J.E.: Games, motivation, and learning: a research and practice model. Simul. Gaming **33**, 441–467 (2002)

Gee, J.P.: What Video Games have to Teach Us About Learning and Literacy. Pelgrave Macmillan, New York (2003)

Hays, R.T.: The effectiveness of instructional games: a literature review and discussion. Technical report, 2005–004, Naval Air Warfare Center Training Systems Division, Orlando, FL (2005)

Hawlitschek, A., Joeckel, S.: Increasing the effectiveness of digital educational games: the effects of a learning instruction on students' learning, motivation and cognitive load. Comput. Hum. Behav. **72**, 79–86 (2017)

Landsberg, C.R., Mercado, A., Van Buskirk, W.L., Lineberry, M., Steinhauser, N.: Evaluation of an adaptive training system for submarine periscope operations. In: Proceedings of the Human Factors and Ergonomics Society 56th Annual Meeting, pp. 2422–2426. SAGE Publications, Los Angeles (2012)

Lister, M., College, M.: Gamification: the effect on student motivation and performance at the post-secondary level. Issues Trends Educ. Technol. **3**(2), 1–22 (2015)

Marraffino, M.D., Johnson, C.I., Whitmer, D.E., Steinhauser, N.B., Clement, A.: Advise when ready for game plan: adaptive training for JTACs. In: Proceedings of the Interservice/Industry, Training, Simulation, and Education Conference (2019)

Mayer, R.E.: Computer games in education. Ann. Rev. Psychol. **70**, 22.1–22.19 (2019)

Mayer, R.E., Johnson, C.I.: Adding instructional features that promote learning in a game-like environment. J. Educ. Comput. Res. **42**, 241–265 (2010)

O'Neil, H.F., Perez, R.S. (eds.): Computer Games and Team and Individual Learning. Elsevier, Oxford (2008)

Plass, J.L., Homer, B.D., Kinzer, C.K.: Foundations of game-based learning. Educ. Psychol. **50**(4), 258–283 (2015)

Plass, J.L., et al.: The impact of individual, competitive, and collaborative mathematics game play on learning, performance, and motivation. J. Educ. Psychol. **105**(4), 1050–1066 (2013)

Prensky, M.: Digital Game-Based Learning. McGraw-Hill, New York (2001)

Ray, J.J.: A quick measure of achievement motivation: validated in Australia and reliable in Britain and South Africa. Aust. Psychol. **14**(3), 337–344 (1979)

Ryan, R.M., Deci, E.L.: Self-determination theory and the facilitation of intrinsic motivation, social development, and well-being. Am. Psychol. **55**, 68–78 (2000)

Shute, V.J., Ventura, M., Kim, Y.J.: Assessment and learning of qualitative physics in newton's playground. J. Educ. Res. **106**(6), 423–430 (2013)

Sitzmann, T.: A meta-analytic examination of the instructional effectiveness of computer-based simulation games. Pers. Psychol. **64**, 489–528 (2011)

Van Buskirk, W.L., Fraulini, N.W., Schroeder, B.L., Johnson, C.I., Marraffino, M.D.: Application of theory to the development of an adaptive training system for a submarine electronic warfare task. In: Sottilare, R.A., Schwarz, J. (eds.) HCII 2019. LNCS, vol. 11597, pp. 352–362. Springer, Cham (2019). https://doi.org/10.1007/978-3-030-22341-0_28

Van Buskirk, W.L., Steinhauser, N.B., Mercado, A.D., Landsberg, C.R., Astwood, R.S.: A comparison of the micro-adaptive and hybrid approaches to adaptive training. In: Proceedings of the Human Factors and Ergonomics Society Annual Meeting, vol. 58(1), pp. 1159–1163. SAGE Publications, Los Angeles, September 2014

van Merrienboer, J.J., Sweller, J.: Cognitive load theory and complex learning: recent developments and future directions. Educ. Psychol. Rev. **17**(2), 147–177 (2005)

Vandercruysse, S., Vandewaetere, M., Cornillie, F., Clarebout, G.: Competition and students' perceptions in a game-based language learning environment. Educ. Tech. Res. Dev. **61**(6), 927–950 (2013). https://doi.org/10.1007/s11423-013-9314-5

Wang, H., Sun, C.T.: Game reward systems: Gaming experiences and social meanings. In: DiGRA Conference, September 2011

Wouters, P., van Nimwegen, C., van Oostendorp, H., van der Speck, E.: A meta-analysis of the cognitive and motivational effects of serious games. J. Educ. Psychol. **105**, 249–265 (2013)

From "Knowing What" to "Knowing When": Exploring a Concept of Situation Awareness Synchrony for Evaluating SA Dynamics in Teams

Baptiste Prébot[1]($\boxtimes$), Jessica Schwarz[2], Sven Fuchs[2], and Bernard Claverie[1]

[1] IMS - Cognitique, UMR 5218, ENSC-Bordeaux INP, Université de Bordeaux, Talence, France
{baptiste.prebot,bernard.claverie}@ensc.fr
[2] Human-System Engineering, Fraunhofer Institute for Communication, Information Processing and Ergonomics, Wachtberg, Germany
{jessica.schwarz,sven.fuchs}@fkie.fraunhofer.de

Abstract. This concept paper presents an initial exploration of measuring Situation Awareness (SA) dynamics in team settings. SA dynamics refer to the evaluation of SA's temporal evolution of one or more teammates. We discuss why current methods are inherently limited by the subjective nature of SA and why it is important to identify measures for the temporal evolution of SA. Most current approaches focus on measuring the accuracy of SA (i.e., What? is known)and the similarity in the context of shared SA, often resulting in rather qualitative assessments. However, quantitative assessments are important to address temporal aspects (i.e., When? and ultimately For how long?). Thus, we propose, as a complementary approach to accuracy and similarity of SA, to consider the concept of SA synchrony as a quantitative metric of SA dynamics in teams. Specifically, we highlight the existence of three latencies with high relevance to shared SA dynamics and discuss options for their assessment.

Keywords: Situation Awareness · SA synchrony · SA dynamics · Teams

1 Introduction

Situation awareness (SA) evaluation has been a central topic in the study of complex operational environments for the past 30 years. Empirical findings show that incorrect SA is a major impact factor on human error. For example, in aviation, 88% of aviation accidents involving human error could be attributed to SA problems [1]. Over the years, there has been a shift in the need to evaluate SA. From accidentology in the late 80's [2], SA became a subject of "in-situ" evaluation in training or interface design contexts [3–6]. Its central place in the decision making process, individually and in teams, makes its assessment a key element in performance prediction and analysis.

© Springer Nature Switzerland AG 2020
R. A. Sottilare and J. Schwarz (Eds.): HCII 2020, LNCS 12214, pp. 505–518, 2020.
https://doi.org/10.1007/978-3-030-50788-6_37

Today, as technology becomes increasingly adaptive, the objectives have evolved towards a real-time evaluation of the user's state, so that technical systems can react to problem states. In operational settings, on-task measures offer the opportunity to mitigate critical user states through adapting levels of automation [7], modes of interaction, or communications. In adaptive instructional systems, real-time measures can be employed to monitor and ensure desired training states, for example to foster the development of coping strategies. An SA-adaptive training system could, for instance, identify SA problems in teams and provide specific training content that focuses on improving communications processes.

To date, despite the unanimously recognized importance of the SA construct, mitigation of SA problems has not yet been a focus of such systems. A look at traditional measures of SA unveils a major limitation that could well be a possible reason for this disregard: designed to detect what is wrong with SA, measures have focused on SA accuracy much more than on when or how fast SA was achieved, often resulting in rather qualitative assessments. However, quantitative assessments are important to know when to adapt. Particularly in team settings a temporal evaluation of SA is necessary to identify when team performance is likely to suffer from asynchronous SA. Multiple researchers agree that the development of unobtrusive objective online measures of SA is the logical and necessary next step [8, 9]. Despite this consensus, we are not aware of any studies that have looked more closely at what it would mean to measure SA dynamics.

To address this demand, this paper explores the concept of SA synchrony as a measure of shared SA temporal dynamics. We propose the use of indicators of when SA is achieved to identify three intervals with relevant shared SA (SSA) problems. We further suggest that it should be possible to effectively mitigate such SSA problems by optimizing the length of these intervals, possibly through adaptive interventions. After a review of current techniques and an exploration of why these are inherently limited by SA's nature, we introduce our conceptual approach, then discuss implications, requirements, and possible approaches to measuring SA synchrony.

2   Measuring Situation Awareness - Knowing What

Measuring SA has traditionally focused on assessing what is wrong with the user's internal representation of a given ground-truth situation. This may originate from SA being commonly defined as the active knowledge one has about the situation he is currently involved in. Notably, Endsley's three-level model [10] describes SA as a product of the situation assessment process on which decision making is based on. Endsley's information processing approach is structured into three hierarchical levels. Level-1 SA comprises the perception of the elements in the environment, level-2 SA is about their comprehension and interpretation, and level-3 SA represents the projection of their evolution in the near future.

At the group level, SA is necessarily more complex to define and evaluate. Although numerous debates also remain regarding its definition, the two concepts of shared SA and team SA tend to be recognized as describing respectively the individual and the system-level of a group situation awareness [9, 11–14]. Given this systemic aspect of SA, most classical measurement methods are not well-suited to account for the higher complexity of the sociotechnical system.

In 2018, Meireles et al. [15] referenced no less than fifty-four SA measurement techniques across eight application fields. (Driving, Aviation, Military, Medical, Sports …). This diversity of assessment techniques illustrates the need for context-specific methods. However, the vast majority of techniques rely on discrete evaluations either during or after the task. Self-rating techniques, performance measurements, probe techniques, observer rating – each of these techniques has particular advantages and disadvantages, as described in the upcoming subsections.

2.1 Post-trial Techniques

In post-trial self-rating techniques, participants provide a subjective evaluation of their own SA based on a rating scale immediately after the task. The situation awareness rating technique (SART) [16], the situation awareness rating scales (SARS) [17], the situation awareness subjective workload dominance (SA-SWORD) [18] and the mission awareness rating scale (MARS) [19] are some of the most used self-rating techniques. Performance measurements have also been explored as a post-trial assessment method. SA is inferred from the subject's performance on a set of goals across the task [20].

Being non-intrusive to the task, post-trial methods seem well suited for 'in-the-field' use and are easily applicable in team settings. However, they suffer from major drawbacks: Self-rating techniques are greatly influenced by subjects' task performance and limited ability to evaluate their own SA [21]. Performance measures are based on the controversial assumption that performance and SA are reciprocally bound.

2.2 In-Trial Techniques

A second category of SA measurement techniques consists of subjects answering questions about the situation during the trial. Called query or probes techniques, these methods can be categorized into freeze probe and real-time probe techniques. The situation awareness global assessment technique (SAGAT) [22] is the most popular and most used among a variety of freeze probe techniques, which also include the SALSA, a technique developed for air traffic control applications [23] and the Situation Awareness Control Room Inventory (SACRI) [24]. The trial is frozen (paused) from time to time while subjects answer questions regarding the current situation. Alternatively, real-time probe techniques push questions to the subject through the interface during the task, without pausing it. The Situation-Present Assessment Method (SPAM) [25] particularly uses response latency as the primary evaluation metric.

Although these techniques allow for an objective evaluation of what subjects know about the situation at critical points in time, they often invoke task interruptions and task-switching issues, they are thus deeply intrusive and less suitable for 'in-the-field' use.

2.3   Potential Continuous Techniques

Observer-rating techniques such as the Situation Awareness Behaviorally Rating Scale (SABARS) [19], are designed to infer the subjects' SA quality from a set of behavioral indicators. Such direct methods require the participation of subject matter experts and often result in a highly subjective evaluation.

Physiological and behavioral measures may also serve as indirect but potential continuous evaluation techniques of SA. However, unlike workload for which numerous psychophysiological and neuropsychological metrics have been proven reliable [26–28], a viable objective continuous measure of SA is still unaccounted for [29, 30].

2.4   In Team Settings

To date, the vast majority of existing measures of team SA (TSA) or shared SA (SSA) are variations of individual SA measurement methods and no measure has been formally validated [13, 31–33]. Shared SA can be seen as a matter of both individual knowledge and coordination, differentiating two levels of measurement [34, 35]: (1) the degree of accuracy of an individual's SA, and (2) the similarity of teammates' SA. The evaluation of SA accuracy is essentially what most objective techniques (cf. Sect. 2.1 and 2.2) are concerned with. One's understanding of the situation is compared to the true state of the environment at the time of evaluation, leading to the assessment of SA as a degree of congruence with reality.

The evaluation of SA similarity is usually based on the direct comparison of teammates' understanding of the situation elements relevant to them. SA on an element is considered shared if they have a similar understanding of it. For example, the Shared Awareness Questionnaire [36] scores teammates SSA on the agreement and accuracy of their answers to objective questions regarding the task. Inherently, these methods suffer from the same limitations than individual techniques and valid and reliable measures are still lacking [37].

2.5   Summary

In summary, methods like post-situational questionnaires or observation are usually unobtrusive but subjective, while objective methods require intrusion in the task to ask the questions (Table 1).

Table 1. Summary of major categories of SA measurements

Type of techniques	When	Characteristics
Self-rating techniques (e.g., SART, SARS, SA-SWORD, MARS)	After task	Unobtrusive Discrete (1-time) Subjective
Performance	After task	Unobtrusive Discrete (1-time) Objective
Probe techniques -Freeze Probes (SAGAT, SALSA, SACRI) - Real-time Probes (SPAM)	During task	Intrusive Discrete (n-times) Objective
Observer-rating techniques (e.g. SABARS)	During task	Unobtrusive Continuous Subjective

Although a one-fits-all technique is not necessarily pertinent due to the diversity of goals and context of evaluation, all measures exhibit a common limitation: they examine SA at certain points in time. As the environment evolves, however, SA has to be built and updated continuously to integrate relevant new events, information, and goals. Thus, SA is inherently dynamic [29, 38] and a continuously evolving construct. The inability to take into account the dynamic nature of SA is the main criticism expressed towards current evaluation techniques [14].

3   The Dynamics of Situation Awareness – Knowing When

In a context where Human-Autonomy Teaming and adaptive systems used in training and operational settings are in dire need for online assessment of the human state, the question of the evaluation of SA's temporal evolution (SA dynamics) has become central [39, 40]. In such operational environments, coherent decision making and team performance rest on a common and accurate understanding of what is going on and the projection of what might happen. Thus, this section addresses the question of why understanding the dynamics of SA is of importance and what might be relevant to measure it in a team context.

According to Endsley's model of Situation Awareness [10] we understand that the building of a shared SA, rests upon the perception and similar integration of the right situational elements by all teammates. In this spirit, shared SA is defined as

> *the degree to which team members possess the same SA on shared SA requirements"* (Endsley and Jones [43], p. 48)

SA requirements are pieces of information needed by individuals to take decisions and act to fulfil their tasks. They may concern the environment, the system, as well as knowledge of and about other team members. In [41], Cain refers to these information items as Necessary Knowledge Elements (NKE). As previously explored by Ososky et al. [42] we propose to extend the concept to Necessary Shared Knowledge Element

(NSKE), defining an information item needed by all teammates to fulfil a collaborative part of their tasks, in other words, the "shared SA requirements" from Endsley & Jones' definition (Fig. 1).

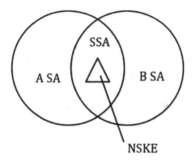

Fig. 1. Illustration of the Necessary Shared Knowledge Element (NSKE).

However, these elements necessary to build the shared understanding of the situation are rarely perceived simultaneously by each individual [41, 43]. Let us assume a hypothetical case where all necessary information is available to two teammates (A and B) and where they have both managed to form the same representation of it, effectively achieving SSA. Whenever a new NSKE appears, it invalidates the current SSA until the NSKE is integrated with A's and B's individual SA, respectively, to achieve an updated SSA (Fig. 2). In this model, three latencies are of interest for temporal SSA assessment, creating four phases of interest for SSA assessment.

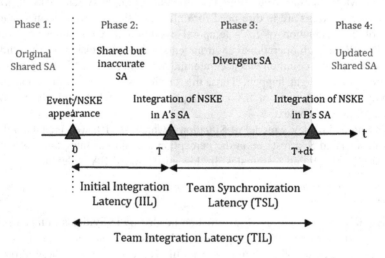

Fig. 2. Illustration of SSA temporal evolution and associated Initial Integration Latency (IIL), Team Synchronization Latency (TSL) and Team Integration Latency (TIL).

The Initial Integration Latency (IIL), the first latency, is the time needed by the first teammate to perceive and integrate the new NSKE into his updated SA. The interval between the appearance of the NSKE and its integration into A's SA (Phase 2 in Fig. 2) represents a situation of shared but inaccurate SA that comes with an increased probability of inaccurate decision making. During this period, teammates still possess a common representation of the situation. Individual decisions are consistent and collective decisions are coherent with the ongoing strategy. However, their representation is no longer up to date. The difference between reality and its representation increases the risk of inappropriate decision making. The duration of this latency is influenced by the same factors concerning attention and the sensory-perceptual system that impact Level-1 SA [32]: Stress, fatigue, workload, or interface complexity.

The second latency, we call Team Synchronization Latency (TSL), represents the time the second teammate needs to perceive and integrate the new NSKE into his updated SA after the first teammate did [Phase 3 in Fig. 2]. Taking into account the first latency, this creates an interval of divergent SA located between the two teammates' SA integrations of the event (Phase 3 in Fig. 2). During this time span, in addition to SA not being accurate for at least one of the teammates, SA is also not shared, increasing the probability of incoherent decision making. In this situation, two teammates, one being up to date with the situation and not the other, could send conflicting instructions to a third one.

Finally, the Team Integration Latency (TIL), is the sum of the first two. It represents the time elapsed between the appearance of the NSKE and its integration by the last team member concerned (Phase 2 + Phase 3 in Fig. 2). It reflects the duration for which not all team members have accurate SA.

Shared SA is re-accomplished once the second teammate acquires the NSKE. (i.e. after the second latency). Two modes of NSKE acquisition can be distinguished: independent and collaborative acquisition of the NSKE. The independent method of synchronization (Fig. 3) consists of both teammates autonomously acquiring the NSKE directly from the environment. As the perception of the new situation element is accomplished without assistance from the teammate, IIL, TSL and by extension TIL are subject to similar influencing factors.

In contrast, collaborative acquisition of the NSKE (Fig. 4) is based on the active exchange of the NSKE between teammates. Research has shown that verbal or electronic communication is central in the process of building and maintaining shared SA [42, 44]. The first individual to perceive an NSKE (teammate A) communicates it to teammate B sometime after having integrated it into his own SA. The communication may comprise the element of the situation itself (e.g. "There is a new unidentified airplane track"; Level-1 SA) or already include higher-level information based on A's processing and sense-making (e.g. "Identification needed on the new track"; Level-2 SA).

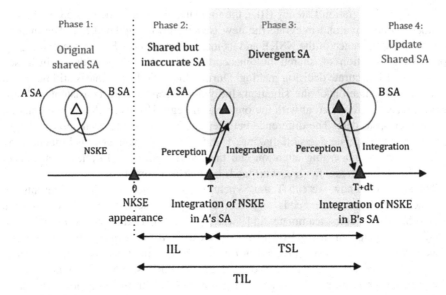

Fig. 3. Independent method of acquiring the NSKE to return to shared SA

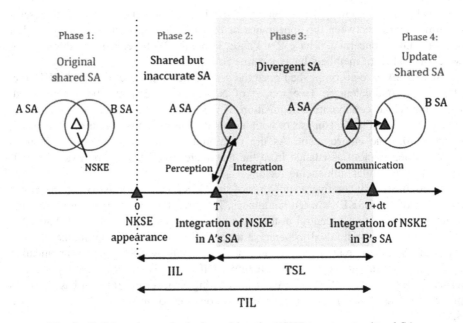

Fig. 4. Collaborative method of acquiring the NSKE to return to shared SA

In this case, B's acquisition of the NSKE depends on its prior acquisition by A, so that the duration of the second latency is influenced by additional factors. While perception and attention can still be impacted by the previously mentioned factors, there are additional factors specific to the exchange of information that can impact the communication and its content. This can be e.g. A's workload, the priority of NSKE over other tasks of A, the quality of shared mental models, or B's ability to receive and process communications. The recognition and effective exchange of NSKE also requires sufficient knowledge of the teammate's tasks and needs of information, as well as an ongoing estimation of the teammate's current SA. This knowledge is commonly referred to as part of the Team SA [9, 11].

By being inherent to the process of SA updating and sharing, these latencies emphasize the importance of SA dynamic properties. As such, we propose their use as a metric to assess SA *synchrony*. The following section addresses possible approaches for measuring these latencies.

4 Perspectives for SA Synchrony Measurement

Direct objective measures of SA have been extensively validated for a wide range of domains; however, they rely on an objective ground truth to compare responses to. They use a methodological standardization to objectify an otherwise subjective representation of the situation. With SA being a cognitive construct, evaluation of the situation model requires the elicitation of its content [4]. Therefore, any direct measure requires the expression or verbalization of an internal construct, making it inevitably intrusive and difficult to apply in fieldsettings. Although in some situations assessing the accuracy of the knowledge possessed can be sufficient, being able to detect and measure the hereinabove latencies through indirect measures would open new ways to quantify, qualify, and respond to shared SA issues in training in real-time.

4.1 Quantifying SA Synchrony

In 1997, Cooke et al. [45] proposed a cognitive engineering approach to individual and team SA measurement including, among others, behavior analysis, think aloud protocols or process tracing. Some of these methods find echoes in today's human monitoring approach in cognitive engineering. Monitoring team members' activities (including cognitive, physiological and behavioral) and comparing them, could provide an indirect way to assess SSA that can help overcome the evaluation constraints inherent to SA's nature.

In this sense, SA Synchrony can be seen as the temporal comparison of SSA-driven reactions and behaviors between two individuals in a collaborative work situation [46].

As illustrated in Sect. 3, the perception of a new situational element defines the three latencies and is central in the shared SA synchronization process. Thus, techniques oriented towards detecting this perception could be suited solutions to measure the three latencies discussed in Sect. 3. In this, some behavioral and physiological measurements present the advantage of being continuous and are already being used for the quantification of the user's state and activity [47–49]. As continuous measures, their temporal evolution can easily be compared and latencies between reactions or behaviors may be observed.

In 2019, de Winter et al.[8] built the case for continuous SA assessment by using a metric derived from the eye movements as a promising, although highly improvable, continuous measure of SA. More generally, eye-tracking is considered a potentially non-intrusive SA measurement tool. Recent applications in aviation [50–52] and driving [53], allowed to infer individual attentional focus and SA from patterns of gaze fixation that can then be compared between teammates. Similarly, reaction times could also be recorded through mouse-tracking or the tracking of other interface-related behaviors, as explored in [54–57].

Given all the techniques already explored and their mixed results, a multi-measurement approach seems to be required to capture complex constructs such as SA [20]. In an exploration of such a usage, we combined eye-tracking and mouse-tracking to extract perception latency and reaction time of individuals during a simplified airspace monitoring task. The first fixation on newly appeared tracks and the first click on them were recorded, allowing for an inference on individual SA actualization moment.

On paper, a multi-dimensional approach to human monitoring provides the basis for continuous and objective real-time assessment. Despite this potential, we recognize that by focusing on the resulting behavior, the measure could be strongly influenced by factors other than SA [45]. In addition, the methods described above still have limitations for field use and many issues need to be considered, such as the "look-but-fail-to-see" phenomenon in which one gazes without necessarily perceiving. As the techniques are already very sensitive and complex, the need to combine them makes their application all the more difficult. Future research should provide insight into how these methods can complement each other in measuring SA synchrony.

4.2   Qualifying SA Synchrony

While SA synchrony is primarily intended to be a purely quantitative objective measure, its interpretation and qualification are nonetheless interesting. Importantly, as communications add an inherent latency, a perfect synchrony of SA across team members is neither realistic nor necessarily desirable [58–60]. We understand that, when collaborating, the interpretation and prioritization of tasks and the relevance of the NSKE is a function of individual strategies and objectives. Thus, in order to identify SA problems, it may be necessary to evaluate the deviation from an expected latency. The interpretation or qualification of SA synchrony requires an in depth understanding of individual and team tasks, processes, and communications. As stated by Salas et al. [61], the qualification of behavioral markers must be contextualized to the environment in which they are being applied. Similarly to theoretical optimal SA [62] a theoretical optimal synchronization could be defined based on team task analysis. In order to be qualified, the link between SA synchrony and performance needs to be studied.

4.3   Using SA Synchrony

As most quantifiable metrics, SA synchrony can be used as descriptor of the collaboration or the performance. It is suited for both posteriori evaluation of overall team behavior during tasks and real-time assessment for an adaptive system or team feedback. Optimized states of synchronization between teammates or with the reality can be defined, aiding in the identification of problematic periods during collaboration processes.

In the specific context of training, scenarios and NSKEs are often known a priori, allowing the definition of anticipated responses to measure IIL, TSL and TIL. Thus, scripted training settings may allow for an easier assessment of SA synchrony than naturalistic situations. Adaptive interventions could then be designed to reduce the problematic latencies.

5 Conclusion

The dynamic nature of SA is unanimously acknowledged and its temporal evolution is the subject of much discussion. However, the assessment of SA dynamics has received little attention compared to SA accuracy.

Thus, we proposed, as a complementary approach to accuracy and similarity of SA, to consider the concept of SA synchrony as an indicator of SA dynamics in teams. We hope that pursuing the opportunities presented by the concept of SA synchrony may help in overcoming current limitations and drafting novel solutions for assessing and improving non-optimal SA dynamics. As discussed, knowing *when?* and *for how long?* SA synchrony is (not) achieved may be a helpful complement for assessing shared SA and preventing human error in a team setting.

We identified three intervals with SA-relevant issues. Future research may focus on measuring the duration of these three latenciesas possible quantitative measures of SA synchrony. SA being an internal cognitive construct has directed measurement techniques towards essentially discrete and intrusive methods. In essence, the measurement of SA content necessarily requires some form of verbalization that does not seem to be compatible with the continuous measurement techniques required today for online assessment. Considering the limitations of current techniques, we suggest the use of indirect measures. Although these are highly criticized for their inability to capture the content of the representation objectively, they seem the best fit for the 'in-the-field' applications required today because of their continuous and unobtrusive characteristics and their potential to be evaluated in real-time. We intend to identify and evaluate a number of candidate measures in upcoming research.

References

1. Endsley, M.R.: Situation awareness in aviation systems. In: Handbook of aviation human factors, pp. 257–276. Lawrence Erlbaum Associates Publishers, Mahwah (1999)
2. Foushee, H.C., Helmreich, R.L.: Group interaction and flight crew performance. In: Wiener, E.L., Nagel, D.C. (eds.) Human Factors in Aviation. Cognition and Perception, pp. 189–227. Academic Press, San Diego (1988)
3. Salas, E., Cannon-Bowers, J.A., Johnston, J.H.: How can you turn a team of experts into an expert team?: Emerging training strategies. In: Naturalistic Decision Making, pp. 359–370 (1997)

4. Endsley, M.R., Bolstad, C.A., Jones, D.G., Riley, J.M.: Situation awareness oriented design: from user's cognitive requirements to creating effective supporting technologies. Proc. Hum. Factors Ergon. Soc. Ann. Meet. **47**(3), 268–272 (2003)
5. Chen, Y., Qian, Z., Lei, W.: Designing a situational awareness information display: adopting an affordance-based framework to amplify user experience in environmental interaction design. Informatics **3**(2), 6 (2016)
6. M. R. Endsley, *Designing for Situation Awareness.* 2016
7. Scerbo, M.W.: Theoretical perspectives on adaptive automation. In: Automation and Human Performance: Theory and Applications, pp. 37–63. Lawrence Erlbaum Associates, Inc., Hillsdale (1996)
8. de Winter, J.C.F., Eisma, Y.B., Cabrall, C.D.D., Hancock, P.A., Stanton, N.A.: Situation awareness based on eye movements in relation to the task environment. Cogn. Technol. Work **21**(1), 99–111 (2019)
9. Nofi, A.: Defining and measuring shared situational awareness. PLoS ONE **5**, 76 (2000)
10. Endsley, M.R.: Toward a theory of situation awareness in dynamic systems. Hum. Factors J. Hum. Factors Ergon. Soc. **37**(1), 32–64 (1995)
11. Sulistyawati, K., Wickens, C.D., Chui, Y.P.: Exploring the concept of team situation awareness in a simulated air combat environment. J. Cogn. Eng. Decis. Making **3**(4), 309–330 (2009)
12. Gorman, J.C., Cooke, N.J., Winner, J.L.: Measuring team situation awareness in decentralized command and control environments. Ergonomics **49**(12–13), 1312–1325 (2006)
13. Salmon, P.M., Stanton, N.A., Walker, G.H., Jenkins, D.P.: What really is going on? Review of situation awareness models for individuals and teams. Theory Issues Ergon. Sci. **9**(4), 297–323 (2008)
14. Stanton, N.A., Salmon, P.M., Walker, G.H., Salas, E., Hancock, P.A.: State-of-science: situation awareness in individuals, teams and systems. Ergonomics **60**(4), 449–466 (2017)
15. Meireles, L., Alves, L., Cruz, J.: Conceptualization and measurement of individual situation awareness (SA) in expert populations across operational domains: a systematic review of the literature with a practical purpose on our minds. Proc. Hum. Factors Ergon. Soc. **2**, 1093–1097 (2018)
16. Taylor, R.M.: Situational awareness rating technique (SART): the development of a tool for aircrew systems design. In: Situational Aware. Aerosp. Oper., no. AGARD-CP-478, pp. 3/1–3/17 (1990)
17. Waag, W.L., Houck, M.R.: Tools for assessing situational awareness in an operational fighter environment. Aviat. Sp. Environ. Med. **65**(5 Suppl), A13–A19 (1994)
18. Vidulich, M.A., Hughes, E.R.: Testing a subjective metric of situation awareness. Proc. Hum. Factors Soc. **2**, 1307–1311 (1991)
19. Matthews, M.D., Beal, S.A.: Assessing situation awareness in field training exercises. ARI DTIC Report No. 1795 (2002)
20. Salmon, P., Stanton, N., Walker, G., Green, D.: Situation awareness measurement: a review of applicability for C4i environments. Appl. Ergon. **37**(2), 225–238 (2006)
21. Endsley, M.R., Selcon, S.J., Hardiman, T.D., Croft, D.G.: Comparative analysis of SAGAT and SART for evaluations of situation awareness. Proc. Hum. Factors Ergon. Soc. Ann. Meet. **42**(1), 82–86 (1998)
22. Endsley, M.R.: Situation awareness global assessment technique (SAGAT). In: Proceedings of the IEEE 1988 national aerospace and electronics conference (NAECON 1988), pp. 789–795 (1988)

23. Hauss, Y., Gauss, B., Eyferth, K.: SALSA-a new approach to measure situational awareness in air traffic control. Focusing attention on aviation safety. In: 11th International Symposium on Aviation Psychology, Columbus, pp. 1–20 (2001)
24. Hogg, D.N., Follesø, K., Volden, F.S., Torralba, B.: SACRI: A measure of situation awareness for use in the evaluation of nuclear power plant control room systems providing information about the current process state (1994)
25. Durso, F.T., Hackworth, C.A., Truitt, T.R.: Situation awareness as a predictor of performance in en route air traffic controllers. Air Traffic Control Q. 6(1), 1–20 (1999)
26. Veltman, J.A., Gaillard, A.W.K.: Physiological workload reactions to increasing levels of task difficulty. Ergonomics 41(5), 656–669 (1998)
27. Kramer, A.F.: Physiological metrics of mental workload: a review of recent progress. In: Multiple-task performance, pp. 279–328 (1991)
28. Roscoe, A.H.: Heart rate as a psychophysiological measure for in-flight workload assessment. Ergonomics 36(9), 1055–1062 (1993)
29. Nofi, A.: Defining and measuring shared situational awareness. 5 (2000)
30. Stanton, N.A., Salmon, P.M., Walker, G.H., Salas, E., Hancock, P.A.: State-of-Science: situation awareness in individuals, teams and systems. Ergonomics 60(4), 1–33 (2017)
31. Cooke, N.J., Stout, R.J., Salas, E.: A knowledge elicitation approach to the measurement of the team situation awareness (2001)
32. Endsley, M.R., Garland, D.J.: Situation awareness analysis and measurement. CRC Press, Boca Raton (2000)
33. Höglund, F., Berggren, P., Nählinder, S.: Using shared priorities to measure shared situation awareness. In: Proceedings of the 7th International ISCRAM Conference–Seattle, vol. 1 (2010)
34. Saner, L.D., Bolstad, C.A., Gonzalez, C., Cuevas, H.M.: Measuring and predicting shared situation awareness in teams. J. Cogn. Eng. Decis. Making 3(3), 280–308 (2009)
35. Bolstad, C.A., Foltz, P., Franzke, M., Cuevas, H.M., Rosenstein, M., Costello, A.M.: Predicting situation awareness from team communications pearson knowledge technologies. Proc. Hum. Factors Ergon. Soc. Ann. Meet. 51, 789–793 (2007)
36. Prytz, E., Rybing, J., Jonson, C.-O., Petterson, A., Berggren, P., Johansson, B.: An exploratory study of a low-level shared awareness measure using mission-critical locations during an emergency exercise. Proc. Hum. Factors Ergon. Soc. Ann. Meet. 59(1), 1152–1156 (2015)
37. Salas, E., Cooke, N.J., Rosen, M.A.: On teams, teamwork, and team performance discoveries and developments. Hum. Factors 50(3), 540–547 (2008)
38. Hjelmfelt, A.T., Pokrant, M.A.: Coherent tactical picture. CNA RM 97(129), 1998 (1998)
39. Adams, M.J., Tenney, Y.J., Pew, R.W.: Situation awareness and the cognitive management of complex systems. Hum. Factors 37(1), 85–104 (1995)
40. Ziemke, T., Schaefer, K.E., Endsley, M.: Situation awareness in human-machine interactive systems. Cogn. Syst. Res. 46, 1–2 (2017)
41. Cain, A.A., Schuster, D.: A quantitative measure for shared and complementary situation awareness. Hfes 60(1), 1823–1827 (2016)
42. Ososky, S. et al.: The importance of shared mental models and shared situation awareness for transforming robots from tools to teammates. In: Proceedings of the SPIE, vol. 8387, p. 838710 (2012)
43. Endsley, M., Jones, W.M.: A model of inter and intra team situation awareness: implications for design, training and measurement. In: McNeese, M., Salas, E., Endsley, M. (eds.) New Trends in Cooperative Activities: Understanding System Dynamics in Complex Environments, pp. 46–67. New trends Coop. Act. Underst. Syst. dyanmics complex Environ. Hum. FActors Ergon. Soc., Santa Monica, CA (2001)

44. Perla, P.P., Markowitz, M., Nofi, A.A., Weuve, C., Loughran, J.: Gaming and shared situation awareness. Center for Naval Analyses Alexandria VA (2000)
45. Cooke, N.J., Stout, R., Salas, E.: Broadening the measurement of situation awareness through cognitive engineering methods. Hum. Factors Ergon. Soc. **41**(4), 215–219 (1997)
46. Delaherche, E., Chetouani, M., Mahdhaoui, A., Saint-Georges, C., Viaux, S., Cohen, D.: Interpersonal synchrony: a survey of evaluation methods across disciplines. IEEE Trans. Affect. Comput. **3**(3), 349–365 (2012)
47. Schwarz, J., Fuchs, S.: Multidimensional real-time assessment of user state and performance to trigger dynamic system adaptation. In: Schmorrow, D.D., Fidopiastis, C.M. (eds.) AC 2017. LNCS (LNAI), vol. 10284, pp. 383–398. Springer, Cham (2017). https://doi.org/10.1007/978-3-319-58628-1_30
48. Jorna, P.: Heart rate and workload variations in actual and simulated flight. Ergonomics **36**(9), 1043–1054 (1993)
49. Tomarken, A.J.: A psychometric perspective on psychophysiological measures. Psychol. Assess. **7**(3), 387 (1995)
50. Kilingaru, K., Tweedale, J.W., Thatcher, S., Jain, L.C.: Monitoring pilot 'situation awareness'. J. Intell. Fuzzy Syst. **24**(3), 457–466 (2013)
51. Moore, K., Gugerty, L.: Development of a novel measure of situation awareness: the case for eye movement analysis. Proc. Hum. Factors Ergon. Soc. Ann. Meet. **54**(19), 1650–1654 (2010)
52. van de Merwe, K., van Dijk, H., Zon, R.: Eye movements as an indicator of situation awareness in a flight simulator experiment. Int. J. Aviat. Psychol. **22**(1), 78–95 (2012)
53. Hauland, G.: Measuring team situation awareness by means of eye movement data. In: Proceedings of HCI International 2003, vol. 3, pp. 230–234 (2019)
54. Calcagnì, A., Lombardi, L., Sulpizio, S.: Analyzing spatial data from mouse tracker methodology: an entropic approach. Behav. Res. Methods **49**(6), 2012–2030 (2017)
55. Frisch, S., Dshemuchadse, M., Görner, M., Goschke, T., Scherbaum, S.: Unraveling the subprocesses of selective attention: insights from dynamic modeling and continuous behavior. Cogn. Process. **16**(4), 377–388 (2015)
56. Kieslich, P., Henninger, F., Wulff, D., haslbeck, J., Schulte-Mecklenbeck, M.: Mousetracking: a practical guide to implementation and analysis (2018)
57. Freeman, J.B., Ambady, N.: MouseTracker: software for studying real-time mental processing using a computer mouse-tracking method. Behav. Res. Methods **42**(1), 226–241 (2010)
58. Salas, E., Prince, C., Baker, D.P., Shrestha, L.: Situation awareness in team performance: implications for measurement and training. Hum. Factors **37**(1), 123–136 (1995)
59. Sonnenwald, D.H., Maglaughlin, K.L., Whitton, M.C.: Designing to support situation awareness across distances: an example from a scientific collaboratory. Inf. Process. Manag. **40**(6), 989–1011 (2004)
60. Salmon, P.M., Stanton, N.A., Walker, G.H., Jenkins, D.P., Rafferty, L.: Is it really better to share? Distributed situation awareness and its implications for collaborative system design. Theory Issues Ergon. Sci. **11**(1–2), 58–83 (2010)
61. Salas, E., Reyes, D.L., Woods, A.L.: The assessment of team performance: observations and needs. In: von Davier, A.A., Zhu, M., Kyllonen, P.C. (eds.) Innovative Assessment of Collaboration. MEMA, pp. 21–36. Springer, Cham (2017). https://doi.org/10.1007/978-3-319-33261-1_2
62. Hooey, B.L., et al.: Modeling pilot situation awareness. In: Cacciabue, P., Hjälmdahl, M., Luedtke, A., Riccioli, C. (eds.) Human modelling in assisted transportation, pp. 207–213. Springer, Milano (2011). https://doi.org/10.1007/978-88-470-1821-1_22

Exploring Video Engagement in an Intelligent Tutoring System

David Quigley[✉], Donna Caccamise, John Weatherley, and Peter Foltz

University of Colorado Boulder, Boulder, CO 80020, USA
david.quigley@colorado.edu

Abstract. This paper presents the results of student engagement with eBRAVO, an Intelligent Tutoring System designed to support students' development of reading comprehension strategies. The eBRAVO curriculum is a personalized experience based on the students' previous engagement with the tool as well as their demonstration of deep comprehension of the current materials. This personalization may include support in the form of video lessons that target the comprehension strategy with which the reader has recently struggled embedded within the chapter context the reader was currently working. This paper outlines the results from a deployment during a summer program supporting students reading ecology content, and shows that students are clearly distinguishable into categories that denote their patterns of engagement with these videos. It also discusses how these results connect to comprehension assessment results within the system and at a unit level and the implications these results have for the design of future classroom intervention systems.

Keywords: Learning analytics · Intelligent Tutoring Systems · Reading comprehension

1 Introduction

Science education is changing. Increasing emphasis is being placed on students in science-as-practice [10] that is helping students understand science not only as a body of knowledge but also as a set of practices for developing and warranting knowledge claims about the natural world. One of the most important aspects of this process is reading scientific texts. The recent report *A Framework for K-12 Science Education* [10] cites "Obtaining, Evaluating, and Communicating Information" (pg 74) as one of the key science and engineering practices. This practice requires students not only to interpret text, but also to compare and evaluate texts in the context of explaining phenomena and solving problems. By twelfth grade, students are expected to be able to read and critique published scientific texts.

In this study, we present the analysis of student engagement with eBRAVO, an ITS designed to support students' reading comprehension in strategies by leveraging the Construction-Integration (CI) model of reading comprehension

© The Author(s) 2020
R. A. Sottilare and J. Schwarz (Eds.): HCII 2020, LNCS 12214, pp. 519–530, 2020.
https://doi.org/10.1007/978-3-030-50788-6_38

[21, 22]. We use a learning analytics [29] approach to understand student activity within eBRAVO using a feature driven sequential analysis approach [27]. We explore the distribution of engagement variables to understand different patterns of use and how they map to in-system measures of student comprehension and unit-level measures of student reading comprehension abilities.

2 Background

2.1 Reading Comprehension and Science Education

Reading to learn [6] is a critical skill to be supported in late primary and secondary education. This represents a significant challenge, since at present many students do not reach basic proficiency in reading comprehension for their grade level, including one third of fourth grade students and one quarter of eighth grade students [9]. Additionally, while great national and international effort has gone into supporting students' reading skills, a significant gap exists in supporting the reading of domain-specific text, especially in science. Reading scientific texts requires skills above and beyond general reading comprehension [13], in part due to the complex nature of the writing style and the importance of synthesizing content across multiple texts, figures, charts, and other sources of information [10]. To be successful in school, students need to be able to read content-area texts well enough to learn and remember new content, and they must be able to apply what they know in future reading and learning situations, as well as in novel contexts. When students begin upper elementary school, they are expected to read content-area texts (often in the form of a textbook); however, they are rarely provided with instruction on how to read informational and expository texts.

Compounding the problem, educators are often ill-equipped to address these domain-specific reading issues. Science teachers are not language arts experts. Their training and expertise focuses on scientific concepts for students to learn to independently examine scientific information. This is especially problematic when students read expository texts, not only because of the unfamiliar subject matter, but also due to the higher density of ideas, lack of coherence, and more complicated reference and structure employed in such texts [23]. There is a sudden jump in the complexity of content area readings in middle and high school, such that many of the popular textbooks are in fact as complex as college-level material in their syntax, vocabulary, and presentation as well as in content [16]. Moreover, there are important differences across disciplines in the way information is presented and represented and in their styles of reasoning, argumentation and inquiry that are best conveyed by teachers within the particular disciplines [14]. The problem that many readers share is not their inability to read the words on a page; instead, their most common problem is their inability to construct a coherent representation of the text meaning that is well integrated into their knowledge base. That is, they fail to deeply comprehend what they read [3].

These difficulties have an impact on science learning beyond the traditional reading activity. The landscape of science education is changing to incorporate disciplinary core ideas, cross-cutting concepts, and scientific practices as three different dimensions of learning [10]. The ability to read for understanding affects one's ability to learn science ideas through the practices that rely heavily on comprehension of text, such as argumentation and modeling, as well as for theory development and dissemination, and even course communication. Thus, it is critical to address these issues for the future of science learning.

2.2 Computer Interventions in Reading Comprehension

To date, the What Works Clearinghouse has evaluated four computer-based literacy programs that had positive effects on comprehension at the middle- or high-school levels: AcceleratedReader [28], Fast ForWord [12], Read180 [20], ReadingPlus [8]. All four programs focus primarily on developing fluency and vocabulary in order to improve comprehension, and are designed to be embedded in language arts or special education classrooms. In contrast, eBRAVO targets deep levels of comprehension in students who are reasonably fluent readers in their science domain classroom. Decoding at a fifth- grade level or higher, these students lack the skills to deeply or even adequately comprehend informational texts.

Recent research supports the development of automated, computer-based interventions that teach students to utilize reading strategies to learn from challenging, complex texts [4,17,25,26,31]. A leading example developed by McNamara and colleagues called interactive Strategy Training for Active Reading and Thinking (iSTART) utilizes natural language processing algorithms to automatically evaluate and provide feedback on students' written self-explanations of text (e.g., [25]). Two newer versions, iSTART extended practice and iSTART-ME, also allow teachers to upload texts [17,18]. However, eBRAVO differs from other online and computer-based programs, such as iSTART, in that it offers a more comprehensive approach to comprehension instruction embedded in the progressive study of content course texts. eBRAVO addresses all levels of comprehension, targeting local and global coherence building, gistmaking and inferencing, as well as metacognitive and problem-solving strategies (e.g., self-explanation) that proficient readers employ to identify and remedy comprehension breakdowns. This comprehensive approach to instructing deep reading comprehension assists students in constructing a coherent textbase and a situation model with multiple connections to the personal knowledge base, thereby ensuring durable and accessible memory for the course content. Furthermore, The pedagogical components of eBRAVO are designed following the CI comprehension model [21,22], a thoroughly researched theory that describes the cognitive processes that contribute to reading comprehension. eBRAVO focuses on instruction of literacy skills together with knowledge-building, using a gradated series of texts contextualized within a content area.

2.3 Intelligent Tutoring Systems and Video Engagement

Intelligent Tutoring Systems (ITS, [1,15]) are a promising approach to supporting learning. These tools provide students with a cohesive experience in a digital learning environment, using their engagement with the problems or tasks in the system to develop an underlying learner model that represents their current understanding of the content as well as relevant situational factors such as engagement or affect [7,11]. ITS then use this model of the learner's mental state to determine the appropriate next action for developing deeper understanding. This approach has been shown to be as effective as one-on-one time with a tutor, providing students with individualized support that can outpace time on task in a larger classroom activity [30].

Videos are increasingly prevalent as a learning tool, but these are primarily studied at a postsecondary level for MOOC and Blended/Flipped Learning environments (see, e.g. [32]). That said, it is important in supporting reading comprehension as a skill in a computer & learner system; when you cannot rely on the learner's deep comprehension of the written word, you have to rely on connections between written words, visual diagramming, and narration. This design consideration inspires the demonstration found in the example screen from the video lesson in Fig. 1.

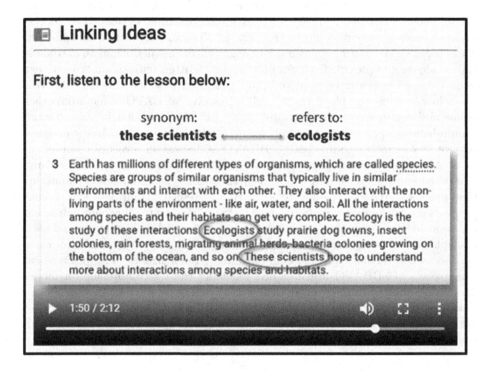

Fig. 1. The video view of a linking ideas lesson.

However, when working with these ITS systems at the secondary level, many different paradigms of motivation are important. Many researches have cited issues with motivation in the use of ITS (e.g., [2]), and different approaches to improving engagement have been explored, including leveraging aspects of gaming directly in the interaction (e.g., [24]).

3 Research Context

Our eBRAVO project builds on BRAVO [5], a connected ecology curriculum with reading comprehension lessons originally designed for deployment in language arts classrooms. BRAVO operationalized the CI model of reading comprehension discussed in the background section above by incorporating five central lessons on the increasingly complex layers of the model, flowing from issues of local cohesion ("Linking Ideas" and "Getting the Gist"), global cohesion ("Summary" and "Graphic Organizers") and situation modeling ("Inference"). These lessons were interspersed among the curriculum chapters, taught by the teacher to the whole class at once.

The eBRAVO curriculum takes the linear process of BRAVO and creates an adaptive reading experience on their web-enabled devices diagramed in Fig. 2 to work through an improved twelve chapter ecology curriculum. This is designed to allow students to encounter lessons as needed, rather than as a class. To accomodate this personalized learning experience in an intelligent tutoring approach, we adapted the five class-level lessons from BRAVO into videos and a practice problem personalized for each chapter, creating 119 lessons (chapter one does not have an inference lesson, since there is no assumed prior experience to draw upon).

As students work within eBRAVO in their browser, they first see a short chapter of 3 to 11 paragraphs of ecology reading content connected to what they have read so far in the curriculum. These readings incorporate in-text highlighting and clickable definitions for key vocabulary, along with embedded figures including images of important components or diagrams of certain systems. Once students have completed their readings, they proceed directly to an open-ended log asking them to record the big ideas found in the text. eBRAVO then probes their deep comprehension with multiple choice questions that target both issues brought up directly in the text as well as inferences and connections to greater ideas from previous texts. If the system determines a student should see a reading lesson based on their comprehension scores, it then gauges which type of reading support (linking ideas, gist, summary, graphic organizer, or inference) with which the student needs help and sends them to the appropriate lesson for that chapter and content, as seen in Fig. 1 above. These lessons incorporate two to five minute videos that outline the key comprehension strategy that is targeted and demonstrate how to apply this comprehension strategy to parts of the chapter that the student has just completed.

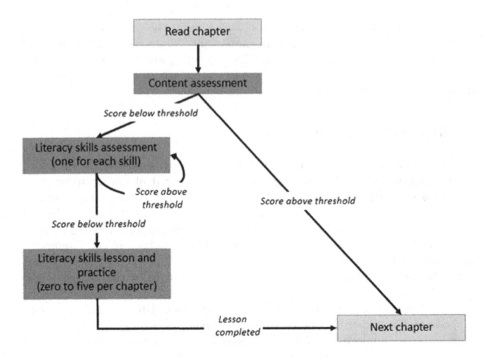

Fig. 2. A diagram of the flow of possible trajectories through chapter content in eBRAVO.

3.1   Data and Analysis

In this paper, we present results from 27 middle school students who provided family consent and used eBRAVO in a four-week summer intensive program. These students used eBRAVO in their 60-min class period four days a week over 12 class periods. We gave them the TORC paragraph reading activity [19] as a pre and post assessment activity in order to independently gauge reading comprehension ability. During this program, students were not assigned grades or other curriculum outcomes, so external motivation for performance was lower than usual for a typical classroom deployment.

We use a learning analytics [29] approach to understand student activity within eBRAVO. We focus our efforts on relating student engagement with the reading lessons as measured by their clickstream with the video content to the resulting outcomes on practice problems in the lesson as well as future questions in the curriculum. We use a feature driven sequential analysis approach [27], creating independent variables of video and lesson engagement. We explore the distribution of these engagement variables to understand different patterns of use.

4   Results

Overall, our student sample demonstrated a wide variety of lesson personalization within eBRAVO, seeing on average 5.44 (SD 3.59) lessons, with two students seeing 11 lessons (almost one lesson every chapter) and four students seeing no lessons.

Our primary division of students is based on patterns of engagement across videos, as seen in Fig. 3. Overall, we see very few students did not reach at least one lesson (No Lesson), a group of students maintained engagement with lessons (Engaged), and a small group of students simply did not engage (Unengaged). However, the largest group of students began the curriculum engaged, but did not maintain their video engagement by their final lesson (Dropoff). Though "Dropoff" students continued to struggle with the deep comprehension questions, they began to show attrition when addressing their issues with the lesson content.

These distinctions demonstrate interesting correlations with a variety of student outcomes. The first outcome of note is the student experience in terms of the average number of lessons encountered within each group, as seen in Fig. 4. The three groups that encountered lessons all demonstrated patterns that trend towards significance on a Kruskal Wallis H Test ($p = 0.099$), with students who demonstrate patterns of dropoff and unengagement trending towards increasing numbers of lessons seen.

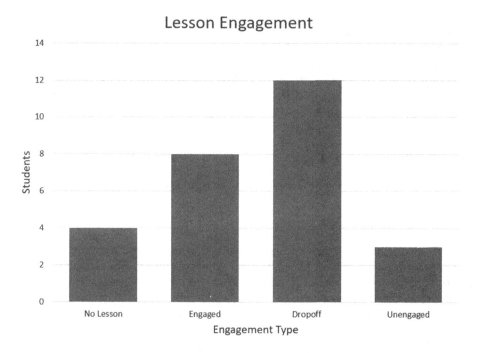

Fig. 3. The distribution of engagement type across students.

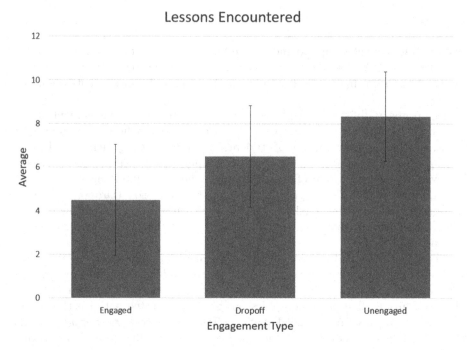

Fig. 4. The distribution of lessons encountered by engagement type.

These groupings also demonstrate interesting implications for demonstrated learning outcomes. In a pairwise t-test analysis of students' comprehension scores within eBRAVO, a significant difference appeared when comparing "No Lesson" students to the "Dropoff" group ($p = 0.0405$), with the No Lesson students doing significantly better on in-system assessments. However, these results did not carry over to the TORC test at significance ($p = 0.15$).

5 Discussion

We see significant differences among each group in our breakdown.

5.1 No Lessons

For our "No Lessons" group, they clearly worked to ensure that they succeeded at the comprehension checks at the end of each chapter. This group demonstrated a mastery of the content within the system, but did not demonstrate a significant difference in the reading outcomes section, which may be due to causes discussed in the limitations section below.

5.2 Engaged

While our "Engaged" group demonstrated a willingness to keep with the program, and an ability to eventually master the abilities needed to complete the comprehension checks, they also did not demonstrate an improvement.

5.3 Dropoff

Our "Dropoff" group showed continued troubles with the comprehension checks within the curriculum - they are consistently diverted to lessons, which could be the source of their frustration and the reasoning behind their transition from engaged to unengaged.

5.4 Unengaged

The "Unengaged" group acted as you might expect - they never watched lesson videos, and they subsequently also never appeared to succeed on comprehension checks which meant they continued to be diverted to lessons. This did not connect to significant differences in in-system or pre/post test measures, which may be attributable to sample size as discussed in the limitations section below.

6 Conclusions

First and foremost, these results have implications for our design, suggesting the need to revisit our approach of repeated presentation of concepts. We found that students quickly found themselves breaking into different patterns of engagement that were easily distinguishable within the clickstreams and formed a distinct set of outcomes.

Moreover, these results should be addressed in other ITS tools that rely on a repeated sampling approach to concept understanding, demonstrating the need for engagement with lesson content to be motivated further. Students in this setting without external motivation from grades or other factors often do not continue to engage with the same content just because it is presented in a new context – they quickly grow tired of the approach.

6.1 Limitations

One important note to consider when discussing this work is the limited scope of this deployment. The first element of scope to consider is the use of 27 students under one teacher, which does not allow us to generalize much beyond the scope of that program. Many of our usage patters also resolved to very small numbers, which impacted our ability to look for significant differences, particularly in course outcome measures among groups such as the "No Lessons" (4 students) and "Unengaged" (3 students) groups. It will require a larger deployment to hone in on differences between these groups and gain further insight. Furthermore, it is important to remember that this was a deployment over a three-week summer program with no formal assessment policies, which did not allow for the teacher to implement any level of external motivation to participate with true fidelity. Many participants may have seen this as an opportunity to "slack off" when faced with learning from video lessons.

7   Future Work

These results and conclusions have motivated some significant changes in the workflow of the eBRAVO system. Some of our changes have already been implemented - we have focused on upgrading our teacher-facing dashboard to better provide a view for how the students are progressing through the materials within eBRAVO and what measures of success they are showing, in order for the teacher to provide just-in-time intervention to a student that may be struggling or showing signs of disengagement. These results have also prompted discussions of more significant redesign of the eBRAVO platform, incorporating intrinsic motivation patterns within the system, such as automated feedback and potential gamification [24] aspects.

Acknowledgements. The research reported here was supported, in whole or in part, by the Institute of Education Sciences, U.S. Department of Education, through grant R305A170142 to the University of Colorado Boulder. The opinions expressed are those of the authors and do not represent the views of the Institute or the U.S. Department of Education.

References

1. Anderson, J.R., Boyle, C.F., Reiser, B.J.: Intelligent tutoring systems. Science **228**(4698), 456–462 (1985)
2. Baker, R.S.: Modeling and understanding students' off-task behavior in intelligent tutoring systems. In: Proceedings of the SIGCHI conference on Human factors in computing systems, pp. 1059–1068 (2007)
3. Biancarosa, G., Snow, C.E.: Reading next: a vision for action and research in middle and high school literacy: a report from Carnegie Corporation of New York. Alliance for Excellent Education (2004)
4. Caccamise, D., Franzke, M., Eckhoff, A., Kintsch, E., Kintsch, W.: Guided practice in technology-based summary writing (2007)
5. Caccamise, D., Friend, A., Groneman, C., Littrell-Baez, M., Kintsch, E.: Teaching Struggling Middle School Readers to Comprehend Informational Text. International Society of the Learning Sciences, Boulder, CO (2014)
6. Chall, J.S.: Stages of reading development (1983)
7. Chaouachi, M., Frasson, C.: Mental workload, engagement and emotions: an exploratory study for intelligent tutoring systems. In: Cerri, S.A., Clancey, W.J., Papadourakis, G., Panourgia, K. (eds.) ITS 2012. LNCS, vol. 7315, pp. 65–71. Springer, Heidelberg (2012). https://doi.org/10.1007/978-3-642-30950-2_9
8. Clearinghouse, W.W.: Wwc intervention report: Reading plus® (2010). Accessed 10 April 2016

9. Council, N.R.: The nation's report card (2017)
10. Council, N.R., et al.: A framework for K-12 Science Education: Practices, Cross-cutting Concepts, and Core Ideas. National Academies Press, Washington (2012)
11. D'Mello, S., Graesser, A.: Dynamics of affective states during complex learning. Learn. Instr. **22**(2), 145–157 (2012)
12. Gillam, R.B., et al.: The efficacy of Fast ForWord language intervention in school-age children with language impairment: a randomized controlled trial. J. Speech Lang. Hear. Res. **51**(1), 97–119 (2008). https://doi.org/10.1044/1092-4388(2008/007)
13. Goldman, S.R.: Discourse of learning and the learning of discourse. Discourse Processes **55**(5–6), 434–453 (2018)
14. Goldman, S.R., et al.: Disciplinary literacies and learning to read for understanding: a conceptual framework for disciplinary literacy. Educ. Psychol. **51**(2), 219–246 (2016)
15. Graesser, A.C., Conley, M.W., Olney, A.: Intelligent tutoring systems (2012)
16. Heller, R., Greenleaf, C.L.: Literacy instruction in the content areas: getting to the core of middle and high school improvement. Alliance for Excellent Education (2007)
17. Jackson, G.T., Boonthum, C., McNAMARA, D.S.: iSTART-ME: situating extended learning within a game-based environment. In: Proceedings of the workshop on intelligent educational games at the 14th annual conference on artificial intelligence in education, pp. 59–68. AIED Brighton (2009)
18. Jackson, G.T., Guess, R.H., McNamara, D.S.: Assessing cognitively complex strategy use in an untrained domain. Top Cogn. Sci. **2**(1), 127–137 (2010)
19. Jongsma, E.A.: Test review: test of reading comprehension (TORC). Read. Teach. **33**(6), 703–708 (1980)
20. Kim, J.S., Capotosto, L., Hartry, A., Fitzgerald, R.: Can a mixed-method literacy intervention improve the reading achievement of low-performing elementary school students in an after-school program? results from a randomized controlled trial of read 180 enterprise. Educ. Eval. Policy Anal. **33**(2), 183–201 (2011)
21. Kintsch, W., Kintsch, E.: Comprehension. In: Children's reading comprehension and assessment, pp. 89–110. Routledge (2005)
22. Kintsch, W., Walter Kintsch, C.: Comprehension: A Paradigm for Cognition. Cambridge University Press, Cambridge (1998)
23. Lee, O., Quinn, H., Valdés, G.: Science and language for english language learners in relation to next generation science standards and with implications for common core state standards for english language arts and mathematics. Educ. Res. **42**(4), 223–233 (2013)
24. McNamara, D.S., Jackson, G.T., Graesser, A.: Intelligent tutoring and games (ITAG). In: Gaming for classroom-based learning: Digital role playing as a motivator of study, pp. 44–65. IGI Global (2010)
25. McNamara, D.S., Levinstein, I.B., Boonthum, C.: istart: Interactive strategy training for active reading and thinking. Behav. Res. Methods Instrum. Comput. **36**(2), 222–233 (2004)
26. Meyer, B.J., Wijekumar, K.: A web-based tutoring system for the structure strategy: theoretical background, design, and findings. In: Reading Comprehension Strategies: Theories, Interventions, and Technologies, pp. 347–375 (2007)
27. Quigley, D., Ostwald, J., Sumner, T.: Scientific modeling: using learning analytics to examine student practices and classroom variation. In: Proceedings of the Seventh International Learning Analytics & Knowledge Conference, pp. 329–338 (2017)

28. What Works Clearinghouse: Accelerated Reader^{TM}. What Works Clearinghouse Intervention Report. Updated. Institute of Educational Sciences (2016)
29. Siemens, G., Gašević, D.: Special issue on learning and knowledge analytics. Educ. Technol. Soc. **15**(3), 1–163 (2012)
30. VanLehn, K.: The relative effectiveness of human tutoring, intelligent tutoring systems, and other tutoring systems. Educ. Psychol. **46**(4), 197–221 (2011)
31. Wijekumar, K.K., Meyer, B.J., Lei, P.: Large-scale randomized controlled trial with 4th graders using intelligent tutoring of the structure strategy to improve nonfiction reading comprehension. Educ. Technol. Res. Dev. **60**(6), 987–1013 (2012)
32. Yousef, A.M.F., Chatti, M.A., Schroeder, U.: The state of video-based learning: a review and future perspectives. Int. J. Adv. Life Sci. **6**(3/4), 122–135 (2014)

Using a Non-player Character to Improve Training Outcomes for Submarine Electronic Warfare Operators

Bradford L. Schroeder[1]([envelope]), Nicholas W. Fraulini[2],
Wendi L. Van Buskirk[1], and Cheryl I. Johnson[1]

[1] Naval Air Warfare Center Training Systems Division, Orlando, FL, USA
{bradford.schroeder, wendi.vanbuskirk,
cheryl.i.johnson}@navy.mil
[2] StraCon Services Group, LLC, Fort Worth, TX, USA
nicholas.fraulini.ctr@navy.mil

Abstract. Previous research has shown that adaptive training (AT) is an effective tool for improving training outcomes relative to non-adaptive approaches. Taking a value-added perspective, in this study we sought to determine whether the presence of an embedded non-player character (NPC) served to improve performance outcomes relative to AT alone. To support this research, we utilized the Submarine EW Adaptive Trainer (SEW-AT) as our testbed, which is a scenario-based AT system that simulates a trip to periscope depth. The submarine EW operator's role is to monitor the radio frequency signals in the environment and submit reports of the contact picture at prescribed intervals (i.e., scheduled reports) and irregular intervals as the environment changes (i.e., unscheduled reports) to the Officer of the Deck (OOD). Sixty-eight U.S. Navy EW operators completed training with one of two versions of SEW-AT: one with an NPC OOD and one without. The NPC OOD was designed carefully to provide realistic immediate feedback to the trainee while also minimizing distraction from the task. In general, all EW operators improved their performance using SEW-AT, but those using SEW-AT with the NPC OOD displayed significantly greater improvement in scheduled report timeliness than those who used SEW-AT without the NPC OOD. These results suggest that the addition of the NPC OOD to provide immediate feedback added an overall benefit over AT alone.

Keywords: Non-player character · Adaptive training · Submarine electronic warfare · Immediate feedback · Immersion · Military training

1 Introduction

1.1 Non-player Characters – History, Design, and Implementation

Non-player characters (NPCs) exist in a variety of media ranging from tabletop board games to computer-based training systems, with roles varying from non-interactive background characters to fully interactive tutors (e.g., "pedagogical agents") that guide end users through advanced learning material. For computer-based media, Warpefelt

This is a U.S. government work and not under copyright protection in the U.S.;
foreign copyright protection may apply 2020
R. A. Sottilare and J. Schwarz (Eds.): HCII 2020, LNCS 12214, pp. 531–542, 2020.
https://doi.org/10.1007/978-3-030-50788-6_39

[1] defined NPCs as "characters within a computer game that are controlled by the computer, rather than the player" (p. 31). Merrick and Maher [2] argued that NPCs support player interaction in video games, essentially facilitating gameplay and guiding the player's interactions with the game. To do this, NPCs are driven by simulation models that plan their behaviors based on changes in the virtual environment, from other NPCs, or from user interactions [3]. These simulations vary in complexity depending on the desired capabilities of the NPC and the anticipated user actions to which the NPC must respond.

In addition to technical programming aspects of NPCs, previous work provides perspective on how NPCs should be designed from a higher level. Researchers have posited that people view their interactions with computer-based characters through a similar lens as face-to-face social interactions with other people [4]. This idea has led researchers to design NPCs as human-like to be effective, particularly in cases where social skills are the training objective (e.g., Moon [5]). Indeed, some have suggested that NPCs must be believable to the end user to be effective characters [6, 7]. Lankoski and Björk [8] borrowed inspiration from cinema in discussing the design of believable NPCs, which includes characteristics such as the ability to use natural language, persistent traits, and titular names. Additionally, Adams [9] argued that NPCs can help facilitate immersion by providing a sense of "tactical immersion" that engages the player to accomplish challenges in tandem with the NPC. Thus, the NPC's actions can elicit changes in the user's behavior [2, 6]. Importantly, Reeves and Nass [4] noted that these characters do not need a great amount of detail to elicit social interpretations from players, and suggested that merely a non-visual interactive voiced character is sufficient to be believable.

Over the past three decades, NPC simulations have grown in complexity to support interactive instructional software facilitated by intelligent NPC tutors, sometimes called "pedagogical agents." Previous work highlights that NPCs can help maintain learner interest and motivation during computer-based training [3, 10, 11], and some have argued that the primary function of an NPC is to deliver educational content to the user [12]. Empirical work supports these assertions. In a series of five experiments, Moreno and colleagues [11] compared the presence and absence of an NPC in an educational computer game and supported that NPCs increase motivation and improve learning as measured through retention and transfer of knowledge. Additionally, they compared visual narrated NPCs against narration-only (i.e., non-visual) NPCs and found they were equally effective in elevating learner interest and learning outcomes. Incidentally, this validates Reeves and Nass's [4] suggestion that voice-only NPCs may be sufficiently effective to aid learning. With the previous literature in mind, the present work describes the design of an NPC for a submarine electronic warfare (EW) adaptive training system. We review data collected from EW operators in the field who used this system with and without an NPC. In the next section, we describe our approach for training submarine EW.

1.2   Real-Time Feedback for Submarine Electronic Warfare

The U.S. Navy recognizes EW's importance for submarine safety, and is currently seeking solutions to improve operator performance. One method that has shown promise in training EW is Adaptive Training (AT). AT has been defined as "training interventions whose content can be tailored to an individual learner's aptitudes, learning preferences, or styles prior to training and that can be adjusted, either in real time or at the end of a training session, to reflect the learner's on-task performance" [13]. Researchers have provided evidence for the benefits of AT compared to non-adaptive forms of training [14–16]. One of the primary benefits of AT is it closely approximates one-on-one tutoring by adjusting instruction based on trainees' performance. Therefore, AT can act as an effective training option for environments in which one-on-one tutoring is not viable [14, 17]. As the definition above suggests, one instructional technique that can be used to approximate human tutors is immediate (or real-time) feedback that can be adapted based on performance.

Bangert-Drowns and colleagues [18] argue that feedback is most advantageous when it immediately corrects erroneous behaviors. In particular, the guidance hypothesis suggests that immediate feedback provides information about errors so that the learner may correct those errors on the next trial [19]. Support for the use of immediate feedback in instructional systems argues that it helps trainees learn appropriate cue-strategy associations [20]. This notion of cue-strategy associations lends itself particularly well to the dynamic environments typical of military training problems. Specifically, immediate feedback should be presented while the environmental cue parameters that were present when the error was made are still available in order to provide context for the feedback [20]. Indeed, there has been empirical support reported for the use of immediate feedback in more complex task environments. For instance, Corbett and Anderson [21] found that presenting immediate feedback resulted in more efficient learning requiring less time on a computer programming task, and Kirlik and colleagues [22] reported an advantage of immediate versus delayed feedback in a simulated military task. Further, Kulik and Kulik [23] performed a meta-analysis where they compared the effectiveness of immediate and delayed feedback on verbal tasks. Their review of 53 studies revealed that immediate feedback showed an advantage over delayed feedback in applied studies, whereas the opposite effect was found in laboratory studies.

Due to the promise of the immediate feedback in complex task environments, we decided to implement that instructional technique in our adaptive training system. However, because the EW task is multi-faceted, the development team took care to provide immediate feedback in a way that would not cognitively overload the operator nor interfere with task requirements. For example, submarine EW is a complex task comprised of visual, auditory, and temporal components that includes multiple subtasks such as auditory and visual change detection, prioritization, decision-making, and signal analysis. More specifically, the EW operators must identify contacts by simultaneously listening to radio frequency signals and navigating cluttered real-time displays while remaining vigilant for counter-detection and threat contacts. Additionally, they must submit a series of reports on their findings to the Officer of the Deck (OOD) in as accurate and timely a manner as possible. We believed that providing a brief auditory cue or hint to the operator would not interfere with their ability to perceive and process contacts in the environment. In addition, we wanted to provide this feedback in a way that would be realistic so as not to be too distracting to the participant. One way that EW operators receive feedback during operations is from the

OOD, usually by verbally alerting the operator of signals in the environment or reports that are incorrect or overdue. Therefore, we determined that providing this feedback using an NPC would create the least cognitive overlap with existing (i.e., visual) aspects of the task. Thus, we decided to provide immediate feedback for critical events by using auditory, verbal cues via an NPC OOD.

1.3   Designing an NPC for Submarine Electronic Warfare Training

The Submarine Electronic Warfare Adaptive Trainer (SEW-AT) was developed to allow trainees to perform the role of an EW operator in a series of 10 to 20 min scenarios, completing tasking and reports as required while using the AN/BLQ-10[1] emulator used in the schoolhouse. Throughout SEW-AT's development, we have incorporated research-inspired design elements that have led to improvements in training outcomes [24]. The present work describes one such element – an NPC OOD that delivers real-time audio feedback to remind operators to complete reporting requirements in a timely manner. SEW-AT's NPC OOD includes many of the characteristics discussed previously. In line with Lankoski and Björk's NPC design recommendations [8], the NPC OOD consistently reminds users of their goal to submit reports in a timely fashion, using a firm tone to prompt trainees much like a real-life OOD. Additionally, the NPC OOD uses tactical language familiar to trainees, promoting a sense of realism during training. To ensure the NPC communicated with operators in a realistic manner, the NPC OOD broadcasts his messages over the communication system consistent with how the OOD communicates with operators on board. Additionally, we recorded the audio messages coming from the NPC OOD with Fleet personnel to maximize authenticity of language and tone. This aligns with recommendations from previous research to design believable NPCs [6, 7] and to use the NPC to facilitate tactical immersion [9].

The NPC OOD provides interaction and feedback to trainees based on a real-time assessment of their activity during training. Our goal is to examine whether the NPC OOD facilitated changes in user behavior in line with previous NPC research [2, 6]. We based our NPC's design on previous research recommendations for effective NPCs, and to determine whether SEW-AT's NPC OOD was effective for training, we examined differences in performance between SEW-AT versions with and without the NPC OOD. Overall, we hypothesized that those training with the NPC OOD would show greater improvements in overall scenario score from pre-test to post-test compared to those training without the NPC OOD (H1). We also aimed to examine the performance components that overall scenario score comprised: accuracy and timeliness. Our second hypothesis was that training with the NPC OOD's feedback would improve users' report accuracy in post-test (H2). Similarly, our third hypothesis was that training with the NPC OOD's feedback would improve users' report timeliness in post-test (H3). If one of these hypotheses is supported, it would provide evidence that the NPC OOD is an effective way to provide immediate feedback in this complex training domain.

---

[1] AN/BLQ-10 is the name of the submarine EW tactical system.

2   Methodology

2.1   Participants

Sixty-eight EW operators' data were collected across separate field data collection events at Submarine Learning Center (SLC) Detachments. The first data collection event (T1) included 27 EW operators from two SLC Detachments from the east and west coast of the United States. The second data collection event (T2) included 41 EW operators from five Submarine Learning Center Detachments from the east and west coasts of the United States and its territories.

2.2   Testbed

As previously mentioned, the testbed used during the two data collection events was SEW-AT. SEW-AT simulates a trip to periscope depth to train EW operators on three main training objectives: (1) keeping the ship safe, (2) identifying changes in the radio frequency environment, and (3) providing accurate and timely reports. Before a scenario starts, a scenario brief is presented and provides the EW operator context for that scenario's mission. Once the EW operator reviews the pre-periscope depth brief, the scenario starts and the operator identifies, analyzes, and classifies emitters and then provides reports to Control. To collect operators' report submissions in SEW-AT (which are verbal reports in the operational environment), we developed a report Graphical User Interface (GUI) that allows operators to generate their verbal reports from drop down menu selections and typed data entries. Once an operator submits a report, the system assesses the accuracy and timeliness of that report. SEW-AT assesses accuracy based on whether the appropriate report was submitted, and whether any content of that report (if applicable) was correct. For timeliness, operators have a brief window of opportunity in which to submit their report, after which they would incur a scoring penalty for late submissions. During these accuracy and timeliness assessments, NPC OOD provides audio feedback if the system detects the operator has made an error. After the scenario ends, SEW-AT adapts the difficulty of the next scenario based on the operator's performance from the scenario they just completed. There are three levels of difficulty based on criteria in submarine training doctrine - easy, medium, and hard. If a trainee performs well, they are moved up into a higher level of difficulty; if a trainee performs poorly, they move down a level of difficulty; if their performance is fair, they stay at the same level of difficulty.

The present report examines two versions of SEW-AT: one version without an NPC OOD and one version with an NPC OOD. The NPC OOD provided the operator with real-time verbal prompts during the scenario. The version of SEW-AT with the NPC OOD assessed trainee performance in real-time and, based on that assessment of performance, would provide verbal prompts in one of two ways. First, the NPC OOD would alert the trainee to high priority errors they just made. Secondly, the NPC OOD would alert them on their report timeliness.

2.3   Procedure

For T1, with coaching from the research team, operators received instruction on how to make verbal reports using the verbal report GUI in SEW-AT and practiced using the GUI in a short familiarization scenario. After the SEW-AT familiarization portion, operators played 10–20 min realistic scenarios in SEW-AT. The first scenario was a medium difficulty scenario that served as the pre-test. After the pre-test, the operators performed additional scenarios in which the difficulty of the next scenario adjusted based on performance during the previous scenario. The objective of all the scenarios was to complete all required searches and submit accurate reports to the OOD on time. Finally, after each scenario operators received performance-based feedback that focused on the three training objectives listed previously.

For T2, operators went through a similar procedure as in T1 with two changes. Instead of a research team-led familiarization portion, these operators received PowerPoint instruction that included SEW-AT tutorial videos. Like T1, the EW operators completed a medium difficulty pre-test scenario, played 10–20 min realistic scenarios in SEW-AT that adapted based on performance, and received performance based feedback after each scenario. The main change in T2 was the addition of the NPC OOD who provided cueing on the lateness of reports.

3   Results

Prior to evaluating performance improvements in each version of SEW-AT, we conducted preliminary tests to ensure both groups were statistically equivalent. Primarily, we did this because our sample was not randomly assigned by condition, was comprised of students at different SLC locations with unequal group sizes, and the data were collected at different times. Before making inferences about whether the NPC helped improve trainee performance, we compared the equivalence of both data collections' pre-test overall scenario scores to each other.[2]

Overall scenario scores are calculated by combining report accuracy (i.e., was a report for this contact submitted correctly?) and report timeliness (i.e., was that report submitted in a timely manner?). We derived both the accuracy and the timeliness measures from submarine EW doctrine. To assess whether each group's scores were statistically equivalent at pre-test, we employed a two one-sided t-test (TOST) procedure as described by Lakens, Scheel, and Isager [25]. First, we conducted a power analysis given our minimum sample size of 27, alpha level of .05, and desired power of .90. We identified that we would be able to detect an effect with Cohen's d of approximately 0.89, yielding equivalence bounds of -0.89 and 0.89. The result of the TOST procedure was significant, $t(57.79) = 2.02$, $p = .024$, providing evidence that both pre-test data collections had statistically equivalent overall scenario scores ($M_{T1} = 35.18\%$, $SD_{T1} = 16.14\%$; $M_{T2} = 28.70\%$, $SD_{T2} = 16.95\%$).

---

[2] When comparing T1 to T2, all analyses were Welch's t tests because of unequal sample sizes.

3.1 Overall Performance

Next, we evaluated changes in overall scenario score from pre-test to post-test for each data collection event. As a reminder, overall scenario score is comprised of both accuracy and timeliness. For T1, there was not a significant improvement in scenario score from pre- to post-test, $t(26) = -1.10$, $p = .14$, $d = -0.43$; however, there was a significant improvement in scenario score for T2, $t(38) = 2.72$, $p = .005$, $d = 0.50$. These differences in improvement were statistically significant when comparing data collection events, such that improvement was greater for those who trained in SEW-AT with the NPC than without, $t(57.24) = 2.63$, $p = .006$, $d = 0.66$ (see Fig. 1).

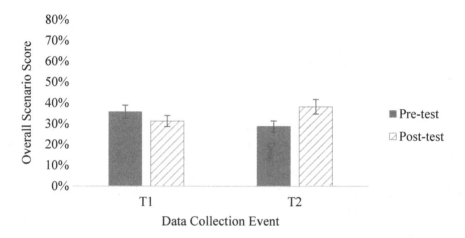

Fig. 1. Mean overall scenario scores at pre-test and post-test for each data collection event.

With our next analyses, we sought to examine the performance components of the overall scenario score further. In doing so, we can better pinpoint what performance aspects the NPC OOD helped trainees improve. The forthcoming analyses examine report accuracy and report timeliness. Additionally, we examine two types of reports: *scheduled reports*, for events that are routine and expected by the OOD by a certain time, and *unscheduled reports*, for events that are unexpected but must be reported as soon as they are detected.

3.2 Report Accuracy

For report accuracy, all participants in both data collections correctly submitted their scheduled reports, save for a single case in post-test for T2. Therefore, all students were generally aware of their scheduled reporting requirements and completed them accurately. For unscheduled reports, we saw significant improvements in accuracy from pre-test to post-test in T1, $t(26) = 3.52$, $p = .001$, $d = 0.53$ and in T2, $t(38) = 1.85$, $p = .036$, $d = 0.42$, but the difference in improvement between data collections was not significant, $t(60.99) = 0.16$, $p = .44$, $d = 0.04$ (see Fig. 2).

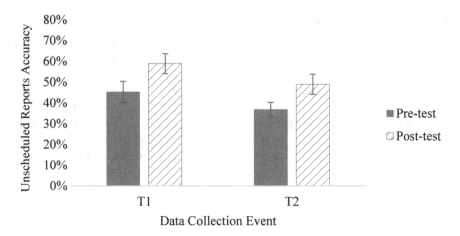

Fig. 2. Mean percentage of unscheduled reports accuracy at pre-test and post-test for each data collection event.

3.3 Report Timeliness

Next, we examined EW operators' improvements in timeliness for scheduled and unscheduled reports. To analyze this performance measure, we scored reports by calculating the percentage they deviated from the required submission time. This yields a percentage of lateness, such that a lower percentage corresponds to a report that is closer to being on time (i.e., less late). For scheduled reports, there was not a significant improvement in lateness from pre- to post-test in T1, $t(54) = -0.72$, $p = .24$, $d = -0.19$; however, there was a significant improvement in lateness for T2, $t(81) = -3.13$, $p = .001$, $d = -0.70$. These differences in improvement were statistically significant when comparing data collection events, such that improvement in lateness for scheduled reports was greater for those who trained in SEW-AT with the NPC than without, $t(127.87) = 1.66$, $p = .049$, $d = 0.29$ (see Fig. 3).

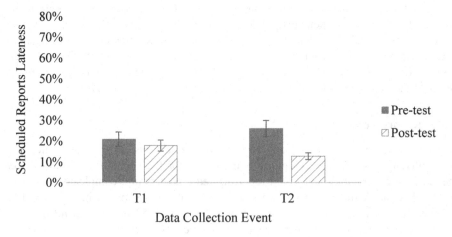

Fig. 3. Mean percentages of lateness for scheduled reports at pre-test and post-test for each data collection event.

For unscheduled reports, there was not a significant improvement in lateness from pre- to post-test in T1, $t(22) = 1.19$, $p = .12$, $d = 0.51$; or T2, $t(25) = -0.68$, $p = .26$, $d = -0.27$. These differences in improvement were not statistically significant when comparing data collection events, $t(45.84) = 1.37$, $p = .099$, $d = 0.39$ (see Fig. 4).

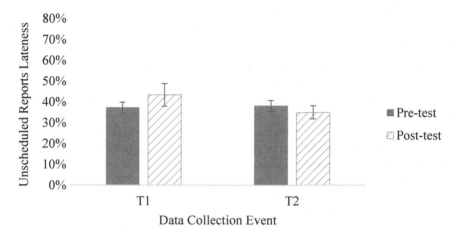

Fig. 4. Mean percentages of lateness for unscheduled reports at pre-test and post-test for each data collection event.

4   Discussion

4.1   NPC OOD Improved Trainee Performance

In our analyses, we identified that those training in SEW-AT with the NPC OOD (T2) displayed greater improvements in overall scenario score than those training without the NPC (T1), supporting H1. Upon further examination, this effect appeared to be driven by improvements in timeliness for scheduled reports. This makes sense, as the NPC OOD provided real-time feedback when reports were late. These results partially supported H3, suggesting that the NPC OOD facilitated a change in our trainees' behavior that led them to improve their performance by submitting their scheduled reports in a timelier manner.

When examining differences in accuracy between T1 and T2, we identified that each group improved from pre-test to post-test, but the difference in improvement was not significant. These results did not support H2. In general, accuracy errors that would trigger the NPC OOD's feedback were rare compared to errors related to timeliness. Therefore, the NPC OOD's accuracy-related feedback messages were probably too infrequent to be helpful in improving trainees' report accuracy.

In addition to performance data, trainees provided positive feedback on the NPC OOD itself. During our conversations with EW operators after the T2 data collection, they commented on the realism of the OOD's commands, noting that the NPC's verbal feedback about missed reports mimicked how an OOD would react during real-life EW exercises. Operators also noted how interactions with the NPC OOD through verbal exchanges occurred similarly in SEW-AT as they would in the real world. Thus, the NPC OOD may have helped to reorient operators to an important goal of the task (i.e., the timely submission of reports) that they may have disregarded briefly during training. These accounts, while anecdotal, still offer converging evidence that the NPC OOD was helpful and effective for training.

4.2 Possible Mechanisms for Performance Improvement

When we designed the NPC OOD for SEW-AT, we had two major considerations in mind. How could we design the NPC to be immersive and believable, and how could we design the NPC OOD to deliver feedback in a useful way? We observed no decrements and some increases in performance after adding the NPC, mostly in timeliness. This could be due to frequency with which trainees received feedback highlighting timeliness errors versus accuracy errors. As mentioned previously, the NPC OOD only alerted trainees when highly egregious mistakes were made. Because these types of mistakes were not often made, participants seldom received accuracy-focused feedback. We did find promising results in timeliness improvements, which we present as evidence that we designed the NPC OOD effectively. However, the question remains as to which of these ideas was responsible for the improvements in performance. Was the NPC OOD believable enough, and did it facilitate tactical immersion to aid in performance as previous research [6–9] suggests? Or, was the NPC merely an effective vehicle for delivering immediate feedback, yielding expected improvements in performance [18–20]? Ultimately, it could be that both of these effects interact in some way to render NPCs effective for training (e.g., the NPC's immediate feedback could have facilitated immersion, which helped trainees maintain their focus on their task objectives). This report cannot answer these questions, warranting future empirical work in this area.

4.3 Limitations and Future Directions

The present results indicate training with a version of SEW-AT that included the NPC OOD helped to improve trainee performance. Despite these positive findings, there were several limitations in the current study that may have influenced these results. The present data were collected in the field and do not represent controlled experimental findings. Future research examining the effects of NPCs during training should be conducted under controlled conditions. Furthermore, the present findings indicate the benefits for the NPC OOD extend only to scheduled events that occurred during training with SEW-AT. Currently, we are unable to explain why these findings do not extend to unscheduled events as well. It may be the case that the underlying mechanisms for attending to unscheduled events differ from those required to attend to scheduled events, and that the NPC OOD addressed only those mechanisms that affect performance on scheduled events. At a more basic level, it could simply be difficult to train for unexpected events. Future research should seek to explain these discrepancies between scheduled and unscheduled events.

We would like to reiterate that the task we examined in this work represents a complex military task comprised of many cognitive processing elements. We observed that an NPC was able to improve operator capabilities along one dimension of performance (scheduled report timeliness), but not others. Previous research emphasizes that immediate feedback is helpful for military tasks and applied studies in particular [21, 22]. With this in mind, it is possible that an empirical investigation of the present study's effects will yield different results with traditional laboratory-based tasks.

In sum, the present work detailed a report of designing adaptive training system elements for military tasks, and how we integrated previous research recommendations to design an effective NPC for training. Despite the limitations we discussed, we argue that the field data analysis we presented offers promising evidence to spark future empirical research and potential application for adaptive training systems.

Acknowledgments. We gratefully acknowledge Dr. Kip Krebs and the Office of Naval Research, who spon-sored this work (Funding Doc# N0001417WX00200). We would also like to thank Marc Prince, Bryan Pittard, and Derek Tolley for their development of the SEW-AT system. Special thanks to Senior Chief Petty Officer Justin Santee for providing the voice recordings of the NPC OOD. Presentation of this material does not constitute or imply its endorsement, recommendation, or favoring by the U.S. Navy or Department of Defense (DoD). The opinions of the authors expressed herein do not necessarily state or reflect those of the U.S. Navy or DoD. NAWCTSD Public Release 20-ORL010 Distribution Statement A – Approved for public release; distribution is unlimited.

References

1. Warpefelt, H.: The non-player character: exploring the believability of NPC presentation and behavior. Diss. Department of Computer and Systems Sciences. Stockholm University (2016)
2. Merrick, K., Maher, M. L.: Motivated reinforcement learning for non-player characters in persistent computer game worlds. In: ACM SIGCHI International Conference on Advances in Computer Entertainment Technology, Association for Computing Machinery, New York (2006)
3. Martens, A., Diener, H., Malo, S.: Game-based learning with computers – learning, simulations, and games. In: Pan, Z., Cheok, A.D., Müller, W., El Rhalibi, A. (eds.) Transactions on Edutainment I. LNCS, vol. 5080, pp. 172–190. Springer, Heidelberg (2008). https://doi.org/10.1007/978-3-540-69744-2_15
4. Reeves, B., Nass, C.I.: The Media Equation: How People Treat Computers, Television, and New Media Like Real People and Places. Cambridge University Press, Cambridge (1996)
5. Moon, J.: Reviews of social embodiment for design of non-player characters in virtual reality-based social skill training for autistic children. Multimodal Technol. Interact. **2**(3), 53–62 (2018)
6. Riedl, M., Lane, H.C., Hill, R., Swartout, W.: Automated story direction and intelligent tutoring: towards a unifying architecture. U.S. Army Research, Development, and Engineering Command (2006). https://apps.dtic.mil/dtic/tr/fulltext/u2/a459187.pdf
7. Warpefelt, H., Johansson, M., Verhagen, H.: Analyzing the believability of game character behavior using the Game Agent Matrix. In: Proceedings of Digital Games Research Association: Defragging Game Studies, pp. 70 – 81 (2013)

8. Lankoski, P., Björk, S.: Gameplay design patterns for believable non-player characters. In: Akira, B. (ed.) Situated Play: Proceedings of the 2007 Digital Games Research Association Conference, pp. 416–423. The University of Tokyo, Tokyo (2007)

9. Adams, E.: Fundamentals of Game Design, 3rd edn. Pearson Education, Peachpit (2014)

10. Lester, J.C., Converse, S.A., Kahler, S.E., Barlow, S.T., Stone, B.A., Bhogal, R.S.: The persona effect; affective impact of animated pedagogical agents. In: CHI, Atlanta, GA, pp. 359–366 (1997)

11. Moreno, R., Mayer, R.E., Spires, H.A., Lester, J.C.: The case for social agency in computer-based teaching: do students learn more deeply when they interact with animated pedagogical agents? Cogn. Instr. 19(2), 177–213 (2001)

12. Bani-Salameh, H., Al-Gharaibeh, J., Jeffery, C.L., Al-Sharif, Z.A.: Collaborative education in a virtual learning environment. IJBIS 25(4), 474–489 (2017)

13. Landsberg, C.R., Astwood Jr., R.S., Van Buskirk, W.L., Townsend, L.N., Steinhauser, N.B., Mercado, A.D.: Review of adaptive training system techniques. Mil. Psychol. 24(2), 96–113 (2012)

14. Landsberg, C.R., Mercado, A., Van Buskirk, W.L., Lineberry, M., Steinhauser, N.: Evaluation of an adaptive training system for submarine periscope operations. In: Proceedings of the Human Factors and Ergonomics Society 56th Annual Meeting, pp. 2422–2426. SAGE Publications, Los Angeles, CA (2012)

15. Romero, C., Ventura, S., Gibaja, E.L., Hervas, C., Romera, F.: Web-based adaptive training simulator system for cardiac support. Artif. Intell. Med. 38, 67–78 (2006)

16. Marraffino, M.D., Johnson, C.I., Whitmer, D.E., Steinhauser, N.B., Clement, A.: Advise when ready for game plan: adaptive training for JTACs. In: Proceedings of the Interservice/Industry, Training, Simulation, and Education Conference (2019). https://s3.amazonaws.co m/amz.xcdsystem.com/44ECEE4F-033C-295C-BAE73278B7F9CA1D_abstract_File4313/ PaperUpload_19105_0820082427.pdf

17. VanLehn, K.: The relative effectiveness of human tutoring, intelligent tutoring systems, and other tutoring systems. Educ. Psychol. 46(4), 197–221 (2011)

18. Bangert-Drowns, R.L., Kulik, C.-L.C., Kulik, J.A., Morgan, M.T.: The instructional effect of feedback in test-like events. Rev. Educ. Res. 61(2), 213–238 (1991)

19. Schmidt, R.A.: Frequent augmented feedback can degrade learning: Evidence and interpretations. In: Requin, J., Stelmach, G.E. (eds.) Tutorials in Motor Neuroscience, pp. 59–75. Kluwer Academic Publishers, Dordrecht (1991)

20. Corbett, A.T., Koedinger, K.R., Anderson, J.R.: Intelligent tutoring systems. In: Helander, M.G., Landauer, T.K., Prabhu, P.V. (eds.) Handbook of Human-Computer Interaction, pp. 849–874. Elsevier, Amsterdam (1997)

21. Corbett, A.T., Anderson, J.R.: Locus of feedback control in computer-based tutoring: impact on learning rate, achievement and attitudes. In: Proceedings of ACM CHI Conference on Human Factors in Computing Systems, pp. 245–252 (2001)

22. Kirlik, A., Fisk, A.D., Walker, N., Rothrock, L.: Feedback augmentation and part-task practice in training dynamic decision-making skills. In: Cannon-Bowers, J.A., Salas, E. (eds.) Making decision under stress: Implications for individual and team training, pp. 91–113. APA, Washington, DC (1998)

23. Kulik, J.A., Kulik, C.-L.C.: Timing of feedback and verbal learning. Rev. Educ. Res. 58(1), 79–97 (1988)

24. Van Buskirk, W.L., Fraulini, N.W., Schroeder, B.L., Johnson, C.I., Marraffino, Matthew D.: Application of theory to the development of an adaptive training system for a submarine electronic warfare task. In: Sottilare, Robert A., Schwarz, J. (eds.) HCII 2019. LNCS, vol. 11597, pp. 352–362. Springer, Cham (2019). https://doi.org/10.1007/978-3-030-22341-0_28

25. Lakens, D., Scheel, A.M., Isager, P.M.: Equivalence testing for psychological research: a tutorial. Adv. Methods Pract. Psychol. Sci. 1(2), 259–269 (2018)

The Impact of Adaptive Activities in Acrobatiq Courseware - Investigating the Efficacy of Formative Adaptive Activities on Learning Estimates and Summative Assessment Scores

Rachel Van Campenhout, Bill Jerome, and Benny G. Johnson[✉]

Acrobatiq by VitalSource, Pittsburgh, PA, USA
benny@acrobatiq.com

Abstract. The purpose of this paper is to explain the learning methodologies behind the adaptive activities within Acrobatiq's courseware, and to investigate the impact of these adaptive activities on learning estimates and summative assessment scores using real course data. The adaptive activities used for this analysis were part of a Probability and Statistics course, which was delivered to college students at a public four-year institution as part of an educational grant. The data were analyzed to identify if the adaptive activities had an impact on learning estimates as well as on summative assessment scores. Results showed that the adaptive activities had a net positive effect on learning estimates. Results also showed that not only did learning estimate states correlate to mean summative assessment scores, but improving learning estimates after completing the adaptive activity practice yielded higher mean summative assessment scores. The implications of this analysis and future research are discussed.

Keywords: Adaptive activities · Doer Effect · Formative practice · Learn by doing · Learning modeling · Learning objectives · Learning outcomes · Scaffolded practice

1 Introduction

One goal of this paper is to illuminate the learning theory used to develop the adaptive activities in Acrobatiq's courseware. The adaptive activities require many inputs from a complex learning environment in order to adapt appropriately for each student. Within the courseware, learning objectives are used to organize both content and formative practice within lessons. As students answer the formative questions, their data are sent to Acrobatiq's predictive model and a learning estimate is generated for each student against each learning objective. The adaptive activities use these learning estimates to select the appropriate scaffolded questions against each learning objective for the students. Each student will receive a set of questions with the appropriate scaffolding specifically selected for their needs.

A second goal of this paper is to analyze data in order to identify the impact these activities have for students. Impact could mean different things in this environment,

© Springer Nature Switzerland AG 2020
R. A. Sottilare and J. Schwarz (Eds.): HCII 2020, LNCS 12214, pp. 543–554, 2020.
https://doi.org/10.1007/978-3-030-50788-6_40

which leads to two different research questions. The first of those questions is: do the adaptive activities increase learning estimates for students? Students have learning estimates for each learning objective included in the module for which the activity is written. The questions within the activity are also formative in nature, and therefore can contribute to that student's learning estimate. This research question could use within-student data as well as between-student data. We will look to see if students increase their learning estimates after completing the adaptive activities. We will also look to see if completion of the adaptive activities changes learning estimates differently between groups of students who have different learning estimates. Students with low learning estimates will have more scaffolded practice and may be more likely to increase their learning estimates than those students who have already been successful and have high learning estimates.

In addition to learning estimates, another measure to investigate is the impact of the adaptive activities on summative assessment scores. These activities are placed immediately before module quizzes as a last scaffolded practice before students take the scored assessment. The second research question is: do the adaptive activities increase student scores on summative assessments? This research question investigates the summative scores of students in different learning estimate categories to identify the differences between groups. This analysis will also look at summative scores for students who increased their learning estimates (after working through the adaptive activity), and students who did not.

The ultimate purpose of the adaptive activities is to assist the learner in their progression through the courseware and in mastery of the content. The significance of the data analysis against both research questions would verify that the purpose of these activities is being met. An increase in learning estimates after completing the activities would indicate that the learning methodology behind the activities is working. While the learning estimate is a metric both created and used by the Acrobatiq platform, improvement in it could indicate the courseware and design of the adaptive activities are functioning as designed. Changes in summative assessment scores after completing the adaptive activities would be a significant finding for these activities. Summative assessments produce scores which are part of the student's gradebook. To assist in improving student scores, and therefore possibly their course grades, would be incredibly valuable to students. The analysis and results of this paper indicate how future research could be conducted to verify results, as well as provide new ideas on how to continue to help students master content through adaptive experiences.

2 Learning Methodology

The purpose of this section is to outline the learning methodology behind the design of the Acrobatiq courseware used in this analysis, as the course features and reasoning for them are key to the investigation. The adaptive activities are integrated into the courseware content and require specific instructional design practices in order for them to properly adapt for each learner.

Formative Practice. The first requirement is the inclusion of formative practice questions for each learning objective in a module of content. The formative practice questions can have a variety of formats (such as multiple choice, text input, equation, drag and drop, etc.), provide immediate targeted feedback for each answer option, and allow students to continue answering until they get the correct answer. Formative practice is a well-established technique shown to increase learning gains for students of all ages, and across subjects [1]. Moreover, studies have shown that formative assessment can raise achievement for low performing students most of all, while improving learning for all [1]. The formative practice questions distributed throughout the text and the adaptive activity also act as no- or low-stakes practice testing. Practice testing increases learning gains and retention, and including feedback has been shown to outperform practice testing without feedback [2].

Formative practice is integrated with the content of the Acrobatiq Probability and Statistics course. The lessons in the courseware begin with the learning objective and are followed by the relevant content and formative practice opportunities, which are interspersed throughout the lesson. This chunking method of following short sections of content with formative practice is key for the learn by doing approach, which produces the Doer Effect [3–5]. Research utilizing interactive courseware from Carnegie Mellon's Open Learning Initiative shows that students who did more interactive activities had a learning benefit approximately six times that of reading text and three times that of watching video [3]. Follow-up analysis showed this relationship between doing and learning to be causal [4], and this finding has been replicated in our previous work [5].

Learning Estimates. While the formative questions do not produce a grade, the student's responses impact his or her learning estimate for that learning objective. The learning estimate is a predictive measure generated by Acrobatiq's analytics engine for each student on each objective to estimate how well a student will perform on the learning objective's summative assessment. This learning estimate is required for the adaptive activity to adapt for the learner (see below).

The machine learning model underlying the learning estimate uses item response theory (IRT) [6, 7] to construct an estimate of the student's ability for the objective, from which a prediction can be made of performance on the objective's summative assessment. An advantage of an IRT-based approach is it can take the psychometric properties of the questions into account when constructing the ability estimate. A two-parameter logistic model is used, which models difficulty and discrimination for each question. A Bayesian approach [8] is used to estimate the posterior distributions of the IRT question parameters from data, as well as the student ability posterior distribution from the formative and adaptive questions answered. From the ability posterior a numerical learning estimate value between 0 and 1 is derived (higher values indicating better expected performance). When the model has sufficient confidence in its prediction based on the data available to it, a category of low, medium or high is also assigned; otherwise the category is labeled as unknown.

Adaptive Activities. The adaptive activities in the Probability and Statistics courseware were designed by instructional designers and subject matter experts to include scaffolded questions against each learning objective in the module. The goal of the adaptive activity is to provide students with the appropriate level of scaffolding for their needs. In this activity, questions are written against the learning objectives from the module at three increasing levels of difficulty (low, medium, and high). By organizing the questions—and content—in this way the adaptive activities align with Vygotsky's zone of proximal development, which structures content and interactions in such a way as to meet the learner at their level of understanding and build upon it [9]. Providing struggling students with foundational questions as scaffolds to more challenging questions helps to reduce cognitive load in a similar way as worked examples [10].

At the start of the adaptive activity, the platform identifies the student's learning estimate for each learning objective used in the activity. The learning estimate determines the level of scaffolding to deliver. A student with a low learning estimate on a learning objective did poorly on the formative practice, and therefore is given the additional scaffolded practice for the learning objective. A student with a high learning estimate did well on the formative practice for the learning objective, and therefore are only delivered the highest difficulty—or core—questions. It is important to note that while the previous formative practice informed the learning estimates which determined how the activity adapted to the student, the adaptive activity itself also contributes to the learning estimate, asthe adaptive activities are also formative in nature.

3   Methodology

The Courseware. The course used for this analysis was a Probability and Statistics courseware developed as an introduction to the subject at the university level. This Acrobatiq courseware was originally developed at the Open Learning Initiative at Carnegie Mellon University and has been substantially revised over the years as an Acrobatiq course. Included in those revisions were the addition of the adaptive elements, new summative assessments, and a new learning model, which are all critical elements to this analysis. The Probability and Statistics courseware included 5 units of content with a combined 10 total content modules within them. The lessons within each module begin with a learning objective and typically have interleaved content and formative questions. Learning objectives appear at the top of the lesson, are student centered and measurable, and all content and formative questions align to and are tagged with them. Formative questions are intended as learning opportunities and therefore do not create a grade. Students receive immediate feedback for formative questions and have the opportunity to continue to answer until they choose the correct response. Each module ends with an adaptive activity and a quiz which contain questions against the learning objectives covered in the module. The adaptive activity is a formative activity as well by providing immediate feedback and multiple attempts, however it does produce a completion score for the gradebook. The quiz is a summative assessment; students do not receive immediate feedback and it produces a score for the gradebook.

The courseware elements necessary for this analysis include each students' formative question attempts and accuracy, learning estimate states, adaptive activity attempts and accuracy, and summative assessment attempts and accuracy. These data points provide a window into each student's journey through the courseware.

The Population. This course was delivered to students at a large public 4-year institution in the fall 2018 semester. There were no experimental manipulations used on this student population, and the platform does not collect demographic information on students, so no analysis according to demographic information would be possible. The data set includes numeric identifiers for individual students, for which all the students' interactions are recorded against. The data collected will be used only for analysis of the relationship of each student's interactions with the adaptive activities in relation to the formative and summative activities.

The Data Set. The data set includes 306 students and 47 learning objectives. The unit of analysis was student-learning objective pairs, *i.e.* the data records corresponded to a single student's work on a single learning objective. Out of the $306 \times 47 = 14{,}382$ possible student-learning objective combinations, there were 12,612 combinations with data. Each data record contained: number of formative questions answered; learning estimate value and category after formative questions; number of adaptive questions answered; learning estimate value and category after adaptive questions; number of summative questions answered; and mean summative question scores. Not all records contained formative, adaptive, and summative data; for example, in some cases students answered adaptive and summative but not formative questions.

This original data set was reduced to include only learning objectives with formative, adaptive, and summative attempts. For some learning objectives, the number of formative questions contained in the course was not consistent with best practices of course design and/or the requirements of the learning model. As such, learning objectives were filtered to those having a minimum of 5 formative questions and a maximum of 45 formative questions. The data set was also cleaned to remove errors in data collection or storage. The final data set included 21 learning objectives, 300 students, and 5,971 total records.

The data analysis was performed on both the full original data set as well as this reduced data set. The reduced data set was chosen for presentation to attempt to obtain the clearest picture of the relationships between student practice and summative assessment performance. However, the qualitative conclusions of the analysis were consistent between both data sets.

4 Results

4.1 Research Question 1

The first analysis done was to address the first research question: do the adaptive activities increase learning estimates for students? The adaptive activities were designed to provide scaffolded questions personalized for each student's learning estimate, with the goal of assisting students who needed additional help before they took the high-stakes summative assessment. Therefore, we hypothesized the adaptive activities would have a positive impact on learning estimates for some portion of students.

Overall Learning Estimate Changes. To answer this question, the data set was analyzed with regard to whether or not student learning estimates before the adaptive activity changed after students completed the adaptive activity questions. There were 3,972 cases in which a learning estimate was available immediately before and after adaptive practice, with a mean learning estimate change of 0.062 (0.169). In 2,550 instances (64.2%), the learning estimate was increased by adaptive practice, with a mean increase of 0.132 (0.167). In the remaining 1,422 instances, the learning estimate decreased by a mean of 0.064 (0.069). A Shapiro-Wilk test showed that the learning estimate differences were not normally distributed, so a one-sample Wilcoxon signed rank test was used to check if the median learning estimate change was of the population was statistically significantly different than 0, which it was ($p \lll 0.001$).

These results support the hypothesis that the adaptive activity had a net positive impact on learning estimates for the majority of students. The smaller portion of students whose learning estimates decreased could be explained by considering those students who may have been near the threshold of a learning estimate category. Getting questions wrong in the adaptive activity could have shifted their learning estimate down to the lower category (Table 1).

Table 1. The descriptive statistics for the increase or decrease of learning estimates after the completion of adaptive questions.

Statistic	Learning estimate increase	Learning estimate decrease
Count	2550.000000	1422.000000
Mean	0.131999	−0.064386
Std	0.167449	0.068799
Min	0.000013	−0.511564
25%	0.023794	−0.086208
50%	0.058838	−0.039807
75%	0.164347	−0.017508
Max	0.806394	−0.000008

Learning Estimate Changes within Categories. In addition to understanding how the student learning estimates increased or decreased as a whole, we also investigated how learning estimates changed for students within different learning estimate categories. The learning estimates for students determine which questions are delivered in the activity—whether or not students need the scaffolded questions, and at which difficulty level. This analysis will reveal if these different groups of students changed learning estimates differently after completing the adaptive activity. There was a total of 3,954 records for which student summative scores were also available for the learning objectives included in this analysis. A Kruskal-Wallis H test was performed on the summative scores in the different groups, which showed the groups do not all have the same median ($p \lll 0.001$) (Table 2).

Table 2. The number of instances of learning estimate changes after completing adaptive questions, grouped by learning estimate category.

Learning estimate category	High (after adaptive)	Medium (after adaptive)	Low (after adaptive)	Unknown (after adaptive)
High (before adaptive)	1511	112	25	NA
Medium (before adaptive)	348	441	129	NA
Low (before adaptive)	47	141	555	NA
Unknown (before adaptive)	339	136	146	24

The first data analyzed were those students who achieved high learning estimates for learning objectives after they completed the formative questions. There was a total of 1,648 (41.7%) instances of students achieving high learning estimates after completing the formative questions. After completing the adaptive activities, there were three possible outcomes based on how they performed: retain high learning estimate, change to medium learning estimate, or change to low learning estimate. Of the total high learning estimate instances, 1,511 (91.69%) remained in the high category after completing the adaptive activity questions. There were 112 (6.8%) instances of students whose learning estimate changed to medium, and 25 (1.52%) instances of students whose learning estimate changed to low. These results were consistent with expectations for this group of students. Students who did well enough on the formative practice to earn high learning estimates similarly did well enough on the adaptive activity questions to retain that learning estimate category. For the less than 10% of instances where learning estimates dropped to medium or low, this means students did poorly enough on adaptive questions to lower their learning estimates. Likely these students were just over the high learning estimate threshold and answering incorrectly moved them to the lower category.

The next category of data analyzed was students who achieved medium learning estimates for learning objectives after they completed the formative activities. There was a total of 918 (23.22%) instances in this category. After completing the adaptive activities, there were three possible outcomes based on how they performed: retain medium learning estimate, change to high learning estimate, or change to low learning estimate. Of the total medium learning estimate instances, 441 (48.04%) remained in the medium category after completing the adaptive activity questions. There were 348 (37.91%) instances of students whose learning estimate changed to high, and 129

(14.05%) instances of students whose learning estimate changed to low. This medium learning estimate category shows more change in learning estimate state than the high category. These results are in line with expectations, as the medium category has thresholds next to both the high and low category, and therefore students near those thresholds could shift their states if they do well or poorly on the adaptive questions.

The next category of data analyzed were those students who achieved low learning estimates for learning objectives after they completed the formative activities. There was a total of 743 (18.79%) instances in this category. After completing the adaptive activities, there were three possible outcomes based on how they performed: retain low learning estimate, change to medium learning estimate, or change to high learning estimate. Of the total low learning estimate instances, 555 (74.7%) remained in the low category after completing the adaptive activity questions. There were 141 (18.98%) instances of students whose learning estimate changed to medium, and 47 (6.32%) instances of students whose learning estimate changed to high. This low learning estimate category had fewer changes to other categories than the medium category previously. However, while nearly 75% of students who struggled on learning objectives continued to do so in the adaptive activity, just over 25% of instances show students who were able to increase their learning estimates to medium or high, which is a positive finding.

The final category of data to be analyzed was students who did not complete enough formative practice against learning objectives to generate a learning estimate. This unknown learning estimate category is not an indicator of ability, but rather a state of the predictive analytics not having enough information to determine a category. Of the 645 (16.31%) instances of an unknown learning estimate, there were four categories of learning estimates after the adaptive activity questions were completed: high, medium, low, or unknown. The change in learning estimate states for these instances after the adaptive activity questions were as follows: 339 (52.56%) changed to high, 136 (21.09%) changed to medium, 146 (22.64%) changed to low, and 24 (3.72%) remained unknown. We cannot determine if the adaptive activity questions helped to shift the final learning estimates, but the activity at least moved all but 3.72% of instances into known categories.

4.2   Research Question 2

The second research question to investigate is: do the adaptive activities increase student scores on summative assessments? While the changes in learning estimates is one indicator that the adaptive activities have an impact on student learning, another measure is the summative assessment scores which correspond with the same learning objectives. In this Probability and Statistics course, the adaptive activity is always placed before a summative quiz, with the goal of trying to help students prepare for this scored assessment. The change for each learning estimate category is compared by looking at the mean summative assessment score for each group (Table 3).

Table 3. Mean summative scores by learning estimate category before and after the adaptive activity questions.

Learning Estimate Category	High (after adaptive)	Medium(after adaptive)	Low (after adaptive)	Unknown (after adaptive)
High (before adaptive)	0.775	0.689	0.617	NA
Medium (before adaptive)	0.716	0.668	0.612	NA
Low (before adaptive)	0.676	0.617	0.543	NA
Unknown (before adaptive)	0.767	0.711	0.709	0.569

The findings of this analysis showed both expected and unexpected results. Students with higher learning estimates generally had higher mean summative scores. Within original learning estimate categories, students who improved their learning estimates after the adaptive questions did better on summative questions than students who maintained their learning estimate category, and students who lowered their learning estimate category after the adaptive questions did worse than their counterparts who maintained their category. Mean summative scores also decreased slightly within the post-adaptive learning estimate category depending on the pre-adaptive learning estimate category. Mann-Whitney U tests—comparing median summative scores of the low and medium category before the adaptive activity to their respective category changes after the activity—found that all changes were significant. This indicates that not only do learning estimates correlate to summative score performance, but students who increase their learning estimates perform better on summative assessment questions.

A surprising finding was the final mean summative assessment scores for the unknown learning estimate category. Recalling the earlier changes in learning estimates for this category: 339 (52.56%) changed to high, 136 (21.09%) changed to medium, 146 (22.64%) changed to low, and 24 (3.72%) remained unknown. Given the findings above, the mean summative scores for the unknown to high, medium, and low learning estimate categories do not align with the other mean summative scores for those categories. The scores for unknown to high, medium, and low are all above 0.7. The only other categories with mean summative scores above 0.7 were high to high, and medium to high. So, despite which learning estimate category the unknown state changed to, all performed as well as those with high learning estimates. The only unknown category who did not perform as well were those who remained unknown, for which they scored the second lowest of all categories.

4.3   Learn by Doing

During the data analysis, there were additional findings which were notable with regard to the learning theory underlying the courseware's design. Learn by doing is a key principle which supported the addition of frequent formative practice. The adaptive activity was similarly expected to help students learn as it was another formative practice activity and gave students one more personalized chance to prepare for a quiz. The analysis of the findings for summative assessment scores showed the correlation between increased learning estimates and increased mean summative assessment scores. This led us to review the mean summative assessment scores for students grouped by whether they participated in formative and adaptive practice.

Table 4. Mean summative scores for students grouped by participation status for formative and adaptive practice.

Formative	Adaptive	Count	Mean summative score
False	False	146	0.5663
False	True	1142	0.5744
True	False	168	0.6098
True	True	4411	0.6935

Table 4 shows the breakdown of students who did or did not participate in formative practice and the adaptive activity practice. We hypothesize that because the adaptive activities produced a completion score, doing the adaptive practice was the largest category for both doing and not doing formative practice. The instances of students who did or did not do the formative practice are also broken down by whether they did or did not do the adaptive activity practice. What we are able to see are the combinations of practice from least to most, and the mean summative scores correlate with the amount of practice completed. Not doing formative or adaptive practice produced the lowest mean summative scores (0.566), while doing both the formative and adaptive practice produced the highest mean summative scores (0.694). A Kruskal-Wallis H test was performed on the groups and there was a statistically significant difference among them (p $\lll 0.001$). These findings are in line with those from previous research [3], which identified correlational relationships between doing formative practice and summative assessment scores. While testing for a causal relationship between practice and outcomes requires additional data not available in this study, the findings of causality from related research lead us to anticipate the same would be true in this instance [4, 5].

5   Discussion

This study was critical in helping to understand the efficacy of the adaptive activities in Acrobatiq's courseware. The learning science and instructional design principles utilized to create the course content were intended to help students better learn the material and prepare them for high-stakes summative assessments. The findings which show that not only do the adaptive activities help increase learning estimates for many students, but that learning estimates correlate to mean summative scores validates the primary function of the adaptive activities.

While not every learning estimate increased after completing the adaptive practice, nearly 38% of students with medium learning estimate instances increased to high learning estimates and over 25% of students with low learning estimate instances increased to medium or high learning estimates. With increased learning estimates correlating to increased mean summative assessment scores, assisting this percentage of students through adaptive practice to increase learning estimates and summative scores is a very positive finding. While final course gradingpolicies are up to instructors, summative assessments produce a grade in the courseware gradebook which is often part of the student's final course grade. If the adaptive practice can improve summative assessment scores for students in the low and medium learning estimate category, that could make a difference in final course grades for those students.

This analysis also supported for the research team the principle that more "doing" is better for students. The more formative practice students completed, the higher the mean summative assessment scores. Students who did not do formative practice but did do the adaptive practice scored slightly higher than those who did no practice at all (note that when no formative practice is done, the adaptive engine has no data to adapt the activity). Yet the adaptive practice had a larger effect when students also completed the formative practice, thereby giving the adaptive practice a basison which to adapt. Instructors could capitalize on the benefits of both the formative and adaptive practice through their expectations and requirements of students when using the courseware. Finding ways to actively enforce the completion of formative and adaptive practice through classroom policies could increase the benefits of these activities for students.

The results of this analysis also show that these findings could be replicated in many other courses. The Probability and Statistics courseware used did not have perfect associations—or tagging—between the formative practice, adaptive practice, and summative assessments. The data set was reduced to only include the data where learning objectives had data for all three. Yet despite the imperfections in the courseware itself, results were still very positive. This is encouraging, as developing perfect courseware is a difficult task. Future research could aim to replicate findings using different courseware for different subject domains, as well as courseware with different instructional design practices.

The data used for the analysis in this paper was also gathered from a course where no experimental controls were used. It is encouraging that this non-experimental, real-world course showed such positive results. Additional validation of results could be found by partnering with instructors in the future to compare variations in classroom controls and practices. Initial plans for data analysis included comparing this data to a course from a different semester which did not include the adaptive activities, but no version could be found where the only substantive change was the adaptive practice.

Future research could also review individual adaptive activities to try to identify the ideal number of scaffolded questions to deliver to students. The analysis of this data revealed support for the Doer Effect, but does not indicate how much practice is ideal to help students increase learning estimates and summative scores. Such research could also analyze the difficulty levels of questions across formative, adaptive, and summative assessments to determine the most beneficial combination and frequency of difficulty levels. The primary function of the adaptive activities is to support student learning. Additional research into ideal number and types of questions to deliver to students could potentially improve learning.

References

1. Black, P., William, D.: Inside the black box: raising standards through classroom assessment. Phi Delta Kappan **92**(1), 81–90 (2010). https://doi.org/10.1177/003172171009200119

2. Dunlosky, J., Rawson, K., Marsh, E., Nathan, M., Willingham, D.: Improving students' learning with effective learning techniques: promising directions from cognitive and educational psychology. Psychol. Sci. Public Interest **14**(1), 4–58 (2013). https://doi.org/10.1177/1529100612453266

3. Koedinger, K., Kim, J., Jia, J., McLaughlin, E., Bier, N.: Learning is not a spectator sport: doing is better than watching for learning from a MOOC. In: Learning at Scale, pp. 111–120. Vancouver, Canada (2015). http://dx.doi.org/10.1145/2724660.2724681

4. Koedinger, K., McLaughlin, E., Jia, J., Bier, N.: Is the doer effect a causal relationship? How can we tell and why it's important. learning analytics and knowledge. Edinburgh, United Kingdom (2016). http://dx.doi.org/10.1145/2883851.2883957

5. Olsen, J., Johnson, B.G.: Deeper collaborations: a finding that may have gone unnoticed. Paper Presented at the IMS Global Learning Impact Leadership Institute, San Diego, CA (2019)

6. Baker, F.: The basics of item response theory. In: ERIC Clearinghouse on Assessment and Evaluation. College Park, MD (2001). http://echo.edres.org:8080/irt/baker/

7. Embretson, S., Reise, S.: Item Response Theory for Psychologists. Erlbaum, Mahwah (2000)

8. Fox, J.: Bayesian Item Response Modeling: Theory and Applications. Springer, Heidelberg (2010). https://doi.org/10.1007/978-1-4419-0742-4

9. Sanders, D., Welk, D.: Strategies to scaffold student learning: applying Vygotsky's zone of proximal development. Nurse Educ. **30**(5), 203–204 (2005)

10. Sweller, J.: The worked example effect and human cognition. Learn. Instr. **16**(2), 165–169 (2006). https://doi.org/10.1016/j.learninstruc.2006.02.005

A Mastery Approach to Flashcard-Based Adaptive Training

Daphne E. Whitmer[1(✉)], Cheryl I. Johnson[2], Matthew D. Marraffino[2],
Rebecca L. Pharmer[1], and Lisa D. Blalock[3]

[1] Zenetex, LLC, Orlando, FL 32817, USA
{daphne.whitmer.ctr,rebecca.pharmer.ctr}@navy.mil
[2] Naval Air Warfare Center Training Systems Division,
Orlando, FL 32826, USA
{cheryl.i.johnson,matthew.marraffino}@navy.mil
[3] University of West Florida, Pensacola, FL 32514, USA
lblalock@uwf.edu

Abstract. Students often use flashcards to study but they do not always use them effectively. In this experiment, we explored different methods of dropping flashcards to inform the development of an adaptive flashcard-based trainer. Forty-seven U.S. Marine Corps students were randomly assigned to one of three groups in an armored vehicle training task. In the Mastery Drop condition, cards were dropped from training based on objective criteria (i.e., accuracy and reaction time). In the Learner Drop condition, cards were dropped based on the learner's choice. In the No Drop condition, cards were not dropped during training, which served as a control group. Using a pre-test post-test design, results showed that the Learner Drop condition had the lowest learning gains on the immediate post-test and the delayed post-test (two days after training), perhaps because participants were unsuccessful at self-regulating their learning and completed training too quickly. Although the No Drop condition had the highest learning gains on the immediate post-test, the gains significantly decreased on the delayed post-test. In contrast, the Mastery Drop condition maintained consistent learning gains from immediate to delayed post-test. Although the No Drop condition completed more training trials than the Mastery Drop condition, this additional practice did not significantly aid long-term retention. Finally, the No Drop condition had the highest immediate transfer test scores, which involved identifying images of real-world vehicles, but there were no group differences on the delayed transfer test. These results suggest that adaptive flashcard training should incorporate mastery criteria, rather than learner-driven decisions about when to drop flashcards from the deck.

Keywords: Adaptive training · Mastery learning · Flashcard training · Learner control

1 Introduction

1.1 Overview

As part of the Sailor 2025 initiative [1], the U.S. Navy and Marine Corps strive to modernize military training and education to make it more effective and efficient for

© Springer Nature Switzerland AG 2020
R. A. Sottilare and J. Schwarz (Eds.): HCII 2020, LNCS 12214, pp. 555–568, 2020.
https://doi.org/10.1007/978-3-030-50788-6_41

today's Sailors and Marines. This includes incorporating more learner-centric and interactive methods, reducing the need for repeated returns to the schoolhouse for training, and reducing delays between training and on-the-job performance. At present, curricula are being revamped to leverage existing and emerging technologies and science of learning principles to make training available at the point of need. Furthermore, there is an increased interest in adaptive training (AT), or training that is tailored to a particular learner's strengths and weaknesses [2], to meet the Sailor 2025 vision. With these goals in mind, the objective of this research was to explore AT techniques for the development of a flashcard trainer that would be suitable for different types of training content for use in military settings.

Flashcards are a commonly used tool for rote memorization of concepts [3] and can be effective for promoting long-term retention. The majority of the previous literature has explored their use in the verbal domain with topics such as GRE vocabulary words and foreign language translations [3–6]. From a military perspective, flashcards could be used to train a variety of concepts from verbal (e.g., acronyms, definitions) to visual (e.g., identifying armored vehicles or aircraft) to conceptual topics (e.g., choosing the right weapon for a given target). In addition, digital flashcards could be loaded on any device and practiced during a trainee's downtime, which may help mitigate knowledge decay.

One important decision for learners to make when using flashcards as a study strategy is whether to drop a card from the deck [3, 7] in order to maximize study time for other items. However, for learners to gauge whether they have mastered a particular flashcard requires metacognitive awareness and self-regulation to decide accurately when to drop that flashcard. Unfortunately, a large body of work has demonstrated that learners are largely unaware of how to regulate their learning effectively [see [8], for a review]. Learners often undervalue effective study strategies [9], overestimate their own learning when making immediate judgements of learning [10], and may drop a concept from study too soon due to poor metacognitive strategies [3]. One way to combat such issues with metacognitive judgements is to apply objective mastery criteria so that learners are no longer forced to make these decisions on their own. Instead, an adaptive flashcard trainer can monitor and assess a learner's performance and retire cards appropriately based on how well the learner is performing on any given concept. Therefore, the goal of this research was to explore different flashcard dropping techniques to determine which one is more effective. In this study, we focused on a visual identification task, which has received less attention in the literature to date.

1.2 Learner-Based Dropping and Self-regulation

Intuitively, it would seem that allowing learners to choose when to drop cards would be advantageous for learning, since it would be more interactive, perhaps more motivating, and would give learners more control over their own learning; however, there is a large body of research against this line of reasoning [see [11], for a review]. In flashcard-based training, self-regulated learning and metacognitive awareness are essential for student success. Self-regulated learning relies on two primary processes: monitoring learning and controlling learning activities in response to monitoring [12, 13]. For instance, learners engage in some type of self-regulation when they evaluate their understanding of the material and adjust their learning strategies based on this appraisal. With the instance of a flashcard trainer, a self-regulated learner would consider which cards to study, how frequently to study them, how to order the cards, and whether or not to remove a card from the deck.

Past research has examined whether dropping flashcards from study is beneficial for long-term retention based on a learner's self-created criteria. Over the course of four experiments using Swahili-English word pairs as the study materials, Kornell and Bjork [3] demonstrated that providing learners with the option to drop flashcards from a deck has a negative effect on learning. In their study, half of the learners were able to drop a concept from a flashcard deck and half studied all concepts without dropping items. The learner drop condition did significantly worse on both an immediate and one-week delayed retention test compared to the learners who were not given an option to drop cards. Kornell and Bjork attributed this difference to poor metacognitive monitoring, with participants undervaluing the benefit of continued study after one correct recall [see also [14]], likely because learners tend to drop items they find easy [3, 7]. This suggests that learners may not see the value in repetition or over-studying material. Furthermore, this highlights a potential advantage to applying AT to flashcard training because the criteria for dropping cards can be objective and predetermined, eliminating the need for learners to regulate their own study.

1.3 Adaptive Training

Adaptive training (AT) provides tailored instruction based on how a student is performing during training [2], and it has been demonstrated to be more effective than traditional training approaches across a variety of domains [15–17]. An AT system can employ any number of instructional techniques, such as providing error-sensitive feedback and adjusting the difficulty of the content based on the performance of the user in a scenario-based trainer [15, 18]. Of particular relevance to flashcard training, mastery learning (i.e., learning to a criterion) is another instructional technique that was found to support positive learning gains when employed in an AT system [19]. By including mastery criteria, the AT system can tailor the pace of instruction so that learners do not advance through a curriculum until they have demonstrated a sufficient level of understanding with the existing content.

Using mastery criteria as an adaptive strategy is one of the more common techniques used in AT systems. Mastery learning is consistent with several cognitive theories of learning which contend that learning gains are maximized when the content is aligned with the current ability level of the individual [20–26]. An AT system can use preset, objective mastery criteria to decide what content to present to the learner and how often the learner should be exposed to study materials. When applied to flashcard-based instruction, this means the AT system would present cards until they are reliably committed to memory and would retire cards that no longer require study.

1.4 Present Research

We aimed to answer the following research question: Which flashcard dropping technique promotes effective learning? We measured the effectiveness of the training by examining learning gains from pre-test to post-test. Previous research has shown that the effects of training tend to be amplified when long-term retention is measured [4, 27]. Therefore, we measured performance immediately after training and two days later. In addition, we used materials that have yet to be explored widely in the existing mastery literature. We examined the visual identification domain, using computer models of armored vehicles as the study materials in the current experiment. We were also interested in training transfer. Therefore, we examined participants' ability to identify real-world images of the armored vehicles after learning from models.

We had four main predictions in terms of learning gains and transfer test performance. First, we predicted that those in the learner-controlled (i.e., "Learner Drop") condition would have the lowest learning gains, followed by those who did not have any cards dropped during training (i.e., the control group or the "No Drop" condition), and those in the AT condition (i.e., "Mastery Drop") would have the highest learning gains (H1). We also hypothesized that this same pattern would appear on the delayed post-test two days later, such that those in the Learner Drop condition would have the lowest delayed learning gains, followed by the No Drop condition, and those in the Mastery Drop condition would demonstrate superior long-term retention (H2). Next, we expected that those in the Learner Drop condition would score the lowest on the transfer test and those in the Mastery Drop condition to score the highest (H3). We expected that some of these differences in learning gains and transfer test performance might be explained by the training data, such that those in the Learner Drop condition would complete the training more quickly in terms of training time and number of trials, and master fewer concepts than those in the Mastery Drop and No Drop conditions (H4a). It was expected that those in the No Drop condition would complete more trials and train longer (in minutes) than those in the Mastery Drop condition (H4b).

2   Method

2.1   Participants

Forty-seven Marines Awaiting Training were recruited from the Marine Corps Intelligence School. One participant was removed from the analysis for failing to follow instructions during training and another participant's post-test data was lost due to a computer error. Participants' ages ranged from 18 to 27 years ($M = 19.12$, $SD = 1.93$) and 38 were male and 6 were female (1 additional participant did not respond to this item). Participants were randomly assigned to one of three between-subjects conditions: Mastery Drop ($n = 15$), No Drop ($n = 15$), or Learner Drop ($n = 15$). During the second session of the experiment, one participant from the Learner Drop and one participant from the No Drop condition did not return. In total, 45 participants were included in the analysis for immediate post-tests and transfer tests and 43 participants were included for delayed post-tests and transfer tests.

2.2   Materials

Training Content. The stimuli used for this experiment consisted of twenty-eight 3D models of armored vehicles taken with permission from the Army Model Exchange. Seventeen of the vehicles were used as learning objectives (i.e., assessed on pre-test and post-test) while the remaining 11 were used as filler items. Each model was presented in the isometric view to show the top, side, and front of the vehicle.

Testbed. We developed a testbed to administer the pre-test, familiarization period, training, post-test, and transfer test. For the pre-test and post-test, participants saw the 3D model image of the vehicle and selected the corresponding name from a list of all the vehicles. Only the 17 learning objectives were included on the tests and feedback was not provided after the pre-test or the immediate post-test. During the familiarization period, the testbed cycled through each of the images twice for five seconds in a random order.

During the training portion, each card depicted one vehicle model along with a list of four possible vehicle names. The participant was instructed to select the name that corresponded to the image as quickly and accurately as possible. Once the participant selected a vehicle name, feedback was provided by highlighting the correct answer in green. If the participant's selection was incorrect, his or her choice was highlighted in red and the correct answer was highlighted in green.

For the transfer test, participants saw a real-world image of the vehicle and selected the corresponding name from a list of all the vehicles. Only the 17 learning objectives were included, and feedback was not provided after the immediate transfer test.

Instruction Reaction Questionnaire (IRQ). The IRQ is a 12-item questionnaire created by the research team to assess participants' opinions about the training. Participants responded with their level of agreement to statements such as "I believe I learned a lot during the training" and "I found this training challenging" on a 1 (strongly disagree) to 6 (strongly agree) Likert scale with an option to select "Does Not Apply."

2.3   Procedure

The experiment consisted of two sessions and participants were run in groups of 4 to 8 individuals. During the first session of the experiment, after consenting to participate, all participants took the pre-test on the 17 armored vehicle models to assess their existing knowledge of the learning objectives. Next, they were presented with passive learning trials (i.e., familiarization period) to gain some exposure to the vehicles to be learned. Participants were then randomly assigned to one of the three conditions and began the training portion of the experiment.

Those in the *Mastery Drop* condition had mastered vehicles that were labeled as learning objectives removed from the deck during training. For a card to be considered "mastered," the participant needed to match the vehicle to its name accurately with a reaction time of less than 6 s for four consecutive presentations of the card. The criteria was determined from pilot testing and previous literature [28, 29]. Participants in this condition completed the training portion when they "mastered" all 17 learning objectives, completed 350 trials (determined during pilot testing), or 45 min had elapsed, which ever occurred first.

Those in the *No Drop* condition were presented with the flashcards in a random sequence until 45 min had elapsed or 350 trials had been completed, which ever occurred first.

Those in the *Learner Drop* condition were prompted to decide whether they wanted to remove a card from the deck or preferred to keep studying the card. Participants in this condition completed the training when they indicated that they had "mastered" all vehicles by dropping all of the learning objectives. During pilot testing, participants in the Learner Drop condition completed the training much faster than those in the other conditions. To ensure they received the same amount of time before the assessment, they completed a distractor task of math problems for approximately 20 min.

After training, all participants were given several questionnaires, which included the IRQ and a demographics questionnaire, which took approximately 20 to 30 min to complete. Lastly, participants completed the immediate post-test and the immediate transfer test on real-world images of the vehicles they learned during training.

Participants returned 48 h after training for the second session of the experiment. During the second session, participants completed the delayed post-test and delayed transfer test.

3   Results

3.1   Immediate and Delayed Post-Test Learning Gains

We aimed to determine if there were group differences based on learning gains at immediate and delayed post-tests. Learning gains were calculated using the following formula ([Post-Test Score − Pre-Test Score]/[Total Score − Pre-Test Score]), which allowed us to measure how much participants learned by taking their pre-test score into account for how much they could have improved. Two learning gain scores were calculated, one using the immediate post-test and a second using the delayed post-test.

A one-way ANOVA was conducted using the condition as the between-subjects factor and the learning gain score (using the immediate post-test) as the dependent measure. As seen in Fig. 1, there was a significant difference between groups, $F(2, 45) = 12.28$, $p < .001$, $\eta_p^2 = .37$. In support of H1, post-hoc analyses indicated that those in the Learner Drop condition ($M = 37.48$, $SD = 30.53$) had the lowest learning gains score compared to the Mastery Drop condition ($M = 62.80$, $SD = 23.80$; $p = .009$, Cohen's $d = 0.93$) and the No Drop condition ($M = 82.41$, $SD = 21.01$; $p < .001$, $d = 1.75$). However, contrary to H1, the No Drop condition had significantly higher learning gains than the Mastery Drop condition ($p = .03$, $d = 0.92$). Therefore, H1 was partially supported.

A one-way ANOVA was conducted using the condition as the between-subjects factor and the learning gain score (using the delayed post-test) as the dependent measure. There was a significant difference between groups (see Fig. 1), $F(2, 43) = 5.66$, $p = .007$, $\eta_p^2 = .22$. H2 was supported as post-hoc analyses indicated that those in the Learner Drop condition ($M = 33.90$, $SD = 28.52$) had the lowest learning gains score compared to both the Mastery Drop condition ($M = 60.87$, $SD = 24.23$; $p = .02$, $d = 1.02$) and the No Drop condition ($M = 69.29$, $SD = 34.56$; $p = .002$, $d = 1.12$). In contrast to the immediate learning gains, there was no significant difference between the Mastery Drop and No Drop conditions ($p = .44$, $d = 0.28$) for delayed post gains. Therefore, H2 was partially supported.

There was a noticeable decrease in learning gains from immediate to delayed post-test gains in the No Drop condition. As a result, we ran paired samples t-tests for each condition comparing the immediate and delayed gain scores. There was a significant

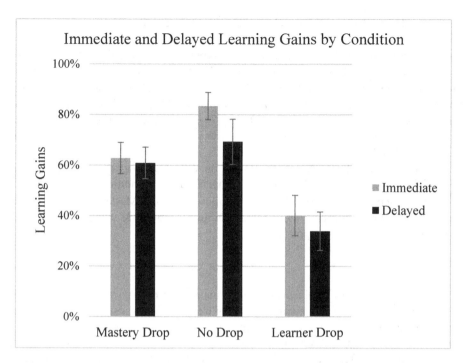

Fig. 1. Learning gains by experimental condition at immediate and delayed post-test

decrease in learning gains from immediate to delayed testing in the No Drop condition, $t(14) = 2.34$, $p = .03$, $d = 0.49$. Although those in the Mastery Drop condition did not have the highest delayed learning gains (contrary to H2), those in the Mastery Drop condition maintained a consistent learning gains score across immediate and delayed post-tests ($t(14) = 0.61$, $p = .55$, $d = 0.08$). Those in the Learner Drop condition also had no change in their learning gains score ($t(14) = 2.13$, $p = .05$, $d = 0.20$).

To interpret the results further, we examined whether the differences between the No Drop and Mastery Drop conditions could be due to an increased exposure to the learning objectives. The learning objectives were the 17 models that could be dropped from the Mastery Drop condition if mastery was achieved. Additionally, these learning objectives were used for all assessments. Therefore, we conducted a post-hoc analysis to determine if the No Drop condition completed more learning objective trials than the Mastery Drop condition. The independent samples t-test showed that participants in the No Drop condition ($M = 192.27$, $SD = 30.48$) completed more learning objective trials than the Mastery Drop condition ($M = 154.80$, $SD = 33.68$), $t(28) = 3.20$, $p = .003$, $d = 1.17$. Therefore, the No Drop condition may have had higher learning gains due to additional exposure to learning objectives.

3.2 Immediate and Delayed Transfer Test Performance

Next, we evaluated differences between training conditions on identifying real-world armored vehicles. Two one-way ANOVAs were conducted using the condition as the between-subjects factor and the immediate or delayed transfer test score as the dependent measure.

There was a significant difference between groups on the immediate transfer test (F (2, 45) = 4.12, p = .02, η_{p^2} = .16). Contrary to H3, those in the No Drop condition had the highest transfer test score (M = 6.27, SD = 2.46), which was significantly higher than the Mastery Drop condition (M = 4.40, SD = 2.32; p = .04, d = 0.78) and the Learner Drop Condition (M = 3.80, SD = 2.57; p = .009, d = 0.98). However, there was no significant difference between the Mastery Drop and Learner Drop conditions (p = .51, d = 0.25).

For the delayed transfer test, there was no difference between conditions F(2, 43) = 2.70, p = .08, η_{p^2} = .12. However, the No Drop condition had the highest transfer test score (M = 7.29, SD = 3.22), followed by the Mastery Drop condition (M = 5.00, SD = 2.56), and the Learner Drop condition (M = 5.00, SD = 3.26). Therefore, there was not support for H3.

3.3   Training Data

The training data were examined in order to understand differences in learning gains between conditions. Three one-way ANOVAs were conducted using condition as the between-subjects factor and total training time (in minutes), number of mastered armored vehicles, and total number of learning trials as the dependent measures. There was a significant difference between groups on total training time, F(2, 45) = 38.64, p < .001, η_{p^2} = .65. Post-hoc analyses showed that those in the Learner Drop condition spent the least amount of time in training (M = 14.18, SD = 12.95) compared to the Mastery Drop condition (M = 39.30, SD = 8.71; p < .001, d = 2.28) and the No Drop condition (M = 40.72, SD = 4.01; p < .001, d = 2.77). There was no difference in the total training time between the Mastery Drop and No Drop conditions (p = .68, d = 0.21).

There was also a significant difference between groups on total number of learning trials, F(2, 45) = 91.27, p < .001, η_{p^2} = .81. Post-hoc analyses showed that those in the Learner Drop condition completed the fewest training trials (M = 82.53, SD = 58.82) compared to the Mastery Drop condition (M = 295.07, SD = 47.78; p < .001, d = 3.97) and the No Drop condition (M = 316.60, SD = 50.10; p < .001, d = 4.28). There was no difference in the number of learning trials between the Mastery Drop and No Drop conditions (p = .27, d = 0.43).

We next examined the number of mastered learning objectives. Mastery was determined during the training trials for the Mastery Drop condition, but calculated post-hoc for the No Drop and Learner Drop conditions (i.e., how many learning objectives were accurately identified with a reaction time of less than six seconds for four consecutive presentations of the card). There was a significant difference between groups on the number of mastered armored vehicles, F(2, 45) = 25.58, p < .001, η_{p^2} = .54. Post-hoc analyses showed that those in the Learner Drop condition mastered the fewest number of armored vehicles during training (M = 0.38, SD = 1.25) compared to the Mastery Drop condition (M = 10.67, SD = 5.66; p < .001, d = 2.55) and the No Drop condition ($M = 10.60$, $SD = 5.67$; $p < .001$, $d = 2.49$). There was no difference in the number of mastered armored vehicles between the Mastery Drop and No Drop conditions ($p = .97$, $d = 0.01$). Together, these results support H4a, such that the Learner Drop condition completed training quickly, completed the fewest number of trials, and mastered the fewest number armored vehicles. However, contrary to H4b, there was no difference between the Mastery Drop and No Drop conditions across these dependent measures.

3.4   Perceptions of the Training Experience

In addition to performance data, we aimed to determine whether there were subjective differences between groups regarding the training experience. Average responses from six items are reported in Table 1. The first three items reflect participants' overall perceptions of the training and the other items gauge some of their metacognitive processes during training. The responses to each item can range in agreement from 1 (strongly disagree) to 6 (strongly agree). Overall, perceptions of the training were positive for all of the items, as the means were all above the midpoint of the scale. Group differences emerged ($F(2, 45) = 3.67$, $p = .03$, $\eta_{p^2} = .15$) for the item "During training, I felt motivated to learn," such that those in the No Drop condition reported feeling the least motivated compared to those in the Learner Drop condition ($p = .01$, $d = 1.00$). There was no difference between the Mastery Drop and the Learner Drop condition on reported feelings of motivation ($p = .20$, $d = 0.52$) or the Mastery Drop and No Drop conditions ($p = .16$, $d = 0.46$). Additionally, there was a significant difference among groups ($F(2, 44) = 3.43$, $p = .04$, $\eta_{p^2} = .14$) for the item "During training, I changed my approach to the task if I noticed it was not working." Those in the No Drop condition had the highest rate of agreement with this statement, which was significantly higher than the Learner Drop condition ($p = .01$, $d = 0.86$). There was no difference between the Mastery Drop condition and the No Drop condition ($p = .30$, $d = 0.48$) or the Mastery Drop and Learner Drop conditions ($p = .12$, $d = 0.55$) on their rate of agreement.

Table 1. Subjective perceptions of the training experience by condition

Item	Condition	M (SD)
I liked the content in this training	Mastery Drop	4.53 (1.25)
	No Drop	4.00 (1.41)
	Learner Drop	4.80 (0.94)
Overall, the training was useful to me	Mastery Drop	4.60 (1.12)
	No Drop	4.07 (1.98)
	Learner Drop	3.79 (1.48)
I would like to use this training to learn other content	Mastery Drop	4.67 (1.23)
	No Drop	3.85 (1.86)
	Learner Drop	5.00 (0.91)
During training, I felt motivated to learn†	Mastery Drop	4.00 (1.41)
	No Drop	3.29 (1.64)*
	Learner Drop	4.60 (0.99)*
I thought about how I was performing during the training	Mastery Drop	5.20 (1.37)
	No Drop	5.57 (1.09)
	Learner Drop	5.27 (1.10)
I expect to remember most of what I learned from the training a few days from now	Mastery Drop	4.13 (1.19)
	No Drop	4.36 (1.45)
	Learner Drop	4.07 (0.96)
During training, I changed my approach to the task if I noticed it was not working†	Mastery Drop	5.00 (0.66)
	No Drop	5.36 (0.84)*
	Learner Drop	4.36 (1.15)*

Note: † indicates a significant group difference at $p < .05$
*indicates a significant difference between pairs at $p < .05$

4 Discussion

4.1 Mastery Learning Leads to Consistent Long-Term Retention

The present research suggests that there may be a benefit of using mastery learning as an AT technique for long-term retention in a visual identification task. When first examining the learning gains using the immediate post-test scores, the data appear to suggest that those in the No Drop condition had superior retention of the armored vehicles compared to the Mastery Drop and Learner Drop conditions. However, examining delayed learning gains showed an important distinction. Although there was no difference between the No Drop and Mastery Drop conditions in terms of delayed learning gains, those in the Mastery Drop condition maintained a consistent learning gain score from immediate to delayed test, whereas the No Drop condition had a significant 13% decrease from immediate to delayed learning gains. This suggests that the No Drop condition had a larger rate of forgetting compared to the Mastery Drop condition. This increased forgetting is despite the fact the No Drop condition completed more learning objectives trials compared to the Mastery Drop condition. This work highlights why measuring long-term retention is a crucial component of the present research, because the memory performance immediately after training was not indicative of future performance for the No Drop condition. The No Drop condition may have had higher immediate learning gains than the Mastery Drop condition due to more trials with the learning objectives, but this did not seem to have a lasting effect on long-term retention.

4.2   Learner Control has Negative Learning Outcomes

Of the three conditions, participants in the Learner Drop group showed the worst memory performance. On average, those in the Learner Drop condition had delayed learning gains 20% lower than the other conditions. Some of these differences can be explained by differences in the training experience. Those in the Learner Drop condition completed training in about a third of the time that those in the Mastery Drop and No Drop conditions completed. Likewise, those in the Learner Drop condition completed less than 100 trials, on average, whereas those in the Mastery Drop and No Drop conditions completed 300 trials, on average. Based on the mastery criteria used in the Mastery Drop condition, those in the Mastery Drop and No Drop conditions mastered approximately 11 armored vehicles whereas those in the Learner Drop mastered less than one armored vehicle, on average. The poor performance in the Learner Drop condition highlights participants' inability to self-regulate their learning, which is consistent with past research [3, 8]. In contrast, providing students with a training system that automatically drops a flashcard based on mastery criteria that operates "behind the scenes" or does not drop cards at all is a more effective training strategy. For flashcard training to be effective, the learner must have strong metacognitive awareness to be in control of the deck or if training time is of concern, the dropping should be done on his or her behalf.

4.3   Transfer Test Performance and Limitations

Although the No Drop condition outperformed other conditions on the immediate transfer test, there was no difference between groups on the delayed transfer test. On average, participants were able to identify about 5 out of 17 of the real-world images correctly, which was a disappointing outcome given that identifying real-world images is a more critical skill for Marines than identifying images of models. This floor effect suggests that perhaps the real-world images were too difficult to compare to the models participants had learned. It may also suggest a need for improved training stimuli. For instance, all of the models were shown at the same angle, whereas there was less methodological control over the real-world images of the armored vehicles (i.e., not all with the same angles and environmental conditions). Perhaps the training models should have been presented at multiple angles to aid identification of the real-world images. It is also possible that any potential difference between Mastery Drop and No Drop is a small effect (particularly after only one exposure to the training) and the present preliminary sample size precludes detection of a significant result. It should be noted that there is limited research to date that has measured training transfer with flashcard training. Additionally, it might be the case that other instructional strategies may improve training transfer with these or other materials, which will be discussed in the future research discussion.

4.4   Perceptions of the Training

In terms of the subjective perceptions of the training experience, opinions of the training were generally positive. However, those in the No Drop condition reported feeling the least motivated to learn during training. Participants in this condition saw the flashcards in a purely random order and training ended when they had completed 350 trials or 45 min had elapsed (whichever occurred first). This finding was surprising, given that there was no statistical difference between training time and number of trials between the Mastery Drop and No Drop conditions. However, having "mastered" cards remain in the deck in the No Drop condition may have reduced levels of motivation during training. This is consistent with notion that matching the training difficulty to learners' performance keeps them engaged [30]. Practically speaking, keeping motivation and engagement levels high may promote a positive learning experience and may encourage students to complete more training.

4.5   Future Research

The adaptive strategy used in the current research was mastery learning. As Durlach and Ray [19] suggested, a mastery learning technique in a new domain will require refinement and iterative testing. In future research, we intend to examine and "fine-tune" the mastery criteria systematically to determine how different criteria influence learning gains and improve long-term retention. It is possible that the mastery criteria used limit the present research because the criteria were too strict (i.e., requiring four consecutive correct recalls with fast reaction times), given that there were no differences in training time, total number of trials, or delayed learning gains between the Mastery Drop and No Drop conditions. Furthermore, we plan to explore the sequencing of flashcards [29, 31, 32] as another adaptive strategy in addition to mastery criteria in future experiments. It may be the case that the interaction of these two strategies enhances learning gains more than a single technique. Finally, we will examine these techniques across multiple domains to determine whether the effectiveness of these techniques is generalizable.

4.6   Conclusions

In the present research, we examined different ways of dropping flashcards in an effort to meet the Sailor 2025 goal of modernizing military training and providing learner-centric training. We presented preliminary evidence that using mastery criteria as an AT strategy to drop cards promotes long-term retention compared to not dropping cards during study. Additionally, the present research showed that learners in control of dropping flashcards from further study results in negative learning outcomes. Moving toward a digital age of training with the learner at the forefront, training must be designed to account for these learner limitations and potentially offload the decision of when something is "mastered" to the technology. AT technologies can be leveraged so that these metacognitive judgments of when to repeat material can be built into the technology in order to provide Sailors and Marines with effective and efficient training. Although it is presently unclear which approach is better for transfer of training, more research is needed to investigate AT solutions that prepare Service members for the real-world task of identifying armored vehicles.

Acknowledgements. We gratefully acknowledge Dr. Peter Squire and the Office of Naval Research who sponsored this work (Funding Doc# N0001419WX00633). We would also like to thank the Marine Corps Intelligence School for their enthusiastic support and help with participant recruitment. Presentation of this material does not constitute or imply its endorsement, recommendation, or favoring by the U.S. Navy or Department of Defense (DoD). The opinions of the authors expressed herein do not necessarily state or reflect those of the U.S. Navy or DoD.

References

1. Burke, R.P.: (2018). https://www.usni.org/magazines/proceedings/2018/march/sailor-2025-navys-strategy-people
2. Landsberg, C.R., Van Buskirk, W.L., Astwood, R.S., Mercado, A.D., Aakre, A.J.: Adaptive training considerations for simulation-based training. Special report No 2010-001, NAWCTSD. Naval Air Warfare Center Training Systems Division, Orlando (2011)
3. Kornell, N., Bjork, R.A.: Optimising self-regulated study: the benefits—and costs—of dropping flashcards. Memory **16**, 125–136 (2008)
4. Karpicke, J.D., Roediger, H.L.: The critical importance of retrieval for learning. Science **319** (5865), 966–968 (2008)
5. Oxford, R., Crookall, D.: Vocabulary learning: a critical analysis of techniques. TESL Canada J. **7**, 9–30 (1990)
6. Oxford, R.L., Scarcella, R.C.: Second language vocabulary learning among adults: state of the art in vocabulary instruction. System **22**(2), 231–243 (1994)
7. Wissman, K.T., Rawson, K.A., Pyc, M.A.: How and when do students use flashcards? Memory **20**(6), 568–579 (2012)
8. Bjork, R.A., Dunlosky, J., Kornell, N.: Self-regulated learning: beliefs, techniques, and illusions. Annu. Rev. Psychol. **64**, 417–444 (2013)
9. Karpicke, J.D., Butler, A.C., Roediger, H.L.: Metacognitive strategies in student learning: do students practise retrieval when they study on their own? Memory **17**, 471–479 (2009)
10. Pyc, M.A., Rawson, K.A., Aschenbrenner, A.J.: Metacognitive monitoring during criterion learning: when and why are judgments accurate? Mem. Cogn. **42**(6), 886–897 (2014). https://doi.org/10.3758/s13421-014-0403-4
11. Scheiter, K., Gerjets, P.: Learner control in hypermedia environments. Educ. Psychol. Rev. **19**(3), 285–307 (2007)
12. Dunlosky, J., Serra, M., Baker, J.M.C.: Metamemory applied. In: Durso, F.T., Nickerson, R. S., Dumais, S.T., Lewandowsky, S., Perfect, T.J. (eds.) Handbook of Applied Cognition, 2nd edn, pp. 137–159. Wiley, New York (2007)
13. Nelson, T.O., Narens, L.: Metamemory: a theoretical framework and new findings. In: Bower, G.H. (ed.) The Psychology of Learning and Motivation, vol. 26, pp. 125–173. Academic Press, New York (1990)
14. Karpicke, J.D.: Metacognitive control and strategy selection: deciding when to practice retrieval during learning. J. Exp. Psychol. Gen. **1238**(4), 469–486 (2009)

15. Marraffino, M.D., Johnson, C.I., Whitmer, D.E., Steinhauser, N.B., Clement, A.: Advise when ready for game plan: adaptive training for JTACs. In: Proceedings of the Interservice/Industry Training, Simulation & Education Conference (I/ITSEC). National Training Systems Association, Orlando (2019)

16. Peirce, N., Wade, V.: Personalised learning for casual games: the 'language trap' online language learning game. In: Leading Issues in Games Based Learning, vol. 159–170 (2010)

17. VanLehn, K., et al.: The Andes physics tutoring system: lessons learned. Int. J. Artif. Intell. Educ. **15**(3), 147–204 (2005)

18. Landsberg, C.R., Mercado, A.D., Van Buskirk, W.L., Lineberry, M., Steinhauser, N.: Evaluation of an adaptive training system for submarine periscope operations. In: 56th International Proceedings on Human Factors and Ergonomics, vol. 56(1), pp. 2422–2426. SAGE Publications, Los Angeles (2012)

19. Durlach, P.J., Ray, J.M.: Designing adaptive instructional environments: insights from empirical evidence. Technical report No. 1297, ARI. U.S. Army Research Institute for the Behavioral and Social Sciences, Arlington (2011)

20. Andrieux, M., Danna, J., Thon, B.: Self-control of task difficulty during training enhances motor learning of a complex coincidence-anticipation task. Res. Q. Exerc. Sport **83**(1), 27–35 (2012)

21. Durlach, P.J.: Fundamentals, flavors, and foibles of adaptive instructional systems. In: Sottilare, R.A., Schwarz, J. (eds.) HCII 2019. LNCS, vol. 11597, pp. 76–95. Springer, Cham (2019). https://doi.org/10.1007/978-3-030-22341-0_7

22. Guadagnoli, M.A., Lee, T.D.: Challenge point: a framework for conceptualizing the effects of various practice conditions in motor learning. J. Mot. Behav. **36**(2), 212–224 (2004)

23. Lintern, G., Gopher, D.: Adaptive training of perceptual-motor skills: issues, results, and future directions. Int. J. Man Mach. Stud. **10**(5), 521–551 (1978)

24. Mayer, R.E.: Cambridge Handbook of Multimedia Learning. Cambridge University Press, New York (2014)

25. Sweller, J.: Implications of cognitive load theory for multimedia learning. In: Mayer, R.E. (ed.) The Cambridge Handbook of Multimedia Learning, 1st edn, pp. 19–30. Cambridge University Press, New York (2005)

26. Vygotsky, L.S.: Interaction between learning and development. In: Gauvain, M., Cole, M. (eds.) Readings on the Development of Children, 4th edn, pp. 34–40. Worth, New York (2005)

27. Roediger, H.L., Karpicke, J.D.: Test-enhanced learning: taking memory tests improves long-term retention. Psychol. Sci. **17**(3), 249–255 (2006)

28. Mettler, E., Massey, C.M., Kellman, P.J.: Improving adaptive learning technology through the use of response times. In: Proceedings of the 33rd Annual Conference of the Cognitive Science Society, pp. 2532–2537. Cognitive Sciences Society, Boston (2011)

29. Mettler, E., Massey, C.M., Kellman, P.J.: A comparison of adaptive and fixed schedules of practice. J. Exp. Psychol. Gen. **145**(7), 897–917 (2016)

30. van Merriënboer, J.J., Sweller, J.: Cognitive load theory and complex learning: recent developments and future directions. Educ. Psychol. Rev. **17**(2), 147–177 (2005)

31. Atkinson, R.C.: Optimizing the learning of a second-language vocabulary. J. Exp. Psychol. **96**(1), 124–129 (1972)

32. Settles, B., Meeder, B.: A trainable spaced repetition model for language learning. In: Proceedings of the 54th Annual Meeting of the Association for Computational Linguistics, pp. 1848–1858. Association for Computational Linguistics, Germany (2016)

Correction to: An Ambient and Pervasive Personalized Learning Ecosystem: "Smart Learning" in the Age of the Internet of Things

Anastasia Betts, Khanh-Phuong Thai, Sunil Gunderia, Paula Hidalgo, Meagan Rothschild, and Diana Hughes

Correction to:
Chapter "An Ambient and Pervasive Personalized Learning Ecosystem: "Smart Learning" in the Age of the Internet of Things" in: R. A. Sottilare and J. Schwarz (Eds.): *Adaptive Instructional Systems*, LNCS 12214, https://doi.org/10.1007/978-3-030-50788-6_2

Chapter ["An Ambient and Pervasive Personalized Learning Ecosystem: "Smart Learning" in the Age of the Internet of Things"] was previously published non-open access. It has now been changed to open access under a CC BY 4.0 license and the copyright holder updated to 'The Author(s)'. The book has also been updated with this change.

The updated original version of this chapter can be found at
https://doi.org/10.1007/978-3-030-50788-6_2

© The Author(s) 2022
R. A. Sottilare and J. Schwarz (Eds.): HCII 2020, LNCS 12214, p. C1, 2022.
https://doi.org/10.1007/978-3-030-50788-6_42

Author Index

Printed in the United States
by Baker & Taylor Publisher Services